http://www.wadsworth.com

wadsworth.com is the World Wide Web site for Wadsworth and is your direct source to dozens of online resources.

At *wadsworth.com* you can find out about supplements, demonstration software, and student resources. You can also send email to many of our authors and preview new publications and exciting new technologies.

wadsworth.com
Changing the way the world learns®

The Wadsworth
Special Educator Series

The following Special Education titles are new for 1998 from Wadsworth Publishing:

- **Special Education Issues Within the Context of American Society**
  Susan McLean Benner, Ed.D., University of Tennessee, Knoxville
  ISBN: 0-534-25230-0

- **Promoting Learning for Culturally and Linguistically Diverse Students**
  Russell M. Gersten, Ph.D., University of Oregon
  Robert T. Jimenez, Ph.D., University of Illinois
  ISBN: 0-534-34417-6

- **Beyond High School: Transition from School to Work**
  Frank R. Rusch, Ph.D., University of Illinois
  Janis G. Chadsey, Ph.D., University of Illinois
  ISBN: 0-534-34432-1

Beyond High School

Transition from School to Work

Edited by

FRANK R. RUSCH

Transition Research Institute
University of Illinois

and

JANIS G. CHADSEY

Department of Special Education
University of Illinois

Wadsworth Publishing Company
An International Thomson Publishing Company

I(T)P®

Belmont, CA • Albany, NY • Bonn • Boston • Cincinnati • Detroit • Johannesburg • London
Madrid • Melbourne • Mexico City • New York • Paris • Singapore • Tokyo • Toronto • Washington

Education Editor: Joan Gill
Editorial Assistant: Valerie Morrison
Print Buyer: Barbara Britton
Permissions Editor: Veronica Oliva
Production: Aksen Associates
Composition: Aksen Associates
Marketing Manger: Jay Hu
Cover Design: Jeanne Calabrese
Cover Photograph: © Tony Stone Images/Peter Samuels
Printer: The Maple-Vail Book Manufacturing Group

Printed in the United States of America
    3 4 5 6 7 8 9 10

For more information, contact Wadsworth Publishing Company, 10 Davis Drive, Belmont, CA 94002,
or electronically at http://www.wadsworth.com/wadsworth.html

International Thomson Publishing Europe
Berkshire House 168-173
High Holborn
London, WC1V 7AA, England

Thomas Nelson Australia
102 Dodds Street
South Melbourne 3205
Victoria, Australia

Nelson Canada
1120 Birchmount Road
Scarborough, Ontario
Canada M1K 5G4

International Thomson Publishing GmbH
Königswinterer Strasse 418
53227 Bonn, Germany

International Thomson Editores
Campos Eliseos 385, Piso 7
Col. Polanco
11560 México D.F. México

International Thomson Publishing Asia
221 Henderson Road
#05-10 Henderson Building
Singapore 0315

International Thomson Publishing Japan
Hirakawacho Kyowa Building, 3F
2-2-1 Hirakawacho
Chiyoda-ku, Tokyo 102, Japan

International Thomson Publishing Southern Africa
Building 18, Constantia Park
240 Old Pretoria Road
Halfway House, 1685 South Africa

Library of Congress Cataloging-in-Publication Data

Beyond high school: Transition from school to work
    Edited by Frank R. Rusch and Janis G. Chadsey
        p.   cm.
    Includes bibliographical references and index.
    ISBN 0-534-34432-1
    1. Handicapped youth—Education (Secondary)—United States.   2. Handicapped youth—Vocational
education—United States.   3. Vocational guidance for the handicapped—United States.   4. School–
to–work transition—United States.   5. Educational change—United States.   I. Rusch, Frank R.
    II. Chadsey, Janis G.
LC4031.B45   1998
371.9'.0473—dc21
                                        97-36935

CONTENTS

11 STUDENT ASSESSMENT AND EVALUATION 265
Martha Thurlow and Judy Elliott

Contributors

Janis G. Chadsey
Department of Special Education
University of Illinois
1310 S. 6th Street
Champaign, IL 61820

R. Brian Cobb
School of Occupational and Educational Studies
Colorado State University
215 Education Building
Fort Collins, CO 80523

Judith Elliott
National Center on Educational Outcomes
University of Minnesota
Department of Educational Psychology
350 ELTH
Minneapolis, MN 55455

Jane M. Everson
LSU Medical Center-HDC
1100 Florida Avenue, Bldg. 119
New Orleans, LA 70119

Anna Gajar
Department of Special Education
The Pennsylvania State University
226B Moore Building
University Park, PA 16802

Thomas E. Grayson
Transition Research Institute
University of Illinois
113 Children's Research Center
51 Gerty Drive
Champaign, IL 61820

Joan D. Guillory
LSU Medical Center-HDC
1100 Florida Avenue, Bldg. 119
New Orleans, LA 70119

David Hagner
Institute on Disability
University of New Hampshire
The Concord Center
10 Ferry Street, #14
Concord, NH 03301

Cheryl Hanley-Maxwell
Department of Rehabilitation Psychology
    and Special Education
University of Wisconsin
432 N. Murray Street
Madison, WI 53706

Carolyn Hughes
Department of Special Education
Peabody College
Box 328
Vanderbilt University
Nashville, TN 37203

Jin-Ho Kim
Department of Special Education
Peabody College
Box 328
Vanderbilt University
Nashville, TN 37203

Paula D. Kohler
Transition Research Institute
113 Children's Research Center
51 Gerty Drive
Champaign, IL 61820

Stephen Lichtenstein
Institute on Disability:UAP
University of New Hampshire
312 Morrill Hall
Durham, NH 03824

Susan Mayfield Pogoloff
Appalachian State University
Department of LRE
124 Edwin Duncan Hall
Boone, NC 28608

Bruce M. Menchetti
Department of Special Education
Florida State University
Room 209, Education Building
Tallahassee, FL 32306-3030

Dorothy M. Millar
Department of Special Education
University of Illinois
1310 S. 6th Street
Champaign, IL 61820

Debra A. Neubert
Department of Special Education
University of Maryland at College Park
1308 Benjamin Building
College Park, MD 20742-1121

Vicky C. Piland
Department of Special Education
Florida State University
Room 209, Education Building
Tallahassee, FL 32306-3030

Frank R. Rusch
Transition Research Institute
University of Illinois
113 Children's Research Center
51 Gerty Drive
Champaign, IL 61820

Jennifer Vander Sande
Institute on Disability
University of New Hampshire
The Concord Center
10 Ferry Street, #14
Concord, NH 03301

Debra Shelden
Transition Research Institute
University of Illinois
113 Children's Research Center
51 Gerty Drive
Champaign, IL 61820

Shepherd Siegel
Career Ladders
Manager, STW Systems
Seattle Public Schools
815 Fourth Avenue, N., MS #AA 304
Seattle, WA 98109

Robert A. Stodden
Department of Special Education
University of Hawaii
Wist Hall 210
1776 University Avenue
Honolulu, HI 96822

Edna Mora Szymanski
Department of Rehabilitation, Psychology,
    and Special Education
University of Wisconsin
432 N. Murray Street
Madison, WI 53706

Martha Thurlow
National Center on Educational Outcomes
University of Minnesota
Department of Educational Psychology
350 ELTH
Minneapolis, MN 55455

Michael L. Wehmeyer
Assistant Director
Department of Research and Program Services
The Arc National Headquarters
500 East Border Street, Suite 300
Arlington, TX 76010

Jean Whitney-Thomas
Institute for Community Inclusion
Children's Hospital—Boston
300 Longwood Avenue
Boston, MA 02115

Reviewers

The editors, authors, and publisher thank the reviewers of the manuscript for their helpful comments and suggestions:

Jim Artesani
University of Maine

Barbara Gartin
University of Arkansas

Diane Bassett
University of North Colorado

John Johnson
University of Cincinnati

Mary Bostick
University of Idaho

Linda Parrish
Texas A&M University

Bob Flexer
Kent State University

David Test
University of North Carolina, Charlotte

Introduction

No country, however rich, can afford the waste of its human resources. Demoralization caused by vast unemployment is our greatest extravagance. Morally, it is the greatest menace to our social order.

FRANKLIN DELANO ROOSEVELT,
September 30, 1934

In 1992, we edited *Transition from School to Adult Life: Models, Linkages, and Policy.* This earlier text was a compilation of chapters that represented the "state of the art" at the time, and we continue to hear from many of our readers who found this text helpful and useful. But much has changed since the publication of this earlier volume. In particular, new legislation has emerged that promises to reshape secondary education as we know it today. We are also bene-fiting from an enormous amount of new information on what appears to be successful in preparing students for employment, a better quality of life, and lifelong learning. In addition, there is a growing understanding that persons with and without disabilities share a common goal, and that goal is attainable: Youth want to see the relevance of their education for their aspirations! Consequently, we must stop believing that every student must experience an education that is loosely designed to accommodate everyone, but serves no one particularly well.

Beyond High School: Transition from School to Work extends our earlier work in several important ways. Foremost, *Beyond High School* presents a large and complex body of research and emerging theories in an attempt to present straightforward solutions to complex problems facing educators today. As such, the text also addresses the fundamental question, "What does existing secondary educational research and theory say about how best to address the genuinely important problems that face youth with and without disabilities as they plan their futures?"

The purpose of this text is to summarize the knowledge acquired from research that has focused on reforming secondary special education and our high schools, and to make recommendations for improving the effectiveness of our nation's high schools.

Most importantly, this text introduces new knowledge that has emerged over a relatively short time period (1985–present). Although much of this research has been focused on students with disabilities, we have attempted to glean from it generalizations that may be made to *all* students who are not college-bound and who form a large network of youths who aspire to graduate and get on with their lives. Consequently, this text is focused on the bigger picture—*preparing adolescents for tomorrow's challenges.*

Beyond High School embodies diverse perspectives of important issues that face everyone associated with secondary education in America. Therefore, this text is appropriate for policy makers and parents, as well as educators. Vocational, rehabilitation, special, and regular educators will find the text useful because in it we have assembled leading researchers, who in addition to their expertise and understanding of the issues, also bring a deep commitment to the value of diversity that once again is beginning to inform educational thinking. As you will learn as you read this text, the problems that face youth today are common to *all* youth—regardless of their color, their disability, or their talents. Our efforts to better understand these youth, the dreams that they share, and our own responsibility as educators can result only in improved educational outcomes for everyone.

To make this text as useful as possible, we have tried to present clear and practical suggestions for individuals charged with varying degrees of responsibilities in providing guidance, direction, and opportunities for youth with and without disabilities. *Beyond High School* is comprised of seventeen chapters on a broad array of topics and issues ranging from adolescent development, on the one hand, to preparation for postsecondary education, on the other. We have divided the text into three parts: introduction to the broader topic of transition, overview of issues and methods that relate to transition planning and student involvement in the schools, and linkages to work and postsecondary education.

INTRODUCTION TO TRANSITION

This text focuses on youth. Consequently, we must examine the literature that addresses these youth as they make the transition from children, to adolescents, and ultimately to young adults. The period that begins around age 12 and ends at approximately 25 is one of the least understood periods in human development. Lichtenstein examines the literature surrounding adolescent development, introducing the reader to the pressures and forces that confront these youth as they prepare to leave a life of parent support and nurturing to a life where they are expected to become autonomous almost overnight. Chapter 1 references all youth with and without disabilities with the understanding that these youth are more alike than they are different. Unless stated otherwise, the reader should understand that youth with and without disabilities enter adolescence; pass through this period experiencing enormous metabolic, psychological, and emotional changes; and enter adulthood in what may be described as one of the most incredible passages undertaken in a lifetime.

Clearly, the high school experience is one of the cornerstones to ensuring success throughout life. Indeed, failure to provide an effective high school experience results in personal short comings, including the failure to attain additional education and training to help mold a career of personal choice. There is ample evidence to suggest that our high schools are failing to achieve desired and expected outcomes for all students, regardless of ability. For example, traditional approaches to special education have often forced students to transfer from the regular classroom to segregated, "special" classrooms, or, worse yet, from the regular classroom to a segregated classroom in a segregated, "special school." The practice of providing an education outside the mainstream of general education is now being challenged because of our better understanding of what should comprise an effective secondary education.

But, there is reason to be optimistic about the potential for improving secondary education in this country. Over the past decade, much research has been sponsored by the U.S. Department of Education, which has addressed the complexities of providing an effective secondary education. Policy makers, parents, and educators from a variety of fields have turned their attention to reform-related issues, including the transition from high school to adult life. The knowledge, technology, and resources are now available to plan a course that would better prepare today's youths for the challenges of the future. If the practices that currently are being validated by federally sponsored model programs throughout the United States could be introduced in every high school in the near future, drastic improvements in secondary special education effectiveness would be realized. Chapter 2 reviews best practices that have emerged in general education, vocational education, and special education over the past fifteen years.

Chapter 3 provides a broad historical overview of legislation that has impacted employment training, rehabilitation, and education. Our country has invested considerable resources in providing education and rehabilitation services for persons with diverse disabilities since the passage of the Smith-Hughes Act in 1917 (P.L. 64-347), which was the first act to create vocational education curricula in secondary schools. Over the course of the past eighty years, legislation has surfaced in diverse areas impacting upon youth, including labor, rehabilitation, and special education. Stodden includes a rich discussion of more recent "transition legislation," showing how legislation from diverse perspectives are beginning to mandate specific practices, which in turn share similar intentions with regard to

definition of services and how these services should be provided.

Tragically, tens of thousands of youth with and without disabilities leave high schools without the skills or the support needed to compete in the marketplace. High schools primarily appear to be a training ground only for our nation's "most promising" students: those who will graduate and pursue a college education. Students who do not aspire to a postsecondary education appear to be left virtually isolated from any unified system that addresses their needs—theirs is an uncertain future, especially as we enter the twenty-first century. In Chapter 4, Grayson discusses how schools are clearly ineffectual in preventing students from dropping out. After focusing on the consequences of dropping out of school, Grayson suggests new strategies for preventing dropping out within the context of educational reform.

TRANSITION PLANNING AND INVOLVEMENT IN SECONDARY SCHOOLS

The first three chapters in this part provide an indepth overview of new models of vocational education (Chapter 5) and career development theories (Chapter 6), and a review of the intent of the School-to-Work Opportunities Act (Chapter 7). Chapter 5 is important reading because Cobb and Neubert develop the goals of vocational education, supporting legislation, and current practices in secondary vocational education. School-based learning practices, including tech-prep programs, career pathways, and career academies, are discussed, as are work-based learning approaches. Work-based learning approaches include cooperative work experiences, youth apprenticeships, and school-based enterprises. Activities that link school- and work-based learning activities also are emphasized.

Chapter 6 provides an overview of career development theories and concepts that form the underlying framework for the transition practices introduced in this text. The ecological model of career development that is introduced by Szymanski includes the interaction of the student in all aspects of planning an effective transition program. Chapter 7 describes several levels of transition services that may be considered when developing a comprehensive transition system. In his chapter, Siegel discusses full engagement in one's community as the primary outcome of providing students the opportunity to be architects of their futures as opposed to being tracked into selected, narrowly defined outcomes.

Importantly, this text introduces new knowledge that has emerged over a relatively short time period (principally from 1985 to the present). In particular, topics related to planning and delivering secondary education and transition services (Chapter 8), involving students in transition planning and program implementation (Chapter 9), including families (Chapter 10), and assessing student outcomes (Chapter 11) are highlighted. These four chapters, as well as the remaining chapters in *Beyond High School,* are based on research that has focused on students with disabilities. As stated earlier, however, the chapter authors have attempted to review available research in search of generalizations that may be made to *all students* who form a larger network of youth who aspire to become meaningfully involved in their communities.

In Chapter 8, Kohler introduces a consumer-oriented paradigm that represents a major shift away from disability-focused, deficit-driven programs toward an educational approach that is based on abilities, options, and self-determination. This paradigm consists of five categories of effective transition-focused practices, including (a) student-focused planning, (b) student development, (c) interagency and interdisciplinary collaboration, (d) family involvement, and (e) program structures and attributes. Important roles for educators are described.

Chapter 9 provides one of the clearer treatments of why student involvement in transition planning is important. After reviewing the history of student involvement in transition, Wehmeyer overviews the benefits of involving students in the major educational decisions that are intended to benefit them. Chapter 10 introduces the reader to practices that are recommended to improve family-school relationships, including reciprocal family education, cultural sensitivity, personal futures planning, and including families in the planning of their children's transition over time. Further, Hanley-Maxwell, Pogoloff, and Whitney-Thomas discuss historical and current family relationships that support the strategies introduced.

Surprisingly, very little has been written about transition assessment and evaluation. In the context of our larger discussion of adolescents and high schools, assessment is introduced to provide the reader with an overview of the procedures that should be used to collect data on students to make decisions about these students in relation to their careers. In addition, evaluation also refers to the process that we undertake to better understand how effective programs are in providing services. Thurlow and Elliott (Chapter 11) offer a broad overview of the purposes of assessment, discussing GEDs and entrance and certification exams. These authors also provide a broader framework for facilitating comprehensive transition assessment and evaluation.

LINKAGES TO WORK AND POSTSECONDARY EDUCATION

Chapter 12 (Everson and Guillory) reviews practices that state, regional, and local-level interagency teams should consider when attempting to build statewide transition services using a network of collaborative interagency teams. Included in this chapter is an overview of the concepts of collaborative, interagency, and team-based service models and ten guidelines for teams to use when implementing a collaborative interagency team-based model. On an individual, personal level, Menchetti and Piland (Chapter 13) illustrate the use of Personal Career

Planning when considering an individual's preferences, goals, and strengths in relation to local employment opportunities. The Personal Career Plan integrates the values and methods of person-centered planning processes described throughout this text with a profile approach to vocational evaluation and assessment that may be used by schools, community rehabilitation facilities, adult education, and other employment service providers.

Emphasizing the importance of relevant, personalized experiences for our youth, Chapter 14 reviews the background and rationale for school-sponsored work experience and examines work experience programs currently prevalent in secondary education. In addition, Hagner and Vander Sande outline considerations for implementing a successful work experience program along with specific job support and instructional components.

Despite advocacy in recent decades for the importance of student support in the transition between school and work, the dismal outcomes facing many adolescents on leaving high school attest to the failure of current models to provide such support. Until recently, little consensus has existed on best practices to support the transition from school to adult life. However, as we have seen in other chapters of this text, applied research is increasingly offering some insight into critical factors that affect successful student outcomes, including paid work experiences during high school, parent involvement, network of family and friends, employment skills training, and so on. Using a practitioner-oriented approach, Hughes and Kim in Chapter 15 present an empirically based, socially validated model of support and illustrate its application through a case study.

Although the major focus in this text has been on the needs of students who do not pursue postsecondary education, it is important to recognize that the number of students with disabilities enrolling in postsecondary education programs, including college, university, vocational and technical school settings, is growing at a faster rate than for nondisabled students. However, services and programs have not kept pace with the needs of this population. After a historical review of postsecondary education for students with disabilities, including legal and legislative mandates, Gajar discusses current practice in general, as well as the characteristics and services cited as necessary for specific disability populations. Despite the success of many students with disabilities in postsecondary environments, many who choose this avenue in their transition to adulthood face inappropriate services and an absence of knowledgeable transition specialist. Chapter 16 concludes with a set of recommended practices, including the need for research, self-advocacy training, training of service providers, and linkages between secondary and postsecondary settings.

It is generally agreed that social interactions and relationships with others are central to happiness and, hence, quality of life. As we approach the final chapter of this text on how to prepare adolescents for employment, a better quality of life and lifelong learning, it becomes clear that no model program, no intervention, is effective without the underlying component of social integration. In Chapter 17, Chadsey and Shelden propose an ecological framework for social inclusion that not only looks to change the individual with the disability, but also involves the environment and others in the environment as part of the intervention focus. A general discussion of social inclusion as an outcome of transition is followed by descriptions of social inclusion in both postsecondary school and employment settings. Finally, based on current intervention studies, a series of recommended practices are offered within the three categories that constitute the ecological framework: individual interventions—those designed to change the individual with the disability; peer interventions—those intended to change others; and contextual interventions—those designed to change the environment or social activities.

Frank R. Rusch
Janis G. Chadsey

PART I

Introduction to Transition

1

⊡

Characteristics of Youth and Young Adults

STEPHEN LICHTENSTEIN

With the goal of achieving a better understanding of the nature and characteristics of youth and young adults with and without disabilities, this chapter examines the literature surrounding adolescent development with special concern for the social ecology and psychology of this age group. Further, the chapter examines the processes and related forces that come to bear on young people. Whereas society has predominantly focused on the differences between adolescents with and without disabilities, the premise of this chapter is that youth and young adults with disabilities are more alike than dissimilar to their peers without a disability. Understanding the pressures and forces confronting youth and their reactions to these influences is critical for the development of strategies to support youth in their education and transition to employment and/or further education in the larger community.

Moving from childhood, through adolescence, to adult life is a transition all people experience with varying degrees of achievement and challenges. As educators and prospective educators, we often ignore the forces that come to bear on our youth and young adults during this period commonly known as "adolescence." Perhaps one reason for the relative absence of attention is that adolescence has often been "viewed as a transitional period between childhood and adulthood rather than as a period of interest in its own right" (Kazdin, 1993:127).

Although it is well documented that this period is a dynamic one, it is a gross oversimplification to assume that it is predictable and easily understood. For this reason and many others, Elliott and Feldman (1990) argue that adolescence is "a confusing blend of the familiar and the unexplored" (p. 1).

The topic of adolescence is rarely linked with opportunities for positive development and outcomes. The majority of the literature and studies, past and present, tend to draw our attention to at-risk behaviors exhibited by youth and young adults (Chang, 1992). Thus, the literature on the high-risk characteristics of adolescents outnumbers books and articles on the positive outcomes by a staggering proportion. For example, all too often, adolescence is characterized in terms of "great vulnerability and turbulence" (Lightfoot, 1983:342) and "juvenile delinquency" (Aseltine & Gore, 1993:247; Feldman & Weinberger, 1994:195). These portrayals say a lot about the current state of affairs with regard to adolescents in our society, but they are also a confession of our inability to understand and empathize with youth (even though all of us have passed through this phase in our lives). Recently, the period has received renewed attention from educators and the research community.

It is probably safe to say that whereas some youth find adolescence difficult, a high proportion, perhaps the majority, do not. Happily, most of the troubles commonly associated with growing up are transient (Schorr, 1988). Even when there is difficulty, problems do not necessarily assume the dire proportions cited in the media (Simmons, 1987). More often than not, our perceptions of adolescents are clouded by reports in the media emphasizing the high rates of violent juvenile crime, school failure, substance abuse, and adolescent childbearing (Schorr, 1988). For adolescents, "The overemphasis on their problematic dimensions of life," according to ethnographer Heewon Chang (1992), "tends to destroy their image as human beings" (p. 3) who are capable of great achievements. The juxtaposition of risk, opportunity, and dynamic change has distracted us and has limited our ability to meet the extraordinary challenges inherent in growing up in our society.

In this chapter, we will examine the literature surrounding adolescent development with special concern for the social ecology and psychology of adolescence. In this examination of the processes and related forces that come to bear on young people, it is my premise that, unless otherwise stated, youth and young adults with disabilities are like any others their age

without a disability. Understanding the pressures and forces confronting youth and their reactions to these influences is critical to the development of strategies to support youth in their education and employment as well as their status in the larger community.

BRINGING CLARITY TO THE PERIOD KNOWN AS "ADOLESCENCE"

Definitions describing adolescence are elusive. One reason is that this crucial transitional period from childhood to adulthood is now very different from what it was in the past. According to David Hamburg (1993), president of the Carnegie Corporation, "the time between childhood and adulthood has grown longer, and the outcomes are less clear. The requirements, risks, and opportunities of this period are now highly ambiguous for most adolescents" (p. 467). One example of the changing times can be found in an examination of how youth select careers. At one time, youth were expected to enter the family business or trade at a young age (or perhaps be apprenticed to a master tradesperson). Today, youth are expected to further their education beyond high school and choose a career that is both fulfilling and economically rewarding. Complicating the process by which young adults transition to adulthood, according to Koenigsburg, Garet, and Rosenbaum (1994), is that it "occurs in different orders and times for females and males and varies for individuals of different races and class groups" (pp. 33–34).

According to a number of scholars in the field, adolescence is a stage of life that is distinct from both childhood or adulthood (Elliott & Feldman, 1990). Ruby Takanishi, executive director of the Carnegie Council on Adolescent Development (1993), portrayed adolescence as a "period of life typically associated with great risk" (p. 460). It is during this time that certain outcomes need to be achieved, among them becoming physically and sexually mature, acquiring skills needed to carry out adult roles, gaining increased autonomy from parents, and realigning social interconnections with members of both the same and the opposite sex (Paul & White, 1990; Furman & Wehner, 1994). In addition, our society places powerful expectations on the adolescent that shape some of these outcomes—for example, by encouraging extended education and postponing an early marriage and entry into the workplace (Elliott & Feldman, 1990).

In modern societies and, in particular, our own, the transition from adolescence to adulthood is defined by an individual's standing in "several different social systems, including education, the family, the economy, and the political/legal system " (Pallas, 1993:412–413). Often, being an adult hinges on multiple roles that individuals perform, for example, as student or nonstudent, worker or nonworker, spouse, or parent. Adolescence as a distinct stage of life, according to Pallas (1993), is defined by a "variety of mechanisms, among them compulsory schooling, child labor laws that regulate when and how one might enter the work force, and a separate juvenile justice system that mandates legal consequences for criminal acts partly on the basis of age" (p. 413). These and other social forces plainly define adolescents as "not adults"; yet neither are they children (p. 413).

Perhaps the most distinctive feature of adolescence is the change that is brought about by puberty. For youth and young adults, the timing of puberty and the timing sequence of sexual maturation are comparable (Schwab, 1995). Nevertheless, a quick glance at middle school students suggests that the onset of puberty is marked by wide variations in timing for the age group.

> Biological changes of puberty transform the size and shape of young people's bodies and evoke new, initially strange feelings. These changes are accompanied by changes in social life: after many years of relatively little interest in the opposite sex, boys and girls begin to find each other attractive, and their interactions with peers and with close friends. (Cole & Cole, 1993:569)

Maturing sexually, becoming increasingly aware of the world around us, beginning to engage in complex reasoning, and dramatically expanding our knowledge of ourselves all occur during this adolescence. "These and many other factors," according to Elliott and Feldman (1990), "foster an urge in them to gain control over how and with whom they spend their time" (p. 4).

WHAT DISTINGUISHES ADOLESCENTS FROM CHILDREN AND ADULTS?

Although adolescence is referred to as a stage of life distinct from either childhood or adulthood, Powell, Farrar, and Cohen (1985) argued that adolescents

> are more like adults than like young children. They have lived long enough, grown enough, and learned enough to express actively the distinct personalities they will possess the rest of their lives. Even more than young children they have minds, feelings, and wills of their own. (p. 2)

It is during adolescence, more so than childhood, that young people "are more involved and intimate with peers, increasingly sharing thoughts and feelings" (Petersen, 1988:600). Their relationship with their parents, though still important, is changing to reflect one of independence and autonomy. Changing relationships with parents and peers and the increasing pursuit of education, employment, and greater consumerism place adolescents squarely on a path to adulthood.

One of the stronger urges felt during adolescence, according to Chang (1992), is the desire to be "treated like adults, rather than children" (p. 126). Young people's conception of adulthood is one in which they exercise "the final word" and assume a level of power and independence. In her study of a typical American high school in Oregon, Chang (1992) found that adolescents preferred the status of adults to that of the child, favoring the label "young adult" (p. 126). Chang (1992) told the story of one young woman who felt comfortable around her father, but did not enjoy being around her mother, who did not trust her judgment. The young woman described a situation as follows:

> This past weekend I went to a gun show with my dad. I had a feeling of freedom. As long as I stayed with the basic rules and asked permission when I wanted out, I could rule my own life. I could eat, sleep, and wander as I wished when my duties were done. This is what it's like with my father. ... Now, my mother—I am very subdued around my mother. She yells a lot and everything is my fault. (p. 127)

DEFINING THE PERIODS OF ADOLESCENCE

The period of adolescence, according to Elliott and Feldman (1990), now extends over so many years that it can be subdivided into early, middle, and late substages. Despite differing conceptions of adolescence in the life span of individuals, in most Western cultures adolescence is now viewed as extending roughly from age 10 or 11 through the late teens and even into the early 20's (Levinson et al., 1978; Elliott & Feldman, 1990). In recent decades, it has been characterized as a time of relative freedom, during which the principal social duty is acquiring an education. The prolonged period of adolescence, according to Pallas (1993), can be partly explained by "the tremendous growth of institutions of higher education in the U.S. in the twentieth century, coupled with the affordability and convenience of long-distance travel" (p. 415), which has resulted in many more youth going away to school. This temporary postpone-

ment of assuming adult roles also creates a distinct subculture of higher socioeconomic young adults who are able to defer adult decision making in favor of increased freedom, exploration, and experimentation.

Most researchers now recognize the following substages of adolescence as *early*, *middle*, and *late*. These substages are depicted in Table 1.1.

In a contrasting view to substages, Yale University's Daniel J. Levinson and colleagues (1978) created an earlier and alternative conceptualization of adolescence by adopting a "life cycle," or seasons-of-our-lives, approach to studying adulthood (males in particular). They viewed both childhood and adolescence as a "formative phase" in preparation for the adult years that follow. Levinson and colleagues' main focus was on the years from late teens to the late 40's among males. Their belief is that "the life cycle evolves through a sequence of eras each lasting roughly twenty-five years" (p. 18). An era is not a stage in development, but a much broader and more inclusive framework. The transition between eras consistently takes 4 or 5 years; not less than 3 and rarely more than 6. Although eras often overlap, the sequence goes as follows:

1. Childhood and adolescence (preadulthood): age 0–22
2. Early adulthood: age 17–45
3. Middle adulthood: age 40–65
4. Late adulthood: age 60–?

Although important changes go on across each era, there are distinctive and unifying qualities of each era that take into account biological, psychological, and social aspects in a holistic manner. Levinson and colleagues (1978) were strongly influenced by the Spanish philosopher José Ortega y Gasset's conception of generations in the history of society. Ortega y Gasset took a broad historical-philosophical view of human life over the last 2,500 years and identified a unique sequence of five generations (Levinson et al., 1978). The salient difference between the sequences of Ortega y Gasset's and those of

Table 1.1 Substages, Ages, and Characteristics of Early, Middle, and Late Adolescence

Stage	Ages	Characteristics
Early adolescence	10 to 14	Typically encompasses the profound physical (e.g., height, weight, reproductive-system development) and social changes (relationships with others, including friends and family; social activities, dating) that occur with puberty, as maturation begins and social interactions become increasingly centered on members of the opposite sex (Elliott & Feldman, 1990; Kazdin, 1993).
		This period has been described as a time of emotional reorientation to the peer group and increasing detachment from the family (Raffaelli & Duckett, 1989). However, although early adolescents want many friends, they still need their families for psychological support, even though the helplessness of childhood has passed (Kagan, 1971).
		It is also a time when gender-role expectations become intensified, "leading to increasing gender differences in social relationships" (Raffaelli & Duckett, 1989:568).
Middle adolescence	15 to 17	Typically, a time of increasing independence; for a significant fraction of American youth, it also marks the end of adolescence (Elliott & Feldman, 1990; Kazdin, 1993).
		Harter (1990), best known for her work on social development and self-concept, reports that most "research studies reveal that during middle adolescence the difference between one's ideal and one's actual self is larger than in early or late adolescence" (p. 360).
		Hauser and Bowlds (1990) report that studies on middle adolescence speak to "the mounting pressure to conform and the heightened temptations to experiment in risky areas" (p. 393).
		Raffaelli and Duckett (1989) report that "Studies of older adolescents find differences in both the amount of time spent talking, and what is discussed with family and friends. ... Topics discussed with parents and friends ... differ; conversations with parents are described as serious and goal-oriented, while conversations with peers are both more lighthearted and more intimate" (p. 568). According to Raffaelli and Duckett (1989), "adolescents use family members and friends to fulfill different needs in their lives" (p. 580).
Late adolescence	18 to mid–20's	Typically occurs for those individuals who, because of educational goals or other factors, delay their entry into adult roles (Elliott & Feldman, 1990).
		This period extends from high school graduation to entry into one or more adult roles (Baumrind, 1987).
		Torney-Purta (1990) reports that "Adolescents aged 17 to 19 ... recognize differences of opinion among groups in society and participate in political discussion" (p. 469). Their ability to resolve contradictions and their advanced cognitive skills allow them to interpret diverse reasoning and opinions more so than in earlier stages of adolescence.

(continued)

Table 1.1   (continued)

Stage	Ages	Characteristics
Late adolescence	18 to mid–20's	According to Paul and White (1990), "late adolescence is typically a time of progress in both identity and intimacy resolution" (p. 379). It is during this stage of adolescence that the individual is more independent and future-oriented in decision making, conflict resolution, and problem solving.

Levinson and colleagues (1978) is that Ortega y Gasset differentiated childhood (age 0–15) from youth (age 15–30) and created two separate generational markers.

According to Levinson and colleagues' conceptualization, extraordinary growth is occurring during the first 25 years as a prelude to adulthood. The major milestones are the birth of the child, the development of the infant into a unique individual, and the child's realization that other people have an enduring existence and character. As time passes, the child grows up and expands his social connections from the immediate family to a larger world that involves school, peer group, and community. The transition from middle childhood to adolescence begins at puberty (usually at age 12 or 13). According to Levinson's life-cycle approach, adolescence is the culmination of the preadult era. The period from 17 to 22 years of age is called "Early Adult Transition" and provides a bridge from adolescence to early adulthood. Given its unique status as a cross-era transition, it is considered a crucial turning point in the life cycle. The growing male is a "boy–man," establishing himself as an adult and making choices through which he makes his place in the adult world.

Their conceptualization rooted in adult development, Levinson and colleagues (1978) believed that the process of entering into adulthood is more lengthy and complex than earlier imagined. Their belief was that a young man needs about 15 years to emerge from adolescence, find his place in adult society, and commit himself to a more stable life. Early Adult Transition presents two major challenges or tasks to achieve. One challenge is to terminate adolescence and leave the preadult world. According to Levinson and colleagues (1978), "a young man has to question the nature of that world and his place in it" (p. 73). Numerous separations, losses, and transformations are required to make this transition. The second challenge is to make a preliminary step into the adult world. This requires an initial exploration of adult possibilities, discovering one's place in the adult world, and making and testing some choices before fully entering it. The first challenge involves a process of termination, the second a process of initiation. Both are considered essential in a transitional period.

THE SOCIAL ECOLOGY OF ADOLESCENCE

Adolescence does not occur in isolation of other factors. It is strongly determined by environmental and individual characteristics present prior to and during this time (Irwin, 1987). Therefore, to best explain adolescent development, we need to study biological, psychological, and social contributors (and their interdependence). Through the study of social ecology, we are able to see the young person "in the context of all the various settings they inhabit on a daily basis" (Cole & Cole, 1993:24).

An ecological approach allows us to get a sense of the whole person and the many influences that act on the individual. According to Irwin (1987), "Serious misrepresentation of adolescence has occurred and will continue to occur if these multiple contexts are not clarified" (p. 8).

The ecological approach teaches us about forces that exert the greatest pressure on youth and young adults and how circumstances might be promoted or modified to foster their positive development (Lesar, Trivette, & Dunst, 1995). Yale University psychologist Alan E. Kazdin (1993) commented that

The emergence of puberty; the impact of maturation on self-esteem, family, and peer relations; parent responses to the emergence of adolescent autonomy; and changes in family life (e.g., parent separation, divorce) that may impact the adolescent are a few of the areas of study essential to understanding adolescent development and adjustment. (p. 138)

One of the more intriguing ecological studies of adolescents, conducted in 1984, was the work of Csikszentmihalyi and Larson (1984), who equipped high schoolers from Chicago with electronic pagers and had them report on what they were doing whenever the beeper went off. Average adolescents in the study divided their activities among schoolwork, maintenance activities, and leisure pursuits. Leisure activities consumed about 40 percent of their waking hours, with the largest proportion devoted to socializing with friends. Not so surprising are the findings that youth and young adults do not devote as much time to schoolwork.

Figure 1.1 and the following sections provide a glimpse into some of the more pressing ecological influences on adolescence, which provide both risks and opportunities.

The Pursuit of Independence

"The transition from adolescence to adulthood in modern societies," according to Pallas (1993),

"involves several interrelated events and role changes" (pp. 412–413). Foremost on the list of major changes for adolescents is the search for independence and the struggle for autonomy. Although elusive in definition, adolescence is often defined as a state of dependency. This dependency takes the form of reliance on parents and the larger family for economic, social, and emotional support. It is in this transition from adolescence to adulthood that dependence gives way to independence.

Chang (1992), in her study of the American high school culture, captured five symbolic markers that signify movement to independence for modern-day adolescents: getting a job, raising funds for activities, being allowed to drive a car, moving away from home, and relying more on peer interactions than on adult authority. "Being independent," in the context of adolescence, according to Chang (1992), is to be taken seriously, to enjoy more freedom, and social privilege. This is a dramatic departure from previous conceptions of independence. The transition to adulthood during earlier periods in our history was "determined directly by family needs, rather than by a more abstract set of social norms governing when children should begin working or leave home" (Pallas, 1993:414). Children were obligated to "contribute to the household through productive work, until they left to start their own families" (Pallas, 1993:414).

"Much more so than in earlier times," according to Elliott and Feldman (1990), "youth seem to be instrumental in molding their own lives." Perhaps nowhere is this more apparent than with one of the more contemporary benchmarks of independence, getting a driver's license. "Obtaining driver's licenses," according to Chang (1992), "changed not only teenagers' life-styles but also patterns of family life" (p. 136). The direct role of the family in moderating current activities and companions, let alone future careers and life-styles, has been greatly reduced" (p. 4). In fact, in the current picture, adolescents often resent the intrusion of their

FIGURE 1.1 Ecological Influences on Adolescence

parents, especially when it pertains to exercising their own judgment. However, the family's significance remains strong as an economic support and as a pivotal factor in career decisions, whereas its role in other areas declines during adolescence (Petersen, Leffert, & Hurrelmann, 1993).

Sometimes, in the case of adolescents with disabilities, parents consciously or unconsciously thwart attempts at independence by being overprotective to the point of promoting childlike behaviors and dependency (Hobart, 1995). The result may seriously impact the young person's self-esteem and search for his or her own identity and natural expressions of independence. Hobart (1995) reported the story of a young adolescent whose parents sought her opinion "because their son had not spoken or listened to them for some months. They were afraid this was some kind of incomprehensible Down syndrome behavior" (p. 41). During discussions with the parents,

the boy went into the next room, and a social worker asked him to help make photocopies that were needed right away. The boy had been treated as if he were a competent adult, and he responded with great efficiency. What is more, he had a long conversation with the social worker, all to the great surprise of the parents. Three years have gone

by since that day, and the young man, who turned out to be very creative in the kitchen, is now writing a cookbook. (p. 41)

Relationships with Parents

It is common knowledge that parents and the family play a critical role in children's academic achievement as well as in their emotional development (Eccles & Harold, 1993). Nevertheless, as children grow into adolescents they seek to establish their own personal identity distinct from their parents and family (Erikson, 1968). Although researchers appreciate the family's powerful impact on adolescent development, how that passage is influenced by family structure and dynamics has not been adequately studied. With the exception of some poignant personal accounts of parents who have young adult children with disabilities, few studies have systematically examined this issue (Greenfeld, 1986; Kaufman, 1988; Kingsley & Levitz, 1994). What is known is that the issues of overprotection, uncertainty surrounding transition from school to adult life, and fear surrounding self-sufficiency and relationships with others often take center stage.

The picture of the family and parental influence has changed dramatically in recent decades (Hanson & Carta, 1995). Over a relatively short time frame, the family and its ability to support and provide guidance has significantly changed. Sweeping changes in the structure of families and competing demands on parents (e.g., employment outside the home) have reshaped how parents relate to their young adult children and vice versa. "Families as social systems," according to Petersen and colleagues (1993), "have become highly susceptible to disturbance, mainly because of an increasing instability in marriage, which is the social heart of the family's relationships" (p. 612). Despite this depiction, family relationships remain the adolescents' emotional and social "home port" (Petersen et al., 1993:612).

In contrast with just two or three decades ago, "today's families are relatively small units of only a few members; increasingly they are households of one or two persons" (Petersen et al., 1993:612). Over the same period of time, Hamburg (1993) found remarkable patterns of change in contact between children and their family. "Not only are their mothers home much less," according to Hamburg (1993),

> but there is very little evidence nationwide of increased time spent by fathers at home to compensate. The general picture across the country is one of mother gone, father gone, and grandparents not there either. The Norman Rockwell family of breadwinner father, mother working at home, and two children now constitutes just 6 percent of all American families. (p. 468)

These demographic features of the family and the steadily declining involvement of parents (and grandparents) during middle and high school years challenge our beliefs about the importance of the nuclear family in providing important safeguards and direction as youth mature into adulthood.

Parent-adolescent relations play a powerful role in young people's choice of pathways in their later teens. In numerous cases, the literature on parent-adolescent relations "viewed severe conflict as normative and the severing of adolescent's relationships with parents as the desirable goal (Steinberg, 1990, cited in Zaslow

& Takanishi, 1993). This popular perception, according to Steinberg (1990), has been challenged and rejected in light of new findings. Although parent-adolescent conflict has been found to increase in early adolescence (Eccles & Harold, 1993), severe conflict has been observed in a small minority of families, and better adjusted adolescents describe greater closeness with their parents (Steinberg, 1990, cited in Zaslow & Takanishi, 1993). In fact, "a variety of researchers have suggested that parent-adolescent relations continue to serve ... a secure base from which adolescents can independently explore and master new environments" (Paterson, Pryor, & Field, 1995:366).

The concept of self-esteem is critical to our understanding of adolescence, because it is a crucial index of mental health and performance (Harter, 1990). Higher self-esteem has been linked to happiness and satisfaction, whereas lower self-esteem has been linked to depression, anxiety, and maladjustment (Cole & Cole, 1993). Research has consistently shown that adolescent attachment to parents is more strongly related to positive growth in self-esteem than attachment to peers (Paterson et al., 1995). In fact, Smith (cited in Nada Raja, McGee, & Stanton, 1992:472) reported that in important situations where values and decisions about the future were required, adolescents were more likely to seek the counsel of their parents rather than that of their peers. Continuing with this theme of parent (and adult) involvement, Gilligan (1987), reporting on the research of Youniss and Smollar (1985), suggested that

> adolescents fare better in situations where adults listen and that mothers and teachers are centrally important in teenagers' lives. Mothers are the parent with whom adolescents typically have the most contact, the one they talk with the most and perceive as knowing most about their lives. Most researchers consider it desirable for fathers to be more involved with adolescents, but they find, in general, that fathers do not spend as

much time or talk as personally with their teenage children. (p. 82)

The importance of mothers and fathers on adolescents' well-being is undeniable; however, relationships with friends appear to be more important for the development of social competence and intimacy (Elliott & Feldman, 1990).

Relationships with Peers

Central to this period of adolescent change is the dynamic nature of interpersonal relationships (Elliott & Feldman, 1990; Cole & Cole, 1993). The establishment of healthy relations with peers and the development of a sense of emotional well-being, security, and intimacy become increasingly important (Paul & White, 1990; Newman, 1991; Chang, 1992; Bukowski, Hoza, & Boivin, 1993). Research has consistently demonstrated that the "strength of adolescent relationships to best friends and peers increases in importance while relationships to either parent decreases over the adolescent decade of life" (Petersen et al., 1993:613). This particular transformation is characteristically associated with adolescence and serves as a "critical interpersonal bridge that moves them toward psychological growth and social maturity" (Savin-William & Berndt, 1990:277).

At the same time that family relationships are in flux, it is one of the developmental markers of adolescence to become increasingly involved with close friends, peers, and others beyond the family. Because "most adolescents did not want to be social loners" (Chang, 1992:115), adolescents typically strive to establish close relationships as a source of security and to help them sort through complex issues of independence, identity, and intimacy (Paul & White, 1990). According to the research conducted by Wagner and her colleagues (Wagner, 1991a) through the National Longitudinal Transition Study (NLTS),

The need to establish relationships with same-sex and opposite-sex peers is no different for youth with disabilities than for their peers without disabilities. Yet previous research has found that youth with disabilities often have problems developing satisfactory social lives and frequently spend their time at home alone. Even those with milder disabilities are often thought to need help with learning about appropriate social interactions. (p. 6-2)

Findings from the NLTS study suggest considerable variation in the frequency with which youth with disabilities were seeing friends (Wagner, 1991a). They found that "a majority of secondary school students with disabilities were socially connected to friends ... a small proportion (14%) of students ... never see friends outside of school or see them less than once a week" (Wagner, 1992b:6-4). Variations were considerable, "ranging from 9% of youth with learning disabilities to 65% of youth who were deaf/blind. Students classified as multiple handicapped (44%) joined those classified as deaf/blind as the least socially involved with friends. Further, youth classified as mentally retarded or visually, orthopedically, or other health impaired were significantly less likely to visit with friends than youth with learning disabilities" (p. 6-5). These variations are very telling of the "limiting influence of more severe disabilities" (Wagner, 1992b:6-5).

The value associated with adolescent peer relations comes from its enormous impact on development. For example, the refinement of interpersonal skills, such as "intimacy, empathy, trust, and cooperation ... develop in the crucible of close relationships with peers" (Greenberger & Steinberg, 1986:218). "Peer groups are important," according to Petersen and colleagues (1993), "in that they offer equal opportunity for participation to their members, which family or school do not provide to the same extent." Friendships and acquaintances allow adolescents "a high degree of autonomy, spontaneity, creativity, and individuality" (Petersen et al., 1993:613), all traits considered important to personal development. Newman (1991) noted that "Young people look to peers to validate self-concepts and to provide behavior models.

Through interactions with friends, youth explore roles and learn social skills that help them make effective transitions to adult roles and responsibilities" (p. 6–3). Further, Newman (1991) cited the results of the *High School and Beyond* study by illustrating her point: "Among sophomores … more than 98% felt that having strong friendships was important to their lives" (p. 6–3).

High Schools and Adolescents

"To attempt to entice and graduate the entire adolescent population, and ensure that most are somehow the better for it, is a monumental and exhausting task " (Powell et al., 1985:1).

High schools are expected to fulfill a multitude of roles in the lives of teenagers. "Virtually no other social institution, " according to Powell and colleagues (1985), "has the task of serving such matured diversity at the same time and in the same place" (p. 2). Besides the traditional roles in instruction and discipline, high schools are now expected to provide citizenship education, nonacademic activities, and a socialization function (Chang, 1992). It is not uncommon to hear that some students come to school to socialize with friends. This includes students with disabilities, who often have fewer opportunities to meet others their own age. Not only is there a long-term economic incentive to completing one's education, there are also, under one roof, support services, such as counseling and job placement services (Wagner et al., 1992). Nowhere else in the typical community can one find the same offerings and activities available in a high school.

It is well known that changes that occur in the lives of adolescents are influenced by the amount of time that they spend away from home. Adolescents spend more time in high school among their peer group and teachers than anywhere else, including time with their families (Eccles & Harold, 1993). In fact, the average adolescent spends at least 7 hours of each weekday in school or approximately 40 percent of his or her week (Simmons, 1987).

Given this set of circumstances, there is every reason to expect the nature of this environmental or ecological context to be influential to the individual's development (Bronfenbrenner, 1979; Simmons, 1987). Compounding the transition from childhood to adolescence is the "transition out of small, intimate elementary schools into larger and more impersonal schools" (Simmons, 1987:36). This change, although not receiving much attention, provides a compelling backdrop to changes happening from within the individual and among the larger social system. For this reason and more, children with disabilities who were successfully integrated into regular classrooms in elementary school, for example, may find middle and high schools to be more segregated with inflexible rules and policies. Further, this may be at the root of the high dropout rate among students with and without disabilities.

For some children, according to Eccles, Lord, and Midgley (1991), entry into adolescence and middle and high school "marks the beginning of a downward spiral in school-related behavior and motivation that often leads to academic failure and school dropout" (p. 521). Behaviors such as a decline in school achievement, overall interest in school (e.g., test anxiety, learned helpless responses to failure, focus on self-evaluation rather than task mastery, and both truancy), self-concepts and/or self-perceptions, and reduced self-confidence erode overall academic success and emotional well-being. Although these behaviors do not affect all youth, there is ample evidence of gradual decline in various indicators of academic motivation, behavior, and self-perception over the adolescent years to make this a major concern for educators, parents, and the larger community (Lightfoot, 1983; Wellesley College Center for Research on Women, 1992).

High school's major role on later educational and career opportunities is intimately associated with the type of high school program in which students are enrolled. In 1990, more 17-year-olds without disabilities reported enrolling in college preparatory and academic programs than reported in 1982. Correspondingly, the number of students enrolling in vocational education declined from 12 percent in 1982 to 9 percent in 1990 (U.S. Department of Education, 1993). These same patterns do not hold true for students with disabilities who are more likely to be tracked into general programs (noncollege prep courses) and vocational education. Although this may be considered an improvement over segregated special education classes or residential institutions, the outcomes associated with general and vocational education programs may be insufficient for meeting the needs of the twenty-first century job market.

Despite years of high dropout rate, high school completion rates are improving. Nevertheless, approximately one in four American teenagers leave high school before receiving a diploma, and dropout rates are higher for minorities (U.S. Department of Education, 1993). Among minority groups, an estimated 40 percent of Hispanic students leave before finishing high school, and in some urban areas, the dropout rate for blacks is climbing toward 50 percent (Ford Foundation Project on Social Welfare and the American Future, 1989). The Committee on Economic Development stated that in 1987, the one million youngsters who leave high school without graduating will be "marginally literate and virtually unemployed" (cited in Schorr, 1988:8). It is not surprising that dropouts are seven and a half times as likely as graduates to be dependent on welfare and twice as likely to be unemployed and to live in poverty (Schorr, 1988:8).

The U.S. Department of Education (1993) reported that among minority groups, African-American students are staying in school longer, with more completing high school and college. Hispanics complete less school than other groups and only 9 percent of 25- to 29-year-old Hispanics completed 4 years of college or more in 1991 compared with 25 percent of whites. With regard to students with disabilities, "It is not surprising," according to Marden (1992), "that past research has found the educational attainment of youth with disabilities considerably lower than that of youth in general"

(p. 3-1). Compared with their peers without disabilities, youth with disabilities are less likely to graduate from high school (Kortering, Haring, & Klockars, 1992; Lichtenstein, 1993). NLTS found that among youth with disabilities who exited high school in a 2-year period, 37 percent dropped out compared with about 21 percent of youth in the general population (Marden, 1992).

Much like the evolution in our thinking about adolescence, the subject of dropping out has changed over time. Today, it "is the single most dramatic indicator of the degree to which schools are failing children" (National Coalition of Advocates for Students, 1985:xi) and a leading indicator of future economic well-being.

> In 1900, nine out of ten youngsters did not graduate from high school, but there was no high school dropout problem. At mid-century, when as many dropped out as graduated, there was no reason for public concern. ... A young person could become a successful, participating adult by quitting school and going to work, as easily as by remaining in school until graduation. But all that has changed in the high-tech last quarter of the century. Today there is only one way to adult self-sufficiency—the school way. (Schorr, 1988:7)

What might lead students to drop out? Finn (1989) cited the influence of an "impaired self-view" (p. 119) resulting from frustration and embarrassment, all of which contribute to early withdrawal from school. The actual behavior for potential dropouts "may take the form of disrupting the instructional process, skipping class, or even committing delinquent acts" (Finn, 1989:119). Finn (1989) believed that preventing youth from dropping out, therefore, requires the development of a positive self-view. To that end, schools need to find ways for youth to earn respect and nurture positive self-esteem, reliable and close relationships, a sense of belonging in a valued group, and a sense of usefulness in some way beyond the self (Finn, 1989; Hamburg, 1989). A more detailed discussion of dropouts and dropout prevention is presented in Chapter 4.

The Expanding Role of Work for Adolescents

Work is an expected part of being an adult in our society and fulfills an important rite of passage for adolescents as they approach adulthood. In fact, adolescence is well recognized as a crucial developmental period in the formation of work-related orientations, career and vocational development, and the development of work identity (Erikson, 1963; Mortimer et al., 1990). It has been said that "until young people can participate in adult work ... they will not gain adult status" (Cole & Cole, 1993:601).

Recent legislative initiatives, such as the School-to-Work Opportunities Act of 1994, have promoted the need for youth and young adults to "acquire the knowledge, skills, abilities, and labor market information they need to make a smooth and effective transition from school to career-oriented work or to further education or training" (*Federal Register*, 1994:5266). For most youth, work experience and the acquisition of knowledge and skills come in the form of jobs held while still in high school. In fact, the rate of employment for American youth and young adults is reported to be the highest in the Western world. The concept of work for youth and young adults in our culture is interwoven with our belief in the "value of hard work, getting ahead, and financial success" (Phillips & Sandstrom, 1990).

In contrast with past generations, the current generation of youth and young adults combine employment and schooling quite freely (Steele, 1991).

According to census data, boys' and girls' employment rates are becoming increasingly similar. In the three decades between 1953 and 1983, the percentage of 16- and 17-year-old boys who were in the labor force while attending school increased from 29 to 36; for girls of the same age, the rate of labor force participation doubled from 18% to 36%. Recent labor force statistics for high school enrollees indicate that 41% of both boys and girls are in the labor force. (Mortimer et al., 1990:203).

Other sources of data suggest even higher levels of employment and a similar profile by gender (Mortimer et al., 1990).

The relationship between high school work experience and later success in the labor force or in college is being debated in the popular press, at school board meetings, and even in the academic literature. The debate centers on the time constraints that are imposed on students who combine school and work. The concern is that jobs held by youth and young adults result in less time devoted to studying and homework, and thus in lowering academic performance and postsecondary education aspirations.

Those who support employment in high school argue that it is complementing educational goals. A number of blue-ribbon commissions hold that employment during high school years enhances behavioral traits in students that can lead to academic success (President's Science Advisory Committee, 1974; Carnegie Commission on Policy Studies in Higher Education, 1980; National Commission on Youth, 1980). Indeed, Powell and colleagues (1985) reported that the President's Science Advisory Committee "argued that schools damaged youth by separating them from work and other realities of adult life" (p. 280).

The empirical evidence related to the effects of work on older high school students suggests that "students who work in excess of 15 to 20 hours per week are absent more often from school, spend less time on homework, and have lower grade point averages" (Lillydahl, 1990:315). The amount of hours worked per week is also related to social class and gender. Cole and Cole (1993) reported that

When teenagers from minority and less advantaged homes find jobs, they tend to work longer hours than middle-class youth. Boys work longer hours than girls. Among boys, sophomores typically work 15 hours a week, while seniors work 21 hours. By comparison, sophomore girls work 11 and senior girls 18 hours a week. Many teenagers work even longer hours during school vacations. (p. 601)

Greenberger and Steinberg (1986) argued that "Extensive part-time employment during the school year may undermine youngsters' education" (p. 6). They also suggested that "teenage employment, instead of fostering respect for work, often leads to increased cynicism about the pleasures of productive labor" (p. 6). These researchers believed that work interferes with the "equally rigorous, but unpaid, work of growing up—work that requires exploration, experimentation, and introspection" (pp. 8–9). In addition to the adolescent development issues, Stern and colleagues (1990) argued that "jobs are usually not related to students' coursework, and there is evidence that this kind of unrelated work experience sometimes actually interferes with students' educational attainment. In short, students are getting more work experience, but less of it is explicitly designed to promote learning" (p. 356). Such findings have fueled debate and further fractionalized groups "for" and "against." Table 1.2 highlights some of these arguments.

The importance of work experience in the lives of students with disabilities is reflected in their high school programs, which have historically featured this option. Thus, high schools have used work experience for students with disabilities as a way to accommodate their functional abilities, promote a smoother transition to adult employment, and as a means of excluding them from schools that have not offered appropriate and suitable coursework to meet their unique educational needs. Within the field of special education, experts continue to place high value on work experience for high school youth and young adults with disabilities (Hasazi,

Gordon, & Roe, 1985; Hasazi et al., 1989; D'Amico, 1991). According to the NLTS study, students with disabilities gain work experience during secondary school, both sponsored by the school and through their own initiative. Findings suggest that 15 percent of students with disabilities in grades 7 through 11 had had work-study jobs, and more than half (56 percent) had had paid jobs of some kind, a rate comparable to that for students without disabilities (D'Amico, 1991).

Extracurricular and Leisure-Time Pursuits

Almost every high school in the United States offers some type of extracurricular activity. Examples include music, academic clubs, and sports. These activities offer opportunities for students to develop the values of teamwork, individual and group responsibility, physical strength and endurance, a sense of community, and enjoyment of leisure time. When structured accordingly, extracurricular activities provide a valuable outlet for reinforcing the lessons learned in the classroom, applying academic skills in a real-world context, and thus may be considered part of a well-rounded education (U.S. Department of Education, 1995b:2).

"An extracurriculum," according to Powell and colleagues (1985), " … is an integral part of the educational program, an often indispensable way to attach students to something that makes them feel successful" (p. 125). It is this component of a student's educational career that may provide an important mechanism for school engagement, especially for those youth and young adults who may feel estranged from their education because of academic and social challenges. In fact, recent research, cited by the U.S. Department of Education (1995b), suggests that participation in extracurricular activities may increase students' sense of engagement or attachment to their school, and thereby decrease the likelihood of school failure and dropping out. If, indeed, participation in extracurricular activities can contribute to success in school, then the

Table 1.2 Arguments "For" and "Against" Youth and Young Adult Employment

Arguments In Favor of Youth and Young Adult Employment
- Provides a means for independent financial support (Pallas, 1993).
- Plays a substantial role in vocational development (Mortimer et al., 1990).
- Improves socialization to work roles (e.g., development of individual maturity and responsibility, enhanced knowledge of available career options, more realistic educational and career aspirations) (Steele, 1991:420).
- Improves educational performance and skill retention during high school (Steele, 1991:420).
- Enhances postsecondary educational and career attainment (Steele, 1991:420).
- Steinberg and his colleagues reported that part-time employment during high school was associated with increased knowledge about the world of work, a more mature individual work orientation, and increased self-reliance (reported by Steele, 1991:421).
- D'Amico (1991) reported that working during high school was not associated with differences in class rank and that moderate levels of work actually increased the probability of high school completion for nonwhite males (Steele, 1991:421).
- The Carnegie Council on Policy Studies in Higher Education (1979) proposed that a combination of school and work would make education more relevant to high school students.
- Builds character and teaches youngsters what "real life" is about (Phillips & Sandstrom, 1990).
- Presumed to teach young people to become more responsible and self-disciplined and to instruct them in accommodations that must be made in the real world (Phillips & Sandstrom, 1990).

Arguments Against Youth and Young Adult Employment
- Typically does not provide students with on-the-job training that will be useful in adulthood (Cole & Cole, 1993:601).
- Usually does not bring adolescents into contact with many adults (Cole & Cole, 1993:601).
- Usually pays minimum wage and offers no job protection (Cole & Cole, 1993:601).
- Provides few opportunities for advancement (Cole & Cole, 1993:601).
- Tends to be segregated in discrete sections of the labor market (e.g., food service, retail sales, clerical, and manual laboring jobs) (Mortimer et al., 1990; Cole & Cole, 1993:602).
- Teenage job opportunities outside the home are more stereotyped than chores carried out within the family (Mortimer et al., 1990).
- Offers little formal instruction in work-related skills (Cole & Cole, 1993:602).
- Is detrimental to schooling and family life and associated with substance abuse (Greenberger, 1983).
- Associated with higher rates of alcohol and marijuana use (Cole & Cole, 1993:602).
- Associated with being absent more and enjoying school less than classmates who did not work (Cole & Cole, 1993:602).
- Highly segregated by sex, with girls frequently in babysitting and clerical jobs, and boys in a wider range of manual and skilled jobs (Mortimer et al., 1990).
- Though boys have more complex work and receive higher hourly wages, they report more stresses on the job (Mortimer et al., 1990).
- Usually not related to students' educational coursework and may interfere with educational attainment (Stern et al., 1990:356).

availability of these activities to all students of all backgrounds becomes an important factor in providing equal opportunity for success.

For most youth and young adults, high schools fill a critical void by providing a source of fun and recreation, especially in small communities with limited outside opportunities. According to Chang (1992), extracurricular pursuits "granted its participants valuable experiences in self-governing, decision making, and cooperating with others" (p. 40). Students who participate in extracurricular activities gain significant advantages (U.S. Department of Education, 1986), including:

- opportunities for recognition, personal success, and broader experience to widen and complement their academic development;

- the chance to develop intellectual, social, cultural, and physical talents to round out their academic education; and

- the opportunity to extend the boundaries of the classroom by acquiring direct experience with the content and concepts of a particular subject area.

Since 1980, the proportion of typical sophomores participating in academic clubs has increased nearly five percentage points. However, at the same time participation in other extracurricular activities has decreased. For example, there has been a significant decline in the percent of students participating in hobby clubs and musical activities. Athletics remains the most popular activity, with more than half of students participating in both 1980 and 1990 (U.S. Department of Education, 1993). Whereas these facts may be true for students without disabilities, the same cannot be said of students with disabilities, who often do not have the same opportunities due to a physical or cognitive challenge. Thus, their extracurricular outlets are significantly limited or relegated to events that are specifically designed for them as a separate group (i.e., Special Olympics).

The greatest competition to participation in extracurricular activities for adolescents as a whole come from part-time employment (discussed later in this chapter) and television viewing. Young adults spend more time watching TV than any other activity except sleeping (Liebert & Sprafkin, 1988). Other variables such as socioeconomic status (SES) have also been negatively linked with achievement and participation. Lower-SES students were more likely to watch 5 or more hours of TV on school nights and less likely to have high

test scores and extracurricular involvement than high-SES students (U.S. Department of Education, 1993).

For students with disabilities, extracurricular activities may be one of their few outlets for social involvement. Thus, there is an inherent problem associated with most extracurricular activities because they operate within the context of schools. That is, organized extracurricular opportunities and the social involvement that results tend to be less common when students leave school. It is well known that social supports, found through friends and group membership, can be "critical in helping young people cope with their changing world and their new and evolving roles" (Wagner, 1992b:6-1). The NLTS reported that 41 percent of secondary school students with disabilities had belonged to school groups, compared with 21 percent of youth who had been out of school up to 2 years (Wagner, 1992b).

In a study related to extracurricular participation, leisure-time activity and behaviors among children with mental retardation, Evans, Hodapp, and Zigler (1995) concluded that "Leisure-time behaviors are important ... in that they seem particularly influenced by such sociocultural factors as age-role expectations. ... The major finding in this study was that specific leisure-time activities develop along similar sequences for children with and those without mental retardation" (pp. 124–125). The researchers concluded that greater attention needs to be given to training children with mental retardation to perform age-appropriate leisure-time activities. According to these researchers, more interactions and friendships would ensue between children with and without mental retardation if age-appropriate leisure-time activities were taught.

An indication of how sociocultural leisure-time activities are may be found in the survey developed by the researchers. The survey, "Questionnaire of Activities and Interests," incorporated the following leisure-time pursuits by early (ages 13–15) and late adolescence (ages 16–18) (Evans et al., 1995):

Early Adolescence:
Ages 13–15 years

Goes to parties, likes to spend time with friends, participates in organized outings, likes to spend time alone, goes to hair stylist, follows the performance of professional athletes, is extremely interested in grooming, goes to concerts, goes on biking trips, dresses like star or hero (e.g., Madonna/Springsteen), "sneaks" beer.

Late Adolescence: Age
16–18 years

Wants to drive a car, curses, tries smoking, expresses an interest in having children, talks about marriage, goes out on double dates, goes steady.

Risk-Taking Behaviors, Juvenile Crime and Punishment

"Risk-taking behavior," according to Baumrind (1987), "characterizes normal adolescent development" (p. 98). However, she cautioned that it is important to distinguish between normal risk taking and those behaviors that are destructive in nature. Experts in the field agree that

> When teenagers take dangerous risks, they don't always stop after just one. With teenagers, trouble comes in bundles. ... A kid who smokes is more likely to drink, too. This clustering of perilous habits is known as "risk behavior syndrome," and it has changed the way public-health experts look at young people. (Drexler, 1996:10)

Dryfoos (1990) delineated adolescents groups on the basis of the seriousness of at-risk behaviors and estimated that among the approximately 28 million adolescents in the United States, 10 percent (2.8 million) are at very high risk (multiple and serious behaviors); 15 percent (4.2 million) are at high risk (two to three problem behaviors); and 25 percent (7 million) are at moderate risk (one problem behavior). The cumulative percentage of youth at high-to-moderate risk is 50 percent. This understanding of

risk behavior and "bundling" has changed the way interventions are being proposed and implemented. Rather than addressing the risk conditions one by one, strategies are increasingly being developed that consider a more comprehensive approach.

Risk behaviors that are not successfully addressed early in adolescence can escalate to much more serious outcomes and result in involvement with the legal system. Unfortunately, no chapter on adolescence is complete without a discussion of delinquency, criminal activity, and its consequences. It is during adolescence that increased types of delinquent behavior occur, such as substance abuse, that are less prevalent at younger ages (Feldman & Weinberger, 1994). Whereas it has been popular in the press to identify race as the leading indicator of criminal activity in this country, it is actually age that "is a more consistent factor in street crime" (Schorr, 1988:5). According to Northwestern University sociologist Welsley Skogan, "Crime is a young man's game. ... So much so that the peak age for arrests for property crimes is sixteen, and for violent crime, eighteen" (cited in Schorr, 1988:5).

Delinquency and criminal behavior are strongly associated with levels of impulse control and self-restraint, and the tendency to inhibit desires in the interest of promoting positive relations with others (Feldman & Weinberger, 1994). Self-restraint and self-regulation skills are formed as a result of family influences in preadolescence. Research in this area supports the notion that effective parenting practices and good overall family functioning predict a significantly reduced likelihood that boys will engage in such delinquent behavior as carrying weapons, substance abuse, and stealing (Feldman & Weinberger, 1994).

In terms of risk-taking behavior and juvenile crime, youth and young adults with disabilities are similar to their peers without disabilities. The NLTS study (Newman, 1991:6-38) found that, overall, 12 percent of youth with disabilities were reported by parents to have been arrested at some time in their lives. Nine percent of secondary school students with disabilities were reported by parents to have been arrested; the rate was significantly higher for youth who were out of school up to 2 years (19 percent). Much of the arrest rate for youth with disabilities overall can be attributed to youth who were labeled as emotionally disturbed or learning disabled. Almost 20 percent of the youth labeled emotionally disturbed and 9 percent of youth labeled learning disabled who were still in secondary school had been arrested. By the time they had been out of school up to 2 years, almost 35 percent of youth labeled as emotionally disturbed and 21 percent of youth labeled learning disabled had been arrested, compared with approximately 19 percent for out-of-school youth with disabilities as a whole.

For comparison purposes, the NLTS research team calculated the rate of arrest for youth in the general population, ages 15 to 20, using data from the U.S. Department of Labor's National Longitudinal Survey of Youth. The comparisons show that youth with disabilities were significantly more likely to have been arrested than were youth in the general population. However, when demographic differences between youth with disabilities and the general population were accounted for, there was no difference in the arrest rate between youth with disabilities and the comparison group (12 percent vs. 10 percent) (Newman, 1991:6-40).

Poverty

It should come as no surprise that many of our social ills, such as crime and substance abuse, are highly correlated to poverty rates. In fact, according to Schorr (1988), "Poverty is the greatest risk factor of all" (p. 3). "Family poverty," cited Schorr (1988), "is relentlessly correlated with high rates of school-age childbearing, school failure, and violent crime—and with all their antecedents" (p. 3). The Children's Defense Fund (1995a) reported that the number of poor children and youth in the United States in 1993 rose to its highest level in 30 years—15.7 million, despite improvements in the nation's economy. In 1991, about 21 percent of

all children and youth and 56 percent of children and youth in female-headed families (with no husband present) lived in poverty. Poverty rates were relatively higher for minority children and youth. About 46 percent of all African-American children and 40 percent of Hispanic children lived in poverty in 1991. The proportion of poor children coming from female-headed households has risen dramatically, from 24 percent in 1960 to 59 percent in 1991 for all children, and from 29 percent to 83 percent for African-American children (U.S. Department of Education, 1993; Hanson & Carta, 1995).

Poverty is not an irreversible fact of life. Nevertheless, since 1969, child poverty has grown by one-half and poverty among Americans over 65 has declined by one-half. According to Carroll (1996), "The burden of poverty in our society has been shifted from the oldest to the youngest" (p. 15). "Wasting America's Future," a report by the Children's Defense Fund (1995b), found that "American children are twice as likely to be poor as Canadian children, three times as likely to be poor as French children, and seven to 13 times more likely to be poor than German, Dutch and Swedish children" (cited in Carroll, 1996:15).

The NLTS study (Wagner et al., 1991a) "demonstrated that students with disabilities were significantly more likely than students as a whole to be from households with lower incomes and less well-educated parents" (p. 11-7). In addition, they were more likely to be African-American and to come from single-parent families. Wagner and colleagues (1991a) argue that "youth from lower-income households had different kinds and levels of service in school and in the postschool years" (p. 11-7). These differences play themselves out in the amount of time spent in regular education classrooms and the variety of support services and adult services students receive (Wagner et al., 1991:11-7). For example,

49% of youth from households with annual incomes of less than $12,000 had received vocational services in the previous year,

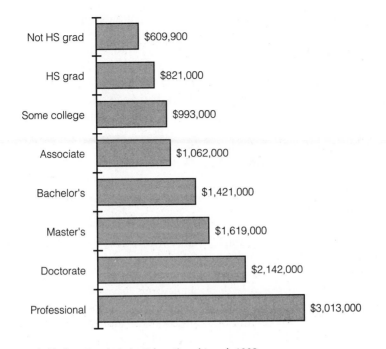

Not HS grad $609,900

HS grad $821,000

Some college $993,000

Associate $1,062,000

Bachelor's $1,421,000

Master's $1,619,000

Doctorate $2,142,000

Professional $3,013,000

FIGURE 1.2 Estimated Lifetime Earnings by Educational Level: 1992

(*Source*: U.S. Department of Commerce, Bureau of the Census, 1994:12).

compared with 58% of youth from households with incomes of $25,000 or more; similarly, figures for occupational therapy were 8% vs. 14%. (Wagner et al., 1991:11-7)

Postsecondary Education

The period after high school is especially important in the lives of young adults. This period typically marks the passage from high school to employment and/or postsecondary education (Koenigsburg et al., 1994). Today, as never before, continuing and higher education are primary indicators of lifetime opportunities and earnings for all students. In fact, the U.S. Department of Commerce (1994) reported that persons with more education can expect higher lifetime earnings. The Bureau of the Census noted that "a person with a professional degree can expect to earn in a lifetime more than twice the amount that a person with a bachelor's

earns—$3,000,000 compared with $1,420,000" (p. 12). Figure 1.2 graphically depicts the estimated lifetime earnings by educational level as reported by the Bureau of the Census: 1992 (U.S. Department of Commerce, 1994).

For a significant segment of the young adult population, entry into further and higher education is difficult to attain as a result of real and persistent barriers (e.g., attitudinal, bureaucratic, financial). Nowhere is this more apparent than for young adults with disabilities. Whereas college attendance for students without disabilities is at an all-time high, the NLTS study found that only 15 percent of students in special education proceeded to any type of postsecondary education following completion of high school (Wagner et al., 1991a; U.S. Department of Education, 1993). The 15 percent included approximately 10 percent in a vocational or trade school, less than 5 percent in a 2-year college, and less than 2 percent in a 4-year college. In each of these situations, the percentages reflect only students who took at least one course, not students enrolled in a program to completion. Moreover, for former students who had been out of school 4 to 5 years, the percentage who had attended a postsecondary technical school in the preceding year dropped to 2.6 percent (Wagner et al., 1991a).

According to the National Center for Education Statistics and the American Association of Community Colleges, 63 percent of students with disabilities attending college in 1989 enrolled in 2-year institutions of higher education (American Association of Community Colleges, 1992). "There can be little doubt," according to Pascarella and colleagues (1995), "that, in an absolute sense, the existence of 2-year institutions has substantially increased both access to higher education as well as the social mobility of numerous individuals whose education would otherwise have ended with high school" (p. 83). This is exceedingly important in light of reports suggesting that 70 percent of the jobs in America will *not* require a college education of 4 years or more. Rather, a majority of these jobs will require only 2 years of postsecondary education (National Center on Education and the Economy, 1990).

Over the past two decades, federal legislation and state legislation have contributed significantly to increased access to postsecondary education for individuals with disabilities. Model demonstration projects and follow-up/follow-along research have strengthened the knowledge base related to young adults in transition from school to work and/or further education and training. This focus by educational and rehabilitation professionals, youth and adult service agencies, parents/guardians, and many other interested organizations has heightened awareness of available meaningful postsecondary education and training opportunities for young adults leaving high schools.

Beyond the fundamental issues regarding access are the pressing problems concerning young adults with disabilities who have not fared well in traditional postsecondary education settings. Recent studies, for example, report that many students with disabilities are having difficulty staying in and completing postsecondary programs (Bruck, 1987; Sitlington & Frank, 1990; Durlak, Rose, & Bursuck, 1994). Students who exit postsecondary education continue to be dependent on society and remain uncertain about their futures in the job market (Ward & Halloran, 1993).

Mass Media

To say that the media have an influence over our daily lives would be an obvious understatement. The media have been so powerful in the late twentieth century that our own beliefs about adolescents have been severely tainted by the frequent media bombardment. Peterson (1988) noted that "adolescents are often portrayed in the media as noisy, obnoxious, dirty, inarticulate, rebellious, and so forth" (p. 584). Such portrayals not only communicate to adolescents how they are expected to behave, but also create an unfair and wholesale lowering of expectations among us all.

The public has grown accustomed to newspaper articles and films (and even government reports) overemphasizing the "pathologies" of adolescence. One does not need to go far to see sensationalism portrayed as commonplace. The fact is most adolescents are not delinquents, nor are they academically underachieving, drug-abusing, sexually active, and violent. "Unfortunately," according to Chang (1992), "the statistical data ... have been overly exposed" and sole "attention to adolescent at-risk behavior has produced misunderstanding of American youth" (p. 2).

Whereas young adults in the general population may not be portrayed in a flattering and realistic manner, the image of youth and young adults with disabilities has improved significantly with the advent of positive TV roles, books that depict positive portrayals, and more balanced newspaper articles. Gone are the days when young adults with disabilities were solely depict-ed as objects of pity and repulsion. The same may not true for adults with disabilities, howev-er, who rarely see true-to-life images of them-selves in the movies (e.g., *Whose Life Is It, Anyway?; Scent of a Woman; Rain Man; Passion Fish; Forrest Gump*) (Norden, 1995). Neverthe-less, change is occurring and with it greater recognition of ability and potential.

In summary, this section has attempted to illuminate the complexity of adolescence by depicting the major issues and ecological influ-ences present in their lives. Although not com-plete, the major influences relate to parent and peer relations, the quest for independence, high school, early employment, extracurricular pur-suits, risk-taking behaviors and juvenile crime, poverty, postsecondary education, and the media. All of these factors shape adolescent thinking and development. They also strongly influence how adolescents are perceived in the larger community.

YOUTH AND YOUNG ADULTS AND HOW THEY THINK

How one thinks is directly related to develop-mental stages. In twentieth-century psychology, Sigmund Freud (and his daughter, Anna Freud), Erik Erikson, and Jean Piaget are the most widely noted behavioral scientists. Whereas Freud's theory has had a profound impact on describing human behavior, it is difficult at times to explain its significance on teaching and learn-ing. In contrast, Erikson, one of Freud's pupils, developed a theory based on the work of Freud that is more directly applicable to explaining personality development among children and adolescents in our culture and society. However, it is important to note that any one theory of cognitive development is not sufficient in explaining human behavior. In fact, there is no single developmental theory that satisfactorily explains behavior. Yet, when Piaget's theory is

integrated with a developmental theory such as Freud's and Erikson's, both of which focus on explanations of personality development and interpersonal relationships, a comprehensive picture of child and youth development begins to emerge.

Jean Piaget's (1896–1980) insights into cog-nitive development have shaped the field for most of the century and has inspired countless followers. As director (1924–1980) of the Institut Jean-Jacques Rousseau in Geneva, Piaget spent many years developing and writing about a comprehensive theory of the intellectual devel-opment of children. His theory describes a number of stages of thinking that children go through as they grow from early infancy to adulthood. The stage of development that coincides with the beginning of adolescence (at approximately age 11), known as formal opera-tions, marks the start of abstract thought and deductive reasoning. Prior to formal operations, the child in the concrete operational stage deals with the present, the here and now; the child who can use formal operational thought can think about the future and hypothetical situa-tions. "Piaget argues that this new mode of thinking changes all aspects of psychological functioning, including adolescents' understand-ing of themselves, their relations with peers, their ability to work, and their attitudes toward social ideals" (Cole & Cole, 1993:575).

Adolescents, with their new way of thinking, can conceive of multiple ways to solve problems. They also can look at a problem from several points of view. It is during this time that adoles-cents search for solutions in a systematic fashion and can think about thoughts, not just concrete objects. Even though adolescents can sometimes deal with mental abstractions representing con-crete objects, most 12-year-olds solve problems haphazardly, using trial and error. It is not until the end of high school years that adolescents are likely to solve problems by first forming hy-potheses, mentally sorting out solutions, and testing possible outcomes. In this way, adolescent thought becomes more flexible, rational, and systematic. They can think about such abstract concepts as space and time.

The theory that is best known for its insights into adolescent development is Erik Erikson's on psychosocial development (Paul & White, 1990). Erikson extended Freudian theory into adolescence and adulthood and is best known for coining the phrase "identity crisis." Emphasizing social relationships, rather than sexual needs, as the key to growing up, Erikson adhered to the view that nature sets the "basic sequence of stages while nurture shapes developmental processes within stages" (Cole & Cole, 1993:20). Based on evidence from many cultures, Erikson emphasized that the prior experiences of the society into which children are born, embodied in its current culture, play a major role in development (Cole & Cole, 1993:20).

According to Erikson, the formation of identity is the developmental issue that is most pronounced during the period of adolescence. Young people are concerned about what kind of people they will become. The trend at this stage is toward development of ego identity and away from role confusion. "The formation of identity becomes crucial during adolescence," in Erikson's view, "because this is the time when the child's beliefs, abilities, and desires must be reconciled with adult norms; that is, individual identity and social identity must be made compatible" (Cole & Cole, 1993:575).

Hobart (1995) provided an excellent illustration of the issues of identity development using the story of a 14-year-old young woman with Down syndrome. Hobart (1995) described how the parents of this young woman were "terrible worried" because she refused to go to school for an entire week. "The daughter would not leave her bed … and even ate her meals in bed. She … would not speak to her parents" (p. 41). The parents were at a loss for solutions and felt that this might somehow be connected to the syndrome. During conversations with the parents, "it emerged that for some time the daughter had wanted to be allowed to go to school by herself. It was a twenty-minute walk, and all her class-

mates went to school on their own" (p. 41). The mother, in an overprotective manner, insisted on walking with her. According to Hobart (1995), "The daughter reacted in a way that we have seen in many cases. It was as if she were saying to her parents, 'if you treat me like a little child, then I'll act like a baby.' The next day the girl went to school by herself" (p. 41).

Interpreting Erikson, Greenberger and Steinberg (1986) argued the importance of a "psychosocial moratorium" for young people to "ponder what sort of person one really is, try out different aspects of the self, and explore ways of fitting oneself into meaningful social roles" (p. 165). Without an opportunity to "develop, practice, and refine newly emerging cognitive abilities, ego skills, and interpersonal strategies," adolescents may lose a valuable sense of themselves (Greenberger & Steinberg, 1986:168). Erikson (1968) believed that if society grants the adolescent a moratorium, the identity crisis will be resolved in a stable sense of identity.

A moratorium for adolescents translates into a period of self-discovery or emancipation. Without this time of self-discovery, there may be "identity foreclosure," a premature end to identity formation. Greenberger and Steinberg (1986) used a number of practical examples to illustrate this phenomenon—"the youngster who is forced to carry on the family business; the adolescent who marries a high-school sweetheart immediately after graduation; the youngster whose parents select a college and a course of study for their child" (p. 169). Again interpreting Erikson, Greenberger and Steinberg (1986) argued that "Without role experimentation, adolescents in modern society either remain locked into roles handed to them by their elders or muddle through adulthood with a confused and incoherent sense of who they are" (Greenberger & Steinberg, 1986:167). Baumrind (1987) went as far as to suggest that adolescents who do not undergo a process of emancipation in some form "remain willing pawns of others, unwilling to accept responsibility for the consequences of their actions" (p. 97).

DECISION MAKING AMONG YOUNG ADULTS

In our fast-paced society, many adolescents are asked to make decisions about a wide range of topics, including sex, drugs, and personal safety. In the past, such topics were either hidden or reserved for adults (Nicholson, 1992). Decisions of this kind are not only potentially life-threatening, but can also have far-reaching consequences that would challenge even individuals who are experienced in decision making.

The ability to make sensible decisions is one of the key characteristics of the mature adolescent (Mann, Harmoni, & Power, 1989). Part of a young adult's need for increased individuality and personal autonomy is demonstrated through a desire to decide what subjects to take in school, to seek out their own friends, to get an after-school job, and to join extracurricular activities. Longer-range decisions that adolescents increasingly make for themselves include furthering one's education, career goals, military service, where to live, and marriage. "What is of concern," according to Feldman and Elliott (1990), "is that most ... adolescents are making such choices while their thinking still tends to focus largely on the here and now rather than on longer-range eventualities" (p. 487).

Commenting on young people's ability to make decisions, Keating (1990) suggested that "their potential for competent decision-making is often greater than their performance in real situations, and that is often determined by a range of social forces" (p. 56). Keating (1990) believed that adolescents' abilities "to make sound and rational decisions are intimately linked to other developmental dynamics, and it is perilous to ignore them" (p. 56). He argued that care must be taken in deciphering "teenagers' decisions that are objectionable to parents or to society at large" (p. 88). What may appear as "incompetent decision-making skills" (p. 88) may actually be the result of strong forces that are coming to bear on the young person.

Keating (1990) cited the following poignant examples:

> The decision of a mathematically talented ninth-grade girl to abandon mathematics may seem to reflect poor decision-making. But it might indicate instead a stronger motivation to maintain peer relationships that would otherwise be threatened. In yet another situation, the decision of an urban teenager to engage in drug trafficking, even at considerable personal risk, is not necessarily the result of failure to consider all the relevant information; it may be the outcome of quite a sophisticated thinking about risk-benefit ratios in oppressive circumstances offering limited or nonexistent options. (p. 88)

In his study of young adults with learning disabilities who dropped out of high school, Lichtenstein (1993) found that the decision to leave school hinged on circumstances that adults often fail to consider.

> Their [students] decision to leave school, in their own view, was singularly the most affirming choice of their high school years. Their leaving had much to do with reclaiming their own lives and attempting to salvage their self-esteem. ... A recurring theme in the interviews with the former ... students was their feeling that their personal opinions were neither sought nor valued in the school setting. (p. 344)

In general, schools, which are entrusted with our children's education, provide few real opportunities for student-centered decision making. According to Powers and colleagues (in press):

> Typically education, and special education in particular, has not emphasized youth empowerment or partnerships. Instead, most efforts have focused on exposing youth to curricula and programs considered essential by professionals and families. Youth have

generally been involved as passive participants in this process.

Nowhere is this passive role more apparent than in the process of developing Individualized Education Programs (IEPs). Although IEPs are intended to be tools for students with disabilities, students are often left out of the decision-making role or relegated to roles that are less empowering. Major decisions, such as course selection and what job or college to pursue after graduation, are not discussed in a manner that allows young people to feel at ease or in control of their destiny. The process is often viewed by students as bureaucratic and assembly-line. (For more specifics about the contents of an IEP, see Chapter 3.)

Many adolescents turn to part-time employment to gain financial independence and to exercise their own decision making. However, according to Greenberger and Steinberg (1986),

> The overall picture of opportunities for developing self-reliance in the adolescent workplace is not impressive. The majority of teenagers have few chances to make major decisions and have little influence over the actions of others. To put it concretely, wrapping fast-food items in paper containers as fast as one can is unlikely to teach a worker very much about self-reliance or decision-making. (p. 67)

As stated earlier in this chapter, the process by which young adults transition to adulthood "occurs in different orders and times for females and males and varies for individuals of different races and class groups" (Koenigsburg et al., 1994:136). "In comparison with the situation in two-parent households," according to Spencer and Dornbusch (1990), "single parents usually have more limited resources of time, money, and energy" (p. 127). Further, they speculated that "this shortage of resources prompts them to encourage early autonomy among their adolescent children. For African-Americans, Asian-Americans, Hispanics, and non-Hispanic whites, granting adolescents more autonomy in decision

making than is typical for their age is associated with negative outcomes such as high rates of deviance and poor grades in school" (Spencer & Dornbusch, 1990:127).

Contrary to such opinions, poignant examples illustrate high levels of perseverance in the face of adversity. One such story, reported in the *Boston Globe* (Valdes, 1996), is about 19-year-old Shahi Smart. Shahi is a senior at English High School, just outside of Boston. His story reflects the lives of many families where supporting the household must be shared by all.

> Shahi has worked since he was 14-years-old, but not like a stereotypical teen-ager earning malt and movie money. He worked because he must, to help his mother and two younger sisters survive. He is not unusual. ... He is one of 3,500 public high school students in the Boston Public Schools' School-to-Work program. (p. 57)

> Shahi's earnings which have ranged over the last four years from $63 to $400 a week, usually goes toward the electric bill and sometimes pays for his sisters' dental visits. He says he is glad after years of homelessness to be able to help ease his mother's strain. On the surface, Smart had the deck stacked against him—son of a teenage mother on welfare, besieged by street gangs, homeless for a time, poor, fatherless. But the briefest conversation with Shahi Smart reveals someone college admissions officers might duel over. His first words to a stranger, "Did you know I'm the managing editor of my school newspaper?" are full of confidence and hope. (p. 60)

> Shahi keeps his mother from slipping into despair, and she helps him ... when he was 17 and starting skipping school and talking about how he didn't want to go to college, his mother picked him up again. According to his mother, I brought home recruiting papers from the Army and the Navy and the Air Force, and I told him I couldn't have a son who was nothing. Then I put myself in college, because I realized that without a

role model he wouldn't think it's important. (p. 60)

Among the issues highlighted by this story is the influence that supportive parents and caring adults can have on guiding adolescents' decision making and awareness of the world around them. The value of positive role models cannot be overstated and has much to do with formation of one's own identity. Whereas infants and toddlers are forming fundamental assumptions about human interactions, adolescents are forming fundamental assumptions about society and their potential role in it (Tierney, Grossman, & Resch, 1995).

GENDER DIFFERENCES IN EDUCATION AND EMPLOYMENT

Prior to puberty girls and boys are much more similar than different in biology and attitudes (Nicholson, 1992). It is after the onset of puberty, during adolescence, that gender differences appear to be most pronounced and distinct. These differences are discussed here because they play an important role in the development of overall mental health (Peterson, 1988), educational achievement (Wellesley College Center for Research on Women, 1992), and employment outcomes (Fulton & Sabornie, 1994).

Peterson (1988) reported that "adolescent boys with psychological difficulties are likely to have had problems in childhood; girls, in contrast, are more likely to first manifest psychological difficulties in adolescence" (p. 590). The striking difference is that "girls appear to increase in depressive affect over the adolescent period, so that by age 17 they have significantly poorer emotional tone and well-being, and more depressive affect than boys" (p. 590). In education, young women, more so in adolescence than childhood, fall behind young men in subject areas strongly associated with higher skill, and higher-paying jobs of the future, such as in the sciences and mathematics (Wellesley College Center for Research on Women, 1992).

In the labor market, while young women are seeking careers in record numbers, a majority continue to be segregated in occupations that pay lower wages than male colleagues and earn only 66% of the wages of similarly educated men (Lichtenstein, 1996; U.S. Department of Education, 1995a).

Education

Until recently, research suggested that boys and girls entered school with equal abilities and self-concepts; yet, females usually fell behind their male peers in both areas upon graduation (Blackhurst & Berdine, 1993; Salend, 1994; Wellesley College Center for Research on Women, 1992). However, "Over the past two decades," according to the U.S. Department of Education (1995a), "women have made substantial educational progress."

> The large gaps between the education levels of women and men that were evident in the early 1970s have essentially disappeared for the younger generation. Although they still lag behind males in mathematics and science achievement, high school females on average outperform males in reading and writing, and take more credits in academic subjects. In addition, females are more likely than males to attend college after high school, and are as likely to graduate with a postsecondary degree. (U.S. Department of Education, 1995a:1)

As we have seen, peer pressure and the desire to be accepted by classmates play a large part in adolescent development, academic choice, and overall performance (Wellesley College Center for Research on Women, 1992; Salend, 1994). For example, issues of self-esteem and self-confidence significantly affect course selection. Some young women, more so than their male counterparts, feel pressure to enroll in less-demanding courses that are consistent with traditional sex-role expectations (Kerr, 1985; Lichtenstein, 1996). This phenomenon can be seen through student course-taking patterns. For example, enrollment in mathematics and science classes is heavily dominated by males. Stereotyping of mathematics and science as domains for males has prompted the National Science Foundation to establish a priority to encourage more girls and women to participate in these subject areas. The foundation cites the following areas of concern:

- the disproportionately high number of girls who lose interest in science during elementary and middle school;

- the low number of women who enroll in college-prep science and math courses in high school;

- the disproportionately low numbers of women entering undergraduate studies in science, engineering, and math, particularly in physical sciences, computer sciences, and engineering;

- the current low number of women completing science, engineering and math graduate degrees; and

- the slow rate of women's advancement to senior rank and leadership positions. (National Science Foundation, 1993)

Whereas women in the general population are narrowing the gap in educational attainment, young women with disabilities are failing to achieve parity with their male counterparts with and without disabilities. The NLTS study (Wagner et al., 1991a) suggests that "young women with disabilities had different experiences in secondary school and followed markedly different transition paths" (p. S-12) after leaving high school. For example, female students with disabilities were found to be less likely than males to have taken occupationally oriented vocational education in high school. The absence of such coursework has been linked to less preparedness for securing better-paying jobs and remaining competitive with their peers (Wellesley College Center for Research on Women, 1992).

The status of young women with disabilities in special education is rather unique. The higher rate of males in special education (males out-

number females by about 2 to 1) makes females a minority group within a minority group. As a result, their education and employment needs have been overlooked in the quest for solutions to the problems of the majority.

Employment

Youth and young adults demonstrate many of the same gender differences in employment as they do in education, except they may be more socially and culturally determined. "Overall, the most noteworthy feature of the observed gender differences in adolescents' work," argue Greenberger and Steinberg (1986), "is their consistency with differences found in the adult labor force" (p. 482). These differences begin "virtually the moment youngsters go to work outside the home, they enter a labor force where the work of males and females is quite distinct; in which males work longer hours than females; and in which males' work is more highly remunerated" (Greenberger & Steinberg, 1986:482). The following list illustrates the gender differences in the job market.

- Whereas the number of women participating in paid employment has increased in the past two decades, it is well documented that fewer women than men are employed and that employed women work fewer hours than men, even if both hold full-time jobs (Wellesley College Center for Research on Women, 1992).

- Working women are segregated in higher proportions than men in lower-paying occupations (Greenberger & Steinberg, 1983). For example, 55 percent of employed women are found in traditional clerical and service occupations (Larwood & Gutek, cited in Matlin, 1987).

- The concentration by women in clerical and service occupations is associated with numerous drawbacks: lower wages, lower status, less-skill requirements, inflexible hours, fewer benefits, fewer training opportunities, and less job security (Sivard, 1985; Matlin, 1987; Koretz, 1990).

- Although major changes have taken place in the selection of occupations and fields of study for women, higher unemployment rates continue to plague women more than men, regardless of educational levels (O'Neill, 1990).
- Young women are "being steered away from the very courses required for their productive participation" in high-skill, high-wage careers (Wellesley College Center for Research on Women, 1992:v).

According to the NLTS study, young women with disabilities were no more likely to complete school than male students or to attend postsecondary schools after high school, even though they may have had better academic performance while in high school. Even among high school graduates, fewer young women found jobs, and, when employed, they earned less than males and were more likely to have jobs in service occupations. When compared with youth in the general population, young women with disabilities lagged further behind their counterparts without disabilities than did young men (Wagner et al., 1991a).

The following list identifies some of the characteristics of employment that illustrate the gender differences among youth and young adults with disabilities.

- Young women with disabilities were significantly less likely than males to be employed, both when they had been out of school less than 2 years, and 3 years later. For example, for the group recently out of school, 32 percent of the young women had been employed compared with 52 percent of the young men. When out of school 3 to 5 years, young women with disabilities lagged even further behind their male counterparts (40 vs. 64 percent) (Wagner, 1992b).
- Part of their relative difficulty in securing jobs may be a result of their lower rate of participation in programs designed to facilitate the transition from school to adult life (Heal & Rusch, 1995). For example, female

students were significantly less likely than males to have been enrolled in occupationally oriented vocational education in high school or to have received it early in their high school careers (Wagner et al., 1991b). Such coursework increases the potential for competitive employment.

- Evidence from a majority of disability-employment studies supports findings that a greater number of young women with mild disabilities will experience prolonged periods and higher rates of unemployment and underemployment than their male counterparts (Fulton & Sabornie, 1994; Lichtenstein, 1996).
- Nationally, using NLTS data, Wagner and colleagues (1992) found that "Young women with disabilities not only differed from males with disabilities, but findings also suggest their experiences differed from their female peers in the general population" (p. 4).
- Typically, the gap in employment between young men and women narrowed with time (Veum & Weiss, 1993); however, in the case of young adults with disabilities, the gap continued to widen between the sexes.

IMPLICATIONS FOR "BEST PRACTICES"

I want to reemphasize my major points that, although supported by considerable research, should not be regarded as proven premises, but rather as an organizer or framework for generating ideas and future activities. Takanishi (1993) said it best when she commented:

All adolescents … have basic needs that must be satisfied: to experience secure relationships with a few adults, to be valued members of groups that provide mutual aid and caring relationships, to become a competent individual who can cope with the exigencies of everyday life, and to believe in a promising future in work, family, and citizenship. (p. 459)

. . . It is not inevitable that adolescents lose self-esteem and interest in learning. . . . It is not inevitable that parents and adolescents experience intense conflict, especially over daily matters, and it is not inevitable that non-college young adults are not prepared adequately for the workplace. (p. 462)

The salient issues and concerns during this period relate to growth, development, and the ability to cope with dramatic changes. The world of adolescence centers on family and peer relations, issues regarding mental health, education, and employment. Although other issues and concerns also play significant roles, they hinge on these major considerations.

Whereas American adolescents now enjoy unequaled freedom of self-determination in many areas of their lives, the same cannot be said for many young people with disabilities, for them whom the transition from adolescence to adulthood is a formidable one. First, it is difficult for some adolescents to be psychologically and emotionally independent of their parents and caregivers when they are often dependent on them for meeting their basic needs. Second, although adolescents without disabilities may encourage and reinforce the expression of differences, a disability may be a difference that they find unacceptable (National Information Center for Children and Youth with Handicaps, 1988).

A cursory examination of the relevant literature (and certainly your own experience) will convince you that adolescence is synonymous with experimentation and change. Other than infancy, there is no other time in life when we experience such rapid transformation and opportunities to "try out" new identities (Eccles & Harold, 1993). If we are to strive to develop the talents of adolescents, we must accept the reality that "the main developmental tasks of the adolescent years is to embark on the unknown—to shape an identity, to gain independence, and, in general, to prepare for adulthood" (Drexler, 1996:10). Taking advantage of this fascinating

and highly formative period requires that youth be challenged in a way that nurtures resiliency and connectedness. The period of adolescence for young people with and without disabilities "provides an exceptional chance for constructive interventions that can have lifelong influence" (Hamburg, 1989:4). These interventions are generally not costly; however, they do demand attention and resources—often at strategic times. This is why families and schools play a significant role and have for centuries.

Sociologist Michael Resnick (cited in Drexler, 1996) suggested that resilient teenagers, those who are able to surmount difficulties, "have a sense of connectedness with something greater than themselves . . . they feel a strong sense of competence and confidence" (p. 10). Resnick presented some practical and attainable suggestions for how young people can, with the help of caring adults, gain a sense of competence and confidence. He argued that youth must be "engaged in the world in a creative, purposeful way. No. 1: Teach them a new skill, something they couldn't do before. No. 2: Teach them to make that skill of help or service to others" (p. 11). In the absence of parents, caring adults and mentors can be instrumental in providing this sense of engagement.

However, it is just when teens need adults that they often push them away as they pursue peer relationships. As a result, adults are often left feeling unconnected to their own children. Harvard University researcher Sara Lawrence Lightfoot (1983) argued that "Adult fears of adolescents stem partially from not knowing them, or not even knowing how to get to know them. Adolescents seem to be our culture's greatest puzzle and uncertainty inspires fear" (p. 342). In her book, Lightfoot (1983) suggested that "high school students need secure and mature attention from adults, a firm regard that offers consistent support, realism, and certainty" (p. 342). When teachers "are apprehensive about, and do not understand, the broad emotional sweeps that send adolescents from vitality and joy into deep moments of sadness, or the sweeps that swiftly carry them from childish impulses to mature adult behavior" (p. 342), the results can produce discomfort, fear, and alienation.

Building on what we know about adolescence as a "naturally occurring time of transition" (Gilligan, 1987:65) and a dynamic period of change can help schools and communities develop resources to both support and challenge youth. All too often, the educational establishment has forgotten that adolescence is a time to question, explore, and experiment with new ideas. The developmental needs of youth and young adults relate to their quest for identity and have implications for current and future pursuits. A logical step in designing and implementing programs and services for youth and young adults is to take into account what they are like, how much they know, and how they think.

QUESTIONS

1. Historically, adolescence as a period of development and growth has changed over time. Discuss the major changes, the origins of that change, and the consequences of that change.

2. During adolescence, young people redefine their relationships with significant others. The value of friendships and peer relations takes on new implications. Discuss the phenomenon of peer relationships in contrast with family and parent relations.

3. Discuss the importance of decision making and identify what opportunities there are for youth and young adults to engage in decision making.

4. How do the substages of adolescence—early, middle, and late—distinguish themselves? Discuss any criticisms you might have about the concept of substages.

5. Adolescence as a distinct stage of life is defined by a variety of biological and social constructs. Discuss these constructs and the notion that adolescence may only be a stage present in Western cultures.

6. What distinguishes the period known as adolescence from childhood and adulthood?

7. The theory that is best known for its insights into adolescent development is Erik Erikson's theory of psychosocial development. Discuss three of his arguments and consider them in relation to the formation of healthy outcomes.

8. The value of work experience for adolescents is a topic of considerable concern and debate. Discuss the arguments "for" and "against" work experience for adolescents and how the experience can promote, rather than detract from healthy, normal development.

9. Discuss at least three gender differences that have been reported between women and men in education and employment.

10. How can we as parents and teachers best support adolescents in their journey toward adulthood?

REFERENCES

American Association of Community Colleges. (1992, December). Serving all. *The Community, Technical, and Junior College Times, IV*, 1.

Aseltine, R., & Gore, S. (1993). Mental health and social adaptation following the transition from high school. *Journal of Research on Adolescence, 3*, 247–270.

Baumrind, D. (1987). A developmental perspective on adolescent risk-taking in contemporary America. In C. E. Irwin (Ed.), *Adolescent social behavior and health. New directions in child development, 37* (pp. 93–121). San Francisco: Jossey-Bass.

Blackhurst, E., & Berdine, W. (1993). *An introduction to special education* (3rd ed.). New York: HarperCollins.

Bronfenbrenner, U. (1979). *The ecology of human development: Experiments by nature and design.* Cambridge, MA: Harvard University Press.

Bruck, M. (1987). The adult outcomes of children with LD. *Annals of Dyslexia, 37*, 252–263.

Bukowski, W., Hoza, B., & Boivin, M. (1993). Popularity, friendship, and emotional adjustment during early adolescence. In B. Laursen (Ed.), *Close friendships in adolescence. New directions for child development, 60* (pp. 23–38). San Francisco: Jossey-Bass.

Carnegie Commission on Policy Studies in Higher Education. (1980). *Giving youth a better chance.* San Francisco: Jossey-Bass.

Carnegie Council on Policy Studies in Higher Education. (1979). *Giving youth a better chance.* San Francisco: Jossey-Bass.

Carroll, J. (1996). Child abandonment: A crime of our own. *The Boston Globe, 249,* 15.

Chang, H. (1992). *Adolescent life and ethos: An ethnography of a US High School.* London: Falmer Press.

Children's Defense Fund. (1995a). *The state of America's children yearbook.* Washington, DC: Author.

———. (1995b). *Wasting America's future.* Washington, DC: Author.

Cole, M., & Cole, S. (1993). *The development of children* (2nd ed.). New York: Scientific American Books.

Csikszentmihalyi, M., & Larson, R. (1984). *Being adolescent: Conflict and growth in the teenage years.* New York: Basic Books.

D'Amico, R. (1991). The working world awaits: Employment experiences during and shortly after secondary school. In M. Wagner, L. Newman, R. D'Amico, E. Jay, P. Butler-Nalin, C. Marder, & R. Cox (Eds.), *Youth with disabilities: How are they doing? The first comprehensive report from the National Longitudinal Transition Study of Special Education Students* (pp. 8-1 to 8-55). Menlo Park, CA: SRI International.

Drexler, M. (1996). Risky business. *The Boston Globe Magazine, 249,* 10–11.

Dryfoos, J. (1990). *Adolescents at risk: Prevalence and prevention.* New York: Oxford University Press.

Durlak, C., Rose, E., & Bursuck, W. (1994, January). Preparing high school students with LD for the transition to postsecondary education: Teaching the skills of self-determination. *Journal of Learning Disabilities, 27,* 51–59.

Eccles, J., & Harold, R. (1993). Parent-school involvement during the early adolescent years. *Teachers College Record, 94,* Spring, 568–587.

Eccles, J., Lord, S., & Midgely, C. (1991). What are we doing to early adolescents? The impact of educational contexts on early adolescents. *American Journal of Education, 99,* 521–542.

Elliott, G., & Feldman, S. (1990). Capturing the adolescent experience. In S. Feldman & G. Elliott (Eds.), *At the threshold: The developing adolescent* (pp. 1–13). Cambridge, MA: Harvard University Press.

Erikson, E. (1963). *Childhood and society* (2nd ed.). New York: Norton.

———. (1968). *Identity: Youth and crisis.* New York: Norton.

Evans, D., Hodapp, R., & Zigler, E. (1995). Mental and chronological age as predictors of age-appropriate leisure activity in children with mental retardation. *Mental Retardation, 33,* 120–127.

Federal Register. (1994, February 3). Notices, Department of Education and Department of Labor, Cooperative Demonstration—School-to-Work Opportunities State Implementation Grants Program. Vol. 59, No. 23.

Feldman, S., & Elliott, G. (1990). Progress and promise. In S. Feldman & G. Elliott (Eds.), *At the threshold: The developing adolescent* (pp. 479–505). Cambridge, MA: Harvard University Press.

Feldman, S., & Elliott, G. (Eds.). (1990). *At the threshold: The developing adolescent.* Cambridge, MA: Harvard University Press.

Feldman, S., & Weinberger, D. (1994). Self-restraint as a mediator of family influences on boys' delinquent behavior: A longitudinal study. *Child Development, 65,* 195–211.

Finn, J. (1989, Summer). Withdrawing from school. *Review of Educational Research, 59,* 117–142.

Ford Foundation Project on Social Welfare and the American Future. (1989). *The common good.* New York: Ford Foundation.

Fulton, S., & Sabornie, E. (1994). Evidence of employment inequality among females with disabilities. *Journal of Special Education, 28,* 149–165.

Furman, W., & Wehner, E. (1994). Romantic views: Toward a theory of adolescent romantic relationships. In R. Montemayor, G. Adams, & T. Gullotta (Eds.), *Personal relationships during adolescence* (pp. 213–234). Thousand Oaks, CA: Sage Publications.

Gilligan, C. (1987). Adolescent development reconsidered. In C. E. Irwin (Ed.), *Adolescent social behavior and health. New directions in child development, 37* (pp. 63–92). San Francisco: Jossey-Bass.

Greenberger, E. (1983). A researcher in the policy arena: The case of child labor. *American Psychologist, 38,* 104–111.

Greenberger, E., & Steinberg, L. (1983). Sex differences in early labor force experience: Harbinger of things to come. *Social Forces, 62,* 467–486.

———. (1986). *When teenagers work.* New York: Basic Books.

Greenfeld, J. (1986). *A client called Noah.* San Diego: Harcourt Brace Jovanovich.

Hamburg, D. (1989). *Early adolescence: A critical time for interventions in education and health.* New York: Carnegie Corporation of New York, Carnegie Council on Adolescent Development.

———. (1993). The opportunities of early adolescence. *Teachers College Record, 94,* 468.

Hanson, M., & Carta, J. (1995). Addressing the challenges of families with multiple risks. *Exceptional Children, 62*, 201–212.

Harter, S. (1990). Self and identity development. In S. Feldman & G. Elliott (Eds.), *At the threshold: The developing adolescent* (pp. 352–387). Cambridge, MA: Harvard University Press.

Hasazi, S., Gordon, L., & Roe, C. (1985). Factors associated with the employment status of handicapped youth exiting high school from 1979 to 1983. *Exceptional Children, 51*, 455–469.

Hasazi, S., Johnson, R., Hasazi, L., Gordon, L., & Hull, M. (1989). Employment of youth with and without handicaps following high school: Outcomes and correlates. *Journal of Special Education, 23*, 243–255.

Hauser, S., & Bowlds, M. (1990). Stress, coping, and adaptation. In S. Feldman & G. Elliott (Eds.), *At the threshold: The developing adolescent* (pp. 388–413). Cambridge, MA: Harvard University Press.

Heal, L., & Rusch, F. (1995, March/April). Predicting employment for students who leave special education high school programs. *Exceptional Children, 61*, 472–487.

Hobart, A. (1995). Aspects of behavior from birth to puberty. In L. Nadel & D. Rosenthal (Eds.), *Down syndrome: Living and learning in the community* (pp. 37–42). New York: Wiley-Liss.

Irwin, C. (1987). Editor's note. In C. E. Irwin (Ed.), *Adolescent social behavior and health. New directions in child development, 37* (pp. 1–10). San Francisco: Jossey–Bass.

Kagan, J. (1971). A conception of early adolescence. *Daedalus, 100*, 997–1012.

Kaufman, S. (1988). *Retarded isn't stupid, Mom*. Baltimore: Paul H. Brookes.

Kazdin, A. (1993, February). Adolescent mental health. *American Psychologist, 48*, 127–141.

Keating, D. (1990). Adolescent thinking. In S. Feldman & G. Elliott (Eds.), *At the threshold: The developing adolescent* (pp. 54–92). Cambridge, MA: Harvard University Press.

Kerr, B. (1985). Smart girls, gifted women: Special guidance concerns. *Roeper Review, 8*, 30–33.

Kingsley, J., & Levitz, M. (1994). *Count us in*. New York: Harcourt Brace.

Koenigsburg, J., Garet, M., & Rosenbaum, J. (1994). The effect of family on the job exits of young adults. *Work and Occupation, 21*, 33–63.

Koretz, G. (1990, December 24). Women still earn less, but they've come a long way. *Business Week, 3193*, 14.

Kortering, L., Haring, N., & Klockars, A. (1992). The identification of high-school dropouts identified as learning disabled: Evaluating the utility of a discriminant analysis function. *Exceptional Children, 58*, 422–435.

Kos, R. (1993). Karen: An interaction of gender role and reading disability. In R. Donmeyer & R. Kos (Eds.), *At-risk students* (pp. 23–42). New York: State University of New York Press.

Lesar, S., Trivette, C., & Dunst, C. (1995). Families of children and adolescents with special needs across the life span. *Exceptional Children, 62*, 197–199.

Levinson, D., Darrow, C., Klein, E., Levinson, M., & McKee, B. (1978). *The seasons of a man's life*. New York: Alfred A. Knopf.

Lichtenstein, S. (1993, February). Transition from school to adulthood: Case studies of adults with learning disabilities who dropped out of school. *Exceptional Children, 59*, 336–347.

———. (1996). Gender differences in the education and employment of young adults: Implications for special education. *Remedial and Special Education, 17*, 4–20.

Liebert, R., & Sprafkin, J. (1988). *The early window: Effects of television on children and youth* (3rd ed.). New York: Pergamon Press.

Lightfoot, S. (1983). *The good high school*. New York: Basic Books.

Lillydahl, J. (1990, Summer). Academic achievement and part-time employment of high school students. *Journal of Economic Education, 15*(2), 307–316.

Mann, L., Harmoni, R., & Power, C. (1989). Adolescent decision-making: The development of competence. *Journal of Adolescence, 12*, 265–278.

Marden, C. (1992). Education after secondary school. In M. Wagner, R. D'Amico, C. Marder, L. Newman, & J. Blackorby (Eds.), *What happens next? Trends in postschool outcomes of youth with disabilities* (pp. 3-1 to 3-40). Menlo Park, CA: SRI International.

Matlin, M. (1987). *The psychology of women*. New York: Holt, Rinehart & Winston.

Mortimer, J., Finch, M., Owens, T., & Shanahan, M. (1990). Gender and work in adolescence. *Youth & Society, 22*, 201–224.

Nada Raja, S., McGee, R., & Stanton, W. (1992). Perceived attachment to parents and peers and psychological well-being in adolescence. *Journal of Youth and Adolescence, 21*, 471–485.

National Center on Education and the Economy. (1990). *America's Choice: High skills or low wages*. Washington, DC: Author.

National Coalition of Advocates for Students. (1985). *Barriers to excellence: Our children at risk*. Boston: Author.

National Commission on Youth. (1980). *The transition of youth to adulthood: A bridge too long*. Boulder, CO: Westview.

National Information Center for Children and Youth with Handicaps. (1988). *Self-determination. Transition Summary, Number 5*. Washington, DC: Author.

National Longitudinal Transition Study. (1991). *Youth with disabilities: How are they doing?* Menlo Park, CA: SRI International.

National Science Foundation. (1993). *Education and human resources activities for women and girls in science, engineering, and mathematics*. Arlington, VA: Author.

Newman, L. (1991). Social activities. In M. Wagner, L. Newman, R. D'Amico, E. Jay, P. Butler-Nalin, C. Marder, & R. Cox (Eds.), *Youth with disabilities: How are they doing? The first comprehensive report from the National Longitudinal Transition Study of Special Education Students* (pp. 6-1 to 6-50). Menlo Park, CA: SRI International.

Nicholson, H. (1992). *Gender issues in youth development programs*. New York: Carnegie Council on Adolescent Development. (ERIC Document Reproduction Service No. ED 362 439.)

Norden, M. (1995). *The cinema of isolation: A history of physical disability in the movies*. New Brunswick, NJ: Rutgers University Press.

O'Neill, J. (1990, November/December). Women & wages. *The American Enterprise*, 25–33.

Pallas, A. (1993, Winter). Schooling in the course of human lives: The social context of education and the transition to adulthood in industrial society. *Review of Education Research, 63*, 409–447.

Pascarella, E., Bohr, L., Nora, A., & Terenzini, P. (1995). Cognitive effects of 2-year and 4-year colleges: New evidence. *Educational Evaluation and Policy Analysis, 17*, 83–96.

Paterson, J., Pryor, J., & Field, J. (1995). Adolescent attachment to parents and friends in relation to aspects of self-esteem. *Journal of Youth and Adolescence, 24*, 365–376.

Paul, E., & White, K. (1990). The development of intimate relationships in late adolescence. *Adolescence, 25*, 375–400.

Petersen, A., Leffert, N., & Hurrelmann, K. (1993). Adolescence and schooling in Germany and the United States: A comparison of peer socialization to adulthood. *Teachers College Record, 94*, 611–628.

Peterson, A. (1988). Adolescent development. *Annual Review of Psychology, 39*, 583–607.

Phillips, S., & Sandstrom, K. (1990). Parental attitudes toward youth work. *Youth & Society, 22*, 160–183.

Powell, A., Farrar, E., & Cohen, D. (1985). *The shopping mall high school*. Boston: Houghton Mifflin.

Powers, L., Wilson, R., Knowles, E., Rein, C, O'Neil, D., & Ginsert, J. (1997). Facilitating adolescent self-determination: What does it take? In D. Sands & M. L. Wehmeyer (Eds.), *Self-determination across the life-span: Theory and practice*. Baltimore: Paul H. Brookes.

President's Science Advisory Committee. (1974). *Youth: Transition to adulthood*. Chicago: University of Chicago Press.

Raffaelli, M., & Duckett, E. (1989). "We were just talking": Conversations in early adolescence. *Journal of Youth and Adolescence, 18*, 568–582.

Salend, S. (1994). *Effective mainstreaming: Creating inclusive classrooms* (2nd ed.). New York: Macmillan.

Savin-Williams, R., & Berndt, T. (1990). Friendships and peer relations. In G. Elliott & S. Feldman (Eds.), *At the threshold: The developing adolescent* (pp. 277–307). Cambridge, MA: Harvard University Press.

School-to-Work Opportunities Act of 1994, P.L. 103–239, 20 U.S.C. 6101 et seq.

Schorr, L. (1988). *Within our reach: Breaking the cycle of disadvantage*. New York: Doubleday.

Schwab, W. (1995). Adolescent and young adulthood: Issues in medical care, sexuality, and community living. In L. Nadel & D. Rosenthal (Eds.), *Down syndrome: Living and learning in the community* (pp. 230–237). New York: Wiley-Liss.

Simmons, R. (1987). Social transition and adolescent development. In C. Irwin (Ed.), *Adolescent social behavior and health. New directions for child development, No. 37* (pp. 33–61). San Francisco: Jossey-Bass.

Sitlington, P., & Frank, A. (1990). Are adolescents with LD successfully crossing the bridge to adult life? *Learning Disability Quarterly, 13*, 97–111.

Sivard, R. (1985). *Women … a world survey*. Washington, DC: World Priorities.

Spencer, M., & Dornbusch, S. (1990). Challenges in studying minority youth. In S. Feldman & G. Elliott (Eds.), *At the threshold: The developing adolescent* (pp. 123–146). Cambridge, MA: Harvard University Press.

Steele, L. (1991). Early work experience among white and non-white youths: Implications for subsequent enrollment and employment. *Youth & Society, 22*, 419–447.

Stern, D., McMillion, M., Hopkins, C., & Stone, J. (1990). Work experience for students in high school and college. *Youth & Society, 21*, 355–389.

Takanishi, R. (1993, February). The opportunities of adolescence—Research, interventions, and policy. *American Psychologist, 48,* 85–87.

Tierney, J., Grossman, J., & Resch, N. (1995). *Making a difference: An impact study of Big Brother/Big Sister.* Philadelphia: Public/Private Ventures.

Torney-Purta, J. (1990). Youth in relation to social institutions. In S. Feldman & G. Elliott (Eds.), *At the threshold: The developing adolescent* (pp. 457–477). Cambridge, MA: Harvard University Press.

U.S. Department of Commerce. (1994). College degree can make you a $ million! *Census and You, 29,* 12.

U.S. Department of Education. (1986). *What works: Research about teaching and learning.* Washington, DC: Author.

———. (1993). *Youth indicators 1993.* Washington, DC: U.S. Department of Education, Office of Educational Research and Improvement.

———. (1995a). *The educational progress of women.* Washington, DC: U.S. Department of Education, Office of Educational Research and Improvement.

———. (1995b). *Educational policy issues: Statistical perspectives—Extracurricular participation and student engagement.* Washington, DC: U.S. Department of Education, Office of Educational Research and Improvement.

Valdes, A. (1996, January 23). The many lives of Shahi Smart. *The Boston Globe, 249,* 57, 60.

Veum, J., & Weiss, A. (1993, April). Education and the work histories of young adults. *Monthly Labor Review,* 11–20.

Wagner, M. (1991a). Reflections. In M. Wagner, L. Newman, R. D'Amico, E. Jay, P. Butler-Nalin, C. Marder, & R. Cox (Eds.), *Youth with disabilities: How are they doing? The first comprehensive report from the National Longitudinal Transition Study of Special Education Students* (pp. 11-1 to 11-16). Menlo Park, CA: SRI International.

———. (1991b, April). *The benefits of secondary vocational education for young people with disabilities.* Paper presented to the Vocational Education Special Interest Group of the American Educational Research Association Annual Meeting, Chicago.

———. (1992a, April). *Being female—A secondary disability? Gender differences in the transition experiences of young people with disabilities.* Paper presented to the Special Education Interest Group of the American Educational Research Association Annual Meeting, San Francisco.

———. (1992b). "A little help from my friends": The social involvement of young people with disabilities. In M. Wagner, R. D'Amico, C. Marder, L. Newman, & J. Blackorby (Eds.), *What happens next? Trends in postschool outcomes of youth with disabilities* (pp. 6-1 to 6-43). Menlo Park, CA: SRI International.

Wagner, M., D'Amico, R., Marder, C., Newman, L., & Blackorby, J. (1992, December). *What happens next? Trends in postschool outcomes of youth with disabilities.* Menlo Park, CA: SRI International.

Ward, M., & Halloran, W. (1993). Transition to uncertainty: Status of many school leavers with severe disabilities, *CDEI, 12,* 71–81.

Wellesley College Center for Research on Women (WCRW). (1992). *The AAUW report: How schools shortchange girls.* Washington, DC: American Association of University Women.

Youniss, J., & Smollar, J. (1985). *Adolescents' relations with mothers, fathers, and friends.* Chicago: University of Chicago Press.

Zaslow, M., & Takanishi, R. (1993, February). Priorities for research on adolescent development. *American Psychologist, 48,* 185–192.

2

Emerging Transition Best Practices

FRANK R. RUSCH and
DOROTHY M. MILLAR

Our nation's high schools remain vested in the primary pursuit of preparing students who intend to pursue a college education. At the same time, we are struggling to determine how best to prepare youth who are not headed to college. Both outcomes are important considerations for educators who are working toward improving the postsecondary options for all students. In this chapter, we review major education reform movements that emerged in the 1980s and continued into the 1990s as a result of mounting criticism from the general public about how we prepare students for their roles as contributing community members. A review of this movement is important because it has almost completely ignored students with disabilities. Clearly, if students with disabilities were not protected by law, leading educators in this country would fund education that would benefit "those students who stand to contribute the most to society," rather than utilize "scarce educational resources" for students with disabilities, ensuring their rights and desires to participate equally in the opportunities provided by our society to all of its members.

It is important to realize that criticism of education is not unique to the past decade. Education was a popular target of reform as early as when Arthur Bestor (1953) called for reform of secondary education. Equally important is the realization that only few among recent reports on educational reform have centered on youth who are not college-bound.

In response to continuous calls for educational reform and our schools' apparent failing marks in providing transition-related services, recent federal initiatives have sought to promote systemic change in the transition process for all youth. Thus, significant and fundamental changes were intended with the passage of recent statutory acts—the Individuals with Disabilities Education Act Amendments of 1997 (IDEA); Carl D. Perkins Vocational Education and Applied Technology Act of 1990; Goals 2000: Educate America; and the School-to-Work Opportunities Act of 1994.

Until 1983, no systematic attempt was made to better understand why youth with disabilities were failing to make the transition from adolescents living at home to young adults striking out on their own. As detailed in Chapter 3, however, Congress signed into law a major shift in educational policy by extending the Individuals with Disabilities Education Act of 1975 to include the use of discretionary monies to improve our understanding of the problems these youth face and to identify solutions to their problems. As a result of legislation introduced in 1984, over 500 model programs were funded. These model programs have introduced innovative services that have enhanced the attainment of postsecondary outcomes for students with disabilities, such as independent living, postsecondary education or training, and employment (Rusch, Kohler, & Hughes, 1992). Importantly, this chapter summarizes common elements across each of the three vocationally focused initiatives that have emerged in the recent past. These "common best practices in transition" are enjoying new recognition as the school curriculum of the future.

Following our review of the reform movement, we describe desired postschool outcomes all youth are expected to achieve. We then review (a) special education "best practices" as identified by model demonstration programs funded by the U.S. Department of Education; (b) general vocational education model programs; and (c) vocational education for special populations exemplary practices. We conclude the chapter by addressing the call for one educational system that supports all youth—with and without disabilities—throughout the transition process.

REVIEW OF REFORM MOVEMENTS

Three separate reports on education reform appeared in 1983, including one of the most popular publications on education reform, the National Commission on Excellence in Education (1983), which identified the problems associated with student performance as a result of standardized test results. In this report, it was suggested that changes were needed in instructional content, instructional time, and teaching in order to improve student performance. Further, reference was made to teacher shortages for youth with disabilities, and it was recommended that the school year be extended to accommodate the special learning abilities of youth with disabilities.

Also, the Twentieth Century Fund (1983) addressed the federal role in supporting the nation's elementary and secondary schools. A background paper in the report prepared by Peterson (1983) mentioned the escalating costs and difficulties associated with identifying and classifying students with disabilities as well as procedural requirements related to the Individual with Disabilities Education Act.

The third report was prepared by Boyer (1983). Different from the National Commission on Excellence in Education (1983) and Twentieth Century Fund (1983), Boyer's foresightful report included specific suggestions for reform, including a "transition school" where students would pursue specialized training in "elective clusters" during their final 2 years of high school. Boyer also suggested the need to establish relationships between high schools and postsecondary institutions as well as with community businesses.

Unfortunately, this report was narrow in its treatment of specific student populations; for example, not a single reference was made to youth with disabilities. Further, none of these three reports referenced youth apprenticeship programs that have evolved over the past three decades or the role that vocational education has played in the preparation of youth (Stern et al., 1995).

Three additional reports published in the 1980s suggested the need for school reform, including reform of secondary education. For example, Goodlad (1984) echoed the sentiments of the three reports published in 1983, suggesting that the "entire education system is nearing collapse" (p. 1). Among his recommendations,

Goodlad noted that secondary special educators felt less adequately prepared to work with students assigned to them than did elementary special educators and that more attention, therefore, needed to be directed to improving their training.

In a metaphorical comparison between shopping malls and high schools, Powell, Farrar, and Cohen (1985) made several references to students with disabilities. For example, they suggested that students with disabilities attend "specialty shops" and "special-need shops," noting that a disproportionate amount of time, energy, and resources are "lavished upon them" (p. 119). In this connection, the authors quoted a counselor as follows, "This is terrible to say," apologized a counselor, "but it's not fair that all the money be put into many youngsters [who] will never be the doctors and lawyers and the leaders of society" (p. 175).

An obvious omission in logic prevails in this report. These authors fail to point out that almost half of all students without disabilities do not attend college, and that 25 percent of those who do attend college do not need a college degree to obtain the job that they acquire after graduation. Remarkably, educational reformists have not addressed the need to shift significant time, energy, and resources away from the prevailing mentality of college preparation for all students, regardless of the students' ambitions. Powell and colleagues (1985) ended their report suggesting that all students have access to "specialty workshops" (p. 316).

In Gardner (1985), some important points were made related to the efficacy of special education. For example, she pointed to the overall effectiveness of special education for students with disabilities and the students' need for specialized attention. At the same time, she cited the proliferation of students labeled as learning disabled as a major threat to education, contending that these students require a disproportionate amount of resources. Further, she concluded that resource rooms and pull-out programs are becoming dumping grounds for regular students, who experience even minor academic difficulties.

Curiously, Gardner (1985) notes that "broad mandates that impose rigid standards and procedures ... dull America's traditional sense of mutual obligation and charity and the resultant capacity for innovative local solutions" (p. 30). Essentially, therefore, she implies that the education of students with disabilities should result from the philanthropy of school districts, thereby making such services optional and considered as charity.

Several reports on school reform are continuing to be published in the 1990s. For example, Toch (1991) and Finn (1992) both addressed classification, categorization, and placement of students with disabilities and the effect that these students are having an undermining reform in Texas and nationally. Specifically, Toch discussed the increasing numbers of students being classified as learning disabled and the lack of movement back to the regular classroom. Finn, in turn, commented on the "politically correct" position of mainstreaming students with widely varying abilities into the regular classroom.

Toch and Finn are two more examples of educators who are fixated on special education as stifling this country's educational reform. Nothing could be further from the truth, however. To date, regular educators have not adequately addressed the needs of students with disabilities. At the same time, special educators have not adequately addressed the needs of students with disabilities in light of the expectations we have for *all* students, including those with disabilities. In essence, by developing separate educational tracks, special and regular educators have ignored the broader goal of developing an educational system that best serves all students versus a system that best serves only students with or without a disability.

Special education suffers from a negative image among many people, including regular educators. Harris (1992) of Louis Harris and Associates compared special education to a "toxic waste dump for those who don't fit into the traditional stereotypes of what a student should be" (p. 14). As is our entire education system, special education is in need of major reform. At the secondary level, the direction of reform efforts will be largely influenced by recent legislation and by the recognition that the problem facing our schools is complex and the solution equally as complex.

In addition to the various reports previously cited, the problems that face our schools have been the topic of numerous reports commissioned by the federal government. One of them, the Secretary's Commission of Achieving Necessary Skills (1991), addresses whether secondary students were being adequately prepared for the demands of the workplace. The Secretary's Commission on Achieving Necessary Skills (SCANS) described the workplace as a place where "workers must be creative and responsible problem solvers and have the skills and attitudes on which employers can build" (p. v). This report delivers the important message that the "business as usual" attitude not only hurts students during their preparation for employment, but ultimately also employers who are counting on a more flexible and problem-solving work force in order to remain competitive in the global marketplace of the twenty-first century. Tables 2.1 and 2.2 display the framework and competencies, respectively, that the SCANS report projects employers will be seeking among its future work-force participants.

As illustrated, the foundation stresses process, higher cognition skills, and learning in context as essential for equipping students with the knowledge, skills, and preparation needed to find meaningful jobs and lead productive lives. SCANS emphasizes the importance of teaching students to perform marketable skills in the real world of work, with its accompanying expectations, as opposed to teaching students to acquire work-related skills in simulated environments.

REVIEW OF REFORM LEGISLATION

As discussed by Stodden in Chapter 3, major legislative acts have emerged since 1983 in support of developing model programs, including the passage and subsequent reauthorizations of the Individuals with Disabilities Education Act.

This legislation highlighted the importance of the transition process, elevating it to a high priority within the U.S. Department of Education, Office of Special Education and Rehabilitative Services (OSERS). Specifically, IDEA mandates that transition services be addressed beginning no later than age 14; earlier, if appropriate. Further, the purpose of such planning is to determine long-range goals relative to the following outcomes: "postsecondary education, vocational training, integrated employment (including supported employment), continuing and adult education, adult services, independent living, and/or community participation" (20, U.S.C. 1401(a)(19). Although sporadic efforts at transition planning could be found prior to IDEA, current legislation requires formal documentation of the transition process for youth receiving special education services (Norman & Bourexis, 1995).

In addition to the special education efforts expressed in IDEA, the Carl D. Perkins Vocational and Applied Technology Education Act of 1990 (P.L. 101-392) places a strong emphasis on the transition process and serves as the basis for current vocational education activities. The purpose of this act is to

> assure that individuals who are inadequately served under vocational education programs are assured access to quality vocational education programs, especially individuals who are disadvantaged, men and women who are entering (with disabilities) non-traditional occupations, adults who are in need of training and retraining, individuals who are single parents or homemakers, individuals with limited English proficiency, and individuals who are incarcerated in correctional institutions. (P.L. 98-524, 98, Stat. 2435)

The Act also mandates that vocational assessment, counseling, support, and transition services be provided for students identified with disabilities and disadvantaged. In short, its goal is successful completion of a vocational education program in the most integrated setting with a clear emphasis on student outcomes (Clark & Kolstoe, 1995).

Table 2.1 SCANS Framework

BASIC SKILLS

Reads, writes, performs arithmetic and mathematical operations, listens and speaks

A. Reading—locates, understands, and interprets written information in prose and in documents such as manuals, graphs, and schedules.

B. Writing—communicates thoughts, ideas, information and messages in writing; creates documents such as letters, directions, manuals, reports, graphs, and flow charts.

C. Arithmetic/Mathematics—performs basic computations and approaches practical problems by choosing appropriately from a variety of mathematical techniques.

D. Listening—receives, attends to, interprets, and responds to verbal messages and other cues.

E. Speaking—organizes ideas and communicates orally.

THINKING SKILLS

Thinks creatively, makes decisions, solves problems, visualizes, knows how to learn, and reasons

A. Creative Thinking—generates new ideas.

B. Decision Making—specifies goals and constraints, generates alternatives, considers risks, and evaluates and chooses best alternative.

C. Problem Solving—recognizes problems and devises and implements a plan of action.

D. Seeing Things in the Mind's Eye—organizes and processes symbols, pictures, graphs, objects, and other information.

E. Knowing How to Learn—uses sufficient learning techniques to acquire and apply new knowledge and skills.

F. Reasoning—discovers a rule or principle underlying the relationship between two or more objects and applies it when solving a problem.

PERSONAL QUALITIES

Displays responsibility, self-esteem, sociability, self-management, and integrity and honesty.

A. Responsibility—exerts a high level of effort and perseveres toward goal attainment.

B. Self-Esteem—believes in own self-worth and maintains a positive view of self.

C. Sociability—demonstrates understanding, friendliness, adaptability, empathy, and politeness in group settings.

D. Self-Management—Assesses self accurately, sets personal goals, monitors progress, and exhibits self-control.

E. Integrity/Honesty—chooses ethical courses of action.

Source: Secretary of Labor's Commission on Achieving Necessary Skills, 1991:16.

In 1994, President Clinton signed into law the Goals 2000: Educate America Act. With its core purpose being educational reform, this act is considered a centerpiece of and framework for restructuring the American education system based on the national education goals. These goals are as follows:

1. *School Readiness.* All students will come to school ready to learn.

2. *School Completion.* The high school graduation rate will be at least 90 percent.

3. *Student Achievement and Citizenship.* Students will demonstrate competencies over challenging subject matter, including the ability to use their minds in order to be prepared for responsible citizenship, further learning, and productive employment in our current and future economy.

Table 2.2 SCANS Competencies

RESOURCES
Identifies, organizes, plans, and allocates resources.

A. Time—selects goal-relevant activities, ranks them,, allocates time, and prepares and follows schedule.

B. Money—uses or prepares budgets, makes forecasts, keeps records, and makes adjustments to meet objectives.

C. Materials and Facilities—acquires, stores, allocates, and uses materials or space efficiently.

D. Human Resources—assesses skills and distributes work accordingly, evaluates performance, and provides feedback.

INTERPERSONAL
Works with others.

A. Participates as Member of a Team—contributes to group effort.

B. Teaches Others New Skills.

C. Serves CLients/Customers—works to satisfy customers' expectations.

D. Exercises Leadership—communicates ideas to justify position, persuades and convinces others, responsibly challenges existing procedures and policies.

E. Negotiates—works toward agreements involving exchange of resources; resolves divergent interests.

F. Works with Diversity—works well with men and women with diverse backgrounds.

INFORMATION
Acquires and uses information.

A. Acquires and Evaluates Information.

B. Organizes and Maintains Information.

C. Interprets and Communicates Information.

D. Uses Computers to Process Information.

SYSTEMS
Understands complex interrelationships.

A. Understands Systems—knows how social, organizational, and technological systems work and operates effectively within them.

B. Monitors and Corrects Performance—distinguishes trends, predicts impacts on system operations, diagnoses deviations in system's performance, and corrects malfunctions.

C. Improves or Designs Systems—suggests modifications to existing systems and develops new or alternative systems to improve performance.

TECHNOLOGY:
Works with a variety of technologies

A. Selects Technology—chooses procedures, tools, or equipment including computers and related technologies.

B. Applies Technology to Task—understands overall intent and proper procedures for setup and operation of equipment.

C. Maintains and Troubleshoots Equipment—prevents, identifies, or solves problems with equipment, including computers and other technologies.

Source: Secretary of Labor's Commission on Achieving Necessary Skills, 1991:12.

4. *Teacher Education and Professional Development.* The nation's teaching force will have access to programs to support continuing improvement of professional skills and acquisition of the knowledge and skills needed to instruct and prepare all American students for the next century.

5. *Mathematics and Science.* American students will be first in the world in mathematics and science.

6. *Adult Literacy and Lifelong Learning.* Every adult American will be literate, will possess the knowledge and skills necessary to compete in a global economy, and will exercise the rights and responsibilities of citizenship.

7. *Safe Schools.* Every school in the United States will be free of drugs, violence, and unauthorized presence of firearms and alcohol, which will result in a disciplined environment conducive to learning.

8. *Parental Participation.* Every school will promote partnerships that will increase parental involvement and participation in promoting the social, emotional, and academic growth of children.

Within the same year, the School-to-Work Opportunities Act of 1994 was signed into law. This Act, in conjunction with Goals 2000, establishes a broad incentive for national education reform by recognizing the importance of systemic reform, thereby offering important advances and opportunities for all youth. For example, the Act calls on states to plan and implement transition systems that will enable all youth to successfully transition from school to postschool environments. Further, it specifies what state plans should include such as basic program components and expected outcomes of students participating in school-to-work transition systems. As outlined in the law, statewide school-to-work systems are to (a) enable all youth to acquire the skills and knowledge necessary to transition smoothly from school to work or further education and training, (b) impact the preparation of all youth for a first job toward a career and to increase opportunities for further education, and (c) expand ways through which school- and work-based learning can be integrated, link occupational and academic learning, and strengthen the linkage between secondary and postsecondary education (Norman & Bourexis, 1995).

REVIEW OF DESIRED STUDENT POSTSCHOOL OUTCOMES

Complete consensus has not been achieved within our society on what constitutes desirable postschool outcomes for all youth as a result of an effective education. Nevertheless, governmental agencies and legislative acts have continually identified employment as one of the most commonly accepted postschool outcomes by which school effectiveness is measured. In special education, an emphasis emerged in the early 1980s on facilitating successful transition from school to work for youth with disabilities (Will, 1984). Assistant Secretary of Education Will (1984) defined the transition process as "an outcome-oriented process encompassing a broad array of services and experiences that lead to employment" (p. 1).

Halpern (1985) expanded the definition of the transition process, suggesting that employment is one of an array of desired postschool outcomes, and that community adjustment, including residential status and establishment of desirable social and interpersonal networks, are also necessary outcomes for which educational services were accountable. These outcomes are briefly described in what follows.

Employment Status. Aspects of the employment outcome typically evaluated in follow-up studies encompass areas such as (a) job attainment, retention, and promotion; (b) earnings; and (c) hours of work. Although employment is a desired postschool outcome, "three-fourths of high school students in the United States enter the work force without baccalaureate degrees, and do not possess the academic and entry level occupational skills necessary to succeed in the changing... workplace" (School-to-Work Opportunities Act, 1994). In addition, youth with disabilities suffer particularly poor postschool employment outcomes, as discussed in Chapter 3 by Stodden.

Living/Residential Status. Residential independence is a well-known societal expectation. However, this outcome has not been as widely evaluated as has employment. Not surprisingly, results from follow-up studies have shown that youth with disabilities live less independently than youth who do not have disabilities (Benz & Halpern, 1987; Blackorby & Wagner, 1996). Also, parents of youth with disabilities have indicated that their children's needs have not seriously been addressed. (Chadsey-Rusch, Rusch, & O'Reilly, 1991).

Social and Interpersonal Status. Social and interpersonal status has only recently received attention as an outcome. Previous follow-up studies have been limited to evaluating just a few aspects of this outcome, including (a) marital status (Wagner, 1989); (b) incarceration (Wagner, 1989); (c) recreational activities (Halpern, Close, & Nelson, 1986); and (d) extracurricular school or community group participation (Halpern et al., 1986). The importance of various aspects associated with satisfactory social and interpersonal relationships is discussed comprehensively in Chapter 17 by Chadsey-Rusch and Shelden.

Quality of Life

The passage of IDEA, in which transition services are defined (P.L. 105-17), established a broad conceptualization of desired student postschool outcomes. In this legislative act, desired postschool outcomes include (a) postsecondary education, (b) vocational training, (c) integrated employment (including supported employment), (d) continuing and adult educa-

tion, (e) adult services, (f) independent living, and (g) community participation. Although employment remains as a highly emphasized outcome, the language in the Act clearly acknowledges the relevance and importance of other desired postschool outcomes. In fact; this legislation acknowledges a broader list of outcomes encompassing the concept of quality of life.

Recently, quality of life has emerged as an essential concept when referenced to postschool outcomes. Numerous definitions of quality of life have been proposed, including the following:

- "Quality of life is a matter of subjective experience. That is to say the concept has no meaning apart from what a person feels and experiences. As a corollary to the first proposition, people may experience the same circumstances differently. What enhances one person's quality of life may detract from another's" (Taylor & Bogdan, 1990:34–35).

- "Quality of life can be viewed as the discrepancy between a person's achieved and their unmet needs and desires. ... Quality of life can also be viewed as the degree to which an individual has control over his or her environment" (Brown, Bayer, & MacFarlane, 1988:111–112).

- "When an individual, with or without disabilities, is able to meet important needs in major life settings (work, school, home, community) while also satisfying the normative expectations that others hold for him or her in those settings, he or she is more likely to experience a high quality of life" (Goode, 1990:46).

Although consensus is lacking on what quality of life is, we can point to common elements among various definitions and subsequently developed a conceptual framework by which transition programs and services can be evaluated. Table 2.3 lists three domains and fifteen outcomes from this framework.

As illustrated, each of the three domains brings in the individual perspective/personal

Table 2.3 Quality-of-Life Domains & Desired Postschool Outcomes

Physical and Material Well-Being

- physical and mental health
- food, clothing, and lodging
- financial security
- safety from harm

Performance of Adult Roles

- mobility and community access
- vocation, career, employment
- leisure and recreation
- personal relationships and social networks
- educational attainment
- spiritual fulfillment
- citizenship (e.g., voting)
- social responsibility (e.g., does not break laws)

Personal Fulfillment

- happiness
- satisfaction
- sense of general well-being

Source: Halpern, A. (1993). Quality of Life as a Conceptual Framework for Evaluating Transition Outcomes. *Exceptional Children*, 59, 486–498.

choice and the societal perspective/social norms. They are briefly discussed in what follows.

Physical and Material Well-Being. According to Halpern (1993), four outcomes in this domain include (a) physical and mental health (prevention of major health problems); (b) food, clothing, and lodging (freedom from severe hunger of homelessness); (c) financial security (regular income to support a life-style above the poverty level); and (d) safety from harm (existing in an environment that is harm-free). Essentially, these outcomes should be viewed as basic entitlements for all individuals.

Performance of Adult Roles. The second domain, often referred to as *independent living or community involvement,* addresses eight outcomes relating to how individuals interact with their environments. These outcomes are (a) mobility and community access (use of transportation); (b) vocational, career, employment (job reflecting career interest); (c) leisure and recreation (use of free time); (d) personal relationships and social networks (social interactions with others); (e) educational attainment (earns a high school diploma); (f) spiritual fulfillment (involved in spiritual activities of choice); (g) citizenship (voting); and (h) social responsibility (obeys laws). For each of the outcomes listed, individuals determine the extent to which they perform the various adult roles. Along with individual choice, societal expectations are to be considered within this domain (Halpern, 1993).

Personal Fulfillment. This third domain, *personal fulfillment,* offered by Halpern (1993), emphasizes person-centered decisions. The three outcomes identified in this domain include (a) happiness, (b) satisfaction, and (c) a sense of general well-being. These outcomes need further clarification.

Using the quality-of-life-outcomes conceptual framework, Halpern applied results from his review of forty-one follow-up and follow-along studies. All studies reported findings pertaining to employment, three-fourths reported information on financial security, and more than half discussed educational attainment (Halpern, 1993). Relationships and social networks were the outcomes addressed by approximately half of the studies reviewed. Not unsurprisingly, the personal-fulfillment domain and related outcomes had been omitted from the studies.

Halpern makes a strong case that many postschool outcomes should be explored, and that a more encompassing and comprehensive approach to evaluate educational practices in relation to postschool outcomes should be implemented. Halpern (1993) suggested that six types of information be collected as part of such a comprehensive approach: (a) student and family characteristics, (b) school services received, (c) school outcomes achieved, (d) quality of life while in school, (e) postschool services received, and (f) quality of life after leaving school. Obviously, the first four types of information would be gathered while this student attended school, the final two once the student has exited the school system and then several times throughout the postschool years. In a preliminary study utilizing these six types of information, Halpern (1993) found that personal/social integration and personal fulfillment were moderately related to youth's quality of life; vocational adjustment and personal/social integration were unrelated.

Summary. Although there is no general societal consensus on what postschool outcomes are desired, employment is consistently regarded as very important. Based on the findings of numerous follow-up studies, it is evident what outcomes are valued by schools, programs, and government agencies. DeStefano and Wagner (1990) identified areas such as attendance rates, standardized test scores, and high school graduation rates as common outcomes that are evaluated to help determine success while students are in school. Once students leave the school environment, common outcomes evaluated to reflect the impact of schooling include employment and residential status.

As the quest for improved postschool outcomes continues, it is essential that we adopt a broader approach to evaluating school impact on youth's quality of life. In the following section, models and practices will be discussed and explored. The quality of such practices must also be evaluated to determine their impact on youths' postschool outcomes. The models and legislative acts, collectively, emphasize outcomes beyond those traditionally associated with schooling (e.g., student attendance and standardized scores). It is no longer sufficient that youth merely read and write, they must also be productive, lifelong learners capable of competing in today's global economy (DeStefano & Wagner, 1992).

MODEL PROGRAM DEVELOPMENT

Federal monies have been made available to fund model demonstration projects with the specific aim of developing and implementing practices that would positively impact the transition process, with the ultimate goal of helping students realize positive postschool outcomes. Whereas these model programs individually have not generated and sustained the energy essential to drive national comprehensive education reform and restructuring, together they direct attention to the issue of transition, focusing policy, practice, and research on educational practices associated with promoting quality adult life for all youth.

Special Education Model Projects

Since 1983, the U.S. Department of Education has supported the transition initiative by authorizing the use of discretionary funding under Part C, in which Congress authorized approximately $5 million annually between 1984 and 1986 to carry out provisions of Section 625, "Postsecondary Education Programs," and approximately $6 million annually for grants under Section 626, "Secondary Education and Transitional Services for Youth with Disabilities." Rusch and Phelps (1987) noted that "the major objectives of Section 626 are (a) to stimulate the improvement and development of programs of secondary special education and (b) to strengthen and coordinate education, training, and related services to assist in the transition process to postsecondary education, vocational training, competitive employment, continuing education, or adult services" (p. 489). Since 1984, OSERS has announced several grant competitions to meet the objectives of Sections 625 and 626. The themes of these competitions are summarized in Table 2.4.

Over 500 model demonstration projects have been developed and implemented as a result of federal funding. Model programs have been funded in every state with the exception of South Dakota, Nevada, and West Virginia. New York, California, and Washington have been the recipients of the highest number of awards, 43, 27, and 23, respectively.

In addition to the model demonstration projects awarded under Section 626, the Rehabilitation Services Administration (RSA), under Section 311 of (P.L. 93-112), also strengthened the transition initiative by awarding grants for "Transition from School to Work Projects" under the Special Projects and Demonstrations for Individuals with Disabilities programs. The purpose of this competition was to establish comprehensive rehabilitation programs in an effort to improve rehabilitation services for persons with severe disabilities, with the primary aim of assisting those individuals in achieving their "optimal vocational adjustment" (Rusch et al., 1992:124).

In 1991, OSERS furthered the transition initiative by allocating federal funds to support a series of 5-year state systems-change programs with the specific purpose that states design and implement a comprehensive process to promote successful transitions for youth with disabilities from school to adult community participation (Norman & Bourexis, 1995).

Aims of these state systems-change grants include (a) increasing the availability of and access to quality transition services for youth with disabilities; (b) improving the ability of professionals, parents, and advocates to work with youth with disabilities throughout the transition process; (c) improving collaborative relations and efforts among stakeholders; and (d) developing incentives for accessing or establishing expertise and resources of programs, projects, and activities related to transition (Norman & Bourexis, 1995).

Kohler (1993) conducted an extensive review of the existing literature aimed at determining which transition practices had been substantiated as *being* a "best practice," as opposed to those *assumed to be* a "best practice." This is a critical issue, because many practices are implemented without sufficient evidence that they are indeed positively impacting postschool outcomes (Peter & Heron, 1993). Kohler reviewed forty-nine transition-related documents, including reports published by model program developers, searching for practices identified as "best" based on substantiating evidence. These practices were then categorized as either substantiated by research or "implied" as being effective by subjective criteria. Vocational training, parent involvement, interagency collaboration, and service delivery were cited in over 50 percent of the documents analyzed. Other practices such as social skills training, paid work experience, and individualized transition planning were supported in at least one-third of the literature reviewed (Kohler, 1993).

Additional practices substantiated by research include (a) early planning, beginning by the seventh grade; (b) team planning and interagency collaboration; (c) incorporating transition and career planning within the IEP process; (d) focusing on integrated employment; (e) utilizing a functional, community-referenced

Table 2.4 Goals of the Fifteen Grant Competitions Funded Since 1983

- Demonstrate innovative approaches to transition using direct service delivery.
- Support new model demonstration projects that link transitioning individuals to community-based training programs and services.
- Stimulate higher education (postsecondary, vocational, technical, continuing, or adult education) possibilities for persons with mild disabilities.
- Focus on special adaptations of postsecondary services/career placement.
- Design, implement, and disseminate practices that facilitate the transition of youth with severe handicaps to employment.
- Support projects that develop and establish exemplary school-community models for specific vocational training and job placement.
- Design cooperative models (State or Local Education Agency) that facilitate effective planning to meet employment needs of exiting students with disabilities.
- Support projects designed to plan and develop cooperative models for activities among SEAs or LEAs and adult service agencies.
- Identify the skills and characteristics necessary for self-determination, as well as the in-school and out-of-school experiences that lead to development of self-determination.
- Identify job-related training needed by secondary students with mild handicaps.
- Support research projects on effective strategies to provide transitional services to youths with disabilities, ages 16 through 21, from one or more of the following special populations: adjudicated youths, youths with severe emotional disturbances, or youths with severe physical disabilities (including traumatic brain injury).
- Support projects that enhance the capacity of local educational agencies by promoting implementation of proven transition models, or selected components of these models, in multiple school districts within a state based on specific needs.
- Encourage follow-up and follow-along studies to document the impact of transition services, and to revise program options based on analysis of outcome data.
- Assist youth with handicaps and their families in identifying, accessing, and using formal and informal networks to obtain needed supports and services to maximize independence in adult life.
- Identify factors that facilitate student involvement in the transition planning process and to develop national dissemination on effective interventions and strategies.

curricula; (f) placing students in jobs that provide opportunities for advancement; (g) providing ongoing inservice personnel training; and (h) evaluating program effectiveness (Heal et al., 1990; Halpern, Benz, & Lindstrom, 1992; Kohler et al., 1994; Benz, Lindstrom, & Halpern, 1995; DeFur & Taymans, 1995; Sands, Adams, & Stout, 1995).

More recently, Kohler (1996) extended the existing research by organizing transition practices into a conceptual framework consisting of (a) student–focused transition planning, (b) family involvement, (c) collaboration, (d) student development, and (e) program integration. Each

of these practices is further reviewed in what follows.

Student-Focused Transition Planning. The practices in this category pertain to the development of educational planning and transition services based on each individual student's needs, preferences, and interests and with students acting as active participants in the design of their education and transition services (Kohler, 1996). As mentioned, IDEA has mandated that transition services be addressed within the IEP, beginning no later than age of 14, earlier if appropriate. Although IDEA specifies that the youth's preferences and interests be the driving force behind transition planning, Wehmeyer and Ward (1995) remind us that "the current reality for many students with disabilities is that they are left out of the transition process, from goal development to placement and instructional decision-making" (p. 108).

An important contribution of IDEA to our understanding of the needs of students was the appearance of language mandating student involvement in transition planning. That is, when transition services are addressed, students *must* be invited to attend planning meetings. This new language heralds recognition of the need to include all students' preferences and interest in the planning and delivery of transition services.

Evidence suggests that students are becoming involved in developing their own education and transition planning as a direct result of the model projects. Thus, students are being provided with opportunities to develop skills associated with being self-determined and are actually directing their own IEP (Martin, Marshall, & Maxson, 1993; VanReusen & Bos, 1994; Wehmeyer & Lawrence, 1995). VanReusen and colleagues (1994) designed a process that teaches students how to inventory their strengths, weaknesses, and goals and to make choices about what they want to learn. The sequence involves orientating students toward active participation in the development of their educational programs through role-playing scenarios. Further, the process provides students with strategies for effectively communicating, taking an active role in making decisions, and self-evaluating.

Another practice that encourages student participation while maintaining a student-oriented focus is the utilization of a person-centered futures planning process. "Person-centered planning" is a term used to describe a variety of processes that focus on an individual. All person-centered planning approaches, such as the McGill Action Planning System (MAPS), focus on the needs, preferences, and interests of an individual based on a recognition of the importance of both formal and informal supports in assisting students in achieving their goals (Mount & Zwernik, 1988; Vandercook, York, & Forest, 1989).

Person-centered futures planning typically consists of three components: (a) a personal student profile and future vision map addressing areas such as employment, living arrangements, and recreation involvement; (b) a group of individuals who provide support to the student in moving toward goal attainment; and (c) a written plan of action specifying who will take responsibility for seeing progress and timeline. In Chapter 9, Wehmeyer expands this discussion to make student involvement in education planning, decision making, and program implementation a reality. Our challenge is to adopt the strategies and practices outlined by Wehmeyer and others to ensure a better future for all students.

Family Involvement. The influence of the family on early development is well known (Szymanski, 1994; Morningstar, Turnbull, & Turnbull, 1996). As discussed by Lichtenstein in greater detail in Chapter 1, the family provides the context and the foundation for all major decisions made by adolescents, including decisions about coursework, early work experiences, and even eventual job selection and career focusing. Despite its undisputed importance, the family is viewed as a paradox. On the one hand, adolescents are struggling for their own identity and desire to "break away" from their "childhood influences," and on the other hand, families are well equipped to help adolescents face the challenges that the future holds.

Parental and family involvement in the planning and delivery of transition services may need facilitation. It is essential, for example, that family members be empowered to actively participate in collaborative teams at all levels (individual student, community, state, and federal levels). Successful participation may require that they receive training in areas similar to those of the students. Topics of training include promoting self-determination and self-advocacy, becoming better informed about agencies and services, and understanding legal issues. In Chapter 10, Hanley-Maxwell, Pogoloff, and Whitney-Thomas further discuss practices designed to facilitate active and meaningful family participation in the transition process.

Collaboration. One of the most important facilitators of a youth's transition from school to adult community participation is collaboration (Benz et al., 1995). In addition to the active participation of the student and family members, many others must become involved. School personnel, peers, employers, local or state agency representatives (such as vocational rehabilitation), and advocates are just a few of the potential collaborators who may be involved in delivering transition services. Due to the vast array of philosophies and opinions represented by various disciplines and professionals, it is critical that all involved with the student come together to clearly understand each other's role. Team values serve to promote common goodwill and direct attention to the primary goal of education.

Collaboration occurs at many interrelated levels, including the *student level,* in which the student is the center; the *organization level,* where it promotes the unification of general and special education services and programs; and the *community level,* where collaboration is necessary to ensure community and business involvement in program development. Later in this text, Everson and Guillory (Chapter 12) identify important characteristics of teaming and collaboration, suggesting that *collaborative interagency teams* be defined as "a group of individuals representing multiple and diverse agencies and organizations who come together to address a common need and agree to pursue a common goal." A critical characteristic of these collaboratives is their early investment in identifying beliefs and principles that bind the team together.

Student Development. According to Kohler (1996) and Chapter 8, best practices related to student development emphasize the importance

of students acquiring the skills and strategies they need to effectively and successfully attain their goals. To enable them to acquire these goals, students must receive academic and vocational curriculum and instruction based on the results of life skills and vocational assessments. Life skills include self-determination and social skills necessary across environments, recreation and leisure skills, and household management skills (i.e., personal finance, personal needs, family responsibility, food preparation) (Kohler, 1996).

Vocational and career curricula and experiences focus on (a) longitudinal career education; (b) community-referenced and community-based training; (c) infusion of career and vocational curricula across academic subject areas, (d) ongoing functional life skills and vocational assessment; (e) infusion of related services into career and vocational development (e.g., occupational therapy, physical therapy, speech therapy); and (f) interagency linkages to continue career education and experiences (Kohler, 1996).

Along with these assessments and curricula and instruction practices, the issue of students meeting the graduation requirements of schools must be considered. As they acquire the skills and knowledge needed to fulfill adult roles, students must have the option of earning course credits in nontraditional manners. For example, students should be able to earn math and science credits through vocational courses or actual work experiences. Further, accommodations and support services, such as peer mentors and access to assistive technology devices, must be available to students (Kohler, 1996).

Program Integration. Program structure, attributes, and integration practices all relate to the efficiency and effectiveness of the educational and transition services provided (Kohler, 1996). To achieve the practices discussed previously (student-focused transition planning, family involvement, collaboration, and student development), educational systems and individual programs must be organized in a manner that best facilitates them. Community-level strategic planning, cultural and ethnic sensitivity, qualified staff, and effective use of resources are but a few of the administrative practices necessary to promote program integration.

Several recent publications have indicated that programs that have been successful in preparing youth for postsecondary involvement and employment maximize every opportunity to integrate youth with disabilities into programs that serve youth without disabilities (DeStefano, 1989; Chadsey-Rusch & Rusch, 1996). Typically, such programs include activities and standards that are applied to all youth, thereby avoiding separate activities, facilities, and groupings. It is important to note that the paths that have been constructed in special education to prepare youth with disabilities to move toward their future goals share the very same ingredients as those used to construct parallel paths emerging outside the disability sphere, including family and student involvement and collaboration (with business, for example). Our challenge is to construct paths for all youth to travel to meet their current needs and future aspirations, because the paths for youth with and without disabilities are more alike than different.

General Vocational Education Model Programs

During the early 1900s, vocational education was comprised predominantly of small-scale programs in such areas as agriculture, home economics, and industrial arts (Cobb & Neubert, 1990). The sole goal of vocational education, as defined in the Smith-Hughes Act of 1917, was to meet the labor needs of local employers. Today, vocational education consists of an extensive and complex infrastructure with a curriculum that typically is comprised of both school- and work-based components (Cobb & Neubert, 1990; Clark & Kolstoe, 1995). This complex infrastructure is a result of the evolved goals of vocational education programs. These goals now encompass the following areas; (a)

acquisition of personal skills and attitudes, (b) computational skills and technological literacy, (c) employability skills, (d) broad and specific occupational skills and knowledge, and (e) foundations for career planning and lifelong learning (National Commission on Secondary Vocational Education, 1984). Additional skills include the development of critical thinking and problem solving (National Council on Vocational Education, 1990–1991).

Historically, the school-based components have evolved around seven major occupational areas: (a) agriculture education and related business, (b) business and office occupations, (c) health occupations, (d) marketing and distributive occupations, (e) home economics, (f) industrial arts and technology, and (g) trades and industrial education. Although some changes have been made to meet the current and future demands of employment, these areas continue to define much of the structure of vocational education (Stern et al., 1990; Smith & Rojewski, 1993; Clark & Kolstoe, 1995).

Among the numerous work-based vocational education approaches, the most common are known as (a) cooperative vocational education, (b) youth apprenticeships, (c) school-based enterprises, (d) career academies, and (e) tech-prep. Table 2.5, adapted from Stern and colleagues (1995), summarizes the common elements of these programs. Further, Cobb and Neubert (Chapter 15) and Hagner and Vander Sande (Chapter 14) provide a more thorough discussion of these programs.

A major emphasis in vocational education research has been on improving the integrity of vocation education and identifying the effects of early work experience on participant outcomes (Stone, 1993; Arum & Shavit, 1995). Results from existing studies of vocational programs generally denote mixed results in terms of benefits for students involved in these programs.

Recently, Charner and colleagues (1995), affiliates of the Academy for Educational Development's National Institute for Work and Learning (NIWL), studied the dynamics of fourteen

Table 2.5 Common Features of Vocational Education Models[a]

Program Feature	Coop	Youth Appren-ticeship	School-Based Enterprise	Career Academies	Tech-Prep
Structured work-based learning is provided while in school	A	A	U	R	R
School curriculum builds on work experience	U	U	S	S	R
Work experience is paid	A	A	R	U	R
Employers provide financial support	A	A	R	A	R
Program arranges student work placement	U	U	A	U	R
Employer is involved in curriculum	S	U	S	U	U
Academic and vocational curriculum is integrated	R	U	S	A	U
Formal link is established to postsecondary education	R	U	R	S	A
Provides employment/college counseling	S	S	R	S	U
Offers pre-11th-grade academic preparation	S	R	R	U	S
Offers pre-11th-grade career exploration	U	U	R	U	S
Model targets students who are at risk	U	S	S	S	R
Model targets students who are not college-bound	U	S	S	S	R
Students have mentors from outside school	S	U	R	U	R
Students receive occupational certification	R	A	R	R	S

Source: Adapted with permission from Stern et al. (1995).

[a]Approximate relative frequency of features in school-to-work programs: A = always; U = usually; S = sometimes,; R = rarely.

vocational programs nationwide in an effort to document and analyze useful models and practices in the hope that others could learn and adapt from these exemplary programs. The authors identified essential practices for building an effective school-to-work transition system, which are listed in Table 2.6.

As shown, effective practices include (a) administrative leaders who, with the support and involvement of their communities, are able to develop a shared vision, articulate goals, and design a comprehensive strategic plan; (b) teachers, counselors, and other professionals who are innovative and flexible, and willing to take risks with instruction, curriculum, and classroom management; (c) collaboration that involves schools, businesses, postsecondary institutions, and other community partners as active participants in all aspects of the educational efforts; (d) self-determination, whereby students take responsibility for their learning and an active role in their education planning; (e) school-based learning where the curriculum and school activities are connected to the world of work with school activities while building a solid academic foundation; (f) work-based learning options where students can be involved in unpaid or paid community-based work

Table 2.6 Key Elements of Successful Programs

- Administrative leadership from educational systems
- Leadership and commitment of program deliverers
- Cross-sector collaboration and partnerships
- Student self-determination
- School-based curriculum and instruction
- Work-based learning strategies
- Integrated career information and guidance
- Progressive system that begins before grade 11
- Access to postsecondary options
- Creative financing
- Application of research

Source: Adapted with permission from Charner et al. (1995).

experiences; (g) integration of career information and guidance support services that are ongoing and individualized, with all students having a career plan that is reviewed and updated on a regular basis; (h) a progressive system that begins before grade 11, recognizing that young students prior to becoming discouraged or disengaged from school need to be informed of the range of available vocational opportunities; (i) access to postsecondary options, while encouraging lifelong learning; and (j) creative financing, looking for in-kind contributions, reallocation of existing resources, as well as additional sources of funding (Charner et al., 1995).

Vocational Education for Special Populations: Exemplary Practice

Since the mid-1960s, the federal government has supported the inclusion of youth with disabilities in vocational education programs by authorizing funding of programs and support services designed to enhance the participation of special populations (Clark & Kolstoe, 1995). Although numerous programmatic approaches have been attempted, few have been rigorously evaluated or researched to determine effective practices or their impact on student postschool

outcomes. An exception is the report by Phelps and Wermuth (1992), who conducted an extensive literature review to determine criteria for identifying exemplary programs and consequently developed a framework that identifies variables and indicators characterizing successful vocational programs serving special populations (see Table 2.7). The framework consists of twenty practices under five major areas (a) program administration (strong administrative leadership and support, sufficient financial support, staff development, formative program evaluation, summative program evaluation); (b) curriculum and instruction (individualized curriculum modifications, integration of vocational and academic curricula, appropriate instructional settings, cooperative learning experiences); (c) comprehensive support services (assessment of individuals' vocational interests and abilities, instructional support services, ongoing career guidance and counseling); (d) formalized articulation and communication (family/parent involvement and support, notification of both students and parents regarding vocational opportunities, vocational educators' involvement in individualized educational planning, formalized transition planning, intra- and interagency collaboration); and (e) occupational experience (work experience opportunities, job placement,

Table 2.7 Framework of Exemplary Practices of Vocational Programs Serving Special Populations

- Program Administration
  Strong administrative leadership and support
  Sufficient financial support
  Staff development
  Formative program evaluation
  Summative program evaluation
- Curriculum and Instruction
  Individualized curriculum modifications
  Integration of vocational and academic curricula
  Appropriate instructional settings
  Cooperative learning experiences
- Comprehensive Support Services
  Assessment of individuals' vocational interests and abilities
  Instructional support services
  Ongoing career guidance and counseling
- Formalized Articulation and Communication
  Family/parent involvement and support
  Notification of both students and parents regarding vocational opportunities
  Vocational educators' involvement in individualized educational planning
  Formalized transition planning
  Intra- and interagency collaboration
- Occupational Experience
  Work experience opportunities
  Job placement
  Follow-up on graduates and nongraduates

Source: Adapted with permission from Phelps & Wermuth, 1992:25–28.

follow-up on graduates and nongraduates). All twenty components of the exemplary vocational special needs programs have received attention in the theoretical literature since the 1970s, however, empirical evidence supporting them is still lacking (Phelps & Wermuth, 1992).

DISCUSSION

Current legislation mandates that states and local school districts be responsible for establishing a comprehensive school-to-work transition system to assist all youth in acquiring the skills and knowledge necessary to make a smooth transition from school to work and/or further education and training. Part of the uniqueness of the School-to-Work Opportunities Act is that it is the first time the importance of developing systemic and noncompeting relationships between special and general education systems has been highlighted. In support of one system, Johnson and Rusch (1993) stated:

> We argue that special and regular educators must begin to understand that they are addressing the same problems in the same schools. If a discrepancy exists it is primarily

an issue of language and communication. While educators talk about problems related to tracking, special educators are concerned about the efficacy of segregated, pull-out, and "special programs." In essence while the context, student populations, and mechanics may differ, the issues are essentially the same. (p. 96)

The challenge facing educators is more than just an issue of several professional groups working together in one school. Recent legislation promotes systemic collaboration among professionals at federal, state, and local education agencies. Although this may seem unachievable, it cannot be dismissed or avoided if an effective transition process is to be established for all youth (Cobb & Hyatt, 1994).

The School-to-Work Opportunities Act of 1994 offers the possibility of creating one system to support all students transitioning from school to adult life so that no youth is neglected, as has been the case with previous school reform. The intent of the Act is for every student to (a) gain access to a relevant education; (b) receive an education that combines classroom, community, and work-related experiences; and (c) realize an education that is individualized and based on the student's needs, interests, and abilities. All students are to receive a high school diploma, a certificate that recognizes 1 or 2 years of post-secondary education, and a certificate that is recognized by business and industry. Although there will be variations in how each state implements school to work, all states will need to include three specific components that are the foundation of the act. These components, also discussed elsewhere throughout this text, include (a) school-based learning, (b) work-based learning, and (c) connecting activities.

According to the School-to-Work Opportunities Act, *school-based learning* includes programs and services designed to help all students meet expected academic and occupational standards. As a result, school-based learning programs are to include programs designed to expose students to an array of career opportunities with the intent of facilitating student selection of a career major. In order to ensure that all students, beginning at the earliest age possible but no later than seventh grade, receive appropriate support, the act provides for career awareness, exploration, and counseling with the intent of enabling students to identify their interests, goals, and career options.

As defined in the act, the *work-based learning* component emphasizes the importance of youth learning from firsthand experience in a workplace that provides an active learning setting. The work-based learning component may include work experience (including paid employment), job training, workplace mentoring, and job shadowing. Additional areas addressed in the work-based learning component include meaningful workplace experiences for all students in the instruction of general workplace competencies and broad instruction in all aspects of a given industry. The intent is for the workplace to be an environment in which youth will not only learn job-specific tasks for entry-level positions, but also acquire work-related skills including positive work habits, social and communication skills, and general knowledge of business operations (Norman & Bourexis, 1995).

Finally, the emphasis of *connecting activities* is to provide support to both the school-based and work-based learning components as well as to encourage the active participation of community members, including employers, parents, students, postsecondary schools, and others, in school-to-work activities. The underlying purpose is to prevent a dichotomy, as has typically occurred in the past, between school- and work-based activities. Connecting activities also are aimed at providing assistance to program participants in finding jobs and/or continuing their education, as well as linking them with community services that may be useful throughout the transition process.

The goal of the School-to-Work Opportunities Act is to serve as a comprehensive national policy aimed at promoting systemic changes in education. This restructuring has the potential to facilitate the development and implementation of quality school-to-work transition processes and thereby enable all youth to successfully enter the workplace and/or obtain further education and training.

Despite numerous attempts to impact the transition process, we have learned that no single program or approach can adequately meet the needs of all youth in every community; however, as reviewed in this chapter, many best-practice elements are shared by researchers and model program developers. Table 2.8 lists "common best practices in transition." These best practices have been identified by special and regular vocational educators, as well as vocational educators who have focused their attention on students with special needs (Brolin, 1995).

These practices are the topic of this text. Each practice is discussed at length throughout this text. Table 2.8 also lists the chapters that provide the most indepth discussion of each of the practices. For example, Wehmeyer provides a thorough overview of "individualized transition and career planning," whereas administrative leadership, professional development, creative financing, research, and program evaluation receive primary treatment in the concluding chapter.

QUESTIONS

1. Recent reports on educational reform have identified problems associated with student performance. Discuss three of the major reports addressed in the chapter.

2. List three legislative acts that have emerged with the specific aim of promoting systemic change in the transition process for all youth.

3. Although consensus has not been reached on what constitutes desirable postschool outcomes for all youths, four outcomes are often mentioned as being desirable. Discuss these four outcomes and how they might be measured.

4. Federal monies have been made available to fund model demonstration projects. Discuss the purpose of the projects as they relate to youth with disabilities.

5. Substantiated "best practices" that promote successful transition of youth from school to postschool adult living has become a critical issue. Discuss what is meant by "best practice" and identify five practices that are essential to the transition process for youth with disabilities.

6. General vocational education models have been in operation since the early 1900s. Identify five of the most common work-based vocational education approaches and discuss their common program features.

7. Since the mid-1960s, youth with disabilities and special populations have been accessing vocational education programs. Identify the five major areas that provide a framework for identifying exemplary programs. Under each of the main areas, identify and discuss two practices.

8. One educational system that supports all youth in the transition process has become increasingly more desirable than having separate systems: one supporting youth in special education and one supporting youth in general education. Discuss the intent of the School-to-Work Opportunities Act as it relates to the creation of one educational system.

9. Although no single program or approach can impact substantially the transition process for all youth, there are many common practices across the three areas explored (special education, general vocational education, vocational education for special populations) that have enabled youth to smoothly and successfully transition from school to postschool settings. List five practices and compare similarities and differences across the three areas discussed in this chapter.

10. Provide specific examples of three "best practices" you have experienced in your life or in the transition from high school to work or postsecondary education.

Table 2.8 Common Best Practices in Transition

Emerging Best Practices	Special Education Models[a]	General Vocational Education[b]	Vocational Education for Special Populations[c]	Chapter Location
Individualized transition and career planning, beginning by the 7th grade	Yes	Yes	Yes	7
Assessment of student vocational interests and abilities	Yes	Yes	Yes	6 and 13
Student involvement and self-determination	Yes	Yes	No	7
School- and work-based, community-referenced curriculum and instruction	Yes	Yes	Yes	5 and 9
Community-based work experiences and/or job placement	Yes	Yes	Yes	8 and 14
Family involvement	Yes	No	Yes	11
Cross-sector collaboration and comprehensive support services	Yes	Yes	Yes	10 and 12
Administrative leadership	Yes	Yes	Yes	5
Professional development	Yes	Yes	Yes	4
Articulation into postsecondary education options	Yes	Yes	Yes	16
Program evaluation	Yes	Yes	Yes	—

Sources: [a]Benz, Lindstrom, & Halpern, 1995; DeFur & Taymans, 1995; Halpern et al., 1992; Heal et al., 1990; Kohler, 1996; Kohler et al., 1994; Sands et al., 1995. [b]Charner et al., 1995. [c]Phelps & Wermuth, 1992.

A "yes" indicates that the practice has been substantiated in the literature as demonstrating a positive impact or influence in the transition process. A "no" indicates that the practice was not explicitly cited as a practice attributed with making a positive impact on the transition practice in the studies reviewed.

REFERENCES

Arum, R., & Shavit, Y. (1995). Secondary vocational education and the transition from school to work. *Sociology of Education, 68,* 187–204.

Benz, M. R., & Halpern, A. S. (1987). Transition services for secondary students with mild disabilities: A statewide perspective. *Exceptional Children, 53,* 507–514.

Benz, M. R., Lindstrom, L. E., & Halpern, A. (1995). Mobilizing local communities to improve transition services. *Career Development for Exceptional Individuals, 18,* 21–32.

Bestor, A. (1953). *Educational wastelands.* Urbana: University of Illinois Press.

Blackorby, J., & Wagner, M. (1996). Longitudinal postschool outcomes of youth with disabilities. Findings from the National Longitudinal Transition Study. *Exceptional Children, 62,* 399–413.

Boyer (1983). *High school: A report on secondary education in America.* New York: Harper & Row

Brolin, D. E. (1995). *Career education: A functional life skills approach* (3rd ed.). Columbus, OH: Prentice Hall.

Brown, R., Bayer, M., & MacFarlane, C. (1988). Quality of life amongst handicapped adults. In R. Brown (Ed.), *Quality of life for handicapped people: A series in rehabilitation education* (pp. 107–123). London: Croom Helm.

Carl D. Perkins Vocational and Applied Technology Education Act. (1990). Public Law 101-392, 104, Stat. 756.

Chadsey-Rusch, J., & Rusch, F. R. (1996). Transition for youth with disabilities: Promising practices. *Contemporary Education, 68,* 9–12

Chadsey-Rusch, J., Rusch, F. R., & O'Reilly, M. F. (1991). Transition from school to integrated communities. *Remedial and Special Education, 12,* 23–33.

Charner, I., Fraser, B. S., Hubbard, S., Rogers, A., & Horne, R. (1995, Spring). Reforms of the school-to-work transition: Findings, implications, and challenges. *Phi Delta Kappan, 40,* 58–59.

Clark, G. M., & Kolstoe, O. P. (1995). *Career development and transition education for adolescents with disabilities* (2nd ed.). Boston: Allyn & Bacon.

Cobb, R. B., & Hyatt, J. (1994). School to work transition for youth with disabilities: Education settings. In National Institute on Disability and Rehabilitation Research (Ed.), *Consensus validation conference—school to work transition for youths with disabilities: Resource papers* (pp. 187–197). Washington, DC: National Institute on Disability and Rehabilitation Research.

Cobb, R. B., & Neubert, D. A. (1990). Vocational education models. In F. R. Rusch, L. DeStefano, J. Chadsey-Rusch, L. A. Phelps, & E. Szymanski (Eds.), *Transition from school to adult life: Models, linkages, and policy* (pp. 93–113). Sycamore, IL: Sycamore.

DeFur, S. H., & Taymans, J. M. (1995). Competencies needed for transition specialists in vocational rehabilitation, vocational education, and special education. *Exceptional Children, 62,* 39–51.

DeStefano, L. (1989). Facilitating the transition from school to adult life for youth with disabilities. In W. E. Kiernan & R. Schalock (Eds.), *Economics, industry, and disability: A look ahead* (pp. 169–178). Baltimore: Paul H. Brookes.

DeStefano, L., & Wagner, M. (1992). Outcome assessment in special education: What lessons have we learned? In F. R. Rusch, L. DeStefano, J. Chadsey-Rusch, L. A. Phelps, and E. Szymanski (Eds.), *Transition from school to adult life: Models, linkages, and policy* (pp. 173–207). Sycamore, IL: Sycamore Publishing.

Dornsife, C., & Bragg, D. (1992, December). An historical perspective for Tech Prep. In D. Bragg (Ed.), *Implementing Tech Prep: A guide to planning a quality initiative* (pp. 2-1 to 2-17) Berkeley: University of California at Berkeley, National Center for Research in Vocational Education.

Finn, C. E. (1992). *We must take charge: Our schools and our future.* New York: The Free Press.

Gardner, E. M. (1985). *A new agenda for education.* Washington, DC: The Heritage Foundation.

Goals 2000: The Educate America Act. (1994). Public Law 103-227, 108, Stat. 125.

Goode, D. (1990). Thinking about and discussing quality of life. In R. Schalock & M. Begab (Eds.), *Quality of life: Perspectives and issues* (pp. 41–58). Washington, DC: American Association on Mental Retardation.

Goodlad, J. I. (1984). *A place called school: Prospects for the future.* New York: McGraw-Hill.

Halpern, A. S. (1985). Transition: A look at the foundations. *Exceptional Children, 51,* 479–486.

———. (1993). Quality of life as a conceptual framework for evaluating transition outcomes. *Exceptional Children, 59,* 486–498.

Halpern, A. S., Benz, M. R., & Lindstrom, L. E. (1992). A systems change approach to improving secondary special education and transition programs at the community level. *Career Development for Exceptional Individuals, 12,* 167–177.

Halpern, A. S.., Close, D. W., & Nelson, D. J. (1986). *On my own: The impact of semi-independent living programs for adults with mental retardation.* Baltimore: Paul H. Brookes.

Harris, L. (1992, Spring). Memo: To the candidates. *America's Agenda,* 13–15.

Heal, L. W., Gonzalez, P., Rusch, F. R., Copher, J. I., & DeStefano, L. (1990). A comparison of successful and unsuccessful placements of youth with mental handicaps into competitive employment. *Exceptionality, 1,* 181–195.

The Heritage Foundation Report. (1984, May 11). *The crisis: Washington shares the blame.* Washington, DC: Author.

Individuals with Disabilities Education Act Amendments of 1990, 20, U.S.C.A. Sec. 1400 et seq.

Johnson, J. R., & Rusch, F. R. (1993). Educational reform and special education: Foundations for a national research agenda focused upon secondary education. In P. D. Kohler, J. R. Johnson, J. Chadsey-Rusch, & F. R. Rusch (Eds.), *Transition from school to adult life: Foundations, best practices, and research directions* (pp. 77–104). Champaign-Urbana: University of Illinois, Transition Research Institute.

Kohler, P. D. (1993). Best practices in transition : Substantiated or implied? *Career Development for Exceptional Individuals, 16,* 107–121.

———. (1996). Preparing youths with disabilities for future challenges: A taxonomy for transition programming. In P. D. Kohler (Ed.), *Taxonomy for transition programming: Linking research and practice* (pp. 1–62). Champaign-Urbana: University of Illinois, Transition Research Institute.

Kohler, P. D., DeStefano, L., Wermuth, T., Grayson, T., & McGinty, S. (1994). An analysis of exemplary transition programs: How and why they are selected. *Career Development for Exceptional Individuals, 17,* 187–202.

Martin, J. E., Marshall, L. H., & Maxson, L. L. (1993). Transition policy: Infusing self-determination and self-advocacy into transition programs. *Career Development for Exceptional Individuals, 16,* 53–61.

Morningstar, M. E., Turnbull, A. P., & Turnbull, H. R. (1996). What do students with disabilities tell us about the importance of family involvement in the transition from school to adult life? *Exceptional Children, 62,* 68–83.

Mount, B., & Zwernik, K. (1988). *It's never too early. It's never too late. A booklet about personal futures planning* (Publication 421-88-109). St. Paul, MN: Governor's Planning Council on Developmental Disabilities.

National Commission on Excellence in Education. (1983). *A nation at risk: The imperative for educational reform.* Washington, DC: U.S. Government Printing Office.

National Commission on Secondary Vocational Education. (1984). *The unfinished agenda: The role of vocational education in the high school.* Columbus: Ohio State University, National Center for Research in Vocational Education.

National Council on Vocational Education. (1990–1991). *Solutions.* Washington, DC: Author.

Norman, M. E., & Bourexis, P. S. (1995). *Including students with disabilities in school-to-work opportunities.* Washington, DC: Council of Chief State School Officers.

Peter, T. L., & Heron, T. E. (1993). When the best is not good enough: An examination of best practice. *Journal of Special Education, 26,* 371–385.

Peterson, P. E. (1983). Background paper. In Twentieth Century Fund (Ed.), *Making the grade. Report of the Twentieth Century Fund task force on federal elementary and secondary education policy.* Washington, DC: Twentieth Century Fund.

Phelps, L. A., & Wermuth, T. R. (1992). *Effective vocational education for students with special needs: A framework* (MDS-112). Berkeley: University of California at Berkeley, National Center for Research in Vocational Education.

Powell, A. G., Farrar, E., & Cohen, D. K. (1985). *The shopping mall high school: Winners and losers in the educational marketplace.* Boston: Houghton Mifflin.

Rusch, F. R., Kohler, P. D., & Hughes, C. (1992). An analysis of OSERS-sponsored secondary special education and transitional services research. *Career Development for Exceptional Individuals, 15,* 121–143.

Rusch, F. R., & Phelps, L. A. (1987). Secondary special education and transition from school to work: A national priority. *Exceptional Children, 53,* 487–492.

Sands, D. J., Adams, L., & Stout, D. M. (1995). A statewide exploration of the nature and use of curriculum in special education. *Exceptional Children, 62,* 68–83.

Secretary's Commission of Achieving Necessary Skills (SCANS). (1991). *What work requires of schools: A SCANS report for America 2000.* Washington, DC: U.S. Department of Labor,

School-to-Work Opportunities Act. (1994). Public Law 103-239, 108, Stat. 569.

Smith, C. L., & Rojewski, J. W. (1993). School-to-work transition: Alternatives for educational reform. *Youth and Society, 25,* 222–250.

Stern, D., Finkelstein, N., Stone, J. R., Latting, J., & Dornsife, C. (1995). *School-to-work: Research on programs in the United States.* Washington, DC: Falmer Press, Taylor & Francis.

Stern, D., McMillion, M., Hopkins, C., & Stone, J. R. (1990). Work experience for students in high school and college. *Youth and Society, 21,* 355–389.

Stone, J. R., III (1993). Debunking the myths: Research offers ammunition to fight misperceptions of voc ed. *Vocational Education Journal, 68,* 26–27, 56.

Szymanski, E. M. (1994). Transition: Life-span and life-space consideration for employment. *Exceptional Children, 60,* 402–410.

Taylor, S., & Bogdan, R. (1990). Quality of life and the individual's perspective. In R. Schalock & M. Begab (Eds.), *Quality of life: Perspectives and issues* (pp. 27–40). Washington, DC: American Association on Mental Retardation.

Toch, T. (1991). *In the name of excellence: The struggle to reform the nation's schools. Why it's failing and what should be done.* New York: Oxford University Press.

Twentieth Century Fund. (1983). *Making the grade. Report of the Twentieth Century Fund task force on federal elementary and secondary education policy.* Washington, DC: Author.

Vandercook, T., York, J., & Forest, M. (1989). The McGill Action Planning System (MAPS): A strategy for building the vision. *Journal of the Association for Persons with Severe Handicaps, 14*(3), 205–215.

VanReusen, A. K., & Bos, C. S. (1994). Facilitating student participation in individualized education programs through motivation strategy instruction. *Exceptional Children, 60,* 466–475.

VanReusen, A. K., Bos, C. S., Schumaker, J. B., & Deshler, D. D. (1994). *The self-advocacy strategy for education and transition planning.* Lawrence, KS: Edge Enterprises.

Wagner, M. (1989). *Youth with disabilities during transition: An overview of descriptive findings from the National Longitudinal Transition Study.* Stanford, CA: SRI International.

Wehmeyer, M., & Lawrence, M. (1995). Whose future is it anyway? Promoting student involvement in transition planning. *Career Development for Exceptional Individuals, 18,* 69–84.

Wehmeyer, M. L., & Ward, M. J. (1995). The spirit of the IDEA mandate: Student involvement in transition planning. *Journal of the Association for Vocational Special Needs Education, 17,* 108–111.

Will, M. (1984). *OSERS programming for the transition of youth with disabilities: Bridges from school to working life.* Washington, DC: Office of Special Education and Rehabilitative Services.

◨

3

School-to-Work Transition

Overview of Disability Legislation

ROBERT A. STODDEN

This chapter presents an overview of federal legislation and other initiatives that have affected the evolution of school-to-work transition programs and services for individuals with disabilities. The first section provides an overview of early legislation in the areas of employment training, rehabilitation, and education, with a focus on policy areas impacting on the needs of persons with disabilities. The second section discusses legislation and policy initiatives leading to the development of the school-to-work initiative within the Individuals with Disabilities Education Act (IDEA). The next section of this chapter discusses major pieces of legislation that support the transition of individuals with special needs from school to employment, postsecondary education, and independent adult life. Lastly, the chapter focuses on the political climate and national policy efforts to consolidate employment, rehabilitation, and education legislation to address the needs of all individuals.

This chapter reviews the historical context of issues and legislation leading to the development of the transition initiative for youth with disabilities, beginning with developments in the 1960s. Further, 10 years of implementation of the "transition initiative" are discussed in relation to resulting changes in definition, policy, and legislation.

1915–1945: SUPPORT AND TRAINING FOR DISABLED VETERANS

Prior to World War I, most education and rehabilitation services for persons with disabilities depended on the interest of private firms, benefactors, and individuals. In 1917, given concern that disabled World I veterans would be a burden on society, the U.S. Congress passed the Smith-Hughes Act (P.L. 64-347), which provided vocational rehabilitation and employment for disabled veterans. This act was the first in a series of federal laws that began to influence the services and lives of persons with disabilities. In addition, the act provided the first federally supported vocational education curriculum in secondary schools in the areas of agriculture, home economics, trade, and industrial education. Soon after, the Congress passed the Smith-Sears Act (P.L. 65-178), providing additional support for disabled veterans. And in 1920, the Smith-Fess Act (P.L. 66-236) was passed, offering vocational training for civilians with disabilities while engaged in civil employment. Although funding and resulting benefits from the programs provided under the three acts were minimal, the legislation did provide a framework and precedence for future legislation.

1946–1965: TRAINING AND REHABILITATION FOR PERSONS WITH DISABILITIES

With the advent of World War II and the need for manpower in war-related industries, the LaFollete Act (P.L. 77-113) was passed to provide vocational training for individuals who did not qualify for military service. For the first time, legislation included medically related services such as examinations, corrective surgery, and prosthetic devices. This legislation further expanded the concept of rehabilitation to include services for people with mental retardation, leading to the development of sheltered workshop services. The Vocational Rehabilitation Amendments (P.L. 83-565) were signed into law in 1954, expanding and improving vocational and rehabilitation programs and providing funds for research and professional training. These research and training programs led to the development of work-study programs,

sheltered workshops, job placement and work-experience activities, and employment follow-up efforts during the late 1950s.

During the 1960s, the President's Panel on Mental Retardation advocated vocational training and supports for all persons with mental retardation. The report was further supported by President Kennedy in his 1962 State of the Union address, which emphasized the findings of the panel and stressed a new program of public welfare, service, and training, rather than prolonged dependence. The Vocational Education Act of 1963 (P.L. 88-210) included provisions for expanded development of vocational programs and training for persons with disabilities.

The 1960s witnessed the passage of two additional pieces of legislation, the Vocational Rehabilitation Amendments of 1967 (P.L. 90-99) and 1968 (P.L. 90-391). The major provisions of these amendments included:

- funding for rehabilitation, research, demonstration, and training projects

- creation of programs for the recruitment and training of rehabilitation service providers

- authorization of up to 10 percent of the funds for vocational and rehabilitation programs for persons with disabilities

Several reviews of programs and services resulting from the legislation of the 1960s have indicated that legislation has had a limited impact on persons with disabilities (Sarkees-Wincenski & Scott, 1995; Kohler & Rusch, 1997). Postschool outcomes for youth leaving secondary school programs failed to improve, fewer youth benefited or were given access to specified training programs or services, and often youth with disabilities were served in separate programs that did not result in competitive employment for them. The Olympus Research Corporation (1974), Weisenstein (1976), and Tindall (1977) also reported that states often did not use the 10 percent set-asides in vocational education funding for youth with disabilities, and in many cases there was a severe shortage of trained personnel in vocational programs who understood how to work with youth with disabilities.

1970s: APPROPRIATE ACCESS AND ACCOMMODATIONS

During the 1970s, several pieces of landmark legislation were initiated to impact the lives of all persons with disabilities. The Rehabilitation Act of 1973, Sections 503 and 504 (P.L. 93-112), provided for significant changes in the training and hiring of persons with disabilities. Specifically, Section 503 stipulated that businesses with federal contracts were to initiate an affirmative action plan for the purpose of hiring, recruiting, training, and promoting persons with disabilities. Section 504 of the act provided for significant changes in the training and hiring of persons with disabilities by ensuring that training institutions and employers not discriminate against persons with disabilities, solely by reason of their handicap or disability. Also, for the first time, emphasis was placed on meeting the needs of those with the most severe disabling conditions.

In 1971, the concept of career education was introduced, "as the totality of experiences through which one learns about and prepares to engage in work as part of his or her way of living" (Hoyt, 1975:4). A federal Office of Career Education was established to guide states in implementing programs, including (a) encompassing the total curriculum of the school and providing a unified approach to education for life; (b) encouraging all members of the community to share responsibility for learning within classrooms, homes, private and public agencies, and the employment community; (c) providing for career awareness, career exploration, and skills development at all levels and ages; and (d) encouraging all teachers to review their subject matter for its career implications. Special educators embraced the concept of career education (Clark, 1979) as a method for linking academic and vocational preparation for

youth with disabilities. Unfortunately, due to a lack of a specific federal mandate and accompanying federal funding, career education programs had minimal impact on the education of adolescents with disabilities (Brolin, 1982).

In 1973, the Comprehensive Employment and Training Act (CETA; P.L. 93-203) took the place of many programs and functions that had been established under employment and job training legislation during the 1960s. The primary purpose of CETA was to provide comprehensive manpower services to alleviate the high unemployment rates of the early 1970s. The act was to address the needs of unemployed youths and adults who had no occupational skills and, thus, were not in a position to contribute to the development of the nation's economy. Although not specifically targeted for youth with disabilities, this legislation provided services, programs, and training opportunities that benefited this population. The Job Training Partnership Act of 1982 (P.L. 97-300), however, reshaped the original CETA programs and provided significant funding for job training and placement programs directly benefiting youth with disabilities.

In 1975, the Individuals with Disabilities Education Act (IDEA; P.L. 94-142) was passed to reduce the disparities in educational opportunity between children with disabilities and other children. This legislation provided partial federal funding to states, which in turn was to ensure that students received a free, appropriate public education (FAPE). One of the indications of FAPE was the development of an Individualized Educational Program (IEP) for each child with a disability; for adolescents and young adults with disabilities, the IEP could include career and vocational objectives if such an education was deemed appropriate by the IEP planning team. Further requirements of P.L. 94-142 centered on guidelines for ensuring the rights of children with disabilities and their parents and guardians. Thus, the law outlined due-process procedures for parents to express concerns or complaints with respect to student identification, evaluation, placement, and educational programming.

In 1976, the Vocational Education Amendments (P.L. 94-482) were revised, resulting in increased funding for vocational education programs, with a 10 percent designated set-aside for youth with disabilities. Further, these amendments established the recognition of a need for cooperative working relationships between vocational education and other job training and employment programs conducted in the Department of Labor. Much of the legislation guiding programs in the 1970s served as a guidepost for more focused and refined legislation to be passed in the 1980s.

1980s: FUNDS TO DEVELOP TRANSITION MODELS AND PRACTICES

During the 1980s, legislation that had been initiated in past years was further refined and refocused on the needs of youth with disability to successfully prepare for and transition from the education years to adult work environments. In 1984, the Carl D. Perkins Vocational and Technical Education Act was passed with the following intent:

> assure that individuals who are inadequately served under vocational education programs are assured access to quality vocational education programs, especially individuals who are disadvantaged, who are handicapped, men and women who are entering non-traditional occupations, adults who are in need of training and retraining, individuals who are single parents or homemakers, individuals with limited English proficiency, and individuals who are incarcerated in correctional institutions. (P.L. 98-524, 98, Stat. 2435)

The act extended the provisions of the Vocational Education Act of 1963 by mandating vocational assessment, counseling, support, and transition services for youth identified as disabled and disadvantaged. Further, the act

mandated planning and coordination with other federally funded programs. Vocational goals and objectives were to be included in each student's IEP, and training was to be provided in the least restrictive environment. Recordkeeping and service delivery under the Perkins Act was to be coordinated in states and local education agencies with special education requirements mandated under P.L. 94-142.

Emergence of the Transition Initiative for Youth with Disabilities

In 1983, P.L. 94-142 was amended with a new Section 626, entitled "Secondary Education and Transition Services for Handicapped Youth," that authorized federal funds for grants to demonstrate support and coordination among education and adult service programs designed to assist youth with disabilities to transition from secondary school to postsecondary education, employment, and community services. The purpose of the section was to stimulate improvement and development of programs for youth with disabilities in secondary schools and to strengthen and link secondary education, training, and related services, thereby assisting the transition to postsecondary education, vocational training, competitive employment, continuing education, or adult services.

Madeliene Will, Assistant Secretary for the Office of Special Education and Rehabilitation Services (OSERS) during the early 1980s, was a key figure in creating a national priority in the area of transition for youth with disabilities. Thus, she was instrumental in establishing the intent of new policy and providing guidance to demonstration projects developing the initiative. (See Chapter 2 for a complete review of this initiative and its impact on youth with disabilities.) The new priority (Will, 1984) was established "to strengthen education, training, and support services for youth with disabilities, and to support their successful transition from school to the adult world of independent work and living" (p. 12). The priority included specific recommendations to create secondary school curriculum with relevancy to the workplace, to improve postsecondary services, and to develop incentives for employers to hire youth with disabilities. The recommendations were based on three areas of perceived need that guided the formulation of OSERS transition policy during the 1980s: (a) a need to focus on all students with disabilities, (b) a need to address the complexity of postschool services, and (c) the goal of employment and independent living.

To address the needs and recommendations of the OSERS transition priority, a model was offered to guide states and local education agencies in planning and designing programs and services (Figure 3.1). The model presented secondary school preparation as the foundation for successful transition, "curriculum content in special education and vocational education affects whether or not students leave school with entry level skills that are salable in the local community" (Will, 1983:5). Employment was depicted as the resulting goal of transition services and supports. The following three levels of intervention were described for youth with disability as they sought to transition from secondary school to adult work environments: (a) transition without special services, (b) transition with time-limited services, and (c) transition with ongoing services.

To begin to operationalize the OSERS transition model, activities concentrated on research, demonstration, and development projects in support of new programs and services in states. As discussed in Chapter 2, numerous research and demonstration projects resulted in refinements of the OSERS transition model, as well as a number of new models that often took a broader perspective of transition, focusing on several quality-of-life issues surrounding youth with disabilities. These projects provided a sense of clarity and definition to the transition initiative, which would guide further policy development in the late 1980s and early 1990s (Table 3.1).

1990s: TRANSITION IS DEFINED AND MANDATED

Emergence of Transition Policy for Youth with Disabilities

Since the passage of the IDEA in 1975, IEPs have been a requirement for all children and youth with disabilities eligible for special education services. Each student's IEP must include (a) a statement of the student's present level of educational performance; (b) annual goals and short-term objectives for reaching the goals; (c) specific special education and related services to be provided, and the extent of participation in general education; (d) projected dates for initiation and duration of services; and (e) criteria and procedures for determining whether short-term objectives had been met.

In 1990, the IDEA was reauthorized as P.L. 101-476 to include a focus on planning for life after the secondary school years, with plans to include participation of adult service agencies and other community services, as applicable. The new legislation and the revised regulations required a statement of needed transition services in the IEP for each student by age 16, and younger, if appropriate. This statement was to include the needed transition services, and, if appropriate, a statement of each public agency's and each participating agency's responsibilities or linkages, or both, before the student leaves the school setting. Additionally, if the IEP team determined that services were not needed in one or more of the areas specified (instruction, community experiences, employment, and other postschool adult living objectives), the IEP must include a statement to that effect and the basis on which the determination was made (Individuals with Disabilities Education Act, P.L. 101-476, 34 CFR, Section 300.18).

Further, transition services in P.L. 101-476 were defined as:

> a coordinated set of activities for a student, designed within an outcome oriented

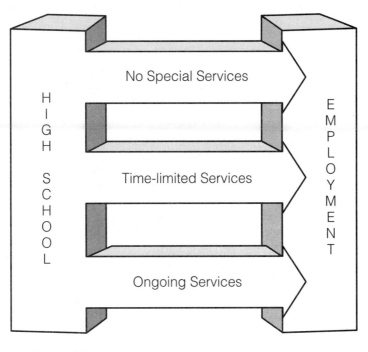

FIGURE 3.1 OSERS Transition Model

(*Source:* Will, 1983.)

process, which promotes movement from school to postschool activities, including postsecondary education, vocational training, integrated employment (including supported employment), continuing and adult education, adult services, independent living or community participation. The coordinated set of activities must: (a) be based on the individual student's needs; (b) take into account student's preferences and interest; and (c) must include instruction, community experiences, the development of employment and other postschool adult living skills and functional vocational evaluation. (Individuals with Disabilities Act, P.L. 101-476, 34 CFR, Section 300.18)

Traditionally, the IEP had been designated as a planning document for a maximum period of 1 year, focusing on annual goals that were broken into short-term objectives. With the addition of the transition services requirements in the IEP, planning for youth with disabilities took on a longer time period, with goals spanning several years. For the first time, therefore, educators at the high school level were being asked to orient their planning toward students' life after secondary school, including statements of needed transition services, agency responsibilities, and linkages to services within other agencies. By defining transition services and by requiring a statement of such services in the student's IEP, the 1990 reauthorization of the IDEA did more than any of previous amendments to promote the development of educational programs focused on postschool goals (Table 3.2). These changes clearly underscored the importance of the transition initiative as a part of the delivery of special education services to youth with disabilities.

Table 3.1 Legislative Path to the Transition Initiative in IDEA

1915–1945 Focus on		
support and	1917	Smith-Hughs Act (P. L. 64-347)
training for	1918	Smith-Sears Act (P. L. 65-178)
disabled	1920	Smith-Fess Act (P. L. 66-236)
veterans	1943	LaFollette Act (P. L. 77-113)
1945–1965 Focus on		
training and	1954	Vocational Rehabilitation Amendments (P. L. 83-565)
rehabilitation	1963	Vocational Education Act (P.L. 88-210)
for persons	1967	Vocational Rehabilitation Amendments (P.L. 90-99)
with disabilities	1968	Vocational Rehabilitation Amendments (P.L. 90-391)
1970s Focus on		
appropriate	1973	Rehabilitation Act (Selections 503 & 504) (P. L. 93-112)
access and	1973	Comprehensive Employment and Training Act (P. L. 93-203)
accommodation	1975	Individuals with Disabilities Education Act (P. L. 94-142)
for persons with	1976	Vocational Education Amendments (P. L. 94-482)
disabilities		
1980s Authorized funds		
to develop	1982	Job Training Partnership Act (P. L. 97-300)
transition models	1983	Individuals with Disabilities Education Act (P. L. 98-199)
and practices	1984	Carl D. Perkins Vocational and Technical Act (P. L. 88-210)
1990s Transition is		
defined and	1990	Individual with Disabilities Education Act (P. L. 101-476)
mandated/	1990	Americans with Disabilities Act (P. L. 101-336)
consistency is	1992	Rehabilitation Act Amendments (P. L. 102-569)
established	1993	Job Training Reform Act (P. L. 102-367)
across other	1994	National Service Trust Act (P. L. 103-82)
legislation	1994	School-to-Work Opportunities Act (P. L. 103-239)

Expansion of Disability Policy in the Early 1990s

IDEA provided important new policy direction to guide the delivery of special education services, including a range of outcomes expected as a result of obtaining an effective education. Other pieces of generic legislation began to reflect the values of the transition initiative as policy and legislation evolved throughout the early 1990s. Further, education, employment, and human service legislation began to complement and embrace common issues and values necessary for cooperation between related government departments and programs to more effectively serve persons with disabilities.

Other federal legislation of the early 1990s followed the direction and intent of IDEA, thereby representing a major shift in public policy with regard to persons with disabilities.

Table 3.2 Progress of the Transition Initiative within IDEA

1975 IDEA (P. L. 94-142)	1983 IDEA (P. L. 98-199) REAUTHORIZATION	1990 IDEA (P. L. 101-476) REAUTHORIZATION	1997 IDEA (P. L. 105-17) REAUTHORIZATION
■ Ensured FAPE for children with disabilities ■ Outlined due-process procedures ■ Established an Individualized Education Planning (IEP) process for each child with a disability	■ Federal funds were provided to demonstrate transition models ■ OSERS transition model was developed ■ Transition outcomes were specified in legislative language	■ Transition services are defined in legislation ■ Legislation included a statement of needed transition services in the IEP for each student, aged 16 or younger ■ Promoted educational planning focused on postschool goals	■ Focused on self-determination for students and families in transition planning ■ Focused on short- and long-range goals rather than objectives within the IEP ■ Focused on student planning and participation in the general education curriculum ■ Focused on integrating transition planning within the process of educational planning starting at age 14 years ■ Based educational planning and programming on postschool results

The Americans with Disabilities Act of 1990 (ADA; P.L. 101-336) and the Rehabilitation Act Amendments of 1992 (P.L. 102-569) further reinforced the shift away from focusing on what people could *not* do, to what persons with disabilities *could* do to contribute to their own quality of life and to society in general. These legislative acts recognized that a disability in no way diminishes the right and desire of persons with disabilities to live independently, make choices, and pursue a meaningful life in their community. The intent across these pieces of major disability legislation was to reflect the broad values of community inclusion, full participation, self-determination with meaningful and informed choices, and the involvement of families and community members as natural supporters in all phases of life.

The ADA, an umbrella civil rights law signed in 1990, prohibited discrimination against people with disabilities in the areas of private employment, public accommodation and services,

transportation, and telecommunications. The Rehabilitation Act Amendments of 1992 (P.L. 102-569) further extended the policy directions of promoting improved quality-of-life outcomes for individuals with disabilities. Developed to be consistent with the Individuals with Disabilities Education Act of 1990, they included several provisions to reinforce the success of youth with disability in the work force. Specifically, the Rehabilitation Act provisions sought to define transition services in the same language as IDEA, and sought to link agencies and services provided by rehabilitation and education programs. Further, the amendments required states to plan and define how the two service systems would collaborate and coordinate in the provision of transition services.

These policy changes have promoted a shift in philosophy and values impacting the way persons providing programs and services perceive individuals with disabilities. Each of the legislative acts supported self-determination and the importance of including individual preferences and desires into service delivery plans. Specifically, the IDEA sought student and family participation in the development of IEPs and stipulated that educational programs must be developed on the basis of postschool transition goals that reflect students' needs, preferences, and interests. Similarly, the Rehabilitation Act Amendments of 1992 focused on consumer-oriented services that supported the needs of persons with disabilities to participate in a satisfying quality of life.

Disability Policy Shifts in the Mid-1990s

The formulation of disability policy and legislation in the mid-1990s was an expansion or broadening of much of the intent established in legislation during the preceding 20 years. Two forces contributed to shifts in thinking about disability policy as major pieces of legislation approached reauthorization in the mid-1990s. These shifts could be attributed to (a) the perceptions of diverse groups of individuals (parents of children with disabilities, general education advocates, and special education and related services advocates), representing more than 20 years of research and experience with disability programs and services; and (b) a changing political climate that affected prevailing perceptions of the federal role in defining education, health, and human services for persons with disabilities. Other chapters in this text will focus on the results of research and experience with disability programs and services. The intent of the following section will be to focus on perceptions drawn from years of research and experience and factors of political climate influencing reauthorization of various pieces of legislation.

The political climate of the mid-1990s could be characterized by the following descriptors:

- a desire to downsize the federal role (mandates for services and funding) in the areas of education, health, and human services, allowing states greater powers to determine eligibility for, and the scope of such services

- a desire to reduce costs at the federal level for education, health, and human services, while also reducing the costs of federal unfunded mandates on states

- a desire to consolidate programs and budgets under single generic authorizations, thereby eliminating conflicting eligibility and funding tracks for numerous employment, training, and education programs

- a desire to focus on broad generic services addressing the needs of all persons eligible for programs and services, and thus removing program earmarks and separate funding floors for programs for persons with disabilities and other special needs groups

- a desire to focus on results and the benefits of federally funded programs on intended individuals

The views of policy groups focusing on services and programs for individuals with disabilities could be characterized by the following descriptors:

- a desire of generic service providers (general education, health, and human services) to impact on disability legislation, which has traditionally been free-standing with separate funding streams and administrative structures

- a desire of legislators to impact on the numerous and conflicting requirements found across pieces of legislation addressing the education and employment needs of persons with disabilities and other special needs groups

- a desire of parents of children with disabilities to reinforce the principle of inclusion and the participation of their children within general education curriculum frameworks and community employment settings, while ensuring the provision of necessary supports and services for children and youth with disabilities to self-determine and succeed in attaining desired goals and outcomes

- a desire of professional advocacy groups to focus on the interests and abilities of persons with disabilities to assume satisfying and productive roles in their schools and communities, instead of focusing on deficits and disability categories

- a desire of legislators to focus on the results or outcomes of programs and services for children and youth with disabilities rather than on the process that was used to conduct the program

Restructuring Employment and Training Legislation

Four pieces of legislation were passed in the mid-1990s that created an impact on the structure of generic education and employment training programs, as well as our thinking about the way we address the needs of special groups. Each of these pieces of legislation reinforced the intent of the transition requirements under IDEA and were inclusive of all youth preparing for graduation and employment, or postsecondary training. Following is a brief overview of the four legislative acts:

- *Job Training Reform Act of 1993* (P.L. 102-367): Provided funds for Job Corps Centers designed to serve disadvantaged young people who need additional education, vocational and social skills training, and other assistance in order to take part in meaningful employment, return to school, or enter the armed forces.

- *National Service Trust Act of 1994* (P.L. 103-82): Created a voluntary national service program offering opportunities for individuals to provide community service in exchange for scholarships to attend college (each individual could receive up to $5,000/year for 2 years maximum time).

- *School-to-Work Opportunities Act of 1994* (P.L. 103-239): Focused on the need for all youth to receive an education that would lead to a high school diploma, a skill certificate, an entry-level position within a career track, college admission, or further skill training.

Key components of the legislation focused (a) the integration of school-based and work-based learning, (b) integrating academic and vocational learning, and (c) linking secondary and postsecondary education. The act sought to build on existing employment and transition programs, such as tech-prep education programs, career academies, mentorship programs, school-to-apprenticeship programs, school-sponsored enterprises, and business-education compacts.

- *Goals 2000: Educate America Act of 1993* (P.L. 103-227): Established eight educational goals that state and local education agencies were expected to achieve by the year 2000. The goals required that secondary school youth become vocationally and technically competent as early as possible. Further, the legislation sought to improve overall literacy, reduce dropout rates, and provide the supports necessary for youth to smoothly connect with employment.

During the 104th Congress (1995–1996), strategies to reform and consolidate federal employment and training programs, such as the Job Training Partnership Act (JTPA), the Carl D. Perkins Vocational and Applied Technology Education Act, the School-to-Work Transition Act, and other employment legislation were considered in both houses. The thinking underlying these strategies included eliminating overlap and duplication, improving performance of programs considered ineffective, and reducing expenditures through program consolidation and elimination. Both the House of Representatives and the U.S. Senate developed bills that sought to repeal several employment and training programs and authorize a consolidation grant to states to develop and promote work-force development systems (Work Force Development Act and CAREERS: Consolidated and Reformed Education, Employment, and Rehabilitation Systems Act). The main activities supported by these pieces of legislation were to be work-force employment activities, work-force education activities, and school-to-work activities. Key features included the creation of state governance structures, provision of one-stop centers in substate areas, and the establishment of goals and benchmarks for program performance. Both bills sought to make fiscal reductions within existing program authorizations, while providing significant fiscal flexibility to states within the new consolidated structure. Many targeted special needs programs and fiscal set-asides found in the Perkins Act and other employment training legislation were to become items for consideration at the state level as needs and programs were restructured.

The Work Force Development Act of 1995 (S. 143) also sought to amend Title I of the Rehabilitation Act, which authorizes rehabilitation programs to assist individuals with disabilities in preparing for and securing employment. Under this legislation, a separate authorization at the federal level would be maintained to continue vocational rehabilitation services under state grant programs. As a job training program, vocational rehabilitation services would be coordinated as much as possible with the comprehensive work-force development system to be established in each state. The bill was to amend Title I of the Rehabilitation Act to achieve coordination of employment training programs within each state. The amendments seek to ensure that the planning processes, timelines, and accountability measures of the vocational rehabilitation system are consistent with the purposes of the Work Force Development Act. Other amendments to the Rehabilitation Act would ensure that vocational rehabilitation representatives participate in the state's overall employment and training efforts and provide technical assistance regarding the provision of services to individuals with disabilities in the overall state system. With these changes, the vocational rehabilitation program is to become a subset of the larger employment and training system in each state, while retaining its own statutory authority and funding stream. The Rehabilitation Act will receive further review and scrutiny as it faces reauthorization prior to October 1, 1997.

Reauthorization of the Individuals with Disabilities Education Act (IDEA) (P.L. 105-17)

During the 104th Congress (1995–1996), and the 105th Congress (1997–1998) the Individuals with Disabilities Education Act also was considered for reauthorization. The U.S. Senate Subcommittee on Disability Policy and Committee on Labor and Human Resources took the lead in reauthorization by working to assemble a bipartisan bill that addressed the concerns of the general education community, as well as families and advocates of children with disabilities. The general education community sought significant changes in the legislation, focusing on concerns over discipline procedures applied to children with disabilities, the high cost of services and supports for children with severe disabilities, and the cost of due process and litigation between school districts and parents. The disability community sought to make minor improvements in the legislation by focusing on the rights of parents, improved transitions from one program to the next, and by clarifying student assessment and planning procedures. Given the overall concern in the 104th and 105th Congress with unfunded mandates, reducing federal involvement and costs, and improved accountability for the use of funds and for producing results for children, the reauthorization process was lengthy and difficult for everyone involved.

Both houses of Congress introduced bills for reauthorization of IDEA, putting forth a number of changes that sought to increase state and local flexibility and reduce the federal burden, while protecting the rights of parents and children with disabilities to a free, appropriate public education. In general, these changes sought to:

- reduce the burden of application and reporting requirements for state and local education agencies

- streamline initial student eligibility evaluations and the reevaluation process to focus on collecting assessment information needed to make instructional decisions and to improve the educational progress of children with disabilities

- reduce redundant and unnecessary paperwork and time within the IEP process

- provide increased flexibility to state and local education agencies to use Part B program implementation funds in ways that will improve educational results for children with disabilities

- restructure the discretionary programs within a functional framework that could be defended within the Appropriations Committee and is linked to accountability for improved services and results for children with disabilities under Part B of the act

Several broad policy shifts were evident in the overall intent of this IDEA reauthorization that would contribute to major changes in the way children with disabilities receive an education. Examples of these shifts were as follows:

1. A shift from focusing on and being accountable for process (steps or procedures applied to implement programs) to focusing on and being accountable for results (educational and transitional results for children with disabilities). Both Senate and House bills required that state and local education agencies focus on improving educational and transitional services and results as they plan, develop, and deliver services to children with disabilities under Part B of the act. Also, state education agency partnerships would be eligible to participate in comprehensive systems-change grants supporting states as they plan for and seek to improve services and results for children with disabilities. Further, the new framework for the discretionary programs placed a requirement on grantees' conducting personnel development, research, technical assistance, and dissemination activities to work cooperatively with state and local education agencies as partners in accountability for improved services and results for children with disabilities.

2. A shift toward focus on the general education curriculum framework when conducting assessments and carrying out planning and instructional activities for children with disabilities. This shift is evident in legislative language reinforcing the participation of children with disabilities in general education assessments and statewide tests, referencing annual instructional goals within the IEP to general education curriculum expectations and requiring the participation of general education teachers within IEP meetings.

3. A shift toward focus on the instructional needs of children with disabilities and the contribution of assessment information and planning processes to address and improve the results of instruction for children with disabilities. In the past, assessment and planning activities had often focused on the child's disability category and efforts to remediate the disability, rather than on determining and planning instructional adaptations and supports for children with disabilities within the general education curriculum.

Changes in IDEA Transition Language

When addressing changes in the transition initiative language of IDEA, the U.S. Senate Committee on Labor and Human Resources considered input from several advocacy groups, as well as feedback from the initial states conducting statewide systems change activities. Numerous recommendations were presented to strengthen the transition language throughout the law and, specifically, within the IEP section of the legislation.

The following information guided improvements to the transition language:

1. State and local education agencies would focus on and be accountable for collecting and using information concerning post-school transition results to improve services and supports to youth with disabilities.

2. Transition activities would be viewed more comprehensively to include movement from early intervention programs to preschool and educational programs, as well as movement from elementary to secondary school, and from school to postschool roles and responsibilities.

3. Planning for postschool transition often begins too late for youth with disabilities; there is significant evidence that many youth drop out of school prior to the initiation of transition planning activities.

4. Youth with mild disabilities often are not included in transition planning activities and/or services; many generic career and vocational educational programs have not been linked or coordinated with transition activities for youth with mild disabilities.

5. Transition planning and service provision activities are often viewed as separate from secondary school academic and vocational curriculum requirements; thus, many of the benefits of the transition initiative have had little or no impact, or perceived relevance, to educational planning activities.

6. Several advocacy and parent/family groups questioned the role of transition services within IDEA, which is viewed by many as educational legislation; thus, transition planning activities and resulting services need to be closely linked to the educational expectations of youth with disabilities during the secondary school years.

Given the conservative political climate surrounding this reauthorization and the input received from the field, the following changes or improvements were made in the legislation:

1. A new focus on accountability for establishing and measuring student results was placed in all parts of the legislation and was specified for state educational agencies as "educational" and "transitional" results. This wording was placed throughout the implementation (Parts B and H) sections and the discretionary programs, seeking to focus administrators, teachers, parents, researchers, trainers, and others in special education to plan for and collect data on student results. The focus should include attention to educational and transitional benchmarks throughout the educational years, as well as attention to the collection of information on postschool results after a student leaves school.

2. The definition of "transition services" remained as it was put forth in the 1990 reauthorization, despite several efforts to expand the definition to include a broader scope (other transitions within the education years) and a more inclusive tone (greater linkage to general education curriculum and school-to-work activities for all youth). The definition was moved to Part A of the legislation, giving it a broader application within all other components of the act.

3. The section of the act concerned with the IEP for youth in secondary school settings underwent several improvements addressing issues that had been raised since the last reauthorization, as follows:

■ Focus on transition planning at an earlier age for youth with disabilities ("beginning at age 14").

■ Focus on integrating planning for the transition needs of students with disabilities within the structure of the individualized education planning process and document ("a statement of the transition service needs of the child under the applicable components of the child's IEP, that focuses on the child's courses of study (such as participation in advanced-placements courses or a vocational education program").

■ Focus on planning within the IEP process for student participation within the general education curriculum, including advanced placement courses, vocational education, and school-to-work programs. The IEP team is instructed to provide a description of modifications to the course of study in which the student will participate and which will lead to a successful transition from secondary school to postschool adult environments.

- Focus on the involvement of postschool agencies in the transition planning and service provision process no later than age 16 for the student with disabilities ("a statement of interagency responsibilities or any needed linkages").

- Requirement that states develop a statement regarding the transfer of rights under IDEA to the student on reaching the age of majority.

4. The section of the act describing the discretionary programs was significantly restructured (including Section 626, which provided authorization of demonstration, outreach, and systems-change grants in the area of transition) with the intent of organizing such programs as supportive activities leading to improved services and results for children and youth with disabilities. Further, the intent was to organize the various discretionary programs in a manner that could be defended as an necessary support package to the implementation of Part B within yearly fiscal Appropriation Committee allocations. To obtain the desired intent, the discretionary programs were described within the following context:

- Discretionary programs were structured with-in functional support areas (program improvement, research and innovation, personnel preparation, and technical assistance and dissemination) rather than by specific disability type or level (serious emotional disturbance, severe disabilities), or specific area of need (transition media and technology).

- Areas of need within each of the functional support areas would be determined by formalized stakeholder partnerships in each of the states. Partnerships would consist of consumers, parents, service providers, and support bodies working to improve services and results for children and youth with disabilities within their state; priorities would be established within each of the support program areas based on needs as determined within the partnerships.

- Coordinated linkages would be created between each of the support programs (program improvement issues within states would serve as the basis for research questions, findings from research projects would be applied within personnel preparation programs, and each funded program would be accountable for dissemination at the classroom level).

- Coordinated linkages would be created between each of the support programs and the implementation of services and improvement of results within states, as described in Part B of the act (each funded support activity would be an accountable partner for improving services and results for children and youth with disabilities).

The restructured discretionary programs within P.L. 105-107 were organized to provide new opportunities for the transition initiative to emerge as a more expansive and powerful force in support of improved educational results for youth with disabilities. Throughout the act, the focus on improving educational and transitional results for children and youth with disabilities was established to guide accountability and quality assurance activities within states as they sought to determine and measure student expectations, including postschool expectations and results. This could serve as an opportunity for those working with the transition initiative to contribute to the development of educational quality assurance and accountability models in states. Further, the new components in the section on IEPs for youth in secondary school provide an opportunity to apply transition postschool expectations to influence and determine educational curriculum decisions when planning for youth with disability.

Disability Policy in the Twenty-First Century

If the education, employment, health, and human service policy shifts of the mid-1990s continue into the next century, major changes in services and supports will be evident for persons with disabilities. Legislators and the general public want a major change in the perceptions held of persons with disabilities and the way programs have been structured and funded to support their equal participation and achievement in education and training programs. New policy initiatives must build on past decades of progress toward equal access and full participation for persons with disabilities, while continuing to promote achievement and excellence for all youth. Efforts to maintain this policy balance in the future raise a number of issues or concerns to be addressed by advocates, policy makers, and others.

1. There is a need for a coordinated system of education and work preparation programs and services implemented under a unified vision and purpose, with a focus on the importance of learning and successful transition into the work force. Such an effort must present a strong and consistent vision of quality education for all children and youth, resulting in an improved range of options and quality of life for all students leaving the secondary school years. Currently, policy, legislation, and funding streams for special programs within education, transition, work preparation, rehabilitation, and special education are separate and autonomous, and often have conflicting purposes and overlapping initiatives. As each legislative initiative and its constituents seek to carve out their own place and identity within the bureaucracy of federal programs, separate boundaries become a sign of success and status. Efforts in the mid-1990s to consolidate and coordi-

nate work preparation programs (The Work force Development Act and CAREERS: Consolidated and Reformed Education, Employment, and Rehabilitation Act) encountered major legislative difficulty because of the inability of policy makers to give up the current separate program structures in favor or visualizing and conceptualizing a service system consisting of a coordinated and integrated sequence of education and training services.

2. There is a need to conduct inclusive discussions and build consensus concerning use of the term "all" when referring to the participation of children and youth with special needs in education and training programs. Because many children and youth with special needs (including youth with disabilities) have traditionally been served under separate funding streams and program models, many policy and program personnel have yet to shift their perception of youth with disabilities as being included in legislative and program language. With the shift away from federal mandated special fiscal set-asides and specific earmarks for different groups of individuals, it will be important that this discussion be inclusive and focus on the broad range of services and supports that will be necessary to achieve equity and excellence for "all" children and youth.

3. There is a need to refocus resources and program agendas from an arena of dependency (i.e., welfare, social work, social services) to the arena of independence and self-determination and sufficiency (i.e., improved education and training programs) in programs for persons with disabilities and other special needs (Kochhar & West, 1995). It is difficult to convince policy makers that persons with special needs should self-determine and be independent when programs continue to distribute funds and follow guidelines that support dependency.

4. There is a need to focus on student results from, and satisfaction with, participation in

education and training programs. As policy makers and the general public become increasing frustrated with the poor outcomes of our educational system, there will be increasingly less advocacy and support for addressing the needs of special populations. As schools and vocational training programs seek to respond to this frustration, it is important that the balance of equity (program access and participation) and excellence (improved outcomes) is maintained for "all" students.

5. There is a need to capture the excellent practices and supports that have been generated through the separate special needs programs and the transition initiative to ensure that such practices are used to improve general education curriculum sequences and generic work preparation programs. Much has been learned about meeting the educational and training needs of children and youth with disabilities; it would be extremely inefficient not to access and apply this knowledge as we move toward serving "all" children and youth within a coordinated and integrated system of education and training.

Summary

Over the past several decades, disability policy concerning education, rehabilitation, training, and preparation for adulthood has been addressed within multiple pieces of legislation, and administered by numerous government departments and programs. Over the years, education, health, employment, and human service legislation has shifted from little or no focus on children and youth with disabilities to a commitment to several special authorizations, and fiscal and programmatic set-asides within more generic legislation.

As many separate government program structures and funding streams evolved to ensure that children and youth with disabilities received special education and training supports, it became increasingly apparent that overlapping and conflicting regulations and services did not support positive and efficient results. Efforts to consolidate legislation and programs meeting the needs of "all" children and youth within a coordinated system of integrated services and supports remain a challenge for policy makers in the twenty-first century.

QUESTIONS

1. Who was impacted by the Smith-Hughes Act (P.L. 64-347)? Why was the act important?

2. What were the major provisions of the Vocational Rehabilitation Amendments of 1967 (P.L. 90-99) and 1968 (P.L. 90-391)?

3. What was the focus of the Rehabilitation Act of 1973, Sections 503 and 504?

4. Describe the OSERS transition model that was developed in 1980.

5. How were transition services defined by the IDEA reauthorized as P.L. 101-476 in 1990?

6. What were the views of policy groups in the mid-1990s concerning services and programs for individuals with disabilities?

7. What were the broad policy shifts in the IDEA reauthorization (P.L. 105-17)?

8. How did IDEA (P.L. 105-17) make improvements in addressing issues with the Individualized Education Program (IEP) for youth in secondary school settings?

9. What was the intent for restructuring the discretionary programs in the IDEA reauthorization of 1997 (P.L. 105-17)? Within what context were the discretionary programs described?

10. What are issues or concerns to be addressed by disability policy in the twenty-first century?

REFERENCES

Brolin, D. (1982). *Vocational preparation of persons with handicaps.* Columbus, OH: Bell & Howell.

Carl D. Perkins Vocational Education Act. (1984). P.L. 98-524, 98, Stat. 2435.

Clark, G. M. (1979). *Career education for the handicapped child in the elementary school*. Denver: Love.

Hoyt, K. B. (1975). *An introduction to career education.* Washington, DC: U.S. Government Printing Office.

Individuals with Disabilities Education Act. (1990). P.L. 101-476, 34 CFR.

Kochhar, C. A., & West, L. L. (1995). Future directions for federal legislation affecting transition services for individuals with special needs. *Journal for Vocational Special Needs Education, 17*(3), 85–93.

Kohler, P. D., & Rusch, F. R. (1997). Secondary education programs: Preparing youths for tomorrow's challenges. In M. C. Wang, M. C. Reynolds, & H. J. Walber (Eds.), *Handbook of special and remedial education: Research and practice* (2nd ed.). New York: Elsevier Science.

Olympus Research Corporation. (1974). *An assessment of vocational programs for the handicapped under Part B of the 1968 Amendments of the Vocational Education Act.* Salt Lake City, UT: Author.

Sarkees-Wincenski, M., & Scott, J. L. (1995). *Vocational special needs* (3rd ed.). Homewood, IL: American Technical Publishers.

Tindall, L. W. (1977). *Vocational/career education programs for persons with special needs in Wisconsin's vocational, technical, and adult districts.* Madison: Wisconsin State Board of Vocational, Technical, and Adult Education.

Weisenstein, G. R. (1976). Vocational education for exceptional persons: Have educators let it drop through a crack in their services continuum? *Thresholds in Secondary Education, 2,* 16–17.

Will, M. (1983). *OSERS programming for the transition of youth with disabilities: Bridges from school to working life.* Washington, DC: Office of Special Education and Rehabilitative Services.

———. (1984). *Supported employment for adults with severe disabilities: An OSERS program initiative.* Washington, DC: Office of Special Education and Rehabilitative Services.

4

◉

Dropout Prevention and Special Services

THOMAS E. GRAYSON

Underlying the discussion in this chapter is the belief that the prevention or reduction of dropouts rests largely with what goes on in schools and the way they are organized, managed, and operated. To prevent students from dropping out of school, therefore, we need to shift the focus from providing traditional predetermined curricula and services to discovering the unique needs and expectations of students and families. The chapter focuses on the consequences of dropping out of school, including students with special needs. After an overview of the current state of school dropout in the United States, we will explore how to intervene and prevent dropping out within the context of educational reform.

In a recent poll, business and industry employers were asked what they valued most in an individual when hiring new employees. Employers responded that they placed the highest values on attitude, communication skills, and work experience (New York Times News Service, April 6, 1995). Other studies have made similar findings. Especially valuable to employers is work experience in which one learns to be disciplined about work hours, to read and communicate, and to accept direction. Research shows that students who graduate from high school are more likely to be employed, especially if they held paid jobs while they were in school or participated in mainstream vocational educational courses or work experience programs (Edgar, 1987; Zigmond, 1990; Zigmond & Miller, 1992; Levine & Edgar 1995). Taken together, these findings suggest that remaining in school until at least high school graduation offers the best chance for all students to acquire basic academic, social, and vocational skills, and to gain exposure to work experience through job training.

Some observers of education, however, are beginning to realize that schools are not meeting the academic and vocational needs of America's youth, and that there is a scarcity of qualified youth entering the nation's work force. Demographers, educators, and business leaders tell us that the total youth population is declining simultaneously with an increase in the proportionate population of students at risk of school failure, and the myriad studies conducted in the early 1980s document that our schools are failing to educate all our children (Boyer, 1983; Goodlad, 1984; Sizer, 1984; Committee for Economic Development, 1985, 1987; Hodgkinson, 1985, 1989; CCSSO, 1987; Charles Stewart Mott Foundation, 1988; William T. Grant Foundation, 1988; Wolfbein, 1988; Natrillo, McDill, & Pallas, 1990). Bennett and McLaughlin (1988) summed up this dilemma succinctly.

> We are rapidly approaching a new century and a vastly different labor market from the one we know. Major changes are already taking place. The number of new jobs is growing, and most experts agree that the skill levels of many of these jobs will be rising. Employers will place a premium on higher levels of reading, computation, communication, and reasoning skills. Such skills will be vital to our domestic economic growth, as well as our ability to compete abroad.
>
> A growing share of our new workers will come from groups where human resource investments have been historically deficient—minorities, women, and immigrants *and individuals with disabilities* [italics added]. Employers will increasingly have to reach into the ranks of less advantaged to obtain their entry-level workforce, frequently those with deficient basic skills. (Bennett & McLaughlin, 1988:ii)

Researchers in education and work highlight several important points relative to school completion. For instance, the Bennett and McLaughlin work suggests that we can expect increasing demands for a much more diversified work force during the next century, that schools must become partners with business and industry, and that teachers must learn how to meet the educational and vocational needs of a very diverse group of students.

Ideally, if schools: (a) connect with students, families, business, and other service providers; (b) develop and implement relevant curricula; (c) provide the necessary supports and services that address the unique needs of all its students; and (d) employ teachers who are competent in their subject matter, have an unconditional respect for all students, and believe that all students can learn, then remaining in school offers the best chance for all students to become self-determined and to lead happy and productive lives. Unfortunately, such an educational ideal is not the norm. Many students continue to drop out of school, and these dropouts continue to be comprised of disproportionate numbers of females, minority students, and students with disabilities.

On a more positive note, there is a current trend in educational reform to bring the student into the center of the educational and training process and to affirm that the educational system is intended to serve all students (Miller, 1990; Lipsky & Gartner, 1992; Norman & Bourexis, 1995). Student-centered planning focuses on the wants and needs of the student and recognizes the importance of supports in assisting students to achieve their dreams (Mount, 1991; Wehman, 1996). Educational programs and services should be based on expected postschool outcomes of students and developed on the basis of student needs, interests, and preferences (IDEA, 1990; Lipsky & Gartner, 1992; Martin, Marshall, & Maxson, 1993; Martin & Marshall, 1995; Wehman, 1996; Grayson, et al., 1997). School-sponsored work experience needs to become part of the student's program, but this will happen only if connections with business and industry are built and curricula are shaped or developed around the expected postschool outcomes of students (Edgar, 1987; Halpern, Doren, & Benz, 1993).

Choice of school, type of job, type of work arrangement, and the nature of instruction are no longer considered appropriately controlled unilaterally by special education teachers and other service providers in the school system (Lipsky & Gartner, 1992; Wehman, 1996). Under the Individuals with Disabilities Education Act

(IDEA) of 1990, transition from school to work or to postsecondary education is to focus on the student rather than the provision of services. This means that student self-determination and choice must be paramount in planning and implementing movement from school to work or postsecondary schooling. It is also clear that students need to become better self-advocates and more engaged in determining their own future and in formulating their own plans for transitioning from school to adult life (Turnbull et al., 1989; Rusch et al., 1992; Wehmeyer, 1992; Grayson et al., 1997).

As discussed in detail in Chapter 3, Congress in recent years has passed major laws related to the preparation of all youth for the work-force demands in the 21st century (i.e., well informed, skilled in basic academic, vocational, and social skills, and practiced with experiential learning). The Americans with Disabilities Act (ADA) of 1990, the Individuals with Disabilities Education Act (IDEA) of 1990, and the Rehabilitation Act Amendments of 1992 pertain specifically to individuals with disabilities. Goals 2000: Educate America Act of 1994 (also known as Goals 2000), P.L. 103-227, and the School-to-Work Opportunities Act of 1994, P.L. 103-239, are broad in nature and pertain to all students in the mainstream. All these laws have far-reaching implications for designing educational programs in such a way that curricula, instruction, and learning experiences are relevant to students' academic and vocational needs and, therefore, should stem the rising tide of dropouts.

CONSEQUENCES OF DROPPING OUT

The phenomenon of students leaving school before high school graduation is a serious national, state, and local problem. The relatively low number of well-educated and well-qualified people in the work force weakens this country's competitive position in an increasingly challenging global marketplace and threatens economic development in our communities (Committee for Economic Development, 1985, 1987; Berlin & Sum, 1988; William T. Grant Foundation, 1988; Thurow, 1996). Moreover, in addition to its economic and social repercussions for society as a whole, dropping out of school has significant impact on a student's well-being (Jay & Padilla, 1990).

The problems associated with dropping out of school are both measurable and immeasurable. For example, there are identifiable costs that result from dropping out: There are costs to the individuals involved and costs to society as a whole (Berlin & Sum, 1988; Jay & Padilla, 1990). Individual costs to dropouts may be recognized in lost income, limited job opportunities, and low self-esteem. On average, individuals with higher levels of education earn more. Dropouts experience higher unemployment rates than their graduating classmates, and they are more likely to suffer periodic losses of employment and to be assigned to lower paying jobs throughout their working lives (Catterall, 1985; Berlin & Sum, 1988; Thurow, 1996).

On a larger, society level according to the Institute for Educational Leadership, dropping out of school costs the nation from $60 to $228 billion each year in lost revenue, welfare and unemployment expenditures, and crime prevention funds (Hahn, Danzberger, & Lefkowitz, 1987). Society loses in the economic realm because dropouts are likely to be less productive due to poor work ethics and lack of basic academic and social skills. National productivity also suffers: dropouts are not likely to be available to contribute to economic growth and development, tend to be more frequent recipients of welfare and unemployment subsidies, and are more likely to engage in criminal activities (Catterall, 1985; Berlin & Sum, 1988). Such individual and social costs are unacceptable.

The bottom line for high school graduates is whether they possess the important basic academic skills and work habits needed in the workplace. Here, basic skills are defined as the ability to read, write, communicate, and compute. Employment in the 21st century will require that individuals demonstrate these necessary skills and have good work habits to function productively on the job (Thurow, 1996). In addition, future workers will need high levels of literacy to make informed choices about their lives, and will need a multicultural perspective that understands and reflects the changing demographic makeup of the work force.

Indications suggest that educators are relying on noneducators to help develop employable high school graduates. For example, work-based and community-based educational approaches such as cooperative education (Barton, 1996), youth apprenticeship, career academies, school-based enterprises, and mentorship programs (Stern et al., 1995) indicate that educators are beginning to form partnerships with "outsiders" from business, the community, and social service agencies in planning, designing, and implementing educational programs.

This chapter will focus on the consequences of dropping out of school, including students with special needs. After an overview of the current state of school dropout in the United States, we will explore how to intervene and prevent school dropout within the context of educational reform.

DROPOUT RATES: WHAT DO THEY MEAN?

One long-standing problem remains with current research on dropouts: the lack of a standardized definition of "dropout." A standardized definition is a prerequisite for consistent accounting procedures across school districts and research studies (MacMillan et al., 1990). It is even more difficult to get a handle on the magnitude of the national and state level special education dropout rates. In addition to the lack of a uniform definition of dropout, special problems arise with the service configurations that exist to serve this population of students, as well as different accounting procedures for reporting graduation and dropout (Padilla & Jay, 1990; MacMillan, 1991).

As an example of how difficult it is to reconcile differing definitions of dropouts and the methods used to calculate dropout rates, consid-

er the way the National Center for Educational Statistics (NCES) analyzes and calculates dropout rates using dropout data collected by the October 1994 Current Population Survey (CPS) of the U.S. Bureau of the Census (NCES, 1996). Three types of dropout rates are calculated: event, status, and cohort rates. The *event dropout rate* provides a measure of recent dropout experiences and shows the proportion of students who leave high school each year without completing a high school program. These rates can be compared from year to year to determine upward or downward trends. Based on the CPS data, the event dropout rate in 1994 was estimated at 5.3 percent; close to one half million students left school without completing a high school program.

The *status dropout* rate includes a count of all young adults who are not enrolled in a high school program and have not completed high school, regardless of when they last attended school. CPS data show that in October of 1994, there were 32.6 million students who were not enrolled in a high school program and report having not completed high school. This results in a status dropout rate of 11.5 percent.

Finally, the *cohort dropout rate* is a statistic that measures what happens to a single group, or cohort, of students over a period of time. This rate is based on repeated measures of a group of students with shared experiences, and reveals how many students starting in a specific grade drop out over time. For example, the cohort dropout rates for the eighth-grade class of 1988 show that 6.8 percent of the eighth graders in 1988 dropped out of school between the spring of 1988 and the spring of 1990. Further, 7.6 percent of the 1988 eighth graders who were enrolled in the spring of 1990 dropped out between 1990 and the spring of 1992; and by the spring of 1992, 11.6 percent of the 1988 cohort of eighth graders were out of school and had not completed a high school program (1996).

To further complicate, NCES also reports a *high school completion rate,* that is, the number of young adults who have completed a high school program and graduated with a regular high school diploma. In 1994, 79.4 percent of young adults, ages 18 through 24, who were not still enrolled in a high school program were graduates holding regular high school diplomas. Thus, we could say that in 1994, the national dropout rate was 20.6 percent (1996).

SPECIAL EDUCATION DROPOUTS

It is safe to say that most research on dropouts has been conducted on the regular general education student population. Research examining dropout rates of students with disabilities is scarce, and one must be cautious in assessing the extent of the special education dropout problem compared with the overall general population dropout rate (Rumberger, 1987; Padilla & Jay, 1990; Wagner, 1991). However, there is research to suggest that the rate of dropping out is higher for certain categories of students with disabilities than for the general student population (Zigmond & Thornton, 1985; Edgar, 1987; Jay & Padilla, 1987; MacMillan, 1991; Wagner, 1991; Blackorby & Wagner, 1996). These rates will be discussed later in detail. In addition, there is evidence to suggest that the negative consequences (e.g., unemployment, loss of opportunity for postsecondary schooling, and lack of engagement in productive activities after high school) of dropping out of high school may be as significant for youth with disabilities as for other youth (Edgar, 1987; Padilla & Jay, 1990; Wagner, 1991; Kortering, Hess, & Braziel, 1996; Wehman, 1996).

Using a completion rate, we know that nationwide the dropout rate of high school youth among the general population is about 25 percent; that is, one in four students drop out. By comparison, the dropout rate for students with disabilities is about 32 percent, or almost one in three students (Wagner, 1991). These rates are higher for both groups when counting only youth between the ages of 15 and 20. In this age group, youth in the general population dropped out at a rate of 31.6 percent, whereas youth with

disabilities dropped out at a rate of 42.9 percent (Wagner, 1991). These statistical comparisons confirm that youth with disabilities are much more likely to drop out of school than youth in the general population.

According to the U.S. Department of Education's, Office of Special Education Programs, 229,368 students with disabilities exited high school during the 1991–1992 school year. Of these, 100,742 (43.9 percent) graduated with a diploma, 30,839 (13.5 percent) received a certificate, and 4,337 (1.9 percent) reached maximum age for staying in school. Table 4.1 displays the number and percentage of students with different disabilities exiting high school without a diploma, certificate, or reaching maximum age. It is important to note that the U.S. Office of Special Education Programs (OSEP) requests states to report only students who formally withdraw from school without completing their educational program to be counted as dropouts. This means that a student who simply stops attending school but fails to formally withdraw is not counted as a dropout. This student is counted by OSEP in the "status unknown" category, which simply means the student left school for other reasons. However, it is relatively safe to assume that many of these students are, in fact, dropouts who simply did not inform anyone in the school district that they were dropping out.

As Table 4.1 indicates, 51,489 students (22.4 percent) dropped out of school during the 1991–1992 school year. An additional 41,961 (18.3 percent) exited school for other unknown reasons. With these rates, and when research tells us that the unemployment rate for individuals with disabilities is somewhere between 50 and 75 percent (Wehman, 1996), it is not difficult to conclude that most of those unemployed individuals are perhaps the same individuals who have dropped out of school.

Other research suggests even higher special education dropout rates than those reported by OSERS. For example, Holsch (1992) and MacMillan (1990) reported dropout rates between 25 and 35 percent; Kortering and Braziel (1992) believed the dropout rate is somewhere

Table 4.1 Number and Percentage of Students with Different Disabilities Exiting School without a Diploma, Certificate, or Reaching Maximum Age: School Year 1991–1992

Disability	DROPOUT		STATUS UNKNOWN	
	Number	Percent	Number	Percent
Specific learning disability	28,257	21.3	23,409	17.7
Speech-language impairments	1,633	20.1	2,230	27.5
Mental retardation	7,650	19.6	4,099	10.5
Serious emotional disturbance	11,894	35.0	9,995	29.4
Multiple disabilities	546	13.6	416	10.3
Hearing impairments	444	13.0	403	11.8
Orthopedic impairments	252	9.2	556	20.2
Other health impairments	606	16.6	584	16.0
Visual impairments	166	11.5	177	12.2
Autism	27	9.3	78	26.8
Deaf-blindness	6	4.2	8	5.6
Acquired brain injury	8	12.5	6	9.4
All disabilities	51,489	22.4	41,961	18.3

Source: U.S. Department of Education, Office of Special Education Programs, Data Analysis System (DANS) (Wehman, 1996). Used by permission of Brookes Publishing Company.

between 30 and 40 percent; and the National Longitudinal Transition Study of Special Education Students (NLTS) found that 32 percent of students with disabilities exit school by dropping out (Wagner, 1991).

MacMillan (1991) found evidence that suggested higher dropout rates for students with mild disabilities, and particularly for students with learning disabilities and with emotional disturbance. Table 4.2 displays the national dropout rates of special education students, broken down for students with learning disabilities, emotional disorders, and cognitive disabilities—the three categories of individuals with disabilities who drop out of school at the highest rate. As is indicated, students with emotional disorders drop out at an significantly higher rate than students with learning disabilities, and students with learning disabilities drop out at a much higher rate than students with cognitive disabilities. The column representing students with cognitive disabilities is added for comparison.

In a study of California's school system, Jay and Padilla (1987) found that students with specific learning disabilities had a higher dropout rate (75 percent of individuals with specific learning disabilities dropped out of school) than students classified as severely emotionally disturbed, mentally retarded, or multiply disabled, each of whom had a dropout rate of 12 percent. Wagner (1991) also found that students with learning disabilities and students with severe emotional disturbances were significantly more likely to drop out of school than students with other disabilities. These studies reinforce MacMillan's findings that two disability groups (e.g., those with learning disabilities and those with emotional disturbances) have a much higher probability of dropping out of school. Similar findings from the works of Pullis (1991), Frank, Sitlington, and Carson (1991), and Kortering & Braziel (1992) verify the high drop out rates of students with learning disabilities and behavioral disorders.

**Table 4.2 National Dropout Rates of
Special Education Students: 1987–1992**

Year	Number of Students with Disabilities	Percentage Who Dropped Out	Percentage Who Left for Other Reasons	Percentage of Students with Learning Disabilities	Percentage of Students with Emotional Disabilities	Percentage of Students with Cognitive Disabilities
1987–1988	238,579	27.4	16.8	43.0	62.5	37.9
1988–1989	248,590	26.6	17.3	41.7	61.5	36.0
1989–1990	221,418	27.0	13.3	37.6	61.0	31.4
1990–1991	223,229	23.3	15.8	36.9	60.1	31.5
1991–1992	229,368	22.4	18.3	39.0	64.3	30.1

Source: U.S. Department of Education, Office of Special Education and Rehabilitative Services, Annual Reports to Congress (Wehman, 1996). Used by permission of Brookes Publishing Company.

Students with singular sensory disabilities are another group who tend to drop out of school at higher rates and who frequently fall through the cracks in transition planning. Allen, Rawlings, and Schildroth (1989) found that about 52 percent of deaf youth graduated with high school diplomas whereas 29 percent dropped out of school. Of these dropouts, none had documented transition plans. Wehman (1996) expects that these results are typical and can be anticipated also for students who are blind or have visual impairments.

These statistics on dropping out of school show the severity and the complexity of the dropout phenomenon from special education populations. Because of this complexity, braided solutions in dropout prevention strategies are required. Solutions must include collaborative partnerships between students, families, educators, other service providers, and business and community leaders. Completion of high school is the first step in the transition process from adolescence to adulthood. Without taking this first step, the next steps of finding a job, getting married, and raising a family may, indeed, prove to be wobbly and quite difficult steps to take toward achieving the transition to adult life.

FACTORS RELATED TO DROPPING OUT OF SCHOOL

Several studies have been conducted to identify and examine the characteristics of high school dropouts. Kortering et al. (1996) recently described an ecological approach to examining the different contexts of a student's environment (e.g., individual, family, peers, school, and community) and to understand the correlates of dropping out of school. Fernandez, Paulsen and Hirano-Nakanish (1989) studied ethnicity as a factor and found that members of minority groups are more at risk of dropping out than the general population. Rumberger (1987), Ekstrom et al., (1986), and Wehlage and Rutter (1986) have identified several factors associated with dropping out, including ethnicity, gender, family, peer groups, school, economic, and student factors. Studying high school students with disabilities who dropped out school, Wolman, Bruininks, and Thurlow (1989) looked at characteristics of dropouts who have received special education services and found similar correlates for dropping out of school (e.g., behavior and disciplinary problems, poor school attendance, low self-esteem, marriage, pregnancy, and substance abuse, as well as other structural and policy-related school factors). Based on interviews with secondary special education students to obtain their perceptions of why they dropped out, Padilla and Jay (1990) reached similar conclusions as to reasons why students drop out.

Lichtenstein (1993) conducted four case studies of individuals with disabilities who had dropped out of school to determine why they dropped out. One of his subjects, Eric, dropped out of high school because he had come to the conclusion that he just did not have the credits to graduate. Fran dropped out of school at the age of 16 as a result of her pregnancy. Steve dropped out of high school three months after starting ninth grade at the age of 16, after a series of suspensions for fighting, smoking in an unauthorized area, and several unexcused absences. Marsha left school midterm into her sophomore year at the age of 16 to work full time. In each of these case studies, students expressed dissatisfaction while their secondary education programming and transition planning. Evidence suggested poorly developed and implemented IEPs and minimal provision of vocational education and career counseling during their early school years. Lichtenstein (1993) came to the conclusion that students leave school because they believe that further academic efforts would be anxiety-provoking and humiliating.

Many other studies have examined demographic factors such as gender, ethnicity, and socioeconomic status; personal factors such as pregnancy, drug abuse, and needing to work; and school factors such as absenteeism and tardiness, discipline, grade retention, academic performance, extra curricular activities, and relationships with teachers (Deschamps, 1992). All have found these factors to be correlates to dropping out of school.

Deschamps (1992) has written one of the most comprehensive reviews of the research on characteristics of dropouts to date. In her review, she identified six major categories associated

with dropping out of school. These categories—social and family, personality, early transition to adulthood, deviant behavior, and in-school variables—are outlined in Table 4.3. Demographic factors associated with each of the six categories are also indicated.

Deschamps (1992) found demographic, social and family, deviant behavior in society, and in-school categories to be most frequently associated with dropping out of high school. Categories of personality and early transition to adulthood were not identified as major areas contributing to dropping out of school. Among the demographic factors, ethnicity and limited English proficiency (LEP) status, low socioeconomic status, coming from a single-parent family, involvement in discipline incidents, and all the in-school factors (i.e., grade retention, school grades/academic achievement, achievement test scores, extra-curricular participation, absenteeism/tardiness, special education status, and poor relationship with teachers) were relatively common precipitators of dropping out of school (Deschamps, 1992).

Recapping, the research shows that although there are some differences between the general student population and students with disabilities as to why students drop out, there are more similarities than differences (MacMillan, 1991; Seidal & Vaughn, 1991; Wagner, 1991; Kortering et al., 1993; Lichtenstein, 1993).

DROPOUT PREVENTION AND INTERVENTION

Unlike in the past when dropout prevention funding was categorical in nature and intervention strategies were supplemental to the general education program, dropout prevention and intervention are now becoming systemic in schools, and this is especially true of inclusive schools. This is due in part to the educational reform movement toward restructuring schools based on the fundamental issues of schooling: learning, curriculum, instruction, and

Table 4.3. Categories and Demographic Factors Associated with Dropping Out of School

Category	Demographic Factor
Demographic	■ Age/grade
	■ Gender
	■ Ethnicity/LEP status
	■ Geographic region
	■ Community type
Social & Family	■ Parents' marital status
	■ Parents' educational/occupational level
	■ Family support received
	■ Socioeconomic status
	■ Peer group influence
	■ Family size
	■ Sibling dropout status
Personality	■ Self-concept
	■ Motivation level/attitude
Early Transition to Adulthood	■ Pregnant
	■ Children
	■ Dating/marital status
	■ Employment
Deviant Behavior in Society	■ Discipline issues/suspension
	■ Substance abuse
In-School Variables	■ Grade retention
	■ School grades/academic achievement
	■ Achievement test scores
	■ Extracurricular participation
	■ Absenteeism/tardiness
	■ Special education status
	■ Poor relationship with teachers

Source: Reprinted with permission from Deschamps (1992):83–84.

assessment. Today, it is assumed that research and experience can help us identify the characteristics of effective learning environments, that the performance of low-achieving students can be significantly modified, and that schools can make a positive difference for all students, including students with disabilities. In the past, on the other hand, it was generally assumed that public schools could optimally serve only the best and the brightest youths. Educational

reform also calls for appropriate support services for students and their families as well as connections with the work force and with communities (NCREL, 1990).

It is important to note that the special education reform movement began shortly after special education's entrance into public education in 1975 with the enactment of the Education for All Handicapped Children Act, Public Law 94-142. Special education reform blended with general education reform during the early 1980s (Ellenberger, 1996). For example, the efficacy of special education programs was discussed in the early 1980s during the Wingspread Conference in 1981 (Hocutt & McKinney, 1995; Ellenberger, 1996). During the period between 1983 and 1986, academic standards were the main priority of reform, and states increased curriculum requirements and tightened teacher certification requirements (Murphy, 1990; Ellenberger, 1996;). Between 1986 and 1989, teacher empowerment and local school district restructuring were emphasized, and from 1989 until the present, there has been a fundamental shift in focus toward meeting the basic academic and vocational needs of *all* students and families through a more collaborative educational service delivery system (Lipsky & Gartner, 1992, 1994; Stainback & Stainback, 1992; Ellenberger, 1996). Chapter 2 presents these shifts in focus in more detail.

Two major reform studies demonstrate how dropout prevention and intervention have become systemic to general education. One of the reform studies reports findings on the progress of the nation's schools toward improving student learning, the other reports on the national agenda for improving outcomes for individuals with serious emotional disorders (SED). These two studies complement each other and make significant contributions toward our understanding of what schools must do to create an environment that is conducive to learning, prepares students for postsecondary outcomes (e.g., work, postsecondary education, and independent community living), and is inherently rewarding so that students are motivated to remain in school until graduation. Although one study focuses on regular education students and the other on students with serious emotional disorders, the findings from each are germane to all schools and all students, including students with a broad range of disabilities.

Preliminary to a fuller discussion of these reports, a brief note on the nature of prevention is offered. The prevention or reduction of dropouts rests largely with what goes on in schools and the way they are organized, managed, and operated. The Prevention Resource Center in Springfield, Illinois (1982), documented some of the essential prevention components in successful educational programs, including

- combined efforts of school, support service agencies, family, community, and business
- personal, social growth, and social skill building activities
- integration of prevention activities into traditional settings
- synthesis of existing materials into other ongoing programs
- community and business input, involvement and ownership in the schools
- integration into existing networks of service delivery systems
- flexibility along with formative self-correcting process
- access to honest, objective feedback from external evaluations.

These components of prevention need to be deliberately and carefully combined with general education practices. Further, the interweaving of these components must be carried out in concert by regular, special, and vocational educators, with help from students, families, businesses, and communities. Key stakeholders involved in this work must possess skills in a variety of areas, including (a) community organization, (b) problem identification, (c) political advocacy, (d) fund raising, (e) human resource identification, (f) human resource development, (g) group facilitation, (h) program organization and management, (i) public relations and marketing, (j) assessment, (k) negotiation, and (l) collaboration. These essential components of prevention and the skills necessary for combining them are likely to be obvious to those who study educational reform, because they are manifested in schools that have achieved successful educational reform.

The following two broad-based reform strategies, School-Based Reform: Lessons Learned from a National Study (OERI, 1995), and The National Agenda to Guide Schools in Achieving Better Results for Children with Serious Emotional Disorders (Chesapeake Institute, 1994) offer a foundation upon which we can build prevention initiatives aimed at keeping all students in school, regardless of race, gender, or exceptionality. Schools that seriously attempt to replicate the lessons learned by other schools should be equally as effective in retaining students with disabilities who are at risk of dropping out as in retaining students without identified disabilities who are at risk of dropping out. In fact, as public schools become a common meeting place for all students in the communities they serve, that is, as they become truly inclusive schools, it behooves them to be deeply concerned about implementing proven strategies that enhance learning for all students (Stainback & Stainback, 1984, 1992; Lipsky & Gartner, 1994). These two school-based reform strategies for improving student learning are discussed in what follows.

School-Based Reform: Lessons Learned from a National Study

The Office of Educational Research and Improvement (OERI) in the U.S. Department of Education provides national leadership for educational research and statistics and, in so doing, studies the progress of schools and their effectiveness in implementing educational reform throughout the nation. OERI recently studied 32 schools in 16 school districts located in five states (California, Connecticut, Kentucky, South Dakota, and Washington) that are undergoing major school-based reform. In their report, School-Based Reform: Lessons Learned from a National Study (1995), OERI described key features of three broad successful reform strategies employed by these schools:

- create challenging learning experiences for all students

- build a school culture that nurtures staff collaboration and participation in decision making
- provide meaningful opportunities for professional growth of teachers.

These broad-based strategies are described in what follows.

Create Challenging Learning Experiences for All Students. Schools can undertake many activities to create challenging learning experiences for all students. OERI recommends at least four. First, schools need to set high expectations for all students. Expectations with clear performance standards that measure student accomplishments against well-defined objectives and identified competencies (what students should know and be able to do) must be a cornerstone in setting challenging learning experiences for students. Second, schools must develop a challenging curriculum that teaches students basic academic, vocational, and social skills, all of which prepare students for work or postsecondary education, and adult living. Third, schools need to be flexible, and they must consider alternative configurations of students and teachers. For example, rather than allocating 40 minutes per day for a particular subject, block scheduling may allow upwards of two hours for students to investigate topics of interest in greater depth. Block scheduling is also conducive to team teaching, and it promotes an interdisciplinary approach to teaching students. The fourth recommendation is to monitor student progress by using a range of outcome measures, including portfolios, authentic assessments, functional assessments or in the case of students with disabilities, for example, individualized outcome measures as prescribed in the student's Individualized Educational Program.

Build a School Culture That Nurtures Staff Collaboration and Participation in Decision Making. Common components of school-based reform found in the OERI study were the organized efforts by schools to increase interaction and communication among teachers and between teachers and school administrators. OERI made three recommendations to assist schools in nurturing teacher collaboration, shared decision making, responsibility, and authority. First, schools must find new ways for teachers to come together through formal or informal arrangements, such as committees and councils to focus on significant and needed changes in the school. Teachers must also feel empowered with ownership in decisions. Second, the roles and authority of teachers and administrators to facilitate shared decision making must be clearly articulated. For example, if teachers are to be empowered with decision-making authority, they need a voice in staff development, curriculum and materials, budgeting, personnel, shared school management, and team teaching. Third, the collaborative work of staff must be promoted by establishing new ways to allocate staff, resources, time, and space. For example, teachers from different disciplines, grades, and specializations could have common planning time; administrators, specialists, and support personnel could be assigned to support classroom teachers; teachers could share classrooms and resource rooms; and class schedules could be revamped to allow for extended team teaching.

Provide Meaningful Opportunities for Professional Growth.

The final broad-based strategy suggested by OERI is for schools to systematically analyze staff development needs, available resources, and staff receptivity and capacity for training. This analysis enables school personnel to prioritize staff development topics and identify the most suitable types of professional development. Many teachers will need not only to update their knowledge but also to acquire new knowledge and skills to deal with the new and varied demands brought about by educational reform. These demands include, among many others: team teaching; cooperative learning; developing curricula that meet specific academic, vocational, and social needs of stu-

dents; using technology effectively; making appropriate accommodations for individuals with disabilities; transition planning; establishing partnerships with business and industry; and engaging parents and members of the community in strategic planning for school activities.

In summary, lessons learned by schools studied by OERI can provide for schools embarking on site-based reform some basic guidelines to create a school climate that will lessen the chance of students leaving before graduation. Three successful school-based reform strategies for improving student learning and, subsequently, preventing students from dropping out are: (a) challenging curriculum for all students, (b) a collaborative school culture, and (c) meaningful opportunities for professional growth by teachers and other school staff. Although schools create varied approaches to implementing these features, the presence and integration of these features in a school characterize successful educational reform efforts that can be modeled by others.

The National Agenda to Guide Schools in Achieving Better Results for Children with Serious Emotional Disorders

Earlier sections of this chapter pointed out that, next to students with learning disabilities, students with emotional disorders drop out of school at a higher rate than any other group of students with disabilities. According to many studies, students with serious emotional disorders (SED) get lower grades, fail more courses, and miss more days of school than other students with disabilities. They also are retained more often at grade level, and they are more apt to encounter the juvenile justice system.

In 1990, Congress authorized a new program for youth with serious emotional disorders under part C of the Individuals with Disabilities Act. In addition, the IDEA mandated a participatory strategic planning process, involving multiple stakeholders to design a national agenda that would focus the attention of educators, parents, advocates, and professionals from a variety of disciplines on what must be done to assist schools in achieving better outcomes for youth with emotional disorders. Based on personal interviews, focus groups, stakeholder meetings, presentations, solicitation of oral and written responses, literature reviews, and an interactive national teleconference, The Chesapeake Institute (1994) prepared a report for the Office of Special Education Programs (OSEP) on how schools could achieve better outcomes for students with serious emotional disorders. Seven "targets" for schools undergoing special education reform were identified. Each target is described in what follows.

Target 1: Expand Positive Learning Opportunities and Results. This target is intended to foster student engagement in culturally responsive, student-centered opportunities to learn basic academic, vocational, and social skills. It is marked by high expectations, and it focuses on meeting clearly identified needs of students. This target supports coordinated efforts of teachers, parents, schools, and other service agencies to contribute to the academic, social, and emotional development of students with serious emotional disorders and those at risk of developing serious emotional disorders. This target calls for providing opportunities for success that will enable students with serious emotional disorders to develop the knowledge, skills, and attitudes essential for educational, social, and workplace achievement.

Target 2: Strengthen School and Community Capacity. This target calls for schools to place students in the least restrictive most appropriate environment. In particular, it asks that schools integrate students with SED into neighborhood schools and regular classrooms. This means that schools must be prepared to provide the resources necessary to improve the readiness and capacity of schools to educate and provide needed support services to students with emotional disorders. The Chesapeake Institute report (1994) strongly

supports active collaborations among regular and special educators, service providers, and families that enable these students to learn and participate in activities with their peers. Existing initiatives that address these goals include: providing field-based training to regular educators; using special educators as consultants; reducing teacher-student ratios; implementing non-traditional methods of dispute resolution; adopting approaches to discipline that keep students in class; teaming special educators in classrooms with regular educators; and bringing health specialists into schools. (p. 9)

Target 3: Value and Address Diversity. This target encourages schools to be culturally competent and to engage in linguistically appropriate dialogue as well as collaborations among families, professionals, students, and communities. These efforts are intended to "foster equitable outcomes for all students and result in the identification and provision of services that are responsive to issues of race, culture, gender, and social and economic status" (p. 10).

Target 4: Collaborate with Families. Family support services are recognized as being crucial to successfully addressing the needs of students with emotional disorders. To improve educational, vocational, and social outcomes for these students, schools and other service providers must collaborate with families and support the active participation of families in planning the students' educational programs and transition services. Examples of how schools can be responsive to families as given in the report include: (a) designating a single person to coordinate services for the family; (b) establishing a single point of entry with clear intake procedures; (c) staffing technical assistance centers with family members; (d) expanding the role of families and caregivers in the student's IEP meetings perhaps by specifically placing a family report on the agenda; and (e) including the family in outreach planning and cultural competency training.

Target 5: Promote Appropriate Assessment Practices. Appropriate assessment practices are essential to improving outcomes for youth with disabilities. Early identification of students in need of special services and supports is possible only through appropriate screening, careful observation, and monitoring. This target promotes assessment practices that are integral to the identification, design, and delivery of services for youth with SED, and that are culturally appropriate, ethical, and functional.

Target 6: Provide Ongoing Skill Development and Support. This strategic target asks that schools provide ongoing support for and professional development of teachers and other service providers in order to: (a) increase their capacity to teach and work effectively with other teachers (e.g., team teaching and interdisciplinary planning of curricular activities), and with individuals outside of the school (e.g., employers, parents, volunteers, and staff from community-based organizations); (b) reduce the sense of isolation that teachers often feel; and (c) rejuvenate the faculty's sense of commitment to meeting the academic, vocational, and social needs of students with SED. Further, developmental training should be extended to all key stakeholders who work with youth with emotional disorders so that they can acquire the knowledge and skills necessary to implement new intervention strategies, and become aware of innovations and promising practices.

Target 7: Create Comprehensive and Collaborative Systems. This target promotes systems change that is built around the academic, vocational, and social needs of students, needs of families, and needs of communities. Systems change, in this context, means service coordination, so that all service providers (e.g., teachers, mental health professionals, vocational educators, substance abuse counselors, career counselors, probation officers, mentors, and others) work in concert without duplication of effort and with maximum efficiency. Such systems respond to local needs and reflect the culture of the communities they serve, provide individualized and family-centered services, respond promptly and flexibly during crises, are outcome-oriented in their planning and decision making, have clear lines of responsibility, and provide systemwide and agency-level accountability.

A Promising Vocationally Oriented Transition Program for Students with Learning Disabilities

According to Grayson et al. (1997), it is past the time for students with learning disabilities to receive an alternative educational option that is entirely vocationally oriented, and that uses teachers and counselors trained in special education as primary providers of job placement, training, and follow-along services before and after students graduate from high school. Such an option would very likely motivate youth with learning disabilities to remain in school and would also allow for flexible reentry into the secondary school, when necessary, even after graduation.

Based on the interpretation by DeStefano and Wermuth (1992) of federal transition requirements, reforming secondary special education programs must involve:

1. developing linkages between school personnel and others involved in the provision of transition services;

2. broadening the scope of secondary special education curricula and programs; and

3. changing the roles and skill requirements of secondary-level special education personnel (p. 538).

These suggested reforms would require secondary-level special education programs to move away from a narrow focus on remedial instruction designed to parallel regular education toward more integrated and vocationally relevant environments of the school and community (Grayson et al., 1997). The following is an example of such an approach, which is identified to be a vocationally oriented model of transition services.

As described by Grayson et al.,(1997), a vocationally oriented model like that being proposed would consist of the following five components: (a) basic skills, survival skills, and academic strategies instruction, and job-related skills taught in a vocationally relevant manner; (b) subject matter (content area) integrated with the vocational education curriculum; (c) in-school mainstream vocational education courses and community-based job experiences beginning in the ninth grade and continuing throughout high school; (d) special educators responsible for job placement, training, and follow-along before students exit high school; and (e) multiple high school reentry points available to all youths with learning disabilities until they reach age 21, whether they have graduated from high school or not.

These components call for dramatic changes in the roles and skill requirements of special education professionals and in the secondary special education curriculum now offered to most students with learning disabilities. Collaboration with vocational educators and employers is the cornerstone of the proposed model. Additionally, the setting in which instruction is provided will expand to include vocational education classrooms and community-based work sites, and the time frame that currently constitutes a normal school day (9:00 A.M. to 3:30 P.M.) or school year (September to June) may no longer be applicable. Briefly described below is an example of such a vocationally oriented education option, the Pathways to Satisfaction program. This program holds promise for keeping youth with learning disabilities in school and in preparing them for work and adult living.

Pathways to Satisfaction (PTS). Since the mid-1980s, secondary-level students with learning disabilities attending West High School in Madison, Wisconsin, have had the opportunity to participate in a comprehensive program designed to facilitate their transition from school to adult life. The program, formally titled Pathways to Satisfaction, was developed by Thomas M. Holub in 1990 and is currently being implemented, in part or wholly, in over 30 school districts in Wisconsin, Illinois, and Minnesota. The PTS program consists of five interrelated phases that students progress through based on their individual needs, interests, and goals for the future. Although these phases are designed to follow a sequential order, they are dynamic in nature, allowing individual students the ability to move flexibly between phases, based on contextual and life-orienting experiences they encounter in educational settings or the community.

The five phases in the PTS program include: (a) focus, (b) synthesis, (c) exploration, (d) connection, and (e) evaluation. Taken together, the phases extend from the point when students are nearing the end of their middle school or junior high school experience and are gathering information about potential high school options or pathways, up to a point after the students have successfully exited from high school. The formal and informal activities and resources that are made available within each of the phases are based on the interests and needs of the students and their parents.

Each phase in the PTS program is student-centered and student-driven. The transition specialists employed by the Madison Metropolitan School District receive continuous inservice training and are provided the option to receive additional training through the Preparing Transition Leadership Cadres for Wisconsin program offered throughout the state by the University of Wisconsin-Madison (Hanley-Maxwell, 1993). Although trained transition specialists work specifically with students with learning disabilities at Madison West High School, students and their parents are expected to be the primary actors throughout the transition process, self-advocating to ensure their desires are programmatically implemented, and managing their own transition plans. Throughout the transition process, students and their parents receive instruction on how to become their own case managers, connecting with postsecondary institutions and agencies, and overcoming common barriers inhibiting successful transitions.

The PTS program is grounded in the philosophical belief that all students should be educated with their chronologically aged peers and should be included to the greatest extent possible in the regular or general education environment. If general education courses and programs offer instructional opportunities for students enrolled in the PTS program, enrollment in those options is explored in preference to creating a separate parallel system serving only students with learning disabilities. If general education opportunities need to be supported by special education teachers in order to meet the educational needs of students enrolled in the PTS program, collaborative instruction involving the general education teacher and special education teacher is implemented. Reasonable instructional accommodations are made for students in such inclusive environments. The accommodations, made with relative ease due to collaborative instruction, include special methodological practices, adaptations for strategy implementation, and alteration of expectations. Regular education staff involved in these collaborative efforts routinely request that PTS strategies be implemented for all enrollees in fully included classes, and parental requests for such participation has been common for students in all grades. The PTS program encourages flexibility and the use of currently available resources and staff to meet the diverse needs of individual students.

Bottom-Up Approach to Dropout Prevention and Building Educational Options for Youth with Disabilities

A number of follow-up studies have been conducted that examine the outcomes of students who were formerly enrolled in special education programs after they exit secondary schools. Most of these studies report high dropout rates for individuals with learning and emotional disabilities, along with high rates of unemployment or underemployment and low rates of enrollment in postsecondary education (Hasazi, Gordon, & Roe, 1985; Mithaug, Horiuchi, & Fanning, 1985; Zigmond & Thornton, 1985; Edgar & Levine, 1986; Sitlington et al., 1989; Wagner, 1989; Harnisch, Wermuth, & Zheng, 1992). Grayson et al. (1997) pointed out that "... results of these studies do not flatter secondary special education programs. Rather, a picture of poor academic preparation and a lack of marketable vocational skills of students served by those supposedly 'special' programs is described...."

Some youths with learning disabilities and emotional disorders leave high school with the necessary academic, vocational, interpersonal, and social skills to successfully continue their education in postsecondary settings or to enter the world of work. Others exit secondary school before graduating only to experience, as Halpern (1992) described, "a period of floundering that occurs for at least the first several years after leaving school as adolescents attempt to assume a variety of adult roles in their communities" (p. 203). The primary goal of secondary-level educational programs designed for individuals with disabilities who are returning to school after dropping out should be to minimize the "period of floundering" by offering a vocationally oriented curriculum that evolves from the transition planning process (Edgar, 1987; Grayson et al., 1997). This curriculum, along with necessary transition support services, must be designed from the bottom-up by individuals who have the most at stake (e.g., students, families, school personnel, other service providers, and businesses).

In addition, returning to school with honor and pride and without encountering bureaucratic barriers must become the routine experiences for all retrieved dropouts. There must be a clearly articulated mechanism of return for youth who have exited school without a diploma or certificate of achievement. Currently, there are few educational options for individuals with disabilities that focus on transition from school to work, and these may not be articulated to the at-risk youngsters, or to those who have left school by choice or force.

Bottom-up programs for students at high risk of dropping out and for retrieved dropouts can be systematically and strategically planned, developed, and implemented (Bickman, 1985, 1987; Galvin, 1989; Trochim, 1989; Grayson, 1992a, 1992b, 1993, 1995; Kolb, 1992; Trochim, Cook, & Setze, 1994). Successful programs of this kind must have strong connections with the community and with locally based business and industry; they need support in the form of leadership, commitment, resources, and training not only from the public schools but also from local community and business leaders. The bottom-up process requires that programs and interventions for dropouts be developed by local stakeholders who have vested interests in their communities and in the development of human resources.

Grayson (1993, 1997), for example, facilitated a group of primary stakeholders representing a broad range of local policy makers, decision makers, and service providers in Fulton, Will, Grundy, and Kendall Counties, Illinois, in conceptualizing a countywide alternative high school for youth at risk of dropping out and for youth who already had dropped out of school. Using nominal group techniques, focus group questioning (Krueger, 1988), and conceptualization methods called "concept mapping" (Trochim, 1989; Grayson, 1992a, 1992b), the group designed an alternative education program plan for youth at risk of dropping out of schools. The plan described the elements and major components of the program, and specified the relative importance of those elements. The plan also provided comparison of the perceptions of various stakeholders (e.g., school administrators, program staff, and support service agencies), relating the importance of various program elements to the financial support given to them, matching expectations of the program with the work accomplished to date, and assessing how well program outcomes met the group's expecta-tions. In other words, this bottom-up

approach resulted in the development of an alternative education program that was designed specifically for its constituency, and that was unique to its community and existing resources.

Bottom-up program development facilitates the empowerment of stakeholders by actively engaging them in the design of program and intervention plans from the very beginning. Specific, concrete ideas that stakeholders are familiar with become the building blocks for program design. The program design represents the thinking and ideas of the stakeholders.

Programs for retrieved dropouts must be built on such principles of empowerment and capacity building. Empowerment involves helping individuals to help themselves (Fetterman, 1993). In this case, the targets for empowerment are students, families, local school district personnel, staff from other support service agencies and community-based organizations, and employers from business and industry. These are the individuals who have vested interests in preparing students for work and independent living. This focus is similar to the W. K. Kellogg Foundation's specific emphasis on empowerment in community settings as a funding strategy:

> We've long been convinced that problems can best be solved at the local level by the people who live with them on a daily basis. In other words, individuals and groups of people must be empowered to become changemakers and solve their own problems, through the organizations and institutions they devise.... Through our community-based programming, we are helping to empower various individuals, agencies, institutions, and organizations to work together to identify problems and to find quality, cost-effective solutions. In doing so, we find ourselves working more than ever with grantees with whom we have been less involved—smaller, newer organizations and their programs. (1992:6)

The work of the Kellogg Foundation in the areas of community-based health services, rural development, leadership, and family and neighborhoods exemplifies this spirit of empowerment and capacity building by putting "power in the hands of creative and committed individuals—power that will enable them to make important changes in the world" (1992:13). This is the spirit that schools must try to emulate. School administrators and teachers must shift their focus from providing traditional predetermined curricula and services to discovering the unique needs and expectations of students and families, and they must then provide the best available staffing and programming to address those needs. Empowerment of key stakeholders means we are helping to build the capacities of various individuals, agencies, institutions, and organizations to be able to work together in order to identify barriers to effective transition, design effective transition services plans, and, finally, to implement those plans.

QUESTIONS

1. The individual and social costs of dropping out of high school are great. Discuss these costs and discuss whether the costs are higher for individuals with disabilities than for individuals without disabilities?

2. The lack of a standardized definition of dropout has been a long-standing problem. The National Center for Educational Statistics calculate three types of dropout rates: (a) event, (b) status, and (c) cohort. How are each of these rates defined, what do they measure, and how might they be used?

3. Research has shown that youth with disabilities are much more likely to drop out of school than students without disabilities. What are some of the difficulties these students might encounter if they do not experience successful transitions from high school to adult living?

4. What is the dropout rate for students with disabilities, and how do the rates vary for youths from different disability groups?

5. Lichenstein (1993) and Deschamps (1992) have identified specific factors that are related to dropping out of school. Discuss those factors.

6. Discuss some of the essential dropout prevention components found in educational reform programs, and describe the skills that key stakeholders must possess in order to carry out the process.

7. Currently, educational reform efforts call for systemic dropout prevention and intervention strategies that are student-centered. Describe the basic features that are espoused by the following two major studies: (a) School-based Reform: Lessons Learned from a National Study, and (b) The National Agenda to Guide Schools in Achieving Better Results for Children with Serious Emotional Disorders.

8. How are the strategies from the studies described in Question 7 similar? How are they different?

9. The Pathways to Satisfaction Program, a vocationally oriented transition program for students with learning disabilities, is a student-centered and student-driven program. Discuss how this program focuses on the student and how it holds promise for keeping youth with disabilities in school.

10. A bottom-up approach to designing curriculum means that individuals who have the most at stake (e.g., students, parents, school personnel, community agencies, and so forth) are actively involved in designing the curriculum. Discuss how such a bottom-up program for students at risk of dropping out of high school might be designed.

REFERENCES

Allen, T. E., Rawlings, B. W., & Schildroth, A. (1989). *Deaf students and the school-to-work transition.* Baltimore: Paul H. Brookes.

Americans with Disabilities Act (ADA) of 1990, P.L. 101-336, 42 United States Congress, 12101 et seq.

Barton, P. E. (1996). *Cooperative education in high school: Promise and neglect.* A policy issue perspective published by the Policy Information Center. Princeton, NJ: Educational Testing Service.

Bennett, W. J., & McLaughlin, A. (1988). *The bottom line: Basic skills in the workplace.* Washington, DC: U.S.

Department of Labor and U.S. Department of Education.

Berlin, G., & Sum, A. (1988). *Toward a more perfect union: Basic skills, poor families, and our economic future.* Occasional paper 3. New York: Ford Foundation.

Bickman, L. (1985). Improving established statewide programs: A component theory of evaluation. *Evaluation Review, 9*(2), 189–208.

———. (1987). *Using program theory in evaluation.* San Francisco: Jossey-Bass.

Blackorby, J., & Wagner, M. (1996). Longitudinal postschool outcomes of youth with disabilities: Findings from the National Longitudinal Study. *Exceptional Children, 62,* 399–414.

Boyer, E. L. (1983). *High school: A report on secondary education in America.* New York: Harper & Row.

Catterall, J. S. (1985). *On the social costs of dropping out of school.* Stanford, CA: Center for Educational Research at Stanford.

Charles Stewart Mott Foundation. (1988). *America's shame, America's Hope: Twelve million youth at risk.* A report prepared by MDC, Inc. Chapel Hill, NC: Author.

Chesapeake Institute. (1994). *National agenda to guide schools in achieving better results for children with serious emotional disorders.* A report prepared for the U. S. Department of Education, Office of Special Education and Rehabilitative Services, Office of Special Education Programs. Washington, DC: Author.

Committee for Economic Development. (1985). *Investing in our children: Business and the public schools.* New York: Author.

———. (1987). *Children in need: Investment strategies for the educationally disadvantaged.* New York: Author.

Council of Chief State School Officers. (1987). *Assuring school success for students at risk: A policy statement of the Council of Chief State School Officers.* Alexandria, VA: CCSSO.

Deschamps, A. (1992). *An integrative review of research on characteristics of dropouts.* Ph.D. dissertation, George Washington University, Washington, DC.

DeStefano, L., & Wermuth, T. R. (1992). IDEA (P.L. 101-476): Defining a second generation of transition services. In F. R. Rusch, L. DeStefano, J. Chadsey-Rusch, L. A. Phelps, & E. Szymanski (Eds.), *Transition from school to adult life: Models, linkages, and policy* (pp. 537–549). Sycamore, IL: Sycamore.

Edgar, E. (1987). Secondary programs in special education: Are many of them justifiable? *Exceptional Children, 53,* 555–561.

Edgar, E., & Levine, P. (1986). *Washington State follow-up studies of post-secondary special education students.* Seattle: University of Washington.

Ekstrom, R. B., Goertz, M. E., Pollack, J. M., & Rock, D. A. (1986). Who drops out of high school and why? Findings from a national study. *Teachers College Record, 87*(3), 356–373.

Ellenberger, D. J. (1996). *Restructuring of the Illinois state board of education: The special education transition standing team.* Master's thesis, University of Illinois, Champaign.

Fernandez, R. M., Paulsen, R., & Hirano-Nakanish, M. (1989). Dropping out among Hispanic youth. *Social Science Research, 18,* 21–52.

Fetterman, D. M. (1993). Empowerment evaluation. *Evaluation Practice, 15,* 1.

Frank, A. R., Sitlington, P. L., & Carson, R. (1991). Transition of adolescents with behavioral disorders: Is it successful? *Behavioral Disorders, 16*(3), 180–191.

Galvin, P. F. (1989). Concept mapping for planning and evaluation of a big brother/big sister program. In M. K. Trochim (Ed.), Special issue: Concept mapping for evaluation and planning. *Evaluation and Program Planning, 12*(1).

Goodlad, J. I. (1984). *A place called school.* New York: McGraw-Hill.

Grayson, T. E. (1992a). *Identifying program theory: A step toward evaluating categorical state-funded educational programs.* Ann Arbor, MI: University Microfilms.

———. (1992b). Concept mapping. In D. D. Bragg (Ed.), *Alternative approaches to outcomes assessment for postsecondary vocational education* (pp. 65-92). Berkeley, CA: National Center for Research in Vocational Education.

———. (1993). *Empowering key stakeholders in the strategic planning and development of alternative school programs for youth at risk of school failure.* Paper presented at the American Evaluation Association Annual Meeting, Dallas, TX.

———. (1995). *Program planning and outcomes through concept mapping.* Paper presented at the Transition: An Investment in the Future Conference, University of Arkansas, Little Rock.

Grayson, T. E. (1997). *Conceptualizing an alternative program for disruptive youth.* Paper presented at the Thirteenth Annual Pacific Rim Conference, Honolulu, Hawaii.

Grayson, T. E., Wermuth, T. R., Holub, T. M., & Anderson, M. L. (1997). Effective practices of transition from school to work for people with learning 8disabilities. In P. J. Gerber & D. S. Brown (Eds.), *Learning disabilities and employment.* Austin, TX: PRO-ED.

Hahn, A., Danzberger, J., & Lefkowitz, B. (1987). *Dropouts in America: Enough is known for action.* Washington, DC: The Institute for Educational Leadership.

Halpern, A. S. (1992). Transition: Old wine in new bottles. *Exceptional Children, 58*(3), 202–211.

Halpern, A. S., Doren, B., & Benz, M. (1993). Job experiences of students with disabilities in their last two years in school. *Career Development for Exceptional Individuals, 16*(1), 63–74.

Hanley-Maxwell, C. (1993). *Preparing transition leadership cadres in Wisconsin.* Madison: University of Wisconsin-Madison, The Center on Education and Work.

Harnisch, D. L., Wermuth, T. R., & Zheng, P. (1992). *Identification and validation of transition quality indicators: Implications for educational reform.* Paper presented at the Third International Conference of the Division on Mental Retardation of the Council for Exceptional Children, Honolulu, HI.

Hasazi, S., Gordon, L., & Roe, C. (1985). Factors associated with the employment status of handicapped youth exiting high school from 1979 to 1983. *Exceptional Children, 51,* 455–469.

Hocutt, A., & McKinney, J. D. (1995). Moving beyond the regular education initiative: National reform in special education. In J. L. Paul, H. Rosseli, & D. Evans (Eds.), *Integrating school restructuring and special education reform* (pp. 43–62). New York: Harcourt Brace.

Hodgkinson, H. L. (1985). *All one system: Demographics of education, kindergarten through graduate school.* Washington, DC: Institute for Educational Leadership.

———. (1989). *The same client: The demographics of education and service delivery systems.* Washington, DC: Institute for Educational Leadership.

Holsch, S. A., Karen, R. L., & Franzini, L. R. (1992). Two-year follow-up of the competitive employment status of graduates with developmental disabilities. *Career Development for Exceptional Individuals, 15*(2), 149–155.

Individuals with Disabilities Education Act (IDEA) of 1990, P.L. 101-476, Title 20, United States Congress, 1400 et seq.

Jay, E. D., & Padilla, C. L. (1987). *Special education dropouts: The incidence of and reasons for dropping out of special education in California.* Menlo Park, CA: SRI International.

———. (1990). Dropping out: A look at the problem in special education. *Readings on Equal Education, 10,* 193–225.

Kolb, D. G. (1992). The practicality of theory. *Journal of Experiential Learning, 15*(2), 24–28.

Kortering, L. J., & Braziel, P. M. (1992). *School dropout among rural youths with and without learning disabilities.* Unpublished manuscript, : Appalachian State University, Boone, NC.

———. (1996). *School dropouts from the perspective of former students: Implications for secondary special education programs.* Unpublished manuscript, Appalachian State University, Boone, NC.

Kortering, L. J., Hess, R. S., & Braziel, P. M. (1996). School dropouts. In G. Baer & K. Minke (Eds.), *Best practices in school psychology.* Bethesda, MD: National Association of School Psychologists.

Krueger, R. A. (1988). *Focus groups: A practical guide for applied research.* Newbury Park, CA: Sage.

Levine, P., & Edgar, G. (1995). An analysis by gender of long-term postschool outcomes for youth with and without disabilities. *Exceptional Children, 61*(3), 282–300.

Lichtenstein, S. (1993). Transition from school to adulthood: Case studies of adults with learning disabilities who dropped out of school. *Exceptional Children, 59,* 336–347.

Lipsky, D. K., & Gartner, A. G. (1992). Achieving full inclusion: Placing the student at the center of education reform. In W. Stainback & S. Stainback (Eds.), *Controversial issues confronting special education* (pp. 3–12). Boston: Allyn & Bacon.

———. (1994). Beyond separate to equal: Changes in rights and rules. *TASH Newsletter, 20*(7), 5.

MacMillan, D. L. (1991). *Hidden youth: Dropouts from special education.* Reston, VA: The Council for Exceptional Children.

MacMillan, D. L., Balow, I. H., Widman, K. F., Borthwick-Duffy, S., & Hendrick, I. G. (1990). Methodological problems in estimating dropout rates and the implication for studying dropouts from special education. *Exceptionality, 1,* 29–39.

Martin, J. E., & Marshall, L. H. (1995). Choice maker: A comprehensive self-determination transition program. *Intervention in School and Clinic, 30*(3), 147–157.

Martin, J. E., Marshall, L. H., & Maxson, L. L. (1993). Transition policy: Infusing self-determination and self-advocacy into transition programs. *Career Development for Exceptional Individuals, 16,* 53–61.

Miller, L. (1990). The regular education initiative and school reform: Lessons from the mainstream. *Remedial and special education, 11,* 17–22, 28.

Mithaug, D. E., Horiuchi, C. M., & Fanning, P. N. (1985). A report on the Colorado statewide follow-up survey of special education students. *Exceptional Children, 55,* 397–404.

Mount, B. (1991). *Person-centered planning: A source book of values, ideals, and methods to encourage person-centered development.* New York: Graphic Features.

Murphy, J. (1990). The educational reform movement of the 1980s: A comprehensive analysis. In J. Murphy (Ed.), *The educational reform movement of the 1980s* (pp. 3–55). Berkeley, CA: McCutchan.

National Center for Education Statistics (NCES).(1996). *Dropout rates in the United States: 1994.* Washington, DC: U.S. Department of Education.

Natriello, G., McDill, E. L., & Pallas, A. M. (1990). *Schooling disadvantage children.* New York: Teachers College Press.

Norman, M. E., & Bourexis, P. S. (1995). *Including students with disabilities in school-to-work opportunities.* Washington, DC: Council of Chief State School Officers.

North Central Regional Educational Laboratory. (1990). *Restructuring to promote learning in America's schools.* Educational Laboratory, Elmhurst, IL: Author.

OERI, U.S. Department of Education. (1995). *School-based reform: Lessons learned from a national study. A guide for school reform teams.* Washington, DC: Author.

Office of Special Education Programs, U.S. Department of Education. (1990). *Twelfth Annual Report to Congress on the Implementation of the Education of the Handicapped Act.* Washington, DC: Author.

Padilla, C. L., & Jay, E. D. (1990). Dropping out: A look at the problem in special education. *Readings on Equal Education, 10,* 193–225.

Prevention Resource Center. (1982). *Prevention: A resource guide for program development.* Springfield, IL: Author.

Pullis, M. (1991). No bridges over troubled waters: Transition services for students with behavioral disorders. *Missouri Lincletter, 14*(2), 1–3.

Rumberger, R. W. (1987). High school dropouts: A review of issues and evidence. *Review of Educational Research, 57*(2), 101–121.

Rusch, F. R., DeStefano, L., Chadsey-Rusch, J., Phelps, L. A., & Szymanski, E. (1992). *Transition from school to adult life: Models, linkages, and policy.* Sycamore, IL: Sycamore.

Seidal, J. L., & Vaughn, S. (1991). Social alienation and the learning disabled school dropout. *Learning Disabilities Research, 6,* 152–157.

Sitlington, P. L., Frank, A. R., & Cooper, L. (1989). *Iowa statewide follow-up study: Adult adjustment of individuals with learning disabilities one year after leaving high school.* Des Moines: Iowa Department of Education.

Sizer, T. R. (1984). *Horace's compromise: The dilemma of the American high school.* Boston: Houghton Mifflin.

Stainback, S., & Stainback, W. (Eds.). (1992). *Controversial issues confronting special education.* Boston: Allyn & Bacon.

Stainback, W., & Stainback, S. (Eds.). (1984). A rationale for the merger of special education and regular education. *Exceptional Children, 51,* 102–111.

Stern, D., Finkelstein, N., Stone, J. R. III., Latting, J., & Dornsife, C. (1995). *School to work: Research on programs in the United States.* The Stanford Series on Education & Public Policy. Washington, DC: The Falmer Press.

Thurow, L. C. (1996). *The future of capitalism: How today's economic forces shape tomorrow's world.* New York: William Morrow.

Trochim, M. K. (1989). An introduction to concept mapping for planning and evaluation. *Evaluation and Program Planning, 12,* 1–16.

Trochim, M. K., Cook, J. A., & Setze, R. J. (1994). Using concept mapping to develop a conceptual framework of staff's views of a supported employment program for individuals with severe mental illness. *Journal of Consulting and Clinical Psychology, 62*(4), 766–775.

Turnbull, H. R., Turnbull, A. P., Bronicki, G. J., Summers, J. A., & Roeder-Gordon, C. (1989). *Disability and the family: A guide to decisions for adulthood.* Baltimore: Paul H. Brookes.

Wagner, M. (1989). *The transition experiences of youth with disabilities: A report from the national longitudinal transition study.* Menlo Park, CA: SRI International.

———. (1991). *Dropouts with disabilities: What do we know? What can we do?* A Report from the National Longitudinal Transition Study of Special Education Students. Menlo Park, CA: SRI International.

Wehlage, G. G., & Rutter, R. A. (1986). Dropping out: How much do schools contribute to the problem? *Teachers College Record, 87*(3), 376–392.

Wehman, P. (1996). *Life beyond the classroom: Transition strategies for young people with disabilities* (2nd ed.). Balitimore: Paul Brookes.

Wehmeyer, M. L. (1992). Self-determination and the education of students with mental retardation. *Education and Training in Mental Retardation, 27,* 302–314.

Wehmeyer, M. L., & Lawrence, M. (1995). *Whose future is it anyway? A student-directed transition planning process.* Arlington, TX: The ARC National Headquarters.

William T. Grant Foundation. (1988). *The forgotten half: Pathways to success for America's youth and young families.* Washington, DC: William T. Grant Foundation Commission on Work, Family, and Citizenship.

Wolfbein, S. L. (1988). America's service economy. *Vocational Research Institute Monograph, 1*(4).

Wolman, C., Bruininks, R., & Thurlow, M. L. (1989). Dropouts and dropout programs: Implications for special education. *Remedial and Special Education, 10*(5).

Zigmond, N. (1990). Rethinking secondary school programs for students with learning disabilities. *Focus on Exceptional Children, 23,* 1–22.

Zigmond, N., & Miller, S. E. (1992). Improving high school programs for students with learning disabilities: A matter of substance as well as form. In F. R.

Rusch, L. DeStefano, J. Chadsey-Rusch, L. A. Phelps, & E. Szymanski (Eds.), *Transition from school to adult life: Models, linkages, and policy* (pp. 17–31). Sycamore, IL: Sycamore.

Zigmond, N., & Thornton, H. (1985). Follow-up of postsecondary age learning disabled graduates and dropouts. *Learning Disabilities Research, 1,* 50–55.

PART II

Transition Planning and Involvement in Secondary Schools

5

◙

Vocational Education

Emerging Vocationalism

R. BRIAN COBB and
DEBRA A. NEUBERT

This chapter describes how traditional and new models of vocational education can support the transition from public school to community life for individuals who are at risk in secondary schools. The introduction describes the goals and purposes of vocational education from an evolutionary perspective. Following this overview, the second section reviews federal legislation and concomitant stages of vocational education. The evolution of the vocational education service delivery system is also discussed in relationship to transition practices. The third section describes current practices in secondary vocational education highlighting the outcomes and benefits of some these practices in the school-to-work arena. Finally, the chapter concludes with a discussion of future or emerging issues in the vocational education system, particularly as they relate to other aspects in the reform of public education.

Transition has existed as a major initiative in special education for nearly a decade and a half; however, the concept of transition from school to work has been embedded within public school vocational education since its inception as a curricular option in the early 1900s. With passage of the School-to-Work Opportunities Act (STWOA) of 1994, and with the associated funding of large-scale, state systems-change grants, interest in the school-to-

work transition concept within vocational education has been rekindled in a much more innovative and comprehensive context than was previously the case.

The scope and curriculum of vocational education, as it is delivered by public secondary schools, has been shaped largely through the influences of federal vocational education legislation. As such, it has evolved to encompass five broad goals:

- acquisition of personal skills and attitudes
- communication and computational skills and technological literacy
- employability skills
- broad and specific occupational skills and knowledge
- foundations for career planning and lifelong learning (National Commission on Secondary Vocational Education, 1984)

In addition, vocational education plays a role in assisting students develop critical thinking and problem-solving skills (National Council on Vocational Education, 1990–1991).

Public school vocational education has not always had this range of goals. For example, Evans and Herr (1978) reported only three goals for vocational education: (a) meeting society's need for workers; (b) increasing the options available to each student; and (c) serving as a motivating force to enhance all types of learning (p. 4). Indeed, the original Smith-Hughes legislation that established public school vocational education set out only one goal—meeting the labor needs of local employers.

Vocational education was most recently defined in the Carl D. Perkins Vocational and Applied Technology Act Amendments of 1990 as

> organized educational programs offering a sequence of courses which are directly related to the preparation of individuals in paid or unpaid employment in current or emerging occupations requiring other than a baccalaureate or advanced degree. Such programs shall include competency-based applied learning which contributes to an individual's academic knowledge, higher-order reasoning and problem-solving skills, work attitudes, general employability skills and the occupational specific skills necessary for economic independence as a productive and contributing member for economic independence as a productive member and contributing member of society. Such terms also includes applied technology education. (Title V, Part B, Section 521)

Interestingly, this is the first significant revision to the legislative definition of vocational education since the original definition appeared in the Smith-Hughes legislation in the early 1900s. The most significant aspect of this revision is in the inclusion of the "softer" skills such as "higher-order reasoning and problem-solving skills, work attitudes, and general employability skills," which have emerged as important facets of vocational learning in recent years, as exemplified by the Secretary's Commission on Achieving Necessary Skills (SCANS; 1991) report. The report summarized the results of a national survey of employers' responses to questions about the most important skills that students should have on leaving high school in order to integrate best into the workplace of the twenty-first century. The results of this survey clearly document the shift in thinking by employers from "meeting the labor needs of local employers" and are summarized in Table 5.1.

As illustrated, the skills (competencies) employers want for the twenty-first century are built on a three-part foundation of "soft" skills, and are much broader than the occupationally specific skills desired in the beginning of the twentieth century. This report received widespread national attention on its release and focused attention on the reform of public school vocational education away from "hard," occupationally specific skills to the more transferable, "softer" skills.

This chapter begins with an overview of the history of vocational education by partitioning it into its major evolutionary periods. Embedded within this overview will be descriptions of how the practice of vocational education has emerged in response to federal and state legislation. We will then present current trends and practices in vocational education (such as a move in focus from occupationally specific "hard" skills to generic and transferable "soft" skills), and end with a view forward to the future of secondary vocational education, with implications for all students who are at risk, including those with disabilities.

Table 5.1 SCANS Foundation Skills and Competencies

Foundation Skills
Basic skills: Reading, writing, arithmetic/mathematics, listening, speaking
Thinking skills: Creative thinking, decision making, problem solving, seeing things in the mind's eye, knowing
   how to learn, reasoning
Personal qualities: Responsibility, self-esteem, sociability, self-management, integrity/honesty

Competencies
Resources: Identifies, organizes, plans, and allocates resources
   Time
   Money
   Materials and facilities
   Human resources
Interpersonal: Works with others
   Participates as member of a team
   Teaches others new skills
   Serves clients/customers
   Exercises leadership
   Negotiates
   Works with diversity
Information: Acquires and uses information
   Acquires and evaluates information
   Organizes and maintains information
   Interprets and communicates information
   Uses computers to process information
Systems: Understands complex interrelationships
   Understands systems
   Monitors and corrects performance
   Improves or designs systems
Technology: Works with a variety of technologies
   Selects technology
   Applies technology to tasks
   Maintains and troubleshoots equipment

FEDERAL LEGISLATION AND THE EVOLUTION OF VOCATIONAL EDUCATION

Although legislation is discussed more broadly in Chapter 3, the following historical view of vocational education legislation provides a basis for understanding the characteristics of vocational education. Specifically, early federal legislation in the 1900s provided the funding and administra-tive structure that created separate tracks for vocational and academic studies. The structure created through this early legislation maintained for approximately half a century, corresponding with the first evolutionary period, the Smith-Hughes period. With the Sputnik threat in the late 1950s and the civil rights emphasis of the Great Society in the Johnson Administration, the first significant reform of vocational educa-tion occurred with the passage of the Vocational Education Act of 1963, creating the second evolutionary period. The last evolutionary period emerged with the Perkins Act in 1984, and targeted practices that attempted to bridge the gap between vocational and academic studies, updated work-force preparation practices, and aligned vocational education with other educational reform efforts. The last 2 years of this period also correspond to the school-to-work period of history, because both federal laws have been in effect during those 2 years. Each of these periods of legislative history will be reviewed in what follows.

The Smith-Hughes Period (1917–1962)

Although federal support for vocational education began with the passage of the Morrill Act of 1862, most historians recognize the beginning of vocational education with the Smith-Hughes Act of 1917 (Scott & Sarkees-Wircenski, 1995). Whereas the Morrill Act provided funding for land grants to colleges to prepare workers for agriculture and mechanic arts, the Smith-Hughes Act of 1917, P.L. 64-347, provided funding for public schools to develop secondary vocational education programs. Vocational education during this period was focused on specific skill training in the areas of agriculture, trade and industry, and home economics.

The Smith-Hughes Act provided many of the administrative structures in vocational education that continue to this day. These include state boards of vocational education, state plans that describe vocational offerings, and annual reports on states' vocational education systems (Scott & Sarkees-Wircenski, 1995). The Smith-Hughes Act also provided funding for separate vocational schools, which furthered the separation of vocational studies from academic studies in secondary settings.

Vocational Education Act Period (1963–1985)

The launching of Sputnik by the USSR in the late 1950s provided the impetus for the first major reform of vocational education since the Smith-Hughes Act nearly half a century earlier. Thus, federal legislation in the 1960s broadened the definition of vocational education, provided funding for cooperative work-study programs, and focused on providing services and training to individuals with special needs.

The Vocational Education Act of 1963, P.L. 88-210. The act sought to improve existing vocational education programs and to develop new programs with a goal of serving all individuals, including those with "special education handicaps" and academic and socioeconomic disadvantages (Bies, 1987). Vocational education programming expanded to include occupational areas such as business education and work-study programs for special needs students (Scott & Sarkees-Wircenski, 1995). This legislation also provided funding for area vocational schools, continuing the separation of the vocational and academic tracks in secondary settings mentioned earlier.

The Vocational Education Amendments of 1968, P.L. 90-576. The amendments canceled and consolidated previous legislation except for the Smith-Hughes Act of 1917. According to Scott and Sarkees-Wircenski (1995), P.L. 90-576 emphasized vocational education in post-secondary schools, broadened the definition of vocational education to bring it closer to general education, earmarked funds for cooperative work-study programs, and strengthened the need to provide access for all in need of training and retraining. Public Law 90-576 initiated the practice of set-aside funding for special populations. For example, 10 percent of a state's basic grant was to be spent on services for individuals with disabilities and an additional 15 percent for individuals with academic or economic disadvantages. Some of the initial vocational assessment (evaluation) units, which resembled those in vocational rehabilitation, were funded with these monies and served individuals with disabilities and disadvantages in vocational education.

The Vocational Education Amendments of 1976, P.L. 94-482. The amendments continued to emphasize the expansion or development of new vocational education programs, and also maintained the focus on providing services to special populations. This legislation kept the set-aside funding structure for special populations by continuing the 10 percent figure for students with disabilities, but increased the set-aside to 20 percent for individuals with disadvantages. Some states used these funds to provide vocational assessment and vocational support services for special needs students. Projects to make facilities accessible to students with disabilities were also funded with set-aside dollars (Scott & Sarkees-Wircenski, 1995).

Other highlights from P.L. 94-482 included development of programs and personnel training to overcome gender discrimination and stereotyping, and improvement of vocational guidance and counseling services. States were required to submit 5-year plans to the federal government and the emphasis on accountability was accentuated with the development of the Vocational Education Data System (Nystrom & Bayne, 1979). This system was to provide data to the federal government on student enrollment, completion of programs, staffing, and expenditures in vocational education. Finally, emphasis was placed on coordinating efforts with other federal occupational training programs, which is a theme that is present in today's legislation and reform efforts.

By the end of this evolutionary period, secondary vocational education had taken on the shape and form that it has today. Largely due to the influences of prior federal legislation, vocational education had maintained a "separateness" from the academic mainstream of public schools—a "separateness" that continues in many local program settings today. Hence, it differs in significant ways from academic and special education, primarily in terms of the environmental context in which it is offered, the background of its instructors, its curriculum, its enrollment patterns, and its funding and administrative

structure. Each of these characteristics will be briefly reviewed in what follows.

Environment. Secondary vocational education is delivered in several different school environments: comprehensive high schools, vocational high schools, and area vocational centers or schools. Most secondary vocational education programs can be found in comprehensive high schools, numbering 15,200 throughout the nation (Boesel et al., 1994a). The majority of comprehensive schools (93 percent) offer vocational courses such as career exploration or technology education, and as of 1992, 74 percent offered other various vocational programs. The distinguishing feature of comprehensive high schools is that they combine an extensive array of vocational education curricular options within the regular high school campus environment.

Vocational high schools (approximately 250 nationwide) are separate public high schools, often found in urban school districts (Boesel et al., 1994a). The dominant curriculum is vocational education, although a full complement of academic curricula is also available. Students apply to and attend vocational high schools for their full high school curriculum, including academic content necessary for a high school diploma.

Finally, there are approximately 1,100 area vocational centers or schools nationwide at the secondary level (Boesel et al., 1994a). Area vocational centers are separate facilities, like vocational high schools, but offer only vocational education curricula. Hence, students must attend a home high school to acquire the necessary academic Carnegie units for graduation. Most often, students attend their home high school for half of the school day and the vocational center for the remainder. Most students attending a comprehensive high school have a choice regarding vocational education programs at the high school or of attending an area vocational school. However, Boesel and colleagues (1994a) reported that less than 29 percent of vocational coursetaking occurs at area vocational schools. Distance and cost are factors associated with a smaller number of students attending area vocational schools.

Instructors. Secondary vocational education instructors often differ in their training background from almost all other groups of public school teachers. For example, vocational educators (particularly in the trades and industrial education) frequently do not have a baccalaureate degree, but gain a credential or a teaching certificate in a specific occupational area of vocational education through their related trade experience. Heaviside, Carey, and Farris (1994) reported that whereas virtually 100 percent of public school academic teachers in the United States have bachelor's degrees, this percentage drops to 88 percent for vocational teachers. More specifically, it appears to depend on the teaching environment in which the vocational teacher works. According to Heaviside and colleagues, whereas 95 percent of comprehensive high school vocational teachers have bachelor's degrees, this proportion drops to only 63 percent of vocational teachers in vocational high schools and area vocational centers. There is some evidence that this trend is on the increase. Levesque and colleagues (1995) noted that whereas the proportion of nonvocational public school teachers with less than a bachelor's degree remained unchanged between 1987–1988 and 1990–1991 (at 0.3 percent), the proportion of vocational teachers increased from 7.4 percent in 1987–1988 to 8.3 percent in 1990–1991. These differences have led to intense discussions regarding the preparation and certification of vocational educators (Hartley, Mantle-Bromley, & Cobb, 1996a; Lynch, 1996), and will be discussed in the last section of this chapter.

Curriculum. The secondary vocational education curriculum is typically comprised of three essential components: in-school skills instruction, out-of-school work experience, and vocational student organizations. Although the names of some vocational programs have changed since the 1990 Perkins Amendments, in-school in-struction and the curriculum at the secondary level can be best conceptualized by three major areas including (a) general vocational courses, such as typing, technology education, business math; (b) specific labor market preparation; and (c) homemaking courses, such as child development and basic food preparation (Boesel et al., 1994a; National Center for Education Statistics, 1992; Scott & Sarkees-Wircenski, 1995). Specific labor market preparation courses best characterize vocational education as we have known it, and center around seven specific occupational areas including agricultural education; business and office education; health occupations education; home economics education or family and consumer sciences education; marketing and distributive education; trades and industrial education; and technical/communication (Boesel et al., 1994a; Sarkees-Wircenski & Scott, 1995). Although the distinctions between many of these programmatic areas are becoming more and more blurred as schools reorient their curricula to meet the employment demands of the twenty-first century (Plihal et al., 1991), these programmatic areas still define much of the structure of vocational education in secondary schools, in state agencies, in vocational teacher education programs, and in state and national professional organizations.

In the past, out-of-school work experience programs were delivered under the rubric of cooperative work education (CWE), which involved placing advanced students from all of the seven specific occupational areas in an employment setting associated with the type of training the student received in school. Often called a capstone program, CWE students are jointly supervised by a cooperative vocational education teacher and an employer. This experience is organized and delivered in a manner similar to student teaching experiences for undergraduate teacher education students. CWE activities have been broadened or accentuated to meet the goals of the 1990 Perkins Amendments and the 1994 School-to-Work Opportunities Act. Now called "work-based learning," examples of these broadened activities include, in addition to traditional cooperative education, youth apprenticeships and school-based enterprises (Stern et al., 1995). They will be discussed in more detail later in this chapter.

Vocational student organizations (VSOs) are also an integral part of vocational education programs. Their place within the secondary vocational education curriculum has been refined with each successive passage of federal legislation. VSOs are essentially leadership clubs for secondary vocational students, and participation in them is frequently required. Each VSO elects its leadership, establishes organizational policies and procedures, and develops an annual program of work. Typically, activities within each program of work revolve around leadership, personal growth, civic and community affairs, social skills development, use of leisure time, fund raising, public relations, and vocational skills development (Sarkees & Sullivan, 1989; Sarkees-Wircenski & Scott, 1995).

Enrollment Patterns. Enrollment in vocational education curricula has been predominantly reserved for senior high school students, although in recent years, adult enrollments have increased as individuals in the community have sought additional training in places where no community college is present. Exceptions to this enrollment pattern exist in vocational high schools and in specialized introductory programs designed to acquaint junior high school students with vocational education options.

Vocational education is generally available to most secondary students; yet it constitutes only a small part of the high school enrollment (Tuma & Burns, 1996). Whereas most students (97 percent) earned some credits in vocational education, only one in four (24 percent) were vocational concentrators and 8 percent were vocational specialists. "Vocational concentrators" are defined as students who earned at least three credits in a specific vocational program; "vocational specialists" earned four credits with at least two credits in upper or advanced level vocational courses. The average high school student earned 3.8 credits in vocational education; African-American and Native-American students earned more vocational credits than other ethnic groups (Boesel et al., 1994).

In 1992, graduating high school students earned approximately 16 percent of their credits in vocational education and about 24 percent concentrated their studies in a vocational education area. This is a relatively sharp reduction in vocational concentrators from 1982 levels of almost 34 percent (Tuma & Burns, 1996). Factors contributing to this decline include increased academic graduation requirements, a declining cohort of high school–aged students, local economic conditions, and increased numbers of special populations in some vocational programs (Boesel et al., 1994a).

Prior to the 1984 Perkins Act, students with special needs were generally underrepresented in vocational education. However, it now appears that there is an overrepresentation of students with special needs in vocational programs (Boesel et al., 1994a; U.S. General Accounting Office, 1995). Special population students take more vocational education courses than other students and are more likely to concentrate their high school program in vocational coursework. Students with disabilities and disadvantages are enrolled predominantly in agriculture, occupational home economics, and trades, with few students enrolled in business, health, and technical education. Boesel and colleagues (1994a) found that "it is unclear to what extent these enrollment patterns represent appropriate matches with students' interests and abilities, or an inappropriate channeling of disabled and disadvantaged students into more limited vocational areas" (p. 32). Other research, although limited, supports the channeling of special needs students into select programs (Adami & Neubert, 1991; Lombard, Hazelkorn, & Neubert, 1992).

Funding and Administrative Structure. Historically, the federal share of secondary vocational education funding has fluctuated around

10 percent of total vocational education expenditures (Phelps, 1984; Scott & Sarkees-Wircenski, 1995), and the remaining 90 percent of funding has varied markedly across states between state and local sources (Benson & Hoachlander, 1981). Although this federal-to-state-to-local share of funding has been proportionately small, it has been significant enough to encourage all but the smallest secondary school districts to seek out those dollars. This federal-to-state-to-local flowthrough funding structure has produced curricula and administrative systems that are, of necessity, consistent with federal guidelines (not unlike the transformation of local special education programs since the passage of P.L. 94-142 in the late 1970s). Hence, administratively, vocational education typically operates separately from mainstream public education, often with separate administrators, clerical personnel, budgets, and staff meetings.

The Carl Perkins Period (1984–1996)

Early federal policy during this period focused on providing special needs students with access to quality vocational education (Phelps et al., 1989) by expanding the use of special set-aside funding for students at risk. In addition, there was a more general focus on reforming and improving the delivery of vocational education programs.

The Carl D. Perkins Vocational Education Act of 1984 (P.L. 98-524) began the process of redirecting states to improve, expand, and introduce innovative programs that would train workers in skilled occupations needed by the existing and future work force. The 1984 Perkins Act also emphasized the need for vocational education to coordinate efforts with community-based organizations, the private sector, and Job Training Partnership Act programs. The 1984 Perkins Act mandated that a National Assessment of Vocational Education (NAVE) be conducted and that the results be reported to Congress. This information included a description and evaluation about the scope and effectiveness of vocational education programs.

A dominant theme in the 1984 Perkins Act was to serve groups traditionally underrepresented in vocational education programs (Cobb & Kingsbury, 1985). Under Title II of the act, each state had to provide vocational education services and activities designed for individuals with special needs, which included individuals with disabilities and disadvantages, adults in need of retraining, individuals who were single parents or homemakers, individuals serving in correctional facilities, and individuals who participated in nontraditional programs. Set-aside funds to provide such services totaled 57 percent of a state's basic grant and included 10 percent of the funds earmarked to individuals with disabilities, 22 percent for individuals with disadvantages, 12 percent for adults in need of retraining due to job loss or late entry into the job market, 8.5 percent to single parents, 3.5 percent to participants in programs to eliminate gender bias and stereotyping, and 1 percent for criminal offenders in correctional facilities (U.S. Department of Education, 1988). Changes in the funding formula of the 1984 Perkins Act helped eliminate separate vocational education programs or facilities for students with disabilities.

Title II, Section 204 of the 1984 Perkins Act specified that individuals with disabilities and disadvantages have equal access to a full range of vocational education activities and be included in recruitment, enrollment, and placement activities. In addition, students with disabilities were to be placed in the least restrictive environment and have vocational education included as a component of their IEPs when appropriate. Finally, students with disabilities and their families were to receive information (both opportunities in vocational education and eligibility requirements) pertaining to vocational education no later than the ninth grade.

In addition to assurances of equal access, students with disabilities or disadvantages who enrolled in vocational education were to receive services or activities that facilitated equal access. The set-aside funds were generally used to provide these supplemental services to individuals with special needs and included: (a) an assessment of interests, abilities, and special needs with respect to completing successfully the vocational education program; (b) the provision of special services, including adaptation of curriculum, instruction, equipment, and facilities; (c) guidance, counseling, and career development activities conducted by professionally trained counselors; and (d) counseling services designed to facilitate the transition from school to postschool employment and career opportunities. During this period, a number of vocational assessment and support models were developed to provide students with such services and to facilitate greater cooperation between vocational and special educators (see, e.g., Maryland State Department of Education, 1984; Cobb & Larkin, 1985; Stodden et al., 1987; Albright & Cobb, 1988; Thomas & Coleman, 1988; Neubert & Leconte, 1990).

The Carl D. Perkins Vocational and Applied Technology Education Act Amendments of 1990 (P.L. 101-392) significantly altered its prior namesake legislation by emphasizing the need to restructure the delivery of vocational education programs. The 1990 Perkins Amendments had two dominant themes: to improve the quality of vocational programs and to provide supplemental services to special populations (Wirt, 1991; Boesel & McFarland, 1994). However, use of special funding set-asides for these special populations was eliminated.

Wirt (1991) summarized the major changes in the 1990 Perkins Amendments, which focused on improving the quality of programs. The first change was to broaden the purpose of vocational education by moving away from the traditional job-skills orientation to focus on integrating vocational and academic skills training. Thus, every basic state grant program was required to support integration of academic and vocational education through coherent course sequences. The second change centered on directing federal resources to school districts with the highest proportions of students from poor families and having the greatest need for reform and improvement of vocational education programs. A third change addressed restructuring of the relationship between the states and local school districts. Local school districts were to provide greater leadership regarding their need for reform and improvement in vocational education. The state's role was to focus on performance assessment, accountability, and outcomes. States were to develop core standards and measures of performance for vocational education programs, which could include students' competency attainment, retention in school, placement into additional training, or job- or work-skill attainment.

Other significant changes in the 1990 Perkins Amendments included the use of apprenticeships to a greater extent and the development and implementation of "technical preparation (tech-prep) programs." Tech-prep programs mandated vertical alignment of curriculum between secondary and postsecondary schools through curriculum articulation agreements between consortia of public schools and junior and community colleges.

Although the intent of serving all students remained in the 1990 Perkins Amendments, the set-aside monies mandated in previous legislation for special populations were removed. Assurances concerning equal access were strengthened throughout the act, and Title II, Section 118, was similar to Section 204 of the 1984 Perkins Act. Therefore, the language regarding the provision of assessment activities, supplemental services, career development activities, and counseling and instructional services designed to facilitate the transition from school to postschool employment and career opportunities remained in the 1990 Perkins Act. Removing the set-aside funding proved to be very controversial, and many professionals cautioned that supplemental services provided to special needs populations would be in jeopardy if set-aside funding initiatives were eliminated (Kochhar & Deschamps, 1992; Leconte & Boyer-Stephens, 1992; West & Meers, 1992). However, recent reports have documented that special needs students continue to have access to vocational education programs at equal or higher rates than pre-1990 levels, defusing fears that removal of set-aside provisions would result in a reversal of the access gains for such groups during the years of set-aside funding provisions (U.S. General Accounting Office, 1993, 1995; Boesel et al., 1994).

The National Assessment of Vocational Education (NAVE) was again mandated under the 1990 Perkins Amendments (Section 403). At this time, it provides the most current data regarding enrollment and outcomes for individuals who participate in vocational-technical education programs. The Final NAVE Report to Congress contained five volumes (Boesel & McFarland, 1994; Boesel et al., 1994a; Boesel, Rahn, & Deich, 1994b; Hudson, 1994; Muraskin, Hollinger, & Harvey, 1994) and offered recommendations for policy development in the future.

The School-to-Work Period (1994–present). The School-to-Work Opportunities Act of 1994 (P.L. 103-239) was passed by the Clinton Administration to establish a national framework for states to create so-called "school-to-work systems." This legislation has set into motion the most significant reform agenda for local vocational education programs in three decades. As of the writing of this book, both the 1990 Perkins Amendments and STWOA are supporting vocational education across the country, albeit in different ways. The 1990 Perkins Amendments continue to provide formula-driven basic grants to states in response to state agency plans, administrative structures, and flowthrough funding initiatives to local districts (i.e., tech-prep). In addition to providing direct model demonstration grants from the National School-to-Work Office to local community partnerships, STWOA provides for large-scale competitive grants to states that are willing to restructure their vocational education delivery system around school-to-work system frameworks. These frameworks are to be aligned with other educational reform movements, prepare youth for high-skilled jobs in the work force, and strengthen partnerships between schools and business and industry. States receive

planning and implementation grants to establish their school-to-work systems and are encouraged to build on existing programs and practices such as tech-prep and the integration of academic and vocational education. Indeed, two of the purposes of STWOA are (a) "to build on promising school-to-work activities, such as tech-prep education, career academies, school-to-apprenticeship programs, cooperative education, youth apprenticeship, school-sponsored enterprises," and (b) "to improve the knowledge and skills of youths by integrating academic and occupational learning, and building effective linkages between secondary and postsecondary education" (p. 5). All states have received their planning grants (Brustein & Mahler, 1994) and twenty-nine received implementation grants as of November 1995. An additional eight to twelve states received funding in late 1996, and the federal budget for fiscal year 1997 includes significant dollars for this remainder of the states to receive funding for systems change activity.

As with prior education-for-work legislation, STWOA addresses the need for all students to have access to programs and specifically mentions individuals with disabilities, low-achieving youth, school dropouts, and those from disadvantaged or diverse racial, ethnic, or cultural backgrounds (Kochar, 1995). It is interesting to note that some of the practices that have been used in vocational special education for the past 20 years such as career awareness and exploration activities, exposing students to broad career opportunities, and matching students' interests, goals, strengths, and abilities with program options are highlighted in STWOA.

OVERVIEW OF CURRENT PRACTICES

This section provides an overview of current practices in vocational education, largely as they have developed in response to the Perkins Amendments of 1984 and 1990, and STWOA. The types of practices discussed follow the concepts of STWOA; however, many of them were in existence prior to passage of STWOA. These current practices include school-based learning, work-based learning, connecting activities, programs and services for students at risk, and performance standards and measures. NAVE provides the most current data on these practices and is cited extensively in this section.

School-Based Learning

School-based learning is a broad term that encompasses a variety of differing practices in the delivery of vocationally oriented curriculum in secondary schools. Although the terminology and even the range of practices subsumed under this "school-based learning" rubric vary somewhat, four types of practices will be described here: tech-prep, the integration of academic and vocational education, career pathways, and career academies.

Tech-Prep. Tech-prep programs in vocational education have received increased attention in the 1990s as one way to elevate academic and vocational skill development, provide competency-based training, and bridge the gap between secondary and postsecondary training opportunities. Title III of the 1990 Perkins Amendments defines tech-prep as

> the 2 years of secondary school preceding graduation and 2 years of higher education, or an apprenticeship program of at least 2 years following secondary instruction, with a common core of required proficiency in mathematics, science, communications, and technologies designed to lead to an associate degree or certificate in a specific career field. (Sec. 344(b)(2))

The NAVE found that nearly half of all secondary districts (5,441 of 11,527) had tech-prep programs, often located in large urban districts or vocational districts (Boesel et al., 1994b). The U.S. General Accounting Office (1995) also reported that between 1990–1991 and 1993–1994 the percentage of students participating in tech-prep programs increased from 9 to 16 percent. Tech-prep programs are found most often in business and office education and in trade and industry programs at the secondary level.

Tech-prep programs can provide an excellent opportunity for all students to extend their vocational training. For example, "2 + 2" tech-prep programs allow students to take a sequence of vocational and academic coursework in high school and the community college, culminating with an associate degree or a certificate of completion at the community college. Although the 1990 Perkins Amendments stated that special populations are to have equal access to the full range of tech-prep programs (Sec.344(b)(6)), special populations face a number of challenges in gaining access to these programs (Brown et al., 1991; Lombard, Hazelkorn, & Miller, 1995). For example, in a study of 368 tech-prep programs across the country, the National Center of Research in Vocational Education (cited in Brown et al., 1991) found that only eighteen provided activities for special populations.

Concern by special needs professionals would appear to be lessening in recent years, however. In a more recent study, Lombard and colleagues (1995) surveyed the tech-prep coordinators in all state departments regarding a number of issues related to tech-prep programs. They found that 83 percent of the respondents had developed accommodations to ensure access to tech-prep programs for special populations, but there was wide variability in the actual practices. Finally, the NAVE found that 70 percent of institutions with tech-prep programs recruited and monitored special populations in their programs. However, the NAVE also reported "special population students are not usually a priority in the development of tech-prep programs, although the majority of programs are making an effort to assure that they are included" (Boesel et al., 1994b:128).

Integration of Academic and Vocational Education. Integration of academic and occupational learning has received increased attention in vocational education and other school-to-work programs as a way to bridge the separation between vocational education, general education, and the workplace. Its appeal is also drawing support, although under different rubrics, from the general education community. For example, Resnick (1987) and Raizen (1989) discussed the concept of *cognitive apprenticeships,* whereas Brown, Collins, and Duguid (1989) and Anderson, Reder, and Simon (1996), among others, have described *situated cognition or learning.* Both of these instructional practices have much in common with the practice of integrated learning as first outlined in the 1984 Perkins Amendments.

Integrated learning efforts were a greater priority in the 1990 Perkins Amendments and are also highlighted in STWOA (Barton & Kirsch, 1990; National Center for Research in Vocational Education, 1990). Integration of academic and vocational education curricula has been described under a curriculum restructuring rubric (i.e., correlated, fused, core, or activity curricula) (Plihal et al., 1991) or an organizational restructuring rubric (Grubb et al., 1991). Organizational restructuring efforts range from simply incorporating some academic content in vocational classes on the one hand to the development of "magnet" vocational schools or "schools-within-schools" efforts on the other.

Secondary schools that attempt to integrate academic and vocational curricula often face a number of challenges. For example, the physical separation of vocational programs (in area vocational schools or wings of comprehensive high schools) from academic programs makes distance and time a problem when implementing integrated learning efforts at the local level. In addition, some vocational and academic teachers continue to view themselves as "separate" from one another (Boesel et al., 1994).

The NAVE reported that by 1993 most secondary state agencies had taken steps to implement the practice of integrating academic and vocational education. The most frequent method of doing this was to make available applied academic course materials from com-

mercial vendors, provide inservice training for vocational educators and academic teachers, and offer technical assistance for administrators on the topic. Whereas the literature contains much descriptive information on integrated learning efforts, the research on the effectiveness of this practice is very limited (Boesel et al., 1994b).

Career Pathways. Career pathways are broad clusters of occupations that revolve around a theme or common element that is shared by all the occupations (i.e., service occupations, health or environmental occupations, or manufacturing occupations). Pauly, Kopp, and Haimson (1995) described career pathways as follows:

> Each pathway uses a sequence of related courses tied to a cluster of occupations. ... Students are usually exposed to a wide variety of careers before choosing an occupational cluster, and they may switch clusters in the course of the program. Each cluster offers occupation-related courses; students receive training in broad, work-related skills after taking introductory career exploration courses. Academic and occupational instruction are integrated and applied learning techniques are sometimes used. (p. 7)

Many of the more innovative vocational education programs across the country have been moving toward the occupational cluster or career pathway approach for a number of years. However, the use of integrated and applied learning within the career pathways practice is far less widespread.

Career Academies. Career academies represent probably the best-researched form of school-based learning that exists to date. Stern, Raby, and Dayton (1992) described career academies as containing the following components:

1. a school within a school, spanning grades 9 to 12 (or sometimes fewer grades)

2. run by a small cadre of teachers from a variety of disciplines

3. recruits students who volunteer for the program and demonstrate their commitment by formally applying for admission

4. focuses on a career theme in a field for which there is good demand and employment opportunities in the local area

5. curriculum combines technical and academic content, usually with one technical and three academic courses each semester

6. maintains the option for the student to attend college

7. students are employed during the summer and often during the year in jobs related to the career theme (pp. 14–15)

The data on career academies, although derived largely from program evaluations, suggest that academies assist in dropout prevention, sustain attendance in postsecondary education, and provide good benefit/cost ratios compared to other work preparation models (see Linnehan, 1996, and Stern et al., 1992: Chapter 4, for summaries of evaluative studies).

Work-Based Learning

Work-based learning in vocational education, such as cooperative work experiences, youth apprenticeships, and school-based enterprises, has received increased attention with school-to-work initiatives. In addition, work-based learning activities must conform to what STWOA calls "all aspects of industry." A description of each follows along with data on the effectiveness of these programmatic components.

Cooperative Education. Work experience has been an integral part of vocational education for several decades, most frequently through cooperative education or cooperative work experience programs. Students work part-time in their field of specialization as they near graduation. These job placements are generally arranged by the vocational educator or placement specialist in the school. The number of students who participate in cooperative work experience is limited. One study reported that 74 percent of the schools they surveyed offered work-study programs, but only 16 percent of vocational education students participated during 1993–1994 (U.S. General Accounting Office, 1995). Using data on 403,000 students from the Omnibus Survey, NAVE reports that 4 percent of students in grades 9 to 12 participated in cooperative work-study programs (Boesel et al., 1994b). Although the research on outcomes is very limited, there is some evidence that these students are more satisfied with school and work and have clearer career goals, increased self-confidence, and increased motivation (Boesel et al., 1994b).

Youth Apprenticeships. Youth apprenticeships are one of the newer work-based learning models designed to prepare students for skilled jobs. Although apprenticeships operated by unions or trade associations have been used for technical training or retraining for decades, Smith and Rowjeski (1993) reported that less than 2 percent of youth enter these programs after graduation from high school. New initiatives for youth apprenticeships have been funded by the U.S. Department of Labor and are characterized by a series of important elements (Jobs for the Future, 1993, cited in Stern et al., 1995):

1. employers provide paid work experience and guided worksite learning

2. schools integrate vocational and academic learning

3. school and workplace learning are coordinated and integrated

4. programs articulate high school and postsecondary learning and are at least 2 years in duration

5. completers receive widely recognized credentials of both occupational and academic skill mastery

6. programs are governed by broad coalitions of institutional partners (p. 24)

Boesel and colleagues (1994b) reported that youth apprenticeships are "found in industries with labor shortages in technician-level occupations, such as hospitals, printing, and other-manufacturing industries" (p. 141). Youth apprenticeships tend to be characterized by active participation of employers, integration of work-based and school-based learning, integration of academic and vocational learning, structured linkages between secondary and postsecondary institutions, and certificates detailing occupation skills (Roditi, 1991). Less than 5 percent of schools offer youth apprenticeships and although promising, it is too early to determine the outcomes and effectiveness of this work-based approach. According to the NAVE report, Arkansas, Georgia, Maine, Minnesota, Pennsylvania, and Wisconsin have apprenticeship demonstration sites.

School-Based Enterprises. School-based enterprises (SBEs) are programs in which students produce goods or services for sale or use by other people; these programs do not directly place students with employers. Examples of SBEs include school restaurants, construction projects, child care centers, and auto shops. According to a 1992 survey, approximately 19 percent of secondary schools had at least one type of SBE (Boesel et al., 1994b). Although there is anecdotal evidence regarding positive outcomes of SBEs, little systematic research has documented the outcomes of SBEs (Stern et al., 1994).

Stern and colleagues (1994) theorized a host of as-yet undocumented benefits of SBEs, however. Within the economic sphere, the authors listed the provision of goods and services at less than market price, community economic development, and crucible testing production and management processes with relatively small risk. Stern and colleagues (1994) also cited social benefits, again based on anecdotal, qualitative data in their case studies of sixteen schools with SBEs. These benefits include a relatively risk-free opportunity to focus on quality, opportunities for community service by workers in SBEs, and

enhanced student retention in school, particularly for students at risk.

All Aspects of Industry. The term "all aspects of industry" appears in Sections 101 and 103 of STWOA, and refers to a requirement, whenever possible, that students who are placed in the various work-based learning opportunities have a chance to experience and understand all of the aspects of the industry or employment setting. This means, for example, that a student placed on a residential construction site would not only have an opportunity to learn or observe construction techniques, but also safety and environmental hazard planning, bidding and estimating techniques, how to work with subcontractors, and how to organize and schedule the timing for delivery of differing kinds of materials. This "all aspects of industry" component clearly elevates this work-based learning element of STWOA to a much higher conceptual understanding of the work setting than has typically been the case with cooperative work experiences and traditional apprenticeships.

Connecting Activities

Connecting activities are designated in STWOA as those activities that serve to link school-based and work-based learning. Section 104 of the act outlines seven broad activities under the rubric of the "connecting activities component," for which the administrative or management functions of school-to-work would be responsible.

1. matching students [interests, abilities, etc.] with the work-based learning opportunities

2. providing a school-site mentor to act as a liaison between the student and key other players in school-based and work-based learning

3. providing technical assistance and services to employers who become involved in the school-to-work process

4. providing technical assistance and training to all key school-based and community-based

personnel on how to integrate academic and vocational education

5. encouraging active participation of employers

6. providing job seeking and placement assistance, or assistance for further education or training, to students who have completed their school-to-work program

7. program evaluation activities (p. 7)

Research on the effectiveness of connecting activities is as yet incomplete, because states and local districts are only developing their approaches to connecting activities at this time. However, Kopp and Kazis (1995) reported the results about connecting activities drawn from student surveys and school administrator interviews at ten sites that are implementing school-to-work programs. These interviews and surveys yielded four connecting activities that were perceived to be most effective:

1. regular, formal relationships between school and worksite personnel

2. opportunities for teachers to get out of the classroom and experience modern work settings first-hand—and for worksite personnel to learn about the realities of high schools as workplaces

3. explicit and clearly delineated expectations of the learning that is to take place at the site

4. classroom-based activities that draw upon and reinforce worksite learning (p. 90)

Stern and colleagues (1995) corroborated much of the findings of Kopp and Kazis (1995) in their research synthesis of work-based learning programs.

Programs for Special Needs Students

Both STWOA and the 1990 Perkins Act require that all vocational education activities be available to youth at risk, usually identified as special needs youth. The literature is relatively well-developed in its descriptions of how to build support systems in vocational education for different types of youth who are at risk. For example, Wermuth and Phelps (1990) identified twenty components of exemplary vocational education programs in their review of research of the vocational special needs literature. These twenty components [of exemplary vocational education programs] are subsumed under five major headings: (a) program administration; (b) curriculum and instruction; (c) comprehensive support services; (d) formalized articulation and communication; and (e) occupational experience, placement, and follow-up. (They appear in Table 5.2 as they appeared in the Wermuth and Phelps (1990) manuscript.)

Comprehensive support services (or supplemental services) were the most consistently identified group of components found across the studies reviewed (Phelps et al., 1989; Wermuth & Phelps, 1990). Three types of services appear in virtually every thorough description of vocational special needs programming: (a) assessment of student's vocational interests and abilities; (b) instructional support services (aides, tutors, and other forms of resource support); and (c) ongoing career guidance and counseling. These are reviewed briefly along with a discussion of transition services for students with disabilities in vocational education.

Vocational Assessment. Vocational assessments of students' interests, abilities, and special needs are typically recommended in descriptions of supplement services for youth with disabilities who enroll in vocational education programs. Less consensus exists, however, in specifications of how these assessments should be subsumed by these services (Cobb & Larkin, 1985; Albright & Cobb, 1987; Leconte, 1994).

In general, the purposes of vocational assessment center on assisting students in exploring vocational options, making recommendations for vocational placement, identifying instructional and other supports that individuals require in vocational settings, and facilitating transition planning in the move from school to adult roles (National Information Center for Children and Youth with Handicaps, 1990).

Table 5.2 Components of Exemplary Vocational Education Programs

Program Administration
  Strong administrative leadership and support
  Sufficient financial support
  Staff development
  Formative program evaluation
  Summative program evaluation
Curriculum and Instruction
  Individualized curriculum modifications
  Integration of academic and vocational curricula
  Appropriate instructional settings
  Cooperative learning experiences
Comprehensive Support Services
  Assessment of individual's vocational interests and abilities
  Instructional support services (e.g., aides, resources)
  Ongoing career guidance and counseling
Formalized Articulation and Communication
  Family/parent involvement and support
  Notification of both students and parents regarding vocational opportunities
  Vocational educators' involvement in individualized planning
  Formalized transition planning
  Intraagency and interagency collaboration
Occupational Experience, Placement, and Follow-Up
  Work experience opportunities
  Job placement services
  Follow-up of graduates and nongraduates (leavers)

Approaches to vocational assessment have also varied over the years and tend to follow into one of the following categories: (a) levels of vocational assessment; (b) curriculum-based vocational assessment; (c) formal or vocational evaluation services; and (d) community-based or ecological assessment (Neubert, 1994; Sarkees-Wircenski & Scott, 1995). However, research documenting the outcomes and benefits of vocational assessment in vocational education is limited.

With the passage of STWOA, the issue of alternative forms of assessment (particularly portfolios) has taken on a new form. A requirement of local partnerships who are reforming their secondary work-force preparation programs is that students who complete vocational education programs will receive portable skills certificates, presumably certifying what they know and are able to do relative to all aspects of the career pathway or industry in which they have been trained. Although there is no statutory language dictating the form this certifying process must take, and although specific assessment processes have yet to emerge from STWOA-funded states, it seems unimaginable that portfolios and other alternative forms of curriculum-based and community-referenced assessments will not be part of overall assessment systems.

Instructional Support. Instructional support services make up the foundation of exemplary vocational education programs for students with disabilities. Support services vary widely and may encompass such forms of tutors, aides, and interpreters for students; instructional material and curriculum modifications; equipment modifications; and referral assistance to other programs and agencies (Gaylord-Ross, 1988; Clark & Kolstoe, 1995; Sarkees-Wircenski & Scott, 1995).

As students with special needs have increasingly gained access to vocational programs, the need for support services has received attention to ensure that students are able to complete vocational programs successfully. In response, a number of vocational support models have been developed throughout the country (e.g., Wisconsin Department of Instruction, 1986, 1993; West, et al., 1992; Lombard et al., 1995). Despite their popularity, there is little empirical evidence that documents the outcomes of providing support services to special populations, provides descriptions of how personnel spend the majority of their time, or describes what support services are most beneficial to specific populations.

Transition Services. Some models of vocational education have been expanded to include specific transition from school to work components (e.g., Danehey, 1986; Eagle et al., 1987; Albright & Cobb, 1988; Neubert et al., 1991). One local education agency's (LEA) approach to extending support to vocational education graduates who were identified as special needs students while in school is depicted in the vocational transition services model displayed in Figure 5.1 (Neubert et al., 1991). Students with disabilities or disadvantages who are in need of continued assistance after they leave school are identified by vocational support personnel as they near graduation. Six months after they exit the school system, they are contacted via a telephone follow-up interview to determine employment and postsecondary outcomes and the need for ongoing services (see Stage II in Figure 5.1). If individuals are unemployed, underemployed, desire assistance in accessing postsecondary programs, or need help accessing

community services (e.g., child care), a transition case manager is assigned.

Case managers, supervised by a part-time project director, are employed on a part-time basis by LEA to work evenings and weekend hours. Case managers' major responsibilities are to continue career planning, revise transition goals, and link participants with appropriate employment or postsecondary opportunities and community services. Monitoring and follow-up are provided periodically once participants have reached their revised transition goals. As participants experience changes in their employment and life situations, the case managers can continue to act in an advocacy/mentor role and link individuals with appropriate opportunities to ensure job advancement and self-sufficiency. Through this approach, graduates can access a variety of postsecondary options and services as dictated by their career development needs.

Career Counseling and Services. The final supplemental service that appears most frequently in the literature on exemplary practices for vocational special needs students involves guidance and counseling services to assist students in making both short- and long-term career choices pertaining to vocational education. The selection of a vocational education program is an integral part of longitudinal transition planning, and career counseling should be geared to providing students and parents with information on a broad range of vocational education programs to comply with Section 118 of the 1990 Perkins Amendments. In addition, information pertaining to how vocational programs can prepare students for postsecondary opportunities, including 2- and 4-year institutions of higher education, should be provided.

Although career counseling is required by federal legislation, and touted as essential in virtually every text in the vocational special needs field, little empirical literature exists in either special or vocational education that documents how well such services are being performed, or

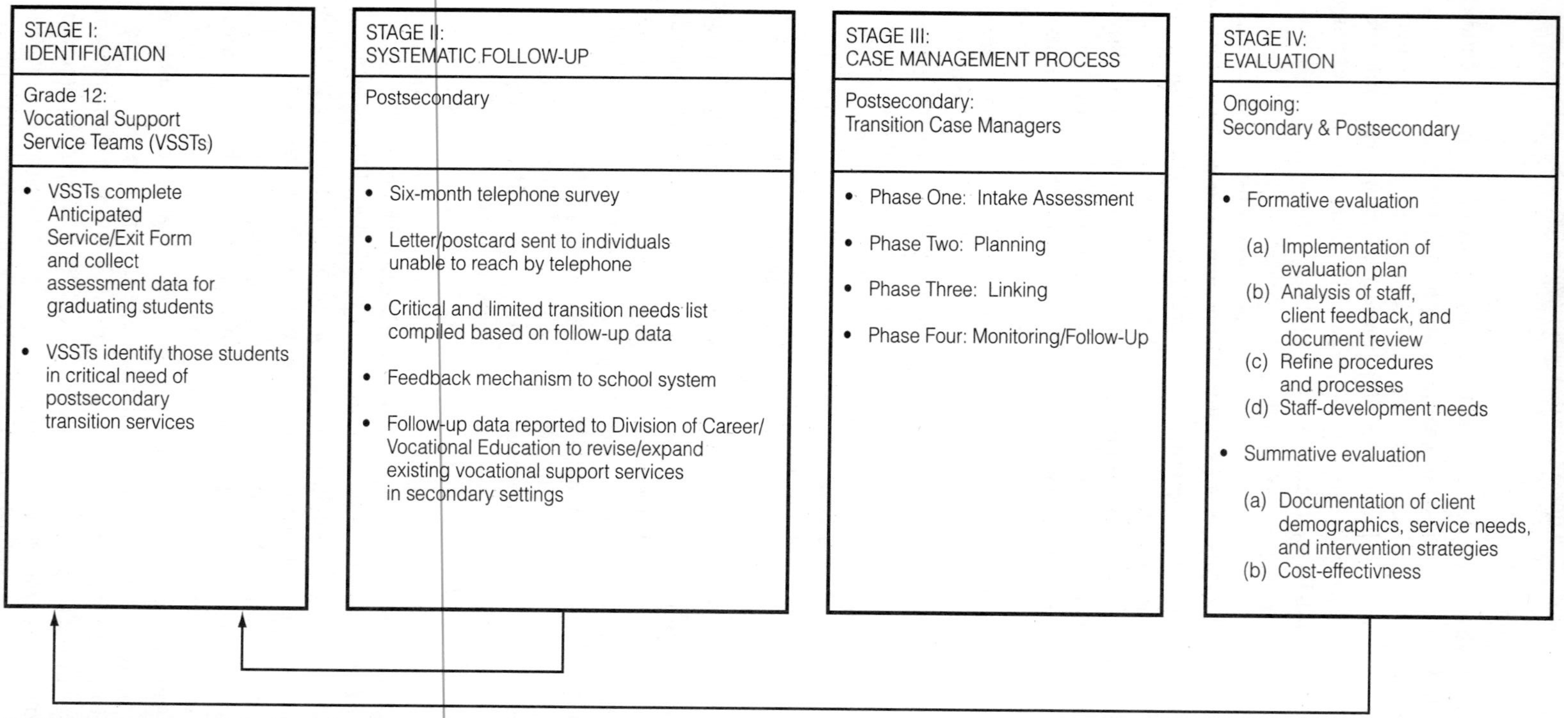

STAGE I:
IDENTIFICATION

Grade 12:
Vocational Support
Service Teams (VSSTs)

- VSSTs complete
  Anticipated
  Service/Exit Form
  and collect
  assessment data for
  graduating students
- VSSTs identify those students
  in critical need of
  postsecondary
  transition services

STAGE II:
SYSTEMATIC FOLLOW-UP

Postsecondary

- Six-month telephone survey
- Letter/postcard sent to individuals
  unable to reach by telephone
- Critical and limited transition needs list
  compiled based on follow-up data
- Feedback mechanism to school system
- Follow-up data reported to Division of Career/
  Vocational Education to revise/expand
  existing vocational support services
  in secondary settings

STAGE III:
CASE MANAGEMENT PROCESS

Postsecondary:
Transition Case Managers

- Phase One: Intake Assessment
- Phase Two: Planning
- Phase Three: Linking
- Phase Four: Monitoring/Follow-Up

STAGE IV:
EVALUATION

Ongoing:
Secondary & Postsecondary

- Formative evaluation
  (a) Implementation of
      evaluation plan
  (b) Analysis of staff,
      client feedback, and
      document review
  (c) Refine procedures
      and processes
  (d) Staff-development needs
- Summative evaluation
  (a) Documentation of client
      demographics, service needs,
      and intervention strategies
  (b) Cost-effectiveness

FIGURE 5.1 Framework for Vocational Transition Service Model

even how extensively (for exceptions, see Cameron, 1989; Feichtner, 1989; Szymanski & King, 1989).

Performance Standards and Measures

Documenting the outcomes and effectiveness of vocational education has been problematic over the years. Since 1963, states have been required to develop state plans and conduct program evaluation in vocational education. Labor market outcomes (placement rates) and employer satisfaction have traditionally been the measures that were collected to document outcomes, along with descriptive data on students, staff, and facilities. However, the recent demand for greater accountability and outcomes-based education has changed the scope of program evaluation in vocational education.

The 1990 Perkins Amendments required states to develop and implement systems of core measures and standards for vocational education. Performance measures can include competency attainment, work-skill attainment, program completion, high school graduation, related placement, any placement, special populations, and gender enrollment. The intent of this mandate is to use performance data to evaluate and improve vocational education programs. In addition, states are to develop and use "learning outcomes—measures of academic and occupational competencies—in assessing program effectiveness" (Boesel et al., 1994b:26). As the NAVE report concludes, it is still to early to assess how these systems are impacting services. However, by 1993, the majority of states had developed performance measures and standards systems although none was complete at that time (Boesel et al., 1994b). In addition, states have taken different approaches in designing their measures; some use specific assessment instruments and others develop local measures. Yet other states are waiting for the development of national industry skill standards to include in their accountability systems.

Local education agencies are to use the systems developed by the states. However, Hoachlander (1995) reported that "local use of performance measures and standards is, at best, sporadic—and in many cases nonexistent" (p. 20). Because responsibility for program improvement and reform has moved from the state to local levels with the 1990 Perkins Amendments, it is critical for local education agencies to participate in newly developed systems of performance measures and standards.

The 1990 Perkins Amendments also mandated states to collect data on individuals including special needs. By 1992, most states were in the process of developing procedures to report performance data (learning and labor outcomes) to measure the performance of special population groups in their accountability systems but no specific data were available (Boesel et al., 1994b).

ISSUES IN EMERGING VOCATIONALISM

To deliver on the ambitious STWOA agenda outlined earlier requires paradigmatic shifts in the thinking of teachers, administrators, parents, community members, and students. Traditional turf boundaries, hierarchical organizational structures, inter- and intraagency policy contexts, and categorical funding limitations must change. Different states and the local partnerships in them will experience vastly different levels of success in addressing these various shifts in the thinking about and the practice of schooling. Literally dozens, perhaps hundreds, of factors will act independently and interactively on the likelihood of success. We will conclude this chapter with a brief discussion of a few of these factors portrayed in the form of school reform issues.

The Design of Secondary Schools

Over the history of public secondary schooling in the United States, very little has changed in the design of schools. The last four decades have seen the construction of area vocational schools and vocational high schools, but the comprehensive high school still dominates the secondary school landscape and is likely to continue as far forward as we can see in the future. But what innovations seem possible and appropriate within the specific design of the comprehensive high school? What would appear to be the most salient design features to enhance secondary schools in general, and the emerging vocationalism of the School-to-Work Opportunities Act in particular?

Copa and Pease (1992) provided hints of these design features in a visioning project supported by the National Center for Research in Vocational Education. Their recommendations, referred to as "characteristics of a twenty-first century high school" are reproduced verbatim from their executive summary:

1. guaranteeing a set of learner outcomes closely linked to present and future life roles and responsibilities for all students

2. learning expectations which include both knowing and applying learning in life situations using authentic assessment

3. multiple ways to learn that are responsive to learning styles and interests

4. integration of high level academic education and modern vocational education for all students

5. partnerships with parents and families, business, industry and labor, community-based organizations, and other schools to diversify learning settings and improve learning effectiveness

6. a special character or focus (learning signature) to the school that gives coherence and spirit to learning

7. operation as a learning community that pays attention to caring, attachments, and expectations often requiring the subdivision of large schools into smaller units

8. alignment and unification of the components of the school in the interests of quality and efficiency

9. decision-making that is consistent with overall aims, yet is located close to the problem at hand

10. costs which are no more than those for existing schools

11. partnership with the larger community as a way to make learning up-to-date and meaningful (p. 16)

These characteristics clearly would be difficult to achieve consistently in any single school; they probably function best as design targets to stimulate discussion about reform in schools.

A second design issue for secondary schools was alluded to by Copa and Pease (1992)—that of education for *all* students in the comprehensive high school. This would suggest a reversal of the practice of building separate vocational schools or area centers, as well as establishing separate work-related programs for subsets of at-risk students, in favor of integrating the physical learning of vocational content directly among those learning academic content.

Finally, the issue of school size appears in the design of comprehensive high schools for the twenty-first century. Although Copa and Pease (1992) designed the archetypal comprehensive high school for 1,600 students, they clearly are sensitive to school size in their design features (schools within schools; basic learning subcommunity within the school of 400 students). The evidence seems to be building that high schools exceeding 1,000 students achieve outcomes for their students that are increasingly negative, although the relationship does not appear to be linear across community socioeconomic status and student ability groups (Friedkin & Neccochea, 1988; Haller, 1992). Lee and Smith (1994) recently elevated the examination of school-size effects with their thoughtful analysis of the relationship between school size and restructured secondary schools. Again, the findings are consistent and seem to tie directly to the design features listed earlier:

We suggest that school size can only have an *indirect* effect on student learning and engagement. Were we to introduce a set of school organization measures such as collegiality, personalized relationships, and the like into our analyses, the magnitude of the direct school size effects seen here would surely decline. ... Given the current fiscal constraints surrounding American education, it is unlikely that new and small high schools will be constructed no matter how strong the empirical link between "smallness" and learning. Rather, we believe that the "school within a school" reform—already embraced by 15% of American high schools—is a feasible and cost-effective way to accomplish this structural reform. (p. 26)

The Curriculum of Secondary Schools

Three curricular issues would appear to warrant discussion here, and are likely to be the subject of repeated debate if school-to-work initiatives begin to take hold in America's high schools. First, it seems increasingly apparent that occupationally specific technical training requiring large laboratories with expensive equipment and supplies will continue to migrate away from secondary schools in favor of community colleges. Part of this issue is the sheer cost of maintaining laboratories that reflect current technologies and systems; part of it is the space such laboratories require, and the highly technical and rapidly changing preparation that instructors will need. Just as the hard sciences (chemistry, physics, biology) are moving to "small-scale science" as a cost-effective means for laboratory experimentation in public schools, so, too, will vocational education.

Second, it seems clear that the community increasingly will be the locus of curriculum and instruction. Special education has found community-referenced curricula and community-based training to be enormously effective in recent years; vocational education and educators, too, must become more willing to make the community their classroom.

Finally, as mentioned earlier, the boundary lines of curricula in the traditionally academic and vocational domains are likely to become more and more blurred as STWOA initiatives become more and more a reality. Model

processes to accomplish this integration are increasingly available (Grubb et al., 1991; Harp, 1993; Stasz, Kaganoff, & Eden, 1993), and it seems inevitable that one or more of these models will find their way into the comprehensive high schools of the twenty-first century.

The Preparation of Teachers for Secondary Schools

One of the features of the school-to-work initiative that distinguishes it from many other systems-change reform initiatives is the breadth of its perspective on the education for work enterprise. Although we have not discussed all of the details of that breadth in this chapter (because elements of elementary and middle school reform are not within the scope of this discussion), one focus of the school-to-work initiative is on the reform of vocational teacher education programs. There is a recognition, here, that the public school "education-for-work" enterprise cannot fully and efficiently engage in reform unless its teachers are prepared for such efforts.

The focus of teacher preparation reform efforts seems to center on two interrelated issues: merging the programs in higher education that prepare both academic and vocational education teachers, and merging the state licensing requirements for both academic and vocational education teachers. The first of these issues will require a major effort on what is unarguably a formidable task. As Hartley, Mantle-Bromley, and Cobb (1996b) stated:

> Administrative, organizational, and professional issues abound in higher education that mitigate against integrating departments of secondary, special, vocational, and professional education, most notably the deep-rooted tradition of specialized departmental structures. With the information explosion and correspondingly exponential increase in the knowledge base of education, the elimination of specialized departments in the preservice education enterprise becomes more and more difficult. However, the conceptual

integrity of integrated teacher preparation programs remains. (p. 48)

With respect to the second issue, teacher licensure, Hartley and colleagues (1996b) again focused directly on the issue:

> vocational education has always had alternative forms of certification, often based on hours of occupational experience. This has … had a detrimental effect on the overall quality of instruction in secondary vocational education, with an equally detrimental effect on the image of vocational education as a viable and co-equal option within the secondary curriculum. … What does seem clear, however, is this: If vocational education is to gain equal stature in the schools, both the perception and the reality of its certifying process must be equal to that of other teachers. (p. 49)

Until the preparation of all teachers in our secondary schools is drawn from the same philosophical and pedagogical base, until preservice vocational teacher education students are educated alongside all of their counterparts with whom they will work in secondary schools, and until the same standards for liberal, subject matter, and pedagogical knowledge are applied to all prospective teachers—it will continue to be extremely difficult to eliminate fragmented and segregated instructional delivery systems in the schools.

The Policy Context for the Reform of Secondary Schools

The defining issue in emerging vocationalism for secondary special education and vocational education in the last two decades of the twentieth century is the transition from school to work. And the policy context for this "new vocationalism," as Grubb (1996) has called it, is the statewide systems-change granting process. Initiated through special education state systems-change grants in supported employment during

the late 1980s, and continued with the secondary transition systems-change grants in the 1990s, this federal-to-state-to-local reform process has been embraced at a much wider level by STWOA in the late 1990s.

Absent from this systems-change/school reform policy context at this time, however, are the regular educators. There has been some similar scale activity, through Goals 2000 grants to states, but the focus of these grants at the secondary education level has not been on school-to-work transition. Whether the U.S. Department of Education will establish a similar state systems-change granting process for academic secondary education focusing specifically on transition is unknown at this time. Were it to do so, focusing on the transition from high school to posthigh school life through integrated curricular programming, the final portion of the loop would be closed on transitional systems-change and secondary educational reform.

SUMMARY

We end this chapter not with answers but with questions: What is the likelihood that the ambitious agenda of STWOA will come to fruition? How many schools, classrooms, teachers, and curricula must be redefined to constitute "going to scale"—that is, to have enough momentum to sustain the reform agenda? The odds are not great. As Pogrow (1996) recently concluded:

> The history of education reform is one of consistent failure of major reforms to survive and become institutionalized… the few that do survive are shorn of their ambitious goals and ideals, becoming instead routinized incremental changes to what exists. (p. 657)

But perhaps the "routinized incremental changes" are enough. It is estimated that only 10 to 12 percent of practice has to change to generate the momentum needed to sustain innovations. We have seen a major shift in the stated purposes of vocational education in successive pieces of legislation—from a narrow interest in fulfilling the needs of local employers in the early Smith-Hughes Act, to an interest in much broader skill development in current legislation. The remaining years of this century without a doubt, will continue to see incremental changes across the K–16 educational spectrum, because interest in school reform continues to be high across that spectrum (Goldberger & Kazis, 1996; Hartoonian & Van Scotter, 1996). And the transition from school to work, for all school-aged youth, will inevitably be a key topic within this reform agenda.

QUESTIONS

1. What do enrollment patterns for students with special needs look like in secondary vocational education?

2. How did legislation during the Vocational Education Act Period (1963–1985) impact the delivery of vocational education and support services to students with special needs?

3. What type of support services and activities became prevalent for students with special needs under the Carl D. Perkins Vocational Education Act of 1984?

4. What major changes took place in vocational education as a result of the Carl D. Perkins Vocational and Applied Technology Education Act Amendments of 1990?

5. How does the School to Work Opportunities Act (STWOA) of 1994 incorporate vocational education programming in current service delivery?

6. How are "connecting activities" designated in STWOA similar to transition activities and services in the field of special education?

7. What are the similarities and differences in cooperative work experience, youth apprenticeships, and school-based enterprises?

8. What types of support of supplementary services are found in exemplary programs for students with special needs?

9. What are the major issues in designing secondary schools in the future?

10. What are the major issues in preparing teachers for secondary schools in the future?

REFERENCES

Adami, H., & Neubert, D. A. (1991). A follow-up of vocational assessment recommendations and placement in secondary vocational education programs for students with disabilities. *Vocational Evaluation and Work Adjustment Bulletin, 24,* 101–107.

Albright, L., & Cobb, R. B. (1987). Curriculum based vocational assessment: A concept whose time has come. *Journal for Vocational Special Needs, 10,* 15–18.

———. (1988). *Assessment of students with handicaps in vocational education: A curriculum-based approach.* Alexandria, VA: American Vocational Association.

Anderson, J. R., Reder, L. M., & Simon, H. A. (1996). Situated learning and education. *Educational Researcher, 25,* 5–11.

Barton, P. E., & Kirsch, I. S. (1990). *Workplace competencies: The need to improve literacy and employment readiness.* Washington, DC: U.S. Government Printing Office.

Benson, C. S., & Hoachlander, E. G. (1981). *Distribution of federal funds for vocational education: Interstate and intrastate allocations* (Substudy B-2). Berkeley: University of California.

Bies, J. D. (1987). The impact of federal legislation on vocational special needs programming. In G. Meers (Ed.), *Handbook of vocational special needs education* (2nd ed.) (pp. 29–46). Rockville, MD: Aspen.

Boesel, D., Hudson, L., Deich, S., & Maston, C. (1994a). *National assessment of vocational education final report to Congress. Volume 2: Participation and quality of vocational education.* Washington, DC: U.S. Department of Education, Office of Educational Research and Improvement.

Boesel, D., & McFarland, L. (1994). *National assessment of vocational education final report to Congress. Volume 1: Summary and recommendations.* Washington, DC: U.S. Department of Education, Office of Educational Research and Improvement.

Boesel, D., Rahn, M., & Deich, S. (1994b). *National assessment of vocational education final report to Congress. Volume 3: Participation and quality of vocational education.* Washington, DC: U.S. Department of Education, Office of Educational Research and Improvement.

Brown, J. M., Asselin, S. B., Hoerner, J. L., Daines, J., & Clowers, D. A. (1991). Should special needs learners have access to tech prep programs? *Journal for Vocational Special Needs Education, 14,* 21–27.

Brown, J. S., Collins, A., & Duguid, P. (1989). Situated cognition and the culture of learning. *Educational Researcher, 18,* 32–41.

Brustein, M., & Mahler, M. (1994). *AVA guide to the School-to-Work Opportunities Act.* Alexandria, VA: American Vocational Association.

Cameron, C. (1989). Accessing services that facilitate transition: Tapping community resources. *Journal for Vocational Special Needs Education, 11,* 25–28.

Clark, G. M., & Kolstoe, O. P. (1995). *Career development and transition education for adolescents with disabilities* (2nd ed.). Boston: Allyn & Bacon.

Cobb, R. B., & Danehey, A. (1986). Transitional vocational assessment: A model for students with handicaps. *Journal for Vocational Special Needs Education, 9,* 3–7.

Cobb, R. B., & Kingsbury, D. E. (1985). The special needs provisions of the Perkins Act. *Vocational Education Journal, 65,* 13–17.

Cobb, R. B., & Larkin, D. (1985). Assessment and placement of handicapped pupils into secondary vocational education programs. *Focus on Exceptional Children, 17,* 1–14.

Copa, G. H., & Pease, V. H. (1992). *A new vision for the comprehensive high school: Preparing students for a changing world.* Executive Summary Report from the National Center for Research in Vocational Education. Minneapolis: University of Minnesota, Department of Vocational and Technical Education.

Eagle, E., Choy, S., Hoachlander, E. G., Stoddard, S., & Tuma, J. (1987). *Increasing vocational options for students with learning handicaps.* Berkeley, CA: Institute for the Study of Family, Work and Community.

Evans, R. N., & Herr, E. L. (1978). *Foundations of vocational education* (2nd ed.). Columbus, OH: Charles Merrill.

Feichtner, S. H. (1989). Counseling to facilitate transition of at-risk students in a postsecondary setting. *Journal for Vocational Special Needs Education, 11,* 19–23.

Friedkin, N. E., & Neccochea, J. (1988). School size and performance: A contingency perspective. *Educational Evaluation and Policy Analysis, 10,* 237–249.

Gaylord-Ross, R. (1988). *Vocational education for persons with handicaps.* Mountain View, CA: Mayfield.

Goldberger, S., & Kazis, R. (1996). Revitalizing high schools: What the school-to-career movement can contribute. *Phi Delta Kappan, 77,* 547–554.

Grubb, W. N. (1996). The new vocationalism: What it is, what it could be. *Phi Delta Kappan, 77,* 535–546.

Grubb, W. N., Davis, G., Plihal, J., & Lum, J. (1991). *The cunning hand, the cultured mind: Models for integrating vocational and academic education.* MDS-141. Berkeley: University of California, National Center for Research in Vocational Education.

Haller, E. J. (1992). High school size and student indiscipline: Another aspect of the school consolidation issue? *Educational Evaluation and Policy Analysis, 14,* 145–156.

Harp, L. (1993). June 23 SREB project helps schools blur line between vocational and academic tracks. *Education Week,* 8.

Hartley, N., Mantle-Bromley, C., & Cobb, R. B. (1996a). A matter of respect. *Vocational Education Journal, 71,* 25, 61.

———. (1996b). Building a context for reform. In N. K. Hartley & T. L. Wentling (Eds.), *Beyond tradition: Preparing the teachers of tomorrow's workforce* (p. 48). Columbia, MO: University Council for Vocational Education.

Hartoonian, M., & Van Scotter, R. (1996). School-to-work: A model for learning a living. *Phi Delta Kappan, 77,* 555–560.

Heaviside, S., Carey, N., & Farris, E. (1994). *Public secondary school teacher survey on vocational education.* NCES Publication 94-409. Washington, DC: U.S. Department of Education, Office of Educational Research and Improvement, National Center for Education Statistics.

Hoachlander, G. (1995). What the numbers really mean. *Vocational Education Journal, 70,* 20–23, 50.

Hudson, L. (1994). *National assessment of vocational education final report to Congress. Volume 4: Access to programs and services for special populations.* Washington, DC: U.S. Department of Education, Office of Educational Research and Improvement.

Jobs for the Future. (1993). *Student apprenticeship news* (No. 6). Cambridge, MA: Author.

Kochhar, C. A. (1995). School-to-work reform: Integrating transition policies for all students. *Journal for Vocational Special Needs Education, 17,* 116–119.

Kochhar, C. A., & Deschamps, A. B. (1992). Policy crossroads in preserving the right of passage to independence for learners with special needs. *Journal for Vocational Special Needs Education, 14,* 9–20.

Kopp, H., & Kazis, R., with Churchill, A. (1995). *Promising practices: A study of ten school-to-career programs.* Boston: Jobs for the Future.

Leconte, P. J. (1994). *A perspective on vocational appraisal: Beliefs, practices, and paradigms.* Ph.D. dissertation, George Washington University, Washington, DC.

Leconte, P., & Boyer-Stephens, A. (1992). Student assessment and support assurances. *Journal for Vocational Special Needs Education, 14,* 54–61.

Lee, V. E., & Smith, J. B. (1994). *Effects of high school restructuring and size on gains in achievement and engagement of early secondary school students.* Madison: University of Wisconsin, Center on Organization and Restructuring of Schools.

Levesque, K., Premo, M., Vergun, R., Emanuel, D., Klein, S., Henke, R., & Kagehiro, S. (1995). *Vocational education in the United States: The early 1990s.* NCES Publication 95-024. Washington, DC: U.S. Department of Education, Office of Educational Research and Improvement, National Center for Education Statistics.

Linnehan, F. (1996). Measuring the effectiveness of a career academy program from an employer's perspective. *Educational Evaluation and Policy Analysis, 18,* 73–89.

Lombard, R. C., Hazelkorn, M. N., & Miller, R. J. (1995). Special populations and tech-prep: A national study of state policies. *Career Development for Exceptional Individuals, 18,* 133–144.

Lombard, R. C., Hazelkorn, M. N., & Neubert, D. A. (1992). A survey of accessibility to secondary vocational education programs and transition services for students with disabilities in Wisconsin. *Career Development for Exceptional Individuals, 15,* 179–188.

Lynch, R. L. (1996). Vocational teacher education: At a crossroads. *Vocational Education Journal, 71,* 22–24.

Maryland State Department of Education. (1984). *Handbook for vocational support service teams in Maryland.* Baltimore: Author.

Muraskin, L., Hollinger, D., & Harvey, J. (1994). *National assessment of vocational education final report to Congress. Volume 5: Funding and administrative issues.* Washington, DC: U.S. Department of Education, Office of Educational Research and Improvement.

National Center for Education Statistics. (1992). *The condition of vocational education: Review edition.* Washington, DC: U.S. Department of Education.

National Center for Research in Vocational Education. (1990). Improving outcomes for students with special needs: Integrating academic and vocational education. *TASSP Brief, 2,* 1–4.

National Commission on Secondary Vocational Education. (1984). *The unfinished agenda: The role of vocational education in the high school.* Columbus: Ohio State University, National Center for Research in Vocational Education.

National Council on Vocational Education. (1990–1991). *Solutions.* Washington, DC: Author.

National Information Center for Children and Youth with Handicaps. (1990). *Transition summary: Vocational assessment—A guide for parents and professionals.* Washington, DC: Author.

Neubert, D. A. (1994). Vocational evaluation and assessment in vocational-technical education: Barriers and facilitators to interdisciplinary services. *Vocational Evaluation and Work Adjustment Bulletin, 27,* 149–153.

Neubert, D. A., & Leconte, P. J. (1990). Vocational assessment: Effective intervention for meeting the vocational needs of rural youth with special needs. *Journal for Vocational Special Needs Education, 13,* 17–22.

Neubert, D. A., Leney, B., Rothenbacher, C., & Krishnaswami, U. (1991). A case management model for providing vocational transition services to at-risk youth. *Journal for Vocational Special Needs Education, 14,* 19–26.

Nystrom, D. C., & Bayne, G. K. (1979). *Occupational and career education legislation* (2nd ed.). Indianapolis, IN: Bobbs-Merrill.

Pauly, E., Kopp, H., & Haimson, J. (1995). *Home-grown lessons: Innovative programs linking school and work.* San Francisco: Jossey-Bass.

Phelps, L. A. (1984). *An analysis of fiscal policy alternatives for serving special populations in vocational education.* Information Series No. 278. Columbus: Ohio State University, National Center for Research in Vocational Education.

Phelps, L. A., Wermuth, T. R., Crain, R. L., & Kane, P. (1989). *Vocational education for special populations: Options for improving federal policy.* Berkeley, CA: National Center for Research in Vocational Education.

Plihal, J., Johnson, M. A., Bentley, C., Morgaine, C., & Liang, T. (1991). *Integration of vocational and academic education: Theory and practice.* Berkeley, CA: National Center for Research in Vocational Education.

Pogrow, S. (1996, June). Reforming the wannabe reformers: Why education reforms almost always end up making things worse. *Phi Delta Kappan,* 656–663.

Raizen, S. A. (1989). *Reforming education for work: A cognitive science perspective.* Berkeley: University of California, National Center for Research in Vocational Education.

Resnick, L. B. (1987). Learning in and out of school. *Educational Researcher, 16,* 13–20.

Roditi, H. F. (1991). *How much does a youth apprenticeship program cost, and who will pay for it? Lessons from some long-standing school-to-work programs and youth apprenticeship programs under development.* Cambridge, MA: Jobs for the Future.

Sarkees, M. D., & Sullivan, R. L. (1989). Learners with special needs in vocational student organizations. *Journal for Vocational Special Needs Education, 12,* 21–26.

Sarkees-Wircenski, M., & Scott, J. L. (1995). *Vocational special needs* (3rd ed.). Homewood, IL: American Technical Publishers.

Scott, J. L., & Sarkees-Wircenski, M. (1995). *Overview of vocational and applied technology education.* Homewood, IL: American Technical Publishers.

Secretary's Commission on Necessary Skills. (SCANS). (1991). *What work requires of schools: A SCANS report for America 2000.* Washington, DC: U.S. Department of Labor.

Smith, C. L., & Rojewski, J. W. (1993). School-to-work transition: Alternatives for educational reform. *Youth and Society, 25,* 222–250.

Stasz, C., Kaganoff, T., & Eden, R. (1993). Integrating academic and vocational education: A review of the literature. Paper prepared for the National Assessment of Vocational Education, National Center for Research in Vocational Education, University of California.

Stern, D., Finkelstein, N., Stone, J. R., Latting, J., & Dornsife, C. (1995). *School to work: Research on programs in the United States.* Stanford Series on Educational and Public Policy No. 17. Bristol, PA: Falmer Press.

Stern, D., Raby, M., & Dayton, C. (1992). *Career academies: Partnerships for reconstructing American high schools.* San Francisco: Jossey-Bass.

Stern, D., Stone, J., Hopkins, C., McMillion, M., & Crain, R. (1994). *School-based enterprise: Productive learning in American high schools.* San Francisco: Jossey-Bass.

Stodden, R., Ianacone, R., Boone, R. M., & Bisconer, S. W. (1987). *Curriculum-based vocational assessment.* Honolulu: Centre Publications.

Szymanski, E. M., & King, J. (1989). Rehabilitation counseling in transition planning and preparation. *Career Development for Exceptional Individuals, 12,* 3–10.

Thomas, S., & Coleman, N. (1988). *Vocational assessment training manual.* Raleigh: North Carolina Department of Public Instruction, Division of Vocational Evaluation.

Tuma, J., & Burns, S. K. (1996). *Trends in participation in secondary vocational education: 1982–1992.* NCES Publication 96-004. Washington, DC: U.S. Department of Education, Office of Educational Research and Improvement, National Center for Education Statistics.

U.S. Congress, Office of Technology Assessment (1995). *Learning to work: Making the transition from school to work.* OTA-EHR-637. Washington, DC: U.S. Government Printing Office.

U. S. Department of Education. (1988). *Second interim report from the national assessment of vocational education.* Washington, DC: U.S. Department of Education, National Assessment of Vocational Education.

U.S. General Accounting Office. (1993). *Vocational education: Status in school year 1990–1991: Early signs of change at the secondary level.* Washington, DC: Author.

———. (1995). *Vocational education: Changes at high school level after amendments to Perkins Act.* Washington, DC: Author.

Wermuth, T. R., & Phelps, L. A. (1990). *Identifying components of effective vocational special needs programs: A preliminary framework.* Berkeley, CA: National Center for Research in Vocational Education.

West, L., Boyer-Stephens, A., Estey, D., & Miller, M. (1992). *Vocational resource educator* (3rd ed.). Columbia, MO: Missouri LINC.

West, L. L., & Meers, G. (1992). An introduction to the Carl D. Perkins Vocational and Applied Technology Act of 1990 for special populations. *Journal for Vocational Special Needs Education, 14,* 4–8.

Wirt, J. G. (1991). A new federal law on vocational education: Will reform follow? *Phi Delta Kappan, 72,* 424–433.

Wisconsin Department of Instruction. (1986). *Designated vocational instruction: A cooperative process for change.* Madison: Author.

———. (1993). *Designated vocational instruction: A resource and planning manual.* Madison: Author.

6

Career Development, School-to-Work Transition, and Diversity

An Ecological Approach
EDNA MORA SZYMANSKI

This chapter provides an overview of the career development theories and concepts underlying the practice of school-to-work transition. An ecological model of career development will be introduced and related to existing career development theories. According to the ecological model, career development is determined by the dynamic interaction of individual, contextual, mediating, environmental, and outcome constructs with congruence, decision making, developmental, socialization, allocation, and chance processes. In addition, career workshops and portfolios will be discussed, and transition interventions will be connected to the ecological model.

School-to-work transition can be considered a road stop on the lifelong career development highway. Thus, career development considerations should underlie transition planning. The purpose of this chapter is to acquaint transition professionals with (a) career development, (b) ecological applications for transition, and (c) career development interventions.

CAREER DEVELOPMENT

The meaning of the term "career development" may vary across populations. For most people,

career development is the "lifelong process of getting ready to choose, choosing, and typically continuing to choose from among the many occupations available in our society" (Brown & Brooks, 1984:ix). However, this definition may not apply fully to people from diverse cultural backgrounds, those who live in poverty, and some individuals with disabilities. "If work is not seen as a central life variable, if options and choices are not seen to be available so that individuals see themselves as having some control over their lives, or if social discrimination operates to distort the effects of individual's characteristics, then theoretically predictable behaviors cannot apply" (Osipow & Littlejohn, 1995:255). At best, therefore, we can say that career development is "the total constellation of psychological, sociological, educational, physical, economic, and chance factors that combine to shape the career of any given individual over the life span" (Herr & Cramer, 1992:27).

Over the years, a wide range of theories have emerged to explain career development. The theoretical landscape has been somewhat disconnected. "Each academic discipline happily develops its own concepts but does not feel obligated to connect them to the concepts that flow from other disciplines" (Schein, 1986:315–316). In addition to being disconnected, the wide range of theories are still at relatively early stages of scientific development (Brown, 1990b).

Some convergence of theories has occurred naturally over time (Osipow, 1994), and the interrelationship of the theories was the topic of a recent edited text (Savickas & Lent, 1994a). However, it has been suggested that multiple theories are necessary in order to address different aspects of vocational behavior (Dawis, 1994; Krumboltz, 1994) and diverse audiences (Holland, 1994). "The theories need each other in order to comprehensively address the complexity of career development. Furthermore, the results of research studies acquire deeper meaning when they are viewed from the perspectives of two or more theories" (Savickas & Lent, 1994b:2).

Although the multiple theories may have scientific value, they make it difficult to connect theory to practice. For this reason, an ecological model has been developed to link the underlying constructs and processes of career development theories and relate them to assessment and intervention. The remainder of this section describes the ecological model and addresses application of theories to people with disabilities and minorities.

Ecological Model of Career Development

All career development theories are based on constructs and processes that describe vocational behavior. During the last few years, I have worked with colleagues to develop a model that uses these constructs and processes to explain career development and facilitate planning interventions. After initial development (Szymanski, Hershenson et al., 1996), the model was applied to people with developmental disabilities (Szymanski & Hanley-Maxwell, 1996) and to school-to-work transition (Szymanski, in press). Most recently, it was significantly extended and applied to rehabilitation counseling (Szymanski & Hershenson, in press).

The model is ecological because it follows in the tradition of Lewin (1936) and Bronfenbrenner (1988) in focusing not only on individuals, but also on the contexts and environments of their lives. "According to this model, career development is determined by the dynamic interaction of individual, contextual, mediating, environmental, and outcome constructs with congruence, decision-making, developmental, socialization, allocation, and chance processes" (Szymanski & Hershenson, in press). Table 6.1 presents the groups of constructs and processes that underlie the model.

The constructs and processes described in Table 6.1 were distilled from career development theories. Table 6.2 shows the relationship of the theories to the constructs and processes. Readers interested in a more complete description of the theories should consult Herr and Cramer (1992), Savickas and Lent (1994a), or Brown and colleagues (1996). In addition, Szymanski and Hershenson (in press) provide an overview of the theories and discuss their applicability for people with disabilities.

Application of Theories to People with Disabilities and Minorities

A number of journal articles and book chapters have discussed the application of career development theories to people with disabilities (see, e.g., Curnow, 1989; Hershenson & Szymanski, 1992; Rojewski, 1994) and minorities (see, e.g., Fitzgerald & Betz, 1994; Vondracek & Fouad, 1994; Osipow & Littlejohn, 1995). Recently,

Table 6.1 Career Development Constructs and Processes

Construct/Processes	Description
Individual constructs	Physical and psychological attributes (e.g., gender; race; physical and mental abilities, including work competencies; predispositions and limitations; interests; needs; values; the aspect of disability that is a personal attribute).
Context constructs	Those aspects of an individual's situation that are external to the person (e.g., socioeconomic status; family; educational opportunities; nonnormative influences such as war or natural disasters; relevant legislation; financial disincentives).
Mediating constructs	Constructs that impact the relationship between people and environments, including individual, social, and environmental mediating constructs.
■ individual mediating constructs	Habits or behavior patterns and personal beliefs about abilities and characteristics (e.g., self-concept, work personality, self-efficacy, task approach skills, career portfolios, career maturity, career decisiveness, adjustment to disability).
■ social mediating constructs	Cultural beliefs or social structures (e.g., culture, religious beliefs, gender or disability role socialization, discrimination, stereotypes, lack of physical access, limited opportunity structures, and attitudes toward people with disabilities).
■ environmental mediating constructs	Beliefs about the environment (e.g., outcome expectations, world-view generalizations).
Work environment	Aspects of the work environment (e.g., types of individuals who work in the environments, task requirements, reinforcement systems, organizational culture, access to work tasks, job accommodation).
Output constructs	Behaviors or states that result from the interactions of the other factors (e.g., job satisfaction, persistence, organizational productivity).
Congruence processes	The process of relative match or mismatch of individuals with their environments.
Decision-making processes	The process by which individuals consider career-related alternatives and formulate decisions.
Developmental processes	The process of systematic changes over time, which are interwoven with the individual's characteristics and perceptions and reciprocally influenced by the environment.
Socialization processes	The process by which people learn work and life roles.
Allocation processes	The process by which societal gatekeepers (i.e., parents, teachers, vocational counselors, school administrators, and personnel directors) use external criteria to channel individuals into or exclude them from specific directions.
Chance processes	Unanticipated events and encounters.

Source: Content adapted from "Career Development of People with Disabilities: An Ecological Model," by E. M. Szymanski & D. B. Hershenson, in press, in R. M. Parker & E. M. Szymanski (Eds.), *Rehabilitation Counseling: Basics and Beyond* (3rd ed.). Copyright by PRO-ED. Adapted with permission.

Table 6.2 Theories, Constructs, and Processes

Theory	Types of Constructs[a]					Types of Process[b]					
	Ind.	Con.	Med.	Env.	Out.	Dev.	DM	Cng.	Soc.	All.	Chnc.
Super's Theory	x	x	x	x	x	x		x			
Holland's Theory	x	x		x	x			x			
Trait-Factor Theory	x	x	x	x	x			x			
Miller-Tiedeman's Theory	x		x				x				
Roe's Theory	x	x		x	x	x			x		x
Krumboltz' Theory	x	x	x	x	x	x	x		x		x
Minnesota Theory	x	x		x	x			x			
Hershenson's Models	x	x	x	x	x	x			x		x
Sociocognitive Approach	x	x	x	x	x	x			x		x
Developmental Contextualism	x	x	x	x	x	x		x	x		x
Sociological Theories	x	x		x	x				x	x	
Organizational Career Theories	x	x		x	x					x	

Sources: Adapted from "Career Development of People with Disabilities: An Ecological Model," by E. M. Szymanski & D. B. Hershenson, in press, in R. M. Parker & E. M. Szymanski (Eds.), *Rehabilitation Counseling: Basics and Beyond* (3rd ed.). Copyright by PRO-ED. Adapted with permission.

Super's Theory (Super, 1990); Holland's Theory (Holland, 1985); Trait-Factor Theory (Brown, 1990c); Miller-Tiedeman's Theory (Miller-Tiedman & Tiedeman, 1990); Roe's Theory (Roe & Lunneborg, 1990); Krumboltz' Theory (Mitchell & Krumboltz, 1990); Minnesota Theory (Lofquist & Dawis, 1969, 1991); Hershenson's Models (Hershenson, 1981, 1996); Sociocognitive Approach (Lent & Hackett, 1994); Developmental Contextualism (Vondracek, Lerner, & Schulenberg, 1986; Vondracek & Fouad, 1994); Sociological Theories (Rothman, 1987; Hotchkiss & Borow, 1990); Organizational Career Theories (Hall, 1990; Gutteridge, Leibowitz, & Shore, 1993).

[a]Ind. = Individual; Con. = Context; Med. = Mediating; Env. = Environment; Out. = Outcome;

[b]Dev. = Development; DM = Decision making; Cng. = Congruence; Soc. = Socialization; All. = Allocation; Chnc. = Chance.

Szymanski, Hershenson, and colleagues (1996) questioned the feasibility of the discussion of theory applicability to special populations for the following reasons.

Theories are explanations of natural phenomena (Kerlinger, 1986). They depend, to some extent, on some homogeneity and predictability of the populations under study.

There is little doubt that people with disabilities comprise a very heterogeneous population (Brodwin, Parker, & DeLaGarza, 1996). Consider, for example, the experiential differences between people with congenital and acquired physical disabilities (Hershenson, 1981). Similarly, consider the differences in experiences and opportunities between people with cognitive and physical disabilities.

Racial and ethnic minority students also comprise very diverse groups (see, e.g., Osipow & Littlejohn, 1995). Not only are there often differences in cultural beliefs and experiences, and relationships with majority society (see, e.g., Sue & Sue, 1990; Lee & Richardson, 1991; Leong, 1995), but acculturation and racial identity also moderate the impact of these factors (LaFromboise, Coleman, & Gerton, 1993). In other words, an individual's ethnic heritage cannot predict the extent to which he or she identifies with minority culture.

The diversity of both individuals with disabilities and racial and ethnic minority groups limits the applicability or inapplicability of career development theories. Both groups are so diverse that it is likely that any given theory will help to explain the behavior of some individuals while omitting critical assumptions necessary to understanding others. Nonetheless, the ecological model described in Tables 6.1 and 6.2, which was distilled from the theories, can provide a framework for assessment and intervention. The caveat here is that no two individuals are the same; the model guides understanding of individuals, their environments, and the contexts in which they live. However, it is only a guide, not an explanation or prescription.

ECOLOGICAL CONSIDERATIONS FOR TRANSITION

The constructs and processes of the ecological model provide conceptual pegs for transition planning. The purpose of this section is to illustrate the application of these pegs to transition planning.

Individual Constructs

As is evident in Table 6.2, most career development theories incorporate individual constructs. Individual constructs were the first part of Parsons' (1909) model of career choice, which required

> (1) a clear understanding of [one's own] ... aptitudes, abilities, interests, ambitions, resources, limitations and their causes, (2) a knowledge of the requirements and conditions of success, advantages and disadvantages, compensation opportunities, and prospects in different lines of work; [and] (3) true reasoning on the relationships of these two groups of factors. (p. 5)

Since Parsons presented his model, individual factors have remained a fairly stable part of the career theory landscape.

There is little doubt that student characteristics are potent variables in planning transition. Skills and abilities as well as the limitations resulting from disability determine, in part, the extent to which individuals will perform satisfactorily in specific jobs (Lofquist & Dawis, 1969, 1991).

Interests also play an important role in transition. For example, they influence options that are pursued (Holland, 1985), although the degree of such influence may be impeded by the lack of opportunities that often accompany disability (Hagner & Salomone, 1989) or poverty (Osipow & Littlejohn, 1995).

Both interests and abilities may pose special problems in planning transition with people with disabilities. Interests are learned (Mitchell & Krumboltz, 1990). For some students, the disability may have limited opportunities for critical learning experiences such as exposure to working role models and accompanying a parent to work. Further, current abilities may not fully reflect future potential (Vygotsky & Luria, 1993). Static assessment approaches, which are unfortunately all too common, do not reflect the fluid nature of both interests and abilities in people with disabilities (Parker, Szymanski, & Hanley-Maxwell, 1989).

Abilities and limitations are often not static in people with progressive disabilities (e.g., muscular dystrophy) (Goldman, 1993). For this population, it is important to consider future potential limitations as well as current conditions.

During transition, therefore, interventions addressing individual attributes should focus on potential. It is important to maximize abilities through education and skills training (Siegel, in Chapter 7). Similarly, functional limitations should be lessened through learning to use assistive technology and practice adaptive behaviors (e.g., learning to request needed accommodations). The ultimate goal of individual interventions is to assist students in being prepared for a wide range of potential future opportunities.

Context

Early career theories often did not reflect sufficient consideration of the influence of the context in which people live on their career development (Vondracek, Lerner, & Schulenberg, 1986; Fitzgerald & Betz, 1994). Perhaps professionals were reluctant to consider influences beyond their control (e.g., poverty, war). Nonetheless, family background (Haveman & Wolfe, 1994), including socioeconomic status (Rothman, 1987), exerts a potent influence in educational and occupational attainment.

The context factor of socioeconomic status is critically important in transition. Students attending poor schools begin their transition at significant disadvantage (Kozol, 1991). Natural disasters (e.g., floods), wars, and other nonnormative events may further influence transition (Vondracek & Schulenberg, 1992).

Unfortunately, poverty and limited opportunities are all too common among racial and ethnic minorities (Kozol, 1991; Trueba, et al., 1993). Thus, for these individuals, context factors may have potent influence in inhibiting career development (Fitzgerald & Betz, 1994).

Transition interventions must consider the contexts of students' lives. For example, families have key roles in planning and implementing transition (see, e.g., Ferguson, Ferguson, & Jones, 1988; Hanley-Maxwell, Pogoloff, & Whitney-Thomas, in Chapter 10).

Mediating Constructs

The connection between individual attributes and environmental possibilities is mediated by a wide range of individual and societal belief structures (Szymanski & Hershenson, in press), which are also important components of transition planning.

Individual mediating structures include work personality, self-efficacy, and outcome expectations. The most general of these constructs is work personality, a personal system of work motivation that develops early in life under the influence of family (Hershenson, 1981). On the more specific level, self-efficacy is belief in the ability to perform a specific task (Bandura, 1982; Hackett & Lent, 1992). It is complemented by outcome expectations, which reflect beliefs about the potential outcome of actions (Lent & Hackett, 1994).

Both disability and diversity can interact with individual mediating constructs. A particular danger is limited exposure to believable (i.e., same gender, race, disability) role models (Betz & Fitzgerald, 1995; Szymanski & Hershenson, in press). That is, if students do not see employed people to which they can relate, they may not believe that they themselves can work. Also, deficit orientations in the early years can compromise work personality and self-efficacy by discouraging personal motivation and belief in abilities (Szymanski, Turner, & Hershenson, 1992).

Culture is another potent societal mediating structure that influences transition. It is the lens or belief structure through which individuals view and make sense of their world (Trueba et al., 1993). The impact of culture is mediated by acculturation (LaFromboise et al., 1993) and racial identity (Rowe, Behrens, & Leach, 1995). In other words, an individual's racial and cultural background does not indicate the extent to which he or she identifies with minority and majority culture.

It is important to recognize that culture influences the relative acceptability of transition goals. Although independence may be an appropriate goal for European-based cultures, interdependence, community membership, and family contributions may be more important in collectivist cultures (Betz & Fitzgerald, 1995).

Environmental Constructs

A wide range of environmental constructs influence career development (Szymanski, Hershenson, et al., 1996), and thus transition. First, the following aspects of the work environment influence opportunities and possible successes: skill requirements and reinforcers (Lofquist & Dawis, 1969), the employee's work interests (Holland, 1985), the occupational structure and organizational culture of the workplace (Rothman, 1987), and the labor market (Ryan, 1996). Second, the physical nature of the workplace is of particular importance for workers with physical disabilities; thus architectural design and job accommodation can impede or facilitate access (Shaw & Linder, 1992).

Job analysis (Weed & Field, 1994) is a potent tool that can aid in transition planning. Similarly, understanding the employer's perspective and the organizational culture is absolutely vital (Millington et al., 1996). "Organizational culture" describes the rituals and customs of the workplace (Rothman, 1987). For workers with disabilities, it is critical that support structures

not impede the individual's socialization into the culture of the workplace.

Outcome Constructs

The interaction between the constructs and processes of career development results in a wide range of behaviors or states (Szymanski & Hershenson, in press). For example, "job satisfaction" characterizes the interaction of individual needs and job reinforcers, and "satisfactoriness" is the match between job requirements and individual performance (Lofquist & Dawis, 1991). Similarly, "work adjustment" is the combined behavioral outcomes for the individual constructs and processes (Hershenson, 1981), whereas "organizational productivity" is the business outcome of the combination of individual career development and human resource management (Hall, 1990).

Job stress is a particular concern for transition planning. Prolonged stress may lead to "strain," which implies physical and emotional consequences such as cardiovascular disease, decreased job performance, or marriage and family problems (Landy, 1992). Although job stress is a very complex phenomenon, there are reasons to believe that it is a major transition concern. Stress is more common in monotonous jobs in which workers perceive little or no control. In addition, social support can limit its impact (Landy, 1992). Thus, students with disabilities could conceivably be at risk both because many of the jobs they obtain afford relatively little control and some may not have well-developed social support networks or social skills to develop such networks. Finally, discrimination and prejudice, when present, may compound this risk for students of color (James, 1994).

Developmental Processes

As evidenced in Table 6.2, developmental processes have been important in many theories (Szymanski & Hershenson, in press). "Career maturity" (Crites, 1978) is an example of a construct developed to quantify a developmental process, which has been found to interact with disability (see, e.g., Biller, 1988).

Disability can interact with developmental processes (Anastasiow, 1986), although the nature of the interaction is very individual. In fact, disability could be considered a risk factor (Rojewski, 1994). Because career development is a lifelong process, disability can impact on any stage (Szymanski et al., 1992). For example, it can restrict the social skills learned from play with nondisabled peers or the work competencies learned from responsibility for chores at home or school (Szymanski, 1994). Further, because interests are learned and depend on a range of experiences (Mitchell & Krumboltz, 1990), disability can restrict interest development and contribute to artificially flattened profiles on interest inventories.

The career development constructs and processes described in this chapter interact in a developmental context throughout life. This process does not begin to stabilize until late adolescence or early adulthood (Lent, Brown, & Hackett, 1994). Thus, it is absolutely critical to ensure that interventions do not contribute to premature foreclosure on career goals (Blustein, 1992). To that end, it is important to recognize that "the transition component of the Individualized Educational Program (IEP) addresses a point in time on the career-development continuum and should expand, not restrict, the range of occupational choices available to a student" (Szymanski, 1994:404).

Decision Making

A variety of decision-making processes have been explored within and outside the context of career development theories (Szymanski & Hershenson, in press). Essentially, these processes assist individuals in developing alternatives (Brown, 1990a). Decision making is a skill that must be learned and nurtured during transition.

Disability or the circumstances associated with disability may limit opportunities to learn or practice decision making. Fortunately, devel-

opments in the area of consumer choice (see, e.g., West & Parent, 1992) and self-determination (Wehmeyer, 1992) have promoted important decision-making skills. Similarly, Hagner and Salomone (1989) have recommended the following approaches to facilitating decision making among persons with developmental disabilities: "(a) guided job experiences, (b) decision making training, (c) technical assistance within the decision-making process, and (d) longitudinal career services" (p. 155).

Career planning is an active process. Successful interventions involve consumers in learning about themselves, exploring occupations and the labor market, generating and evaluating alternatives, and making and implementing a plan of action (Oliver & Spokane, 1988; Ettinger, 1995; Szymanski, Hershenson et al., 1996). Unfortunately, in the quest to keep students from falling through the cracks, they are often "placed" in jobs, provided with printouts of matched jobs, and otherwise made passive participants in the process. In the long run, such passive interventions are likely to backfire.

It is important to remember that

> any particular career decision … is merely a single instance in a lifetime of career choice points. Unless we plan to work with an increasingly dependent client again and again across the decades, *our professional responsibility is to assure that each person learns the* [career planning] *process.* (Mastie, 1994:37)

All career planning is not deliberate decision making. Chance is a potent force. If students learn good planning skills, they will be able to see and evaluate the opportunities that come by chance in order to obtain or advance in employment (Cabral & Salomone, 1990).

Congruence

Trait factor or person–environment interaction theories rely on the correspondence or congruence of individual attributes with environmental characteristics (Szymanski & Hershenson, in press). As noted in Table 6.2, this group includes the Minnesota Theory of Work Adjustment (Lofquist & Dawis, 1969), Holland's Theory (1985), and Trait and Trait-Factor Theory (Brown, 1990c).

Congruence processes have been prevalent in rehabilitation and special education (Hershenson & Szymanski, 1992). For example, the job-matching processes that are common in rehabilitation and supported employment are direct applications of this process. Unfortunately, however, there some limitations in the application of these processes to people with disabilities. First, they are dependent on valid measurement of individual traits, which may present a challenge for some individuals with disabilities (Parker et al., 1989) when not considered in an ecological framework (Parker & Schaller, 1996). Similarly, in considering environments, it is important to include consideration of barrier removal and job accommodation.

One final consideration in the application of congruence processes is warranted. As mentioned, culture influences the relative acceptability of transition goals. Similarly, for some Latinas, self-efficacy and social class may limit the extent to which they consider career opportunities that are otherwise tenable (Arbona, 1995). It is possible that the same limitations exist for people with disabilities.

Socialization

Socialization is a powerful career development process that has been overlooked in some theories (Szymanski & Hershenson, in press), despite considerable evidence of its potency (see, e.g., Haveman & Wolfe, 1994). It "includes both deliberate attempts to inculcate values and perspectives as well as the unintentional but systematic differences in experiences associated with structural position and group membership—parental occupation and social class, gender, and race and ethnicity" (Rothman, 1987:254).

Both disability itself and the attitudes of parents and professionals can impact socialization

(Gove, 1976; Salifos-Rothschild, 1976). In planning transition, it is important to examine the extent to which students have been socialized to expect or pursue less than their potential.

Allocation

Allocation is a related process, which is important to career development and reflected in some theories (Szymanski & Hershenson, in press). It is the process by which gatekeepers (e.g., parents, teachers, counselors, personnel directors) channel people "in certain directions on the basis of externally imposed criteria such as gender, race, and social class" (Rothman, 1987:254). Special education, in itself, is an allocation process that impacts on later opportunities. Similarly, teachers, counselors, and other professionals serve as gatekeepers, who may, at times, enforce societal norms by channeling people with disabilities into specific types of opportunities (McKnight, 1977; Szymanski et al., 1995). It is important that transition professionals recognize the potency of their gatekeeper role and work to assist students and their families to take active control over their career plans.

Chance Processes

As is evident from Table 6.2, the impact of chance on career development has been addressed in some career development theories. Chance events and encounters contribute to career development and thereby to transition. The extent and direction of their impact are determined by the context in which they occur and their timing in relationship to development (Cabral & Salomone, 1990). "The ability to cope successfully with unforeseen events or encounters depends, in large part, on the strength of the individual's self-concept and sense of internal (or enabling) control" (Cabral & Salomone, 1990:14). Transition interventions, especially those that support self-efficacy and teach planning skills, can help students to recognize and capitalize on chance.

CAREER DEVELOPMENT ASSESSMENT AND INTERVENTION

It is not sufficient to understand career development. Transition professionals must also work to facilitate their students' positive career development. The chapters in the last part of this book provide excellent guides for assessment and career development intervention. The purpose of this section is to complement those chapters by illustrating the connection between assessment and interventions and the ecological model of career development through a discussion of (a) career workshops and portfolios, and (b) connecting assessment and intervention to the ecological model.

Career Workshops and Portfolios

Career workshops and portfolios are interventions that integrate the gains from both skills training and counseling interventions. The Rehabilitation Research and Training Center (RRTC) on Career Development and Advancement at the University of Wisconsin–Madison tested these interventions with a wide range of consumers with physical and learning disabilities (Szymanski, 1995). Initial results were favorable, suggesting further study and potential applications in school-to-work transition. For this reason, the interventions are briefly described in the following paragraphs.

Career Workshops. Research has suggested that career workshops can be effective for people without disabilities (Oliver & Spokane, 1988) as well as people with disabilities (Bolton & Ackridge, 1995). Studies at the RRTC demonstrated that such workshops were considered beneficial by independent living consumers (Enright, 1997) and college students with and without disabilities (Conyers & Szymanski, in press). In addition, college students with and without disabilities decreased their career indecision and increased career decision making self-efficacy (Conyers & Szymanski, in press).

Workshops can vary in length from 10 hours to a full semester or year. Generally, longer workshops have been found to be more effective (Oliver & Spokane, 1988). In the college setting, Conyer's 10-hour workshop, which was presented over 4 weeks, included the following elements:

(a) exercises for interest and value assessment; (b) introduction to academic and career resources; (c) use of the Career Visions [Wisconsin Career Information Systems, 1994] program for exploration of interests and their relation to possible occupations; (d) consideration of career beliefs and transferable and self-management skills; and (e) instruction and practice in goal setting, decision-making, and problem-solving. (Conyers & Szymanski, in press)

Keys to effective career workshops are *active involvement* of consumers in (a) gathering information, including self-assessment and learning about occupations and the labor market; (b) generating alternative courses of action and weighing those alternatives (i.e., decision making); and (c) formulating plans of action (Oliver & Spokane, 1988; Phillips, 1992). Homework and group activities are also vital.

Workshops must actively involve students in learning to understand themselves and the world around them. In addition, career workshops offer valuable opportunities for students to engage parents, relatives, and friends in discussions about career possibilities.

The content of career workshops can be divided into three broad sections: self-assessment, learning about work, and decision making and planning. Self-assessment topics can include interest inventories, summaries of work histories, consideration of assets and transferable skills, assessment of work values, development of financial goals, and consideration of potential incentives and disincentives (e.g., social security work incentives). In addressing the labor market, students can explore print or computer occupational information, interview friends and families about work requirements, do job shadowing, and engage in informational interviews. Potential decision-making and planning topics include strategies for generating alternatives, decision-making processes and worksheets, evaluation of barriers, planning strategies, planning for advancement, and guarding against demoralization (Szymanski, Fernandez, et al., 1996).

There are some excellent sources of materials that can be adapted for career workshops with students with disabilities. I do not recommend a "canned" curriculum. Rather, I suggest reviewing materials within the parameters of the three sections (i.e., self-assessment, learning about work, decision making and planning). Two particularly potent sources for workshop materials are Hecklinger and Black's (1994) *Training for Life* (Kendall/Hunt Publishing Company; 4050 Westmark Drive; P.O. Box 1840; Dubuque, IA 52004-1840) and the wide range of materials and curricula (e.g., Ettinger, 1995) available from the Center for Education and Work; University of Wisconsin-Madison; Room 964, 1025 W. Johnson Street; Madison, WI 53706.

It is not possible to emphasize too heavily the importance of active student involvement in career planning. In order for students to learn the skills necessary for their future planning, they must learn and practice the component skills included in career workshops. As teachers and counselors, we are responsible for ensuring that these critical planning skills are learned, practiced, and maintained.

Career Portfolios. The use of student portfolios for assessment has been a topic of considerable discussion in education. Similar discussion has emerged in career counseling (McDivitt, 1994). In addition, some discussion of career portfolio assessment has emerged in special education (Sarkees-Wircenski & Wircenski, 1994).

The career portfolio concept can be applied both to planning and assessment. Integrating experiences, skills, values, and potential alternatives is a challenge for everyone, not just students with disabilities. Portfolios have long served as integrative repositories of the work of artists.

Similarly, in higher education, professors assemble compilations of many aspects of their work in preparation for tenure reviews or merit evaluation. In addition to providing evidence for others of specific accomplishments, portfolios help individuals to review their own work in a broader context.

The RRTC workshops have included use of a career portfolio. The primary purpose of career portfolios used by the RRTC has not been assessment. Rather it has been to assist consumers in assembling and integrating relevant career information. In addition, the portfolios have served as tangible evidence of the career planning process that has been learned in the workshops and hopefully will be practiced for many years to come.

Sections of the portfolio can be organized around the same sections as the career workshops (i.e., self-assessment, learning about work, decision making and planning). Other sections (e.g., community resources) can be added as needed, with the specific organization and contents guided by the teacher or counselor. In addition, the portfolio can include samples of student work, résumés, sample employment applications, and names and addresses of references (Koch & Johnston-Rodriguez, in press; Szymanski, Fernandez, et al., 1996). In essence, the portfolio is a flexible tool that provides students with tangible evidence of the career planning process, and in so doing, facilitates continued self-assessment and planning.

Connecting Assessment and Intervention to the Ecological Model

The major impetus for developing the five-factor and six-process ecological model for career development was to provide practitioners with conceptual pegs for planning intervention (Szymanski, Hershenson, et al., 1996; Szymanski & Hershenson, in press). Although researchers (including this author) enjoy the scientific benefits afforded by multiple theories, this complex theoretical landscape has presented many obstacles to practitioners. Indeed, it may have limited the extent to which critical theoretical considerations (e.g., the developmental process and the consequent importance of not forcing early career goals) have been incorporated into practice.

The ecological model provides a guide for understanding and planning transition. Because individuals are so very different, it cannot offer a blueprint. Rather, each part of the model is an aspect of the ecological system surrounding a student's transition from school to work. The five groups of constructs and six processes provide focal points for assessment questions and interventions. Table 6.3 illustrates some questions and interventions according to the components of the model.

It is important to note that the questions and interventions included in Table 6.3 are not exhaustive. Rather they are illustrative. In other words, for each group of constructs and each process, there are four basic questions:

1. How can the student's current and past situation be described according to this construct or process?

2. What are the student's goals in relationship to this construct or process?

3. How can the student take active ownership of career planning and positive career development in relationship to this construct or process?

4. How can we help and empower without creating dependence?

CONCLUSION

Career development is a lifelong process. Although transition is but a road stop on the career development highway, it is one in which the services can either promote or impede the rest of the journey. The role of transition professionals is to facilitate the career development journey by teaching the skills and planning processes that promote self-determination and positive career development.

QUESTIONS

1. Describe the relationship between career development and transition.

2. Describe the constructs that underlie career development theories.

3. Describe the processes that underlie career development theories.

4. Discuss the applicability of career development theories to people with disabilities and minorities.

5. Explain why it is important for students to learn career planning processes.

6. Discuss career portfolios and their potential uses in the setting in which you work or plan to work.

7. Discuss career workshops and their potential uses in the setting in which you work or plan to work.

8. Career planning requires active consumer involvement. Explain this statement and discuss ways in which interventions in your current or potential future setting facilitate or impede this active involvement.

9. Explain why it is important for transition professionals to understand career development processes.

10. Based on our understanding of career development, what considerations should guide the transition component of IEP?

REFERENCES

Anastasiow, N. J. (1986). *Development and disability: A psychobiological analysis for special educators.* Baltimore: Paul H. Brookes.

Arbona, C. (1995). Theory and research on racial and ethnic minorities: Hispanic Americans. In F. T. L. Leong (Ed.), *Career development and vocational behavior of racial and ethnic minorities* (pp. 37–66). Mahwah, NJ: Lawrence Erlbaum.

Bandura, A. (1982). Self-efficacy mechanism in human agency. *American Psychologist, 37,* 122–147.

Betz, N. E., & Fitzgerald, L. F. (1995). Career assessment and intervention with racial and ethnic minorities. In F. T. L. Leong (Ed.), *Career development and*

Table 6.3 Assessment Questions and Interventions According to the Constructs and Processes of the Ecological Model of Career Development

INDIVIDUAL CONSTRUCTS

Questions	Possible Interventions
What are current abilities, interests, and limitations?	Active involvement in self-assessment
How are these perceived by the consumer and family?	Career portfolio
What skills have been learned as a result of education or work experience?	Career portfolio
What values are considered important to career planning by the consumer and by the family?	Career portfolio
Has the consumer had sufficient experiences to foster interest development?	Volunteer and paid work experience
How can individual abilities be enhanced?	Skill training, further education, job supports
How can limitations be lessened?	Assistive technology, job accommodation

CONTEXTUAL CONSTRUCTS

How have family background and neighborhood influenced perception of opportunities and responsibilities?	Work role models, mentors, chores, work experience, community empowerment
How has education facilitated or impeded realization of potential?	Remedial education
What are the financial incentives or disincentives perceived by the individual nd family as associated with work?	Inclusion of financial considerations in career planning

MEDIATING CONSTRUCTS

How does the consumer perceive her or his work-related abilities?	Career counseling, successful work experiences
What outcomes does the consumer expect from employment preparation or rehabilitation?	Appropriate role from models, mentors
What are the consumer's abilities in career planning?	Career classes and workshops, career counselng
What are the consumer's and family's cultural and religious beliefs that relate to education and work?	Culturally sensitive career planning, culturally sensitive career portfolios
How has the consumer been impacted by discrimination or stereotypes?	Advocacy

ENVIRONMENTAL CONSTRUCTS

How physically accessible are various target environments?	Consultation on barrier removal, assistive technology, job accommodation, consideration of alternate environments
What is the organizational culture of the target work environment? Does the consumer understand how to get along in such a culture?	Job analysis, social skills training

(continued)

Table 6.3   *(continued)*

Questions	Possible Interventions
ENVIRONMENTAL CONSTRUCTS	
How has the consumer gotten along in previous work or school environments?	Social skills training, job coaching
What are the tasks of the environment?	Job analysis
What are the reinforcements?	Job analysis, planning for career advancment
OUTCOME CONSTRUCTS	
How well do the consumer's skills and behaviors meet the requirements of possible work environments?	Additional training, on-the-job training, social skills training
How well do the reinforcements of the work environment meet the consumer's needs?	Additional training for career advancement, possible job change
Has the consumer experienced job-related stress?	Stress-reduction techniques
How well is the student equipped to cope with job-related stress?	Wellness planning, encouragement to use social support, leisure and life-style planning
CONGRUENCE OR CORRESPONDENCE PROCESSES	
Is the consumer aware of potential job accommodation or assistive devices? Have these possibilities been considered?	Discussion and exploration of acommodations possibilities and assisted devices
Have ability scores been lowered by problems of construct validity?	Ecological or qualitative problems of approaches to measurement
Is social class or self-efficacy limiting the types of occupations considered?	Enrichment experiences, occupations role models
DECISION-MAKING PROCESSES	
What are the cultural practices of the consumer and her or his family relating to decision making and indepencence?	Incorporate the consumer's culture into interventions and goals, involve appropriate family members if appropriate
What are the consumer's skills and experiences related to making choices	Decision-making training, assistance with identifying alternatives and making choices, multiple-trial work experiences
DEVELOPMENTAL PROCESSES	
Has disability limited developmental experiences?	Longitudinal approach to career planning, cautious approach to interpretation of interest measures
Has social skill development been limited?	Social skill training
Has work personality and work competency development been impeded?	Chores, supervised work experiences
SOCIALIZATION PROCESSES	
How have socialization processes affected the consumer's current role or consideration of future roles?	Enrichment experiences, role models, psychoeducational interventions

(continued)

Table 6.3   *(continued)*

Questions	Possible Interventions
ALLOCATION PROCESSES	
Have opportunities been limited by gatekeeping functions in education, rehabilitation, or other services delivery systems?	Remedial education, mentoring, enrichment programs, special recruitment programs
Do the requirements or processes of current service delivery programs restrict options, create dependency, or otherwise disempower?	Empowerment evaluation, capacity-building intervention
CHANCE PROCESSES	
Is the consumer prepared to recognize and capitalize on chance opportunities?	Career-planning workshops, career portfolio

Sources: Reprinted from "Career Development of People with Disabilities: An Ecological Model," by E. M. Szymanski & D. B. Hershenson, in press, in R. M. Parker & E. M. Szymanski (Eds.), *Rehabilitation Counseling: Basics and Beyond* (3rd ed.). Copyright by PRO-ED. Reprinted with permission.

Content was also adapted from "Career Development: Planning for Placement" by E. M. Szymanski, D. Fernandez, L. Koch, & M. Merz, 1996. University of Wisconsin-Madison, Rehabilitation Research and Training Center on Career Development and Advancement.

vocational behavior of racial and ethnic minorities (pp. 263–279). Mahwah, NJ: Lawrence Erlbaum.

Biller, E. F. (1988). Career decision-making attitudes of college students with learning disabilities. *Journal of Postsecondary Education and Disability, 6*(4), 14–20.

Blustein, D. L. (1992). Applying current theory and research in career exploration to practice. *Career Development Quarterly, 41,* 174–184.

Bolton, B., & Akridge, R. L. (1995). A meta-analysis of skills training programs for rehabilitation clients. *Rehabilitation Counseling Bulletin, 38,* 262–273.

Brodwin, M., Parker, R. M., & DeLaGarza, D. (1996). Disability and accommodation. In E. M. Szymanski & R. M. Parker (Eds.), *Work and disability: Issues and strategies in career development and job placement* (pp. 165–207). Austin, TX: PRO-ED.

Bronfenbrenner, U. (1988). Foreword. In A. R. Pence (Ed.), *Ecological research with children and families: From concepts to methodology* (pp. ix–xix). New York: Teachers College Press.

Brown, D. (1990a). Models of career decision-making. In D. Brown, L. Brooks, & Associates, *Career choice and development: Applying contemporary theories to practice* (2nd ed.) (pp. 395–421). San Francisco: Jossey-Bass.

———. (1990b). Summary, comparison, and critique of the major theories. In D. Brown, L. Brooks, et al., *Career choice and development: Applying contemporary theories to practice* (2nd ed.) (pp. 338–363). San Francisco: Jossey-Bass.

———. (1990c). Trait and factor theory. In D. Brown, L. Brooks, et al., *Career choice and development: Applying contemporary theories to practice* (2nd ed.) (pp. 13–36). San Francisco: Jossey-Bass.

Brown, D., & Brooks, L. (1984). Preface. In D. Brown, L. Brooks, et al., *Career choice and development: Applying contemporary theories to practice* (pp. ix–xii). San Francisco: Jossey-Bass.

———. (1990). Introductions to career development: Origins, evolution, and current approaches. In D. Brown, L. Brooks, et al., *Career choice and development: Applying contemporary theories to practice* (2nd ed.) (pp. 1–12). San Francisco: Jossey-Bass.

Brown, D., Brooks, L., et al., (1996). *Career choice and development* (3rd ed.). San Francisco: Jossey-Bass.

Cabral, A. C., & Salomone, P. R. (1990). Chance and careers: Normative versus contextual development. *Career Development Quarterly, 39,* 5–17.

Conyers, L., & Szymanski, E. M. (In press). The effectiveness of an integrated career intervention for college students with and without disabilities. *Journal of Post Seconday Education and Disability.*

Crites, J. O. (1978). *Career maturity inventory.* Monterey, CA: CTB/McGraw-Hill.

Curnow, T. C. (1989). Vocational development of persons with disability. *Vocational Guidance Quarterly 37,* 269–278.

Dawis, R. V. (1994). The theory of work adjustment as convergent theory. In M. L. Savickas & R. W. Lent

(Eds.), *Convergence in career development theories: Implications for science and practice* (pp. 33–43). Palo Alto, CA: CPP.

Dawis, R. V., & Lofquist, L. H. (1984). *A psychological theory of work adjustment.* Minneapolis: University of Minnesota Press.

Enright, M. S. (1997). The impact of a short-term career development program for people with disabilities. *Rehabilitation Counseling Bulletin, 40,* 285–300.

Ettinger, J. M. (1995). *A guide to planning and implementing effective career development programs for school-to-work transitions.* Madison: University of Wisconsin, Center for Education and Work.

Ferguson, P. M., Ferguson, D. L., & Jones, D. (1988). Generations of hope: Parental perspectives on the transitions of their children with severe disabilities from school to adult life. *Journal of the Association for Persons with Severe Handicaps, 13,* 177–187.

Fitzgerald, L. F., & Betz, N. E. (1994). Career development in cultural context: The role of gender, race, class, and sexual orientation. In M. L. Savickas & R. W. Lent (Eds.), *Convergence in career development theories: Implications for science and practice* (pp. 103–117). Palo Alto, CA: CPP.

Goldman, J. (1993). Neurological conditions. In M. G. Brodwin, F. Tellez, & S. K. Brodwin (Eds.), *Medical, psychosocial, and vocational aspects of disability* (pp. 421–437). Athens, GA: Elliot & Fitzpatrick.

Gove, W. R. (1976). Social reaction theory and disability. In G. L. Albrecht (Ed.), *The sociology of physical disability and rehabilitation* (pp. 57–71). Pittsburgh: University of Pittsburgh Press.

Gutteridge, T. G., Leibowitz, Z. B., & Shore, J. E. (1993). *Organizational career development: Benchmarks for building a world-class workforce.* San Francisco: Jossey-Bass.

Hackett, G., & Lent, R. W. (1992). Theoretical advances and current inquiry in career psychology. In S. D. Brown & R. W. Lent (Eds.), *Handbook of counseling psychology* (2nd ed.) (pp. 419–451). New York: Wiley.

Hagner, D., & Salomone, P. (1989). Issues in career decision-making for workers with developmental disabilities. *Career Development Quarterly, 38,* 148–159.

Hall, D. T. (1990). Career development theory in organizations. In D. Brown, L. Brooks, et al., *Career choice and development: Applying contemporary theories to practice* (pp. 422–454). San Francisco: Jossey-Bass.

Haveman, R., & Wolfe, B. (1994). *Succeeding generations: On the investment in children.* New York: Russell Sage Foundation.

Hecklinger, F. J., & Black, B. M. (1994). *Training for life: A practical guide to career and life planning* (5th ed.). Dubuque, IA: Kendall/Hunt.

Herr, E. L., & Cramer, S. H. (1992). *Career guidance and counseling through the lifespan: Systematic approaches* (4th ed.). New York: HarperCollins.

Hershenson, D. B. (1981). Work adjustment, disability, and the three r's of vocational rehabilitation: A conceptual model. *Rehabilitation Counseling Bulletin, 25,* 91–97.

———. (1996). A systems reformulation of a developmental model of work adjustement. *Rehabilitation Counseling Bulletin, 40,* 2–10.

Hershenson, D., & Szymanski, E. M. (1992). Career development of people with disabilities. In R. M. Parker & E. M. Szymanski (Eds.), *Rehabilitation counseling: Basics and beyond* (2nd ed.) (pp. 273–303). Austin, TX: PRO-ED.

Holland, J. L. (1985). *Making vocational choices: A theory of vocational personalities and work environments.* Englewood Cliffs, NJ: Prentice Hall.

———. (1994). Separate but unequal is better. In M. L. Savickas & R. W. Lent (Eds.), *Convergence in career development theories: Implications for science and practice* (pp. 45–51). Palo Alto, CA: CPP.

Hotchkiss, L., & Borow, H. (1990). Sociological perspectives on work and career development. In D. Brown, L. Brooks, et al., *Career choice and development: Applying contemporary theories to practice* (2nd ed.) (pp. 262–307). San Francisco: Jossey-Bass.

James, K. (1994). Social identity, work stress, and minority worker's health. In G. P. Keita & J. J. Hurrell, Jr. (Eds.), *Job stress in a changing workforce: Investigating gender, diversity, and family issues* (pp. 127–145). Washington, DC: American Psychological Association.

Kerlinger, F. N. (1986). *Foundations of behavioral research* (3rd ed.). New York: Holt, Rinehart & Winston.

Koch, L., & Johnston-Rodriguez, E. M. (In press). The career portfolio: A vocational rehabilitation tool for assessment, planning, and placement. *Journal of Job Placement,* Madison: University of Wisconsin.

Kozol, J. (1991). *Savage inequalities: Children in America's schools.* New York: Crown.

Krumboltz, J. D. (1994). Improving career development theory from a social learning perspective. In M. L. Savickas & R. W. Lent (Eds.), *Convergence in career development theories: Implications for science and practice* (pp. 9–31). Palo Alto, CA: CPP.

LaFromboise, T., Coleman, H. L. K., & Gerton, J. (1993). Psychological impact of biculturalism: Evidence and theory. *Psychological Bulletin, 114,* 395–412.

Landy, F. J. (1992). Work design and stress. In G. P. Keita & S. L. Sauter (Eds.), *Work and well being: An agenda for the 1990s* (pp. 119–158). Washington, DC: American Psychological Association.

Lee, C. C., & Richardson, B. R. (Eds.). (1991). *Multicultural issues in counseling: New approaches to diversity.* Alexandria, VA: American Counseling Association.

Lent, R. W., Brown, S. D., & Hackett, G. (1994). Toward a unifying social cognitive theory of career and academic interest, choice, and performance. *Journal of Vocational Behavior, 45,* 79–122.

Lent, R. W., & Hackett, G. (1994). Sociocognitive mechanisms of personal agency in career development: Pan theoretical prospects. In M. L. Savickas & R. W. Lent (Eds.), *Convergence in career development: Implications for science and practice* (pp. 77–101). Palo Alto, CA: CPP.

Leong, F. T. L. (Ed.). (1995). *Career development and vocational behavior of racial and ethnic minorities.* Mahwah, NJ: Lawrence Erlbaum.

Lewin, K. (1936). *Principals of topological psychology.* New York: McGraw-Hill.

Lofquist, L. H., & Dawis, R. V. (1969). *Adjustment to work: A psychological view of man's problems in a work-oriented society.* New York: Appleton-Century-Crofts.

———. (1991). *Essentials of person environment correspondence counseling.* Minneapolis: University of Minnesota Press.

Mastie, M. M. (1994). Using assessment instruments in career counseling: Career assessment as compass, credential, process and empowerment. In J. T. Kapes, M. M. Mastie, & E. A. Whitfield (Eds.), *A counselor's guide to career assessment instruments* (3rd ed.) (pp. 31–40). Alexandria, VA: National Career Development Association.

McDivitt, P. J. (1994). Using portfolios for career assessment. In J. T. Kapes, M. M. Mastie, & E. A. Whitfield (Eds.), *A counselor's guide to career assessment instruments* (3rd ed.) (pp. 361–371). Alexandria, VA: National Career Development Association.

McKnight, J. (1977). Professionalized service and disabling help. In I. Illich, I. K. Zola, J. McKnight, J. Caplan, & H. Shaiken, *Disabling professions* (pp. 69–91). London: Marion Boyars.

Miller-Tiedeman, A., & Tiedeman, D. V. (1990). Career decision-making: An individualistic perspective. In D. Brown, L. Brooks, et al., *Career choice and development: Applying contemporary theories to practice* (2nd ed.) (pp. 308–337). San Francisco: Jossey-Bass.

Millington, M. J., Asner, K. K., Linkowski, D. C., & Der-Stepanian, J. (1996). Employers and job development: The business perspective. In E. M. Szymanski & R. M. Parker (Eds.), *Work and disability: Issues and strategies in career development and job placement* (pp. 277–308). Austin, TX: PRO-ED.

Mitchell, L. K., & Krumboltz, J. D. (1990). Social learning approach to career decision-making: Krumboltz's theory. In D. Brown, L. Brooks, et al., *Career choice and development: Applying contemporary theories to practice* (2nd ed.) (pp. 145–196). San Francisco: Jossey-Bass.

Oliver, L. W., & Spokane, A. R. (1988). Client-intervention outcome: What contributes to client gain? *Journal of Counseling Psychology, 35,* 447–462.

Osipow, S. H. (1994). Moving career theory into the twenty-first century. In M. L. Savickas & R. W. Lent (Eds.), *Convergence in career development theories: Implications for science and practice* (pp. 217–224). Palo Alto, CA: CPP.

Osipow, S. H., & Littlejohn, E. M. (1995). Toward a multicultural theory of career development: Prospects and dilemmas. In F. T. L. Leong (Ed.), *Career development and vocational behavior of racial and ethnic minorities* (pp. 251–261). Mahwah, NJ: Lawrence Erlbaum.

Parker, R. M., & Schaller, J. L. (1996). Issues in vocational assessment and disability. In E. M. Szymanski & R. M. Parker (Eds.), *Work and disability: Issues and strategies in career development and job placement* (pp. 127–164). Austin, TX: PRO-ED.

Parker, R. M., Szymanski, E. M., & Hanley-Maxwell, C. (1989). Ecological assessment in supported employment. *Journal of Applied Rehabilitation Counseling, 20*(3), 26–33.

Parsons, F. (1909). *Choosing a vocation.* Boston: Houghton Mifflin.

Phillips, S. D. (1992). Career counseling: Choice and implementation. In S. D. Brown & R. W. Lent (Eds.), *Handbook of counseling psychology* (2nd ed.) (pp. 513–547). New York: Wiley.

Roe, A., & Lunneborg, P. W. (1990). Personality development and career choice. In D. Brown, L. Brooks, et. al., *Career choice and development: Applying contemporary theories to practice* (2nd ed.) (pp. 68–101). San Francisco: Jossey-Bass.

Rojewski, J. W. (1994). Applying theories of career behavior to special populations: Implications for secondary vocational transition programming.

Issues in Special Education and Rehabilitation, 9(1), 7–26.

Rothman, R. A. (1987). *Working: Sociological perspectives.* Englewood Cliffs, NJ: Prentice Hall.

Rowe, W., Behrens, J. T., & Leach, M. M. (1995). Racial/ethnic identity and racial consciousness: Looking back and looking forward. In J. G. Ponterotto, J. M. Casas, L. A. Suzuki, & C. M. Alexander (Eds.), *Handbook of multicultural counseling* (pp. 218–235). Thousand Oaks, CA: Sage.

Ryan, C. P. (1996). Work isn't what it used to be: Implications, recommendations, and strategies for vocational rehabilitation. *Journal of Rehabilitation, 61*(4), 8–15.

Salifos-Rothschild, C. (1976). Disabled persons' self-definitions and their implications for rehabilitation. In G. L. Albrecht (Ed.), *The sociology of physical disability and rehabilitation* (pp. 39–56). Pittsburgh: University of Pittsburgh Press.

Sarkees-Wircenski, M., & Wircenski, J. L. (1994). Transition planning: Developing a career portfolio for students with disabilities. *Career Development for Exceptional Individuals, 17,* 203–214.

Savickas, M. L., & Lent, R. W. (Eds.). (1994a). *Convergence in career development theories: Implications for science and practice.* Palo Alto, CA: CPP.

Savickas, M. L., & Lent, R. W. (1994b). Introduction: A convergence project for career psychology. In M. L. Savickas & R. W. Lent (Eds.), *Convergence in career development theories: Implications for science and practice* (pp. 1–6). Palo Alto, CA: CPP.

Schein, E. H. (1986). A critical look at current career development theory and research. In D. T. Hall et al. (Eds.), *Career development in organizations* (pp. 310–331). San Francisco: Jossey-Bass.

Shaw, L., & Linder, G. C. (1992). Resources for accommodation. In N. Hablutzel & B. T. McMahon (Eds.), *The Americans with Disabilities Act: Access and accommodations* (pp. 273–290). Orlando, FL: Paul M. Deutsch Press.

Sue, D. W., & Sue, D. (1990). *Counseling the culturally different: Theory and practice* (2nd ed.). New York: Wiley.

Super, D. E. (1990). A life-span, life-space approach to career development. In D. Brown, L. Brooks, et. al., (Eds.), *Career choice and development: Applying contemporary theories to practice* (2nd ed.) (pp. 197–261). San Francisco: Jossey-Bass.

Szymanski, E. M. (1994). Transition: Life-span, life-space considerations for empowerment. *Exceptional Children, 60,* 402–410.

———. (1995). *Project report.* Madison: University of Wisconsin, Rehabilitation Research and Training Center on Career Development and Advancement.

———. (In press). School to work transition: Ecological considerations for career development. In W. E. Martin & J. L. Swartz (Eds.), *Applied ecological psychological for schools within communities: Assessment and intervention.* Hillsdale, NJ: Lawrence Erlbaum.

Szymanski, E. M., Fernandez, D., Koch, L., & Merz, M. A. (1996). *Career development: Planning for placement.* Training materials. Madison: University of Wisconsin, Rehabilitation Research and Training Center on Career Development and Advancement.

Szymanski, E. M., & Hanley-Maxwell, C. (1996). Career development of people with developmental disabilities: An ecological model. *Journal of Rehabilitation, 62*(1), 48–55.

Szymanski, E. M., & Hershenson, D. B. (In press). Career development of people with disabilities: An ecological model. In R. M. Parker & E. M. Szymanski (Eds.), *Rehabilitation counseling: Basics and beyond* (3rd ed.). Austin, TX: PRO-ED.

Szymanski, E. M., Hershenson, D. B., Enright, M. S., & Ettinger, J. (1996). Career development theories, constructs, and research: Implications for people with disabilities. In E. M. Szymanski & R. M. Parker (Eds.), *Work and disability: Issues and strategies in career development and job placement* (pp. 79–126). Austin, TX: PRO-ED.

Szymanski, E. M., Hershenson, D. B., Ettinger, J., & Enright, M. S. (1996). Career development interventions for people with disabilities. In E. M. Szymanski & R. M. Parker (Eds.), *Work and disability: Issues and strategies in career development and job placement* (pp. 255–276). Austin, TX: PRO-ED.

Szymanski, E. M., Johnston-Rodriguez, S., Millington, M. J., Rodriguez, B. H., & Lagergren, J. (1995). The paradoxical nature of disability services: Illustrations from supported employment and implications for rehabilitation counseling. *Journal of Applied Rehabilitation Counseling, 26*(2), 17–22.

Szymanski, E. M., Turner, K. D., & Hershenson, D. (1992). Career development of people with disabilities: Theoretical perspectives. In F. R. Rusch, L. DeStefano, J. Chadsey-Rusch, L. A. Phelps, & E. M. Szymanski (Eds.), *Transition from school to adult life: Models, linkages, and policy* (pp. 391–406). Sycamore, IL: Sycamore.

Trueba, H. T., Rodriguez, C., Zou, Y., & Cintron, J. (1993). *Healing multicultural America: Mexican immi-*

grants rise to power in rural California. London: Falmer Press.

Vondracek, F. W., & Fouad, N. A. (1994). Developmental contextualism: An integrative framework for theory and practice. In M. L. Savickas & R. W. Lent (Eds.), *Convergence in career development: Implications for science and practice* (pp. 207–214). Palo Alto, CA: CPP.

Vondracek, F. W., Lerner, R. M., & Schulenberg, J. E. (1986). *Career development: A life span developmental approach.* Hillsdale, NJ: Lawrence Erlbaum.

Vondracek, F. W., & Schulenberg, J. (1992). Counseling for normative and nonnormative influences on career development. *Career Development Quarterly, 40,* 291–301.

Vygotsky, L. S., & Luria, A. R. (1993). *Studies on the history of behavior: Ape, primitive, and child* (V. I. Golod & J. E. Knox, Trans. and Ed.). Hillsdale, NJ: Lawrence Erlbaum. (Original work published in 1930.)

Weed, R. O., & Field, T. F. (1994). *Rehabilitation consultant's handbook* (rev. ed.). Athens, GA: Elliot & Fitzpatrick.

Wehmeyer, M. L. (1992). Self-determination and the education of students with mental retardation. *Education and Training in Mental Retardation, 27,* 303–314.

West, M. D., & Parent, W. S. (1992). Consumer choice and empowerment in supported employment services: Issues and strategies. *Journal of the Association of Persons with Severe Handicaps, 17,* 47–52.

Wisconsin Career Information System. (1994). *Career visions.* Madison: University of Wisconsin, Center on Education and Work.

7

◉

Foundations for a School-to-Work System That Serves All Students

SHEPHERD SIEGEL

This chapter presents a review of the intent of the School-to-Work Opportunities Act. A model is then proposed that describes five intensity levels of transition services that a comprehensive school-to-work system must have if it is to serve all students. By using the guiding principle of citizenship in a democracy, school-to-work transition is discussed in the context of the broader educational mission. The chapter concludes with a discussion of the concept of full *engagement* (versus full employment) as one that will better serve the needs of citizens and society in the twenty-first century. If students can articulate a sense of identity, of place in the community, and a means of engagement, then we can embark on a path to the future where young citizens are not tracked into job placement in a predetermined future economy, but are the self-determined architects of that future.

When addressing the issues surrounding school-to-work transition for students with special needs, it is tempting and convenient to view the subject as a separate niche in the field of education, a neat compartment, a specialty. But a just explanation of how to serve the career needs of youths in special populations taps into the crux of what public education is all about. "What is the purpose of education?" "How shall all students be served?" and "What are the criteria for a universal pedagogy?" are questions that must be addressed before building a school-to-work system. Consciously or unconsciously, all social institutions are built on paradigms that, for better or worse, answer these questions. School-to-work is no exception. The exceptionalities special needs students bring to the educational arena provide a test of the justice, viability, and usefulness of any educational reform movement. They present the possibilities that must inform any attempts to create a system for all students.

In this chapter, we will address the immediate tasks facing educators and society at large. A review of the principles of the School-to-Work Opportunities Act and the challenges it presents is followed by a model that proposes five intensity levels of transition services that, if implemented, would improve the school-to-adult life transitions of all students. A brief discussion of the overall purpose of education prepares the way for a curriculum postulate whereby the educational experience expects the student to be able to answer three questions: "Who am I?" "What is my community?" and "How do I engage in a meaningful way?" This chapter will make the case that the core of a superior education is not academics or vocational skills, rather it is the preparation of all students to assume the mantle—the responsibilities and privileges—of full citizenship in a democracy.

PREPARING FOR THE THREE SECTORS OF WORK LIFE

Drucker (1994) described the public, private, and social sectors as the three critical functions for the progress of our society. Neither the public nor the private sector alone can provide adequately the social capital necessary to bind together communities in modern times. The United States has the unique advantage of having one of the most developed social sectors: independent churches, charities, and nonprofit organizations that dedicate themselves to the task of creating human health and well-being (Rifkin, 1995). Increasingly, they serve a second and equally important purpose. Through opportunities for full participation in public life, they create citizenship for both the providers and the recipients of services, most often through volunteer activities.

Drucker (1994) discussed how U.S. society creates unprecedented wealth but also unprecedented failures. The social sector provides opportunities for workers in the public and private sectors to directly participate in the amelioration

of these failures, and opportunities of empowerment for marginalized populations. "The emergence of a strong, independent, capable social sector—neither public sector nor private sector—is thus a central need of the society of organizations. But by itself it is not enough—the organizations of both the public and the private sector must share in the work" (p. 80).

Public education must prepare youth to participate in all three sectors. Perhaps an ideal situation would be one where all citizens had three jobs: a profit-making venture; time spent participating in our government and public institutions, where everyone pitched in to make our government work; and a community service or volunteer activity, whereby all citizens contributed to the common good, whether through service to elders, environmental cleanup and maintenance, working with youths facing risky circumstances, or support in the community for persons with significant disabilities.

Economist Jeremy Rifkin (1995) assures us that full employment will never occur, hence entrepreneurship (the oft-recommended panacea) must be encouraged but has severe limitations. As an alternative, community service or service learning offer *engagement,* as opposed to *employment.* There is plenty of (currently unpaid) work yet to be done in our society—and the reward is the social capital it provides. Community service functions to maintain our ethical balance, our societal self-esteem if you will, that neither the public nor private sectors can supply. Rifkin also explores systems for using tax dollars to promote community service in a manner that would reduce federal budgets, by paying people who might otherwise be in the military or on welfare for contributing to social capital. This proposal would put tax dollars directly into the nonprofit sector in lieu of welfare, and it would support solutions to other social and environmental problems that these third-sector organizations address. A question worth considering is whether the school-to-work movement will aspire to a harmony with this new age of social transformation.

IMPLEMENTING THE SCHOOL-TO-WORK OPPORTUNITIES ACT

The School-to-Work Opportunities Act (STWOA) of 1994 will eventually be replaced by a new work-force development act that combines the activities of adult job training with activities of the public schools. Nonetheless, STWOA provides a model that should be continued into the era of the newer act. As discussed in Chapter 5, STWOA divides its operations into three components: work-based learning, school-based learning, and connecting activities. This model has been well received and accommodates the tech-prep movement that preceded STWOA. STWOA also makes clear provisions for serving all students:

> both male and female students from a broad range of backgrounds and circumstances, including disadvantaged students, students with diverse racial, ethnic, or cultural backgrounds, American Indians, Alaska Natives, Native Hawaiians, students with disabilities, students with limited-English proficiency, migrant children, school dropouts, and academically talented students. (Sec. 4.2)

Specific guidelines for providing these services and an assessment of progress so far are described in the next section.

Work-Based Learning

The work-based learning component of STWOA has generated the most excitement and has had the greatest impact in the field. Thousands of schools across the nation are offering a wide variety of internship and work-experience opportunities to an increasing number of students. Organized labor has joined successfully with business and education in this new initiative. After some initial wrangling over paid versus unpaid internships, the Departments of Labor and Education have agreed to guidelines for unpaid internships, though continued vigilance by the Department of Labor is needed

to ensure that students are not exploited and that employees are not replaced by any unpaid interns. Leaders in special education (Simon et al., 1994) have investigated the issue and developed guidelines that support the development of work-experience policies for all students.

Internships and mentoring are at an all-time high, with numerous examples of corporations entering into partnerships with schools. For example, the Boeing Company sponsors tech-prep internships to students every summer; Career Partners, Inc., of Tulsa, Oklahoma, facilitates career pathways capable of graduating 5,000 students per year; many large corporations have jobs and scholarship programs that target youth from the inner city; and hundreds of employers support quality-work internships for students with special needs in Jobs for America's Graduates and Career Ladders–type programs. Nationally, there are thousands of examples of business/school partnerships. More and more students are spending more and more time learning at the workplace, and the School-to-Work Opportunities Act has catalyzed and validated this movement. Job shadowing, especially when provided for middle school students, is a highly effective means of introducing youth and the work world to each other. As it becomes more common, we can expect even more work-experience options to unfold for students, equipping them to make better career choices.

Two impediments arise in the course of implementing this concept, however. First is the concern that students facing the highest risks (i.e., those with significant disabilities or those with arrests or convictions in their history) will not be included in these essential activities, or will be required to engage through separate programming. We need to adequately plan for and fund the levels of supervision necessary to give these students successful and integrated work-based learning opportunities. STWOA funds a special competition for Urban/Rural Opportunity grants that may foster programs that provide more intensive services cost-effectively. The future challenge will be whether these model programs will be maintained after STWOA's "venture capital" is exhausted, and whether exemplary programs for students at higher risk can be successfully replicated.

Second, heavy class loads may impede our most academically talented students from participating in these opportunities. This would be regrettable, as these students need early exposure to the work world (too many of them languish in college for interminable lengths, wasting vital resources), and to develop a conscious sense of who fills the ranks of the worker positions, as many of them will eventually assume business leadership positions.

School-Based Learning

It is in the realm of school-based learning that many battles are yet to be fought. It is too likely that implementing this component will either be left to vocational education, or that vocational education will be left out of the process. Either scenario is unacceptable. The school-based component of a school-to-work system should have opportunities for all students to prepare for work through their course selection; and not at the cost of their college eligibility. Special education is an example of an education initiative that has been moving to a functional curriculum since 1975. In many cases, special education has partnered with vocational education, through the support of students with disabilities in the vocational classroom, the development of new courses that are more congenial to special abilities, or through team-teaching arrangements between the two departments. In Chapter 2, Rusch and Millar give an overview of the types and numbers of programs where collaboration across disciplines has increased the options for integrating students with disabilities.

General education must learn from this example, integrating its curricula with that of vocational education and developing new team-taught options for students. Examples might

include combining a chemistry course with internships at a chemical firm, and a course on careers in that field; teaching technical reading and writing for English credit; deriving academic objectives from community-based internships and service learning courses; and so on. There is a movement and there are regular conferences that address the integration of vocational and academic curricula.

To suggest this closer collaboration among disciplines brings up all kinds of old issues regarding turf in the high school curriculum offerings. It reopens wounded feelings of inferiority and false assertions of superiority among the staffs and students who are enrolled in regular, special, or vocational education, and it calls into question (again) the relevance and value of a general educational program that at best produces a 20 percent college graduation rate. However, continued separation of school-to-work goals from the academic for *every* curriculum is a disservice to students. Regular education must allow vocational education to share leadership. Vocational education, for its part, must adopt a broad view of what successful adult engagement is, fully participate in discussions with representatives of the Goals 2000: Educate America Act, break out of any constricting habits regarding where and how vocational skills must be taught, and remember its obligation to create offerings for all students. These are the serious challenges facing the development of the school-based learning component of the School-to-Work Opportunities Act.

Connecting Activities

The School-to-Work Opportunities Act lists eight main connecting activities. It includes matching students with work-based learning opportunities and providing mentors at the school site who act as liaisons between the student, school, family, and work world. It is about working with employers and garnering their participation in developing school-based and work-based learning opportunities. And it describes the linkage between students and other community services, conducting follow-up studies, and linking youth development activities with employer and industry strategies for upgrading skills.

This is the weakest and least developed aspect of STWOA, and the least fully implemented component of most school-to-work systems. In the American Vocational Association's (AVA) official manual for building a school-to-careers system, ten chapters are devoted to school-based learning, six chapters are devoted to work-based learning, and no chapter is devoted to connecting activities (Thiers, 1995). There are at least two reasons for this neglect.

The more benign explanation is that the leaders of the school-to-work movement, vocational educators, have never had to address the impact and outcomes of their work. They are unfamiliar with the nature of adult service in the employment realm. Whereas counselors, for better or worse, have always been judged on the number of successful college placements they make, vocational educators have never had to do any serious follow-up on the employment rate or educational level of "their" graduates. High school was a matter of closing the case with the award of the diploma, and the not-conscious philosophy was, "if we inject students with curriculum A, and then graduate them, outcome B (employment or college enrollment) will occur." Though educators recognize that this is not how life progresses, nor is it the way we should approach education for careers, behavior and curriculum have not yet shifted.

The second reason for a weak concept of connecting activities is rooted in the American tradition of "pulling oneself up by the bootstraps," that is, that students should be able to navigate their own course after they leave high school. Not only do we lack the infrastructure and the resources to support them beyond high school, but we have not had the will or the intention of doing so.

Those who have worked with youth with disabilities (of all levels) know that the diploma is no guarantee of self-determination and have developed linkages with rehabilitation and other adult service professionals. Those who have worked with adjudicated and youth with high-risk behaviors know painfully well that their "rehabilitated" students are most often unprepared for life on their own, where they confront a void of services indicative of a national denial of their problems. Our social service systems neglect the crucial need for follow-along after the initial interventions.

Highly successful internships and work experiences have been developed, both historically and recently, and these experiences sometimes evolve into competitive employment opportunities for high school graduates. Vocational areas are required to have advisory boards that include business/employer representatives, and many educators develop viable networks for job placement through these relationships. But this is not enough. School-based teachers generally are not trained nor do they have the time to develop services, in particular for students at risk who need more than just a subsidized summer job or a job lead, but who need ongoing support throughout the job-getting and -keeping process.

As students' relationships in the community and the question of academic relevance to the economy finally take hold in American schools, we may see effective solutions. The *educateur* approach (Hobbs, 1982), developed in post–World War II France and recreated by the Re-ED (Re-education of the Emotionally Disturbed) group in the United States in the 1960s, posited two separate roles for teachers: those teachers who teach content area in the school building, and teacher-liaisons whose role it is to coordinate all manner of activities—jobs, volunteering, social services—in the community. Though there are work-experience coordinators, counselors, social workers, and transition specialists in our high schools who perform these functions, an ideal scenario that takes a more earnest approach to connecting activities would provide such liaison personnel at a much smaller teacher-to-student ratio, and for more students.

Examples of connecting activities in the current movement given in the AVA handbook (Clifford & Flores, 1995) include an interdisciplinary team among educators, employers, and community members for the purpose of dialogue; staff awareness of real-world business; more work-based learning in academic courses; enhanced communication with colleges; increased articulation between secondary and postsecondary curricula; increased employer and community participation in designing curricula; and increased public awareness of school-to-careers programs. STWOA addresses these types of activities, but also calls for

> providing assistance to participants who have completed the program in finding an appropriate job, continuing their education, or entering into an additional training program ... linking the participants with other community services that may be necessary to assure a successful transition from school to work; collecting and analyzing information regarding post-program outcomes ... on the basis of socioeconomic status, race, gender, ethnicity, culture, and disability ... linking youth development activities under this Act with employer and industry strategies for upgrading the skills of their workers. (Secs. 104.6 to 104.8)

Somehow, this key aspect of the law was omitted from the AVA guide, perhaps for the reasons described earlier (it has never before been required of vocational educators, and it runs counter to some of our cultural mores about making it on your own).

School-to-college transition is one area where connecting activities have been more sufficiently addressed, particularly those where tech-prep articulation agreements have been made. Under these agreements, students may take courses during their last 2 years of high

school that advance their placement and are coordinated with certificate programs at their local community and technical colleges. Tech-prep was a burgeoning movement before STWOA was passed, and has blended well into the new framework. It has been a boon for students who are ready and capable of completing such a program.

STWOA heralds an unprecedented collaboration between two federal departments, Labor and Education. Logic would infer that connecting activities would relate more directly to the contributions of the Department of Labor. In fact, this has manifested itself in greater participation of union leadership in developing school-to-work systems, and may increase coordination between union apprenticeships and exiting high school students. Private Industry Councils, faced with legislation that would eliminate their usual lock on funding, have stepped forward as applicants for STWOA grants.

Regrettably, the results of this federal collaboration usually offer up proposals that are "juiced-up" versions of old programs that have only been moderately successful. Only rarely do we see new programs that address the diverse backgrounds of students, provide more intensive follow-along, or are flexible enough to shape services to the needs of students. In short, the school-to-work movement has thus far supported the expansion and installation of existing services, many of them very good; but we have seen very few examples of new or innovative approaches to delivering more intensive services to students who are at greater risk (or in need of Level 4 and Level 5 services, described in the next section).

One of the core challenges facing youth job-training programs is that they are not prepared to deal with the complexity of problems presented by many of today's students. They are programs that are typically less expensive to operate, but ultimately less effective. Thus, we often obtain a poor fit between the program and the recruited youth, and the results are disastrous. It is agonizing to watch dedicated professionals burn out as they try to wrestle with problems that their programs (caseload, duration of services, intensity of services) are not equipped to handle. It is doubly agonizing to see employers feel "burned" by such programs when the students cannot deliver and the school or agency personnel cannot supervise. But the greatest anguish is that students fail in programs that do not offer enough structure, attention, and shaping to their special needs. It is imperative that educators alert the public that more preventive programs, even at quadruple the costs of a current service, will create enormous savings by offering more intensive connecting and follow-along services, and likely turn a taxeater (incarceration, institutionalization, welfare, disability payments) into a functioning taxpayer.

A related "blind spot" is the refusal of the school-to-careers movement to develop programming that can acknowledge and accommodate the inevitable "floundering period" of anywhere from 1 to 10 years that often youths go through after high school. It is during this period that most students who are at risk of chronic unemployment fall through the "cracks" of the system. This *is* the proverbial "crack/canyon" of the system through which youth fall, never to be fully included again. Services to address this issue are proposed later in this chapter. Despite its glossy and new overtones, most school-to-work philosophies and programs still view the student as a passive vessel somehow able to select a career by age 16 and move smoothly from high school to postsecondary training or a job in that specific field. Although there is great merit to giving students the opportunity to make career choices at an earlier age, it is doubtful that the lability of the floundering period will be dramatically reduced. The solution is follow-along services that are in contact with the youth as they exit school and experiment in their adult life, and the effective and cost-effective ongoing availability of transition services.

The sector most capable of delivering this type of service is that which Drucker calls the social sector, not the community college system, nor organized labor. The social (nonprofit) sector has the capability to cost-effectively provide follow-along services that can take the floundering period into account and maintain contact with young adults through failures and successes. Agencies that already perform youth job placement and support, recreation, counseling, and social services to special populations are best equipped to make the paradigm shift to ongoing availability of service and community building through peer networks, solutions that will prevent harmful floundering. Ironically, these types of agencies have been practically excluded from the master plans of school-to-careers systems. When they have been included, it has been to deliver "business-as-usual" services (predicated on closing cases and producing numbers) that show only moderate gains in improving the outcomes of students most at risk of underemployment.

FIVE LEVELS OF TRANSITION SERVICES

There is no such thing as a school-to-work *program* that can serve all students, but all programs should strive to maximize accessibility. The only way to serve all students is through a multiple-option school-to-work *system* so students may adjust their individualized program as their interests and needs change and develop over time.

Special education has completed a necessary phase by developing the means for addressing special needs. Whether we now call it "mainstreaming," "inclusion," or "integration," the time has come for our educational system to serve all students, without the need to label and create special and segregated programs. To the greatest extent possible, all courses should strive to serve all students who enroll in them. What we do need are multiple options that include opportunities for students to congregate according to like activities and interests, and programs that deliver varying intensities of service. The taxpayer, the teacher, the student, and the family alike care less about whether a student has an attention deficit disorder or a learning disability. They care more that the student receives the level and type of service that is suitable to growth. It is education's job, and it is now within education's reach, to deliver this broad range of services and incorporate a system that allows students to flow to where they are served best.

Many schools have adopted career pathways models where coursework is clustered among five or six career areas, for example: communications and arts, agriculture, marketing and business, health occupations, and human services. This is a highly successful approach in that it provides a career-application context for an entire school's curriculum, and it allows students to meaningfully shape their courses of study. What such a model sorely lacks is the flexibility to serve the entire range of abilities and needs that students present.

A "career quilt" is proposed that crosses each career pathway, such that the student with a profound intellectual disability, the student who is profoundly gifted and capable, and every student in between can find themselves served and appropriately challenged within the same career pathway. For example, an Introduction to Health Occupations course might be taught in an inclusive environment where a student whose intentions are to become a surgeon, a student seeking a nursing license, a student who is to volunteer or do entry-level work in a hospital, and a student who has not yet figured out which health occupation to pursue, all take this same course. As their respective career pathways take shape, they would each attend other, more specialized courses that serve their individual needs. Thus, the value of inclusive environments is promoted and experienced, and students get the specialized knowledges they will need.

As graduation approaches, students will find themselves needing different levels of transition services. Five levels of transition services are described forthwith, and students, through

counseling and guidance services, should be able to exercise choice, and locate and receive appropriate services. The level of service is not determined by the student's label, but by the intensity of service needed by that particular student, so the student can successfully participate. When we view students in terms of what intensity of service they need instead of some internal condition or imposed label, some striking insights emerge. Students who we might not expect to be served together are found to be in need of the same intensity of service. These five levels are summarized by Table 7.1, and are now discussed in order, from most to least intensive. The reader is reminded that these are not permanent tracks, but multiple options, and the same student may use combinations of all levels over the course of secondary education and postsecondary experience.

Level 5: Services for Youths at the Greatest Risk of Unemployment and Marginalization

Youths who need Level 5 services most often comprise two broadly defined groups: those with significant and profound disabilities, and those with excessively challenging behaviors who have been adjudicated or are at greatest risk of adjudication. A possible third group of students is those with serious conduct disorders who evade both the judicial system and special education identification; nonetheless, they can be well served by Level 5.

For students with disabilities, there is a highly developed infrastructure of supported employment services. Even these services are threatened by budget cuts, however, and we are still far from fully serving the transition needs of all of these youths. Current levels should be viewed as a floor from which adequate Level 5 services can rise.

The second group—youths whose behaviors challenge the norms and can be physically threatening to others—has failed to stimulate an adequate response from the community

Table 7.1 Five Intensity Levels of Transition

Youth	Service Needs	STW System Should Provide ...
LEVEL 5 Low-achieving or with significant disabilities and/or at high risk of chronic unemployment/illegitimate career paths	Early intervention; immersion programs; intensive follow along services	Middle school–initiated programs; Job Corps; Conservation Corps; supported employment; model community programs; new and experimental models under the Americorps and other initiatives
LEVEL 4 Low to average achievers; at risk of dropping out, school failure, illegitimate career paths; need all of Level 3, but with more intensity	Early interventions; supervised work-experience internships; paced training options; assistance with college education; intensive follow-along services	Intensified community-based agencies and programs; new and innovative school programs; new and innovative vocational rehabilitation and other state/regional programs
LEVEL 3 Low to average achievers; some college-bound; lower socioeconomic status; need reasonable opportunities and career counseling; advocacy and some monitoring	Early interventions; monitored work-experience internships; paced training options; assistance with college education	Vocational/special education cooperatives, tech-prep; existing community-based agency programs; school district; Private Industry Council; adult education; community and technical colleges
LEVEL 2 Average to high achievers; some college-bound; more from a low socioeconomic status; lack only reasonable job opportunities	Job and job-training opportunities; unsupervised work-experience internships; targeted college scholarships and options	Tech-prep, private sector; school district; academies; adult education, community college, college and university
LEVEL 1 Average to high achievers; many college-bound; average to high SES; have social and professional connections	Existing college and employment options	Tech-prep, existing education, and employment institutions

and schools. These youths need elaborate and well-designed day treatment, residential, and immersion programs that remove them from their usual settings and give them an opportunity to rebuild their identity in a productive, prosocial, and personally satisfying fashion. Such services cannot be injected like a medicine with the expectation that the youths will be "fixed" within 6 months or even a year. Many of the young people utilizing Level 5 will need follow-along/wraparound services for up to 5 years; they must be supported as they reenter the community.

It is this author's guess that significantly more resources—fiscal and human—have been dedicated to the employment of people labeled disabled than to those who are otherwise disadvantaged. Deriving reliable figures to support this assertion is not yet possible, given the complex web of funds transferred among federal, state, and local governments, private foundations, and the social capital accrued through volunteer and other goodwill activities (Dawson & Stan, 1995). Note, however, that the 20 percent crime reduction rate achieved by California's "three strikes and you're out" law could be matched by cash incentives to encourage disadvantaged youth to complete high school at less than one-fifth the cost (Greenwood et al., 1996). Suffice it to say, the programs supported throughout this book argue for greater investment in programs that direct youth from incarceration and institutionalization, and data to support their cost-effectiveness are available (Gladwell, 1996; Greenwood et al., 1996).

Investigation of no other level brings into relief so dramatically the difference a label makes. It is a reflection of our national conscience that youths with significant disabilities evoke perceptions of victimization and subsequently a chain of compassionate advocacy and legislation that translates into an infrastructure of reasonably effective services. Youths with significantly insubordinate behaviors have fewer advocates, and the national response has been less one of transforming their experience to prosocial ends and empowering them, and more one of fear that translates into an infrastructure of expensive and ineffective incarceration and punishment, and elaborate security measures. But when we view students according to need instead of condition or label, we may be able finally to adopt policies that match epidemic violence and alienation with the intensity of service it deserves, raising its funding level and type of service to one more commensurate with others receiving Level 5 services.

Educators and communitarians from around the nation have sought to develop solutions for students whose serious behaviors preclude attendance at school. The term "boot camp" has been used, which is unfortunate, but the concept of immersion programs has merit. The superior solution for adolescents with high-risk behaviors is powerful prevention and early interventions, from Head Start to elementary and middle school programs. However, comprehensive day treatment, residential and immersion programs may be the best we can deliver until the situations of adolescents at high risk are reduced to nominal levels. Students presenting high-risk behaviors can be more successfully served through Re-ED concepts (Hobbs, 1982), military organization, character education and citizenship education, rites of passage that serve adolescent needs, technical skills instruction, planned reentry into the community, and job development with ongoing support.

Many states are developing "boot camps" that possess some of the features just described. Some lean toward the punitive; others retain a more rehabilitative mission. The current approach is to operate these camps through subcontracts with private corporations who hire ex-military personnel and who make claims of delivering the services for less money, due in part to their salary structures. Community-based approaches to Level 5 services that can help individuals one at a time, but also create positive movements in the neighborhood may hold more promise (see Case Study 1).

Proposals being discussed in several states call for financial incentives to use prevention and preincarceration programs. Under such proposals, disbursement formulas are changed so that school districts are financially rewarded for reducing the incarceration rates of students, and, conversely, their budgets are reduced if incarceration rates increase. Alternatively, the state will match the school's annual expenditure when incarceration-preventing options, such as day treatment or boot camps, are used. In the state of Minnesota, for example, juvenile corrections and education have been combined into a single department. This creates a flow of funds between the corrections and education budgets, making it possible for the more cost-effective solutions where a school could underwrite a more expensive intervention sooner, rather than writing off the student and passively deferring to the justice system, which must bear the problems and expenses of more costly and less effective interventions.

Planning successful programming for these youths will require utmost care and exceptional talent, with the understanding that it will not be inexpensive. We must be prepared to spend $20–35,000 per year per youth on prevention services. However, this is still considerably less that the $40,000 per year it now costs to incarcerate (*San Francisco Focus*, 1995). Residential treatment should be offered for at least 18 months, and perhaps for as long as 5 years. The key to long-term success for youths exiting these programs is intensive follow-along and support, such as what is offered by Career Ladders transition specialists (see Level 4).

These challenges cannot be addressed haphazardly; they present an opportunity for unique approaches that will engage the community in

CASE STUDY 1   Level 5: The Omega Boys Club

"We're not a program, we're a family."

Joe Marshall and Jake Jacqua were teachers in the San Francisco public school system in 1987. As they saw more and more of their students suffer the consequences of drug abuse and violence, they left their teaching jobs to found the Omega Boys Club, serving primarily African-American youths aged 11 to 25. By leaving the school system, they gave themselves the freedom to create a more intensive service and evolve their program more quickly than a large bureaucracy could allow:

> I could take the kids to visit college campuses without going through a major bureaucratic hassle. I could use a great book like *Before the Mayflower*, a history of African-American people, which I couldn't even bring into the classroom because it wasn't a state-approved text. But probably the biggest thing is that … we could keep the kids around us, we could guide them to where they wanted to go. And we know that whatever worked, we could keep, and what didn't work, we could drop like a hot potato—unlike the school system, which clings to a lot of anachronistic practices. (*San Francisco Focus,* 1995)

What the program has evolved to is a four-pronged approach: peer counseling for incarcerated youths, violence prevention through a 4-hour weekly call-in radio show on San Francisco's most popular FM music station (and simulcast in Los Angeles), academic help, and job training. A youth who is taking full advantage of all that the Omega Boys Club offers could be considered to be receiving Level 5 services. Since 1987, over 140 Omega members have gone from the streets and jails to college. Hundreds of others have quit their gang affiliations. One of the most important distinctions of Omega Boys Club is the conduit to other immersion programs that, in the context of a youth exiting a street life, could be considered Level 5. For example, they make great use of black colleges, and have developed a strong, positive relationship with the courts system in San Francisco such that they have been able to get a release of two inmates from detention to go on the Club's annual tour of southern colleges. Probation has been granted to youths who go on to college under the custodial eye of the Club. They have successfully advocated for court referrals to strict reform schools in lieu of lockup. They also meet the definition of Level 5 services through intensive follow-along and long-term commitment to youths. "Cases" are never opened or closed. Simply put, youths come to the organization and the organization reaches out to them.

Numerous stories tell of violent revenges that have been averted through the persistent intervention of the Club's staff. Omega brought the Crips and Bloods together after two decades of warfare to talk peace, leading to a gang truce following the Rodney King riots. They persuaded one of Los Angeles' most notorious gangsters to lay down his weapons. By making its services available in the community and on the community's terms, so to speak, the Omega Boys Club can have a cultural impact, fostering a healthy change in the streets. Reliance solely on removal of youths and placement in immersion programs works as a strategy only if there are enough placements to "starve" out a drug or violence problem—not likely.

> [W]e have a growing [prison] industry here that's based on primarily black and brown people going into institutions. What you really need to do is to get people not to become criminals. To do that you have to do much more intervention and prevention and rehabilitation. If you're not putting at least the same amount of money into that as you are into locking people away, you're not really interested in stopping or deterring crime but in fighting a never-ending war. (*San Francisco Focus,* 1995:54)

Versions of Omega are being replicated in Los Angeles, Detroit, and Chicago, and replication will be the Club's most critical challenge. By developing the Club at the street level, responding creatively and improvising based on the circumstances of the contrast between life on the streets and what the system imposes, Marshall and Jacqua have shaped a unique program within a turbulent setting. But just as supported employment emerged as the intensive, yet only successful, means of integrating people with significant disabilities into the work world, so the Omega Boys Club is an analogous approach for other youths in need of resource-intensive—Level 5—services (see Chapter 5 for a detailed description of the supported employment approach).

solving one of the most serious problems it faces. Ultimately, the solution for students in such dire straits has to be earlier intervention.

The solution for students with significant disabilities is the permanent incorporation of environments ergonomic and human—congenial to them throughout the work world and the community, such that the need for separately operated Level 5 services evaporates altogether. This means that the capacity for supported employment must be built into the infrastructure of the employer, and the natural supports of the workplace allow a greater diversity of citizens to successfully work there.

Level 4: Services for Youths at Moderate Risk of Unemployment and Underemployment

Students and youths needing this level (Level 4) of service tend to be at risk of dropping out or failing in school, are academically behind, may have mild learning or emotional disabilities, have been arrested once or twice, are in the foster care system, have mild drug involvement, are parenting, or are of a sexual minority—or any combination of these factors. Many come from low-income families. They are truly "at-risk" youths in the sense that if their challenges are left unaddressed, they soon may be youths in the less tractable position of needing Level 5 services. However, when they receive quality services, their need often can be greatly reduced.

These youths need early identification and intervention, as well as constant opportunities for involvement in the community. Vocationally, an ideal program offers job-shadowing opportunities by the seventh grade, if not earlier, and coordination of these experiences with classroom learning (see Table 7.2; Siegel, 1992; and Thiers, 1995, for more details on this option). Job shadowing helps students make their first career choices, and is followed by a series of once-weekly mini-internships in the ninth and tenth grades.

During the last 2 years of school, students needing Level 4 services benefit from daily 3-hour supervised work experiences (community classroom), weekly seminars where the work experience is processed, and a support network of peers. On graduation, many of these students will need the ongoing availability of a wide array of adult transition services. Such services work on an empowerment basis of providing as little service as possible and as much as is necessary for the graduates to sustain their own interdependent network of peers facing similar work, education, and life challenges. A well-run career/work-experience program of this type can deliver a very high success rate. This is the essence of the Career Ladders model (Siegel et al., 1993).

About thirty school districts in seven states have begun replicating Career Ladders. Many employers (Safeco Insurance, ATL, Media Technologies, AAA Insurance, Sam's Warehouses, McDonald's, City of Bellevue) and hospitals (five in the Puget Sound region, two in San Francisco) are offering community classroom internships. Teachers and staff from these districts provide on-the-job supervision and carefully orchestrated weekly seminars. Coordinators meet regularly to compare notes and organize their efforts. These school districts have already committed and are scheduled to commit several million dollars to these efforts. In partnership with adult services, nonprofit funding is being sought to continue Career Ladders services for graduates of these programs. With community support, leaders in the various projects are making efforts to put together federal, state, county, private, and other funds to pilot and begin the steps to institutionalize this critically needed service. Career Ladders strives to minimize categorical requirements and maximize flexibility; if funding efforts are successful, this innovative approach to postsecondary transition services will become a social service reality.

At a one-time cost of $4,000 to $6,000 per graduate, ongoing availability of transition services can be provided. Career Ladders adult services are shaped to the lives of its participants, which means that resources are "banked" in preparation for a 3- to 5-year unpredictable

Table 7.2 Features of Comprehensive Career and Life-Skills Education

Middle (Ages 11–14)	High (Ages 15–16)	Transition (Ages 17–22)
Law and Government	Law and Government	*Law and Government*[a]
	Job-Skills Training	*Job-keeping Skills*
		Job-Skills Training
		Job Placement
		Transition Services
		Community Internships
		Support Groups
		Job-Search Skills
Affective Education	*Affective Education*	Affective Education
Consumer Economics	*Consumer Economics*	Consumer Economics
Job-Keeping Skills	*Job-Keeping Skills*	Job-Keeping Skills
	Community Internships	
	Community Resources	
	Regular Job Tasks	
	Career Exploration	
	Job-Search Skills	
Working for Product	Working for Product	Working for Product
Working in Groups	Working in Groups	Working in Groups
Academic Remediation	Academic Remediation	Health Education
Health Education		
Role Models		
Career Awareness		

[a]Emphasized curriculum in italics type.

floundering period. A case is never closed, and Career Ladders' unique approach to case management—continuous cyclical triage, development of cohorts, and building of peer communities—makes this effective and cost-effective style of services work.

The key to previously reported successes with graduates of Career Ladders is that the transition specialists stay with a limited case-load—a cohort—over an extended period of time. Services are not predicated on a principle of marketing graduates to employers, sustaining a minimum number of days on the job, and closing the case. Instead, Career Ladders transition services aim to build community, with the transition specialists facilitating a cohesiveness that includes the program participants. As the weave of community takes hold, the participants experience success and integration. An efficient method of managing cases—continuous cyclical triage—designates service time and resources to the persons and situations where the highest impact is likely; this allows transition specialists to provide intensive services to many youths (actual size of caseloads depends on the special circumstances of the group served: teen parents, drug-involved, on probation, etc.). Using this community approach, as opposed to a case-open/case-closed operation, has resulted in a combined employment/college attendance rate of 92 percent (Siegel et al., 1991, 1992).

Unfortunately, this is still considered an expensive service, and there are no established funding streams or national commitments to provide such services. Funding for students in need of Level 4 services is generally low and only offered on a numbers basis (*x* number of job placements by *y* date) or is time-limited. This is despite the postsecondary floundering period, where periods of success are delayed or intermittently interrupted, is a generally accepted phenomenon (Wilson, 1987). Level 4 services can benefit a wide range of students, averting higher-risk, less tractable situations, reducing dropout rates, engaging students in the community, engaging the community in the educational process, and forging the necessary linkages between the schools and the adult service networks. (See Case Study 2.)

Level 3: Services for Youths in Need of State-of-the-Art Education for Careers

Youths in need of Level 3 service are often achieving at low to average academic levels. Many come from low-income families. Some successfully set their sights on a college education and achieve it. Many attend community colleges. Students needing this level of service often present disabilities, behaviors, or learning problems that a congenial school environment can reasonably and easily accommodate.

Many public schools have vocational programs that are exemplary in their successful inclusion of students with special needs. Configurations include team teaching, vocational special education programming, community-based work experiences, partnerships with adult service agencies, support in community college programs, support for participation in vocational service organizations, and use of vocational resource instructors (an instructor, teacher, or aide who is specially trained in supporting students with special needs in the vocational setting and facilitating collaboration between vocational and special education—IEP process, assessment, course selection, etc.) (Hazelkorn & Lombard, 1991; Prickette, 1995).

In Wisconsin, Georgia, and Washington, vocational and special education have set up cooperatives to support and enlarge these collaborative programs. They provide site visits and consultation on integrating special needs students into the schoolwide school-to-work systems; seminars and workshops where staff develop the skills of accommodating special needs youth in the vocational classroom; educational resources on vocational/special education topics; an annual event recognizing excellence in service to students with special needs; and support of liaisons among students, their families, adult service agencies, and the employment community. These teams of vocational and special education directors have a significant history of collaborating, blending resources, striving for state-of-the-art programming, and sharing ownership for the education of all students.

In North King County, for example, students are able to cross school district lines without cost in order to take courses that may not be offered in their own district, and designated vocational instructors travel and provide support to students who need it. Throughout our nation, different forms of Occupational Skills Centers and adult education offer vocational training on a regional basis; many provide services to students with special needs as one of their strongest features. School administrators have created strong relationships with the region's businesses and community colleges through tech-prep programs (see Gajar in this volume, Chapter 16, for more on the school-to-postsecondary education transition). As these collaborative programs provide full access to all students and take responsibility for the mission of the vocational/special education co-op, they realize their potential for being ideally matched to students needing Level 3 services.

In the community, students receiving Level 3 services are able to take advantage of conventional or mainstream job training and placement programs, from community college courses to Private Industry Council and other job placement programs. One highly visible and successful provider of Level 3 adult services for special needs youth is the IAM-CARES project of the International Association of Machinists. Nationally, the Department of Labor has funded Projects with Industry that provide Level 3

CASE STUDY 2   Level 4: Career Ladders

"Services are shaped by the needs of the youths served."

Jimmy was recruited into the Career Ladders program at his school during his senior year of high school. He had aphasia, and his syntax was often confused and confusing. This condition amplified conflict situations when his desire to be respected among his peers was threatened by his inability to communicate well. In other words, he tended to get into fights a lot.

Jimmy's community classroom was in a large office building where he was placed on the custodial crew; he did well there for several weeks. However, eventually there was a misunderstanding and a conflict with his supervisor. He was terminated from that placement, and completed his internship with another employer.

After graduation, Jimmy seemed startled to see Vince, his transition specialist from the program, show up at the "mom-and-pop" grocery store where he had a part-time job. In fact, he initially resented the connection. However, when the transition specialist gently persisted, dropping in a couple of times a month, Jimmy came to appreciate and even look forward to the visits. As their dialogue progressed, Vince learned that Jimmy had always wanted to work on cars. They developed a plan whereby Jimmy would attend a Private Industry Council–sponsored program where he could learn a variety of car maintenance skills, and eventually get placed in a job that was more challenging, paid more, and had better benefits than the grocery store job.

In the midst of planning for this transition, Vince received a call one day from Jimmy, saying that he had had a disagreement with his employer at the grocery store and had been fired. Vince rushed down to plead with the employer, but to no avail. Less than 2 weeks later, however, Jimmy was back on the job.

In the meantime, Jimmy enrolled in the Auto Maintenance program, but dropped out after less than a month, with no apparent explanation. A few months later, he had another fight with his boss and quit. Again Vince pleaded his case; again to no avail. Less than 2 weeks later, Jimmy was back on the job.

Eventually, Vince was educated as to the (dys)functional (you make the call!) nature of Jimmy's relationship with his boss; firing, quitting, and rehiring was a dance they had worked out. Vince at least learned to stay clear of it, but his relationship with Jimmy matured. Vince's plan was for Jimmy to reenroll in the Auto Maintenance class and then give notice when he finally completed the course and had a new job offer waiting. But clearly, Vince could manage and influence only certain aspects of this situation; Jimmy was his own captain.

Pretty much on schedule, Jimmy quit his job for about the third time in 2 years (he had also been fired and rehired about three times). Only this time, he called Vince and said he was ready to reenroll in the class. He did, this time not returning to his old job; he completed the course and was placed in a high-paying (over $10/hour) job in an outlet for a major tire company. He experienced no friction with his boss or co-workers in this situation and continued to climb the career ladder.

Over 3 years elapsed from the time Jimmy entered his Career Ladders internship to the time he was hired in the tire outlet. Though he received continuously available services (his case was never closed), the cost of the services to the taxpayer was minimal. Due to the very common, yet unique nature of Jimmy's posthigh school floundering period, it took 3 years for Vince to build the trust level with him whereby Jimmy would have the courage to leave his more limiting job and make multiple attempts to pursue his dream and climb a career ladder. The trust and community building that is intrinsic to this style of adult services are critical to the success of people like Jimmy who have skills but do not know how to develop the networks and resources that can help them get ahead. Thus, the case is made for Level 4 services that at first glimpse may seem costly, but ultimately, as they are shaped to the lives of the youths receiving the services, will foster success.

services to youths with disabilities. Students who succeed in Level 3 programming often are able to make good use of community agencies. Programming for postsecondary Level 3 services is carried out to a large extent by nonprofit organizations with public and private foundation funding. It has been easier for postsecondary institutions and unions to collaborate on this level.

Jobs for America's Graduates (JAG) is a good example of a Level 3 service specifically designed for students at risk. This highly successful program originated with the support of the governor of Delaware in 1980; today, the model is in use in over twenty-four states. Similar in principles to Career Ladders, JAG provides a job specialist, a student-led organization, access to remedial education and social services, job placement, 9 months of follow-up, and a curriculum based on thirty-seven job-related competencies (Koeninger, 1995). The competencies, based on employers' input on desired worker behaviors, are divided into six areas: Career Development (identify occupational interests, aptitudes and abilities, develop a career path for a selected occupation, describe the conditions and specifications of the job goal, etc.); Job Attainment (construct a résumé, conduct a job search, use the telephone to arrange an interview, etc.); Job Survival (demonstrate appropriate appearance, identify problems of new employees, appropriately quit a job, etc.); Basic skills (comprehend verbal communications, communicate in writing, etc.); Leadership and Self-Development (demonstrate team membership, compete successfully with peers, demonstrate commitment to an organization, etc.); and Personal Skills (understand types of maturity, base decisions on values and goals, develop healthy self-concept for home, school, and work, etc.) After the 9-month period, JAG offers extended follow-up to students who fail to graduate or who have not attained a positive outcome. JAG is distinguished from Career Ladders by its greater demands for student competency, more latitude on the format for work-based learning, more limited follow-up, and lower costs. Compared to Career Ladders, it provides a good example of how the same principles can be applied at different levels of intensity.

Programming for students needing Level 3 services can be most easily enhanced by increasing the coordination of many services that are already available. Whereas the provision of services at Levels 4 and 5 often require intensification of existing approaches or the invention of completely new models, Level 3 marks the domain where existing services, more scrupulously applied and with a mind toward accommodation, can have maximum impact. (See Case Study 3.)

Areas for development, then, include achieving the maximum possible integration of academic, special, and vocational programming on the school campus. Also, the connection between secondary vocational programs and job placement programs in the community could be increased, so that even students who do not need the intensive kind of follow-along that Level 4 and Level 5 services provide are still connected to job placement and career development services. Tech-prep addresses the high school to community college/adult vocational connection and could provide Level 3 services, but that is still in need of advocacy and development. The U.S. Department of Education's Office of Special Education and Rehabilitative Services has been sponsoring numerous postsecondary grants to develop consummate approaches to maximize postsecondary opportunities for students with disabilities. Self-advocacy has been the cornerstone of this developing movement.

Level 2: Services for Youths in Need of Career Opportunities

Students and youths in need of Level 2 services are average to high achievers. Many are college-bound, and probably many more could be. These students come from lower-income families and lack only reasonable opportunities. (See Case Study 4.)

CASE STUDY 3   Level 3: The King County Vocational/Special Education Cooperative

---

"Making the employment of challenged youths everybody's business."

I'll never forget the first day Charlie Winter enrolled in my Nursing Assistant class during the fall of 1991. He was strong, healthy, and wanted to be a doctor. He listened and watched carefully. He was a visual/auditory learner with a learning disability. His reading was slow-paced and he required a calculator in order to do his math work.

He came to class with skills he had learned as an Explorer Scout. He loved his work assignment at the Sea-Tac Fire Station. After he discovered and realized that his math and reading skills were not high enough to get him into medical school, he was able to reshape his dreams and reset his sights on becoming a firefighter or an emergency medical technician. It was part of my job as his teacher and counselor to gradually and kindly ease him into this realization.

Our class ran an active VICA Club and Charlie joined the first year he was with me. He needed to be coaxed into participating in the school district's leadership contest held in November of 1991. With persistence and a lot of raised and risked self-esteem, Charlie prepared a winning job demonstration. He won first place, which kindled his desire to be a winner. In the spring of 1992, he won first place in the regional VICA Nursing Assistant Contest and fourth place in the state's VICA Nursing Assistant Contest.

He returned to my class in the fall of 1992. This time he came back to participate as a leader. Mary McGee was assigned as a vocational resource instructor to our school, and I was fortunate enough to have her work with me in my program. She helped Charlie continue on the path he had forged thus far, and that year, he was the first place winner in the state in Nursing Assisting, and sixth place in the nation. He had never traveled far before, and he was elated to make the trip to receive his award.

Mary developed an exemplary teacher/student relationship with Charlie. She would not let Charlie make any excuses for not doing excellent work. With her guidance, he developed into a leader. Mary insisted that he set goals, make a plan, and do his best to carry them out. He was elected president of the VICA club. He headed up the fund raisers and encouraged active participation by others. At the same time he was attending the Realistic Transition Program (RTP), a job placement service for transitional special education students, where he was further encouraged. His attendance sometimes was sporadic and his energy was low. He needed to learn how to manage all the activities in his life. Joint conferences were held to discuss his educational commitments. It worked. In 1993, he was awarded Student of the Year by the King County Vocational/Special Education Cooperative.

During his senior year in high school, Charlie moved on to the Medical Assistant Program at Sea-Tac Occupational Skills Center, where he had some difficulty with follow-through and attendance. He maintained his interest in VICA, but the reading and language requirements of his courses were too much for him, and it was only his VICA involvement that kept him in school. With the help of Mary, he developed an excellent résumé and won first place in the state in Job Interview skills. That same year he won second place in the state in Nursing Assistant.

Charlie was recognized on his graduation night at Satellite High School. His mentor from the Sea-Tac fire station was there, as well as the teachers from RTP and Mary. Charlie is presently employed at the Highline Community Hospital where he works with patients who have chronic and acute respiratory problems. He continues to live at home with his family. He is a true champion!

Contributed by Bea Lorentzen

Earlier identification of students with these needs could increase the size of this group while reducing the numbers of students needing Level 3, 4, and 5 services. Students requiring Level 2 services are primarily in need of the funding and the means to obtaining the highest quality training, education, and employment or entrepreneur opportunities. Sometimes this means increasing funding to their schools and delivering excellent teaching. Sometimes it is a matter of directly offering them resources to further and enhance their education, training, and job/career opportunities. Students receiving quality Level 2 services also can move on to benefit from Level 1 services (see what follows).

The most glaring deficiency in this category is the correction of funding inequalities between school districts. This is a complex problem, beyond the scope of this chapter. The issue has been analyzed most carefully by Kozol (1991); public dialogue and action on the issue of equitable funding formulas are crucial.

Barring the ability to affect school-funding formulas on a broad scale, there are at least four areas where educators can make a contribution to youths in need of Level 2 services. The first is to raise money and provide scholarships for school materials and special courses for exemplary students from low-income families; college scholarships for students from the same group could be developed and awarded as well. The Omega Boys Club in San Francisco (see Level 5 Case Study) has made its mission the encouragement and college placement of high-achieving inner-city youth. The Zion Academy Prep School of Seattle does similar work and has a special job-training arrangement with Starbucks Coffee. Such work could be broadened and public schools should be partners in the enterprise. Intelligently approached, public schools may find a new role as the trusted distributors of corporate donations, ensuring that scholarship monies go to students who are most in need, most deserving, and most able to benefit from the bestowal.

Second, there is a lack of adequate counseling for students due in part to the general attrition of this role in the high schools over the last 20 years. Schools need to have quality career-counseling centers. Such services would be open to all students, but they would be most effective as a Level 2 service. School districts may be willing to work together to cooperatively fund such a center or centers. One-stop career-counseling centers, promoted by the Clinton Administration for dislocated workers and welfare-to-work citizens, should expand to provide better linkage

between school and work; they are a key mandate of the Workforce Development movement to be implemented in 1997.

Third, Level 2 services should include numerous opportunities for community service. High-achieving students can exemplify commitment to their local communities and show that service to the environment, health, and less able members constitutes a worthy application of their talents.

And, finally, academically successful students from low-income families need highly public recognition for their achievements. This type of attention will increase the chances of them becoming empowered, prosocial members of their communities.

Level 1: Services for All Students, Including High-Achieving, High-Income Youths

Level 1 services are for all students, and include academically average to high achievers. Most of them are college-bound. They come from higher-income families, and a significant majority of them likely will become the leaders, employers, power brokers, and decision makers of the future.

Level 1 services are designed to assist the students for whom the system of high school to college, graduate studies, professional, and executive positions has worked well. But these students also can benefit from work experiences during their teen years—many of them do work—and they should take advantage of career linkage programs, perhaps at Levels 2 and 3.

Students and youths needing Level 1 services must be educated to understand that the opportunities afforded them are not universally shared, and that they have a responsibility for the welfare of their community. In terms of successful school-to-work transitions, the system is already arranged to their advantage. School-to-work programs can help to develop the social consciousness of these students through intensive education in democracy.

Citizenship education must occur for all students, but there is a particular need for it in

---

CASE STUDY 4   Level 2: Urban Scholars

"Providing Students with a Real Career Opportunity"

Sixteen-year-old Thuy Nguyen is having a summer she will never forget. Thuy is working as a physical therapy aide for the University Medical Center and plans to study medicine when she graduates from high school.

But a good high school internship and college aspirations were not always a part of Thuy's plans. Born in Vietnam, Thuy's family immigrated to the United States when she was 2 years old. Two weeks later, her father died of a heart attack. Without any other options, Thuy, her mother, two sisters, and brother moved in with her father's relatives; 15 people living in a tiny apartment.

Cramped living arrangements and poverty were only two of many obstacles for Thuy. She was often sick, and her mother would take an entire day off from work to get her to doctors' appointments. This compounded the troubles they had with her father's relatives. Often, they would degrade her and label her as worthless.

Thuy and her mother knew she was not worthless. Frequently, her mother would tell her that "we are in a situation where the family thinks that you are not worth schooling. We have to prove them wrong." And they did! Thuy's mother raised the family, worked full-time, and went to night school to earn her accounting degree. Thuy worked hard in school to get good grades.

As a high school junior, Thuy began to consider pursuing a medical career. A friend recommended that she apply to the Urban Scholars program so she could explore the profession further. The career center in Thuy's school held an informational meeting especially for students of color, young women, and economically disadvantaged youth interested in exploring the world of work. Thuy was excited at what the program had to offer, especially the promise of computer training, a summer job, and possible scholarship money. She knew the program would not be easy, but she resolved to finish what she had begun.

Through the rest of her junior year, every 2 weeks Thuy would travel to job-skills workshops at different business locations throughout the downtown area. The workshops were taught by business people, not school teachers. The business people told Thuy and her peers what businesses are looking for when they hire employees.

Thuy learned a lot that year. She learned about communication and interpersonal skills. She learned how to talk with her supervisor and co-workers. The business trainers informed her about the habits and attitudes that would make her effective and successful on the job. Finally, Thuy attended several workshops on résumé writing and interviewing skills. Those workshops were her favorite. "The job-search skills section was the best," she said. "It instilled and reinforced a sense of responsibility that I needed to look for and get a job."

That summer, while many of her friends enjoyed the weather, Thuy attended a computer technology camp. "I loved it," Thuy reflected. "They didn't 'baby' us. We were in the same facilities that they teach adults in, and that was the way they treated us, like adults." Thuy learned how to use business software and even how to design a web page. At the end of the camp, Thuy had to present a mock business World Wide Web presentation to her fellow students and the business volunteers.

Finally, it was time for Thuy to get a job. The program provided her with the names and phone numbers of business people who were willing to give her a job interview. Using the phone skills she had learned, Thuy arranged three job interviews. "I was so scared, I had 'butterflies' in my stomach," she said, "but I had a professional-looking résumé and had practiced interviewing, so I felt prepared." Thuy was prepared. She was offered two summer jobs, both in hospitals.

"My internship at the University Medical Center has given me more insight into what the world of work is like. It's not bliss, I had to get up at 6:00 A.M. every day to get to work by 8," Thuy said. "At first I was a bit resentful, but then I realized that this was the same thing my parents and sisters learned to do. I guess it was my first real experience as an adult."

Thuy's successful school-to-work experience has strengthened her resolve to go to college and medical school and become a pediatrician or an obstetrician. Her grades and attendance in school have improved, and she has matured and grown in self-confidence. Urban Scholars and the many people involved in the program have helped give Thuy the tools to compete and succeed in the increasingly challenging world of work.

Contributed by Todd Snider

Level 1. Here, students are positioned to examine, rather than avoid, issues of social stratification, looking at the real struggles of people who seek to improve their lives. They can learn to question various myths that make the status quo seem legitimate and fair, and envision alternatives to current arrangements of work and justice (i.e., creating new kinds of livelihood, ensuring medical care for all, and equalizing career opportunities). It is their responsibility to fashion a truly cooperative plan between those in command of our economy and its workers, such that the school and the workplace become places where all variations of ability, age, and culture can contribute and grow.

Full employment may not be a viable goal; but full engagement in meaningful community-oriented activity is something that makes good sense and is honorable and realistic. We will need the ideas and energy of everyone—especially the most gifted of today's youth—to resourcefully meet the challenge of fully engaging the population in meaningful activities when there are "jobs" as we know them only for a diminishing percentage of the general population.

The task of educating future leaders of democracy represents a huge deficiency in our schools. Curriculum reform could deliver this level of service through forums, symposia, and workshops that would attract tomorrow's leaders and put them to work on the social, cultural, educational, and economic problems they are about to face. Developing team- and consensus-building skills, disability, and diversity awareness are all activities that can empower these students to help build a future society where the school-to-adult life transition is a smoother and more enriching process for all citizens. Level 1 services also would help students begin the work of tackling the real-life problems of school-to-work transition such as taxation, wages, profits, skills, distribution of jobs, and alternative means of livelihood.

Citizenship education should include the responsible use of power and the development of a social conscience. Historically, education has been conceptualized as preparation of citizens for public life in a democracy. John Dewey (1938), for example, agreed with Thomas Jefferson's 1779 observation that

> Even under the best of forms, those entrusted with power have, in time, and by slow operations, perverted it into tyranny: … the most effectual means of preventing this would be, to illuminate, as far as predictable, the minds of the people at large. (Chap. 79, Sec. I)

Economically and socially privileged students need to learn how to honor and understand the perspectives of those who have been at a disadvantage. Most people assume that education generally functions in an ideologically neutral manner, and that schools as we know them have the potential to equally prepare everyone to be civic-minded citizens. However, a growing body of literature originating in the "new" sociology of education, critical theory, and multicultural education argues that education actively reproduces the status quo and teaches students to view social injustices as "natural." A more complete education may inspire students to envision and create new economies more conducive to diversity.

For example, despite the passage of the Americans with Disabilities Act, disturbing trends persist in the workplace. The rising costs of benefits and insurance have caused management to seek ways to reduce labor-intensiveness—the fewer employees, the better. The direction of workplace technology has focused primarily on the economic goal of streamlining and downsizing, ignoring the social and cultural need for more jobs. This is a dangerous trend. As long as our society continues to value work as a badge of citizenship and prefers to pay only people who work, we need to make the workplace more, not less, labor-intensive. If effective incentives could be devised, then more jobs that can be performed by a more diverse work force might be created.

If we are not going to create more jobs for people, then we must develop a national attitude that begins to value engagement in terms that are not usually thought of as jobs (care of infants and toddlers, elderly, the environment, etc.). The students receiving services at Levels 1 and 2 are in the best position to forge this new philosophy and give it a pragmatic base.

A Level 5 service that would be appropriate for all students provides an example. In Redmond, Washington, the concept of fully including individuals with disabilities has moved beyond employment with the establishment in 1995 of the ROSE, or Redmond Organization for Supportive Environments. This group of advocates for inclusive communities is developing a fully accessible community garden and has a project whereby persons with significant disabilities can develop their own empowered identity as more than a worker by building the garden as a public work and interacting with nondisabled individuals, as a fully participating member in the community.

Five Levels of Transition Services: Another Version of Tracking?

All five levels of services should be made available to all students. Individualization is one of the subtleties of exemplary educational practices, and has been the foundation of special education for over 30 years. The opposite of tracking is to provide a single, standardized curriculum for all students that does not account for students' unique backgrounds and aspirations. Such a "general track" does the majority of youth a grave injustice. When students are tracked by means of the current system, we maintain current social inequalities. But if we can individualize and customize services within the broad guidelines described earlier with the intention of leveling the playing field, we stand a chance of mitigating, reducing, and ultimately eliminating the differences that necessitated these services in the first place.

The appropriate goal is not to develop state-of-the-art Level 5 services, but to create and support healthy and inclusive families, communities, and elementary schools that help young students grow such that the need for Level 5

services becomes a thing of the past. Schools, communities, and workplaces that naturally accommodate diversity will eventually obviate the need for Level 4 services. Further, full adoption and a deep understanding of democratic principles and a society striving for greater equality would preclude the specific need for overt Level 1 services as well. In the meantime, education's job is to design programs that address inequality and provide opportunities for those at a disadvantage—to thrive, improve their station in life, and climb a career ladder.

Education is one of the linchpins of our democratic society. Its mission is to act as a peaceful equalizer, evenly distributing opportunities for success, wealth, happiness, and growth to all students. Yet nowhere are the virtues and flaws of our educational systems more apparent than in the measure of outcomes of students making the transition from school to adult life.

Educational efforts create currents that can have dramatic effects on these outcomes. Though victories are won one student at a time, and nothing can replace the efforts of instructors and staff who successfully shepherd students through this difficult time, certain systemic factors can either enhance or impede those efforts. The five levels of transition services presented here are a framework for channeling educational effort in a way that is likely to have the greatest positive impact on the greatest number of students. The classroom, the school, special programs, principals, families, employers, labor, and communities make a difference by creating the conditions—multiple options like the five levels of service—under which that student will strive for adult citizenship. In the next section, we discuss how the five-level approach fits into the broader scheme of the educational mission.

CITIZENSHIP AND THE SCHOOL-TO-WORK MOVEMENT

Until our society reaches greater agreement on what the purpose of our educational system is, debate over what to teach, who to teach, and how to teach it will be endless. Until we find ways to provide a consummate education to all students, the social and economic injustices that perpetuate poverty, abuse, alienation, underemployment, and unfulfilled lives will persist. School-to-work and the needs of special populations cannot be treated as add-ons to an educational system that is présuméd to be functioning smoothly. To adopt school-to-career goals for all students requires a renewal of the entire educational mission. Rather than addressing the needs of special populations as a separate activity, we have a pressing obligation to define the universal qualities of education for all students, so that curriculum does not perpetuate social stratification. We are learning that the answers to these problems facing U.S. students and society today do not lie in a system that only prepares the best for a college education. They do not lie in a movement to prepare most or all for a college education. And they do not lie in the 1990s' version of the American dream—that all students exit high school or even community college with a marketable skill. These are all necessary but insufficient goals. The answer is an educational system that, in partnership with the public, private, and nonprofit sectors, prepares students to be fully engaged in the process of being a citizen in a democracy and in their communities at the local, regional, state, national, international, and cybernetic levels—through work, learning, and service in the community.

If we can successfully teach students what it means and how to be a full citizen in a democracy, then many of the issues surrounding postsecondary education and work—at least in terms of student motivation—can be much more successfully addressed. Students should have a strong and growing sense of self, a sense of place in the community, and ways to meaningfully engage themselves in nurturing the health of that community through participation in the governmental processes, work, leisure, and volunteer activities.

If we can teach citizenship, then students will care about being productive and meaning-producing members of their local communities and society at large, and will be motivated to pursué options. For educators to simply promote college and work as atomized "good things" that our children and students "should" pursue is to perpetuate the alienation of youth that plagues both so-called successes and dropouts and continues to hinder the mending of our society. As obvious as the preceding definition of citizenship seems, it is not what television, street warfare, dead-end jobs, computer-based games, or two-career families teach. For educators to simply teach students to conform to the skills set that the latest futurist tells us a future economy will demand means forfeiting the next generation's control of their economic destiny, which, in a true democracy, is part of their birthright.

Finally, for such a citizenship-driven curriculum to be successful, we must acknowledge and provide transition services in the context of a rite of passage from adolescence to adulthood. This, at a bare minimum, addresses youths' underlying need to belong, which may be expressed though a desire to have career training. The archetypal resonance and seriousness of this passage is what ultimately attracts students' interest, provides relevance to them, and produces a mature adult who is enthusiastic about being accepted and included in the world of adults.

WHAT CONSTITUTES A "UNIVERSAL PEDAGOGY"?

The national community is acknowledging the flaws and problems of using the public schools exclusively as places from which to skim the best college material. To move toward a system that makes best efforts to endow all students with marketable skills is a step in the right direction, but it will ultimately fail as a standard of what a public education should provide. The certificate of mastery—a "one-size-fits-all" requirement of the learning objectives all high school graduates in a particular state must meet—is an example of educational reform that has moved from the college-preparation to the "marketable-skills" model. As a reform, it brings to light three of the problems of this model.

States that have required a certificate of mastery soon realized that *certain individuals (i.e., students with developmental disabilities), through no fault of their own, could not reach levels of mastery,* but were still entitled to a free and appropriate public education. The original concept of universal standards quickly breaks down as proponents of certificates of mastery jimmy and duct-tape special cases in order to uphold the standards of mastery without damaging the lives of individuals who cannot meet them. And by cornering itself without adequately considering the special case of students with developmental disabilities, this so-called reform only serves to reinvent the segregated system we have been seeking to outgrow for the past generation.

Although there may have been efforts at collaboration when certificates of mastery were developed, the glaring fact that the standards lack universal application demonstrates that *we have not yet achieved the levels of collaboration nor the skills of consensus necessary to author this scope of reform.* Educators in many school districts, regions, and states have worked hard to develop collaboration between vocational and special education, but when the School-to-Work Opportunities Act of 1994 created a new source of funds and mandated that school-to-work systems serve all students, special education was often left out of the planning, even at the federal level.

The third reason why certificates of mastery reflect an incomplete approach to educational reform is that they are predicated on *the false assumption that all high school graduates will go to work, and the standards of such certificates are based too restrictively on skills needed at the workplace.* If this educational reform moves our system from 50 years behind to 20 years behind, we have made progress, but the job is clearly left undone and the problems remain unsolved. Now that we have awakened to the reality that not every student will attend college, it is time to face the fact that not every student will go to work. Like it or not, technology and capitalism have moved us into an economy that requires fewer and fewer

workers. Any truly contemporary educational reform must adapt to the emerging reality that we will never have full employment. All reform proposals must look to the future, not just catch up with the present. They must balance the economic demands of the current society with the need to educate students to have the vision and means to recreate a better society.

What we can have, in contrast to full employment, is *full engagement.* Public education can and should prepare all students to be fully engaged in a productive and meaningful life, and fully prepared to participate in U.S. democracy. Education toward these goals will produce leaders and citizens, workers and volunteers, independent and interdependent community members.

If we have learned any lesson at all, it is that a single curriculum cannot serve all students. Students need multiple options if all are to succeed. A curriculum that answers three questions *for all students* can nurture and sustain this process: *Who am I in the world? What is my community?* Having answered these first two questions with some degree of satisfaction, *How do I then engage myself and fully participate at all levels of community?*

If we structure reform around these three basic questions, then we can serve all students, and we can support their pursuits of meaningful lives. The following principles for a universal curriculum are intended to provide a context for teaching all subjects and providing a quality education for all students. It is based on the assumption that every comprehensive high school in the United States will offer the finest academic and technical skills education available. However, without the broader context that addresses citizenship and multiple levels of individual abilities, not enough students will care to avail themselves of courses of study and be successfully engaged in their own education and adult life.

To return briefly to the certificate-of-mastery example, it has become clear that this reform was weighted too heavily in the direction of serving the economy and not the diverse needs of students. An alternate proposal that blends economic needs with student interest is that of career majors. STWOA and Gary Clark (Clark & Kolstoe, 1990) have proposed this more sensible reform, that of having high school students select career majors and subsequently coursework that corresponds to those selections. The National Center for Research in Vocational Education is conducting the first survey of high schools with exemplary career majors systems. It is hoped that (a) students with all levels of abilities will be able to have a wide and varied selection of majors and an appropriate course of study, and (b) such high schools will get full cooperation from their states and from postsecondary institutions in obtaining recognition for and accreditation for students from these high schools.

Thus, a student might major in a science, a technical field, the humanities, functional life skills, service occupations, and so on. The diversity of student interest and ability is served by offering a menu of career majors. If, on graduation, the high school diploma itself lists the competencies a student has, future employers will have the benefit they seek: an accurate description of what the student can do.

Who Am I in the World?

Students need activities that build a sense of self. They need practice and conceptual rationales for living with sensitivity to others, and they need to develop values and value systems for which they take full ownership. As this learning accumulates, students develop a positive identity, the sine qua non for moving forward toward citizenship and a full, rich adult life. Despite the gibing it receives, self-esteem is essential to students' readiness to learn, their immunity to drug abuse and violence, and their ability to commit to a career for themselves and the welfare of others. "Love thyself" and "know thyself" are educational precepts altogether accordant with the mission of public education in a democracy.

Field and Hoffman (1994) viewed this process as self-determination: "the ability to define and achieve goals based on a foundation of knowing and valuing oneself" (p. 164). Thus, self-knowledge is actualized and operationalized by self-advocacy and being able to implement a plan. This process will be taken up again in the section, "How Do I Engage?"

Many alternative education, vocational education, special education, and rehabilitation programs attempt to help young people develop a positive feeling about themselves. They provide experiences in which students succeed, receive praise for their accomplishments, and are granted pay or personal attention that fosters self-worth and builds relationships. Ultimately, many students also need to develop a positive image of themselves as members of special groups. This means not just focusing on their individual and unique attributes as a person with a disability or member of a special group, but facing their identity squarely and learning to feel proud of themselves and of others who are members of the same group. Just as minority students can move from a position of being limited by the system to one where their educational experience is an empowering one (Cummins, 1986), so can students with disabilities or members of all special groups.

Banks (1981, 1991) proposed several stages of ethnic identity that can be applied to other groups. In the first stage, *Psychological Captivity,* the individual accepts the negative stereotypes of his or her group that abound in society. Such stereotypes could be that African-Americans are lazy, musical, criminal, highly sexual, and so forth, or that people with disabilities are dumb, happy, undeserving, pathetic, "goody-goody," asexual, and so forth. Children who are members of oppressed groups often believe these stereotypes, and as a result think they are incapable of success, or that their needs and interests are not important. Sometimes they look down on other members of their own group. Often they try to dissemble to the outside world that they are not really members of this group, engaging in impression management (Goffman, 1959).

The second stage, *Encapsulation,* is the reverse of the first stage. Individuals at this stage believe that their group is superior to others and does not need to interact with other groups. Members have learned positive accomplishments of their group, and if their group is oppressed, how it has been victimized by others. Deaf children, for example, can learn that "Deaf is Beautiful," and much about other deaf people that supports this claim.

Finally, the third stage is *Identity Clarification,* in which the person understands and values the group identity, but also understands and values other groups. Banks argued that, this third stage is preferable for all people, but that the second stage is an important transition for those who begin at the first stage.

Frank (1988) provided a fascinating description of the development of the personal identities of three people with severe congenital limb deficiencies, over their life spans. Although she did not use Banks' stages for her discussion, it is clear how two of these individuals dealt with Psychological Captivity issues, and how all three arrived at the stage of Identity Clarification. Frank shows how these three people rejected the stigma nondisabled people often attribute to disabilities in a healthy and empowering way. One also sees how arrival at the stage of Identity Clarification is not automatic, but could be facilitated through education (Siegel & Slecter, 1992).

As students gain a greater and more formed sense of self, the time comes for them to address the social task of becoming sensitive to others. The technical curriculum that directly addresses this is *social skills training,* a prominent feature of cooperative learning. The numerous curricula on the market offer approaches that range from the behavioral (Goldstein et al., 1980; Walker et al., 1993) to peer-counseling models (Varenhorst, 1980; Gibbs, 1987; Palomares, 1990). Chadsey and Shelden in Chapter 17 in this volume offer a look at this component of career education. Curriculum approaches need to account for the complexity of social skills (including conflict resolution and peer mediation), and the diversity of adolescent needs, ranging from what adolescents need to present to their peer groups, to the high school environment, to the work and adult community world.

Schools create a social schism by secluding children into elementary and middle schools, where they are kept out of the way of market-economy settings, except as consumers. By the time they enter secondary school, the process of living in their own peer culture zone is at an advanced stage, and many youth have created an oppositional culture deliberated to fly in the face of what a workplace social skills curriculum might look like. Certain youth peer groups disdain study and punish youth members who attempt to achieve in school (*San Francisco Focus,* 1995). Dress codes and slang are developed that challenge the straight-laced expectations of a workplace setting. Clearly, there is a structural issue that inhibits connection to the community. This issue could be partly addressed by a greater use of community-based education in the earlier grades—service learning, job shadowing, and volunteer opportunities (Corporation for National Service, 1996). But we must also remain open to the probability that students who do not behave as we would like them to are trying to tell us something worth hearing (Kohl, 1994).

As youths discover and develop their interests and values, there is a consequential *need* to advocate for them. Affective education opens up the process of honestly identifying feelings. From there, values develop and take shape. In the workplace, conflicts over values are certain to occur, and the better students are able to identify and express their feelings and values, the more competently they are likely to resolve or at least come to grips with those conflicts. They must be able to identify the feelings that accompany the behavior changes that are necessary to succeed in the workplace.

Thus, education is faced with a complex task: first, to teach students to behave so that they will be employable, gaining the rights that come with employment and income; and second, to help them recognize—not rationalize or repress—the feelings that come with many employment situations, and to make wise decisions based on that recognition. For example, troublesome relationships with a manager must be resolved by a young employee in a non-antagonistic, yet sincere fashion if the youth is to retain employment and avoid harboring hostility.

It will be workers and citizens with character and well-developed value systems who will be able to shape the future's economy and society to the will of the people. Students will apply their strengthened sense of self and the ability to be socially skillful when they see that they are tools for advancing their own developing values. There is great controversy in the United States regarding the teaching of values in the public schools. The most strenuous objections to values education come from those who would prefer that their specific set of values be taught. The most suitable role for public education in a democracy is not to teach values per se, but to staunchly defend and aggressively pursue effective curricula that teach students and engage them in the *act of valuing*. Students, in the context of their families, their peers, their religious groups, or their own individual quests, are free to develop personal values. And there are processes by which a community can agree on values that should be taught in the schools (Berreth & Scherer, 1993; Huffman, 1993). As part of its campaign for essential learnings, the state of Washington's Commission on Student Learning, formed in 1992, said:

> The legislature also recognizes that certain basic values and character traits are essential to individual liberty, fulfillment, and happiness. However, these values and traits are not intended to be assessed or be standards for graduation. The legislature intends that local communities have the responsibility for determining how these values and character

traits are learned as determined by consensus at the local level. These values and traits include the importance of

- Honesty, Integrity, and Trust
- Respect for Self and Others
- Responsibility for Personal Actions and Commitments
- Self-Discipline and Moderation
- Diligence and a Positive Work Ethic
- Respect for Law and Authority
- Healthy and Positive Behavior
- Family as the Basis of Society

(Washington State Commission on Student Learning, 1994)

For these values to be expressed and lived in a civilized and responsible fashion, all students need public education. This is the definition of civic responsibility in a democracy. Specific to career education, students must explore their values if our system has any hope of producing workers with reasonably high levels of job satisfaction.

What Is My Community?

As students develop a stronger internal sense of self, they gain the means of better relating to and understanding the world around them. This translates to the need to educate all youth for democratic citizenship and social responsibility. In the old model, these issues were addressed through history and civics curricula. Today, students need to interact with the community around them and explore questions of their own personal ancestry and ethnicity; understand the local, regional, state, national, international, and cybernetic communities; and develop a deeper understanding of economics and political systems.

Certainly, academic skills are critical to competent engagement for an aspiring worker, citizen, and human being seeking a rich and full life. The same Commission on Student Learning (see earlier) summarized and mandated four essential learning goals for all students in the state; they include academic and employment skills. Though they have the attribute of being applicable to the capabilities of *almost* all students, the theme of citizenship is still relegated to a minor aspect of Goal 2:

> Goal 1: Read with comprehension, write with skill, and communicate effectively and responsibly in a variety of ways and settings.
>
> Goal 2: Know and apply the core concepts and principles of mathematics; social, physical, and life sciences; civics and history; geography; arts; and health and fitness.
>
> Goal 3: Think analytically, logically, and creatively, and integrate experience and knowledge to form reasoned judgments and solve problems.
>
> Goal 4: Understand the importance of work and how performance, effort, and decisions directly affect career and educational opportunities.

(Washington State Commission on Student Learning, 1994)

In a curriculum developed by Parker (Edgar et al., 1994) for noncollege-bound middle and high school students from the Belief Academy, the "What is my community"? question was elegantly and meaningfully addressed. Students were expected to investigate the environment, historical accounts, geography, taxes, the arts, their family histories, and occupations, all in the interest of developing a deepening sense of their place in the world and learning the means of gathering information. This set of activities increased students' sense of self and their knowledge of their environment, and prepared them to enter into the third and final phase of public education, full engagement in the community.

How Do I Engage?

The first stage of engagement is for students to take their heightened sense of identity and place and put it into action through self-advocacy and self-determination. This is discussed earlier in this chapter, and is addressed by Wehmeyer in Chapter 9 as well. Five components, when included as part of citizenship training, facilitate this process.

Self-Determination. First is *problem ownership,* where students learn which problems are in fact theirs, so that they can begin to discriminate when they are unfairly attributing problems to other players in their lives. Problem ownership is a requirement for competent decision making. Second is *problem-solving skills,* where students identify feelings, specific problems, and broader issues, generate and test alternatives, and, finally, plan and act on strategies. These skills give students a positive presence and enable them to cope, advocate for themselves, and to negotiate competently when they do eventually go to work. Third is the actual rehearsal of *social skills,* which increases the likelihood that students will experience social acceptance on the job. Social-skills training has received substantial attention in the special education literature (Bullis & Foss, 1986; Lignugaris/Kraft et al., 1986; Kazdin et al., 1987; Chadsey-Rusch & Rusch, 1988), and is addressed by Chadsey and Shelden in Chapter 17 of this book. Fourth is *team building,* where the ability to gather support for a career from the players and resources in a school-based ecosystem (peers, family, community, teachers, etc.) is generalized and transferred to an adult ecosystem (peers, family, co-workers, employers, community, rehabilitation professionals, etc.). Finally, *ecosystematic intervention* and ongoing support, with the services of an external trainer and advocate eventually fading out, permit job placements to succeed and provide a margin of insulation so that the first steps toward self-advocacy might be successful.

Skills. The employment skills most essential to the technical aspects of a successful transition are very easily summarized as attendance, social skills, job-keeping (or employer-pleasing) skills, the job skills themselves, and job-search skills. Lesson plans that elaborate on these skills can be found in Siegel and colleagues (1993). The thirty-seven job-related competencies taught by Jobs for America's Graduates provide a reasonable summary of employability skills. Also, the Life-Centered Career Education curriculum published by the Council for Exceptional Children (Brolin, 1995) offers a complete curriculum on employability skills. Finally, there are numerous other quality products on the market. Academic skills are summarized by the four essential learning goals enumerated earlier.

Engagement. Work and work experience constitute the most common form of adult engagement in societal activity. But community service and service learning are other critical forms that are gaining in usage in public schools. Schools that implement a community service program require students to volunteer in the nonprofit sector. Many school districts now require a community service project from every graduating senior in which they must apply their academic skills by contributing to and documenting their experience. One *Goals 2000: Learn and Serve America* grant includes projects such as elementary school students working with a forest agency to track and document salmon migrations; a middle school group mending clothing and donating it to a homeless shelter; a high school group volunteering in an AIDS hospice center; and a group of Native-American students preparing a multimedia presentation on their culture and sharing it with other schools in their region.

As the engagement experience builds, students can be expected to participate in groups of citizens that form around the concerns and aspirations represented by the site of their community service. Youths need to learn to analyze their status and the status of others in the social structure in order to understand precisely the manner and to what extent they are affected by external forces. Why do the elderly and infirm live where they do? How did an endangered species become endangered? Why are so many people homeless? How did this river become polluted?

For example, despite the great strides made in the technology for employing people with disabilities, the full-time employment rate of people with disabilities is not yet on par with that of the rest of the population. Sheltered employment has been shown to be a self-sustaining system that delays the entry of citizens with developmental disabilities into the competitive workplace, yet this system persists today. In many communities, zoning laws limit housing for people with developmental disabilities to certain areas. Furthermore, few people with disabilities are ever elected to public office. These are areas of life where most people with disabilities have limited choices and resources, whereas the average citizen regards them as a natural right. These are examples of issues students can learn to investigate and analyze.

Group Membership and Advocacy. Youths need to learn both to utilize existing advocacy groups and to organize collectively to accomplish specific advocacy tasks. Many people experience collective needs and frustrations. For example, a person hired into a job that has no benefits, or who attempts to use social institutions that are poorly accessible, experiences a collective problem. Collective problems need to be addressed collectively, not just individually. Collective organization around social problems can bring about social changes. For example, ADAPT (American Disabled for Accessible Public Transit), a national organization that works to make public transportation more accessible to people with disabilities, has won several victories against transportation facilities as large as the Chicago Transit Authority ("Chicago Transit Violates Illinois Law," 1988). An organization project in Wisconsin has had several successes, including impact on "policy formation, program implementation, and service delivery" (Checkoway & Norsman, 1986).

People First, the National Association of the Deaf, and the National Foundation for the Blind are examples of other advocacy groups. Whereas individuals working alone may not be able to effect such changes, individuals working collectively can.

Groups do not always exist to serve specific needs. For example, a person with a learning disability may work for an employer who requires reading and writing tasks that are unnecessary to the job itself; yet the employer periodically fires or refuses wage increases on that basis. That individual would need to find out whether other employees are experiencing the same difficulty. If the individual is skilled in organizing a group, developing a collective statement and examination of the problem, negotiating differences, and devising collective action strategies, he or she will be in a position to advocate for themselves and others. Cooperative learning in school helps young people develop many of these skills necessary to do this. Role plays that address political analysis of and collective action on problems develop pertinent skills and attitudes and help put them into a social context (for an excellent resource, see Scheidewind & Davidson, 1983).

How might this look on the "work" end of the school-to-work transition? The self-directed work groups used in Japanese and some American auto manufacturing plants have assumed a form of collective action in concert with employers that allows for diversity in the workplace. These work groups, in which the manufacture of the product is delegated to the workers, and the production tasks distributed and renegotiated on the front line, have unfortunately been limited to an elite stratum of the work force. But the model has enormous potential, as it implicitly views people with disabilities as simply a few workers among many who all bring different strengths to the tasks at hand.

This final curriculum strand must give students of all abilities an opportunity to synthesize their sense of self with their sense of place, and develop their vision of the future and the belief that they have the power to create that vision. Although it is not often couched in such grand terms, this is precisely the role of the career counselor: to view each student as an active creator of the world, and not a passive peg to be placed in the appropriate hole. To achieve this more complex task means making the entire curriculum of the school relevant to the student's past (Who am I?), present (What is my community?), and future (How do I engage?) life. It means involving all aspects of the student's being in the equation of making and pursuing career choice.

Although career education in the elementary years is not the focus of this chapter, it is important. Clark (1979) has developed a career education curriculum for elementary school students. One example of how the school-to-work movement is beginning to make an impact at that level is *2001: A Career Odyssey* where partners from education, labor, business, and the community have come together to prepare a 2-hour presentation on the changing economy and how schools can prepare students to succeed. The presentation is made before PTAs of elementary and middle schools, and concludes with a process whereby the schools develop their own school-to-work plan.

Table 7.2 summarizes a curriculum for career and life skills. It serves as a guide to all teachers such that aspects of education for adult life always occupy a prominent place in the curriculum. In the middle grades, students need strong and varied role models; this is an age where it is so important and so rare for a student to be connected to the work and lives of adults. If we were to fully implement job-shadowing and job-mentoring programs, we could avert much of the disenfranchisement that confounds our best efforts in later years. Students at this age must stay healthy; they must maximize their literacy, math, and learning skills; and they must make working in groups and working for product daily events.

The freshman and sophomore years are times for developing emotional responsibility (affective education), a sense of what a dollar buys, what the work world expects, and work routines. Now is the time for students to do work internships on a regular basis. This is one of the best ways for students to discover the career paths that will inspire their passion and discipline.

In the transition time, 1 and 2 years before graduation, students are ready to hold down some type of part-time job and begin serious training, perhaps in a tech-prep program. They should be developing a deeper understanding of law and government, and letting it temper their own social vision. They need to connect with adult service agencies that are likely to be providing service after graduation. They need to develop support groups among their peers to minimize the need for other services.

CONCLUSION

One of the most serious shortcomings of a narrow view of the school-to-careers transition is the looming reality of fewer jobs. Many school-to-work programs still operate on the notion that there are enough jobs out there or that entrepreneurship will create enough new jobs. With its admirable zero-reject philosophy, American schools will seek successful school-to-work transitions for all of its students. But this is never going to happen.

What is possible is that some day all students will make successful transitions from school to *adult life,* and they will be meaningfully *engaged,* but not always in a job as we know it now. Educators must be active participants in a national dialogue on the development of relevant public educational systems and workforce development. Issues such as redistribution of labor, the end of jobs as we know them, and the growth of the third sector are paramount. Some of the writers who are addressing these questions are Juliet B. Schor (1991) in *The Overworked American,* Peter Drucker (1994) in *The Third Sector,* Matthew Fox (1994) in *The Reinvention of Work,* and Jeremy Rifkin (1995) in *The End of Work.*

Job sharing remains a cutting-edge reform that gives more work opportunities to more people. In Europe, nations are redistributing work and moving toward more flexible scheduling and 4-day workweeks. In exchange for accepting unusual shifts, workers receive the same pay for 20 percent fewer hours on the job. The increased productivity more than compensates. The educational field can participate in the move to more fully distribute labor throughout the population by modeling the best of these ideas within their own schools, promoting redistribution concepts, and keeping these ideas vital through educational activities for students, teachers, and employers.

Engagement activities and "jobs" of the future must include community service as a viable option. Our society must support work activities that build community and the social health of citizens. This is a daunting challenge that all sectors of society will have to address. Rifkin (1995) has suggested tax deductions and credits for time volunteered in community organizations. Education's role is to promote and require community service of its students, and to promulgate this concept as it gains acceptance and provides a new and growing arena where youth in transition can find meaningful engagement in society at large.

Jobs as we now know them are ending. Though the school-to-work movement signals a huge attempt at having U.S. schools catch up, it will not be enough if broadened concepts of engagement do not further propel that movement. There are ideas for full engagement that our adult community has not even considered. We need our students—the adult community of the future—to be equipped to create those visions and ideas. If school-to-work is narrowly interpreted to mean training in job skills for the current and predicted economy, the movement will have built a cul-de-sac from which we are not likely to escape. That is why school-to-work transition and education for citizenship in a democracy must be viewed, implemented, and taught as the same endeavor.

All students are capable of learning, all students are capable of making a contribution to their local community, and all students are capable of having a sense of self, of place, and how they can fit into the big picture of our national and global communities. To so merge the curriculum and instruction of school-to-career education with the entire educational enterprise is a natural fit, one that should be pursued, and should engage the efforts of all students, families, and educators concerned with the quality of education.

The risk of making this argument is that it begins to sound like support for the liberal arts, general education track that a strong school-to-work movement was meant to supersede. But there is a huge difference. To develop a strong school-to-work movement is essential, and it should take a leading role. But it should not leave the main virtue of the liberal arts education—the creation of free-thinking citizens—in its wake. Nor should it ignore the huge trends of an ever-changing labor market. Nor should it be a slave to those trends. The school-to-work movement is an opportunity to create a curriculum and instructional opportunities that are relevant, directly tied to the community, and academically challenging. Such a curriculum has the potential of empowering all students to help revitalize our democratic society through the full engagement of their talents and abilities.

QUESTIONS

1. Describe the three components of the School-to-Work Opportunities Act, and discuss the potential problems with implementing each component.

2. Describe the five levels of transition services and the type of student circumstances under which each level might be most appropriate.

3. What are some of the problems encountered when designing school-to-work transition services for youths who are coming out of the juvenile justice system? What would a good program look like?

4. What does it mean to "shape services to the lives of the youths served?"

5. Describe the four areas, and give examples, of where educators can make a contribution to youths in need of Level 2 services.

6. Are school-to-work services necessary for students who are baccalaureate-bound? Why or why not?

7. Describe what is meant by "citizenship education."

8. What is the difference between providing services at five levels of intensity and an educational system that "tracks" students?

9. What is the difference between "engagement" and "employment"? Why is this an important distinction?

10. Summarize the curriculum that best answers the three questions that constitute a universal pedagogy. What is your opinion of this model?

REFERENCES

Banks, J. A. (1981). *Multiethnic education: Theory and practice.* Boston: Allyn & Bacon.

———. (1991). A curriculum for empowerment, action, and change. In C. E. Sleeter (Ed.), *Empowerment through multicultural education* (pp. 125–142). Albany: SUNY Press.

Berreth, D., & Scherer, M. (1993). On transmitting values: A conversation with Amitai Etzioni. *Educational Leadership, 51*(3), 12–15.

Brolin, D. (1995). The Life Centered Career Education Curriculum. Reston, VA: Council for Exceptional Children.

Bullis, M., & Foss, G. (1986). Guidelines for assessing job-related social skills of mildly handicapped students. *Career Development for Exceptional Individuals, 9*(2), 89–97.

Chadsey-Rusch, J. & Rusch F. R.,(1988). Ecology of the workplace. In R. Gaylord-Ross (Ed.), *Vocational education for persons with handicaps* (pp. 234–256). Palo Alto, CA: Mayfield.

Checkoway, B., & Norsman, A. (1986). Empowering citizens with disabilities. *Community Development Journal, 21,* 270–277.

Chicago transit violates Illinois law with separate bus service, judge rules. (1988, March/April). *Disability Rag,* p. 9.

Clark, G. M. (1979). *Career education for the handicapped child in the elementary classroom*. Denver: Love.

Clark, G. M., & Kolstoe, O. P. (1990). *Career development and transition education for adolescents with disabilities.* Boston: Allyn & Bacon.

Clifford, M. A., & Flores, R. (1995). Creating a partnership agreement. In N. Thiers (Ed.), *Successful strategies: Building a school-to-careers system* (pp. 11–18). Alexandria, VA: American Vocational Association.

Corporation for National Service. (1996). *Expanding boundaries: Serving and learning.* Columbia, MD: Cooperative Education Association.

Cummins, J. (1986). Empowering minority students: A framework for intervention. *Harvard Educational Review, 56*(1), 18–36.

Dawson, J. E., & Stan, P. J. E. (1995). *Public expenditures in the United States: 1992–1993.* Santa Monica, CA: RAND Corporation.

Dewey, J. (1938). *Experience and education.* New York: Macmillan.

Drucker, P. F. (1994). The age of social transformation. *Atlantic Monthly, 274*(5), 53–80.

Edgar, E., Parker, W., Siegel, S., & Johnson, E. (1994). Curricula options at the secondary level: Preparing youth for the 21st century. *Preventing School Failure, 38*(2), 7–12.

Field, S., & Hoffman, A. (1994). Development of a model for self-determination. *Career Development for Exceptional Individuals, 17*(2), 159–169.

Fox, M. (1994). *The reinvention of work.* New York: HarperCollins.

Frank, G. (1988). Beyond stigma: Visibility and self-empowerment of persons with congenital limb deficiencies. *Journal of Social Issues, 44,* 95–115.

Gibbs, J. (1987). *Tribes: A process for social development and cooperative learning.* Santa Rosa, CA: Center Source Publications.

Gladwell, M. (1996, June 3). The tippling point. *The New Yorker,* pp. 32–38.

Goffman, E. (1959). *The presentation of self in everyday life.* Garden City, NY: Doubleday.

Goldstein, A. P., Sprafkin, R. P., Gershaw, N. J., & Klein, P. (1980). *Skillsreaming the adolescent.* Champaign, IL: Research.

Greenwood, P. W., Model, K. E., Rydell, C. P., & Chiesa, J. (1996). *Diverting children from a life of crime: Measuring costs and benefits.* Santa Monica, CA: RAND Corporation.

Hazelkorn, M. N., & Lombard, R. C. (1991). Designated vocational instruction: Instructional support strategies. *Career Development for Exceptional Individuals, 14,* 15–25.

Hobbs, N. (1982). *The troubled and troubling child.* San Francisco: Jossey-Bass.

Huffman, H. A. (1993). Character education without turmoil. *Educational Leadership, 51*(3), 24–27.

Kazdin, A. E., Esveldt-Dawson, K., French, N. H., & Unis, A. S. (1987). Problem-solving skills training and relationship therapy in the treatment of antisocial child behavior. *Journal of Consulting and Clinical Psychology, 55*(1), 76–85.

Koeninger, J. G. (1995). A model for serving at-risk students. In N. Thiers (Ed.), *Successful strategies: Building a school-to-careers system* (pp. 227–236). Alexandria, VA: American Vocational Association.

Kohl, H. (1994). *"I won't learn from you" and other thoughts on creative maladjustment.* New York: New Press.

Kozol, J. (1991). *Savage inequalities: Children in American schools.* New York: Crown.

Lignugaris/Kraft, B., Salzberg, C. L., Stowitschek, J. J., & McConaughy, E. K. (1986). Social interacting patterns among employees in sheltered and nonprofit business settings. *Career Development Quarterly, 35*(2), 123–135.

Palomares, V. (1990). *Magic circle.* San Clemente, CA: Magic Circle.

Phelps, L. A., & Wermuth, T. R. (1992). *Effective vocational education for students with special needs: A framework.* Berkeley: University of California, National Center for Research in Vocational Education.

Prickette, K. (1995). *Designated vocational instruction: A cooperative process for change* (2nd ed.). Madison: Wisconsin Department of Public Instruction.

Rifkin, J. (1995). *The end of work: The decline of the global labor force and the dawn of the post-market era.* New York: Putnam.

San Francisco Focus. (1995, January). Marshall Plan: The interview, pp. 52–56.

Scheidewind, N., & Davidson, E. (1983). *Open minds to equality.* Englewood Cliffs, NJ: Prentice Hall.

School-to-Work Opportunities Act of 1994, P.L. 103-239, 20, U.S.C. 6101 et seq.

Schor, J. B. (1991) *The overworked American.* New York: HarperCollins.

Siegel, S. (1992). *Job shadowing as career exploration for young teenagers.* Unpublished manuscript, San Fransisco.

Siegel, S., Robert, M., Avoke, S. K., Paul, P., & Gaylord-Ross, R. (1991). A second look at the adult lives of participants in the Career Ladder Program. *Journal of Vocational Rehabilitation, 1*(4), 9–23.

Siegel, S., Robert, M., Greener, K., Meyers, G., Halloran, W., & Gaylord-Ross, R. (1993). *Career ladders for challenged youths in transition from school to adult life.* Austin, TX: PRO-ED.

Siegel, S., Robert, M., Waxman, M., & Gaylord-Ross, R. (1992). A follow-along study of participants in a longitudinal transition program for youths with mild disabilities. *Exceptional Children, 58*(4), 346–356.

Siegel, S., & Sleeter, C. (1991). Transforming transition: Next stages for the school-to-work transition movement. *Career Development for Exceptional Individuals, 14*(1), 27–41.

Simon, M., Cobb, B., Norman, M., & Bourexis, P. (1994). *Meeting the needs of youth with disabilities: Handbook for implementing community-based vocational education programs according to the Fair Labor Standards Act,* cooperative agreement H158G0002. Washing-ton, DC: U.S. Department of Education, Office of Special Education and Rehabilitative Services, National Transition Network.

Thiers, N. (Ed.) (1995). *Successful strategies: Building a school-to-careers system.* Alexandria, VA: American Vocational Association.

Varenhorst, B. B. (1980). *Curriculum guide for student peer counseling.* Palo Alto, CA: Author.

Walker, H. M., Todis, B., Holmes, D., & Horton, G. (1993). *Adolescent curriculum for communication and effective social skills.* Austin, TX: PRO-ED.

Washington State Commission on Student Learning. (1994). *High standards: Essential learnings for Washington's students. A work in progress.* Olympia: Author.

Wilson, W. J. (1987). *The truly disadvantaged.* Chicago: University of Chicago.

8

◉

Implementing a Transition Perspective of Education

A Comprehensive Approach to Planning and Delivering Secondary Education and Transition Services

PAULA D. KOHLER

This chapter presents a transition perspective that represents a comprehensive approach to educational program development consisting of an alignment of student goals with educational experiences and services. With a focus on implementing the transition perspective, five categories of effective transition-focused practices are identified and described: (a) student-focused planning, (b) student development, (c) interagency and interdisciplinary collaboration, (d) family involvement, and (e) program structures and attributes. Results of a research study to identify who should be responsible for implementing the practices are then presented. Specific roles are described for special, vocational, and regular educators; transition specialists; school counselors; rehabilitation counselors and other community service providers; school and school district administrators; parents and family members; and students. Implications for professional development are also introduced.

The most frequently asked questions related to transition planning focus on the *what, who,* and *how* of developing and delivering transition-related instruction and services. The answers to these questions depend primarily on one's perspective of transition planning and, subsequently, on the particular local context of schools, students, and community resources and opportunities. This chapter will start with a rationale for adopting a broad perspective of transition planning and subsequently present a research-based model for planning, developing, and evaluating transition-focused education programs. Finally, based on recent research, specific suggestions will be offered for delivering transition-related instruction and services.

A TRANSITION PERSPECTIVE

The concept of *transition planning* means different things to different people. Many in the field of special education view transition planning from a narrow perspective that focuses specifically on a student's movement from school to immediate postschool activities. When viewed in this manner, transition planning typically refers to those linking activities that occur primarily during a student's final year or two of high school. During this period, the school or educational agency refers the student to adult service providers who then pick up service provision on the student's exit from school. Edgar (1987) illuminated this concept of transition planning in his discussion of sending agencies, receiving agencies, and the event/process of the handoff. Indeed, the famous "bridges" transition model formulated by the Office of Special Education and Rehabilitative Services (Will, 1983) focused primarily on the bridges—or service routes—that students utilize when moving from high school to employment. Although a high school foundation was a primary component of the Will (1983) model, much attention was directed to the connecting activities or bridges that lead from school to employment.

A number of problems have emerged that can be attributed to a narrow interpretation of transition planning. Prior to 1990, one problem was local education agencies' tendency to use a "check-off" procedure on a student's IEP to indicate that transition issues or services had been addressed. Again, the focus was on connecting students with postschool service providers. With the mandate for transition services by the Individuals with Disabilities Education Act (IDEA) of 1990, this check-off process was modified in many cases, but not forsaken. Many local education agencies' tendency to meet the letter of the law rather than the intent has resulted in expanded IEP forms that include lists of outcomes, services, and agencies that purportedly represent a coordinated set of activities developed through an outcome-oriented process. Typically, IEP developers check off specific outcomes, identify disability-specific curricula, and indicate referral to adult agencies to meet the transition requirements (Kohler & Rusch, 1996). Thus, although more specific than pre-IDEA practice, this practice reinforces the notion that transition planning represents primarily the *process* or actual movement of students from school, rather than the *preparation* for that movement.

Closely related to the "check-off" problem, perhaps as a result of it, is the problem that transition planning has yet to become institutionalized as a primary aspect of education. That is, transition planning has been *added on* to the educational process of students with disabilities, rather than becoming the fundamental basis of that education. Stodden and Leake (1994) noted that past attempts to include transition planning and services in educational programs have met with resistance and have achieved limited success because they have been "hampered by a pervasive tendency to add programs to the core of the education system, rather than infusing essential changes into the core itself" (p. 65). In practice, secondary special education teachers have assumed most of the transition planning burden, as they are the ones typically responsible for developing students' IEPs (Wagner, 1993; Wagner, Blackorby & Hebbeler, 1993a). As a result, transition planning has become an added responsibility requiring substantial supporting documentation and paperwork to those who are already overwhelmed by the daily demands of teaching, planning, and record keeping (Gajar, Goodman, & McAfee, 1993; Kohler, 1996a). Again, therefore, transition planning is perceived often to be a *process* that focuses on a *process*.

A number of authors (e.g., Rusch et al., 1992a; Gajar et al., 1993; Clark & Kolstoe, 1995; Kohler, 1996a; Kohler & Rusch, 1996) have suggested the need for a much broader interpretation of transition planning and services. This definition includes the notion that *all* educational programs and instructional activities should be (a) based on the postschool goals of students and (b) developed on the basis of individual needs, interests, and preferences.

As an example, let us review the educational program of a typical college-bound student enrolled in college-preparation curricula during high school. This student takes 2 years of foreign language instruction and academic coursework required by most 4-year universities; registers for and takes the SAT or ACT exams, also required for admission; identifies and applies to selected colleges and universities; identifies and applies for appropriate scholarships or financial aid; and participates in extracurricular activities that develop personal, social, and leadership skills that enhance one's ability to succeed. Many individuals within the school and community setting work with this college-bound student to see that these various tasks are accomplished and somewhat personalized, including teachers, guidance counselors, coaches and other club sponsors, administrators, parents, and even employers. Importantly, this student is actively involved in planning his or her schedule each year, choosing electives, identifying careers and colleges of interest, and choosing the clubs and sports in which to participate.

The new broader interpretation of these interrelated activities considers these events, this process, as *transition planning*. Kohler and Rusch (1996) refer to this interpretation as a *transition perspective* of education. Thus, transition services are defined as they are by IDEA, but the "coordinated set of activities" (34 C.F.R., Section 300.18) is interpreted to mean *all* the educational activities and programs in which a student participates. This transition perspective does not view "transition planning" as an add-on activity for students with disabilities once they reach age 16, but as a fundamental basis of education that guides the development of all educational programs.

With respect to specific postschool goals, transition planning occurs for students who plan to go on to postsecondary education. As illustrated earlier, their educational programs and instructional activities are designed to help them attain their postschool training goal related to employment—a college education. Our educational systems are set up to facilitate this transition planning process for students who are college bound, albeit informally. Generally, the system has been effective for this population of students (Berliner, cited in Edgar & Polloway, 1994). However, the statistics suggest that for students who are not college-bound—both students with and without disabilities—the system has not been very effective (Hasazi, Gordon, & Roe, 1985; Mithaug, Horiuchi, & Fanning, 1985; Wagner, 1989, 1993; Wagner et al., 1992).

To summarize, the transition perspective views the educational planning process as consisting of the following steps:

- postschool goals are identified based on student abilities, needs, interests, and preferences

- instructional activities and educational experiences are developed to prepare students for their postschool goals

- a variety of individuals, including the student, work together to identify and develop the goals and activities

This transition perspective reinforces an emerging consumer-oriented paradigm that provides an outcome-oriented structure for educational planning (Kohler & Rusch, 1996). This emerging paradigm represents a shift from disability-focused, deficit-driven programs to a new education and service-delivery approach that is based on abilities, options, and self-determination (Szymanski, Hanley-Maxwell, & Parker, 1990b; Wehman, 1992a; Kohler & Rusch, 1996). Our challenge is to build educational systems and structures that make the transition perspective operational for *all* students.

BUILDING A FRAMEWORK: A TAXONOMY FOR TRANSITION PROGRAMMING

In order to promote student-oriented outcome planning, secondary education programs must be transformed from deficit-based, disability-driven programs to outcome-based, ability-driven programs (Rusch et al., 1992a; Gajar et al., 1993;

Clark & Kolstoe, 1995; Kohler & Rusch, 1996). The IDEA Amendments of 1990 and 1997, the Rehabilitation Act Amendments of 1992, the Carl D. Perkins Vocational Education and Applied Technology Act of 1990, and the School-to-Work Opportunities Act of 1994 provide a policy framework for structuring secondary education. Research on effective transition practices provides the substance with which to build these programs.

Kohler and colleagues (e.g., Rusch, Kohler, & Hughes, 1992b; Kohler, 1993a, 1996a; Kohler et al., 1994;) developed a Taxonomy for Transition Programming (Kohler, 1994b, 1996b), which presents a comprehensive, conceptual organization of practices that represent the transition perspective of secondary education. Education practices that define the taxonomy are organized into five categories that are relevant for organizing schools and instruction to facilitate transition: student-focused planning, student development, interagency and interdisciplinary collaboration, family involvement, and program structure and attributes (see Figure 8.1). The conceptual framework represented by the taxonomy operationalizes the transition perspective and depicts the consumer-oriented paradigm that serves as its foundation. As such, the taxonomy represents the things we need to *do* to provide transition-focused education.

Student-Focused Planning

Individualized planning is the key to effectively matching a student's educational program and school experiences to his or her postschool goals, and is an essential construct of the transition perspective and the consumer-oriented paradigm. Theoretically, an IEP was intended to serve as a means of adapting education to meet the needs of students with disabilities. Over the years, however, individual planning has been characterized by disability-based planning with little student involvement.

The IEP is the planning vehicle for implementing the transition requirements specified in the IDEA Amendments of 1990 and 1997. In defining transition services, the legislation

focused on outcomes, activities, students' preferences and interests, and student, parent, and service provider involvement. As indicated in Figure 8.1, a comprehensive approach to developing outcome-focused educational programs, therefore, must address IEP development, student (and family) participation, and specific planning strategies. Student participation in this process is essential, and self-determination skills may be fundamental for participation (Van Reusen & Bos, 1990; Wehmeyer, 1992; Schloss, Alper, & Jayne, 1994).

As illustrated in previous discussion, a number of individuals participate in helping nondisabled college-bound students achieve their long- and short-term goals. For example, teachers, counselors, coaches, parents, and peers typically work in concert with the student to ensure that he or she engages in curricular and extracurricular activities that are associated with the goal of postsecondary education.

By contrast, special education teachers traditionally have taken on the primary role of educational planner for students with disabilities, often with little cooperation from or collaboration with general or vocational education teachers, school administrators, or community service providers (Wagner, 1993; Wagner et al., 1993a). In addition to the student, an effective IEP team must include other individuals relevant for ascertaining student needs and preferences and providing instruction and services. Members of a student's planning team will vary across time and from student to student, depending on the student's needs as well as age and grade level (Stodden et al., 1987; Gajar et al., 1993; Clark & Kolstoe, 1995). Members might include, but are not limited to (a) special, vocational, and regular education teachers; (b) speech, occupational, or physical therapists; (c) adult service providers, including rehabilitation or independent living counselors; (d) educational program support staff and guidance counselors; and (e) employers or postsecondary education representatives.

The underlying purpose of the IEP is to specify the goals and objectives of a student's - educational program and the mechanisms for achieving and evaluating progress. The IEP

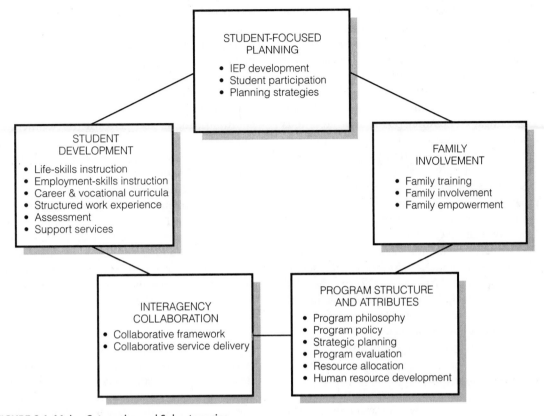

FIGURE 8.1. Major Categories and Subcategories
of the Taxonomy for Transition Programming

Source: Taxonomy for Transition Programming, by P. D. Kohler, 1996b, Champaign: University of Illinois, Transition Research Institute. Copyright 1996 by the University of Illinois.

document should reflect activities and services relevant to achieving postschool goals in the areas of postsecondary education and vocational training, residential, recreation and leisure, community participation, and employment, as well as the persons or agencies responsible for conducting the activities and providing the services. Further, the IEP should reflect student needs and interests and be based on assessment information that reflects the student's current level of functioning. As a result, there is a fundamental relationship among the IEP content as reflected in the document, assessment data on student abilities and interests, the educational activities in which a student participates, and student outcomes. Unfortunately, research indicates that all too often, one or more of these variables are

missing in the IEP document (Stodden et al., 1989; Benz & Halpern, 1993; Trach, 1997).

Practices relevant to effective planning also include those related to facilitating such planning. For example, preparation and meeting times must be adequate to allow information gathering, evaluation of progress, input by all involved, brainstorming for creative solutions, and identification of specific goals, objectives, and responsibilities. Meeting times and places must also be conducive to student, family, and agency involvement. Importantly, in order to truly implement the transition perspective, transition-focused planning must begin early in the student's secondary education years. Beginning transition planning at age 16 or later is a characteristic of the narrow perspective of transition, and does not allow time for developing substantive educational programs and activities.

In summary, if we expect to improve the adult outcomes of individuals with disabilities, it is essential that we improve the IEP process and IEP content (Stodden et al., 1989; Benz & Halpern, 1993; Martin, Marshall, & Maxson, 1993; Edgar & Polloway, 1994). Educators must begin early to assist and guide students in developing appropriate education programs based on individual transition goals (Newman & Cameto, 1993). As required in the legislation, educational program planning must become outcome- rather than disability-focused (Wehman, 1992a; Edgar & Polloway, 1994). As a student's IEP is the primary vehicle for identifying educational objectives, activities, services, and service providers, educators must reform the IEP process to include student involvement and so that it includes the development of relevant assessment information and identification of valued and attainable postschool goals.

Student Development

During their secondary education experience, students need to gain skills that enable them to live and work as independently as possible in their adult lives, including academic, life, and employment skills. To teach these skills, schools must provide academic and vocational instruction through a number of curricular options, identify and provide the supports that facilitate learning by all students, conduct and utilize assessment related to instructional planning, and, where appropriate, provide structured work experience (Rusch et al., 1992; Gajar et al., 1993; Clark & Kolstoe, 1995; Kohler, 1996a).

Research indicates that work quality, attitude, social skills, living and academic skills, and the absence of asocial behavior are related to postschool employment (Heal et al., 1989, 1990; Heal & Rusch, 1995). On-the-job training that includes work-based and school-based learning enhances employment rates (Goldberg et al., 1990; D'Amico & Marder, 1991) and increases employment-related skills and behav-

iors (Kohler, 1994a). Further, student self-esteem and self-advocacy are considered essential to the success of students with disabilities in postsecondary education programs (Kohler, 1993b). Thus, it is essential that secondary education programs provide curricula that focus not only on academic skill development, but enhance the vocational, social, and personal development of students. These issues are discussed in more detail elsewhere in this text, particularly in Chapters 5, 14, and 17.

If state credit requirements for high school graduation remain the same, course and program content must be reevaluated so that competency development in the areas described here can be adequately addressed within the framework of the graduation requirements. For example, students must have the option to earn specific academic credits related to math, science, and writing through career and vocational curricula, as provided for in the School-to-Work Opportunities Act of 1994. And self-determination, social, and living skills development must be included in curricula related to health and social studies. In other words, instructional or educational maps must be drawn, indicating those competencies identified in research as being important for students' postschool success along with opportunities for students to develop such competencies within their schools. Based on individual needs and abilities, students will gain these competencies through differing curricular options and experiences. Therefore, rather than organizing instructional opportunities rigidly within schools by disability category, educational offerings should be flexible and adaptive to individual students. Individual needs and student choices must be a paramount consideration. (See Case Study 1.)

Interagency and Interdisciplinary Collaboration

Current legislation (e.g., Individuals with Disabilities Education Act Amendments of 1997, School-to-Work Opportunities Act, Rehabilitation Act Amendments of 1992) requires

---

CASE STUDY 1   Sarah

Sarah is a junior at East Side High School. She was in an accident in 3rd grade that left her with a learning disability and without the use of her legs; she uses a wheelchair for mobility. Sarah has use of both arms and hands, but she experiences weakness in them after prolonged use. Sarah is interested in a career in the retail fashion industry, both in sales and clothing design. She plans to live independently and wants to work with youth programs in her spare time.

Her IEP team this year is headed by one of the school's guidance counselors and consists of Sarah, her parents, her LD teacher, a vocational rehabilitation counselor, the OT/PT, her marketing and distributive education (DE) teacher and the district's transition specialist. Based on an assessment of Sarah's needs, goals, and preferences, her educational program for 11th grade will consist of the following courses: art (drawing), computers (graphic design), marketing and distribution (two class periods), English, math, and physical education.

The guidance counselor and LD teacher are working with the general academic teachers to assist Sarah in applying strategies to facilitate her learning in these classes. Through her marketing and distributive education class (a regular vocational education cooperative program), Sarah will begin working at the Gap store in the local mall. She will leave school at the end of sixth period and will work 20 hours per week. She will ride the transit system bus from school to work. Her parents will provide transportation home, although Sarah expects to arrange rides with co-workers in the mall once she gets to know them.

The DE teacher has worked with Sarah and her new supervisor to develop a training plan that identifies her work tasks and the competencies she is to develop through the work experience. The VR counselor is helping the employer modify the cashiering station to accommodate Sarah's wheelchair, as well as the storage areas and store aisles. In the future, the VR counselor will assist Sarah in developing a PASS plan (Plan to Achieve Self-Support) to purchase a computer needed for the graphic arts program at the community college—her immediate postschool training goal. The DE teacher has also invited and encouraged Sarah to join the DE club that meets every Wednesday after school.

Through the help of her parents and the district transition specialist, Sarah worked half days during the previous summer, and will do so next year, in the summer youth program doing arts and crafts activities with elementary school children. To help Sarah gain strength in her hands and arms, the OT/PT is working with Sarah and her PE teacher to develop a weight-lifting program. She has also helped to identify strategies that Sarah can use when drawing and working on the computer so that her arms and hands become less fatigued.

At home, Sarah has specific chores and responsibilities involving cleaning, cooking, laundry, and helping to care for the family pet. With her parents' assistance and cooperation, Sarah developed a schedule that fits together school, work, and home responsibilities as well as provides time to just hang out with her friends.

---

collaboration on both the individual planning level and the community level. Collaboration at the individual planning level was discussed in the previous section. The Interagency Collaboration practices in Figure 8.1 address collaboration at the community level and focus on programs, systems, and service delivery.

Research indicates that effective transition programs include a strong collaboration and cooperation component, whereas lack of collaboration and cooperation can serve as a barrier to program implementation and effectiveness

(Rusch, Kohler, & Hughes, 1992b; Kohler, 1993a; Kohler et al., 1994). With respect to transition planning at the community level, collaboration focuses on eliminating service gaps, avoiding service duplication, and increasing efficient use of scarce resources; it also reduces professional territoriality and increases holistic planning and service delivery (Everson & Moon, 1990). An interagency coordinating body that includes consumers, parents, service providers, and employers facilitates these collaborative outcomes.

Various transition-related service providers often come to the table with little knowledge about each other's systems and their inherent missions or procedures, defensive about increased demand for finite resources, and unclear about their role in an emerging transition-focused network. Establishing methods of communication among service providers is a key practice in developing a collaborative framework. By developing a structured way to address problems, share information, and identify solutions, the various education and community service providers are more likely to be successful in coordinating their services, addressing consumer needs, and maximizing their limited resources.

Friend and Cook (1996) identified an evolving sense of community as an emergent characteristic of a collaborative style of interaction that is distinguished by a willingness to work toward a common goal. The focus on a common goal (e.g., to improve postschool options and adult outcomes of youths with disabilities) decreases the focus on individual differences (Friend & Cook, 1996). Thus, collaboration emerges as a process as well as an outcome that is valued by those who engage in a collaboration and that results in trust among the collaborators (Friend & Cook, 1996). Further, a coordinating body and established methods of communication were identified by transition-state, systems-change project directors as necessary for systems change to occur (Wallace, Kohler, & Wiltrout, 1996).

Halpern, Benz, and Lindstrom (1992) and Brito and colleagues (1995) presented systems-change models designed to support improvements in program capacity to address service needs identified through individual-focused planning. Both models, Community Transition Teams (Brito et al., 1995) and the Community Transition Team Model (CTTM) (Halpern et al., 1992), provide structured methods for groups of educators, service providers, and other transition stakeholders to assess their present levels of services and programs and to plan where they want to go in the future. Through the process, participants are able to view a community

picture of (a) programs, services, and options; (b) overlaps as well as gaps in services; and (c) barriers to systems interface and to students and parents negotiating the systems. With this knowledge, stakeholders can set both short- and long-term goals and subsequently identify resources and take action to achieve their goals. For example, working with local school and school district personnel, vocational rehabilitation counselors, and other transition stakeholders in Champaign, Illinois, this author applied a similar process to address community concerns about collaboration and postschool options. Through a series of meetings, participants summarized goals and assessed both existing strengths and needs with respect to these goals. Subsequently, the group identified short-term goals (e.g., earlier involvement from and additional meeting time for input by adult service providers), long-term goals (i.e., increasing supported employment services for individuals who require more extensive supports than currently available), and corresponding action plans. (See Case Study 2.)

Family Involvement

As discussed more thoroughly in Chapter 10, several reasons exist for involving parents, guardians, or other family members in planning educational programs for students with disabilities. First, students and their families are those whose lives are most impacted by transition-focused education and services (Wehman, 1992b). They have ongoing service needs during and after their son's or daughter's exit from school and hold the knowledge about the true nature of these needs (Wehman, 1992b; Hanley-Maxwell, Whitney-Thomas, & Pogoloff, 1995). Further, parents and family members can lend keen insight into a student's interests, abilities, history, and preferences. In addition, parents or family members typically remain in close contact or continue to serve in supportive roles after the student's exit from school. Most often, they represent the one consistent source of support throughout childhood and into

---

CASE STUDY 2   Community-Level Transition Planning

The XYZ school district, in collaboration with other community organizations, established curricula and services to provide both school-based and community-based vocational training and paid work experiences to secondary education students. These curricula and experiences are educational options that are considered during the individual program planning and development for each student.

To provide the services that enable a wide range of students to participate in these experiences, the school district developed partnerships with a number of community organizations and employers through the district's Transition Planning Council. Using the Council as a platform for collaboration, the organizations joined in a formal interagency agreement that specifies the Council's mission, philosophy, and operating procedures, as well as each organization's agreed-upon responsibilities. The chair of the Council is an individual with a disability, and members include parents of and youths with disabilities.

Community- and school-based vocational exploration and skills-training programs were developed by teams representing business and industry, the school district, and the community college. Business involvement was established through the Chamber of Commerce Business-Education Committee and tied to their work focused on developing industry skill standards. Through the vocational exploration and skills-training curricula and experiences, student-assessment information is collected relevant to their interests, preferences, and support needs. This information is subsequently used to identify and develop paid work experiences that coincide with student-identified career goals.

A variety of services are available to facilitate student participation in the paid work experiences, depending on their abilities and support requirements. For many students, either the student or the teacher provides the primary contact with an employer. In other cases, a vocational rehabilitation counselor works with the student, teacher, and employer to identify and develop worksite accommodations or provide an on-the-job training subsidy during the initial training period. Employment specialists, employed by an adult services agency and funded through the local Private Industry Council, join the team to work with students who have moderate and severe disabilities to provide on-site training and more intensive support.

Through collaboration, community service organizations, schools, employers, parents, and students have developed this working model that includes both individual-level, student-focused planning and community-level planning and service delivery. Individual-level planning is characterized by student- and parent-identified planning teams; career exploration and vocational-skill development; identification of student abilities, interests, and preferences; and individualized work experiences that include both school-based and community-based learning. Results of the community-level planning include programs that reflect diverse, yet equally important perspectives; shared use of relevant and meaningful student-assessment information; shared service delivery and resource allocation; ongoing interdisciplinary and interagency staff development; and program evaluation and long-term planning that include projected service needs.

---

adulthood (Steere et al., 1990). Thus, the family members serve as a sustaining factor as educators fade away and are replaced by adult service providers, and in some cases, by no service providers. Finally, research indicates that students with higher levels of family involvement are more successful in school than students with little or no family involvement. Specifically, students whose parents are very involved in their education miss significantly fewer days of school and are significantly less likely to fail a class than their peers whose parents are not at all involved in their schooling (Wagner et al., 1993a). High parental expectations and high parental involvement are also associated with residential independence and full community participation (Wagner et al., 1993), as well as student enrollment in postsecondary vocational and academic programs (Newman & Cameto, 1993).

An additional benefit of continuing parental involvement in the school program relates to the problem of unrealistic parental expectations. Cummings and Maddux (1987, cited in Gajar et al., 1993) found that parents' expectations for their sons or daughters with a disability ranged from being much too low to, more often, unrealistically high. In conjunction with their expectations, parents often advocate for an educational program that does not support realistic postschool goals; as a result, adequate time to provide training and experiences associated with more realistic goals may not be available. Continued participation of parents in the schooling of their children provides for ongoing opportunities to assess student abilities and progress toward specified postschool goals (Gajar et al., 1993).

Those involved in planning and developing transition-focused educational programs cannot realistically expect all parents to participate fully in their son's or daughter's education, however. Time constraints, personal problems or conflicts, or a lack of transportation can hinder parent participation (Steere et al., 1990). Further, previous negative experiences with education or agency personnel can serve as barriers to family involvement (Steere et al., 1990). Parents and students may feel uncomfortable with their roles as active participants and the planning process. Through a series of focus group sessions, Benz and colleagues (1995) found that parents and students often felt uncomfortable and dissatisfied with transition planning activities and meetings. Reasons for such feelings included (a) ambiguous and confusing rehabilitation and education assessment requirements and practices; (b) the requirement to discuss disabilities and needs with professionals with whom they were not familiar; (c) intimidating and difficult-to-understand language and application procedures; (d) a lack of clear, relevant, and timely information about transition services and resources; and (e) the tendency of school staff to dominate transition planning meetings (Benz et al., 1995).

In light of the identified barriers, educators and service providers must make a concerted effort to evaluate their beliefs and behaviors to ensure they are conducive to parent involvement. Often, preconceived notions on the part of teachers and service providers send signals that parent involvement is unwarranted or unwanted. In this case, specific training is necessary to teach skills that facilitate parent involvement. In other cases, specific training for parents may be desirable to develop their skills and knowledge related to promoting self-determination, advocacy, the transition-related planning process, or legal issues (Kohler, 1997). In the Benz and colleagues (1995) study, parents suggested that the following would improve the transition planning process and the quality of parent involvement in that process: better informational materials; joint training for vocational rehabilitation and school staff, parents, and students; resource fairs; a single, knowledgeable contact person; and support groups and networking opportunities.

Program Structure and Attributes

In order to achieve the practices featured in Figure 8.1 and described previously—student-focused planning, student development, collaboration, and family involvement—schools and programs must be organized in a way that promotes these activities. In other words, to implement the transition perspective, fundamental change must occur in two areas: (a) educational programs (i.e., curricular decisions) for all students must be based upon postschool goals, and relevant to these goals, (b) a variety of curricular options must be made available to students (Gajar et al., 1993; Edgar & Polloway, 1994; Stodden & Leake, 1994). The "check-off" procedure highlighted at the beginning of this chapter is inadequate for planning and delivering transition-focused education. Instead, schools must adopt and infuse

> transition values that would guide the decision-making of teachers regarding, most importantly, *why* they teach what they do: to prepare students for the day when they

leave the school system, whether that is one year or twelve years down the road. Once the *why* of teaching is established, it guides *what*, *when*, *where*, and *how* to assess, plan, and teach…. (Stodden & Leake, 1994:69)

Practices that promote outcome-based education and expanded curricular options include community-level strategic planning, cultural and ethnic sensitivity, a clearly articulated mission and values, qualified staff, and sufficient allocation of resources (Kohler, 1996a, 1996b). Transition-oriented schools must focus also on systematic community involvement in the development of educational options, community-based learning opportunities, systematic inclusion of students in the social life of the school, and increased expectations related to skills, values, and outcomes for all students (Edgar & Polloway, 1994).

Reflect again on the example that described the transition planning process for students who are preparing for postsecondary education. The school structure has been established to facilitate this planning—the curricula and curricula requirements are focused on the outcome of postsecondary education, the course scheduling and guidance counseling processes provide the coordinated set of activities, and teachers and other school personnel operate from a college-focused paradigm. This very same process must be adopted and expanded for *all* students. For this to happen, the targeted outcomes must include options other than a 4-year college degree, and the coordinated set of activities must include other than college-prep curricula. In this effort, we must be careful to truly expand the options. In the past, by focusing on our perceptions of the "needs" of individuals with disabilities, we limited their opportunities by herding them into "functional" life-skills curricula (Szymanski et al., 1990b; Wehman, 1992a).

A transition-focused school would begin early to facilitate student-driven postschool goal setting, align students with school day and extracurricular activities, and work as a collegial

unit that perceives the education of noncollege-bound youths as equally important as that of college-bound youths. The structures and attributes of a school provide the framework for a transition perspective—the other categories of practices in Figure 8.1 provide the substance. A transition-focused school is a community of leaders, teachers, counselors, supporting staff, students, and parents that work in concert to ensure that *all* students develop valued and appropriate postschool goals, participate in school-based and community-based curricula, develop academic and other needed skills, and are fully engaged in the process of learning. By operating from the transition paradigm, schools put in place those structures and policies that reflect the notion that outcomes and activities of 100 percent of the students are important.

IMPLEMENTING THE FRAMEWORK: WHO DOES WHAT?

Subsequent to the development of the taxonomy, Kohler (1996c) investigated who was responsible for implementing it. Using survey methodology, Kohler asked a national group of over 600 individuals to identify who might be responsible, from among eleven options, for doing each of the practices; over 300 individuals (50 percent) responded. Results of this study indicated that it takes more than the secondary special education teacher or a transition specialist to implement the transition perspective; the entire school community must be involved. As Figure 8.2 illustrates, responsibility for doing the practices within each of the five taxonomy categories varied across the eleven options: special, vocational, and regular education teachers; transition specialist; school and rehabilitation counselors; community agency personnel; school and school district administrators; parents or guardians; and others.

This information tells us two important things relevant to individual program planning

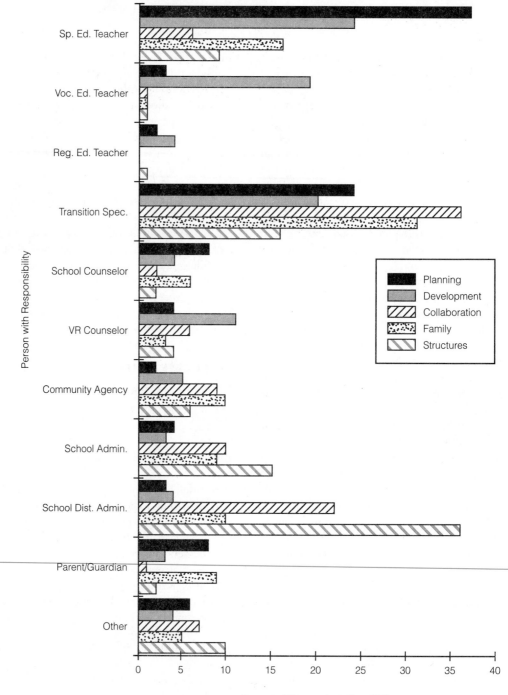

FIGURE 8.2. Percent of Respondents Who Identified Specific Transition Stakeholders as Having Primary Responsibility for Doing the Transition Practices within Each of Five Practice Categories

Source: Transition-Related Instruction and Services: Who Does What?, by P. D. Kohler, 1997, Champaign: University of Illinois, Transition Research Institute.

and school- or community-level planning: (a) who might be involved in planning and providing specific instruction or services to individual students, and (b) who might be involved in the broader task of curricula or program development and implementation. This section examines the results of the Kohler (1997) study and provides specific suggestions for roles and responsibilities of particular transition stakeholders (see Table 8.1).

Special Education Teachers

As discussed previously, secondary special education teachers have had to assume the burden of transition planning as it has typically been implemented (Gajar et al., 1993). They have been held responsible for connecting with regular and vocational education teachers, referring students to community service agencies, developing IEPs, scheduling and conducting IEP meetings, conducting student assessment, controlling classroom behavior, and developing and delivering instructional programs. In sum, they have been expected to develop transition "programs," to direct planning for individual students, and to conduct the daily business of teaching. Results of the Kohler (1997) study indicated that special education teachers were more appropriately responsible for specific student development and planning activities than for program development and coordination. Gajar and colleagues (1993) concurred with this finding, indicating that targeting the special education teacher as the transition "facilitator" misrepresents the complexity of the transition process and represents an "overload" for the teachers and for special education.

In working with individual students, special educators will teach specific skills such as self-determination (e.g., decision making, goal setting, self-awareness) and social skills, learning strategies, and academic subjects, depending on the extent to which the student is included in regular education classes. They will help identify and develop accommodations that students might need in school or community activities

and in academic and vocational classes, and will participate in determining specific goals and objectives in these areas. Due to fiscal constraints in many schools, the special education teacher might remain the primary coordinator of a student's IEP planning process, and as such take responsibility for scheduling, coordinating, and conducting the meeting. When possible, however, someone else should assume this responsibility. By doing so, the coordination burden would be removed from the teacher on a daily basis, allowing him or her to focus directly on student-specific activities such as modifying behaviors, teaching, and consulting with other service providers and teachers.

Program-level planning requires teacher participation as well; however, *responsibility* for such should rest on other individuals. Specific special education teachers should participate in program and curriculum development and evaluation by serving on curriculum- or program-development teams and interagency councils or community bodies. Teachers can also participate in parent or family training and in technical assistance or staff-development activities. Finally, special education teachers should play a role in strategic planning and resource allocation.

Vocational and Regular Education Teachers

Regular or general and vocational education teachers will participate in similar roles as the special education teacher. That is, they will teach students specific subjects and address specific skill development. For example, the general educator will teach reading, writing, and math skills, as well as other topics such as art, music, language, and physical education. The vocational educator will focus on vocational skill development and integration of academic skills relevant to the vocational program. Further, both general and vocational educators should address self-determination, social skills, and work-related behaviors within the context of their classroom and particular subject. Both can use group learning activities and involve students with disabilities in extracurricular clubs and activities that

Table 8.1 Planning, Instruction, and Service Responsibilities for Transition Stakeholders

			TAXONOMY PRACTICES CATEGORY		
Stakeholders	**Student Development**	**Student-Focused Planning**	**Collaboration**	**Family Involvement**	**Program Structure & Attributes**
Special education teacher	■ Teach self-determination ■ Teach social skills ■ Teach learning strategies ■ Identify and develop accommodations	■ Identify measurable transition-related goals and objectives ■ Develop educational experience that corresponds with goals and objectives ■ Document student preferences ■ Teach students to participate in planning activities	■ Participate on interagency coordinating body ■ Collaboratively consult with regular and vocational educators ■ Provide information about upcoming service needs ■ Provide student-assessment information	■ Provide pre-IEP planning activities for parents ■ Identify and present information about program options ■ Facilitate parent attendance at IEP/ITP meetings ■ Actively include parents and family members in planning and decision making	■ Develop outcome-based programs ■ Provide flexible program options to meet student needs ■ Participate in program evaluation ■ Teach students in integrated settings
Vocational teacher	■ Teach vocational skills ■ Provide apprenticeships and other work-based training ■ Teach work-related behaviors ■ Provide career information	■ Participate on student planning team ■ Identify measurable vocational goals and objectives ■ Develop educational experiences that correspond with goals and objectives ■ Provide career counseling	■ Participate on interagency coordinating body ■ Collaboratively consult with regular and special educators ■ Provide student-assessment information	■ Identify and present information about program options ■ Participate in parent/family training ■ Involve parents in student assessment	■ Develop outcome-based programs ■ Provide flexible program options to meet student needs ■ Participate in program evaluation ■ Teach students in integrated settings

Table 8.1 *(continued)*

Stakeholders	Student Development	Student-Focused Planning	Collaboration	Family Involvement	Program Structure & Attributes
Regular education teacher	■ Teach academic skills ■ Provide career-awareness activities ■ Teach self-determination skills ■ Teach social skills	■ Participate on student planning team ■ Teach students to participate in planning activities ■ Document student interests ■ Provide assessment information	■ Participate on interagency coordinating body ■ Collaboratively consult with special and vocational educators ■ Provide student-assessment information	■ Identify and present information about program options ■ Participate in parent/family training ■ Involve parents in student assessment	■ Develop outcome-based programs ■ Provide flexible program options to meet student needs ■ Participate in program evaluation ■ Teach students in integrated settings
Transition specialist	■ Identify community worksites ■ Coordinate transportation services ■ Assess job opportunities and requirements ■ Develop work-experience programs	■ Schedule adequate meeting time ■ Coordinate referral to adult service providers ■ Monitor fulfillment of responsibilities identified in IEP ■ Identify financial issues to be addressed in planning	■ Chair and/or participate on interagency coordinating body ■ Coordinate collaborative program planning and development ■ Coordinate shared delivery of transition-related services ■ Coordinate development and use of student assessment data among agencies	■ Develop parent/family training activities ■ Develop and implement structured method to identify parent/family needs ■ Develop and provide a directory of transition-related services ■ Identify and facilitate specific parent/family roles	■ Develop and provide transition-related resource materials and technical assistance to educators, service providers, parents/families, and employers ■ Evaluate student outcomes ■ Identify postschool services or program needs ■ Implement longitudinal approach to transition (early childhood to adult)

(continued)

Table 8.1 *(continued)*

Stakeholders	Student Development	Student-Focused Planning	Collaboration	Family Involvement	Program Structure & Attributes
School counselor	■ Provide career education experiences ■ Teach self-advocacy ■ Conduct assessment ■ Teach self-determination	■ Identify and communicate information on postsecondary education institutions and services ■ Provide career counseling ■ Facilitate student self-determination in planning process ■ Identify student interests and preferences	■ Develop and provide student-assessment data relevant to other service providers ■ Coordinate contact with post-secondary education institutions ■ Provide information about community resources ■ Coordinate requests for information with other service providers	■ Participate in parent/family training activities ■ Include parents/family members in student assessment ■ Collect information about parent/family needs ■ Provide information about parent/family support network	■ Provide information for program evaluation ■ Participate in student follow-up and follow-along ■ Identify postschool service and program needs
Vocational rehabilitation counselor	■ Conduct job placement ■ Conduct assessment for assistive technology ■ Provide assistive technology devices ■ Conduct assessment	■ Initiate student contact prior to student's exit from school ■ Complete referral process prior to student's exit from school ■ Provide career counseling ■ Identify postschool goals and objectives	■ Participate on interagency coordinating body ■ Establish methods of communication ■ Identify and fund specific services ■ Establish collaborative procedures for collecting assessment data and sharing student information	■ Participate in parent/family training activities ■ Collect information about parent/family needs ■ Utilize parents/family members in specific roles ■ Involve parents in student assessment	■ Restructure system to include transition planning and services as integral components ■ Provide information for program evaluation ■ Participate in student follow-up and follow-along ■ Identify postschool service and program needs

(continued)

Table 8.1 *(continued)*

Stakeholders	Student Development	Student-Focused Planning	Collaboration	Family Involvement	Program Structure & Attributes
Community service agency personnel	■ Provide assistive technology devices ■ Provide or fund transportation ■ Develop environmental adaptations ■ Teach independent living skills	■ Participate in student planning team ■ Identify postschool goals and objectives ■ Provide support services to individual students as identified	■ Participate in interagency coordinating body ■ Establish methods of communication ■ Identify and fund specific services ■ Establish collaborative procedures for collecting assessment data and sharing student information	■ Participate in parent/family training activities ■ Collect information about parent/family needs ■ Utilize parents/family members in specific roles ■ Involve parents in student assessment	■ Restructure system to include transition planning and services as integral components ■ Transfer resources from sheltered and/or segregated facilities to community-based and/or integrated facilities ■ Participate in community-level strategic planning ■ Identify postschool service and program needs
School/district administrator	■ Facilitate curriculum development ■ Facilitate community-based structured work experience ■ Provide career education curriculum ■ Facilitate provision of related services (e.g., occupational, physical, or speech therapy)	■ Establish accountability for identification and fulfillment of participant responsibilities ■ Establish assessment-based planning ■ Establish annual review of student progress ■ Establish student-centered planning framework	■ Establish formal interagency agreement ■ Participate on interagency coordinating body ■ Develop specific funding and staffing patterns in collaboration with other service providers ■ Reduce system barriers to collaboration	■ Include parents/families in policy development ■ Facilitate parents/family members as the decision makers ■ Participate in parent/family training activities ■ Provide services that facilitate family involvement (interpreters, child care)	■ Provide ongoing staff development ■ Allocate sufficient resources and personnel ■ Restructure education system to include transition-related planning and services as integral components ■ Clearly articulate a transition perspective and mission

(continued,

Table 8.1 (continued)

Stakeholders	Student Development	Student-Focused Planning	Collaboration	Family Involvement	Program Structure & Attributes
Parent or guardian	■ Teach rights and responsibilities ■ Teach leisure skills ■ Teach independent living skills ■ Teach self-determination	■ Take initiative in the planning process ■ Address medical issues during planning process ■ Address guardianship during planning process ■ Provide assessment information	■ Participate in interagency coordinating body ■ Participate in development of policies and procedures to release and share student information	■ Participate in family support network ■ Participate in and/or attend parent/family training ■ Exercise decision making ■ Identify and participate in specific roles or activities (e.g., mentors, trainers, program development, student assessment)	■ Participate in decisions regarding resource allocation ■ Participate in strategic planning ■ Participate in program evaluation ■ Provide information for student follow-up
Student	■ Participate in extracurricular activities ■ Take responsibility for learning ■ Seek assistance ■ Identify necessary supports	■ Identify goals ■ Indicate interest and preferences ■ Evaluate progress ■ Participate in decision making	■ Participate on interagency coordinating body ■ Provide input for information-release and sharing procedures	■ Provide information to parents ■ Identify parent/family roles ■ Participate in parent/family training ■ Identify parent/family needs	■ Participate in program evaluation ■ Participate in human resource development ■ Participate in resource-allocation decisions ■ Participate in program planning

will do much to address social and leadership skill development, connection with the school community, and application of self-determination skills. Further, they will involve students in career-awareness activities through which students learn about career and occupational options, requirements, and pathways.

Too often, special education students "dabble" in vocational education courses, rather than receiving occupation-specific training that is associated with higher rates of postschool employment (Wagner, 1991). Concurrently, too few students with disabilities leave school prepared to attend postsecondary education (Fairweather & Shaver, 1990, 1991), a pathway to employment associated with significantly higher wages (National Center for Educational Statistics, 1994). General and vocational educators can play key roles in addressing these issues by working with students, their parents, and special education teachers to identify specific postschool goals and corresponding educational programs and experiences that directly relate to postsecondary education or training and specific occupations. By gathering relevant assessment information and providing it to student planning teams, regular and vocational educators can guide the development of goals, objectives, and informed decisions. Vocational educators also can provide key information to both student- and program-planning teams relevant to industry-referenced curricula, apprenticeship requirements and programs, and validated work-related behaviors. Finally, both academic and vocational educators should participate in strategic planning, program evaluation, and parent training.

Transition Specialist

The transition specialist is a relatively new position that has emerged with the advent of transition programs and related legislation. Competitions for the preparation of transition personnel sponsored by the Division of Personnel Preparation, Office of Special Education and Rehabilitative Services (OSERS), in 1984 and 1987 resulted in funding for twenty-eight programs to train transition leaders and specialists (Baker & Geiger, 1988). With reference to several of these programs, deFur and Taymans (1995) investigated and validated competencies for transition specialists and in so doing concluded that their role was emerging as one that provides coordination of transition services, rather than as direct service provider. Results of the Kohler (1997) study reinforced this finding. It is the transition specialist who may be necessary to link services and instruction provided by specific teachers and service providers with broader program issues of schools and community.

For example, with respect to student development, the transition specialist may play a crucial role in identifying job opportunities and competency requirements, developing community worksites and work-experience programs, and identifying or coordinating transportation (see Table 8.1). Related to individual student planning, the transition specialist will serve as facilitator to identify postschool options, coordinate referral to adult service providers, schedule meetings and contact participants, and monitor fulfillment of participant responsibilities as agreed upon in the IEP.

Collaboration among different types of educators, educators and service providers, and educators and parents appears repeatedly as a crucial aspect of effective transition programs (Szymanski, Hanley-Maxwell, & Asselin, 1990a; Rusch et al., 1992b; Kohler, 1993a, 1996a; Kohler et al., 1994; deFur & Taymans, 1995; Kohler & Rusch, 1996). Someone must take responsibility for establishing, coordinating, and monitoring these collaborative efforts. In such a role, the transition specialist might chair (at the minimum, participate in) an interagency coordinating body and in this capacity coordinate collaborative program planning, development, and service delivery. Specific efforts must focus on (a) agreed-upon communication strategies and procedures; (b) methods to collect, release, and share student assessment information; and (c) future service needs of individuals and families. Specific to families, the transition specialist in collaboration with others should develop materials about transition services, resources, and referral processes. The results of the Benz and colleagues (1995) focus groups indicated that students and parents are clearly

(a) confused about the transition process and the different transition resources in the community; (b) intimidated by the VR [vocational rehabilitation] application process; (c) frustrated with the number of assessments that must be conducted for eligibility determination, and the lack of meaningful information about the reasons for these assessments; and (d) overwhelmed by, and even somewhat embarrassed about, the variety of professionals with whom they must discuss their needs in order to obtain transition information and resources. (p. 143)

A transition specialist also can take the lead in providing transition-related resource materials and technical assistance to educators, service providers, employers, and other community resources. As the transition "expert," he or she can help others integrate transition issues and concepts into curricular areas and programs. The transition specialist should also play a key role in program evaluation and, subsequently, provide essential information for use in strategic planning. Specific evaluation roles might include coordination of student follow-up or follow-along information, identification of specific targeted program outcomes, and analysis of student outcomes relevant to targeted outcomes. Also, through the transition-planning process for individual students, a transition specialist should compile information relevant to identifying postschool service or program needs for cohorts of students. These data, in turn, provide essential information about projected service needs for adult service organizations.

A transition specialist is not likely to be commonplace in a majority of schools and districts for some time. Unfortunately, due to limited educational resources, many local schools or small districts might perceive a transition specialist as a luxury rather than a necessity.

Importantly, it is the role of the transition specialist—rather than the position itself—that is critical. Again, the responsibilities outlined here provide an important linkage between services and instruction provided by specific teachers and service providers, and broader program issues of schools and community. If it is not the transition specialist, *someone* must provide this linkage.

School Counselor

For students without a disability, the school counselor typically plays a key role in providing career information and scheduling advice. Too often, the special education teacher takes over these roles for their students with disabilities, and by doing so removes these students from natural information pipelines about postsecondary training and career options. Rather than play a decreased role with students with disabilities, school counselors should become more involved. Through their resources and interactions with students with disabilities, they can provide career education experiences, conduct assessment, and teach self-advocacy and self-determination skills.

With respect to planning individual educational programs, counselors should work with students to identify their interests and preferences, identify and communicate information about postsecondary education institutions and services, provide career counseling, and facilitate student self-determination in the planning process. Corresponding to these roles, counselors should collaborate with teachers and service providers to develop and provide student assessment data, to coordinate requests with other service providers for information relevant to students and their families, and to provide information about community resources. As mentioned, Benz and colleagues (1995) found that students and families are frustrated and confused about assessment procedures and requirements, and by having to deal with a number of people to obtain transition information and resources. School counselors typically coordinate standardized assessment efforts and provide linkages to postsecondary education institutions and community services. Thus, their role in the transition-planning process for students with disabilities should be a natural extension of their typical involvement and interactions with other students.

Rehabilitation Counselors and Other Community Service Providers

The similarity between the definition of *transition services* in the IDEA amendments of 1990 and 1997, and the Rehabilitation Act Amendments of 1992 was no accident. Clearly, the intent was to remove barriers to and facilitate a seamless transition from school to postschool services when those services are appropriate. As a result, legislative and system barriers to early involvement of rehabilitation counselors with secondary students with disabilities were removed with the two pieces of legislation. This early involvement, beginning at least 2 years prior to a student's exit from school, is essential for a seamless transition from an entitlement-based education program to eligibility-based adult services.

Active involvement on IEP and transition-planning teams is crucial for the maximum impact of service agency participation to be realized. Vocational counselors and other service providers bring their expertise about rehabilitation technology, employment training, workplace demands and opportunities, independent living supports, and available services to the student-focused planning process. Based on this expertise, they are instrumental in helping to identify postschool goals and objectives and the supports necessary to achieve them. Also, by initiating the referral process long before a student leaves school, this process can be facilitated by routine contact among students, families, teachers, and agency representatives.

The school-to-community connection should be the primary focus of rehabilitation counselors and other adult service providers such as developmental disabilities and community mental health agencies. Specifically, adult service providers must address the supports and services that individuals with disabilities require to live, work, and recreate as independently as possible in their community. For example, vocational rehabilitation counselors or employment specialists must work with educators to identify and develop specific assistive technology, accommodations, or modifications of worksites relevant to the student's employment and postsecondary education or training needs. Further, they should be involved in job development and placement when appropriate. Concurrently, a developmental disabilities or other community service provider should address the same issues with respect to independent living and community involvement. By identifying and providing direct services to students prior to their exit from high school, community service agencies reduce the possibility of students "falling through the cracks" and hasten the move to independence.

To facilitate a collaborative working relationship with educators and others involved in the transition-planning process, vocational counselors and other service providers should participate on interagency coordinating bodies and work specifically to develop interagency and family communication strategies and procedures. Other major tasks include identifying common assessment information needs, sources of assessment information, and by working with parents, procedures for sharing assessment information among collaborators.

The linkages with parents are as critical as those with educators, as most often the interactions with parents and families continue beyond the student's exit from school, particularly for students with severe disabilities. To strengthen these linkages, community service providers should participate in parent- or family-training activities, collect information about family needs in relation to student needs, involve parents or family members in specific roles, and include parents or family members in student assessment.

Vocational counselors and community service providers also play a critical role in policy development, program planning and evaluation, and resource allocation. To facilitate implementation of the transition-focused paradigm, adult service systems must restructure themselves so that transition planning and services are integral components. These agencies must develop philosophies and policies that promote the intent of the legislation; that is, they must operationalize the notion of a seamless transition. For example, vocational rehabilitation agencies must identify specific school liaisons and vocational rehabilitation counselors must meet with students in schools, rather than require them to meet at their offices. Further, funding for rehabilitation and developmental disabilities services must be aligned with the outcomes we expect students to achieve. If community-based employment outcomes are targeted, then funds must be shifted from sheltered workshops to supported employment services. A primary barrier to achieving successful outcomes for many students with moderate or severe disabilities is that community-based service supports are often lacking. Thus, it is essential that postschool service options are aligned with targeted postschool outcomes.

To accomplish this goal, vocational and community service agencies must participate in student follow-up and follow-along studies, and provide information for program evaluation. Through these efforts, as well as the individual transition-planning process, they must collect and compile information to project postschool service and program needs for local areas. Finally, they must synthesize this information to project regional and state needs, and allocate resources accordingly, both human and financial.

School and School District Administrators

As illustrated throughout this section, although it is often perceived that teachers and other direct service providers have the primary responsibility for transition planning and transition programs, results of the Kohler (1997) study indicated otherwise. In fact, school or school district administrators were identified as the ones who should have primary responsibility for over 70 percent of the practices included in the Program Structures and Attributes category (see Figure 8.2). Importantly, it was this category of practices that received the highest mean rating of all categories in both Kohler studies (i.e., Kohler, 1996a, 1997) in which participants rated the Taxonomy practices for importance. As discussed previously, without the underlying elements of philosophy, policy, planning, evaluation, and resource development and allocation, transition-focused schools cannot exist. School and school district administrators must take the leadership role in the development of these elements.

School leaders must clearly articulate a transition perspective and mission for *all* students, which means restructuring schools and educational programs to include transition-related planning and services as integral components. As with community service agencies, they must ensure that fiscal and human resources are adequate and aligned with services and programs that promote targeted outcomes. School leaders' expectations must include accountability based on program evaluation and needs assessment that include input from students, parents, employers, and other transition stakeholders. Their behaviors and policies must reflect a commitment to integrated learning environments, accessibility for all students to all educational options, sensitivity to cultural and ethnic differences, and flexibility in programs relative to student needs. To ensure that schools operate from a transition-focused paradigm, school leaders must work to develop shared principles and consistent policies with partner community agencies and postsecondary education programs. Thus, school leaders must model a commitment to and expectation that *all* educational programs and instructional activities be (a) based on the postschool goals of students and (b) developed on the basis of individual needs, interests, and preferences.

When school leaders take responsibility for implementing the transition perspective of education, they facilitate the development of outcome-oriented curricula that include career exploration and education, and community-based structured work experiences, as well as the related services that students need to excel in these experiences. As a framework for students' educational activities, they must adopt a student-centered planning approach that builds on student-assessment information, is reviewed at least annually, and that establishes accountability for the identification and fulfillment of various participant responsibilities. They also must take responsibility for establishing formal interagency agreements and coordinating bodies and, in collaboration with partner community agencies, develop funding and staffing patterns and reduce system barriers that inhibit collaboration or shared delivery of services. An effective transition-focused leader must adopt the perspective that collaboration is focused on what each participating service provider—educational or otherwise—can do to improve the postschool lives of the community's young people, and thus, of the community as a whole. This perspective is in contrast to one that propels the notion that partners with education focus on how to forward the mission of the educational community, although, in the end, a transition perspective will result in accomplishing education's mission.

Finally, with respect to families, school leaders must send the message that parent and family involvement is valued and expected. To reflect this intent, they must include family members in policy development, decision making, and program evaluation and must enjoin their staff to take a proactive approach to facilitate family input and participation in all aspects of their schools. Also, in order to realize family involvement, they must provide specific services or accommodations that enable families to become involved, such as interpreters or flexible meeting times and places.

Parents and Family Members

School and agency personnel must recognize that parent and family participation can take many forms and should be perceived as an asset rather than a liability in the education- and transition-planning process. Parents and family members should assume roles in program and policy development and evaluation, provide information about student abilities and support needs, and participate in a natural supports network (Kohler, 1996a). Some parents also can work as trainers and mentors, and participate in staff development, strategic planning, and resource allocation. All parents must pay a key role in identifying and evaluating options, and in making decisions. Importantly, parents and other family members can help extend transition-focused education to home and community environments by encouraging student self-determination and independence at home; teaching and giving responsibility for daily living and personal-social goals; assisting the student in developing personal and social values, self-confidence, and self-esteem; and by reinforcing work-related behaviors (Clark & Kolstoe, 1995). Other chapters included in this text address specific roles for parents and family members, including those of advocate and case manager.

Students

In the example of the college-bound student, a primary participant in the "transition planning process" was the students themselves. Students with disabilities—both college-bound and non-college-bound—must also assume a primary role in planning and preparing for their postschool lives. As with parents, active participation and self-advocacy come natural for some students, whereas for others, these behaviors must be developed and nurtured. The level of involvement of particular students will vary, depending on their abilities and interests. Some students will participate as consumer representatives on interagency councils and provide important input about interagency procedures for developing and sharing information about individual students. Others will participate in program planning, development, and evaluation. Students should also participate as trainers, and as such provide an important perspective that is often overlooked.

Students must think about, identify, and in some way express their interests and preferences, and from these develop their goals. Students must make decisions about their educational programs and evaluate their progress, identifying both successes and problems. In developing IEP teams, students should identify specific individuals they want to attend and participate. All students must take responsibility for learning, seek assistance when they encounter problems, and work with teachers, family members, and others to identify the supports they need to succeed. Students must take advantage of opportunities, such as joining school clubs and becoming involved in other extracurricular activities. In sum, students must become *engaged* in school. Educators and others can teach specific skills associated with self-determination, but, ultimately, students must take responsibility for applying these skills.

IMPLICATIONS FOR PROFESSIONAL DEVELOPMENT

Effective transition-practices research has direct implications for both the content and process of professional development. In addition to content about specific academic disciplines, we must teach teachers and other educators about self-determination, social skills, career planning and development, transition-focused goals and objectives, other service systems, collaboration with each other as well as with community service representatives, facilitating family involvement, and both student and program assessment and evaluation. In essence, personnel competencies—those of educators and other service providers—must reflect the ability to *do* the "practices" that have emerged as important for improving the postschool outcomes of our young people.

Instruction on methods of teaching must include methods for collaborating, for involving students in educational planning, and for facilitating parent involvement. With respect to process, if educators and other service providers are to participate effectively in the roles described in this chapter, they must have opportunities to do so during preservice and inservice training. Typically, teacher-training experiences, especially for educators training to work with students with mild disabilities, focus on teaching academics. To these experiences, we must add (a) teaching self-determination skills; (b) recruiting and including students in extracurricular activities; (c) conducting community-based assessment and vocational skill training; (d) identifying and developing academic, vocational, and independent living supports and accommodations; and (e) collaborating among special, vocational, and general educators.

The education of school leaders, counselors, and other educators must also include instruction and experience related to the roles outlined herein—both content and process. Most importantly, preservice, inservice, and graduate training must foster a view of education from a transition perspective. A transition perspective of education for all students is essential for developing the knowledge and skills necessary to be effective leaders, educators, and service providers that in turn foster quality postschool outcomes for *all* students.

QUESTIONS

1. Describe what is meant by a "narrow perspective" of transition planning.

2. Describe what is meant by a "transition perspective of education."

3. Why should transition planning begin early in the secondary education of students, as compared to beginning at age 16?

4. Identify and describe the five categories included in the taxonomy.

5. Describe the focus of community-level transition planning. Why is community-level planning important?

6. Identify two strategies that might be used to facilitate parent and family involvement in IEP development.

7. Identify five specific behaviors that a school principal might model to facilitate implementation of the transition perspective.

8. Describe three roles of a general educator in planning and delivering education to students with disabilities.

9. Identify and explain five competencies that might be included in training for transition specialists.

10. Should transition-related competencies be included in the certification requirements for educators, school leaders, and community service providers who work with adolescents with disabilities? Why or why not?

REFERENCES

Baker, B. C., & Geiger, W. L. (1988). *Preparing transition specialists: Competencies from 13 programs.* Paper distributed by Dissemin/Action. (ERIC Reproductions Services ED 306 755.)

Benz, M. R., & Halpern, A. S. (1993). Vocational and transition services needed and received by students with disabilities during their last year of high school. *Career Development for Exceptional Individuals, 16,* 197–211.

Benz, M. R., Johnson, D. K., Mikkelsen, K. S., & Lindstrom, L. E. (1995). Improving collaboration between schools and vocational rehabilitation: Stakeholder identified barriers and strategies. *Career Development for Exceptional Individuals, 18,* 133–144.

Berliner, D. C. (1992, February). *Educational reform in an era of disinformation.* Paper presented at the American Association of Colleges for Teacher Education, San Antonio, Texas.

Brito, C., Davis, K., Blalock, G., & D'Ottavio, M. (1995, October). Community transition teams as a foundation for transition services for diverse learners. Paper presented to the 1995 Division on Career Development and Transition International Conference, Raleigh, North Carolina.

Clark, G. M., & Kolstoe, O. P. (1995). *Career development and transition education for adolescents with disabilities* (2nd ed.). Boston: Allyn & Bacon.

Cummings, R. W. & Maddux, C. D. (1987). *Career and vocational education for the mildly handicapped.* Springfield, IL: Thomas.

D'Amico, R., & Marder, C. (1991). *The early work experience of youth with disabilities: Trends in employment rates and job characteristics. A report from the National Longitudinal Transition Study of Special Education Students.* Menlo Park, CA: SRI International.

deFur, S. H., & Taymans, J. M. (1995). Competencies needed for transition specialists in vocational rehabilitation, vocational education, and special education. *Exceptional Children, 62,* 38–51.

Edgar, E. (1987). Secondary programs in special education: Are many of them justifiable? *Exceptional Children, 53,* 555–561.

Edgar, E., & Polloway, E. A. (1994). Education for adolescents with disabilities: Curriculum and placement issues. *Journal of Special Education, 27,* 438–452.

Everson, J. E., & Moon, M. S. (1990). Developing community program planning and service delivery teams. In F. R. Rusch (Ed.), *Supported employment: Models, methods, and issues* (pp. 381–394). Sycamore, IL: Sycamore.

Fairweather, J. S., & Shaver, D. M. (1990). A troubled future? Participation in postsecondary education by youths with disabilities. *Journal of Higher education, 61,* 332–348.

———. (1991). Making the transition to postsecondary education and training. *Exceptional Children, 57,* 332–348.

Friend, M., & Cook, L. (1996). *Interactions* (2nd ed.). White Plains, NY: Longman.

Gajar, A., Goodman, L., & McAfee, J. (1993). *Secondary schools and beyond: Transition of individuals with mild disabilities.* New York: Charles E. Merrill.

Goldberg, R. T., McLean, M. M., LaVigne, R., Fratolillo, J., & Sullivan, F. T. (1990). Transition of persons with developmental disability from extended sheltered employment to competitive employment. *Mental Retardation, 18,* 199–304.

Halpern, A. S., Benz, M. R., & Lindstrom, L. E. (1992). A systems change approach to improving secondary special education and transition programs at the community level. *Career Development for Exceptional Individuals, 15,* 109–120.

Hanley-Maxwell, C., Whitney-Thomas, J., & Pogoloff, S. M. (1995). The second shock: A qualitative study of parents' perspectives and needs during their child's transition from school to adult life. *Journal of the Association for Persons with Severe Handicaps, 20,* 3–15.

Hasazi, S. B., Gordon, L. R., & Roe, C. A. (1985). Factors associated with the employment status of handicapped youth exiting high school from 1979 to 1983. *Exceptional Children, 51,* 455–469.

Heal, L. W., Copher, J. I., DeStefano, L., & Rusch, F. R. (1989). A comparison of successful and unsuccessful placements of secondary students with mental handicaps into competitive employment. *Career Development for Exceptional Individuals, 12,* 167–177.

Heal, L. W., Gonzalez, P., Rusch, F. R., Copher, J. I., & DeStefano, L. (1990). A comparison of successful and unsuccessful placements of youths with mental handicaps into competitive employment. *Exceptionality, 1,* 181–195.

Heal, L. W., & Rusch, F. R. (1995). Predicting employment for students who leave special education high school programs. *Exceptional Children, 61*(5), 472–487.

Individuals with Disabilities Education Act of 1990, 20, U.S.C. Sec. 1400 et seq.

Kohler, P. D. (1993a). Best practices in transition: Substantiated or implied? *Career Development for Exceptional Individuals, 16,* 107–121.

———. (1993b). Serving students with disabilities in postsecondary education settings: A conceptual model of program outcomes. Ph.D. dissertation, University of Illinois at Urbana-Champaign.

———. (1994a). On-the-job training: A curricular approach to employment. *Career Development for Exceptional Individuals, 17,* 29–40.

———. (1994b). *Taxonomy for transition programming.* Champaign: University of Illinois, Transition Research Institute.

———. (1996a). Preparing youths with disabilities for future challenges: A taxonomy for transition programming. In P. D. Kohler (Ed.), *Taxonomy for transition programming: Linking research and practice* (pp. 1–62). Champaign: University of Illinois, Transition Research Institute.

———. (1996b). *Taxonomy for transition programming* (rev. ed.). Champaign: University of Illinois, Transition Research Institute.

———. (In press). *Transition-related instruction and services: Who does what?* Champaign: University of Illinois, Transition Research Institute.

Kohler, P. D., DeStefano, L., Wermuth, T., Grayson, T., & McGinty, S. (1994). An analysis of exemplary transition programs: How and why are they selected? *Career Development for Exceptional Individuals, 17,* 187–202.

Kohler, P. D., & Rusch, F. R. (1996). Secondary educational programs: Preparing youths for tomorrow's challenges. In M. C. Wang, M. C. Reynolds, & H. J. Walberg (Eds.), *Handbook of special and remedial education: Research and practice* (2nd ed.) (pp. 107–130) Tarrytown, NY: Elsevier.

Martin, J. E., Marshall, L. H., & Maxson, L. L. (1993). Transition policy: Infusing self-determination and self-advocacy into transition programs. *Career Development for Exceptional Individuals, 16,* 53–61.

Mithaug, D. E., Horiuchi, C. N., & Fanning, P. N. (1985). A report on the Colorado statewide follow-up survey of special education students. *Exceptional Children, 51,* 397–404.

National Center for Education Statistics. (1994, March). *Annual earnings of young adults,* NCES 94-407. Washington, DC: U. S. Department of Education, Office of Educational Research and Improvement.

Newman, L., & Cameto, R. (1993). *What makes a difference? Factors related to postsecondary school attendance for young people with disabilities.* Menlo Park, CA: SRI International.

Rusch, F. R., DeStefano, L., Chadsey-Rusch, J., Phelps, L. A., & Szymanski, E. (1992a). *Transition from school to adult life: Models, linkages, and policy.* Sycamore, IL: Sycamore.

Rusch, F. R., Kohler, P. D., & Hughes, C. (1992b). An analysis of OSERS-sponsored secondary special education and transitional services research. *Career Development for Exceptional Individuals, 15,* 121–143.

Schloss, P. J., Alper, S., & Jayne, D. (1994). Self-determination for persons with disabilities: Choice, risk, and dignity. *Exceptional Children, 60,* 215–225.

Steere, D. E., Pancsofar, E., Wood, R., & Hecimovic, A. (1990). Principles of shared responsibility. *Career Development for Exceptional Individuals, 13,* 143–153.

Stodden, R. A., Ianacone, R. N., Boone, R. M., & Bisconer, S. W. (1987). *Curriculum-based vocational assessment: A guide for addressing youth with special needs.* Honolulu: Centre Publications.

Stodden, R. A., & Leake, D. W. (1994). Getting to the core of transition: A re-assessment of old wine in new bottles. *Career Development for Exceptional Individuals, 17,* 65–76.

Stodden, R. A., Meehan, K. A., Bisconer, S. W., & Hodell, S. L. (1989). The impact of vocational assessment information and the individualized education planning process. *Journal for Vocational Special Needs Education, 12,* 31–36.

Szymanski, E. M., Hanley-Maxwell, C., & Asselin, S. (1990a). Rehabilitation counseling, special education, and vocational education: Three transition disciplines. *Career Development for Exceptional Individuals, 1,* 29–38.

Szymanski, E. M., Hanley-Maxwell, C., & Parker, R. M. (1990b). Transdisciplinary service delivery. In F. R. Rusch (Ed.), *Supported employment: Models, methods, and issues* (pp. 199–214). Sycamore, IL: Sycamore.

Trach, J. S. (In press). *Impact of curriculum on student postschool outcomes.* Champaign: University of Illinois, Transition Research Institute.

Van Reusen, A. K., & Bos, C. S. (1990). I Plan: Helping students communicate in planning conferences. *Teaching Exceptional Children, 22*(4), 30–32.

Wagner, M. (1989, May). *Youth with disabilities during transition: An overview of descriptive findings from the national longitudinal transition study.* Menlo Park CA: SRI International.

———. (1991). *The benefits associated with secondary vocational education for young people with disabilities: Findings from the National Longitudinal Transition Study of special education students.* Menlo Park, CA: SRI International.

———. (1993). *The secondary school programs of students with disabilities.* Menlo Park, CA: SRI International.

Wagner, M., Blackorby, J., Cameto, R., Hebbeler, K., & Newman, L. (1993a). *The transition experiences of young people with disabilities.* Menlo Park, CA: SRI International.

Wagner, M., Blackorby, J., & Hebbeler, K. (1993b). *Beyond the report card: The multiple dimensions of secondary school performance of students with disabilities.* Menlo Park, CA: SRI International.

Wagner, M., D'Amico, R., Marder, C., Newman, L., & Blackorby, J. (1992). *What happens next? Trends in postschool outcomes of youth with disabilities. The second comprehensive report from the National Longitudinal Transition Study of Special Education Students.* Menlo Park, CA: SRI International.

Wallace, T., Kohler, P., & Wiltrout, D. (1996, July). *Strategies for sewing all students in School-to-Career Transition: Lessons learned at the system and program levels.* Paper presented to the National Leadership Forum on School-to-Career Transition, Long Beach, California.

Wehman, P. (1992a). Transition for young people with disabilities: Challenges for the 1990's. *Education and Training in Mental Retardation, 27,* 112–118.

———. (1992b). *Life beyond the classroom.* Baltimore: Paul H. Brookes.

Wehmeyer, M. L. (1992). Self-determination and the education of students with mental retardation. *Education and Training in Mental Retardation, 27,* 302–314.

Will, M. (1983). *OSERS programming for the transition of youth with disabilities: Bridges from school to working life.* Washington, DC: U.S. Department of Education.

9

◨

Student Involvement in Transition-Planning and Transition-Program Implementation

MICHAEL L. WEHMEYER

This chapter reviews the history of student involvement in transition as well as the numerous benefits. A number of different curricula have emerged in the education marketplace, and these curricula share important dimensions. These dimensions, or characteristics, are reviewed, including tracking student self-awareness, increasing awareness of the transition process, goal setting, decision making and planning, learning self-advocacy and acquiring leadership skills.

As mentioned in previous chapters, IDEA (P.L. 101–476) contained language that made the delivery of transition services to students with disabilities more than just a good idea or a best practice, but the law. In addition to requiring that transition services be provided to students 16 and older, IDEA also mandated student involvement in transition planning by stating that needed transition services *must* be based on student *preferences* and *interests*. The intent of this language is that students become actively involved in transition planning and decision making (Martin, Marshall, & Maxson, 1993; Wehmeyer & Ward, 1995).

Mithaug, Wolman, and Campeau (1992) suggested that the requirements in IDEA transition services language "comprise a logical sequence or causal flow [as depicted in Figure 9.1] *beginning with* student-determined and -defined needs, which lead to plans for coordinated services, which, in turn, result in community-based experiences that culminate in postschool adjustments" (p. 7). As Mithaug and colleagues (1992) pointed out, "For the first time, the mandated condition is for *student preferences* to drive service delivery" (p. 7).

However, there is a significant gap between the recognition, indeed the requirement that students should be involved in transition planning, decision making, and program implementation, and current practice in education and transition. Too frequently, promoting student involvement has been misinterpreted as equivalent to giving students absolute control over the educational process. Involvement in educational planning and decision making can take many forms, from students generating their own IEP goals and objectives to introducing members of the IEP team. The degree to which students can participate in educational planning and decision making, when provided adequate support, will vary significantly across students.

Zimmerman (1994) described student self-regulated learning as the degree to which students are metacognitively, motivationally, and behaviorally active in their own learning process. Agran (1997) defined student-directed learning as instructional activities in which students have control over their learning, experience opportunities to set goals, define actions based on those goals, implement those actions, evaluate their outcomes, and adjust their performances. Student involvement in transition planning and decision making is the intuitive antecedent to student-directed learning; students are actively involved in their own educational planning and decision making. As such, the definitional criterion for student involvement, be it in planning and decision making or program implementation, is not that students have absolute control, but that they are active participants, indeed equal partners, in the process.

A HISTORICAL REVIEW OF STUDENT INVOLVEMENT

Student Involvement in Transition Planning and Decision Making

The emphasis on participatory planning and student involvement in planning and decision making is in response to, and in contrast with, the historical role of students, which was one of passivity and inactivity. This shift in emphasis represents what Bersani (1995) referred to as the "third wave" of the disability movement. The first wave involved the delivery of disability services with only professionals participating in the decision-making process. The parent movement of the 1940s and 1950s constituted the second wave, with parents rightly demanding that they be included when professionals met to discuss their children's needs (Bersani, 1995). In the 1970s and 1980s, spurred on by the successful civil rights movements of preceding decades for women's suffrage and racial equality, disability activists and advocates began organizing and demanding that consumers of disability services be invited to the table where and when decisions were made. This third wave has been referred to as the consumer, self-help, or self-advocacy movement; Driedger (1989) characterized this movement as the "last civil rights movement."

This progression has parallels in the history of special education. Prior to the passage of the Education for All Handicapped Children Act (P.L. 94-142), decisions about the educational program a student with a disability received were made by educational and psychological professionals, typically the school psychologist or diagnostician (Yoshida et al., 1978). P.L. 94-142 opened the door for parental and family involvement in educational planning and decision making, and although the actual implementation of this component remains inconsistent (Wehmeyer & Davis, 1995), parental involvement has become a more visible factor in educational placement and program decisions.

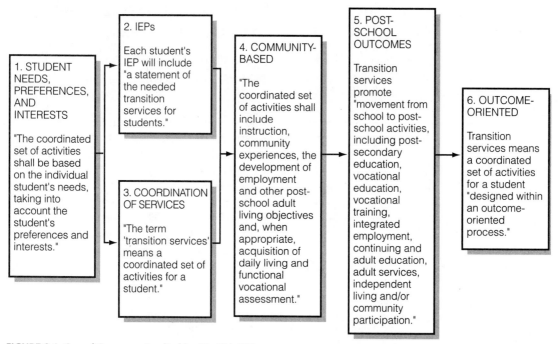

FIGURE 9.1 Causal Sequence Implied by P.L. 101-476

Source: Adapted from Mithaug et al., 1992.

P.L. 94-142 left students' involvement in IEP decisions to "whenever appropriate" and, as Gillespie and Turnbull (1983) have pointed out, this was too frequently interpreted to mean that student involvement was not appropriate or necessary. As a result, student involvement in educational planning and decision making became haphazard at best, and students were essentially outsiders to the educational decision-making process (Van Reusen & Bos, 1990, 1994; Wehmeyer & Lawrence, 1995a; Martin & Marshall, 1996). Van Reusen and Bos (1990) concluded that "student involvement [in educational planning], even at the secondary level, is for the most part either nonexistent or passive" (p. 30). This is in spite of evidence that student involvement can have positive effects on student achievement, outcomes, and motivation, and that, for the most part, educators agree that students can benefit from greater involvement in transition planning. Walker and Shaw (1995)

found that special educators perceived student involvement in transition planning to be low, but felt such involvement to be desirable.

Unfortunately, there is very little empirical evidence concerning the degree to which students with disabilities participate in transition or, for that matter, educational planning meetings. Field, Hoffman, and Sawilowsky (1994) conducted a pilot study of student involvement in transition planning. They interviewed forty-one students, classified as having a disability and eligible for special education services, regarding their involvement in their last educational planning meeting. Seventy-one percent of these students indicated that they attended their last IEP meeting. However, 56 percent noted they had not been told the purpose of the meeting, 63 percent commented that they had not been told things to think about before the meeting, 76 percent said they had not prepared for the meeting, and only 41 percent responded that they had helped identify goals that were included in their IEP.

Student Involvement in Transition-Program Implementation

There is also very little information documenting the degree to which students are involved in transition-program implementation. Student involvement in transition-program implementation is achieved by applying models of teaching and learning that enable students to become active participants in assessment, instructional, and program-evaluation activities. Student-directed learning incorporates the use of self-management methodologies, typically using self-monitoring, self-instruction, and self-reinforcement procedures to place students in roles traditionally held by educational personnel. So, for example, instead of the teacher keeping track of a student's progress on a specific goal or objective by marking scores in a grade book, a self-directed program might enable students to self-direct their program by graphing, charting, or otherwise marking scores to track progress.

Although there is limited documentation of the degree to which teachers use student-directed strategies, there is a general agreement that such strategies are underutilized in special education (Wehmeyer, 1992; Agran, 1997). A comprehensive reading of the literature leads to several conclusions. First, self-directed learning techniques are most likely to be used with low-incidence populations, such as students with severe mental retardation. Second, student-directed learning seems to be a treatment of last recourse, in that it is frequently applied in circumstances where traditional teaching models have failed. For example, self-management procedures are frequently used to address challenging or problematic behaviors. In essence, despite evidence that student-directed learning strategies have potential to benefit all students across a broad range of subjects and settings, these procedures are "marginalized" and too frequently employed only with low-incidence

populations or in circumstances where all else has failed.

BENEFITS OF STUDENT INVOLVEMENT

Benefits of Student Involvement in Planning and Decision Making

A number of benefits are gained by involving students in educational planning and decision making, including benefits to the student and the educational process itself. Table 9.1 highlights some of these benefits, which include enhanced motivation to learn, improved educational outcomes, and opportunities to learn and practice self-advocacy skills. The last is a particularly important, given the increasing number of studies that have found that students leave school without the self-determination and self-advocacy skills they need to succeed as young adults (Wehmeyer & Metzler, 1995; Wehmeyer & Schwartz, 1997).

McTaggert and Gould (1988) suggested that secondary-age instruction in self-advocacy includes instruction and practice in some or all of the following areas:

- assertive behavior
- public speaking skills
- leadership skills
- decision-making skills
- problem-resolution skills
- legal and citizenship rights and responsibilities
- transition planning
- goal setting and attainment
- use of community resources
- communication

Each of these topics is important in the transition-planning meeting. The educational planning meeting can be a setting in which

Table 9.1 Benefits of Student Involvement in Educational Planning and Decision Making

Benefits to Student

Students may be more motivated to pursue goals that they have helped select.

Students have the opportunity to learn and put in use already learned self-advocacy, leadership, teamwork, effective communication, and other important skills.

Students who are involved in setting goals have more positive outcomes related to achieving those goals than with goals selected by others.

Benefits to Other Team Members and the Process

Students can contribute firsthand information regarding areas that present the greatest and the least amount of difficulty for them and identify strategies that enable them to overcome these difficulties (from Strickland &Turnbull, 1990).

The student's presence at the IEP meeting can personalize the meeting for team members, particularly if they do not know the student. It also enables other team members to ask the student directly about interests, skills, accommodations, and so forth (from Strickland & Turnbull, 1990).

By including students in the decision-making process, team members communicate to students that they are expected to behave maturely and responsibly (from Strickland & Turnbull, 1990).

to practice both self-advocacy and self-determination skills that students have been working on throughout the year, like problem solving or effective communication skills, and a means of introducing students to the importance of such skills.

In addition to the impact of student involvement on student self-advocacy and self-determination, research consistently indicates that students who have the opportunity to participate in choosing school activities show enhanced motivation to learn (Swann & Pittman, 1977; Koestner et al., 1984). A similar line of research has demonstrated that opportunities to express preferences and make choices lead to greater motivation and enhanced outcomes. In fact, Kohn (1993), reviewing the evidence to support the view that choices lead to learning, found it so compelling that "it is frankly difficult to understand how anyone can talk about school reform without immediately addressing the question of how students can be given more say about what goes on in their classes" (p. 12). Perlmutter and Monty (1977) showed that students' opportunities to make choices about educational activities improved student performance. Realon, Favell, and Lowerre (1990) noted that when individuals with

profound levels of mental retardation were allowed to make choices regarding leisure-time activities, the amount of time they spent interacting with the chosen leisure materials increased.

In addition to increased motivation, evidence from research examining student participation in goal setting suggests that active student involvement in educational decision making can improve educational outcomes. This conclusion has strong face validity because, as Schunk (1985) pointed out, participation in goal setting can result in higher commitment to the goal and, consequently, increased performance. This assumption has also been borne out by research. For example, Schunk (1985) found that students with learning disabilities who participated in setting goals related to mathematics activities showed greater improvement in this area than did students who participated in the same instruction but either had goals selected for them or had no goals identified.

In addition to benefits accrued by the student, active student involvement in educational planning and decision making benefits other team members and the process as well. As Strickland and Turnbull (1990) pointed out, student participation provides team members a chance to hear about student needs, interests, and preferences and to talk with the student about how he or she learns best. Such participation also tends to personalize the decision-making process for team members.

Benefits of Student Involvement in Program Implementation

Similar findings permeate the research on student self-directed and self-regulated learning, which typically examines components of individual self-monitoring, self-instruction, self-evaluation, and self-reinforcement. (See Martin et al., 1988, for a comprehensive overview of the research literature prior to 1986.)

Self-Monitoring and Self-Recording Procedures. These procedures have been shown to improve the motivation and performance of students with disabilities. For example, Malone and Mastropieri (1992) determined that under a self-monitoring condition, middle school students with learning disabilities performed better on reading comprehension transfer tasks than peers who did not self-monitor. McCarl, Svobodny, and Beare (1991) found that teaching three students with mental retardation to record progress on classroom assignments improved on-task behavior for all students and increased productivity for two of the three.

Kapadia and Fantuzzo (1988) used self-monitoring procedures to increase attention to academic tasks for students with developmental disabilities and behavior problems. Further, self-recording activities enabled adults with mental retardation to improve task completion of daily living activities (Lovett & Haring, 1989). Similarly, Chiron and Gerken (1983) found that students with mental retardation who charted progress on school reading activities showed significant increases in reading level. Trammel, Schloss, and Alper (1994) found that self-recording (graphing) and student-directed goal setting enabled students with learning disabilities to increase the number of assignments they completed.

However, application of self-monitoring procedures is not a panacea for improvement. Effects on outcomes depend on the type of self-monitoring procedure used. For example, Misra (1992) found that self-monitoring procedures assisted in the generalization of social skills across settings and students for youth with mental retardation, but that there was variability in the degree to which these procedures contributed to the maintenance of these skills. Reid and Harris (1993) found that students with learning disabilities who were taught to self-monitor their performance and attention to task showed enhanced on-task behavior in both conditions, compared with a baseline spelling study procedure, and that correct practice was higher in the self-monitoring of performance condition. However, spelling achievement was lower in the self-monitoring of attention condition than at baseline, and spelling maintenance was lower in this condition than at baseline or the self-monitoring of performance condition.

Self-Instructional Strategies. These strategies also have been shown to be beneficial. Self-instruction generally refers to "verbalizations an individual emits to cue, direct or maintain his or her own behavior" (Agran, Fodor-Davis, & Moore, 1986:273); however, several authors report self-instructional strategies where students think through the strategies instead of verbalizing them. A number of studies have found that self-instruction training is a useful technique for increasing job-related skills of individuals with mental retardation (Agran et al., 1986; Rusch et al., 1988; Hughes & Petersen, 1989; Salend, Ellis, & Reynolds, 1989). Graham and Harris (1989) found that a self-instructional strategy improved the essay composition skills of students with learning disabilities. Agran, Salzberg, and Stowitschek (1987) noted self-instructional strategies increased the percentages of initiations with a work supervisor when employees, five individuals with mental retardation, ran out of work materials or needed assistance.

Self-Evaluation or Self-Judgment. This is the third common component of self-directed learning. Schunk (1981) showed that students who verbalized cognitive strategies related to evaluating their study and work habits had increased math achievement scores. Brownell and colleagues (1977) found that students who determined their performance standards demonstrated increased time on-task compared with students operating under imposed standards.

Self-Reinforcement. This fourth component of self-regulated learning also leads to increased performance. Lagomarcino and Rusch (1989) used a combination of self-reinforcement and self-monitoring procedures to improve the work performance of a student with mental retardation in a community setting. Moore, Agran, and Fodor-Davis (1989) similarly applied a combination of student-directed activities, including self-instructions, goal setting, and self-reinforcement, to improve the production rate of workers with mental retardation. Finally, Shapiro and Klein (1980) found that students who self-reinforced maintained high levels of on-task behavior.

These studies represent only a sample of the research showing positive educational benefits of the use of student-directed learning techniques. Taken as a whole, it seems evident that it is beneficial to both the student and the educator to involve students in all aspects of transition-related programming. Given that this is not the case, what barriers exist to the adoption of such practices?

BARRIERS TO STUDENT INVOLVEMENT

As already suggested, many students are left out of the transition process, from goal development and instructional decision making to placement and program implementation. One common factor that too often has led to the assumption that student involvement, particularly in educational planning and decision making, was not

appropriate was the presence of a severe disabling condition. Thus, until recently, issues of student choice and preference for students with severe, multiple disabilities have been largely ignored (Guess, Benson, & Siegel-Causey, 1985). For example, in a study of students with severe disabilities, Houghton, Bronicki, and Guess (1987) determined that classroom staff responded with very low rates to student-initiated expressions of preference or choice during the school day.

The assumption that students with severe disabilities cannot be involved in educational planning and decision making is not consistent with findings from the student-directed learning literature, which show that these students can self-direct learning. Many of the studies highlighted previously showed that students and adults with severe disabilities can self-regulate all or a portion of the learning process. The primary barrier for students with severe disabilities is the assumption, discussed earlier, that student involvement is equated with absolute student control.

However, exclusion from educational planning and decision making is not the experience only of students with severe disabilities. Students with learning disabilities, emotional disorders, mild mental retardation, and other higher-incidence populations have not gained adequate access to the planning process. For example, when Gilliam and Coleman (1981) conducted a survey of participants in IEP meetings for students with learning disabilities and emotional disorders to determine who most influenced IEP committee decisions, students were not even included in the survey!

A number of additional issues stand as barriers to student involvement. One such issue is a societal distrust of the competence of most minors to make decisions in an informed and effective manner (Adelman et al., 1990). Many educators also point to the lack of student motivation to participate in the educational process, particularly the IEP meeting, as a barrier to student involvement. Finally, there is a pervasive belief that the educational planning and deci-sion-making process, inherently, is too complex for students and, thus, requires someone with specific expertise in control. However, there is sufficient evidence to discount these objections and to actively involve students in the transition process.

Student Capacity to Make Informed Choices and Decisions

An underlying assumption held by many educa-tors and parents, which constitutes a significant barrier to student involvement, is that minors do not have the capacity to make informed choices and decisions. This assumption is also frequently made about individuals with disabilities, so the overwhelming assumption about adolescents with disabilities is that they are incapable of par-ticipating in the decision-making process. How-ever, research, including research with students with disabilities, has shown that minors are indeed competent to make important decisions.

Adelman and colleagues (1990) conducted a series of studies showing that students demon-strate the ability to make competent decisions. Taylor, Adelman, and Kaser-Boyd (1983) found that the majority of adolescents referred for special support services wanted to participate in a decision-making meeting regarding those ser-vices, knew what outcomes they wanted, believed they were capable of participating in the meeting, followed through on actions agreed to at the meeting, and, subsequently, rated their involvement in the meeting as effective. A repli-cation with students identified as having a learn-ing disability or severe emotional disorder also found that these students were interested in im-proving the skills they would need to participate more effectively (Taylor, Adelman, & Kaser-Boyd, 1985). Adelman and colleagues (1985) ob-served that youth with school-related problems were competent to understand, evaluate, and communicate their psychoeducational problems.

Other researchers have determined that when provided the opportunity to participate in

educational decision making, students with dis-abilities do as well as other team members. Specifically, Salend (1983) noted considerable congruence between student self-selected IEP objectives and those selected by the interdiscipli-nary team. Phillips (1990) and Van Reusen and Bos (1994) found that students with learning disabilities were able to participate in the deci-sion-making process, a finding duplicated by Wehmeyer and Lawrence (1995a) with students with mental retardation.

The belief that minors and students with dis-abilities cannot take into account the degree of risk involved with various options has con-tributed to the misperception of minors as being incapable of making competent decisions. How-ever, this assumption is not supported by research in developmental psychology. Based on a review of the cognitive and behavioral charac-teristics of minors in relation to the question of competence to consent to treatment, Grisso and Vierling (1978) concluded that "there is no psy-chological grounds for maintaining the general legal assumption that minors age 15 and above cannot provide competent consent, taking into account risk-related factors" (p. 424). In fact, these authors contended that there are "circum-stances that would justify the sanction of *inde-pendent* consent" (p. 424) by minors between the ages of 11 and 14. It should be reiterated that although Grisso and Vierling (1978) were inter-ested only in the degree to which adolescents without cognitive impairments should be allowed to independently consent to treatment, their review provides guidelines for the degree to which students with disabilities should be allowed to make *independent* decisions. And, if taken a step further, it suggests that students could become involved in and a part of, though not solely responsible for, such decisions as a team member at a much earlier age.

Kaser-Boyd, Adelman, and Taylor (1985) confirmed this suggestion. Students ages 10 to 20 who were identified as having a learn-ing or behavior problem in school were asked to list potential risks and benefits of entering psychoeducational therapy. As expected, there was a relationship between age and efficacy in this task. However, even young students were able to identify relevant concerns that were appropriate to their situation and their developmental needs.

Student Motivation for Participation

Another frequently cited barrier to student involvement is a perceived lack of student motivation to participate in meetings and educational programs. Although it is true that student motivation to participate has been linked negatively to participation in the educational decision-making process (Adelman et al., 1990), the assumption that students should not or cannot participate in planning meetings because they lack the necessary motivation seems incongruous with findings, presented before, that student involvement in all aspects of the educational process increases motivation. The reality is that student lack of motivation to participate is often a direct result of their lack of control over the process. And as such, student involvement is one solution to the problems with student motivation. Discussing the state of education today, Kohn (1993) concluded:

> Much of what is disturbing about students' attitudes and behavior may be a function of the fact that they have little to say about what happens to them all day. They are compelled to follow someone else's rules, study someone else's curriculum and submit continually to someone else's evaluation. The mystery, really, is not that so many students are indifferent about what they have to do in school, but that any of them are not. (p. 10)

Complexity of the Transition Process

A final barrier to student involvement is the assertion that the transition process is too complex. Although this has some face validity, given the complexity of most school processes and the often emphasized paperwork associated with educational planning, the fact is that students can, and do, participate in all aspects of their transition program with considerable success. The assumption that the transition process is too complex for students to be involved rests on the related, and incorrect assumptions, that student involvement means total control over the process and that students are not competent to make decisions. As discussed previously, both of these assumptions have been shown to be erroneous.

Perhaps the strongest evidence against the assumption that the transition process is too complex for students to be actively involved, is that a number of researchers have shown that students can be involved effectively in the transition process, in either planning, decision making (Van Reusen & Bos, 1994; Martin & Marshall, 1995; Wehmeyer & Lawrence, 1995a), or, as highlighted earlier, program implementation. Turnbull and colleagues (1996) showed that students with severe cognitive and multiple disabilities could be involved in transition planning and decision making. These programs succeed because they actively involve students to participate maximally. In many cases, maximal participation is achieved by use of the principle of *partial participation,* introduced by Baumgart and colleagues (1982). This principle was originally forwarded in relationship to the participation of students with severe disabilities in educational programs. Simply put, it suggests that most students can be at least partially involved in virtually any activity. In the case of transition planning, a student with mental retardation, for example, may not be able to complete the complicated IEP form mandated for use by the school district, but could introduce his or her team members, be responsible for listing the previous year's goals, and identify new goals or objectives.

In summary, there seems to be clear evidence that student involvement in transition planning, decision making, and program implementation can have multiple benefits. Yet, despite this evidence, it appears that such involvement is minimal and marginalized. Traditional barriers to student involvement are based primarily on beliefs about minors and students with disabilities that are, at best, incorrect and serve to limit the degree to which educators and family members seek to involve students in transition programming.

CURRENT PRACTICES IN STUDENT INVOLVEMENT

Through impetus from the student involvement requirements in the IDEA, the self-determination movement, and the increased visibility of people with disabilities in society, a set of promising practices have emerged promoting student involvement in the transition process. The following sections provide an overview of key elements that are present across programs and procedures that support student involvement, and describe promising practices and specific programs supporting student involvement in transition planning, decision making, and program implementation.

A series of federally funded projects (Ward, 1996; Ward & Kohler, 1996) developed and made available materials to promote self-determination for youth with disabilities. Many of these projects applied principles introduced by Mithaug and colleagues (1987b), who proposed that students should learn to become "more independent in understanding what they need and want, how to set personal goals ... and to select action plans that will lead to desired outcomes" (Mithaug, Horiuchi, & McNulty, 1987a:59).

The Adaptability Model, forwarded by Mithaug and colleagues (1987b) and depicted in Figure 9.2, was among the first to incorporate findings from problem-solving, self-management, and self-regulation literature (Bandura, 1986; Kanfer & Goldstein, 1986; Agran & Martin, 1987; Martin et al., 1988; Mithaug, 1993) to provide a framework through which student involvement could be achieved. The core tenets of the Adaptability Model were that students should be involved in activities promoting decision making, independent performance, self-evaluation, and adjustment. This model operationalizes, and thus exemplifies, the key

elements of student involvement in transition programming. Students involved in activities based on the Adaptability Model identify their own needs, interests, and abilities; consider options and alternatives for transition-related outcomes; and select goals and objectives related to the selected outcomes. Students then work with teachers to design and implement student-directed learning activities that enable them to achieve these goals and objectives, including self-instruction and other antecedent procedures like picture cues, written prompts, and verbal labeling (Wehmeyer, Martin, & Sands, 1997).

While working on these tasks, students self-evaluate by monitoring and recording performance outcomes, and then compare their results with goals and performance objectives set during the decision-making process. Students adjust their performance by using their self-evaluations to decide what to do next time. These adjustments "are the essential component of the Adaptability Model. They connect future actions with past performance. Before beginning another task or project, students review feedback from previous adjustment decisions and select goals, plans and performance objectives accordingly" (Wehmeyer et al., 1997).

Perhaps the key ingredient of student involvement across virtually all programs is that students' preferences, interests, abilities, wants, and needs are the starting point for all activities. Although some students with more severe disabilities may have considerable difficulty with the decision-making, goal-setting, or problem-solving aspects of student involvement, all students express some preferences and can become involved from that aspect. The degree to which student preferences and interests are used to enable students to make meaningful choices for educational programs depends essentially on the creativity and motivation of educators and family members.

However, it should not be taken for granted that all students will automatically be able to identify their own interests, abilities, limitations, and strengths. This may be especially true for students receiving special education services,

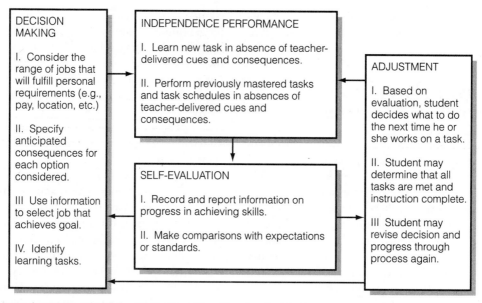

FIGURE 9.2. Adaptability Model Applied to Transition Planning for Employment

Source: Mithaug, Martin & Agran, 1987b.

where a deficits model has too frequently emphasized student weaknesses (Wehmeyer, 1992). Consequently, most programs to promote student involvement focus on enabling students to identify interests based on their preferences, understand their unique abilities and limitations, and learn to apply these strengths and interests to identify future plans and goals. Additional themes common to student-involvement programs, and illustrated by the Adaptability Model, include having students learn to identify problems, identify and evaluate options or solutions to these problems, and identify and contact resources that enable them to implement selected options. Student involvement programs frequently teach students how to generate, evaluate, and track educational goals and objectives; express leadership and self-advocacy skills; communicate effectively using negotiation, compromise and persuasion; and self-regulate behavior. The last includes the employment of student-directed learning strategies like self-instruction, self-modeling, self-evaluation, and self-reinforcement.

A final element of such programs is that they emphasize student responsibility for achieving

goals and following through on promised activities. This is an important issue, but one that is relevant only when the other key elements of student involvement are in place. Too frequently, students are held accountable and responsible for outcomes even though they do not experience any real opportunities to contribute to educational planning and decision making.

Student Involvement in Transition Planning and Decision-Making Programs

Several programs apply these key elements to involve students in transition planning. These programs employ two basic strategies, *student-directed, transition-planning programs* and *self-advocacy programs,* although most programs incorporate aspects of both strategies. Student directed, transition-planning programs emphasize student direction of the educational planning process, are often written expressly for students to implement, and typically use the IEP or transition-planning meeting as the fulcrum for activities. Self-advocacy programs tend to emphasize the development of skills related to leadership, assertive communication, individual rights and responsibilities, and advocacy efforts; are less likely to use the IEP meeting itself as a central focus; and are generally implemented by someone other than the student, such as the classroom teacher.

ChoiceMaker Self-Determination. Transition Curriculum and Program. The ChoiceMaker program (overviewed in Martin & Marshall, 1996) emerged from a federally funded self-determination grant and teaches self-determination through student self-management of the IEP process. The *ChoiceMaker Self-Determination Transition Curriculum* (Martin & Marshall, 1995) consists of three sections: (a) Choosing Goals, (b) Expressing Goals, and (c) Taking Action. Each section contains from two to four teaching goals and numerous teaching objectives that address six transition areas. Examples include: (a) an assessment tool, (b) Choosing Goals lessons, (c) the Self-Directed IEP, and (d) Taking Action lessons. The program also includes a criterion-referenced, self-determination, transition-assessment tool that matches the curricular sections.

ChoiceMaker materials are built around a socially validated transition curriculum. The first step in the validation process involved a comprehensive literature review and interview process, which resulted in a list of thirty-seven self-determination concepts, grouped by the authors into seven areas:

- self-awareness
- self-advocacy
- self-efficacy
- decision making
- independent performance
- self-evaluation
- adjustment

Table 9.2 lists the thirty-seven self-determination concepts in the seven areas. After this initial identification phase, the concepts were defined, expanded, and placed into a curriculum matrix. At this time, teachers, adults with disabilities, parents, and university-based transition experts from around the country validated the concepts and the matrix. Finally, a comprehensive field test of the materials was conducted. Figure 9.3 gives a graphic example of the flow between the transition domains of the Choice-Maker IEP process. *ChoiceMaker Self-Determination Curriculum* sections, goals, and lessons are provided in Table 9.3.

Choosing Goals lessons enable students to learn the necessary skills and personal information needed to articulate their interests, skills, limits, and goals across one or more self-selected transition areas. Self-Directed IEP lessons enable students to learn the leadership skills necessary to manage their IEP meeting and publicly disclose their interests, skills, limits, and goals as identified through the Choosing Goals lessons. Rather than be passive participants at their IEP meetings, students learn to lead their meeting to the greatest extent of their ability. These lessons teach students eleven steps for leading their own staffing, as shown in Table 9.4.

The Taking Action materials enable students to learn how to break their long-range goals into specific goals that can be accomplished in a week. Students learn how they will attain their goals by deciding (a) a standard for goal performance; (b) a means to get performance feedback; (c) what motivates them to do it; (d) the strategies they will use; (e) needed supports; and (f) schedules. Rather than teachers, parents, or support staff telling students what to do, when to do it, and how they did, students assume these responsibilities. This requires a learning process that fades teacher instruction as students learn the crucial skills. Martin and Marshall (1995) reported that the ChoiceMaker materials were field-tested and revised with students with behavioral and learning disabilities across several school districts.

Whose Future Is It Anyway? A Student-Directed, Transition-Planning Program. The Arc, a national organization on mental retardation, with funding from the U.S. Department of Education, has developed and

Table 9.2 ChoiceMaker Self-Determination Constructs

Core Area	Self-Determination Construct
Self-Awareness	■ Identify needs ■ Identify interests ■ Identify and understand strengths ■ Identify and understand limitations ■ Identify own values
Self-Advocacy	■ Assertively state wants ■ Assertively state rights ■ Determine support needs ■ Pursue needed support ■ Obtain and evaluate needed support ■ Conduct own affairs
Self-Efficacy Decision Making	■ Expect to obtain goals ■ Assess situational demands ■ Set goals ■ Set standards ■ Identify information needed to make decisions ■ Consider past solutions for new situations ■ Generate new, creative solutions ■ Consider options ■ Choose best option ■ Develop plan
Independent Performance	■ Initiate tasks on time ■ Complete tasks on time ■ Use self-management strategies ■ Perform tasks to standard ■ Follow through on own plan
Self-Evaluation	■ Monitor task performance ■ Compare performance to standard ■ Evaluate effectiveness of self-management strategies ■ Determine if plan is completed and goals met
Adjustment	■ Change goals ■ Change standards ■ Change plan ■ Change strategies ■ Change support ■ Persistently adjust ■ Use environmental feedback to aid adjustment

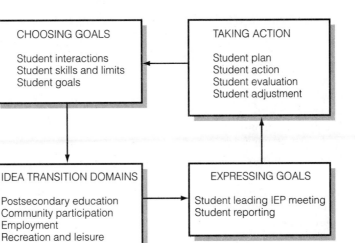

FIGURE 9.3. The Flow Between Transition Domains and the ChoiceMaker IEP Process

Source: Adapted from Martin & Marshall, 1996. Used by permission of James E. Martin.

field-tested a student-directed, transition-planning program for adolescents with mental retardation and other cognitive and developmental disabilities, titled *Whose Future Is It Anyway?* (Wehmeyer & Kelchner, 1995b). This curriculum consists of thirty-six sessions introducing students to the concept of transition and transition planning, and enabling students to self-direct instruction related to (a) self-awareness and disability awareness, (b) making decisions about transition-related outcomes, (c) identifying and securing community resources to

Table 9.3 ChoiceMaker Self-Determination Transition Curriculum Sections, Goals, and Lessons

Section	Goals	Lessons
1. Choosing Goals	A. Student Interests	■ Choosing Employment Goals
	B. Student Skills and Limits	■ Choosing Personal Goals
	C. Student Goals	■ Choosing Post-High School Goals
		■ Choosing Secondary School Goals
		■ Choosing Housing and Daily Living Goals
		■ Choosing Community Participation Goals
2. Expressing Goals	D. Student Leading Meeting	■ Self-Directed IEP
	E. Student Reporting	
3. Taking Action	F. Student Plan	■ Take Action
	G. Student Action	
	H. Student Evaluation	
	I. Student Adjustment	

Source: Adapted from Martin & Marshall, 1996. Used by permission of James E. Martin.

Table 9.4 Eleven Steps for Transition Planning

Step	Activity
1	Begin the meeting by stating the purpose.
2	Introduce everyone.
3	Review past goals and performance.
4	Ask for others' feedback.
5	State your school and transition goals.
6	Ask questions if you do not understand.
7	Deal with differences in opinion
8	State the support you will need.
9	Summarize your goals.
10	Close meeting by thanking everyone.
11	Work on IEP goals all year.

Source: Martin & Marshall, 1996. Reprinted by permission of James E. Martin.

support transition services, (d) writing and evaluating transition goals and objectives, (e) communicating effectively in small groups, and (f) developing skills to become an effective team member, leader, or self-advocate.

The materials are student-directed in that they are written for students as end users. The level of support needed by students to complete activities varies a great deal. Some students with difficulty reading or writing need one-on-one support to progress through the materials, others can complete the process independently. The materials make every effort to ensure that students retain this control while receiving the support they need to succeed. For example, although there is a Coach's Guide (Wehmeyer & Lawrence, 1995b) to assist teachers in providing adequate support, the identification of the person to serve as coach is left to the student. Students are instructed to identify a teacher or other person to serve as a coach and to take the Coach's Guide to that person.

Section 1 of *Whose Future Is It Anyway?* (titled Getting to Know You) introduces the concept of transition and educational planning, provides information about the transition requirements in IDEA, and enables students to identify who has attended past planning meetings, who is required to be present at such meetings, and who they want involved in their planning process. Later in the section, students are introduced to four primary transition outcome areas (employment, community living, postsecondary education, and recreation and leisure). Throughout the process, activities focus on these transition outcome areas.

The remainder of the sessions in this first section discuss the topic of disability and disability awareness. Students are encouraged to identify their unique characteristics, including their abilities and interests. They then identify unique learning needs related to their disability, beginning with a discussion of stereotypes associated with disability and the possible negative impact of such stereotypes. Finally, students identify their unique learning needs resulting from their disability.

The second section (Making Decisions) introduces a decision-making process called DO IT! (see Table 9.5) that students apply making decisions about the four transition outcome areas mentioned earlier. Students learn a simple problem-solving process by working through each step in the process to make a decision about a potential living arrangement, and then apply the process to make decisions about the

Table 9.5 DO IT! Problem-Solving Strategy from *Whose Future Is It Anyway?*

Initial	Activity
D	**D**efine the problem
O	**O**utline your options
I	**I**dentify the outcome of each option
T	**T**ake action
!	Get excited!

three other transition outcome areas. In the final session in this section, students learn to use the process to give informed consent with specific application to the transition-planning meeting.

The third section (How to Get What You Need, Sec. 101) enables students to locate community resources identified in previous planning meetings that are intended to provide supports in each of the transition-outcome areas. After identifying such supports, if available, students then gather information about each community resource. Section 4 (Goals, Objectives and the Future) enables learners to apply a set of rules to identify transition-related goals and objectives that are currently on their IEP or transition-planning form, evaluate these goals based on their own transition interests and abilities, and develop additional goals to bring to their next planning meeting. For example, students learn what goals and objectives are, how they should be written, and ways to track progress on goals and objectives.

The fifth section (Communication) introduces effective communication strategies for small-group situations, like the transition-planning meetings. Students work through sessions that introduce different types of communication (verbal, body language, etc.) and how to interpret communicative behaviors, the differences between aggressive and assertive communication, how to effectively negotiate and compromise, when to use persuasion, and other skills that will help them to be more effective communicators during transition-planning meetings.

The final session (Thank You, Honorable Chairperson) enables students to learn types and purposes of meetings, steps to holding effective meetings, and roles of the meeting chairperson and team members. Students are encouraged to work with school district personnel to play a meaningful role in planning for and participating in the meeting, including eventually chairing a transition-planning meeting.

As they work through the program, students are encouraged to work on one session per week during the weeks between their previous transition-planning meeting and the next scheduled meeting, as illustrated in Case Study 1. The final two sessions review the previous sessions and provide a refresher as students head into their planning meeting.

After all materials development activities had been completed, the *Whose Future Is It Anyway?* process was field-tested with almost sixty students with cognitive disabilities attending high school (Wehmeyer & Lawrence, 1995a). Analysis of pre- and postintervention student assessments indicated significant changes in students' scores on self-efficacy and outcome expectancy for educational planning, indicating that students believed they possessed more skills necessary to participate in their planning meeting and felt that if they exhibited these actions, preferred outcomes related to their involvement in the meeting would occur. In addition, students provided consistently positive feedback about the process and its importance to their lives, a finding replicated with these students' teachers.

CASE STUDY 1   Whose Future is it Anyway?

Marcus' last transition-planning meeting had been held almost 1 year ago. It was his first transition-planning meeting and his teacher had told him that he had to be there. Marcus did not really see why, because there would be people just like his parents and his teacher who would talk about what they wanted him to do! Had he been asked, he would have admitted that he really did not even know what the meeting was about or what a "transition" was. On the other hand, it got him out of social studies for an hour, so he had agreed to go. Just as he figured, the meeting was to talk about him. However, he was surprised when his teacher said that the meeting was to create a plan about his future, like where he would live or work after he graduated, and that he really needed to become involved in making some of those decisions. Sure, he had agreed, but how?

The following week Marcus began working on a program called *Whose Future Is It Anyway?* His teacher had ordered a copy of the program for him and some of his peers at school. He spent an hour looking at the materials, and reading through the first section. That section told him that this was something he could work on pretty much by himself, and that it would help him learn how to become more in control of some of the decisions made at his transition planning meeting. One of the first things he had to do was to pick someone to be his coach as he worked through the sessions. Marcus figured that because Ms. Palmer had given him the book and because she was around most the time, she would probably be the best coach. He then went up to her desk and asked her to be the coach. Marcus then asked when he could work on *Whose Future Is It Anyway?* Ms. Palmer suggested that he take an hour from her class each week and work on the program through the school year.

During the first 6 weeks, Marcus learned that there was a law that guaranteed him an education that fit his needs. He learned that "transition skills" are skills you need to get from one point in your life to another, and that "transition planning" means making decisions about what you need to learn to be successful as an adult. He also learned that transition plans are made at meetings. His meeting was called an Individualized Educational Planning meeting. He also found that there were a lot of times that his coach (Ms. Palmer) was a lot of help!

After Marcus learned who had to be at planning meetings, he identified people from other areas of his life whom he might want to invite to his next planning meeting. He remembered that the only people at the previous meeting was him, Ms. Palmer, the assistant principal, his mom, and a person called a "vocational adjustment coordinator" whom he had never met before. He decided that was probably enough people, although he had decided he might invite his boss from the grocery store to the next meeting. He spent the rest of the 6 weeks learning about his unique learning strengths and needs and figuring out the types of supports he would need to learn best.

In the second 6-week period, Marcus learned how to DO IT! DO IT! is a decision-making process that he had memorized and then used to make decisions about things like where he might want to work, go to school or live, or how he might spend his free time. He also learned to use the same process to decide if he wanted to sign his IEP form. After the decision-making sessions, Marcus worked through a series of activities that showed him how to locate and access community resources that would provide support for him when he needed it. That was followed by 6 weeks of sessions in which he learned what a goal was, how to set goals, and how to track how well he was doing on goals. He looked at some of the goals from his last IEP and wrote some of his own goals about what he would need to learn to work, live, learn, or play where he wanted.

In the last two 6-week periods, Marcus learned how to communicate with others assertively, but not aggressively, how to negotiate and compromise, and how to persuade others that what he wanted was important. He also learned some things about leading meetings, being a good participant and team player, and what had to happen to make sure the meeting went well.

For the last 2 weeks, Marcus had been reviewing all of the things he had learned over the year. His meeting was scheduled for tomorrow afternoon at 3 o'clock. He had decided that he didn't really want to lead the meeting, but instead had written three goals that he would like included in the transition plan. Two of the goals were employment-related; one was a leisure goal. He had already met with Ms. Palmer,

(continued)

CASE STUDY 1   *(continued)*

who was very supportive of his goals. He had also talked to the vocational adjustment counselor, who had agreed to help him work on those goals. Finally, he already knew how he would track them if they got on the IEP form.

Marcus was a little nervous, but also felt pretty good. He did not see any reason why the goals would not be on his plan ... he had already talked with everyone about them and they agreed they were important. He thought back to the last meeting. He felt very different about his role in the upcoming meeting. In some ways, he felt more grown up and responsible. So, while he was a little nervous, he felt confident that tomorrow's meeting would go well. In fact, he would never admit it to his folks or Ms. Palmer, but he was kind of excited about the meeting! After all, he thought, whose future is it anyway!

Next S.T.E.P.: Student Transition and Educational Planning. A third student-directed transition planning program is the Next S.T.E.P. curriculum (Halpern et al., 1997). The two main purposes of this curriculum are to "teach students the skills they need to do transition planning" and "engage students successfully in this process" (Halpern et al., 1997:1). The curriculum uses video and print materials developed for specific audiences (students, teachers, family members) to help students become motivated to engage in transition planning, self-evaluate transition needs, identify and select transition goals and activities, assume responsibility for conducting their own transition-planning meeting, and monitor the implementation of their transition plans.

The curriculum consists of sixteen lessons, clustered into four instructional units designed to be delivered in a 50-minute class period. These lessons include teacher and student materials, videos, guidelines for involving parents and family members, and a process for tracking student progress. Unit 1 (Getting Started), which introduces and overviews transition planning, is intended to enable students to understand the transition-planning process and to motivate them to participate. Unit 2 (Self-Exploration and Self-Evaluation) includes six lessons that focus on student self-evaluation. Students work through activities that identify unique interests, strengths, and weaknesses in various adult-outcome-oriented areas. At the end of this unit, stu-

dents complete the student form of the *Transition Skills Inventory,* a seventy-two item rating instrument assessing how well the student is doing in four transition areas: (a) personal life, (b) jobs, (c) education and training, and (d) living on one's own. The student's self-evaluation of these areas is combined with similar evaluations by his or her teacher and a family member to form a basis for future transition-planning activities. Students are encouraged to discuss differences of opinion between the teacher or family member evaluations and their own self-evaluation and to resolve any discrepancies either before or during the transition-planning meeting.

Unit 3 (Developing Goals and Activities) contains five lessons regarding transition goal identification in the four areas comprising the *Transition Skills Inventory.* Students identify their hopes and dreams, then select from a broad range of potential goals in each area, narrowing the total set of transition goals to four or five goals that they prefer. In addition, students choose activities that will help them pursue the goals they have selected. Unit 4 ("Putting a Plan into Place") includes three lessons that prepare students for their transition-planning meeting. The lessons emphasize the implementation of their plan and work with students to ensure that they monitor their progress and, if necessary, make adjustments. Halpern and colleagues (1997) have field-tested the curriculum with more than 1,000 students with disabilities.

The Self-Advocacy Strategy for Education and Transition Planning. Van Reusen and colleagues (1994) have developed a procedure that incorporates both types of strategies, student-directed transition planning and self-advocacy instruction. The program stresses the importance of self-advocacy to enhance student motivation and is "designed to enable students to systematically gain a sense of control and influence over their own learning and development" (p. 1). Students progress through a series of lesson plans focusing on seven instructional stages. Stage 1, Orient and Make Commitments, broadly introduces education and transition-planning meetings, the program itself, and how participation can increase student power and control in this process. Stage 2 (Describe) defines and provides detailed information about transition and education meetings and the advantages students experience if they participate. In this stage the "I PLAN" steps of student participation are introduced. These steps provide a simple algorithm that students can use to chart their participation in planning meetings. Table 9.6 illustrates the I PLAN steps.

In Stage 3 (Model and Prepare), the teacher models the I PLAN steps so that students can see the process in action. Students complete an Inventory, step 1 in the I PLAN process, resulting in a completed inventory that they can use at their conference. Stage 4 is Verbal Practice, during which students are asked questions to make sure they know what to do during each step of the I PLAN strategy, and then verbally rehearse each of the steps. In Stage 5 (Group Practice and Feedback), once students have demonstrated mastery of the steps in I PLAN, they participate in a simulated group conference. The student receives feedback from the teacher and other students, and the group generates suggestions on where the student might improve. The simulated conference is audio- or videotaped for future reference.

Stage 6 (Individual Practice and Feedback), allows the student to meet independently with the teacher for practice, feedback and, eventually,

mastery. The audio- or videotape from the previous stage is reviewed and students provide a self-evaluation of their performance. The student and instructor work together to improve areas of self-identified need and engage in another simulated conference, which is also audio- or videotaped and used to document improvement and reevaluate performance. Finally, Stage 7 (Generalization) is intended to generalize the I PLAN strategy to actual conferences. This stage has three phases: (a) preparing for and conducting the planning conference, (b) preparing for other uses of the strategy, and (c) preparing for subsequent conferences. Van Reusen and colleagues (1990, 1994) have shown that the I PLAN strategy can be successfully implemented with students with disabilities and that it results in increased motivation and participation.

TAKE CHARGE for the Future. This student-directed, collaborative model (Powers, 1996) is designed to promote student involvement in educational and transition planning. The model is an adaptation of a validated approach, referred to as *TAKE CHARGE,* that promotes the self-determination of youth (Powers et al., 1996). TAKE CHARGE uses four primary components or strategies to promote adolescent development of self-determination: skill facilitation, mentoring, peer support, and parent support. For example, youth are introduced to three major skills areas needed to take charge in ones life: achievement skills, partnership skills, and coping skills. Table 9.7 shows the skills addressed in each of these areas.

Youth involved in the *TAKE CHARGE* process are matched with successful adults of the same gender who experience similar challenges and share common interests, and are also involved in peer-support activities throughout (Powers et al., 1996). Parent support is provided via information and technical assistance and written materials.

TAKE CHARGE for the Future uses the same set of core strategies described for the other programs to enable students to participate

Table 9.6 I PLAN: A Self-Advocacy Strategy

Initial	Activity
I	Inventory your strengths, areas to improve or learn, goals and choices for learning or accommodations
P	Provide your inventory information
L	Listen and respond
A	Ask questions
N	Name your goals

in their planning meeting. Student receive self-help materials and coaching to identify their transition goals, to organize and conduct transition-planning meetings, and to achieve their goals through application of problem-solving, self-regulation, and partnership management strategies. Concurrently, they participate in self-selected mentorship and peer-support activities to increase their transition-focused knowledge and skills. Their parents also receive information and support to enhance their ability to encourage their son's or daughter's active involvement in transition planning.

Group Action Planning. Turnbull and colleagues (1996) developed the Group Action Planning procedure (Anderson et al., 1995) to help youth with severe mental retardation and developmental disabilities become involved in their educational planning. Group Action Planning incorporates strategies from futures-planning models to achieve this end. Students, family members, professionals, and others complete a process that begins with the student's dreams and hopes, to identify goals, resources, and obstacles to achieving the student's desired outcomes. Using this information, the student with a disability, supported by the group, formulates action plans across eight areas of daily life: domestic, transportation, employment, financial, recreational, social relationships, behavioral, and community participation.

Table 9.7 Strategies and Skills in TAKE CHARGE Model

Skill Category	Skills
Achievement	Dream
	Set goals
	Problem solve
	Prepare
	Do it!
Partnership	Schmooze
	Be assertive
	Negotiate
	Manage help
Coping	Think positively
	Focus on accomplishments
	Manage frustration
	Track and reward progress

Summary of Current Practices in Student Involvement in Transition Planning and Decision Making. The programs discussed in this section provide both specific programming that may be implemented directly with students. More importantly, they are guides for teacher-initiated efforts to improve student involvement. Current practices in student involvement in transition planning and decision making share common activities, including efforts to increase student self-awareness; awareness of the educational and transition process; goal-setting, decision-making, and planning skills; self-advocacy; and leadership skills. They take as their basic vision the importance of getting students actively involved to the greatest extent possible.

Current Practices in Student Involvement in Transition-Program Implementation

Students become involved in the implementation of their educational program through the use of self-management strategies. Self-management strategies, according to Heward (1987), are "personal and systematic application of behavior change strategies that result in the desired modification of one's own behavior" (p. 517). Agran (1997) identified several core self-management strategies, three of which, self-monitoring, self-instruction, and self-reinforcement, seem particularly relevant to student involvement in transition-program implementation and, therefore, will be presented here.

Student Self-Monitoring. Student self-monitoring strategies involve students in assessing, observing, and recording their own behavior. As such, self-monitoring is most frequently used to improve work-related activities, like attention to task, task completion, and task accuracy (Hughes, Korinek, & Gorman, 1991)—all important aspects of transition-related programs. Agran and Martin (1987) pointed out that, in addition to the benefits of self-monitoring to increase the efficacy of educational interventions, asking a student to monitor a target behavior may, in and

of itself, produce a desired change, without any other intervention. For example, for a student who is self-monitoring in-seat behavior by marking whether he is seated in his chair at set intervals, the act of recording each occurrence serves as a reminder that he is to remain seated unless otherwise instructed and may decrease out-of-seat behavior simply as a function of the monitoring behavior.

The first function of self-monitoring, *self-assessment,* places the student in the role of evaluator. To the extent that evaluation activities are used to gather information to develop educational plans and programs, such self-assessment belongs in the category of student-directed transition planning. If, on the other hand, assessment is being used as a means to document ongoing progress on goals and objectives, such activities fall in the realm of self-monitoring. In either case, it is important that educators involve students in the assessment of their transition skills, needs, interests, and preferences.

Several models incorporate student self-assessment into transition planning. For example, the *Transition Skills Inventory* (Halpern et al., 1997) is completed by all stakeholders in the transition-planning process, including students, their family members, and educators. Data from these participants are compared and discussed to provide a broader picture of a student's transition needs and skills. Although instruments like the *Transition Skills Inventory* provide a systematized way to achieve such self-evaluation, the same could be accomplished through teacher-generated checklists or by completing other transition and vocational assessments with students as equal partners in the process, instead of just the "subject" of assessment. An overview of transition-related assessments for use with students with disabilities is beyond the scope of this chapter, but certainly instruments like the *SLD Behavior Checklist* (Goyette & Washburn, 1984) or the *Functional Skills Inventory* (Wisconsin Division of Vocational Rehabilitation Counselors, 1988) can be used to involve students in assessing their own transition skills, needs, and interests.

Several federally funded projects have developed assessments of self-determination that include student self-report versions and provide critical information for transition planning and tools for documenting progress. For example, Wehmeyer and Kelchner (1995a) developed *The Arc's Self-Determination Scale,* a student self-report measure of self-determined behavior that makes operational the definitional framework of self-determination as an educational outcome as discussed earlier (see also Wehmeyer, 1996). This instrument provides students a vehicle to self-assess transition needs in the area of self-determination. The scale identifies student strengths and limitations in four "essential characteristics" of self-determined behavior: autonomy, self-regulation, psychological empowerment and self-realization (Wehmeyer, 1996, 1997). The *AIR Self-Determination Scale* (Wolman et al., 1994) yields a profile of students' level of self-determination, identifies specific educational goals and objectives that may be incorporated into the IEP or transition program, and evaluates the degree to which students' opportunities to be self-determined and their capacity to do so contribute to their level of self-determination. This scale includes student, family, and teacher forms. Information from these respondents is combined to provide an overall picture of student self-determination.

Student involvement in transition-program implementation should also include systematic strategies to enable students to track and evaluate their progress on goals and objectives. This frequently involves self-recording procedures in which the student graphs, charts, or otherwise documents progress on a goal or objective. Such progress is typically determined through some form of self-observation, during which the student discriminates (a) that a given target behavior has occurred and then (b) compares this with some previously determined standard or expected outcome (Agran, 1997). Students can be taught to score worksheets, identify the occurrence of a target behavior, track time intervals for the occurrence or nonoccurrence of a

target behavior, and record this information in a graphic or chart format or through some other means of tracking, including the use of tokens.

Self-Instruction. Self-instructional strategies involve teaching students to "provide their own verbal prompts for solving an academic or social problem" (Hughes, et al., 1991:272). This technique has been used successfully to solve job- and work-related problems (Agran et al., 1986; Hughes & Rusch, 1989) and to teach skills, like social skills, that are critical to independence (Agran et al., 1987; Hughes & Agran, 1993). In essence, self-instruction strategies move the responsibility for providing verbal prompts and cues from an external source, typically the teacher, to students themselves.

Self-Reinforcement. A third self-managment strategy that is particularly useful for promoting student involvement in transition-program implementation is self-reinforcement. Agran (1997) defined self-reinforcement as the self-administration of consequences, either positive or negative, contingent on the occurrence of a target behavior. He suggested that self-reinforcement should have two functions: self-identification of reinforcers and delivery of the reinforcer. Student involvement in the former, self-identification of reinforcers, can enhance the efficacy of the latter. Self-reinforcement can be more effective than having another person deliver the reinforcer, especially because self-reinforcement almost always can be immediate.

Summary of Current Practices in Student Involvement in Educational Program Implementation. The efficacy of self-management strategies to promote more positive educational, motivational, and transition outcomes for youth is firmly established. At the very least, educators should incorporate aspects of self-monitoring, self-instruction, and self-reinforcement into day-to-day activities of youth with disabilities. This is particularly important for educational programs to promote transition outcomes.

CONCLUSIONS

The intent of the IDEA transition mandate was that students become actively involved in their transition planning, decision making, and program-implementation process (Wehmeyer & Ward, 1995). Likewise, the intent of the School-to-Work Opportunities Act is to promote an educational process that prepares young people to become self-determined young adults. As shown in this chapter, there is ample evidence from the educational and psychological literature that student involvement in the totality of their educational program has significant educational benefits.

Few practices in education seem as compelling and justified, and yet are as infrequently implemented, as student involvement and self-determination strategies. Wehman (1993) identified student choice as one of five critical transition issues for the field as we head into the twenty-first century. Pointing out that the earliest transition models did not focus enough on "student choice, family choice and self-determination" (p. 189), Wehman identified the implications of a student involvement approach to transition as:

> students being directly involved in writing IEPs and individual transition plans, going out to the workplaces and identifying the jobs they want and vetoing unfair vocational evaluation practices. They further involve student directly picking the type of skills that they believe will be useful. (Wehman, 1993:189–190)

The strategies and practices needed to make student involvement in educational planning, decision making, and program implementation a reality exist. Outcomes like those presented in Case Study 2 are not unrealistic, but readily achievable. It is now incumbent on practitioners in the field to put them into place and make student involvement the norm, not the exception!

QUESTIONS

1. What does the Individuals with Disabilities Education Act mandate with regard to student involvement in transition planning?

2. What is meant by student involvement in transition planning, decision making, and program implementation?

3. What are some of the factors contributing to the increased attention to student involvement in transition?

4. What are some of the benefits to student involvement in transition planning, decision making, and program implementation?

5. What are some of the barriers to student involvement in transition planning and decision making?

6. Describe some of the key elements of student involvement in transition programming.

7. Define self-monitoring strategies and describe how they can be used to involve students in the transition process.

8. Define self-instruction and identify ways such strategies have been used to promote transition outcomes.

9. How does a focus on student involvement differ from traditional transition models?

10. Write a rationale and a strategy for involving students in transition planning that would convince a school administrator to implement such a plan.

REFERENCES

Adelman, H. S., Lusk, R., Alvarez, V., & Acosta, N. K. (1985). Competence of minors to understand, evaluate and communicate about their psychoeducational problems. *Professional Psychology: Research and Practice, 16,* 426–434.

Adelman, H. S., MacDonald, V. M., Nelson, P., Smith, D. C., & Taylor, L. (1990). Motivational readiness of children with learning and behavior problems in psychoeducational decision making. *Journal of Learning Disabilities, 23,* 171–176.

Agran, M. (1997). *Student-directed learning: Teaching self-determination skills.* Pacific Grove, CA: Brooks/Cole.

CASE STUDY 2   Getting Involved in Transition Planning

Cheryl is 16 years old and has been identified as having mild mental retardation. Although she was aware that her parents attended an annual meeting with her teachers, she had no interest in this meeting. This year, however, she moved to the high school campus. At the beginning of the school year, her teacher told her about a new type of meeting, called a "transition-planning meeting," at which goals would be set that would help her get a job that she liked, help her find a place to live, and become involved in the activities she enjoyed when she graduated. Her teacher asked Cheryl if she wanted to become involved with that meeting and help plan what she would learn so that she could graduate to all those outcomes. Cheryl readily agreed that she did.

The meeting, Cheryl was told, would be held in April. She had a number of questions about the meeting, like who would be there and what she would be expected to do, but was hesitant to ask. However, when she indicated that she was interested in being involved, her teacher showed her a set of materials that helped her learn more about transition and transition planning. Cheryl worked through these materials, sometimes on her own and at other times with her teacher, and after several months, she had learned what transition meant, what the transition meeting was for, and what she could do in the transition meeting. Cheryl also used the materials to identify what she was good at doing and what she needed help with, and talked with her family, teachers, and some friends about what kinds of job she might like best, where she might want to live, and how to make that happen. She learned how to write goals and objectives, what goals and objectives were in her educational program from the last year, and, together with her teacher, identified some goals she would like to work toward. She also learned how meetings work, how to communicate in small groups, and what responsibilities team members have in the meeting.

In April, Cheryl attended her transition-planning meeting. Included in the meeting were her teachers, parents, and the school assistant principal, as well as a friend she had asked to be invited. Cheryl had made up a list of goals and objectives that she and her teacher had identified. Cheryl introduced her friend and her parents to her teachers and the assistant principal, and then introduced them to her family members and friend. As they had discussed, her teacher identified her goals from the previous year and talked about Cheryl's progress. Cheryl talked briefly about how she had done and what she thought she had done best. The teacher then asked her to read to the team the goals and objectives she would like to see included in her educational program for the coming year. Cheryl did this, talking about her interests and abilities and the outcomes the goals were designed to reach. She asked the team to generate additional goals, and together, they identified six goals that were priority. There were some disagreements and not all the goals on Cheryl's list were included. But she successfully negotiated with her father to get one recreation goal included even though he thought she should be working only on math at that time.

After the meeting, Cheryl and her teacher sat down and discussed the outcome of the meeting. Her teacher outlined several ways that Cheryl could take more responsibility for meeting the goals. In the end, it was decided that Cheryl could keep track, using a chart, of her progress on each of the goals. Cheryl left the meeting with her teacher with a sense of pride and a commitment to show her teacher, and herself, that she could reach the goals.

Agran, M., Fodor-Davis, J., & Moore, S. (1986). The effects of self-instructional training on job-task sequencing: Suggesting a problem-solving strategy. *Education and Training of the Mentally Retarded, 21,* 273–281.

Agran, M., & Martin, J. E. (1987). Applying a technology of self-control in community environments for individuals who are mentally retarded. In M. Hersen, R. M. Eisler, & P. M. Miller (Eds.), *Progress in behavior modification* (pp. 108–151). Newbury Park, CA: Sage.

Agran, M., Salzberg, C. L., & Stowitschek, J. J. (1987). An analysis of the effects of a social skills training program using self-instruction on the acquisition and generalization of two social behaviors in a work setting. *Journal of the Association for Persons with Severe Handicaps, 12,* 131–139.

Anderson, E. L., Seaton, K., Dinas, P., & Satterfield, A. (1995). *Group Action Planning: An innovative manual for building a self-determined future.* Lawrence, KS: Full Citizenship.

Bandura, A. (1986). *Social foundations of thought and action: A social cognitive theory.* Englewood Cliffs, NJ: Prentice Hall.

Baumgart, D., Brown, L., Pumpian, I., Nisbet, J., Ford, A., Sweet, M., Messina, R., & Schroeder, J. (1982). Principle of partial participation and individualized adaptations in educational programs for severely handicapped students. *Journal of the Association for Persons with Severe Handicaps, 7,* 17–27.

Bersani, H. (1995, Summer). Leadership: Where we've been, where we are, where we are going. *Institute on Community Integration IMPACT, 8*(3), 2–3.

Brownell, K. D., Colletti, G., Ersner-Hershfield, R., Hershfield, S. M., & Wilson, G. T. (1977). Self-control in school children: Stringency and leniency in self-determined and externally imposed performance standards. *Behavior Therapy, 8,* 442–455.

Chiron, R., & Gerken, K. (1983). The effects of a self-monitoring technique on the locus of control orientation of educable mentally retarded children. *School Psychology Review, 3,* 87–92.

Driedger, D. (1989). *The last civil rights movement: Disabled Peoples' International.* New York: St. Martin's Press.

Field, S., Hoffman, A., & Sawilowsky, S. (1994). *Student involvement in transition planning: A proposal submitted to the U.S. Department of Education.* Detroit: Wayne State University.

Gillespie, E. B., & Turnbull, A. P. (1983). It's my IEP! Involving students in the planning process. *Teaching Exceptional Children, 29,* 27–29.

Gilliam, J. E., & Coleman, M. C. (1981). Who influences IEP committee decisions? *Exceptional Children, 47,* 642–644.

Goyette, C. H., & Washburn, C. (1984). *Vocational rehabilitation of learning disabled adults: Participant's manual.* Pittsburgh: Vocational Rehabilitation Center of Allegheny County.

Graham, S., & Harris, K. R. (1989). Improving learning disabled students' skills at composing essays: Self-instructional strategy training. *Exceptional Children, 56,* 214–231.

Grisso, T., & Vierling, L. (1978). Minors' consent to treatment: A developmental perspective. *Professional Psychology, 9,* 412–427.

Guess, D., Benson, H. A., & Siegel-Causey, E. (1985). Concepts and issues related to choice-making and autonomy among persons with severe disabilities. *Journal of the Association for Persons with Severe Handicaps, 10,* 79–86.

Halpern, A. S., Herr, C. M., Wolf, N. K., Lawson, J. D., Doren, B., & Johnson, M. D. (1997). *NEXT*

S.T.E.P.: Student transition and educational planning. Teacher's manual. Austin, TX: PRO-ED.

Heward, W. L. (1987). Self-management. In J. O. Cooper, T. E Heron, & W. L. Heward (Eds.), *Applied behavior analysis* (pp. 515–549). Columbus, OH: Charles E. Merrill.

Houghton, J., Bronicki, G. J. B., & Guess, D. (1987). Opportunities to express preferences and make choices among students with severe disabilities in classroom settings. *Journal of the Association for Persons with Severe Handicaps, 10,* 87–95.

Hughes, C., & Agran, M. (1993). Teaching persons with severe disabilities to use self-instruction in community settings: An analysis of applications. *Journal of the Association for Persons with Severe Handicaps, 18,* 261–274.

Hughes, C. A., Korinek, L., & Gorman, J. (1991). Self-management for students with mental retardation in public school settings: A research review. *Education and Training in Mental Retardation, 26,* 271–291.

Hughes, C. A., & Petersen, D. L. (1989). Utilizing a self-instructional training package to increase on-task behavior and work performance. *Education and Training in Mental Retardation, 24,* 114–120.

Hughes, C., & Rusch, F. R. (1989). Teaching supported employees with severe mental retardation to solve problems. *Journal of Applied Behavior Analysis, 22,* 365–372.

Individuals with Disabilities Education Act of 1990, P.L. 101–476, 20, U.S.C.A., Section 1400 et seq.

Kanfer, F. H., & Goldstein, A. P. (1986). *Helping people change: A textbook of methods* (3rd ed.). New York: Pergamon Press.

Kapadia, S., & Fantuzzo, J. W. (1988). Training children with developmental disabilities and severe behavior problems to use self-management procedures to sustain attention to preacademic/academic tasks. *Education and Training in Mental Retardation, 23,* 59–69.

Kaser-Boyd, N., Adelman, H. S., & Taylor, L. (1985). Minors' ability to identify risks and benefits of therapy. *Professional Psychology: Research and Practice, 16,* 411–417.

Koestner, R., Ryan, R. M., Bernieri, F., & Holt, K. (1984). The effects of controlling versus informational limit—setting styles on children's intrinsic motivation and creativity. *Journal of Personality, 52,* 233–248.

Kohn, A. (1993). Choices for children: Why and how to let students decide. *Phi Delta Kappan, 75*(1), 8–20.

Lagomarcino, T. R., & Rusch, F. R. (1989). Utilizing self-management procedures to teach independent performance. *Education and Training in Mental Retardation, 24,* 297–305.

Lovett, D. L., & Haring, K. A. (1989). The effects of self-management training on the daily living of adults with mental retardation. *Education and Training in Mental Retardation, 24,* 306–307.

Malone, L. D., & Mastropieri, M. A. (1992). Reading comprehension instruction: Summarization and self-monitoring training for students with learning disabilities. *Exceptional Children, 58,* 270–279.

Martin, J. E., Burger, D. L., Elias-Burger, S., & Mithaug, D. (1988). Application of self-control strategies to facilitate independence in vocational and instructional settings. In N. W. Bray (Ed.), *International review of research in mental retardation* (vol. 15, pp. 155–193). San Diego: Academic Press.

Martin, J. E., & Marshall, L. H. (1995). ChoiceMaker: A comprehensive self-determination transition program. *Intervention in School and Clinic, 30,* 147–156.

————. (1996). ChoiceMaker: Infusing self-determination instruction into the IEP and transition process. In D. J. Sands & M. L. Wehmeyer (Eds.), *Self-determination across the life span: Independence and choice for people with disabilities* (pp. 211–232). Baltimore: Paul H. Brookes.

Martin, J. E., Marshall, L. H., & Maxson, L. (1993). Transition policy: Infusing self-determination and self-advocacy into transition programs. *Career Development for Exceptional Individuals, 16,* 53–61.

McCarl, J. J., Svobodny, L., & Beare, P. L. (1991). Self-recording in a classroom for students with mild to moderate mental handicaps: Effects on productivity and on-task behavior. *Education and Training in Mental Retardation, 26,* 79–88.

McTaggert, N., & Gould, M. (1988). *Choices and empowerment toward adulthood: A self-advocacy manual for students-in-transition.* Baltimore: Self-Advocacy Training Project of Maryland.

Misra, A. (1992). Generalization of social skills through self-monitoring by adults with mild mental retardation. *Exceptional Children, 58,* 495–507.

Mithaug, D. E. (1993). *Self-regulation theory: How optimal adjustment maximizes gain.* Westport, CT: Praeger.

Mithaug, D. E., Horiuchi, C. N., & McNulty, B. A. (1987a). *Parent reports on the transitions of students graduating from Colorado special education programs in 1978 and 1979.* Denver: Colorado Department of Education.

Mithaug, D. E., Martin, J. E., & Agran, M. (1987b). Adaptability instruction: The goal of transitional programs. *Exceptional Children, 53,* 500–505.

Mithaug, D. E., Wolman, J., & Campeau, P. (1992). *Research in self-determination in individuals with disabilities: Technical proposal.* Palo Alto, CA: American Institutes for Research.

Moore, S. C., Agran, M., & Fodor-Davis, J. (1989). Using self-management strategies to increase the production rates of workers with severe handicaps. *Education and Training in Mental Retardation, 24,* 324–332.

Perlmutter, L. C., & Monty, R. A. (1977). The importance of perceived control. Fact or fantasy? *American Scientist, 65,* 759–765.

Phillips, P. (1990). A self-advocacy plan for high school students with learning disabilities: A comparative case study analysis of students', teachers', and parents' perceptions of program effects. *Journal of Learning Disabilities, 23,* 466–471.

Powers, L. E. (1996). *TAKE CHARGE transition planning project.* Grant H158U50001, U.S. Department of Education and Oregon Health Sciences. Portland: Oregon Health Sciences University.

Powers, L. E., Sowers, J., Turner, A., Nesbitt, M., Knowles, E., & Ellison, R. (1996). TAKE CHARGE: A model for promoting self-determination among adolescents with challenges. In L. E. Powers, G. H. S. Singer, & J. Sowers (Eds.), *On the road to autonomy: Promoting self-competence for children and youth with disabilities* (pp. 291–322). Baltimore: Paul H. Brookes.

Realon, R. E., Favell, J. E., & Lowerre, A. (1990). The effects of making choices on engagement levels with persons who are profoundly mentally handicapped. *Education and Training in Mental Retardation, 25,* 248–254.

Reid, R., & Harris, K. R. (1993). Self-monitoring of attention versus self-monitoring of performance: Effects on attention and academic performance. *Exceptional Children, 60,* 29–40.

Rusch, F. R., McKee, M., Chadsey-Rusch, J., & Renzaglia, A. (1988). Teaching a student with severe handicaps to self-instruct: A brief report. *Education and Training in Mental Retardation, 23,* 51–58.

Salend, S. J. (1983). Self-assessment: A model for involving students in the formulation of their IEPs. *Journal of School Psychology, 21,* 65–70.

Salend, S. J., Ellis, L. L., & Reynolds, C. J. (1989). Using self-instruction to teach vocational skills to individuals who are severely retarded. *Education and Training in Mental Retardation, 24,* 248–254.

Schunk, D. H. (1981). Modeling and attributional effects on children's achievement: A self-efficacy analysis. *Journal of Educational Psychology, 73,* 93–105.

Schunk, D. H. (1985). Participation in goal setting: Effects on self-efficacy and skills of learning-disabled children. *Journal of Special Education, 19,* 307–316.

Shapiro, E. S., & Klein, R. D. (1980). Self-management of classroom behavior with retarded/disturbed children. *Behavior Modification, 4,* 83–97.

Strickland, B. B., & Turnbull, A. P. (1990). *Developing and implementing individualized education programs.* Columbus, OH: Charles E. Merrill.

Swann, W. B., & Pittman, T. S. (1977). Initiating play activity of children: The moderating influence of verbal cues on intrinsic motivation. *Child Development, 48,* 1128–1132.

Taylor, L., Adelman, H. S., & Kaser-Boyd, N. (1983). Perspectives of children regarding their participation in psychoeducational decisions. *Professional Psychology: Research and Practice, 14,* 882–894.

———. (1985). Minors' attitudes and competence toward participation in psychoeducational decisions. *Professional Psychology: Research and Practice, 16,* 226–235.

Trammel, D. L., Schloss, P. J., & Alper, S. (1994). Using self-recording, evaluation and graphing to increase completion of homework assignments. *Journal of Learning Disabilities, 27,* 75–81.

Turnbull, A., Anderson, E., Turnbull, H. R., Seaton, K., & Dinas, P. (1996). Enhancing self-determination through group action planning: A holistic emphasis. In D. J. Sands & M. L. Wehmeyer (Eds.), *Self-determination across the life span: Independence and choice for people with disabilities* (pp. 233–252). Baltimore: Paul H. Brookes.

Van Reusen, A. K., & Bos, C. S. (1990). I Plan: Helping students communicate in planning conferences. *Teaching Exceptional Children, 22*(4), 30–32.

———. (1994). Facilitating student participation in individualized education programs through motivation strategy instruction. *Exceptional Children, 60,* 466–475.

Van Reusen, A. K., Bos, C. S., Schumaker, J. B., & Deshler, D. D. (1994). *The self-advocacy strategy for education and transition planning.* Lawrence, KS: Edge Enterprises.

Walker, J. H., & Shaw, S. F. (1995, October). *Perceptions of team members regarding the involvement of students with learning disabilities in transition planning.* Paper presented at the International Conference of the Division on Career Development and Transition, Raleigh, North Carolina.

Ward, M. J. (1996). Coming of age in the age of self-determination: A historical and personal perspective. In D. J. Sands & M. L. Wehmeyer (Eds.),

Self-determination across the life span: Independence and choice for people with disabilities (pp. 1–14). Baltimore: Paul H. Brookes.

Ward, M. J., & Kohler, P. D. (1996). Promoting self-determination for individuals with disabilities: Content and process. In L. E. Powers, G. H. S. Singer, & J. Sowers (Eds.), *On the road to autonomy: Promoting self-competence in children and youth with disabilities* (pp. 275–290). Baltimore: Paul H. Brookes.

Wehman, P. (1993). Transition from school to adulthood for young people with disabilities: Critical issues and policies. In R. C. Eaves & P. J. McLaughlin (Eds.), *Recent advances in special education and rehabilitation* (pp. 178–192). Boston: Andover Medical.

Wehmeyer, M. L. (1992). Self-determination and the education of students with mental retardation. *Education and Training in Mental Retardation, 27,* 302–314.

———. (1996). Self-determination as an educational outcome: Why is it important to children, youth and adults with disabilities? In D. J. Sands & M. L. Wehmeyer (Eds.), *Self-determination across the life span: Independence and choice for people with disabilities* (pp. 15–34). Baltimore: Paul H. Brookes.

———. (1997). Self-directed learning and self-determination. In M. Agran (Ed.), *Student-directed learning: Teaching self-determination skills* (pp. 28–59). Pacific Grove, CA: Brooks/Cole.

Wehmeyer, M. L., & Davis, S. (1995). Family involvement. In D. Brolin (Ed.), *Career education: A functional life skills approach* (pp. 91–116). Columbus, OH: Charles E. Merrill.

Wehmeyer, M. L., & Kelchner, K. (1995a). *The Arc's self-determination scale.* Arlington, TX: The Arc National Headquarters.

———. (1995b). *Whose future is it anyway? A student-directed transition planning process.* Arlington, TX: The Arc National Headquarters.

Wehmeyer, M. L., & Lawrence, M. (1995a). Whose future is it anyway? Promoting student involvement in transition planning. *Career Development for Exceptional Individuals, 18,* 69–83.

———. (1995b). *Whose future is it anyway? Coach's guide.* Arlington, TX: The Arc National Headquarters.

Wehmeyer, M. L., Martin, J. E., & Sands, D. J. (1997). Self-determination for children and youth with developmental disabilities. In A. Hilton, & R. Ringlaben (Eds.), *Best Practices in Educating Students with Developmental Disabilities* (pp. 545–579). Austin, TX: PRO-ED.

Wehmeyer, M. L., & Metzler, C. A. (1995). How self-determined are people with mental retardation? The national consumer survey. *Mental Retardation, 33,* 111–119.

Wehmeyer, M. L., & Schwartz, M. (1997). Self-determination and positive adult outcomes: A follow-up study of youth with mental retardation or learning disabilities. *Exceptional Children, 63,* 245–255.

Wehmeyer, M. L., & Ward, M. J. (1995). The spirit of the IDEA mandate: Student involvement in transition planning. *Journal of the Association for Vocational Special Needs Education, 17,* 108–111.

Wisconsin Division of Vocational Rehabilitation Counselors. (1988). *Best practices: Successful vocational rehabilitation of persons with learning disabilities.* Madison: University of Wisconsin.

Wolman, J. M., Campeau, P. L., DuBois, P. A., Mithaug, D. E., & Stolarski, V. E. (1994). *AIR self-determination scale and user guide.* Palo Alto, CA: American Institutes for Research.

Yoshida, R. K., Fenton, K. S., Maxwell, J. P., & Kaufman, M. J. (1978). Group decision-making in the planning team process: Myth or reality. *Journal of School Psychology, 16,* 237–244.

Zimmmerman, B. J. (1994). Dimensions of academic self-regulation: A conceptual framework for education. In D. H. Schunk & B. J. Zimmerman (Eds.), *Self-regulation of learning and performance: Issues and educational applications* (pp. 3–21). Hillsdale, NJ: Lawrence Erlbaum.

10

◉

Families

The Heart of Transition

CHERYL HANLEY-MAXWELL,
SUSAN MAYFIELD POGOLOFF,
and JEAN WHITNEY-THOMAS

Families play a variety of roles during the transition-time period for young adults with disabilities. The purposes of this chapter are to discuss these roles and changing familial relationships (historic and current), and to suggest practices that enhance family–school collaboration. The review of history includes the historical roles of families of children with disabilities and the legal requirements related to family involvement in special education. Current issues in family involvement include the reality of adolescence for families of children with disabilities and the status of family involvement in special education, and, more specifically, transition. Finally, four practices are recommended to improve current family–school relationships as they relate to transition: reciprocal family education, cultural sensitivity, personal futures planning, and a longitudinal framework for including families in transition planning.

Adulthood is represented by a variety of markers in our society: employment, completion of formal schooling, moving out of the family home, increased independence, and marriage (Marini, 1984). One of these markers, the completion of high school (Buchmann, 1989; Pallas, 1993) has taken on increasing prominence in the past few years. This event is the most visible aspect of the time period that we have come to know as "transition from school to work" (e.g., School to Work Opportunities Act;

Will, 1984) or "transition from school to adulthood" (Hanley-Maxwell & Collet-Klingenberg, 1997). Examination of the events of this developmental stage has focused on the skills of the adolescent, the changes he or she must make to be a successful adult, and the services available to the adolescent (e.g., schools) compared to those available to the adult (e.g., residential service, employment services). Families have tended to be viewed as tangential or even inhibiting to the development of the growing young adult

(Ferguson, Ferguson, & Jones, 1988). However, this view is gradually changing as professionals become aware of the critical roles that the family plays in this stage of development (Alper, 1994; see also Lichtenstein in this volume, Chapter 1).

The family provides both foundation and the context for the decisions made during the transition-time period. As a part of the foundation, the family has impacted on the career development of the adolescent (Szymanski, 1994). As the context, choice making during this time period reflects the past and current influences that the family has on the young adult (see Lichtenstein, this volume). Morningstar, Turnbull, and Turnbull (1996) described a variety of formal and informal family influences that are active in the lives of teenagers with disabilities. Using qualitative methods of inquiry, Morningstar and colleagues (1996) documented the effect that informal role models provided by family members had on career selection. Furthermore, these students demonstrated the desire and the need for continued active involvement with their families after they had moved out of the family home. Many of these students actively acknowledged the need for family as a source of social support. Finally, the students in this study identified their families as primary sources of assistance in planning for their futures. However, these positive views of family support were tempered by the comments of the students who felt that family members tried to exert too much control over decisions and current responsibilities.

The tension between the need for family and the desire to break away reflects the continuing redefinition of the parent–child relationship that occurs throughout the life of a child. Ideally, this relationship results in increasing independence for the child while emotional bonds and positive social influences are maintained (Baumrind, 1991; see also Lichtenstein in this volume, Chapter 1). Finding the balance in this relationship is known as "modulation of dependency" (Collins & Russell, 1991:100). That

is, the end of this process is not the complete detachment of young people from their family, but the development of a sense of self and independence by the young adults, and the continuing support and encouragement of their family (Ryan & Lynch, 1989; see also Lichtenstein in this volume, Chapter 1).

As a part of normal development, all families struggle with the "modulation of dependency." However, more questions are raised about the process when the child involved experiences a nonnormative sequence of events (Pallas, 1993) or is an individual for whom independence is more complicated. Poor transition outcomes for individuals with disabilities indicate that the sequence of events that lead to adulthood is disrupted for these people because of their disability status (Wagner et al., 1991; see also Lichtenstein in this volume, Chapter 1). Furthermore, families of students with disabilities express fears and concerns that reflect the fact that these families are also affected by the transition problems experienced by young adults with disabilities (Whitney-Thomas & Hanley-Maxwell, 1996). Although families of adolescents with disabilities seek to develop independence in their child (Hanley-Maxwell, Whitney-Thomas, & Pogoloff, 1995), sometimes this independence is modified by their child's ongoing need for support and assistance. Furthermore, this assistance may be unavailable (Ferguson et al., 1988; Dempsey, 1991; Hanley-Maxwell et al., 1995). Fear of limited services and decreased expectations for independence alters the process of "modulating dependency" (Collins & Russell, 1991:100).

The purpose of this chapter is to explore family roles and relationships as they relate to the transition-time period for young adults with disabilities. Family roles and relationships fluctuate from family to family, and may vary based on the severity of the child's disability. However, many family roles and responsibilities are remarkably similar across all types of families and disabilities or lack of disability (Whitney-Thomas & Hanley-Maxwell, 1996). As a result, the focus of this chapter is on those roles and responsibilities that are assumed by most families of children with disabilities. In the first section, the history of family involvement in education is explored as a foundation for understanding the current status of family relationships with schools and other service systems discussed in the next section. Finally, recommended practices are suggested as ways to improve the current family–school relationships.

HISTORICAL REVIEW

Family–school relationships are difficult to describe because each interaction is impacted by the multitude of individual differences that compromise the family unit. Every family is a unique array of characteristics forming the complex patterns of the family. Family characteristics include socioeconomic status, cultural background, personal interaction among family members, individual reactions to exceptionality, coping strategies employed, amount and type of social support received by the family, integration of past experiences with professionals, and the manner in which these characteristics change, develop, and interact over time (Turnbull & Turnbull, 1990). Furthermore, in recent years, the concept of family has changed from a societally imposed definition to an individually determined unit. Accordingly, Hanson and Lynch (as cited in Hanson & Carta, 1995) describe the characteristics of a family as individuals who see themselves as a unit, are associated with each other, and are committed to caring for each other.

Family involvement in the transition process is further complicated because this involvement is not static, but an evolving process defined not only by the aforementioned family characteristics, but also by changing professional attitudes and practices. Due to the layers of complexity surrounding family involvement, it is impossible to provide a concise definition that applies to all families who participate in the transition

process. An individualized definition that applies to family involvement evolves for each family as it participates in the process. In addition to the array of characteristics and issues listed before, it is imperative to understand the influence of history on family involvement. Historical roles cast on families of children with disabilities and a brief review of legal requirements related to family involvement in special education are discussed in this section.

ROLES

The historic roles that families of students with disabilities have been burdened with, or willingly assumed, impact the interactions of families and professional today. It is important to know that, like transition, these roles do not occupy a discrete moment in time or apply universally to all families. Roles interact and overlap with each other. Many that appear to be outdated may continue to impact attitudes, behaviors, and relationships. As shown in Table 10.1, Turnbull and Turnbull (1990) and Alper (1994) described several roles for parents or other family members. Assumption or imposition of any one of these roles on families impacts the quality and type of family involvement in the transition process. Each of these roles is discussed in what follows.

Problem Source

One of the oldest and most devastating roles for family members is that of being considered the source of their child's problem (Turnbull & Turnbull, 1990). This role has its roots in superstitions as well as biological and psychological beliefs (Alper, 1994). Views reflecting the biologically and psychologically based beliefs resulted in the eugenics movement of the early 1900s and the therapeutic treatment of mothers by Bruno Bettleheim and others in the 1950s and 1960s. Recent research has confirmed the connection of genetic anomalies with some disabilities and the impact that prenatal exposure to

Table 10.1 Historic Roles for Family Members

- Problem source
- Advocate
- Service developer
- Decision recipient
- Learner and teacher
- Decision maker
- Family member

drugs and alcohol has on the developing child (Alper, 1994). However, these discoveries have not resulted in a return to the parent–blaming practices of the earlier part of the century.

Despite increased understanding of the sources of disabilities and the complexity of factors that effect their manifestation, family blaming continues to plague the family–professional relationship. Overt blaming of families for the difficulties children experience has declined and changed in focus, but has not disappeared in the last 20 years. For example, Ferguson and colleagues (1993) confirmed that variations of this belief continue today. In their examination of the triadic relationship of parents, professionals, and the individual with a disability, Ferguson and colleagues (1993) found that professionals often view parents as a barrier to developing effective working relationships with the individuals they are attempting to serve. This barrier is viewed as particularly problematic in that the professionals from the Ferguson study felt that the influence of family often diminished the adult status of the person with a disability. Families reported that they felt estranged from their loved one and were concerned that professionals had more influence on life decisions than they did.

Imposition or assumption of this role by family members can result in several barriers to family–professional relationships. These include resentment, low self-esteem, and lack of trust or defensiveness. These barriers can be manifested in the relationship between parents and professionals when parents do not attend meetings or conferences initiated by school personnel for any of the reasons previously listed.

Organization Member and Political Advocate

The second role for families is that of members of support or advocacy organizations. For this discussion, this role is coupled with the role of family member as political advocate. These roles grew out of inadequate or absent public and professional response to the needs of children with disabilities, as well as familial need for emotional support (Turnbull & Turnbull, 1990). Parent groups started, banded together, and became a formidable source of power (Alper, 1994). For example, parent groups have had a monumental impact on service delivery and political advocacy and have been the catalysts behind educational legislation as well as improvement of standards for treatment in institutions and community agencies (Turnbull & Turnbull, 1990; Yancey, 1993). Examples of organizational member and political advocates can be seen at the local level through school committees and organizations such as the Association of Retarded Citizens, at the state level through governor's commissions and within disability-specific groups, and at the national level through organizations that engage in advocacy such as the Association for Persons with Severe Handicaps and the William's Syndrome Association, to name two.

Service Developer

The third role is that of service developer. Families have started and administered organizations to deliver services to children and adults with disabilities. These same individuals also have assumed the role of catalyst for services from public and private organizations (Turnbull & Turnbull, 1990). Kirk (as cited in Turnbull & Turnbull, 1990) attributed most of the advancements for children with disabilities to parental leadership and effort. Many professionals continue to expect families to create their own services. This is an unreasonable burden to place on families. Nevertheless, there have been examples where families came together and designed services when none previously existed. This is especially true in the areas of residential and respite services and in rural areas of the country where access to services is difficult.

Decision Recipient

The fourth role identified by Turnbull and Turnbull (1990) is that of the recipient of professional decisions. Roos (as cited in Alper, 1994) identified the pervasive belief by many professionals that they "know best." This belief is based on the assumption that because of their training and unique expertise, they have superior knowledge. One of the problems that arises from this type of family–professional relationship is that families, the student, and professionals may identify different needs and priorities for the individual student. Family members are focused on achieving the personal needs and desires of their family and the individual members of the family. Professionals, on the other hand, often focus on what services various systems provide or can sustain and on achieving those outcomes identified at the "macrolevel" as appropriate outcomes for all individuals as they grow into adulthood. Professionals operating at the systems level make important life decisions *for* students with disabilities, rather than *with* them and their families. This can result in outcomes that are not desir-

able to the individual or the family, outcomes that fail once continuous supports are removed (Hill et al., 1987), uncoordinated planning, and reciprocal blame when problems occur (Turnbull & Turnbull, 1990; Alper, 1994). Although this passive role expectation has decreased over the past 10 to 15 years, it continues to exist in practice. Educators, directly or indirectly, communicate this expectation, which, in turn, builds and maintains barriers to positive partnerships (Dettmer, Dyck, & Thurston, 1996).

Teacher and Learner

Next is the role of family member as learner and teacher. This twofold role depicts families as the recipients of professional training designed to improve their performance as caregivers, role models, and home teachers. As home teachers, family members are expected to extend the school-based learning experiences of the child into the home and community activities in which the family engages. During the 1960s and 1970s, families were viewed as the key ingredient for increasing progress for children. Documented success for parents as teachers reinforced this role and increased pressure on parents and other family members to perform as learners and teachers (Turnbull & Turnbull, 1990; Alper, 1994). Examples of how parents are teachers and learners can be seen in instances where parents attend continuing education or inservices offered to staff in their local school districts. Parents, in turn, often teach school personnel procedures and routines that their child is accustomed to at home and that need to be carried over into school settings. Likewise, parents are often taught by school personnel to implement strategies and programs at home that have been designed at school.

Family Member

"Family member" is a role that is based on the premise that a happy family life depends on balancing the needs of all family members. This is a relatively new concept in special education and a difficult one to achieve in light of competing need and pressures involved in parenting a child with a disability (Turnbull & Turnbull, 1990). Turnbull (1988) admitted that, as a parent, she became "consumed by the need to establish services" (p. 16) and was forced to understand the problems with past practices as well as the wisdom of a family systems model for family involvement. Within the context of the family, parents find that they need to help siblings understand the special needs of their sister or brother with a disability and work to assimilate these needs into the family system. Additionally, as siblings grow into adulthood, they are faced with unique and critical roles in the life experiences of their brother or sister with a disability. For example, the experiences of older siblings as they move through their own transitions help them serve as role models and information keepers for their brother or sister with a disability (McLouglin & Senn, 1994).

Decision Maker

The last role described by Turnbull and Turnbull (1990) is "decision maker." The role was legally established with the passage of the Education for All Handicapped Children Act, P.L. 94-142, in 1975 and expanded by subsequent amendments to P.L. 94-142 (i.e., P.L. 99-457 and P.L. 101-476, the Individuals with Disabilities Education Act). Through these laws, families were given a vehicle to ensure that professionals listen to their input and provide an appropriate education for their children. As decision makers, parents are asked to sign off on Individualized Education Programs (IEPs) and Individualized Transition Plans (ITPs). As the child grows, however, there is a need to balance the role of family member as decision maker with the need for the young person with a disability to become his or her own primary decision maker.

Although some of these roles appear more relevant than others today, it is valuable to understand that they all impact current relationships with families. Turnbull and Turnbull (1990) portrayed the impact of these roles as a pendulum that swings back and forth. For example, professionals vary in their perceptions of families from (a) the problem's source to its primary solution; (b) expecting passivity, to expecting an active central role; and (c) focusing on the mother–child relationship, to balancing the needs of all family members. Avis (as cited in Turnbull & Turnbull, 1990) described the confusing position many family members find themselves in as being in "time-zone changes" such as "deinstitutionalization jet lag" and "parent-role jet lag." These terms refer to the contradicting messages professionals have given parents over the years. The same family members who were told during the 1970s to passively accept the advice of professionals are now being told that they need to be leaders in programs and services for their family member with a disability. Clearly, best practices for family involvement have changes.

LEGAL REQUIREMENTS

The role of family members as decision makers is mandated in federal law. The Education for all Handicapped Children Act of 1975 (EHA), P.L. 94-142, was the first law to require that family members be part of the evaluation and planning process that determines the Individualized Education Program (IEP). Additionally, this law established the due-process rights of family members. With the passage of P.L. 94-142, family members became entitled to procedural and informational safeguards that protect their decision-making rights. The rights established by P.L. 94-142 were expanded by P.L. 99-457 to children ages 3 to 5. Additionally, this law required the use of the IFSP, the Individualized Family Service Plan, in which services were planned around the family as well as the young child. Finally, the 1990 amendments to P.L. 94-142, the Individuals with Disabilities Education Act (IDEA), reaffirmed the federal requirements for active family participation in the planning and decision-making process, and more specifically transitional planning.

Schriner and Bellini (1994) stressed the importance of IEP (and, subsequently, participation in the process) by identifying IEP as "the tool which 'drives' the process by which the student is prepared for, and becomes engaged in, adult living" (p. 20). The cumulative effect of the IEP process is directly demonstrated in postschool outcomes for students. Given the importance of the IEP process, it is critical to find ways to actively involve families and their needs and desires in the process.

CURRENT PRACTICES

In recent years, there has been considerable discussion about the family's role during the transition process (Nisbet, Covert, & Schuh, 1992). Current recommended practices include having families and professionals working as a team (Jamison, 1993). In fact, Everson and McNulty (1992) specifically identified parental involvement as a vital component of successful transition programming as it is also viewed in several chapters of this text. Additionally, because they often assume future responsibility for or with the family member with a disability, other family members should also be included in this process (Brotherson et al., 1988; McLoughlin & Senn, 1994). Brothers and sisters should be actively involved in all aspects of transition planning and activities, from assessment to decision making, as they work in conjunction with their sibling who has a disability to create an acceptable future (McLoughlin & Senn, 1994).

Nisbet and colleagues (1992) emphasized that although actual participation varies from family to family, professionals should act on the assumption that family members are leaders and decision makers in the transition process. This is especially important because these individuals often remain actively involved throughout the life span of the individual by providing information, acting as advocates, acting as a safety net

(Yancey, 1993), and offering or obtaining supports and services (Ferguson et al., 1993). Additionally, active family involvement is often desired by students with disabilities. As previously discussed, adolescents report that family members play at least three roles in their lives as they make decisions for the future: career-selection guide and role model, source of social support, and source of assistance in planning of the future (Morningstar et al., 1996).

The roles identified by adolescents are echoed in the work of Irvin, Thorin, and Singer (1993), who described current types of active involvement as five roles that family members often assume in the transition process: provider of ongoing support, mediator of connections between the service provider and the adult child, developer of work-support behaviors, de facto case manager, and primary care giver. Table 10.2 summarizes the positive roles that families play in the transition from school to adult life. Families may also serve the negative role of transition and adult role-adaptation impeder, however. This role may manifest itself as limited expectations. For example, Gallivan-Fenlon (1994) found that adults had more limited expectations for the individual with a disability than the individual had for him/herself. Such lowered expectations may have been the result of poor transition planning and decisions based on limited information, however.

Understanding the reality of adolescence for families of children with disabilities is a critical piece of the foundation from which best practices are recommended. Additionally, understanding the current involvement of families in the special education, and more particularly the transition process, and the barriers they face as they attempt to plan for the child's future, provide the final foundational pieces. This section is a discussion of those foundational pieces.

REALITY

Families of adolescents with disabilities face multiple types of transitions as the adolescent becomes an adult. Ferguson and colleagues

Table 10.2 Transition Roles for Family Members

- Career selection guide and role model
- Social support source: current and future
- Future planning assistance source
- Child/adult child-service system mediator
- Developer of adult support skills
- De facto case manager
- Primary caregiver

(1988) identified three major types of transitions faced by these families: bureaucratic, family functioning, and status. Each of these types of transition is an important consideration in and of itself, so they will be discussed separately in this section. In reality, however, they are faced simultaneously. The final topic of this section is a discussion of how these distinct types of transition overlap and create unmet needs for families.

Bureaucratic Transition

Bureaucratic transition involves the change from the regulated and *required* system of family involvement and school services to unstable, unknown, *unmandated*, and often unavailable adult services (Ferguson et al., 1988). Unlike families of adolescents without disability, families of children with disability are part of a "miniuniverse" (Lesar, Trivette, & Dunst, 1996:197), which is composed of the settings and people of the social service and disability service systems (Lesar et al., 1996). Navigation of these systems becomes increasingly difficult as families face the complex and seemingly less welcoming adult service system (Hanley-Maxwell et al., 1995; Whitney-Thomas & Hanley-Maxwell, 1996). Families whose children have participated in inclusive educational settings and services seem to have particular difficulty with the adult service systems and their lack of entitlement (Gallivan-Fenlon, 1994).

Regardless of their child's educational setting, families report relying on the transition coordinator within the school to provide them with assistance and all they need to know to enter the adult service world. In fact, families report that they could not have made the move from school to adult services without the help of school transition coordinators or teachers (Gallivan-Fenlon, 1994; Hanley-Maxwell et al., 1995). Parents expressed to Whitney-Thomas and Hanley-Maxwell (1996) that schools were partners in preparing the young person for adult life. Nevertheless, many parents expressed great concern for service availability and their child's future in world of adult service delivery (Hanley-Maxwell et al., 1995; Thorin, Yovanoff, & Irvin, 1996).

Families of children with significant disabilities are also faced with questions related to legal competence and guardianship (Quadland, et al., 1996). For example, questions arise in relation to the growing child's ability to make legal and often self-preserving decisions. At age 18, all adolescents reach the age of legal majority. Therefore, families who believe that their adolescent is incapable of making the required legal or self-sustaining decisions must take legal action to establish a guardianship relationship for the now adult child (Quadland et al., 1996).

Transition in Family Functioning

In the second type of transition, the transition of family functioning described by Minuchin (1991), families are forced to deal with disrupted family routines (Ferguson et al., 1988). A family provides organized and stable life patterns to its members through the shared contexts of the family. As members of the family experience life events, other family members are affected. That is, when one family member experiences change, family functioning and daily routines change. This often causes disequilibrium, forcing the family to use trial and error to establish new patterns of functioning. Once new patterns are developed, the equilibrium of the family is reestablished until the next life event. Because of such change, families are not static units, but are in constant development. The developmental cycle of the family is equilibrium followed by disequilibrium caused by change, and reorganization leading to the reestablishment of equilibrium. Life events that effect the equilibrium of a family are unique to each family and are dependent on a given family's perception of the event (Minuchin, 1991).

The approaching adulthood of a child within the family system is one example of family disequilibrium. And for families of adolescents with disabilities, the approaching life change is often perceived as a crisis and a major readjustment of family functioning patterns (Ferguson et al., 1988; Hanley-Maxwell et al., 1995; Whitney-Thomas & Hanley-Maxwell, 1996). Additionally, many families are continuing to face more immediate problems and often choose to deal with these instead of the elusive future discussed in transition planning (Yancey, 1993). Faced with uncertain services and critical deadlines, these families attempt to reestablish equilibrium, often through the normative trial-and-error process (Hanley-Maxwell et al., 1995; Whitney-Thomas & Hanley-Maxwell, 1996). One question that arises in the family functioning transition is whether or not one parent quits work to be with a son or daughter who leaves school without a job or adult services.

Status Transition

Finally, families deal with the meanings of the status transition that the child is making, moving from childhood to adulthood. In this transition, parents and other family members must resolve conflicting needs related to the growing child's independence and potential ongoing support needs. Family members are attempting to ensure that they can achieve the visions that have been developed for the future of the child: (a) friends/support networks, (b) constructive and satisfying free time, (c) a safe and homelike residence, and (d) independence that frees the child from the constraints of the family and the family from the demands of the child (Hanley-Maxwell et al., 1995). One parent told Whitney-Thomas and Hanley-Maxwell (1996) that this status transition makes her feel like "I'm between clenching and letting go."

Families and professionals may have different future visions as the result of holding different meanings of "adulthood" for the individual with a disability. Professional views tend to reflect general social markers and symbols of adulthood. As a result, enhancing the adulthood status of the individual requires decreasing family influence as the skills of the individual increase. Families are usually more reluctant to release their influence. Family assessment of adulthood is intertwined with the ability of the individual to make "self-preserving decisions of all types" (Ferguson et al., 1993:20). Decisions to decrease assistance or influence are the result of judgments made about the individual's skills, needs, past experiences, and other personal variables (Ferguson et al., 1993). To cope with frustrations, varying perspectives, and to obtain desired outcomes, individuals with disabilities and their families should be encouraged to play central roles in the transition process (Nisbet et al., 1992; Stineman et al., 1993).

Intersection

Emphasis on the full participation of families has grown partially because of the increased understanding of the interaction among the types of transitions that families face. This intersection results from a combination of stresses inherent in the move from childhood to adult life and the need for services that may or may not be available (Singer & Irvin, 1991; Thorin & Irvin, 1992; Irvin et al., 1993). Families of children with disabilities frequently face the dilemma of having to choose between their desire for their child's independence and the need to establish ongoing adult services to sustain their child in the community. Furthermore, many families are faced with limited or no services. For example, families report residential options to be a priority (Brotherson et al., 1986; McDonnell, Wilcox, & Boles, 1986; Thorin & Irvin, 1992). However, they are often faced with few services and long waiting lists (Nisbet et al., 1992). The results are compromised plans for independence and the perpetuation of family-child roles that would normally have ended (Ferguson et al., 1988; Nisbet et al., 1992; Irvin et al., 1993; Stineman et al., 1993). Lack of residential and social opportunities means that although many young adults wish they could move out, they continue to live at home (Haring & Lovett, 1990). Additionally, current reality for these young adults is social isolation (Lichtenstein & Michaelides, 1993), inactivity (Mithaug, Horiuchi, & Fanning, 1985), and continuing dependence on the family for social and community interaction (Scuccimarra & Speece, 1990; Sitlington & Frank, 1990).

Although families rarely complain about the transition services they receive, when pressed, they associate their frustrations with lack of adult services, lack of transportation, poor service coordination, and failure of professionals to listen to them (Yancey, 1993; Hanley-Maxwell et al., 1995). Parents who participated in a study by Hanley-Maxwell and colleagues (1995) discussed their desires to increase the independence of their child by engaging in an educational program that provides functional skill development in the broader scope of life (i.e., extending the concept of transition beyond vocational development). More specifically, they identified five broad categories of need:

1. reliable, accessible, and high quality services that address *all* aspects of adult life (e.g., transportation, adult education, recreation, residential, vocational)

2. physical separation of adult child from family through the provision of *home-like* residential alternatives

3. support networks for parents, families, and adult children (e.g., respite, friendships, natural supports, parental assistance)

4. service systems that respond to family and individual needs and goals in the time frame determined by the family and the adult with disability (e.g., flexible service beginning and ending time frames, broadening the definition of transition beyond the employment focus, increasing availability of services, providing nontraditional supports to families, refocusing the end goal to be the happiness and fulfillment of the adult with disability)

5. multiple and diverse experiences for students prior to leaving high school (pp. 12–13)

Despite their clear identification of needs, these same parents reported patterns of involvement that reflected the passive role of decision recipient, as well as the roles of "waiting" decision maker and quality control (Hanley-Maxwell et al., 1995). As discussed in the next section, this passive involvement is not unusual.

INVOLVEMENT

Despite mandated family participation in the special education process (e.g., EHA, IDEA), current research indicates that families tend to be passively involved. This passivity seems to be even greater in families from minority backgrounds (Harry, Allen, & McLaughlin, 1995). Thus, many reports suggest that family involvement in transition is submissive participation (Ferguson et al., 1988; Harry, 1992; Gallivan-Fenlon, 1994; Hanley-Maxwell et al., 1995). Unfortunately, passive participation does not appear to be the ideal or most productive role, because family members are generally the one constant in the lives of individuals with disabilities (Brotherson et al., 1986).

Passive participation is particularly ironic given the emphasis on family involvement for the past decade or more. Unfortunately, contradictions often exist between professional espoused values related to family involvement and the reality of daily practices when interacting with families (Harry, 1992). For example, in contrast with increasing stress on significant family involvement in the transition process (Gallivan-Fenlon, 1994), Panzer, Pratt, and Wilcox (as cited in Gallivan-Fenlon, 1994) found in statewide survey of parents and professionals, that the parents reported that they (a) were not getting transition-related information (even though schools and agencies reported having disseminated this information); (b) similar to other team members, were dissatisfied with their participation in transition teams; (c) viewed the existing scope and amount of transition planning accomplished differently than other team members; and (d) had different "wished for" services for their children that they thought were unavailable. Furthermore, research by Gallivan-Fenlon (1994) found that in practice transition planning was occurring much later than required by law or recommended, there was little evidence of family or student involvement in transition-related activities (e.g., job development, transition meetings), and families were being provided with late and limited information. These combined factors appeared to result in family confusion and anxiety, and possibly limited future options. Perhaps an even clearer indication of family disengagement from the process was the finding that parents from this study could not identify the other members of the transition team.

Given that family participation in transition planning is passive at best, and given that family participation in the process is viewed as a critical element, it is ironic that current transition services seem to supplement rather than support the family (Ferguson et al., 1988). Gallivan-Fenlon (1994) recommended supportive actions for professional and active involvement of fami-

lies. These include providing families with multiple ways to obtain information for informed decision making, ensuring that families direct the transition exploration and planning processes, and including families in systems-level committees that develop policies and service system practices. However, families and professional seeking to have active engagement of families face a variety of barriers.

Barriers to Involvement

Harry and colleagues (1995) identified four possible sources of reduced involvement of families in the special education process: knowledge, personal resources, authority and power, and communication. More specifically, many families, especially minority families, lack critical knowledge about their rights, the processes and procedures of the educational system, and the system policies that affect them and their children. Without such knowledge, they cannot engage the system in a way that is effective and beneficial. Furthermore, lack of knowledge puts families at a disadvantage in terms of authority and power (Harry et al., 1995). The traditional source of power in educational decisions lies usually with the educational professionals (Giangreco et al., 1995). Professional authority coupled with lack of communication (especially during the assessment and placement process) and lack of sensitivity to cultural variations often result in families who are alienated by the very system that is intended to solicit and value their input (Harry et al., 1995). Minority families may also face personal resource issues, including difficulties in arranging transportation and child care, and work conflicts. Some families even may be engaged in a daily battle to survive. Expecting follow-through on system-imposed commitments and roles, therefore, is unrealistic for these families (Hanson & Carta, 1995). Many families are unfamiliar with such questions as who can help their son or daughter get a job once schools are no longer the service agency, how long their son or daughter can stay in school after age 18, and the difference between formal plans like the IEP and ITP and personal futures planning.

Factors that appear to be specially related to reduced family involvement in the transition planning process have been identified by Stineman and colleagues (1993). These include the perception of appropriate family involvement (type and degree) held by professionals, the amount of family involvement encouraged in past educational decisions, confusion related to expectations, limited or inaccessible opportunities to participate, and stresses experienced by the family in relation to the realities of the adult service world, and the typical renegotiation of the parent–child relationship. These barriers, summarized in Table 10.3, give rise to identification of practices that can enhance family involvement. Examples of how to help families engage in the transition process include

- build and sustain natural support systems for the family and the student

- have the family participate in the development of a personal profile of their son or daughter and their family interests

- give family members opportunities to share in the responsibility of accomplishing action plans

Professionals engaged in transition planning need to help families build and sustain natural support systems, LISTEN to family needs and concerns, provide a range of options in an attempt to reduce the obstacles that families face (Hanson & Carta, 1995), avoid assumptions about what family participation should be, enhance communication about expectations for participation, share information and solicit family input, change the professional role from expert to facilitator, ensure access to opportunities to participate, and INVITE participation (Stineman et al., 1993). Practices such as these result in more family-centered planning and active parent involvement. Current family- and person-centered approaches to educational decision making are based on the beliefs that collaborative work is essential to quality education and

that the family, as part of the team, is critical to longitudinal, relevant planning (Jamison, 1993; Giangreco et al., 1995). Furthermore, "[p]ractices that are family centered and that actively involved parents in decision-making and resource mobilization roles resulted in better outcomes, compared with practices more aligned with a professionally centered approach" (Lesar et al., 1996:198). Practices that build on person-centered planning and collaborative work are discussed in the final section of this chapter.

RECOMMENDED PRACTICES

From birth to age 18, the children spend 87 percent of their time under the control of the home environment (Bevivino, as cited in Dettmer et al., 1996). Given this fact and the positive effect of family involvement in educational outcomes, practitioners have to find ways to enhance family–school collaboration. Collaboration, working together, and establishing a mutually respectful relationship is preferable to simply involving families in the educational processes (Dettmer et al., 1996). Dettmer and colleagues (1996:288) identified the five principles on which family–school collaboration is based:

1. Families are a constant in children's lives and must be equal partners in all decisions affecting the child's educational program.

2. Family involvement includes a wide range of family structures.

3. Diversity and individual differences among people are to be valued and respected.

4. All families have strengths and coping skills that can be identified and enhanced.

5. Families are sources of wisdom and knowledge about their children.

Clearly, individualization is the key to implementing best practices for family–school collaboration. The type and extent of collaborative relationship should be individualized according

Table 10.3 Barriers to Family Involvement

- Lack of knowledge, personal resources, authority and power, and communication
- Professional perceptions of appropriate family involvement (type and degree)
- Amount of past discouragement of family involvement in educational decisions
- Confusion related to expectations
- Limited or inaccessible opportunities to participate
- Normal familial stress

to family preference. Despite the importance of individualization, however, it is imperative that passive participation is not interpreted as a preference. As mentioned, passivity in this process could be due to several factors, including professional devaluation of family input (Turnbull & Turnbull, 1990; Harry, 1992; Dettmer et al., 1996), lack of understanding about school system and processes, feelings of inferiority, and intimidation by school personnel (Turnbull & Turnbull, 1990; Harry, 1992).

Much of the transition literature focuses on the need for a collaborative family–school relationship resulting in the family being an integral part of the transition process (Ferguson et al., 1988; Thorin & Irvin, 1992; Hanley-Maxwell et al., 1995). Families are urged to assume a leadership role in their child's transition process. Perhaps by utilizing the best practices for including families, families will become the center of the process regardless of whether they are capable or choose to assume a traditional leadership role. Applying best practices may help families assume individualized central roles. Becoming the center of the process can be explained by visualizing the family as the center of the universe with professionals, agencies, and informal support systems revolving around the family, providing support when it is needed (Turnbull, 1988). In essence, professionals initiate and sustain the collaborative and supportive relationships with families.

Collaborative relationships are enhanced if professionals focus on the needs and interests of the children and their families, not on the value

differences that may exist between the family and the professional. Sometimes the beginning of a collaborative relationship starts by a simple invitation to family members to participate and providing them with positive feedback about their efforts (Dettmer et al., 1996).

The literature regarding best practices for family involvement provides more complex ways to solicit and maintain ongoing individualized, collaborative relationships. Four identified best practices include (a) reciprocal family education, (b) cultural sensitivity, (c) personal futures planning, and (d) a longitudinal framework for including families in transition planning. These practices incorporate many of the collaborative behaviors recommended when working with families in transition.

Individualization Through Reciprocal Family Education

The outdated concept of family education as a one-way transmission process from the all-knowing, expert professional is insulting to families and creates a major barrier to student progress and family professional partnerships by reinforcing the roles of family members as students and the family as recipient of professionals' decisions (Turnbull & Turnbull, 1990).

The concept of family education as a reciprocal process, one of exchanging information, pooling resources, and learning from each other, is the key to facilitating effective family–professional partnerships and promoting positive transition outcomes for students and families

(Turnbull & Turnbull, 1990; Hanley-Maxwell et al., 1995; Dettmer et al., 1996).

Described in this section and summarized in Table 10.4 are ways to individualize family involvement. This individualization is accomplished via the four components involved in implementing a reciprocal family–education process: (a) establishing trusting relationships, (b) getting to know families, (c) restructuring family and professional roles, and (d) exchanging information. Each of these components is also illustrated in the case studies for Shawna and Chou Do Houa later in this chapter.

Establishing Trusting Relationships

The primary component in creating a reciprocal family–education process is to establish a trusting relationship. "Building a trustful and respectful relationship with families is an interactive process that involves mutual sharing of ideas, information and feelings" (Margolis & Brannigan, as cited in Turnbull & Turnbull, 1990:158). Margolis and Brannigan suggested several ways for professionals to build relationships, including (a) accepting families unconditionally by respecting their right to have their own opinions and values (Dettmer et al., 1996); (b) listening empathetically for the cognitive and emotional content of messages communicated; (c) increasing the family's comfort level by sharing information and resources whenever possible; (d) preparing for meetings so that knowledge of *family* meanings is communicated; (e) focusing on family visions, needs, and concerns; (f) actively responding to families (Dettmer et al., 1996) by keeping promises, returning calls, and sharing materials; (g) allowing the family's expertise to shine (by developing and utilizing family strengths and knowledge; Dettmer et al., 1996); and (h) being available when needed.

Major strides will be made when professionals learn to truly listen to family members (Dettmer et al., 1996). Listening is the "language of acceptance" (Turnbull & Turnbull, 1990:162). There are two ways to establish trusting relationships. One is to meet with families in nonthreatening, neutral, and convenient locations such as their home or a setting within their community. The second is for professionals to share relevant personal stories from their own life in order to establish common ground with the families. Shawna's case study (Case Study 1) provides an illustration of how one teacher worked to establish trusting relationships by enhancing her knowledge of the family and meeting with them in settings that were most comfortable to them.

Getting to Know Families

A second component involved in creating a reciprocal family–teacher education process is to get to know families. Two ways to get to know families identified in this section are *learning to listen* and *determining relevant information*.

Learning to Listen. Listening is considered by many to be one of the most essential ingredients in an effective relationship. As defined by Webster (1970), listening is "to make a conscious effort to hear; attend closely so as to hear" (p. 825). For listening to become the "language of acceptance," it must go beyond the dictionary definition, however. For example, Gordon (1970) described active listening as an activity that promotes problem solving and encourages acceptance and expression of thoughts and feelings. Hence, the process of active listening means adopting a strategy for communicating basic attitudes. The six attitudinal prerequisites for active listening are (a) wanting to hear what the other person is saying; (b) wanting to help the other person with his/her problems; (c) being able to genuinely accept the other person's feelings, even when drastically different from your own; (d) trusting the other person's capacity to find solutions to his/her problems; (e) realizing and appreciating that feelings are transitory; therefore, you do not need to fear them; and (f) viewing the other person as separate, with alternative perceptions of the world. When listening is utilized to communicate these attitudes, it will

Table 10.4 Professional Behaviors That Support Family Involvement

Building Relationships	Getting to Know Family	Restructuring Roles	Exchanging Information
Accept families unconditionally	Learn to listen	Develop collaborative relationships	Share information resources
Listen empathetically	Identify:	Prepare families for new roles:	Listen empathetically
Share information/ resources	family characteristics family interactions family functions family life cycle communication preferences	families as assessors families as presenters of reports	Use multiple methods
Communicate family meanings		families as policy makers	Use multiple formats for resource access
Focus on family identified issues	Determine what is relevant	families as advocates and peer supports	Ensure reciprocity in communication
Actively and reliably respond to families	Information by profiling family priorities and dreams	Increase flexibility in hours and locations	
Highlight families' expertises			
Be available			
Meet in family- friendly locations			
Use personal stories for common ground			

not only enhance the acquisition of information, it will also communicate acceptance. Many parents express relief and pleasure when they can tell their stories to someone who they feel is listening and could help. Shawna's case study reveals that her teacher, Nancy, was still struggling with learning to listen. This was especially true when she held opinions about Shawna's future that were different than her family's views.

Determining Relevant Information. The second stage of getting to know families and individualizing involvement is determining relevant information. Professionals need to determine what information is important to obtain through discussions with families. Family characteristics, family interactions, family functions, family life cycle, and home–school communication preferences are general categories from which professionals may need to gain detailed information. Selecting the general categories and specific topics within those general categories is

equally important. Topics should be selected that are important for establishing a positive initial rapport and should be determined by their relevancy to the particular individual and family. Maintaining flexibility within discussions is imperative. Allowing the discussion to be directed by the family facilitates discovery of the issues important to them (Turnbull & Turnbull, 1990). One way to determine relevant information is to develop with the family a profile of their priorities and dreams.

Restructuring Roles

Restructuring roles is the third component of individualization through reciprocal family education. Open-ended dialogue may promote relaxation of traditional family and professional roles. Harry (1992) argued that the major problem in family–professional discourse is the way the educational system structures interactions and communication. Thus, the legalistic framing

CASE STUDY 1   Shawna Johnson

Shawna is 17 years old and within 1 year of leaving school. Because she is in special education, transition planning was started for her several years ago. Fortunately for Shawna and her family, the transition coordinator at Shawna's school, Nancy, took the role of Shawna's family very seriously. When Shawna was 14, Nancy requested a time to meet with Shawna and her family so that they could start actively planning for Shawna's future. Nancy came to the house one Saturday afternoon and stayed for several hours of coffee, phone ringing, door slamming, and general family mayhem. When she left, she knew she was just starting to understand the dynamics of Shawna's family and the visions that they and Shawna had for the future. She left behind information she felt that Shawna's family needed to help them think about what the future might hold for Shawna. She also left behind promises to Shawna and her family that this was just the beginning of an ongoing planning process and that their opinions and wishes would be the most important considerations in these discussions.

Subsequent formal and informal discussions were held during the next 3 years. It became apparent early in the planning process that if Shawna's family was going to feel comfortable with the process, the involved professionals would have to change their behavior. Shawna's mother, grandmother, older brother, and minister attended most of the meetings if they were held at Shawna's home in the evening. A few initial meetings were held during the day and at school. These meetings were occasionally attended only by Shawna's grandmother, who clearly felt uncomfortable at these meetings. The decision was made to hold all meetings and informal gatherings at Shawna's home at a time that was convenient for the family.

In getting to know Shawna's family, Nancy had to learn to monitor her use of professional language, her jargon, and her assumptions about various cultural aspects of Shawna's family. At first it was hard, but after she and the family felt they could trust each other, the cultural "barrier" became an ongoing source of amusement for them. Nancy had to confront other cultural differences. Initially, she had to make a conscious decision to respect the rights of Shawna's family to their own values and opinions, even when these conflicted with her own. But, as she really listened to the family, she found it easier to understand their perspectives, even when she did not agree. It also became easier to identify their strengths, resources, and knowledge, and to use these as the foundation for longitudinal planning.

Because Nancy knew that it was important to ensure that Shawna and her family felt that they were the most important part of the process, she helped them prepare for all meetings, involved them in all assessment and job-development activities, and assisted them in shaping and communicating their visions of Shawna's future. Sometimes she felt uncomfortable with the family's view and pressed them to develop more "realistic" options. Other times, she felt that Shawna's family was underestimating Shawna's skills and, therefore, pushed harder to have them consider other options. But, each time she pushed too hard, Shawna's minister reminded her that because it was Shawna and her family who would have to make these plans work after she left school, they had to feel comfortable with them.

At first, the planning process seemed controlled mostly by the professionals and dealt more with immediate needs than future plans. And, when the plans did deal with the future, they seemed too vague to be real. But, as the process changed over the years, so did the plans. They became more future-oriented, more specific, and more organized. Nancy made sure that Shawna and her family knew many of the potential pitfalls the future holds. To help them face the future realistically, she nurtured a mentoring relationship between a former student's family and Shawna's family.

Three years later, Shawna and her family are facing her imminent departure from school with both excitement and nervousness. Armed with the knowledge of what they all want for Shawna, what resources they need to get to that vision, and a plan for how to get there, they feel more confident they can face the future.

of family and professional roles tends to ritualize interactions. Collaborative relationships in which professionals and families combine their knowledge and skills to plan and intervene often produce the best results for the child and the family (Dettmer et al., 1996). To achieve this collaborative relationship, participation roles must be altered.

Family Role Changes. According to Harry (1992), it is the responsibility of the professional to "provide communication structures that will make dialogue possible and mutual understanding likely" (p. 239). Harry outlined four roles that need to be developed for families in the special education process. Proposed roles are as follows:

1. *[Families] as assessors:* [Families] would be included in the entire assessment process, with professionals relying on [families'] intimate knowledge of their children and of historical and cultural features that may account for children's development, learning, and behavioral patterns. Under the present system, by the time [families] are invited to the placement meeting the power and legitimacy of professional expertise have already been established by the exclusion of [families] from the assessment process. Example: Families should be engaged in working with other's to develop a profile of their son or daughter in order to fully assess his or her likes, dislikes, and dreams.

2. *[Families] as presenters of reports:* [Families] would be expected to be present at conferences in order to give an oral or written family report which would be an official document, part of the child's educational record. This would signal to [families] that their input is not only valued, but needed; currently, [families] have virtually no

role in placement conferences. Example: family member presentations should take place within schools and communities, at the regional and state level, and at national conferences for the benefit of policy and knowledge dissemination at multiple levels.

3. *[Families] as policy makers:* [Families] would elect their own representatives to advisory committees at the building, or, at least, the neighborhood level, with responsibility for participating in decision-making about special education programming and cultural or community concerns.

4. *[Families] as advocates and peer supports:* [Family] groups within schools, perhaps overlapping with the advisory committees, would provide peer advocacy, support at IEP meetings, and perhaps most important, serve as mutual interpreters between the cultures of the community and of the school. (pp. 239–240)

If families are to participate in evaluation, intervention, and meetings, they must be prepared for this participation. Preparing families to participate in meetings and other activities means providing information about who will be attending the meeting or working with the family and child, how the meeting or activity will be conducted, what the family can contribute, how they can prepare to contribute, and what to expect in relation to meeting or activity followup (Dettmer et al., 1996). As can be seen in Case Study 1, Nancy developed actions to ensure the participation of Shawna and her family in all aspects of the assessment and planning processes.

Professional Role Changes. Teacher role changes are also suggested as a way to facilitate individualization through reciprocal family education. Removing the traditional ritualistic structure of interactions and developing the central roles for families listed previously will result in a less traditional role for teachers. New roles involve working flexible hours and in alternative settings that extend beyond traditional school concerns. For example, teachers need to go into the homes of students, getting to know the personal context of each student/family's transition. This role change facilitates trusting relationships and gives families the personal connection they desire (Hanley-Maxwell et al., 1995). Professional role change may be evident in such simple alterations as those described in Shawna's case study: conducting planning meetings on evenings and weekends to be more convenient to nonschool-related participants and holding meetings in settings that are comfortable and accessible to all who wish to participate in planning or educational process.

Exchanging Information

The final component of the reciprocal education process of professionals and families involves exchange of information. As we adjust our perceptions of ourselves, it is important not to disregard the need to communicate information to families. A lack of knowledge/facts leads to disempowerment (Gallivan-Fenlon, 1994). Parental intimidation and discomfort have been identified as reasons for low parental involvement (Everson & McNulty, 1992). Families are typically unprepared to participate knowledgeably in discussions. Professionals frequently utilize the technical jargon of their field rather than speaking plain English (Brotherson et al., 1986; Harry, 1992). Furthermore, families report relying almost exclusively on school staff to provide information. In some cases, such exclusive reliance on professionals for information can result in a limited vision of future possibilities for their child. Limited vision is consistent with limited knowledge and information made available to them (Gallivan-Fenlon, 1994). Topics covered in the following section are related to exchanging information and include (a) content areas, (b)

methods, and (c) formats. An illustration of the quality aspects of exchanging information can be found in Shawna's case study. Additionally, Case Study 2, of Chou Do, introduces creative ways to ensure that information is getting to the family as well as from the family to the school.

Content Areas. From the previous discussion of the need for professionals to communicate information to families emerge several content areas that need to be addressed during the transition process. Gallivan-Fenlon (1994) asserted that families need information regarding (a) existing and potential quality adult services, (b) opportunities to observe students train for supported jobs, and (c) opportunities to observe adults working in supported employment. Additionally, basic facts about transition and follow-up information should be communicated to families (Nisbet et al., 1992). Turnbull and Turnbull (1990) suggested that families need information relating to behavior management, advocacy, and planning for the future.

According to Thorin and Irvin (1992), the areas most frequently mentioned by family members are sexuality, self-care, getting along, and taking responsibility. As mentioned, concerns about residential placement are overwhelmingly the most stressful issues faced by families.

Family-to-family manuals and newsletters provide some clues about the information needs of families. Table 10.5 summarizes ten informational needs identified in a transition manual developed by parents for families (Quadland and colleagues, 1996). Although not all parents may want or need information in all of these areas, or may, in fact, need information in areas not identified by Quadland et al. (1996), manuals and newsletters help professionals identify potential needs and may provide a starting point from which to begin the discussion with each family.

Professionals should obtain actively information about all of these areas and, in turn, make that information available to families. Content areas should be selected based on the needs and

CASE STUDY 2   Chou Do Houa

Chou Do Houa is 13 years old and in the seventh grade. He has multiple disabilities. He has been enrolled in special education since his family moved to the United States when he was 4 years old. Carol is his special education teacher at the middle school and feels it is important to begin planning immediately for Chou Do Houa's life after school.

Carol feels somewhat overwhelmed by the task. Chou Do Houa's former teacher, Dan, is very negative about the family's involvement. Dan feels that the language and cultural barriers make the collaboration with the family almost impossible. The school social worker expressed frustration with the situation also, noting that changing interpreters ten times in 9 years has contributed to communication problems. She said that the family will attend meetings and politely agree to whatever the professionals suggest, but they rarely follow through with suggestions and do not seem to understand what the team feels is important.

Carol believes that what happens in Chou Do Houa's future depends on how well his family and transition team collaborate. She is determined to build a more positive, collaborative relationship with his family in order to enhance his education and preparation for life. After all, his family will be involved with him long after school district personnel are out of the picture.

It is obvious that Chou Do Houa's family members are not expressing their true opinions, feelings, and needs, and probably do not feel comfortable doing so at this time. No plans can be created for his future as long as the family will not even express what they want or think.

Carol realizes that establishing and maintaining a trusting relationship with Chou Do Houa and his family will take flexibility, creativity, and lots of time. First of all, Carol enrolled in a minicourse about Chou Do Houa's culture and cultural history. She feels this will facilitate an understanding of any value differences. Then Carol arranged to spend a day with the family and the interpreter. Part of the day was spent with the interpreter obtaining information such as (a) where they were born, (b) how long they have been in the United States, (c) what they think about school, (d) familial dreams and hopes for their children, (e) children's past school experiences, and (f) information about health, nutrition, employment and education of parents. The remainder of the day was spent observing daily life, where they live, what they eat, what they do for entertainment, and how Chou Do Houa integrates into the day-to-day life. After spending this day with the family, Carol summarized what she had learned and her interpretation of her observations.

Carol began to notice that some of her colleagues made derogatory comments about Chou Do Houa's family. She felt the comments were unfair and based on inaccurate assumptions and biases. Carol's concern over these comments and their impact on Chou Do Houa prompted her to reflect on the major cultural differences and her own biases. She asked herself the following questions: What in the lives of this family is the most difficult to accept, understand, and justify? What are the most important child-rearing values demonstrated by this family? What do I find in these values to be in conflict with my own values? What do I know about their country of origin, their life-style there, relatives, traditions, and values? What do I know about their culture's views on the meaning of disability? By answering these questions Carol was able to develop a deeper understanding of Chou Do Houa and his family, as well as her own values, biases, and prejudices.

Subsequent communication involved not only interaction through the interpreter, but also more informal daily communication utilizing the interpreting skills of Chou Do Houa's brother and sister, who also attend the middle school. Carol found that establishing a relationship with Chou Do Houa's siblings was a tremendous help in daily communication and in understanding cultural differences and family dynamics and preferences. If Chou Do Houa's brother and sister could develop an understanding of the school and service systems, they could assist their parents in the future. Carol facilitated opportunities for Chou Do Houa's siblings and parents to observe students with severe disabilities working in supported jobs, so they could begin to understand and visualize some of the possibilities for Chou Do Houa's future. She made plans to continue to expand their opportunities for observations of additional supported employment sites as well as community living and recreational possibilities for Chou Do Houa.

By the end of her first year as Chou Do Houa's teacher, Carol felt she had learned much about herself, Chou Do Houa, his family, and culture. She realized the transition-planning process would be a complicated, constantly changing process that would last throughout his school years. Carol looked forward to growing in her understanding of Chou Do Houa and his family and facilitating their visions for the future.

Table 10.5 Transition Information Needs of Families

- Transition foundations (definitions and processes)
- Role descriptions of IEP committee members (especially parents and students)
- Criteria for evaluating IEP
- Identification of postsecondary options and connection strategies
- Agency access information (including eligibility requirements and contact persons)
- Social security (including eligibility and access information)
- Legal issues of guardianship and estate planning
- Assistive technology information (including legal mandates and resources)
- Example forms used for evaluation, planning, and visioning
- Listing of addresses and phone numbers for local, regional, and state "disability" services

preferences of individual students, parents, and family members, and should not be viewed as an inclusive list.

Methods. Methods for exchanging information should be individualized according to the preferences of the family. McCarney's study of parental involvement preferences (as cited in Turnbull & Turnbull, 1990) indicated that families preferred direct communication with professionals, such as family–teacher conferences, telephone contacts, open house at school, notes sent home by teachers, classroom observations, and informal teacher contacts. Other nonconference methods include written communication, such as handbooks, newsletters, personal letters, notes or logbooks, progress notes, occasional messages, handouts for specific situations or circumstances (Turnbull & Turnbull, 1990), and family-to-family mentoring. For example, Chou Do's teacher found that establishing a communication link with his siblings was critical for effectively working with his family.

Formats. The format in which information is presented to families is also significant. The importance of quality information cannot be overemphasized. It is essential to transmit information to families in various formats (Goodall & Bruder, 1986). Turnbull and Turnbull (1990) suggested that professionals provide information that include print, media, and computer tech-

nology. Keeping a file of state, local, and national resource information and resource persons is also proposed as an avenue for accessing and communicating information.

When communicating and exchanging information, it is necessary to maintain a reciprocal communication process. This two-way communication is even more important when interacting with individuals from diverse cultural backgrounds. Hence, the best practice described in the next section involves cultural sensitivity.

INDIVIDUALIZATION THROUGH CULTURAL SENSITIVITY

Considering the increasingly diverse population of students in our schools, cultural diversity, and how to deal with it, must not be neglected. The issues being faced are complex and multifaceted. Teachers must not only deal with the conflicts and problems of their students, they must also deal with their own role in creating those problems the degree to which the teacher reflects the dominant culture and how this impacts the empowerment of their students and student families.

A comprehensive discussion of cultural diversity and its implications for educators is beyond the scope of this review. Thus, cultural diversity issues will be addressed here only as one facet of individualization for families and students. Ten ways educators can impact the success of culturally different students are identified and cultural therapy exercises for teachers are outlined.

Culturally Competent Attitudes and Behaviors

It is important to recognize the role educators play in the success or failure of culturally diverse students and families. Trueba and colleagues (1993) outlined ten culturally competent attitudes and behaviors teachers can demonstrate.

1. Professionals must demonstrate cultural understanding and sensitivity to enable students to develop their maximum potentials.

2. Teachers and other service providers must have a powerful ethnic identity of their own (Trueba et al., 1993) and must couple this identity with a devotion to assisting minority students in understanding their own ethnic identity and cultural values (Zeichner, as cited in Trueba et al., 1993).

3. Professionals must understand the dynamics of racism and prejudice and be able to help minority students deal with demonstrations of prejudice and racism, while maintaining self-respect and self-esteem (Zeichner, as cited in Trueba et al., 1993).

4. Professionals who are culturally competent must display a spirit of cooperation, paired with a willingness and a capacity to facilitate cooperative learning among teachers and students to acquire new knowledge.

5. Teachers must possess the information and competence necessary to correct historical accounts that often omit the contributions of ethnic and other minority groups, including individuals with disabilities.

6. Growth in this and other areas requires that culturally competent teachers have the desire and ability to continually develop additional professional skills to improve teaching performance.

7. Continuing professional development may include the development of their own capacity and responsiveness to proactively involve themselves with families of ethnic-minority students, and to engage these families in the cultural and academic activities of the school.

8. Teachers can demonstrate culturally competent attitudes and behaviors by maintaining positive expectations for student achievement both in school and outside of school.

9. Teachers must be willing to try creative strategies when dealing with instructional difficulties or challenges (Trueba et al., 1993).

10. Culturally competent teachers must hone their "bicultural skills to assist children in their adjustment to school and society" (Trueba et al., 1993:138).

In seeking to understand a family's cultural background and experience, professionals should express their interest and respect for the family's customs and traditions by asking them which are important to them rather than assuming which aspects are most important.

Cultural Therapy Exercises

Cultural therapy is defined as a "process of healing" (Trueba et al., 1993:155). The fundamental assumption behind cultural therapy is that interaction between and among people with diverse backgrounds is subject to misunderstanding and ethnocentrism. Cultural therapy raises our awareness of our own cultural values while also heightening our capacity for tolerance of the life-styles of others. Cultural therapy involves efforts at building the necessary cultural knowledge and understanding of our own values, ethnohistory, and enduring self (Trueba et al., 1993). According to Trueba and colleagues (1993), exercises in cultural therapy "will help obtain cultural knowledge that guides informed judgement, providing contextual cultural knowledge of their own lives and of the people with whom we live or work" (p. 156).

Based on Trueba and colleagues' assumptions regarding cultural therapy, cultural therapy exercises can be used as a tool for individualizing interactions, services, and supports for families. Three exercises recommended for practitioners involve acquiring knowledge about students and their families through (a) gathering general information, (b) reflecting on salient cultural differences, and (c) reflecting on personal values and summarizing. These exercises, described in what follows, are also illustrated in Case Study 2 of Chou Do Houa and example questions for each exercise are provided in Table 10.6.

Gathering General Information. General information can be gathered by spending time with the student and family. It is important to visit students and their family in their home. When appropriate, arranging to bring an interpreter allows for communication with family members to obtain important information such as the items identified in Table 10.6. Careful observations should be included in the information-gathering exercise. Observations should include where they live, what they eat, and how they manage income. After the information has been gathered, teachers should summarize the information and their understanding of it (Trueba et al., 1993).

Reflecting on Salient Cultural Differences. Reflecting on the lives of students is the second recommended exercise in cultural therapy. Examples of questions that teachers may ask themselves are listed in Table 10.6. By answering these questions, teachers develop a deeper understanding of the family and themselves. This understanding is the basis for the next exercise (Trueba et al., 1993).

Reflecting on Personal Values and Summarizing. It is essential that professionals examine their own lives. Examples of areas for self-examination are identified in Table 10.6. Again, knowledge and insights gained from the self-examination process should be summarized (Trueba et al., 1993).

Cultural differences can be major barriers and sources of misunderstandings between families and professionals. Cultural therapy can be utilized by educators to better individualize support and collaborative relationships with families. Steps in cultural therapy are also essential aspects of personal futures planning strategies, the individualized planning process described in the next section.

Individualization Through Personal Futures Planning Strategies

Recently, a major focus has been directed toward different and innovative ways of planning. Such strategies are ways to further individualize family involvement. Numerous alternative approaches to planning have been developed, including personal futures planning, whole life planning, life-style planning, vision-building strategies, or outcome-based planning (O'Brien, 1987; Mount & Zwernik, 1988; Vandercook, York, & Forest, 1989; Steere et al., 1990; Bolles, as cited in Butterworth et al., 1993).

These strategies are based on the following assumptions about the rights that individuals with disabilities have to

- community presence
- community participation
- consideration of competence
- respected and valued community roles
- choices about everyday and life-defining matters (O'Brien & Lovett, 1992)

Additionally, these strategies capitalize on the beliefs that (a) it is essential that the individual and family create a vision of the future based on their desires and that they identify how to get there; and (b) individuals, families, friends, and neighbors are key members of the vision planning processes (Vandercook et al., 1989).

Table 10.6 Examples of Questions Asked in Cultural Therapy Exercises

Gathering General Information	Reflecting on Salient Cultural Differences	Reflecting on Personal Values
Where were they born?	What in the lives of these families is the most difficult to accept, understand, and justify?	What are my values, biases, and prejudices?
What are their thoughts about school?	What are the most important child-rearing values demonstrated by these families?	What is my background?
What are the dreams and hopes for the children in the family?	What do you find in these values to be in conflict with your own values?	What is my life-style?
What are the past school experiences of the children?	What do you know about their country of origin, their life-style there, relatives, traditions and values?	What customs, traditions, and rituals are important in my family?
Are their issues related to health and nutrition?	What do you know about their culture's views on the meaning of disability?	What languages are spoken in my family?
Where do they currently live?		Who have been important role models in my family?
What are the role expectations for family members?		

The Lifestyle Planning process (O'Brien & Lyle, 1987) is one example of a personalized planning strategy. This process is used to describe a desirable future for the individual and define the necessary steps and resources needed to achieve that future.

Another strategy, the McGill Action Planning Systems (MAPS; Vandercook et al., 1989) focuses on seven areas identified by Smull (as cited in Vandercook et al., 1989): These include the description of a person's (a) nonnegotiables, (b) strong preferences, and (c) highly desirables. The remaining areas include specification of (a) the descriptors, folklore, and characteristics used to describe the person by people who know and care about the person; (b) the person's reputation, concerns, issues, and labels; (c) needed supports and strategies; and (d) action steps, time frames, and responsibilities. MAPS also includes discussion of the child's history; the dreams and nightmares that participants have for the child; a description of the child; and a description of the child's strengths, gifts, abilities, and needs.

Choosing Options and Accommodations for Children (COACH; Giangreco, Cloninger, & Iverson, 1993) is a more recent addition to individualized planning strategies. This tool moves beyond the others to include the student's and family's values and dreams in the student's IEP planning process. Consequently, IEP goals and objectives are selected and prioritized within the context of the valued life outcomes, activity preferences, and preferred curricular areas identified by the family.

Finally, the Personal Futures Planning process (Mount, 1992, 1995) involves dreaming, describing, and doing with the individual and his or her support system. Mount proposes a mapping process to develop a personal profile that is subsequently used to develop a vision for the person's future. Brainstorming of possibilities becomes the basis for identifying common themes or categories, which then are prioritized. Finally, implementation strategies are identified to accomplish the vision. These include opportunity and barrier identification, development of an action plan, and solicitation of follow-through commitments from participants. Unlike the others, Mount and Zwernick (1988) are adamant that personal futures plans be totally separate from the IEP process.

Despite differences, Butterworth and colleagues (1993) have identified content and procedural commonalities in all of these approaches.

First, all approaches reflect changing emphases. For the individual with a disability, this change reflects a shift in emphasis from needs and limitations to talents, strengths, preferences, and dreams. For families, the changing emphases are evident in the planning process. Further, the emphasis is shifted from professionals to the contributions and participation of the individual with a disability and his/her family, friends, and peers. Next, the planning process is accomplished within a group format in which an unrestricted vision for the individual's future is developed. Goals are developed and supports and resources are identified to support achievement of that vision. Finally, in all strategies, resources and supports are organized. They are intended to be as local, informal, generic, and "nonprofessional" as possible to carry out the plans.

Turnbull (1988) supported the use of the IEP with personal futures planning, arguing that the past failures of the IEP process were due to the "rush to have paper compliance and signed documents in files [that] resulted in an artificial and superficial planning process that has not been sufficiently upgraded in quality in ten years of implementation" (p. 263). Turnbull (1988) also noted, "The potential of individualized planning has been masked by the legalistic scurry for compliance" (p. 263).

As implementation of personal futures planning expands, families and professionals are learning about the advantages and disadvantages that accompany this style of planning (summarized in Table 10.7). One of the most frequently cited advantages of personal futures planning is the building or strengthening of social support networks around the focal person. Thus, Mount (1994) saw personal futures planning as a mechanism for what she called "community-building" (p. 100). This can happen both through greater participation and involvement in the community at large and through strengthened personal relationships on a more individualized basis. Hagner, Helm, and Butterworth (1996) found that parents were pleasantly surprised by their son's or daughter's social support networks, which either gained focus and strength through

the process or developed over the course of consecutive planning meetings. Another frequent advantage or benefit of personal futures planning is the opportunity to clarify the focal person's vision for his or her future. The group structure of most personal futures planning processes allows significant others to help the focal person articulate his or her hopes and dreams (Hagner et al., 1996). One more advantage is that personal futures planning can contribute to or inform more bureaucratic plans such as the IEP, ITP, and ISP. Although proponents of personal futures planning often maintain that these plans should remain distinct from the IEP and ISP process (Hagner et al., 1996), personal futures planning can contribute to the more formal and mandated plans. These contributions may be indirect such as increased individual participation or input from a broader support network in the formal planning. The contributions of one planning process to the other may also be more direct such as including in the IEP, ITP, or Individualized Service Plan (ISP) the systems' commitments to action steps that will help the individual achieve his or her desired future.

Although for many the advantages of personal futures planning seem enough to justify its use, the model presents logistical disadvantages or drawbacks that cannot be ignored. First, personal futures planning processes are time-consuming to implement. The planning process is just that: a process and should not be confused with a meeting (Mount, 1994). Most processes involve multiple meetings or gatherings and a group of supporters who are close to the focal person. Nevertheless, once a carefully designed planning process has been completed, the heightened meaning of the plan to the focal person compensates for the time commitment of the support group. Another drawback to personal futures planning is that the focal person is often overwhelmed by a group process and, therefore, may not participate to the maximum extent possible (Hagner et al., 1996). Ongoing research as part of the Massachusetts Natural Supports Project at the Institute for Community Inclusion in Boston has documented instances

Table 10.7 Advantages and Disadvantages of Personal Futures Planning

Advantages	Disadvantages
■ Building or strengthening of social support networks around the focal person	■ Time-consuming to implement
■ Greater participation and involvement in the community at large	■ Contributing to or informing more bureaucratic plans
■ Opportunity to clarify the focal person's vision for his or her future	■ The focal person is often overwhelmed by a group process and, therefore, may not participate
■ Contributing to or informing more bureaucratic plans	■ Tendency to standardize rather than individualize the planning processes

in which transition-aged students sat quietly through their planning meetings, left the room, or fell asleep. These same students were much more engaged when the facilitator sat down with them individually and talked directly to them about the process and their visions. The lesson to be learned is that personal futures planning needs to be individualized in the same way any process or learning experience is. Indeed, Mount (1994) warned against the tendency to standardize planning processes and thereby lose the personal characteristics.

Considering the large commitments of time, effort, and energy involved in futures planning, it appears to be logical to combine the legal requirements of the IEP process with the more idealistic strategies or futures planning. Building personal visions for the future is closely related to utilizing a longitudinal framework for transition planning and services.

LONGITUDINAL FRAMEWORK FOR TRANSITION SERVICES

Viewing transition from a longitudinal perspective is the final best practice for including families in the transition process to be discussed in this chapter. To maximize the effectiveness of a longitudinal approach to transition, it should be utilized in conjunction with all other best prac-

tices. In other words, individualization, reciprocal family education, and personal futures planning should all begin when the child enters school and continue throughout the school years to prepare the student for the ultimate transition from school to adult life. Individualized family planning during the transition from preschool to elementary school programs is one way to initiate longitudinal collaboration with family members. For example, the McGill Action Planning Systems and COACH both have been used with families of young students to design inclusive education programs and address students' needs and parents' priorities during the early school years. In addition to addressing transitions that occur throughout the educational process, such as from preschool to elementary school and into middle school, there needs to be greater acknowledgment of the transition from childhood to adult life as a lifelong process.

Transition is a lifelong process. "Transition is not a discrete time in life affecting only the individual and one aspect of their functioning. Rather, transition is a part of career development, which is known to be a life-long process that begins at birth, and relates to all life roles, not just work" (Super, as cited in Szymanski, 1994:402). Examples of how this transition is manifested throughout childhood include children engaging in adult role playing, children dreaming of what they will be when they grow up, and the attention children pay to role models in careers and roles that interest them. These types of activities need to be encouraged in all children and opportunities to engage in them should be systematically provided through educational programs, at home, and with peers.

Turnbull (1988) supported this longitudinal view of transition by referring to the second goal of Part H of the Education of the Handicapped Act Amendments of 1986, which is "to enhance the capacity of families to meet the special needs of their infants and toddlers" (p. 261). Turnbull argued that most citizens agree that the goal of education is to prepare individuals to live and work in society throughout their life. Therefore, considering that early intervention is the child's and family's first educational experience, this goal can be interpreted as "teaching critical skills that will evolve over time leading to adult competence and community integration" (Turnbull, 1988:261). Some of these critical skills include problem solving and daily living skills that promote a child's independence. Independence is another critical element that needs to be encouraged in all children so that autonomy and self-determination can develop in the teens and as young people make the transition to the adult world.

One reason for the limited success of transition programs is their shortsightedness and narrow focus (Szymanksi, 1994). Literature written for families argues that transition education should become part of a school system's family education programs so that families are introduced to the issues during their child's elementary school years (e.g., Hanley-Maxwell & Collet-Klingenberg, 1997). If families are equipped with the necessary information, they will be able to participate more knowledgeably and fully in their child's transition process (Goodall & Bruder, 1986). It is important to take a longitudinal approach toward including families in transition planning by beginning individualization of supports, reciprocal family education processes, cultural sensitivity, and personal futures planning strategies in the early years. The critical considerations in longitudinal planning for transition are summarized in Table 10.8.

SUMMARY

Family participation in the transition process is crucial to the success of the individual with a disability (Brotherson et al., 1986; Everson & McNulty, 1992; Nisbet et al., 1992; Jamison, 1993). This chapter was designed to enhance professional understanding of what is meant by family involvement, how families are currently involved, and how family involvement can be enhanced and increased.

In the first section, the review of the history of family involvement identified traditional family roles and the legal foundation developed in Public Law 94-142 and extended by subsequent amendments. Family roles were affected by the passage of federal laws stressing active involvement of families in the education of their children with disabilities. Despite this mandate, many families assumed or were forced into roles that were detached or became only passively involved in the educational enterprise.

Parental involvement and the reality of facing the life transitions of adolescents with disabilities was discussed in the second section. The literature reviewed in that section suggests that professionals need to recognize that families are deeply affected by the impending transition of their children from school to adulthood. Furthermore, professionals must remain cognizant that these families are dealing with transition on many levels. As families face the future, teachers and other service providers must help them negotiate the effects of changing role relationships with their children; changing security for daily care from known, unified, and mandated school services to unknown, diverse, and difficult-to-access adult services; and changing family patterns of daily living and interactions. As these types of changes overlap, they create unmet needs for families. These needs and the

Table 10.8 Considerations in Longitudinal Transition Services

- Begin when the child enters school; continue throughout the school years
- Address other transitions that occur throughout the educational process
- Introduce families to transition issues during child's elementary school years
- Begin early to individualize supports, use reciprocal family education processes, develop cultural sensitivity, and utilize personal futures-planning strategies

barriers to active engagement of family members are discussed in the final portions of this section.

Finally, based on knowledge of the past and the issues that parents face as they look to the future, recommended practices are suggested in the final section of this chapter. Recommended practices, predicated on the need to develop collaborative family–school relationships, include reciprocal family education, cultural sensitivity, personal futures planning, and a longitudinal framework for including families in transition planning. Each recommended practice was accompanied by specific suggestions for teacher behavior or formal planning structures.

Table 10.9 depicts the unifying framework the underlies the multiple ideas presented in this chapter. The critical element of the framework is that the roles, transitions, and strategies discussed in the literature can be characterized as occurring at an *intrafamily level* (i.e., within individual families and between family members), at an *interfamily level* (i.e., between families and peers), and at an *extrafamily level* (i.e., between families and the community at large or between families and professionals who do not share the direct experiences of families with children who have disabilities). A framework such as this is important because professionals working with families through transitions need to consider the simultaneous contexts in which family members operate. Additionally, it is important to consider the context of the service strategies in order to meet the specific needs of families. For example, cultural sensitivity strategies should be used as a mechanism to build bridges between families and professionals. Personal futures planning is

used to address the visions and needs of one individual within his or her family. Conversely, simply implementing one strategy does not necessarily address all the needs that families have during a transition process. For example, a family who needs and has expressed an interest in sharing experiences with others who have gone through the same process does not necessarily feel that this need is met if a personal futures process is implemented to identify integrated job opportunities for their son or daughter. This need will not be met until strategies with an interfamily design are initiated.

Transition from childhood to adulthood is a complex, stressful time for individuals with disabilities and their families. As their children age, these families are faced with conflicting needs, uncertain services, and the emotions related to letting the child grow up. It is up to teachers and other service providers to support and facilitate actions that families and children must take to help them move forward during this life cycle.

QUESTIONS

1. Identify and discuss three types of transitions for families of adolescents with disabilities.

2. Why is it important to include the input of family members in the transition–planning process?

3. What is "modulation of dependency"? How does this concept interact with transition planning for individuals with disabilities?

4. What are six roles that family members play in the transition process?

Table 10.9 A Framework for Considering Family Roles, Transitions, and Service Strategies

Longitudinal framework: The following should be taken into consideration across the life span.

Intrafamily	Interfamily	Extrafamily
ROLES		
Family member	Teachers and learners	Political advocates
Decision maker	Service developers[a]	Service developers
Assessor	Presenters of reports[a]	Decision recipient
Career role model	Peer supports	Presenter of reports
Source of social support		Policymaker
Planning assistance source		Child-service system mediator
Primary care giver		De facto case manager
TRANSITIONS		
Family functioning		Bureaucratic
Status		
SERVICE STRATEGIES		
Personal futures planning		
Reciprocal family education	Family-to-family information exchange	Cultural sensitivity and therapy
Individualized supports	Peer support	

[a]Some of these roles can be thought of as both interfamily and extrafamily, depending on the audience or the context in which these roles take place

5. What five broad area of secondary and post-secondary needs have been identified by parents of adolescents with disabilities?

6. What are the barriers to family participation in the transition process?

7. What are the components of reciprocal family education?

8. What are 10 ways educators can impact the success of culturally different students and their families?

9. What is cultural therapy and how does it fit into the transition-planning process?

10. How do personal futures–planning strategies impact on transition planning?

REFERENCES

Alper, S. (1994). Introduction and background: The role of parents. In S. K. Alper, P. J. Schloss, & C. N. Schloss, *Families of students with disabilities: Consulta-tion and advocacy* (pp. 1–16). Needham Heights, MA: Allyn & Bacon.

Baumrind, D. (1991). Effective parenting during the early adolescent transition. In P. A. Cowan & E. M. Hetherington (Eds.), *Family transitions: Advances in family research series* (pp. 111–163). Hillsdale, NJ: Lawrence Erlbaum.

Brotherson, M. J., Backus, L. H., Summers, J. A., & Turnbull, A. P. (1986). Transition to adulthood. In J. A. Summers (Ed.), *The right to grow up: An introduction to adults with developmental disabilities* (pp. 17–44). Baltimore: Paul H. Brookes.

Buchmann, M. (1989). *The script of life in modern society: Entry into adulthood in a changing world.* Chicago: University of Chicago Press.

Butterworth, J., Hagner, D., Heikkinen, B., Farris, S., DeMello, S., & McDonough, K. (1993). *Whole life planning: A guide for organizers and facilitators.* Boston: Children's Hospital and University of Massachusetts.

Collins, W. A., & Russell, G. (1991). Mother–child and father–child relationships in middle childhood and adolescence: A developmental analysis. *Developmental Review, 11,* 99–136.

Dempsey, I. (1991). Parental roles in the postschool adjustment of their son or daughter with a disability. *Australia and New Zealand Journal of Developmental Disabilities, 17,* 313–320.

Dettmer, P. A., Dyck, N. T., & Thurston, L. P. (1996). *Consultation, collaboration, and teamwork for students with special needs.* Boston: Allyn & Bacon.

Education for All Handicapped Children Act of 1975, P. L. 94-142, 20, U.S.C., Sections 1401 et seq.

Everson, J. M., & McNulty, K. (1992). Interagency teams: Building local transition programs through parental and professional partnerships. In F. R. Rusch, L. DeStefano, J. Chadsey-Rusch, L. A. Phelps, & E. M. Szymanski (Eds.), *Transition from school to adult life: Models, linkages, and policy* (pp. 341–351). Sycamore, IL: Sycamore.

Ferguson, P. M, Ferguson, D. L., Jeanchild, L., Olson, D., & Lucyshyn, J. (1993). Angles of influence: Relationships among families, professional, and adults with severe disabilities. *Journal of Vocational Rehabilitation, 3*(2), 14–22.

Ferguson, P. M., Ferguson, D. L., & Jones, D. (1988). Generations of hope: Parental perspectives on the transition of their children with severe retardation from school to adult life. *Journal of the Association for Persons with Severe Handicaps, 13,* 177–187.

Gallivan-Fenlon, A. (1994). Their senior year: Family and service provider perspective on the transition from school to adult life of young adults with disabilities. *Journal of the Association for Persons with Severe Handicaps, 19*(1), 11–23.

Giangreco, M. F., Cloninger, C. J., & Iverson, V. S. (1993). *Choosing options and accommodations for children.* Baltimore: Paul H. Brookes.

Giangreco, M. F., Edelman, S. E., Dennis, R. E., & Cloninger, C. J. (1995). Use and impact of COACH with students who are deaf–blind. *Journal of the Association for Persons with Severe Disabilities, 20,* 121–135.

Goodall, P., & Bruder, M. (1986). Parents and the transition process. *The Exceptional Parent, 53*(1), 22–28.

Gordon, T. (1970). *Parent effectiveness training.* New York: New American Library.

Hagner, D., Helm, D. T., & Butterworth, J. (1996). "This is your meeting": A qualitative study of person-centered planning. *Mental Retardation, 34,* 159–171.

Hanley-Maxwell, C., & Collet-Klingenberg, L. (1997). Curricular choices related to work: Restructuring curricula for improved work outcomes. In P. Wehman & J. Kregel (Eds.), *Teaching independent living skills: A longitudinal curriculum for individuals with special needs* (pp. 155–184). Austin, TX: PRO-ED.

Hanley-Maxwell, C., Whitney-Thomas, J., & Pogoloff, S. (1995). The second shock: Parental perspectives of their child's transition from school to adult life. *Journal of the Association for Persons with Severe Handicaps, 20*(1), 3–16.

Hanson, M. J., & Carta, J. J. (1995). Addressing the challenges of families with multiple risks. *Exceptional Children, 62,* 201–212.

Haring, K., & Lovett, D. C. (1990). A follow-up study of special education graduates. *Journal of Special Education, 23,* 463–477.

Harry, B. (1992). *Cultural diversity, families and the special education system: Communication and empowerment.* New York: Teachers College Press.

Harry, B., Allen, N., & McLaughlin, M. (1995). Communication versus compliance: African-American parents' involvement in special education. *Exceptional Children, 61,* 364–377.

Hill, J. W., Seyfarth, J., Banks, P. D., Wehman, P., & Orelove, F. (1987). Parent attitudes about working conditions of their adult mentally retarded sons and daughters. *Exceptional Children, 54*(1), 9–23.

Individuals with Disabilities Education Act of 1990, P. L. 101-476, 20, U.S.C., Sections 1400 et seq.

Irvin, L. K., Thorin, E., & Singer, G. H. S. (1993). Family-related roles and considerations: Transition to adulthood by youth with developmental disabilities. *Journal of Vocational Rehabilitation, 3*(2), 38–46.

Jamison, S. D. (1993). Vocational rehabilitation: A risky business when family matters. *Journal of Vocational Rehabilitation, 3*(2), 11–13.

Lesar, S., Trivette, C. M., & Dunst, C. J. (1996). Families of children and adolescents with special needs across the life span. *Exceptional Children, 62,* 197–199.

Lichtenstein, S., & Michaelides, N. (1993). Transition from school to young adulthood: Four case studies of young adults labeled mentally retarded. *Career Development for Exceptional Individuals, 16*(2), 183–195.

Marini, M. M. (1984). The order of events in the transition to adulthood. *Sociology of Education, 57,* 63–84.

McDonnell, J., Wilcox, B., & Boles, S. M. (1986). Do we know enough to plan for transition? A national survey of state agencies responsible for services to persons with severe handicaps. *Journal of the Association for Persons with Severe Handicaps, 11*(1), 53–60.

McLouglin, J. A., & Senn, C. (1994). Siblings of children with disabilities. In S. K. Alper, P. J. Schloss, & C. N. Schloss (Eds.), *Families of students with disabilities* (pp. 95–122). Needham Heights, MA: Allyn & Bacon.

Minuchin, P. (1991). When the context changes: A consideration of families in transitional periods. In R. Cohen & A. W. Siegel (Eds.), *Context and development* (pp. 235–252). Hillsdale, NJ: Lawrence Erlbaum.

Mithaug, D. E., Horiuchi, C. N., & Fanning, P. N. (1985). A report on the Colorado statewide follow-up survey of special education students. *Exceptional Children, 51,* 397–404.

Morningstar, M. E., Turnbull, A. P., & Turnbull, H. R. (1996). What do students with disabilities tell us about the importance of family involvement in the transition from school to adult life? *Exceptional Children, 62,* 249–260.

Mount, B. (1992). *Person-centered planning: Finding directions for change using personal futures planning.* New York: Graphic Futures.

————. (1994). Benefits and limitations of personal futures planning. In V. Bradley, J. Ashbough, & B. Blaney (Eds.), *Creating individual supports for people with developmental disabilities* (pp. 97–108). Baltimore: Paul H. Brookes.

————. (1995). *Capacity works: Finding windows for change using personal futures planning.* New York: Graphic Futures.

Mount, B., & Zwernick, K. (1988). *It's never too early. It's never too late: A booklet about personal futures planning,* Publication Number: 421-109. St. Paul, MN: Metropolitan Council.

Nisbet, J., Covert, S., & Schuh, M. (1992). Family involvement in the transition from school to adult life. In F. R. Rusch, L. DeStefano, J. Chadsey-Rusch, L. A. Phelps, & E. M. Szymanski (Eds.), *Transition from school to adult life: Models, linkages, and policy* (pp. 407–424). Sycamore, IL: Sycamore.

O'Brien, J. (1987). A guide to life-style planning. In B. Wilcox & T. Bellamy (Eds.), *A comprehensive guide to the activities catalogue: An alternative curriculum for youth and adults with severe disabilities* (pp. 75–189). Baltimore: Paul H. Brookes.

O'Brien, J., & Lovett, H. (1992). *Finding a way toward everyday lives: The contribution of person centered planning.* Harrisburg: Pennsylvania Department of Public Welfare, Office of Mental Retardation.

O'Brien, J., & Lyle, C. (1987). *Framework for accomplishment.* Decatur, GA: Responsive Systems Associates.

Pallas, A. M. (1993). Schooling in the course of human lives: The social context of education and the transition to adulthood in industrial society. *Review of Educational Research, 63,* 409–447.

Quadland, C., Rybacki, S., Kellogg, A., & Hall, S. (1996). *A parent's guide to transition for youth with disabilities.* Madison: Wisconsin's Design for Transition Success,

Department of Public Instruction and Division of Vocational Rehabilitation.

Ryan, R. M., & Lynch, J. H. (1989). Emotional autonomy versus detachment: Revising the vicissitudes of adolescence and young adulthood. *Child Development, 60,* 340–346.

Schriner, K. F., & Bellini, J. L. (1994). Analyzing transition policy implementation: A conceptual framework. *Career Development for Exceptional Individuals, 17*(1) 17–27.

Scuccimarra, D. J., & Speece, D. L. (1990). Employment outcomes and social integration of students with mild handicaps: The quality of life two years after high school. *Journal of Learning Disabilities, 23,* 213–219.

Singer, G. H. S., & Irvin, L. K. (1991). Supporting families of persons with severe disabilities: Emerging findings, practices, and outcomes. In L. H. Meyers, C. A. Peck, & L. Brown (Eds.), *Critical issues in the lives of people with severe disabilities* (pp. 271–312). Baltimore: Paul H. Brookes.

Sitlington, P., & Frank, A. (1990). Are adolescents with learning disabilities successfully crossing the bridge into adult life? *Learning Disability Quarterly, 13,* 97–111.

Steere, D. E., Wood, R., Pancsofar, E. L., & Butterworth, J. (1990). Outcome-based school-to-work transition planning for students with severe disabilities. *Career Development for Exceptional Individuals, 13*(1), 57–69.

Stineman, R. M., Morningstar, M. E., Bishop, B., & Turnbull, H. R. (1993). Role of families in transition planning for young adults with disabilities. *Journal of Vocational Rehabilitation, 3*(2), 52–61.

Szymanski, E. M. (1994). Transition: Life span and life-space considerations for employment. *Exceptional Children, 60,* 402–410.

Thorin, E. J., & Irvin, L. K. (1992). Family stress associated with transition to adulthood of young people with severe disabilities. *Journal of the Association for Persons with Severe Handicaps, 17*(1) 31–40.

Thorin, E., Yovanoff, P., & Irvin, L. (1996). Dilemma faced by families during their young adults' transitions to adulthood: A brief report. *Mental Retardation, 34*(2), 117–120.

Trueba, H. T., Rodriguez, C., Zou, Y., & Clintrón, J. (1993). *Healing multicultural America: Mexican immigrants rise to power in rural California.* Washington, DC: Falmer Press.

Turnbull, A. P. (1988). The challenge of providing comprehensive support to families. *Education and Training in Mental Retardation, 23,* 261–272.

Turnbull, A. P., & Turnbull, H. R. (1990). *Families, professionals and exceptionality: A special partnership* (2nd ed.). Columbus, OH: Charles E. Merrill.

Vandercook, T., York, J., & Forest, M. (1989). The McGill Action Planning System (MAPS): A strategy for building a vision. *Journal of the Association for Persons with Severe Handicaps, 14*(3), 205–215.

Wagner, M., Newman, L., D'Amico, R., Jay, E. D., Butler-Nalin, P., Marder, C., & Cox, R. (1991). *Youth with disabilities: How are they doing?* Menlo Park, CA: SRI International.

Webster's new world dictionary. (1970). New York: World Publishing.

Whitney-Thomas, J., & Hanley-Maxwell, C. (1996). Packing the parachute: A survey of parents' experiences as their children prepare to leave high school. *Exceptional Children, 63,* 75–87.

Will, M. (1984). *OSERS programming for the transition of youth with disabilities: Bridges from school to working life.* Washington, DC: U.S. Department of Education, Office of Special Education and Rehabilitative Services.

Yancey, G. (1993). Importance of families in transition from school to adult life: A rehabilitation practitioner's perspective. *Journal of Vocational Rehabilitation, 3*(2), 5–8.

11

◉

Student Assessment and Evaluation

MARTHA THURLOW
and JUDITH ELLIOTT

Student assessment and evaluation are critical for all students, including students with disabilities. Students with disabilities traditionally are assessed for eligibility for services and reevaluated to determine the need for continued services in special education. However, up to now little has been written that addresses the need for assessment in relation to transition planning and programming for students with disabilities. In this chapter, we provide a framework to facilitate comprehensive transition assessment and evaluation. Using the framework of outcomes and indicators, we describe a levels approach to transition assessment, types of assessment, layers to be involved in the assessment process, and how to use the information to plan and adjust transition programming. Other transition-related assessments, including GEDs, entrance and certification exams, are also discussed.

Students who receive special education services are assessed frequently during their school careers. The purposes for these assessments vary, as do the consequences of the students' participation in them. Most educators agree that the initial assessment to determine eligibility for special education services is the most critical of all assessments of students with disabilities. Second in importance are transition assessments.

The Individuals with Disabilities Education Act (IDEA) suggests that assessment and evaluation are a part of transition services (see Box 11.1). In addition, states are to include students with disabilities in general state and districtwide assessment programs, many of which occur during transition ages. The role of assessment and evaluation has been defined in the School-to-Work Opportunities Act, which clearly is intended to include students with disabilities. In

---

BOX 11. 1

"Transition services" means a coordinated set of activities for a student with a disability, designed within an outcome-oriented process, that promotes movement from school to postschool activities, including, but not limited to, postsecondary education; vocational training, integrated, competitive employment (including supported employment); continuing and adult education; adult services; independent living; or community participation. The coordinated set of activities must be based on the individual student's needs, taking into account the student's preferences and interests, and shall include needed activities in the following areas:

1.   instruction
2.   community experiences
3.   the development of employment and other postschool adult living objectives
4.   if appropriate, acquisition of daily living skills and functional vocational evaluation
     (34 CFR 300.18)

---

this act, assessment and evaluation are mentioned in both the school-based learning and connecting activities components (of which there are three: school-based learning, work-based learning, and connecting activities). With respect to the school-based component (Section 102), the act requires:

(5) regularly scheduled evaluation involving ongoing consultation and problem-solving with students and school dropouts to identify their academic strengths and weaknesses, academic progress, workplace knowledge, goals, and the need for additional learning opportunities to master core academic and vocational skills.

For the connecting activities (Section 194), the act requires:

(7) collecting and analyzing information regarding post-program outcomes of participants in the School-to-Work Opportunities program to the extent practicable, on the basis of socioeconomic status, race, gender, ethnicity, culture, and disability, and on the basis of whether the participants are students with limited English proficiency, school dropouts, disadvantaged

students or academically talented students.

These requirements reinforce the importance of assessment and evaluation during transition.

OVERVIEW

The purpose of this chapter is to explore the role of assessment and evaluation at the time of transition and transition planning. In doing this, we have chosen to consider both traditional transition-related assessments, those used for the purpose of making decisions about individual students, and other assessments that students of transition age will encounter.

After defining the terms "assessment" and "evaluation" within the context of the different purposes of assessments that may be used during the transition years, we examine (a) why assessment and evaluation are important during transition, (b) the components of comprehensive transition assessments, (c) the use of assessments to evaluate and adjust programs, and (d) the participation of students with disabilities in other transition-related assessments. As we explore these topics, we address their relevance for the diversity of students receiving special education services in today's schools, from students with "invisible" disabilities to those with the most severe cognitive and physical disabilities. At the same time, we keep in mind the ethnic and socioeconomic diversity reflected in these students.

Definitions

The terms "assessment" and "evaluation" are sometimes defined very specifically to mean different things, yet at other times they are used interchangeably. Consistent with Salvia and Ysseldyke (1995), we use the term "assessment" to mean collecting data to make decisions. Salvia and Ysseldyke (1995) defined thirteen types of decisions that can be made, ranging from prereferral decisions to decisions about program effectiveness. The decisions can be made in relation to individual students (e.g., What are the student's strengths? What instructional procedures does the student need? Is the program meeting the student's needs?) or to programs (e.g., Are the overall goals of the program being achieved?).

Evaluation experts (cf. Worthen & Sanders, 1987), while recognizing the many alternative evaluation approaches, generally define "evaluation" to mean the procedures used to determine the *worth* of something. For example, program evaluation usually refers to the process of holding a program up to a set of standards to determine where the standards are met and where they are not met.

In this chapter, we talk about data collection that covers both "assessment" and "evaluation." When we discuss "assessment," we are referring to the collection of data on students to make decisions about students. When we talk about "evaluation," we are referring to the collection of data to make decisions about programs. We believe it is not the specific term that is important, however, but rather the act of collecting data to make decisions. And, we argue that there are many types of decisions that educators do not typically consider that would influence the nature of assessment during transition.

Why Assessment and Evaluation Are Important During Transition

Transition through school or out of school occurs regardless of whether there is good assessment-based planning about how it should occur. For a long time, educators were not required to document a plan for the student's movement through school to a postschool environment of work, postsecondary education, or other activity. Without a plan, there was nothing against which success could be measured. In fact, it is the poor postschool outcomes of students with disabilities, the lack of planning for the transition of these students, and the failure to define what the important outcomes of education for these students are that probably best explain why assessment and evaluation are so important during transition.

Poor Postschool Outcomes. For some time, questions have been raised about the efficacy of schooling for students graduating from American schools (see International Association for the Evaluation of Educational Achievement, 1987; Secretary's Commission on Achieving Necessary Skills, 1991). These concerns also have been raised for students with disabilities, who in adulthood have been found to be unemployed or underemployed, dependent on others, and dissatisfied with their social lives (Chadsey-Rusch, Rusch, & O'Reilly, 1991; Wagner et al., 1991, 1995; Chadsey-Rusch & Heal, 1995; Wagner, 1995).

Lack of Planning. Before 1990, when transition plans were first required for all students with disabilities, transition was discussed almost exclusively in relation to students with low-incidence disabilities (severe cognitive delays, multiple disabilities). However, findings of poor postschool outcomes made it evident that students with mild disabilities also were having difficulties after completing school, with few graduates finding adequate employment or assuming adult responsibilities (Wehman, Kregel, & Seyfarth, 1985; Rusch & Phelps, 1987). In fact, these students were found to be among the most likely to leave school before graduating, joining the ranks of the dropouts (Wolman, Bruininks, & Thurlow, 1989; Wagner et al., 1991) and leading to many questions about the appropriateness of secondary programs for students with mild disabilities (Edgar, 1987).

Failure to Define Educational Outcomes. Regardless of label or type of disability, it is now clear that the traditional curriculum of basic skill remediation, although perhaps necessary, is not sufficient to prepare students to meet the challenges of society. The traditional secondary program has been shown to be heavily academic-oriented and too often focusing on basic skill remediation for students with disabilities (Edgar, 1987). Why so many students' schooling was unrelated to their postschool success has been attributed to some degree to the failure to define what the important outcomes of their education were, and to the associated lack of information about how students were progressing toward those outcomes (DeStefano & Wagner, 1992).

A Framework for a Comprehensive Transition Assessment and Evaluation

IDEA refers to a variety of postschool activities that could be targeted when thinking about transition assessment and evaluation. Some say that the essential components of successful transition are employment, independent living, and community integration. Others go into much more detail about what the important components are. Overall, however, there is agreement that, as indicated in IDEA, the focus must be on the outcomes of the process rather than the process itself.

Outcomes of Education. In 1990, the National Center on Educational Outcomes (NCEO) was funded to work with states and federal agencies to develop a conceptual model of educational outcomes for students with disabilities. Very early in its efforts to do so, NCEO

staff met with numerous general and special educators, policy makers, and parents. Despite the diversity of the individuals involved, they all supported a unified system of educational outcomes and indicators (National Center on Educational Outcomes, undated). NCEO then proceeded to pull together hundreds of stakeholders to first reach agreement on what outcomes and indicators were (Ysseldyke & Thurlow, 1993a), and then to identify the important outcomes and indicators for youngsters at age 3, age 6, grade 4, grade 8, school completion, and postschool.

The basic model of outcomes developed through the work of NCEO, which is portrayed in Figure 11.1, includes eight domains:

1. Presence and Participation—opportunities for physical presence as well as active and meaningful participation in school and the community by all individuals.

2. Accommodation and Adaptation—availability and use of adjustments, adaptive technologies, or compensatory strategies that are necessary to achieve outcomes.

3. Physical Health—extent to which the individual demonstrates or receives support to engage in healthy behavior, attitudes, and knowledge related to physical well-being.

4. Responsibility and Independence—extent to which the individual's behavior reflects the ability to function, with appropriate guidance or support, independently or interdependently, and to assume responsibility for oneself.

5. Contribution and Citizenship—individual gives something back to society or participates as a citizen in society.

6. Academic and Functional Literacy—use of information to function in society, to achieve goals, and to develop knowledge.

7. Personal and Social Adjustment—individual demonstrates socially acceptable and healthy behaviors, attitudes, and knowledge regarding mental well-being, either alone or with guidance and support.

CONCEPTUAL MODEL OF OUTCOMES

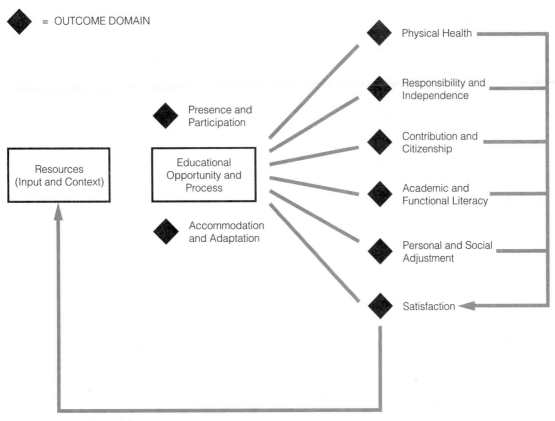

FIGURE 11.1 NCEO Model.

Sources: Ysseldyke, Thurlow, & Gilman (1993b). Reprinted by permission.

8. Satisfaction—favorable attitude is held toward education.

The specific outcomes for the three levels directly relevant for transition planning (grade 8, school completion, and postschool) are listed in Table 11.1.

On one hand, the NCEO model provides a framework for evaluating how well transition programs are meeting students' needs. On the other hand, it also can provide a framework for thinking about the assessment of students for transition planning. In general, what we know about transition outcomes has not evolved from a theoretical framework (DeStefano & Wagner, 1992). It is likely, therefore, that the numerous guides, pamphlets, and books available on transition planning also lack a framework for thinking about the important domains.

After reaching agreement among stakeholders on a set of outcomes, NCEO continued to work with them to identify indicators of those outcomes. Indicators are needed so that data requirements and possible sources of data can be identified. For each of the outcomes identified in the NCEO documents, indicators of those outcomes were also identified, anywhere from one to six per outcome. For example, for the

Table 11.1 Outcomes in NCEO Model at Grade 8, End of School, and Postschool

Domain	Grade 8	School Completion	Postschool
Presence and participation	(A1) Is present in school	(A1) Is Present in school	(A1) Is in community
	(A2) Participates	(A2) Participates	(A2) Participates in the community
		(A3) Completes school	(A3) Is employed
Accommodation and adaptation	(B1) Uses enrichments, adaptations, accommodations, or compensations necessary to achieve outcomes in each of the major domains	(B1) Makes adaptations, accommodations, or compensations necessary to achieve outcomes in each of the major domains	[No outcomes were identified for this domain at the postschool level.]
	(B2) Demonstrates the presence of family	(B2) Demonstrates family support and coping skills	
Physical health	(C1) Makes healthy life-style choices	(C1) Makes healthy life-style choices	(C1) Makes healthy life-style choices
	(C2) Is aware of basic safety, fitness, and health care needs	(C2) Is aware of basic safety, fitness, and health care needs	(C2) Is aware of basic safety, fitness, and health care needs
	(C3) Is physically fit	(C3) Is physically fit	(C3) Is physically fit
Responsibility and independence	(D1) Demonstrates age-appropriate independence	(D1) Gets about in the environment	(D1) Gets about in the environment
	(D2) Gets about in the environment	(D2) Is responsible for self	(D2) Is responsible for self
	(D3) Is responsible for self	(D3) Functions independently	
Contribution and citizenship	(E1) Complies with school and community rules	(E1) Complies with school and community rules	(E1) Complies with school and community rules
	(E2) Knows the significance of voting	(E2) Knows the significance of voting and procedures necessary to register to vote	(E2) Votes
	(E3) Volunteers	(E3) Volunteers	(E3) Volunteers
			(E4) Pays taxes
Academic and functional literacy	(F1) Demonstrates competence in communication	(F1) Demonstrates competence in communication	(F1) Demonstrates competence in communication
	(F2) Demonstrates competence in problem-solving strategies and critical thinking skills	(F2) Demonstrates competence in problem-solving strategies and critical thinking skills	(F2) Demonstrates competence in problem-solving strategies and critical thinking skills
	(F3) Demonstrates competence in math, reading, and writing skills	(F3) Demonstrates competence in math, reading, and writing skills	(F3) Demonstrates competence in math, reading, and writing skills used in daily life
	(F4) Demonstrates competence in other academic and nonacademic areas	(F4) Demonstrates competence in other academic and nonacademic areas	(F4) Demonstrates competence in other academic and nonacademic areas
	(F5) Demonstrates competence in using technology	(F5) Demonstrates competence in using technology	(F5) Demonstrates competence in using technology

(continued)

Table 11.1 *(continued)*

Domain	Grade 8	School Completion	Postschool
Personal and social adjustment	(G1) Copes effectively with personal challenges, frustrations, and stressors	(G1) Copes effectively with personal challenges, frustrations, and stressors	(G1) Copes effectively with personal challenges, frustrations, and stressors
	(G2) Has a good self-image	(G2) Has a good self-image	(G2) Has a good self-image
	(G3) Respects cultural and individual differences	(G3) Respects cultural and individual differences	(G3) Respects cultural and individual differences
	(G4) Gets along with other people	(G4) Gets along with other people	(G4) Gets along with other people
Satisfaction	(H1) Student satisfaction with school experience	(H1) Student satisfaction with high school experience	(H1) Individual's satisfaction with high school experience
	(H2) Parent/guardian satisfaction with education that student is receiving	(H2) Parent/guardian satisfaction with education that students received	(H2) Parent/guardian satisfaction with education that students received
	(H3) Community satisfaction with education that student is receiving	(H3) Community satisfaction with education that students received	(H3) Community satisfaction with current status of individual

Sources: Grade 8: Ysseldyke, Thurlow, Erikson (1994a). School completion: Ysseldyke, Thurlow, & Gilman (1993b). Postschool: Ysseldyke, Thurlow, & Gilman (1993a). All reprinted with permission.

outcome "Gets about in the environment" within the Responsibility and Independence domain, four indicators were identified at the school completion level:

D1a Percent of students who can get to and from a variety of destinations

D1b Percent of students who know how to access community services (e.g., rehabilitation, counseling, employment, health, etc.)

D1c Percent of students who complete transactions (shopping, banking, drycleaning, etc.) in the community

D1d Percent of students with a driver's license

These indicators are designed for programs, but could easily be applied to individual students according to need (e.g., "student can get to and from a variety of destinations"). Additional documents prepared by NCEO identify possible sources of data for each of the indicators identified within its model (e.g., Ysseldyke, Thurlow, & Erickson, 1994b; Ysseldyke, Thurlow, & Vanderwood, 1994; Ysseldyke, Thurlow, & Erickson, 1995).

Developing Individualized Outcomes. The NCEO model is not the only model that could be adopted. In fact, NCEO argues that it is necessary for local programs and their constituents to be involved in defining the important outcomes and strongly recommends that they use a consensus-building process to develop their own outcomes to be targeted during transition planning for students (Vanderwood, Ysseldyke, & Thurlow, 1993; Ysseldyke & Thurlow, 1993b). This personalized model then can be used to help design an assessment plan that complements the requirements identified in law and meets the needs of individual students. It is very important to identify what stakeholders consider to be the important outcomes, and then design assessments to address those domains.

ASSESSMENT APPROACHES

In order to plan thoroughly for transition, appropriate assessments must be conducted. According to federal law, all students receiving special education services must receive IEP transition planning no later than age 14. Assessment for transition takes many forms and varies from state to state. Some state regulations require that planning start earlier. For example, New York requires that transition assessment and planning begin "for those students age 15 (and at a younger age, if determined appropriate)" (8 NYCRR 200.4(c)(2)), and preplanning or screening as early as age 12. Not only do the age requirements vary state to state, so do the levels of assessment that are required. Regardless of these specific requirements, in order to maximize planning and use of available instructional time, instructional content and activities must be coordinated among elementary, middle, and secondary programs.

Furthermore, consideration must be given to the level of support a student needs in both current and future environments. For example, a student with a mild learning disability or speech/language impairment may require a different level of assessment and planning timeline than a student with moderate to more involved disabilities. Postschool environments (social, vocational, community, employment) will vary from student to student regardless of skill and ability. Therefore, it is important that assessment for transition be individually tailored, ongoing, and include input from all the players involved in the student's postsecondary school life.

The purpose of this section is to review transition-assessment options, including who to involve, formal and informal assessments, and evaluation of the process itself. In order to be effective, planning for transition services must (a) involve the student and other stakeholders to the greatest extent possible; (b) use relevant data for developing instruction and services; and (c) provide natural sustained supports that truly meet the needs of the student. Furthermore, it is extremely important to evaluate the degree to which the transition IEP is moving the student toward the ultimate test—living in society. Exactly how well is the student being prepared? How do we know? Much is written on the process of transition IEP development for stu-

dents with disabilities. However, there is little or nothing that addresses evaluation of the process itself.

Levels of Assessment

Assessment for transition can be divided into three levels (Maxam, 1985). The movement from level to level depends on individual student needs. All students do not need to progress from level to level. In fact, some stay at Level 1 for their entire transitional school-based planning. Other students who need more intense services and supports may move to Levels 2 and 3. All levels, however, have the same end purpose—to identify a student's potential, needs, functional abilities, interests, skills, aptitudes, and achievement relative to what is needed to be successful in both current and future environments (Berkell & Brown, 1989).

Level 1. Level 1 is the initial process of screening to arrive at a decision for providing transitional services or instruction. Several domains are examined. At a minimum, they include instruction, community experience, development of employment and/or postsecondary living objectives, and acquisition of daily living skills (if appropriate). Information about the student's interests, strengths, needs, and preferences is gathered. Level 1 assessment typically consists of collecting information via:

- Interviews with the student
- Interviews with the parent/guardian or other family members
- Interviews with teachers
- Compilation of existing information
- Review of records

This assessment or information-gathering stage can be performed by anyone who knows the student. Often, this level of assessment falls within the role of the school counselor as part of a required annual guidance review or is performed by the classroom teacher. For many students with disabilities, this is the level they maintain throughout their schooling career. Information gathered at this level is specific enough to allow for instructional plans, experiences, and IEP goals to be developed.

Level 2. Level 2 (see Case Study 1) involves a more indepth study of student needs. Thus, vocational counseling and/or additional psychoeducational assessment may be completed. Level 2 may also include skills analysis or job matching (see "Informal Assessment," this chapter) that considers the transferability and alignment of student skills and interest in a vocation. Level 2 information, which is added to Level 1 information, can be obtained by examining:

- Vocational evaluation
- Educational evaluation
- Additional psychological evaluation
- Present levels of performance
- Degree of involvement in community and respective agencies

Level 3. This is a systematic and comprehensive process that involves the vocational assessment, also known as a vocational evaluation. Level 3 assessment is considered formal and should be performed by personnel trained in such assessments. The vocational evaluation has been described from various perspectives (Vocational Evaluation and Work Adjustment Association, 1975; Peterson, Madden, & Ley-Siemer, 1981; Sitlington et al., 1985), and defined as:

> a holistic approach which considers an individual's total career development [whose purpose] is to collect and provide objective career information for parents, educators, the student, and others to use in planning appropriate education experiences to enhance the student's employability. (Peterson & Hill, 1982:1)

This vocational assessment is performed with the goal of identifying individual interests, strengths, education, and training needs. This information, in turn, provides the basis for plan-ning an individualized, comprehensive transition program. (See Case Study 2.)

Who Is Involved in the Transition Assessment?

In the traditional sense, multidisciplinary teams have been responsible for processing referrals for assessment in order to ascertain the need for special education services. The major purpose of this assessment has been to identify or diagnose problems and prescribe appropriate services to meet the students educational needs. The IEP meeting that is held for this purpose must include (according to Public Law 105-17) parents, at least one regular education teacher if the student participates in regular education, at least one special education teacher or provider, an LEA representative knowledgeable about specially designed instruction, general curriculum, and availability of resources, a person who can interpret the instructional implications of evaluation results, and, at the discretion of the parents, others who have knowledge or expertise.

For transitional assessment and planning, information is obtained from these and many other individuals. Additional potential players could include the student, peers, parents and other family members, people from a receiving agency, community service personnel, admissions department personnel, and/or family services people. The timing and intensity of the involvement of other people are directly related to the intensity of need and the planning timeline for the student. For example, these people may not be involved in an initial Level 1 assessment of a 12-year-old. However, an ongoing or initial Level 1 assessment of a 15- or 16-year-old, depending on transition goals and the number of school years left, might precipitate their active participation. A transition-planning process referred to as "personal futures planning" (Amado & Lyon, 1991), in which a group of people work together to bring about social change for one individual, generally involves only those individuals intimately linked to the focus individual, and thus may involve a limited

CASE STUDY 1

This case study highlights the transition planning process of a student with mild to moderate learning disabilities. It illustrates the assessment and planning process over the middle school and high school years.

Jamaal is a seventh-grade student with disabilities. Jamaal attends a first-ring suburban school and receives resource room services on a daily basis. Jamaal was originally diagnosed with learning disabilities in reading comprehension and expressive writing in grade 4. At the conclusion of grade 7, Jamaal and his guardian met with his resource room teacher to complete a Level 1 assessment. As a result of this screening, Jamaal's initial career interests and immediate transition needs were identified. Jamaal indicated he would "like to be a veterinarian." Relevant areas in need of further development included developing general independence, task perseverance, and a greater awareness of what is required of someone planning to attend a postsecondary veterinarian school. Although Jamaal was interested in this career, his guardian wondered how realistic it was, given Jamaal's disabilities. It was felt that by having Jamaal "look into" the career, he might gain a better perspective on whether he was "capable" of pursuing it. As a result of the assessment and meeting, transition goals for Jamaal's IEP included increasing his independence in the school setting, exploring the career of a veterinarian by reading and gathering information, increasing task perseverance and completion of independent assignments, homework and projects, and developing the ability to make his needs known and access support for them.

The resource room teacher created an academic goal that integrated Jamaal's interest in becoming a vet, the need to increase independence and task perseverance, and the continued need to remediate and instruct expressive writing skills. The IEP goal stated:

> Jamaal will increase his career awareness of Veterinarians by gathering information about the career and respective requirements and write an informational report summarizing his findings.

Three years later, as a tenth grader and as a part of an annual process, Jamaal's current transition goals were reviewed. Jamaal's needs were still within the Level 1 assessment process. He did not require any further assessment. Information gathered from his current progress reports, report cards, and stakeholders was sufficient to warrant continued comprehensive planning for Jamaal's transition to postsecondary life. During this IEP meeting, specific needs were identified that Jamaal needed for a smooth transition into a local university to start his path of schooling to become a veterinarian. At this conference, with both Jamaal and his guardian in attendance, the guardian indicated that he could not believe how the time had flown by. The guardian reflected on the initial Level 1 meeting at which time Jamaal announced he wanted to be a veterinarian. And, here it was 3 years later, actually planning for that career. "I really thought he would have changed his mind several times. Even though he did think of other careers he always came back to this one."

In reviewing the current accommodations stated on Jamaal's IEP, it was clear that the need for a reader, clarifying directions, and extended time for written assignments continued and had to be integrated into his postsecondary schooling. As a result of this meeting and assessment, Jamaal's transition goals were written as follows:

1. Jamaal will go to the career center and begin to identify geographic locations and schools with veterinarian programs.
2. Upon locating a school of choice, Jamaal, with assistance of his school counselor, will contact the admissions office to obtain an application and gather more specific information about the school and available supports for students with special needs.

As an eleventh grader, Jamaal's last high school IEP was developed. Jamaal would graduate from high school as a twelfth grader, age 17. Transition goals for Jamaal's IEP included:

1. Jamaal will independently enroll and complete a preparation course for the SAT offered by the school district.
2. Jammal will, with assistance from his school counselor, sign up for and take the SAT.
3. Jamaal will actively participate in the application process to several schools of choice.

(continued)

CASE STUDY 1   *(continued)*

---

4. Jamaal will learn how to access postsecondary education support services at the school of acceptance.

   Jamaal successfully completed his transition IEP goals, was accepted into a program, and is currently completing his second year of schooling. With the coordinated support of the campus services for special needs students, Jamaal has been able to maintain the level of support and assistance needed to be successful in his program.

---

number of people. This type of planning is discussed in Chapter 10.

Students. Students are central to the entire transition-assessment process. They directly provide the team with information to use in collaboratively pursuing a student-focused direction for both assessment and planning for program instruction. Based on a student's skills, abilities, and testimony, the team can tailor assessment to these, as well as to identified short- and long-term goals and objectives. Chapter 7 discusses in detail the various areas of student involvement in the overall transition process.

Parents and Other Family Members. Input and observations from parents and other family members are an important part of the transition-assessment and -planning process. In many cultures it is not just the biological parent who has responsibility for rearing a child. Extended family members may also be integral participants in the life of the student. It is important to find this out and include them as equal members in the planning process. Parents and other family members have the unique perspective of seeing how the student functions outside the school environment.

Peers. A student's peers often can provide a rich pool of information valuable to the transition-planning process. Information about the development and daily use of social skills, self-advocacy and work habits, to name a few, can be gleaned directly from the participation of one or more of the student's peers.

Agency Personnel. Vocational counselors, social workers, case workers from Family Services and Social Security, and mental health providers are among the many agency personnel who can assist in an assessment. They also can help determine eligibility and next steps in applying for services. These personnel can provide information about their domain of services that pertain to transition needs and planning for a student.

Employers. Both current and past employers can provide information about the skills needed to be successful in specific work settings. This type of information can be used in direct instruction on skills needed for success in work settings. If the student is currently working, the employer can report on the student's work habits, strengths, and areas of needed remediation.

Community Personnel. Community agency personnel can provide information on services such as transportation, available support services, advocacy services, housing, recreation, and leisure activities within the community or area of potential residence of the student.

Postsecondary Personnel. Personnel from postsecondary education settings such as community colleges, universities, and technical colleges provide a valuable perspective. They can

CASE STUDY 2

This case study highlights the transition-planning process of a student with moderate mental retardation. It illustrates the assessment and planning process over the middle school and high school years.

Kim is a fifth-grade student with disabilities. Kim was initially diagnosed with mental retardation at birth. She received self-contained special education services until grade 2, when she began the inclusive schooling process. At the end of her sixth year of school, at the middle school, a Level 1 assessment was conducted with Kim's parents, current teacher, school counselor, and school psychologist. The result of the screening revealed several areas of concern and need. Kim's future environments, both daily living and vocational, were discussed. Kim's parents indicated that they believed that Kim would need much assistance in preparing for postsecondary school life. In fact, they were not aware of what options were available to her. With assistance from the school psychologist and counselor, vocational programs within the district were explained. External support services were discussed. Appointments were made for the parents to visit the vocational programs and meet with agency personnel to gain an awareness of available supports. As a result of the initial Level 1 screening, the immediate transition need areas for Kim included developing the skills to ask for assistance when confronted with a problem-solving situation, continuing to develop the social skills needed to work cooperatively on tasks, reaching a level of automaticity on functional money skills, and developing skills to allow her to be an office volunteer.

Three years later, as an eighth grader, a Level 2 assessment was completed by Kim's special education teacher, school counselor, and school psychologist. Level 2 assessment included an observation of Kim in her current educational program and her volunteer office work. The school psychologist administered an interest inventory and a functional assessment in the area of reading and writing and math. In addition, the special education teacher, in collaboration with Kim's general education teachers, completed a survey checklist of work behaviors and attitudes. At the transition-planning meeting, input from IEP members and the assessment results were used to write transition goals. It was decided that Kim would participate in a 20-week vocational orientation program as a ninth grader. During this time Kim would be exposed to a variety of career and vocational opportunities. At the end of the 20 weeks, Kim would select one program in which she would major for the remainder of her school years. Transition goals were written reflecting the skills Kim needed in order to successfully participate in the program:

1. Kim will participate in a vocational exploratory program.
2. Kim will develop the skills necessary to independently ride the bus to and from the vocational center.
3. Kim will continue to develop communication skills to allow her to make her needs known in an age-appropriate manner.
4. Kim will develop the skills necessary to work a task or job to completion, stopping only when directed by the teacher or supervisor.

At the conclusion of ninth grade, Kim decided that she wanted to major in horticulture. In preparation for her grade 10 annual review and continued transition planning, Level 2 and Level 3 assessments were conducted. For the Level 2 assessment, the school psychologist conducted a situational assessment of Kim's functioning within the horticulture program. These results were shared not only with immediate stakeholders, but also with the assessor for the Level 3 vocational assessment. As a result of these assessments, specific strengths and needs were identified. Although Kim was meeting with success in her vocational program, she lacked the knowledge, experience, and mobility skills to take a metro bus to a potential work site. Kim also showed needs in the areas of asking for assistance, initiating tasks unsupervised, personal hygiene, and the ability to adjust to new requests or task assignments. As a result of the assessments, transition IEP goals focused on skills and domains in the areas of responsible and independent functioning, personal and social adjustment, physical health, and academic and functional literacy. The immediate needs of mobility and specific task-related areas were addressed by a community-based trainer who taught Kim how to ride a metro bus independently. While under the guidance of a job coach, Kim began working two half-days per week in a local florist shop. The job coach used a functional checklist to document Kim's progress and development of skill independence.

Kim successfully completed her high school vocational program and secured a job with the florist where she had trained. Kim independently transports herself on a metro bus and has received "excellent" work reviews from her boss.

help clarify available disability services as well as requirements for documentation of disability by the student and information needed to identify reasonable accommodations for the postsecondary setting. Input from potential post-secondary institutions provides realistic and grounded perspectives about what skills are expected and the natural supports the student will need to be successful in those settings.

Any and all of the preceding potential team members should be considered for input involvement at the assessment and transition IEP development stages. Based on individual student needs and intensity of support, these players will vary in terms of their input and involvement. For college- or vocational educa-tion–bound students, for example, the school counselor, parent, student, and teacher may be key players. For those moving toward more supported environments, others likely to be involved include agency and community per-sonnel. Assessment for transition planning and IEP development should be based on input from team members selected according to what the student needs to be prepared for transition to postschool environments.

Types of Assessment

Assessment is the process of gathering informa-tion about a student in order to make decisions. Assessment processes range from those that are relatively informal to those that are quite formal.

Formal Assessment. Formal assessment can include any standardized battery that yields targeted information. This is over and above the traditional psychoeducational testing that the student experienced for initial classification. Unfortunately, it is not uncommon to find fragmented evaluations in files of students with disabilities. One of the most significant criticisms of most formal assessment is the inability to translate results into useful planning information.

For transition planning, most psychometric tests have limitations. They tend to focus on large groups of students and the student's relative position in a "normal" population, rather than on individual strengths and abilities. Even indi-vidual psychometric tests have questionable reliability and validity for transition planning because their use for transition planning frequently is not aligned with the purpose of the tests. For example, an achievement test, although yielding important information, may have little predictive validity for how well a student will function in a work setting or in the community. Similarly, it provides limited information on the kind of instruction needed to achieve success in the work environment.

In contrast, *formal vocational assessment* gener-ally takes a holistic approach to assessment. An important component of the vocational assessment is the development of learner profiles that delineate the skill and attributes of the student being assessed (Berkell & Brown, 1989). Learner profiles typically contain information about the following areas: academic, psychologi-cal, psychomotor, medical, social, and vocational information. With the assessment tailored to individual students, it is likely that some, but not all, of these components will be required.

Standardized work samples also are a part of a formal vocational assessment. These work sam-ples are vocational activities that simulate real job tasks and focus on hands-on performance. The success of using work samples is dependent on each student's readiness for this type of assess-ment, the content assessed, and the usability of the information it provides to personnel respon-sible for transition planning. Work sample assess-ments have been published commercially and frequently are locally developed. Work samples are project- or product-oriented and allow for systematic observation and recording of actual on-the-job task requirements.

In sum, formal vocational assessments take on many forms and processes. They are tailored to individual students. Vocational-assessment services may not be available at all schools or districts, but can be obtained usually through contract with a local agency or cooperative. (See also Chapter 5.)

Informal Assessment. Informal assessments can be developed by and for any number of individuals (parents, teachers, students, agencies, employers). Because transition planning is long-range planning, informal assessment is a valuable method to use on an ongoing basis. Informal assessment includes, but is not limited to

- Curriculum-based vocational assessment
- Interviews and questionnaires
- Observations
- Ecological inventories
- Situational assessments
- Interest inventories
- Teacher-made assessments or checklists

There are numerous informal evaluations, both teacher-made and commercially produced. An informal evaluation can be developed to inventory almost any target area. Because these measures are informal and not standardized, it is important that they be directly related to the desired purpose. Informal measures can provide functional information about what a student knows and is able to do. In the same manner, these measures provide the opportunity for instruction in a functional curriculum that is directly aligned with what the student needs to demonstrate in order to be successful in future settings. And the use of informal assessment measures should be guided by student needs that are ultimately linked to outcome domains. Each of these assessments is described briefly here.

Curriculum-Based Vocational Assessment (CBVA). CBVA is an assessment procedure that is directly linked to the curriculum, both school- and job-specific. CBVA provides integrated information from and within multiple service environments. The strength of this type of assessment is its direct relevance to the student's existing curricula and alignment to needed instruction and skill

development for the targeted setting (West et al., 1992). CBVA is driven by the collection of performance-based information that is needed in order to make informed decisions about programming and placement for individual students.

A fundamental premise of CBVA is that valuable vocational-assessment information can be gathered by effectively using the existing resources within an environment. It can be administered via a performance-based activity within a vocational framework. This entails collecting targeted information over time and in a variety of settings. By synthesizing this assessment information, we are able to obtain a complete picture of the student's current strengths, needs, and characteristics specific to both the current curriculum and that which is expected of the student in other environments. For example, independence is an important skill, regardless of setting. Skills of independence might include attendance, punctuality, following a schedule, hygiene, initiation of tasks, working with others, and taking a break. A CBVA can be performed within the student's current setting and curriculum to assess which of these skills are present and which need to be further developed. In turn, these skills can be assessed again in any specific environment where they are needed for success.

For example, a student working in a retail clothing store's receiving department may be responsible for placing incoming clothes on hangers and then onto racks, to be later sorted by size. In this vocational environment, the student needs independent skills to complete the task of hanging clothes, as well as those needed to promptly take mid-morning, late-afternoon, and lunch breaks. This is a difficult task for many individuals. It is not uncommon for a student to work through the day without any formal break unless told to take one, for example. Nor is it uncommon for a student to become distracted by something in the work environment that impedes job completion.

With CBVA, we can use the actual setting, the clothing receiving department, to assess whether the student has the skills needed to work in the environment independently, while following the state labor board mandates. This job also could be simulated and assessed within the student's classroom. CBVA allows us the opportunity to assess and plan, in a variety of settings, for what skills need to be learned and how they can be developed to promote student success.

Interviews and Questionnaires. Different people are part of different circles of a student's life and are able to provide important information from different perspectives. These individuals include parents and other family members, students, friends, physicians, counselors, employers, neighbors, extracurricular leaders or supervisors, agency personnel, and so forth. Interviews or questionnaires can be developed to elicit specific information regarding transition needs.

There are unlimited numbers of questions that could be asked, it is important to tailor the questions to the specific student and settings. It is often also a good idea to organize questions within broad areas of interest (see Box 11.2). Questions for parents/guardians should reflect a recognition of both the student's age and level of disability involvement (see Box 11.3).

Observations. The immediate setting in which a student participates in various activities is rich with important and valuable information. It may be important to prioritize the many settings students participate in, so that the one that will yield the most information directly relevant to the ultimate goals of transition assessment and instruction is known. For example, if the student will be working in a video store reshelving videos, it is important to observe that student or others completing the required task. In doing so, one can gather information on the scope and sequence of skills required to successfully function in a public business.

Another means of observation is job shadowing. Job shadowing provides students with the opportunity to "shadow" or follow in the footsteps of another person doing the job-related task. Information about the student's accuracy, ability to understand directions, problem solving, motivation, and general skill for the job can be observed. Checklists often are developed from both of these observation methods and are used to instruct the student in preparation for transition into the work setting (see Box 11.4).

Ecological Inventories. Along the same line, ecological assessment or inventories help to further delineate the needs of the student within the community. Ecological assessment looks holistically at the student's environment, including variables such as physiological factors (health, allergies, medications); reinforcement history; self-help skills; interactions with community members, teachers, employers, and other employees; as well as physical aspects of the environment (spatial density, seating and working arrangements) (Boyer-Stephens, 1992).

The purpose of an ecological inventory is to assess the characteristics of a community environment in relation to student abilities. By analyzing current and future environments in which a student spends time and the needed skills, one can determine the abilities that are required to be successful there. For example, in analyzing a community college program, a potential future environment for a variety of students with disabilities, issues surrounding course requirements and/or mobility could be identified. Other areas could include those associated with dormitory living, library use, or socializing. A common inventory use is to identify ecologically or environmentally specific mobility needs of incoming freshmen (see Box 11.5). By using ecological inventories, we can consider levels of skill development and experience relative to those needed to be successful in the future campus environment and tailor needed instruction accordingly.

Situational Assessments. Situational assessments in community jobs, general community, and school environments allow systematic observation of students in the real environment (see Box 11.6 for an example of a situational assessment of the communication skills of a person in a cashier

---

BOX 11.2

Defining a Vision

1. What are your greatest dreams?
2. What are your greatest fears?
3. What barriers might get in the way of you accomplishing your goals?

Employment/Vocational

1. What would you like to be doing 2 years (5 years, 10 years) from now?
2. What career are you interested in?
3. What would your ideal job look like?

Education

1. How do you learn best?
2. What modifications or accommodations do you need in your classes in order to succeed?
3. What are you experiencing difficulty in?

Living Options

1. Where do you want to live after graduation?
2. If you moved to a new community, how would you locate housing?
3. How will you manage your money after you graduate from high school?

Medical/Legal

1. Do you have a doctor and dentist?
2. Who would you contact in case of an emergency?
3. What community persons/agencies can help with medical or legal needs?

Leisure/Recreation

1. What do you like to do for fun?
2. Is there anything you wish you could learn how to do that you don't know now (e.g., bowling, swimming, skiing, painting, knitting, etc.)?

Personal/Family

1. What kinds of things are stressful for you?
2. Who do you include in your circle of friends?
3. How do you resolve conflicts or problems?

BOX 11.3   Parent/Guardian Questionnaire

1. What is your concern for your son/daughter after graduation?
2. What type of employment situation do you think would be most appropriate for your son/daughter?
   _____ Competitive part-time
   _____ Competitive full-time
   _____ Other _____
3. Does your son/daughter have age-appropriate friends?
4. Does your son/daughter communicate needs and disappointments in an age-appropriate manner?
5. Will your son/daughter require assistance in obtaining employment?
6. What kind of assistance will your son/daughter need in a postsecondary academic setting?

BOX 11.4

Observation Checklist

Name: Betty B.   Job: Dishwasher/Kitchen Aide
Date/Time: November 1, 1999   Job Site: Jones College kitchen
Task: Upon arrival to site, Betty will perform and maintain the following skills independently with 100% accuracy for no less than three consecutive sessions.

M—model, V—verbal, I—independent	Dates			
1. Greets co-workers				
2. Hangs coat				
3. Signs/punches in				
4. Locates and puts on apron				
5. Checks dish room for dirty dishes				
6. Loads dirty dishes/trays				
7. Rinses off with sprayer				
8. Pushes through machine				
9. Stacks clean dishes				
10. Checks pot area				
11. Washes dirty pots (rinse/soak)				
12. Stacks pots to dry				
13. Continues with Nos. 6–13 until complete				
14. Checks with boss for other duties				

position). Situational assessments attempt to evaluate general work skills rather than job-specific skills and takes place in the actual education, rehabilitation, employment, training, or community setting (Berkell & Brown, 1989). Assessment activities may be real or simulated. Either way, they provide information about work skills within the targeted environment or setting.

Interest Inventories. Commercially developed interest inventories are available that can be used easily without excessive preparation by teachers. Teacher-developed interest inventories are also appropriate (see Box 11.7 for an example). As with the other types of assessment, interest inventories should be used in combination with other assessments in order to obtain a complete

---

BOX 11.5 Inventory for Campus Mobility Needs

(Y = Yes / N = No / NI = No Information)

1. *Bill* can successfully use the metro bus lines to get to campus.
   Y N NI
2. *Bill* knows how and where to obtain exact change for roundtrip fare.
   Y N NI
3. *Bill* is aware of the appropriate dress needed for waiting at the bus stop in different weather conditions.
   Y N NI
4. Once on campus, *Bill* is able to locate on a map buildings where classes are.
   Y N NI
5. *Bill* is able to physically find the buildings on campus.
   Y N NI
6. Once in building, *Bill* can locate classroom.
   Y N NI
7. After class, *Bill* is able to find his next class and building, arriving on time.
   Y N NI
8. *Bill* is able to find the library from any point on campus.
   Y N NI
9. *Bill* is able to find the Student Union from any point on campus.
   Y N NI
10. *Bill* is able to read a metro bus schedule in order to catch the bus from home or campus, at varying times throughout the day.
    Y N NI
11. *Bill* is able to locate the emergency center, bursars/student records, and recreation center from anywhere on campus.
    Y N NI

BOX 11.6

Name: Patricia

Date:

Job Site: USA Market

Area: Communication Skills

A = Outstanding   B = Satisfactory   C = Marginal   D = Not Satisfactory

Interpersonal Skills

A	B	C	D	
A	B	C	D	1. Tone of voice is age-appropriate, not too loud or too soft.
A	B	C	D	2. Establishes eye contact with customer/person speaking.
A	B	C	D	3. Spoken grammar is free from slang and profanity.
A	B	C	D	4. Listens to questions and directions and follows through correctly.

BOX 11.7   Student Interest Inventory

1. What school subject(s) do you like best?
2. What school subject(s) do you like least?
3. List two strengths you have.
4. List two areas you would like to improve.
5. List the kind of job(s) you would like to have in the future.
6. What would be your dream job?
7. What are your activities and hobbies outside of school?
8. How do you like to spend your free or leisure time?

---

picture of a student's skills, capabilities, and needs.

Teacher-Made Assessments/Checklists. Information can be gathered from observations or systematic task-analysis checklists developed by teachers. Both methods reflect an informal assessment of skills required in target settings—work, social, daily living, or community. Functional checklists can be developed that are directly related to successful functioning in outcome domains. Once administered, teachers can use the information to develop lessons geared toward remediating or expanding needs on the checklist.

New Forms of Assessment. Recently, two forms of assessment have been touted as providing more "authentic" assessments of what students know and are able to do:

- Portfolios
- Performance assessments

These forms of assessment have caught the attention of educational reformers as ways to merge assessments used for program accountability and instructional relevance. Although not really all that "new," we discuss them separately here because of their widespread appeal.

Portfolios. For a long time, portfolios have been an integral part of the evaluation process in the fields of art, music, photography, journalism, commercial arts, and modeling (Winograd & Gaskins, 1992). Portfolios go beyond the simple display of sample products as a means of facilitating judgments about student performance. They serve several purposes: to document student effort, to document student growth and achievement, to augment information from other assessment methods, and to provide a public accounting of the quality of educational programs (Salvia & Ysseldyke, 1995). The use of portfolios is one attempt to provide more relevant assessment to enhance instructional decision making and evaluation of student progress.

This method of assessment may prove useful for transition. In providing employers or postsecondary schools with actual products of student learning, informed decisions can be made about what needs to be done to maintain support or extend learning in the new environment. Obviously, the content of the portfolio should reflect the nature of the plans for transition. That is, if a student is college-bound, a portfolio may be used to support and document the student's capability over and above the admissions process for the school. For those students who are entering directly into the world of work, portfolios can be developed to support and document both the acquired skills needed in the work setting and the quality of the student's work. Aligning the portfolio contents with the targeted work setting is important. For example, the ability to write a five-sentence paragraph may have little to do with the actual job of reshelving videos.

Educators and assessment specialists are far from reaching consensus about what constitutes a portfolio or how one should be used in assessment. We offer it here as a viable option to consider in the process of planning and assessing for transition.

Performance Assessments. The desire to ensure that students graduate with more than basic skills has fueled an interest in performance assessment. Students taking part in performance-based assessment may be asked to write an essay, perform a group experiment, define in writing how they answered a math problem, or keep a portfolio of their best work. Increasingly, states are looking to portfolio and performance assessment systems to get a more complete picture of students' abilities (Thurlow, 1994). It has been argued that American students are the "most tested" and the "least examined" (Resnick & Resnick, 1985). Performance-based assessment provides educators with a means to both measure and tailor instruction to help students meet learning outcomes.

If performance assessments, also referred to as Work Experience Performance Evaluations, are to be used in transition assessment, then they must be used with a specific purpose in mind. As previously noted, for some students, a writing or math performance is rich in information that is directly related to postsecondary plans and settings. For others, assessments will need to be tailored. For example, one performance assessment might entail a student orally describing what steps to take after having missed a metro bus. Another might be demonstrating how to safely cross a street or call for help. Personal Adjustment Training (PAT) is one such performance-based assessment. Used extensively in the city schools of Buffalo, New York, PAT covers the first 40 days on a job site. During this time students are evaluated for skills and strengths and are directly trained in areas that are critical to job success. If after 40 days the student has passed the PAT assessment, the student stays on the job and is paid. If the student is unsuccessful, the student receives additional training, with the cost paid by the state.

Transition planning can be assisted dramatically by putting it within a framework like that mentioned in the previous section. In fact, by organizing the transition IEP around the critical outcome domains, assessment needs for planning and ongoing assessment are facilitated. Furthermore, with this type of organization, IEPs across students can serve as the basis for program evaluation.

Using Assessment to Evaluate and Adjust Programs

Within the past decade, the concept of "accountability" has come to the forefront in education. Assessment for transition is not only about accountability, but program effectiveness. Is the student prepared for the ultimate transition—entering the postsecondary community? Are the program and planning doing what they were intended to do? How do we know? It is not enough to assess, plan, and write transition IEP goals and review them annually. If the ultimate goal of transition planning is to ready students with disabilities for postsecondary life, then we need to evaluate whether students are, in fact, successful in postsecondary life. The notion of conducting an evaluation of the planning process may seem monumental, but then so was the idea of transition itself when it was initially introduced. Unfortunately, despite the need for evaluation, especially of the transition-planning process, such evaluations are often not done or are conducted only in response to requests or legal mandates.

If we do not know for sure what works, how do we decide what programs to continue? Because we are required by law to assess and plan for students with disabilities, which in turn involves multiple players and time to assess, plan, write, and develop IEPs, all of which use taxpayers money, it only makes sense to check whether we are on the "right" course.

There are many pragmatic reasons to initiate and conduct evaluations of the transition-planning process. Such evaluation yields information that can be used to document needs and support requests for additional resources. More importantly, evaluation of the transition-planning process can provide information about what is effective, what is not, and what can be done to improve the process that directly impacts planning for individual students.

Program evaluation needs to be practical and designed to answer questions about students' progress, programming, planning, and respective effectiveness. For example, if we want to know whether community-based instruction and mobility training lead to productive employment and on-time arrival at the job site or other setting, we need to gather information about how to define "productive employment" and how to measure it. In other words, we need to evaluate whether instruction is producing the outcomes we said it would for the individual student.

Evaluation of the process can help determine the effectiveness of individual transition plans and the process itself. It can help identify areas of the process that need reorganizing or restructuring and those that are effective as is. Further evaluation of the transition-planning process can help determine the relationship of the secondary curriculum or student preparation to the success of students with disabilities in postsecondary settings. Is there a correlation between the student's transition IEP plan and success in the targeted setting? If not, why not? For example, does the self-esteem or social skills program used really help the student learn socially acceptable behavior and generalize them to postschool settings? If not, why not? One discovery might be that certain skills need to be taught and retaught throughout a student's career. Evaluation of the planning process can help determine the need for service or program expansion to meet the wide spectrum or continuum of student needs.

One of the most difficult steps in program evaluation is deciding where to begin. If a program has started from a framework like that identified at the beginning of this chapter, then that framework can be used to direct the evaluation process. If a framework has not been used to guide transition planning, one must be developed for its evaluation. Several principles should be kept in mind when beginning to plan for an evaluation of the transition-planning process (Vallecorsa, deBettencourt, & Garriss, 1992).

1. Evaluate only a few indicators of quality at a time. Do not attempt to simultaneously evaluate every aspect of the process.

2. Select a data collection method that is within available resources and timetable. Avoid complex, jargon-filled designs and/or those that create the perception of "extra work." Consider those who will be involved in the evaluation process.

3. Collect information from everyone involved—from students, respective stakeholders to teachers and administration. Consumer satisfaction, perceptions, and achieved outcomes are all vital to the process of such an evaluation.

4. Gather information that will identify strengths and weaknesses of the process, while focusing on how this information may guide actions for improvement. Get specific information that can be operationalized into action plans.

Because transition planning is a process that occurs over several years, we suggest that both formative and summative evaluations be considered. For example, some formative areas could include the following:

1. What do the student's parents or other significant family members think about the process? Do they perceive the transition-planning process to be on the "right track"? What are the bases for these perceptions?

2. What suggestions do parents and/or teachers have about the process and progress the student is making toward the targeted outcomes?

3. What do the students think? How is the plan working for them? Is it helping them?

Providing them with necessary learning experiences? What suggestions do they have?

For those students who age-out (continue in school until the maximum age allowed by state law), leave, or graduate, summative questions need to be asked of the students, parents, and other stakeholders. For example:

1. How did the planning process help? If indication is given otherwise, find out what suggestions or changes would have been helpful in the process. We want to avoid after-the-fact information, so evaluate early and in an ongoing manner. Document what has worked well and which areas are in need of change.

2. Find out how students have adjusted to their targeted postsecondary school settings. What are the indicators of success? What are areas and indicators that are problematic? Find out how to proactively plan for these.

Evaluation questions are endless. Although we recognize that the nature and scope of individual students' needs may vary dramatically, evaluation of the overall transition-planning process is the key. Collaboration, assessment, planning, and writing of transition goals for any student's IEP will take on a similar format. That format or framework is what needs to be evaluated. Is it effective? Does it allow for the best planning possible for each student?

The School-to-Work Act has provided students and educators with the responsibility of long-range planning for postschool life. School personnel are responsible for monitoring and evaluating the quality of instructional programs and service delivery in their schools, districts, and state. We encourage you to think of evaluation of the transition-planning process as more than an externally mandated activity, however. The notion of evaluation goes well beyond the issue of legal compliance. It is a moral and ethical obligation. We need to continually identify and evaluate whether the transition planning meets the needs of students, is in need

of improvement, and provides students with the support needed to achieve their intended outcomes.

OTHER TRANSITION-RELATED ASSESSMENTS

As a result of the implementation of recent educational reform initiatives, students with disabilities of transition age (typically those with "mild" disabilities) are increasingly participating in large-scale assessment programs of one type or another. Large-scale assessments are those given to many students, usually for the purpose of describing how groups of students perform or for making decisions about many individuals. Several large-scale assessments will be important for some students with disabilities of transition age—assessments that are used to verify successful completion of programs, to determine acceptance into new programs, and to certify the attainment of skills needed for some jobs. Under Public Law 105-17, states also will require students to participate in assessments that have no direct consequences for them, but that are important for evaluating the effectiveness of their educational system.

Perhaps the most common large-scale assessments in which transition-age students with disabilities might want to participate include

- Graduation or GED exams
- Entrance exams
- Certification exams

Assessments that have no direct consequence for the student, but in which it is important for students to participate, include

- School reward/sanction exams
- State report exams
- National assessments

These assessments now are directly relevant because they are recognized in Public Law 105-17 as a mechanism of accountability for the results of education for students with disabilities. States are required to encourage the participation of students with disabilities in general state assessments, and to develop an alternate assessment for those students not able to participate in the general assessment. States also are required to report on the number of students with disabilities participating in each type of assessment and to report on performance, in the same manner and with the same regularity as for other students.

There are many reasons why students with disabilities should participate in school, state, and national assessments. At the same time, a number of considerations must be made for students with disabilities who do participate.

Graduation Exams

Increasingly, students are being required to demonstrate that they have attained certain levels of competence before they can receive a graduation diploma (Thurlow, Ysseldyke, & Anderson, in press). The focus on graduation exams follows a decade or so during which students had to demonstrate attainment of specific minimal competencies before they would be considered eligible to receive a diploma (DeStefano & Metzer, 1991).

At the end of 1995, seventeen states required that students pass some kind of exam in order to obtain a standard high school diploma (Bond & Roeber, 1995; Thurlow et al., in press). Three additional states (Arizona, Indiana, and Minnesota) had plans to start using graduation exams within another 1 to 3 years (Thurlow et al., in press). Yet another two states used an exam to add some kind of endorsement to the standard diploma. For example, Oregon recently started to use certificates to verify either initial mastery or advanced mastery in addition to the standard diploma. Students must pass exams to earn these certificates in addition to the standard diploma, which is earned for taking a specific distribution of courses. In West Virginia, students may earn a "warranty" when they receive a diploma. This "warranty" provides employers with certification that the student has achieved a certain level of proficiency; if the employer determines within 5 years that a student is not performing up to that level of proficiency, the student can go back to the school for further education at no cost to the employer. In order to receive the "warranty," students must achieve an acceptable score (defined by the county) on the *California Test of Basic Skills* during the eleventh grade.

For students with disabilities whose transition plans include attainment of a standard diploma (rather than a certificate of attendance or completion), the role of the graduation exam must be considered, and this must be done with consideration of the state in which the student lives. In Table 11.2 we have listed, for those states with graduation exams, the requirements for students with disabilities to obtain the standard diploma. It should be noted that local education agencies sometimes have the option of establishing more stringent requirements than those mandated by the state.

As is evident in Table 11.2, for the seventeen states with existing graduation exams, five indicated that the student with disabilities could be exempted from the test. When this happens, the student still can earn a standard diploma in these states. In the twelve other states, the student shifts into a special diploma or certificate option when exempted from the test. Increasingly, it will be important for those concerned with the transition of students with disabilities to know exactly what their state (and local) requirements are for graduation from high school. Although there are many who argue that all students with disabilities should receive a standard diploma for successful completion of their programs (Smith & Puccini, 1995), many state policies do not reflect this viewpoint. State and local requirements will affect the transition plans that are made for the majority of students with disabilities.

What do we know about graduation exams? We know that they cover an array of content areas (see Table 11.3), most focusing on reading,

Table 11.2 States with Exit Exams and Requirements for Students with Disabilities

State	Requirements for Students with Disabilities to Earn Diploma
Alabama	Same—Must have required Carnegie units plus pass the exam. Get certificate if (a) only pass exam, (b) only have required Carnegie units, or (c) complete IEP.
Florida	Courses to meet coursework requirements can be modified, but must pass High School Competency Test in reading, writing, and math. Otherwise, eligible for special diploma.
Georgia	Same—Must have required Carnegie units, plus adequate attendance, plus pass the exam. Get High School Performance Certificate if only meet attendance and Carnegie unit requirements. Get Special Education Diploma if complete IEP, but do not meet other requirements.
Hawaii	Same—Must have required Carnegie units plus pass the exam. Get Certificate of Course Completion when all courses are completed but do not pass exam, or when complete IEP.
Louisiana	Courses to meet coursework requirements can be modified, but must pass Graduation Tests in English, language arts, writing, math, science, and social studies. Otherwise, eligible for Certificate of Achievement.
Maryland	Same—Must have required Carnegie units plus pass the exam. Get Certificate if adequate attendance for 4 years beyond grade 8 or 4 years beyond grade 8 and 21 years of age.
Mississippi	Same—Must have required Carnegie units plus pass the exam. Get Certificate of Attendance if complete IEP.
Nevada	IEP may define different standards for obtaining standard diploma.. Adjusted diploma is a local education agency prerogative.
New Jersey	IEP may exempt student from graduation requirements, including exemption from the proficiency test; student still receives a standard diploma.
New Mexico	Student may receive standard diploma for completion of IEP if approved by the local education agency and state superintendent (student may be exempted from the exam). Certificate of Completion is an option for local education agencies, but the state does not recommend it.
New York	Same—Must have required Carnegie units plus pass the exam to receive a Regents diploma. Get a local diploma if coursework is completed and pass the Regents Competency Tests (RCTs). Get an IEP diploma if only complete IEP.
North Carolina	Same—Must have required Carnegie units plus pass the exam. Get Certificate of Graduation if coursework is completed, but do not pass the exam.
Ohio	IEP may excuse student from taking a specific test. Get standard diploma if complete courses, or IEP, plus pass exam or get exempted.
South Carolina	Courses to meet coursework requirements can be modified, but must pass Exit exam for reading, math, and writing. Get Special Education Certificate if only earn credits.
Tennessee	Same—Must have required Carnegie units, satisfactory attendance and behavior, plus pass the exam. Get Certificate if meet all requirements except passing exam. Get Special Education Diploma if complete IEP plus have satisfactory attendance and conduct.
Texas	IEP may exempt student from all or part of exams. Only one diploma available, but three types of seals—regular, advanced, and honors.
Virginia	Same—Must meet required Carnegie units plus pass the exam. Get Special Diploma if complete IEP. Get Certificate for Completion if complete prescribed course of study and do not qualify for diploma.

mathematics, and writing. We do *not* know how many students with disabilities take these exams, nor what percentage pass them. Nor do many of the states in which they are administered know this information. We do know that the extent to which accommodations are allowed during these exams varies and that the types of accommodations allowed vary as well (Thurlow, Scott, & Ysseldyke, 1995a; Thurlow, Ysseldyke, & Silverstein, 1995b). For example, Box 11.8 is an example of guidelines from one of the states with graduation exams that require students

Table 11.3 Content Areas Assessed in Exit Exams[a]

State	Reading	Language Arts[b]	Math	Writing	Science	Social Studies	Other
Alabama	X	X	X				
Florida	X		X	X			
Georgia		X	X	X	X	X	Health
Hawaii	Hawaii State Test of Essential Competencies includes 16 competencies						
Louisiana		X	X	X	X	X	
Maryland	X		X	X			Citizenship
Mississippi	X		X	X			
Nevada	X		X	X			
New Jersey	X		X	X			
New Mexico	X	X	X		X	X	
New York	X		X	X	X		Global Studies, U.S. History, & Government
North Carolina	Currently devising new standards						
Ohio	X		X	X			Citizenship
South Carolina	X		X	X			
Tennessee	X	X		X	X	X	
Texas	X		X	X			
Virginia	Literacy Passport Test (content undefined)						

[a]Information in this table is from 1996 assessments.

[b]Language arts is sometimes combined with English. At other times, English is listed separately. Both alternatives have been coded here simply as Language Arts

with disabilities to pass them in order to receive a diploma.

GED Exams

The General Educational Development (GED) exam is now a widely accepted avenue for documenting mastery of high school-level requirements. This exam assesses performance in reading, mathematics, writing, social studies, and science. Although there has been some evidence that the postschool outcomes of males who receive a GED are not as good as those of males who receive standard high school diplomas (Cameron & Heckman, 1993), there is also evidence that males who earn a GED do derive economic (wage growth) benefits (Murnane, Willett, & Boudett, 1995). The most recent report on this exam (Baldwin, 1995) revealed that of the more than 800,000 individuals tested, nearly 2,000 took special editions of the GED tests (audiocassette, braille, large print), and more than 5,500 accommodations (e.g., extended time, use of reading/optical device, alternative answer recording methods) were used.

Entrance Exams

Increasingly, students with disabilities are taking advantage of a variety of postsecondary education opportunities. To gain access to these experiences, students with disabilities, like other students, must take a variety of entrance exams. These exams can pose significant challenges for students with disabilities, challenges that appear to go above and beyond the typical challenges faced by students without disabilities (see Shokoohi-Yekta & Kavale, 1994).

The ACT and SAT assessments are used by colleges to determine whether students are

---

BOX 11.8

In the Tennessee Comprehensive Assessment Program (TCAP), the following guidelines address the use of accommodations for the competency test:

"Standards and testing procedures concerning the TCAP/CT have been established by the Competency Test Advisory Committee in compliance with provisions established by the Tennessee General Assembly. Allowable test modification(s) may be provided for appropriate students in the actual testing situation. In no case should the modification(s) give the student assistance in interpreting or solving any test item. Modifications in testing may include the following:

- *Flexible Scheduling.* Administer the test in shorter sessions. *If testing within a subtest is to extend beyond one school day, contact your System Testing Coordinator and State Testing for special instructions.*
- *Flexible Setting.* Have the test administered individually or in small groups by a person familiar to the student.
- *Recording Answers.* Allow students to mark answers directly in the test booklet (to be transcribed by school personnel onto an answer sheet), type answers by machine, or indicate answers to a Proctor who will transcribe them onto an answer sheet. If a student marks his/her answers directly in the booklet and the answers are then transcribed onto an answer sheet, have the student write his/her name on the test booklet. *Separate the marked test booklets from unmarked test booklets when packing test materials for return so that the booklets with the student's names and answers will serve as an original record.*
- *Alternative Test Editions.* Administer large-print or Braille tests, provide magnifying devices, or use templates to reduce the amount of visible print on a page.
- *Signing Directions.* Provide signing for hearing-impaired students only on directions normally read aloud to students.

NOTICE: No part of the TCAP/TC, including internal test directions and test items, may be read to students. Extraordinary circumstances may justify special accommodations for the needs of certain students (i.e., blind children who cannot read Braille). However, permission to provide a tape recording of any portion of the test must be obtained from the Director of State Testing through a written request from the local superintendent. All requests will be reviewed in conjunction with the office of Special Education Programs." (Thurlow et al., 1995a:112)

---

eligible for consideration for admission to their programs. These exams usually are administered while the student still is in high school. Both of these exams recognize that some of their test takers have disabilities, and both have a set of guidelines for the use of accommodations during the assessments. Recently, some states have been developing and adopting their own assessments to determine whether students have mastered the skills necessary to enter their higher education institutions. For example, Oregon is developing a proficiency-based admission standards system, involving criterion-referenced tests, common assessment tasks, and teacher verifications, designed to tie admission "directly to a student's demonstrated proficiency, not 'seat time,' credit hours, or other indirect measures of learning" (Conley & Tell, 1995:2; see also Conley, 1994).

When thinking about assessments of students with disabilities during transition planning, it is important to consider the possible participation of students in these exams, and to determine what training experiences are needed, and what types of accommodations are needed by individual students.

Credential Exams

Transition is an appropriate time to begin considering other kinds of exams that the student may face before entry into the world of work.

An increasing number of exams are designed to determine whether an individual can enter a certain line of work, including exams required for individuals to become teachers, realtors, and members of the civil service. It is important to consider these during transition, rather than wait until it is too late.

School Reward/Sanction Exams

The focus on school accountability has increased tremendously in the past decade. What this means is that schools and their staff are increasingly being held accountable for the performance of their students. In several states, accountability is carried out by giving rewards (such as increased funding) or sanctions (removing school leaders, closing the school) to schools whose performance is exceptional in either direction. South Carolina does this by identifying (in a published list) the 300 worst-performing schools in the state. Texas does it by listing both exceptional schools and poorly performing schools. Kentucky gives cash awards to schools that meet their performance targets, with the cash to be used however the staff and site-based councils decide.

Whenever rewards or sanctions are given to schools on the basis of the performance of their students, there is the potential for inappropriate exclusion of students whom the schools see as producing scores that pull down the average performance levels. As soon as some students are not allowed to participate in the assessment, the problem of variable participation rates emerges. This point is illustrated in the scenario presented in Box 11.9, a scenario that is not uncommon according to administrators, teachers, and parents.

Why do we need to worry about this type of exclusion when a student is of transition age? Many unintended consequences can occur when a student is excluded so that school performance levels will be higher. Of most concern is the frequent finding that when a student is not part of an accountability system that is seen as important, concern about the education of that student becomes less than it otherwise would be (Ysseldyke, Thurlow, & Geenen, 1994; Geenen, Thurlow, & Ysseldyke, 1995). If teachers know that a student will not take an accountability test or that how a student performs on the accountability test will not be counted, that teacher is less likely to have a sense of urgency to make sure that the student will master the concepts to be tested. Furthermore, the student is denied the opportunity to benefit from the testing experience. The trauma of assessment is a threat that does not apply more to the student with disabilities than to others. It is something that needs to be dealt with through proper preparation, training in test-taking skills, and feedback.

It is easier for most people to understand how students with relatively mild disabilities could be included in an accountability system, particularly when appropriate accommodations are provided, than it is for them to understand how an accountability system can include all students. Kentucky has taken an approach that provides for the participation of all students in the statewide accountability system, by allowing some small percentage of students to participate in an alternate portfolio system. Most students in the state of Kentucky participate in the regular assessment, which consists of performance items and portfolios, both relatively new forms of assessment. All students must participate in this system, unless it is determined that they have a cognitive or other disability that is so severe that they are unable to participate. The latter students may participate in the alternate portfolio, which does not have the same requirements as the regular portfolio, but which counts into the school score the same as that of any other student (see scenario in Box 11.10). Students who do not participate either through the regular assessment or the alternate portfolio receive a score of zero, which then counts toward the average school score.

It is important also to know whether students' scores count in accountability systems if

BOX 11.9

In a large urban school district, the scores of students on the state achievement test are used to determine which schools receive rewards for high achievement. Every year at this time, the principal makes an extra effort to call the parents of those students who are not performing well. He suggests to these parents that on the day for which the test is scheduled, they might want to have their child stay home because of the stress that the assessment is likely to place on the child. The principal conveys concern for the emotional well-being of the students, indicating at the same time that the students would be much better off studying at home than taking the test.

they take the tests. Some states have decided that students in special education should take an assessment, but that their scores do not count into the accountability scores. Sometimes the scores of students with disabilities are excluded if they have used an accommodation during the assessment. There is much variability in practice from state to state, again leading to concerns about the policies that drive these systems. When students' scores are excluded, their scores may or may not be aggregated in other ways so that the information is available.

Other Statewide and National Exams

Not all exams are used for accountability. Both at the state and the national level, exams are administered to students so that scores can be used to describe the status of students' educational performance. It is important for students with disabilities to be included in these tests as well as the tests already discussed. Participation

in such exams prepares students for other exams in which it is important for them to participate, and ensures that educators and policy makers know that schools really are responsible for all students.

CONCLUSIONS

The role of student assessment and evaluation in transition planning and *process* is increasing in importance. Today, we recognize perhaps more than ever before the need to identify the student's skills, the characteristics of the desired future environments, and the skills needed to be successful in those future environments. Consequently, we must devise plans to assist the student to move from current skills to skills needed in the identified future environments, and then keep track of the student's progress toward the desired skills. As we do all this, there are certain things we need to remember.

BOX 11.10

In a small rural state, all students participate in some type of assessment, and their scores are entered into a school score for the school they would attend if they were living at home. This procedure in the state accountability system means that if a student is in a residential educational placement, that student's score is sent back and counted with those of all the other students attending the school. School officials soon realized that they would rather be responsible for what the student was taught, so that they were not dependent on some educational placement to do a good job teaching the student whose score they would have to assume. With this kind of thinking, the school pulled the student back home from the residential placement and is now serving the student within its own building.

Need for Individualization and Consideration of Severity of Disability

Transition planning *is not* a canned curriculum. Likewise, assessment for transition must be student-tailored. The need for individualization in student assessment and evaluation is paramount in the area of transition planning. Along with the need for individualization, however, is the recognition that the assessment must take into consideration the severity of the student's disability.

Need for Comprehensiveness and Knowledge of Future Environments

In order to contribute to effective and efficient transition planning, the transition assessment needs to be comprehensive. This does not mean, however, that every possible approach to assessment, involving every possible stakeholder, has to be used. Rather, it means that it is necessary to define a framework within which student assessment and evaluation is planned and conducted.

Interconnected with the need to be comprehensive is the need for the transition planners and the assessment developers to be knowledgeable about the characteristics of the future environments. Furthermore, it is important to know about the skills that are required to be successful in that future environment, so that it is possible to design instructional programs that will help students move from their current skill level to that needed in future environments.

Need for Evaluation of the Transition-Planning Process

Students receiving special education services have IEPs. Within the IEP is a transition component. All IEPs are reviewed annually, but what about the time in between? Public Law 105-17 suggests that parents will be regularly informed, through interim reports, of their child's progress toward annual goals. Still consideration needs to be given to the extent to which stakeholders and students are successfully and actively involved, how programs and instruction are selected, the effectiveness of these with respect with the students' transition goals, what is working well to ready students for school to work, and what needs to change. The answers to these questions only can be addressed accurately by evaluating the process itself.

Need for Participation in Larger Context of Student Assessment

In this chapter, we have also spoken of some assessments that are not used for transition planning, but that are part of transition itself. These are the assessments that most students encounter as they move through their school years, assessments such as graduation exams, college entrance exams, and other exams that qualify an individual to proceed with training, to enter a job, and so on. Some of these are exams the student will choose to take; others are exams that the student must take to do something that he or she desires to do. Still others have no direct consequence for the student, but have an indirect impact on the educational context. It is important for students with disabilities to be included in these assessments to ensure that educators and policy makers realize that they are accountable for *all* students in the educational system.

QUESTIONS

1. Discuss in some detail why assessment and evaluation are important during transition.
2. Why is it important to use an outcomes framework to organize assessments for transition planning?
3. Differentiate among Level 1, 2, and 3 assessments. Tell when and how each is used.
4. Identify three to five people who should be involved in transition planning, and indicate how assessment procedures might be applied to them.

5. When and/or why would informal rather than formal assessment methods be used for transition planning?

6. What are some commonly used informal assessments, and what is the primary purpose for using each of them?

7. What is the purpose of evaluating the transition-planning process? Explain how this evaluation is different from the evaluation of IEP goal progress.

8. What are some common transition-related assessments in which students with disabilities may want to participate?

9. Why might a student with a disability be advised to take an assessment that has as its purpose the reporting of information on how students are performing in a particular district?

10. In addition to being individualized, what are three other key aspects of effective transition assessments?

REFERENCES

Amado, A. N., & Lyon, P. J. (1991). *"Listen, lady, this is my life:" A book of stories about personal futures planning in Minnesota.* St. Paul, MN: Human Services Research and Development Center.

Baldwin, J. (1995). *Who took the GED? GED 1994 statistical report.* Washington, DC: American Council on Education.

Berkell, D. E., & Brown, J. M. (1989). *Transition from school to work for persons with disabilities.* White Plains, NY: Longman.

Bond, L. A., & Roeber, E. D. (1995). *The status of state student assessment programs in the United States.* Oak Brook, IL: North Central Regional Educational Laboratory.

Boyer-Stephens, A. (1992). *Transition implementation guide. Instructor materials.* Columbia: University of Missouri, Department of Special Education.

Cameron, S. V., & Heckman, J. J. (1993). The nonequivalence of high school equivalents. *Journal of Labor Economics, 11*(1), 1–47.

Chadsey-Rusch, J., & Heal, L. (1995). Building consensus from transition experts on social integration outcomes and interventions. *Exceptional Children, 62*(2), 165–186.

Chadsey-Rusch, J., Rusch, F. R., & O'Reilly, M. F. (1991). Transition from school to integrated communities. *Remedial and Special Education, 12*(6), 22–33.

Conley, D. T. (1994). *Proficiency-based admission standards study (PASS).* Eugene: Oregon State System of Higher Education, Office of Academic Affairs.

Conley, D. T., & Tell, C. A. (1995). *Proficiency-based admission standards system (PASS).* Eugene: Oregon State System of Higher Education, Office of Academic Affairs.

DeStefano, L., & Metzer, D. (1991). High stakes testing and students with handicaps: An analysis of issues and policies. *Advances in Program Evaluation, 1A,* 281–302.

DeStefano, L., & Wagner, M. (1992). Outcome assessment in special education: What lessons have we learned? In F. R. Rusch, L. DeStefano, J. Chadsey-Rusch, L. A. Phelps, & E. Szymanski (Eds.), *Transition from school to adult life* (pp. 173–207). Sycamore, IL: Sycamore.

Edgar, E. (1987). Secondary programs in special education: Are many of them justifiable? *Exceptional Children, 53,* 555–561.

Geenen, K., Thurlow, M., & Ysseldyke, J. (1995). *A disability perspective on five years of educational reform.* Minneapolis: University of Minnesota, National Center on Educational Outcomes.

International Association for the Evaluation of Educational Achievement. (1987). *The underachieving curriculum. Assessing U.S. school mathematics from an international perspective.* Champaign, IL: Stipes.

Maxam, S. (Ed.). (1985). *Informal assessment: A handbook for LEAs serving special needs students in vocational education.* Columbia: Missouri LINC, Instructional Materials Laboratory.

Murnane, R. J., Willett, J. B., & Boudett, K. P. (1995). Do high school dropouts benefit from obtaining a GED? *Educational Evaluation and Policy Analysis, 17*(2), 133–147.

National Center on Educational Outcomes (NCEO). (Undated). *Foundations for NCEO's Outcomes and Indicators series.* Minneapolis: University of Minnesota.

Peterson, M., & Hill, P. (1982). *Vocational assessment of students with special needs: An implementation manual.* Commerce: East Texas State University, Occupational Curriculum Laboratory.

Peterson, M., Madden, B., & Ley-Siemer, L. (1981, December). *Issues and recommendations concerning vocational assessment of special needs students.* Paper presented at the American Vocational Association Convention, Atlanta.

Resnick, D. P., & Resnick, L. B. (1985). Standards, curriculum, and performance: A historical and comparative perspective. *Educational Researcher, 14,* 5–21.

Rusch, F. R., & Phelps, L. A. (1987). Secondary special education and transition from school to work: A national priority. *Exceptional Children, 53,* 487–492.

Salvia, J., & Ysseldyke, J. E. (1995). *Assessment* (6th ed.). Boston: Houghton Mifflin.

Secretary's Commission on Achieving Necessary Skills (SCANS). (1991). *What work requires of school: A SCANS report for America 2000.* Washington, DC: U.S. Department of Labor.

Shokoohi-Yekta, M., & Kavale, K. A. (1994). Effects of increased high school graduation standards on college entrance examination performances of students with learning disabilities. *Learning Disabilities Research & Practice, 9*(4), 213–218.

Sitlington, P. L., Brolin, D., Clark, G., & Vacanti, J. (1985). Career/vocational assessment in the public school setting: The position of the Division on Career Development. *Career Development for Exceptional Individuals, 8*(1), 3–6.

Smith, T. E., & Puccini, I. K. (1995). Position statement: Secondary curricula and policy issues for students with mental retardation. *Education and Training in Mental Retardation and Developmental Disabilities, 30*(4), 275–282.

Storms, J., DeStefano, L., & O'Leary, E. (1996). *Individuals with disabilities act: Transition requirements. A guide for states, districts, schools, and families.* Stillwater, OK: National Clearinghouse of Rehabilitation.

Thurlow, M. L. (1994). *National and state perspectives on performance assessment and students with disabilities* (CEC mini-library, performance assessment and students with disabilities). Reston, VA: Council for Exceptional Children.

Thurlow, M. L., Scott, D. L., & Ysseldyke, J. E. (1995a). *A compilation of states' guidelines for accommodations in assessments for students with disabilities,* Synthesis Report 18. Minneapolis: University of Minnesota, National Center on Educational Outcomes.

Thurlow, M. L., Ysseldyke, J. E., & Anderson, C. (In press). High school graduation requirements for students with disabilities. *Journal of Learning Disabilities.*

Thurlow, M. L., Ysseldyke, J. E., & Silverstein, B. (1995b). Testing accommodations for students with disabilities. *Remedial and Special Education, 16*(5), 260–270.

Vallecorsa, A. L., deBettencourt, L. U., & Garriss, E. (1992). *Special education programs: A guide to evaluation.* Park, CA: Crown Press.

Vanderwood, M., Ysseldyke, J., & Thurlow, M. (1993). *Consensus building: A process for selecting educational outcomes and indicators,* Outcomes and Indicators Report Number 2. Minneapolis: University of Minnesota, National Center on Educational Outcomes.

Vocational Evaluation and Work Adjustment Association. (1975). *Vocational evaluation project: Final report.* Menomonie, WI: Stout Vocational Rehabilitation Institute, Materials Development Center.

Wagner, M. M. (1995). Outcomes for youths with serious emotional disturbance in secondary school and early adulthood. *The Future of Children. Critical Issues for Children and Youths, 5*(2), 90–112.

Wagner, M., D'Amico, R., Marder, C., Newman, L., & Blackorby, J. (1992). *What happens next? Trends in postschool outcomes of youth with disabilities.* Menlo Park, CA: SRI International.

Wagner, M., Newman, L., D'Amico, R., Jay, E. D., Butler-Nalin, P., Marder, C., & Cox, R. (1991). *Youth with disabilities: How are they doing?* Menlo Park, CA: SRI International.

Wehman, P., Kregel, J., & Seyfarth, J. (1985). Employment outlook for adults with mental retardation. *Rehabilitation Counseling Bulletin,* 90–99.

West, L. L., Corbey, S., Boyer-Stephens, A., Jones, B., Miller, R. J., & Sarkees-Wircenski, M. (1992). *Integrating transition planning into the IEP process.* Reston, VA: Council for Exceptional Children, Division on Career Development.

Winograd, P., & Gaskins, R. (1992). Improving the assessment of literacy: The power of portfolios. *Pennsylvania Reporter, 23*(2), 1–6.

Wolman, C., Bruininks, R. H., & Thurlow, M. L. (1989). Dropouts and dropout programs: Implications for special education. *Remedial and Special Education, 10*(5), 6–20.

Worthen, B. R., & Sanders, J. R. (1987). *Educational evaluation: Alternative approaches and practical guidelines.* New York: Longman.

Ysseldyke, J. E., & Thurlow, M. L. (1993a). *Developing a model of educational outcomes,* Outcomes and Indicators Report Number 1. Minneapolis: University of Minnesota, National Center on Educational Outcomes.

———. (1993b). *Self-study guide to the development of educational outcomes and indicators.* Minneapolis: University of Minnesota, National Center on Educational Outcomes.

Ysseldyke, J. E., Thurlow, M. L., & Erickson, R. N. (1994a). *Educational outcomes and indicators for grade 8.* Minneapolis: University of Minnesota, National Center on Educational Outcomes.

———. (1994b). *Possible sources of data for postschool level indicators.* Minneapolis: University of Minnesota, National Center on Educational Outcomes.

———. (1995). *Possible sources of data for grade 8 indicators.* Minneapolis: University of Minnesota, National Center on Educational Outcomes.

Ysseldyke, J. E., Thurlow, M. L., & Geenen, K. (1994). *Implementation of alternative methods for making educational accountability decisions for students with disabilities.* Minneapolis: University of Minnesota, National Center on Educational Outcomes.

Ysseldyke, J. E., Thurlow, M. L., & Gilman, C. J. (1993a). *Educational outcomes and indicators for individuals at the postschool level.* Minneapolis: University of Minnesota, National Center on Educational Outcomes.

———. (1993b). *Educational outcomes and indicators for students completing school.* Minneapolis: University of Minnesota, National Center on Educational Outcomes.

Ysseldyke, J. E., Thurlow, M. L., & Vanderwood, M. L. (1994). *Possible sources of data for school completion indicators.* Minneapolis: University of Minnesota, National Center on Educational Outcomes.

PART III

Linkages to Work and Postsecondary Education

12

◉

Building Statewide Transition Services Through Collaborative Interagency Teamwork

JANE M. EVERSON AND
JOAN D. GUILLORY

Although many states have embraced regional- and local-level teams as important components of comprehensive, statewide transition services, few states have systematically addressed the training and support necessary to initiate and maintain these teams. If collaborative interagency teamwork models are to be realized on a statewide basis, the large body of applied literature associated with teaming must be merged with "best practices" transition literature and reports from transition projects. The purpose of this chapter is to provide leadership and team members with the tools necessary to build statewide transition services. Ten guidelines, suggested by research on teams as well as the authors' experiences, are presented as a guide for teams to use when implementing a collaborative interagency team-based model.

As discussed in previous chapters, especially Chapter 2, the decade spanning the mid-1980s through the mid-1990s yielded multiple transition demonstration models, research findings, state-level policies, and, ultimately, federally mandated transition services. As a result of these efforts, transition services, which we once thought consisted of a relatively simple individualized planning process culminating in a written statement of transition services, are finally being recognized as much more complex. Comprehensive transition services are now viewed as a longitudinal and multilevel array of interagency and interdisciplinary services designed to prepare and support young adults with disabilities in a variety of community-inclusive adult settings and opportunities.

In most communities across the United States, however, the programmatic, personnel, and fiscal resources necessary to achieve comprehensive transition services statewide are seriously lacking. To address this deficiency, many reports from federally funded projects, "best practices" literature, research outcomes, as well as federal and state policies, have suggested collaborative interagency teamwork as one mechanism for responding to the needs raised by transition services. Indeed, the need for interagency teams to pursue multilevel systems-change activities and to provide comprehensive transition services has been recognized not simply as a "best practice," but as an essential practice (e.g., Kohler et al., 1994).

As a result, most transition models include a network of state-, regional-, and local-level teams, as well as individualized student planning teams as salient features (e.g., Minnesota Department of Education and Institute on Community Integration, 1990; Bates et al., 1992; Everson, 1993). Unfortunately, very little literature exists to systematically guide teams through the activities associated with team-based transition systems-change. Minnesota (Minnesota Department of Education and Institute on Community Integration, 1990) and Oregon (Halpern et al., 1991) have played a leadership role in these efforts, but even their reports and resources fail to address maintenance of pilot projects and expansion of efforts statewide. In effect, although agreeing that teams and teamwork must constitute important components of comprehensive statewide transition services, few of us have the experience or the skills to make collaborative interagency team-based models a reality. In addition, little to no literature has established an empirical basis for the use of teams or discriminated between effective and ineffective teams (Guzzo & Dickson, 1996). Thus, team facilitators must borrow heavily from psychology literature conducted in organizational settings in which dependent variables are indicative of process and performance effectiveness.

The purpose of this chapter is to merge findings from the empirical literature, the "best practices" literature, and the reports of transition projects in an attempt to identify the tools necessary to build statewide transition services using a network of collaborative interagency teams. The chapter begins with an overview of the concepts of collaborative, interagency, and

team-based service model, followed by a rationale for using this model. We conclude by presenting 10 guidelines for teams to use when implementing a collaborative interagency team-based model.

DEFINING CONCEPTS

Collaborative

"Collaborative" is defined as a relationship between two or more agencies or organizations that is mutually beneficial and well-defined. The purpose of such a relationship is to achieve common goals. Thus, a relationship is collaborative if it includes (a) articulation of the mutual goals; (b) jointly developed operating structures; (c) shared roles and responsibilities; (d) mutual authority and accountability for success; and (e) sharing of resources and rewards (Mattessich & Monsey, 1992).

Interagency

Specific to educational *services,* much discussion has been directed toward differentiating among "interdisciplinary," "transdisciplinary," and "multidisciplinary." However, very little focus has been directed toward these three prefixes when attached to *agency.* Because "interagency" is the term most frequently used, it will be used in this chapter. However, one can make a strong argument for the adoption of "transagency" as a more desirable term, borrowing heavily from the recognized definitions of transdisciplinary. "Interagency," as used here, is defined as a group of individuals representing multiple and diverse agencies and organizations who come together and commit themselves to teaching, learning, and working with each other across traditional agency and organizational boundaries to better serve individuals with disabilities. Their activities may include assessment, planning, service delivery, and evaluation at both the consumer and community levels.

Team

Larson and LaFasto (1989) studied teams over a 3-year time period to determine the characteristics of effective teams. Eight characteristics were identified as distinguishing effective teams from ineffective teams: (1) a clear, elevating goal; (2) a results-driven structure; (3) competent members; (4) unified commitment; (5) a collaborative climate; (6) standards of excellence; (7) external supports and recognition; and (8) principles of leadership. In a similar vein, Varney (1989) noted that successful teams embrace four concepts: (1) team member roles are clear to each individual as well as to other team members; members are committed to their jobs, and accept the roles of others; (2) individuals have goals and the sum of individual goals adds up to the team goals; (3) structure, practices, and systems are understood and agreed to by all team members; and (4) working relations are seen as an essential part of an effective team.

RATIONALE FOR USING A COLLABORATIVE INTERAGENCY TEAMWORK MODEL

For the purposes of this chapter, a "collaborative interagency team" is defined as a group of individuals representing multiple and diverse agencies and organizations who come together to address a common need and agree to pursue a common goal. Over time and with much effort, the group becomes a team if its members agree to common values and a mission, set clear goals and objectives, design an organizational structure and operating procedures, develop common communication patterns, and pursue agreed-upon roles and activities. If the team maintains these characteristics and self-monitors and assesses its activities and outcomes, it will become an effective team that may accomplish improved transition services, improved student outcomes, and other systems-change results.

In order for comprehensive statewide transition services to be operational, a state must support a state-level interagency team as well as a network of regional- and/or local-level teams serving all communities and students within the state. In addition, partnerships among the state-, regional-, and local-level teams must support data-based decision making associated with policy changes, funding streams, program development, professional training, and family and student outreach efforts.

GUIDELINES FOR USING A COLLABORATIVE INTERAGENCY TEAMWORK MODEL

In one of the earliest attempts to understand the growth and development of teams, Tuckman (1965) described four stages of teaming. Tuckman's work serves as a conceptual model for many team initiators and leaders and was used as a foundation for the development of the collaborative interagency teamwork model presented in this chapter.

During the first stage, *forming,* team members seek a shared sense of the team's values and mission as well as their own individual roles on the team. Trust is not fully developed and individual members are more concerned with personal agendas than with team needs. During the second stage, *storming,* team members seek group norms and operating procedures. The team may need to revisit its values and mission and review its membership. It is at this stage that additional training or consultants are most frequently requested, but it is also at this point that teams are most likely to become frustrated and abandon their efforts. The third stage, *norming,* occurs when the entire team evidences a shared sense of its mission, operating procedures, roles, and traditions or culture. For the first time, the team is able to balance its team initiation and maintenance concerns with activities designed to accomplish its mission. Finally, the fourth stage, *performing,* brings the team to its highest level of effectiveness—attendance is high, leadership has emerged, roles are clear, goals and objectives are accomplished, members are willing to take risks, and they take pride in their accomplishments. Also, at this stage, teams are willing to self-monitor and evaluate their efforts and use this information to make necessary changes.

Effective teams may be defined broadly (e.g., Hackman, 1987; Sundstrom, DeMeuse, & Futrell, 1990) as those teams that evidence: (a) team-produced outcomes such as consumer satisfaction and quality services; (b) consequences for team members such as recognition and other tangible reinforcers; and (c) performance capability that enables the team to maintain itself over time.

When viewed in this fashion, that is, as a developmental process, teams can plan appropriate team activities and anticipate potential problems by recognizing team developmental milestones. The authors' work with more than 200 teams in 25 states suggests that collaborative interagency teams addressing comprehensive and statewide transition services are most effective if they acknowledge this developmental framework of forming, storming, norming, and performing while pursuing activities within the 10 guidelines described in what follows.

Existing teams first need to identify the stage at which they are currently functioning by documenting their team activities to date, diagnosing any pressing team problems, and evaluating their satisfaction with team activities and outcomes. Next, they must determine which critical activities occurring at the current stage or at an earlier stage need to be completed or reviewed in order to enhance team effectiveness. Some teams will be able to complete this self-assessment themselves; however, others, especially those functioning at the storming stage or those who need to return to the storming stage in order to complete or revisit activities, will most likely benefit from the assistance of an external consultant. Figure 12.1 is an example of a team self-assessment instrument that many

teams have found useful—determine the stage in which they are currently operating. Newly forming teams need to begin with the first stage—forming—and systematically progress through the designated stages and activities.

To aid the reader in understanding and implementing each of the following guidelines, two case studies representing composites of the activities and experiences of typical teams are provided. Case Study 1 illustrates a highly effective team whose activities took them from the forming stage through the performing stage, whereas Case Study 2 illustrates a less effective team whose activities took them from the forming stage to the storming stage where they have been operating for an extended period of time.

FORMING STAGE

Guideline 1: Initiate and Organize a Team

Initiate a Team. The obvious first step within the forming stage is for one or more individuals to recognize the potential use of a team and to suggest that it be initiated. The initiators should ask themselves three questions and reach consensus on the answers: *What is the need? Who are the people impacted by this need? How will a team address this need?*

Teams can be self-initiated by any one or more potential team members; they can be externally initiated by consultants or supervisory agency staff; or they can be initiated by formal directives such as legislative mandates or grant or project funding requirements. Brager and Holloway (1978) suggested that teams should be initiated by direct service personnel instead of managers because they have the closest contact with students and clients and thus the clearest understanding of their needs. In a 4-year study of state and local team partnerships in seventeen states, Everson and Rachal (1996) found that when team initiators included individuals with disabilities, parents, and family members, they were more likely to achieve changes in

Louisiana Statewide Transition Project
INTERAGENCY TEAM SELF-ASSESSMENT INSTRUMENT

Names of Team Members Completing Assessment: (Please list contact person first.)

_____

_____

Telephone Number for Contact person: _____

Location of team: _____ Date of Assessment Completion: _____

As a member of an interagency team addressing local interagency transition services, please indicate the extent to which you agree that this team has addressed the following activities.

Forming Stage	Strongly Agree	Agree	Disagree	Strongly Disagree
1. We have defined the need(s) to be addressed.				
2. We have defined the people/agencies impacted by the need.				
3. We have defined the geographical area to be served by the team.				
4. We have defined the core stakeholders to serve as team members.				
5. We have held at least one organizational meeting.				
6. We have held at least one follow-up meeting.				
7. We have confirmed team membership and have a written membership list.				

Storming Stage	Strongly Agree	Agree	Disagree	Strongly Disagree
8. We have developed a written value statement.				
9. We have developed a written mission statement.				
10. We have conducted needs assessments of our community and refined our targeted need(s) accordingly.				
11. We have developed written team goals (both long-term and short-term).				
12. We have developed written team structural procedures (e.g., use of "core" team, "resource" team, subcommittees, etc.)				
13. We have a written description of the role of the chair(s).				
14. We have written roles defined for other team members.				
15. We have determined a process/timelines for filling the chair(s) and other team positions.				

(Developed by the Louisiana Statewide Transition Project, April 1997)

FIGURE 12.1 Sample Team Self-Assessment Instrument (_continued_)

	Strongly Agree	Agree	Disagree	Strongly Disagree
16. We have determined an annual meeting schedule.				
17. We have delineated ground rules.				
18. We have developed consensus on voting and decision-making procedures				
19. We have developed an annual action plan with goals, activities, timelines, and responsible personnel identified.				
20. We have addressed communication skills and conflict resolution skills.				
21. We have addressed meeting effectiveness skills.				

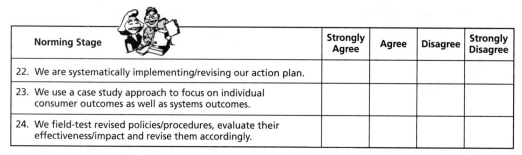

Norming Stage	Strongly Agree	Agree	Disagree	Strongly Disagree
22. We are systematically implementing/revising our action plan.				
23. We use a case study approach to focus on individual consumer outcomes as well as systems outcomes.				
24. We field-test revised policies/procedures, evaluate their effectiveness/impact and revise them accordingly.				

Performing Stage	Strongly Agree	Agree	Disagree	Strongly Disagree
25. We use action planning to maintain our team's direction and focus.				
26. We use self-monitoring and evaluative procedures to maintain our team's direction and focus.				
23. We field-test revised policies/procedures, evaluate their effectiveness/impact and revise them accordingly.				

Comments: _____

_____

_____

_____

_____

_____

FIGURE 12.1 (*continued*)

consumers' lives and changes in systems. Regardless of who the team initiators are, they must be authorized, either formally or informally, as well as committed to completing all the necessary organizational activities, summarized in the following section. Those teams that pursued these organizational activities were more likely to stay together during their first 2 years and were less likely to experience problems of membership, commitment, and goal setting than teams that failed to address these activities (Everson & Rachel, 1996).

Organize a Team. The team initiators must make various preliminary organizational decisions before holding the initial team meeting. First, they must define the geographical area they will be serving. The geographical boundaries of the team's activities may be as broad as a region, city, county, or township or as specific as a single high school or school district. The geographical boundaries will be dictated in part by the identified need, but the team also must consider such issues as service catchment areas across key agencies, population size, and transportation and travel requirements. In some cases, the geographical boundaries of the team are dictated by the authorizing body or by mandates. The team initiators must have a clear understanding about the team's geographical boundaries before they can answer a fourth question: *What are the appropriate agencies and organizations to invite to become team members?*

For teams addressing transition needs, the key stakeholders are the collective agencies and organizations that deliver total life services to young adults with disabilities. These include education and adult services agencies, as well as organizations representing individuals with disabilities, families, employers, and other general community services. Once identified, all stakeholders should be invited to send a representative to an initial organizational team meeting. The method of inviting stakeholders to the initial meeting requires careful planning. Everson and Moon (1990) suggested that team initiators

address these questions: (a) Who should send the letter? (b) Who should sign it? (c) Should it be written on one agency's letterhead? (d) Where is the most appropriate location to hold the meeting? (e) What is the best time for all key stakeholders to attend? (f) How should the letter be followed up?

Hold an Organizational Meeting. The agenda for the initial meeting also requires some careful planning. Everson (1993) recommended a brief 2-hour meeting with these nine agenda items: (1) welcome and introduction by the team initiators; (2) rationale for organization of a team; (3) description of the identified needs; (4) description of the geographical boundaries of the team; (5) rationale for involvement of all stakeholders; (6) introductory or ice-breaker activity; (7) discussion of similar team efforts in other communities or states; (8) group discussion of team needs, goals, and membership issues; and (9) group discussion of next steps.

Plan Follow-Up Meetings. By the end of the initial meeting, team initiators must ensure that stakeholders are willing and interested in participating in a second meeting to be held within 45 days and that any overlooked stakeholders are invited to participate in this second meeting. The agenda for the second meeting should address (1) confirmation of membership, (2) commitment of membership, (3) consensus on the need or needs to be addressed by the team, and (4) consensus on geographical boundaries and target population to be served.

Guideline 2: Confirm Membership

Confirmation of membership is a critical forming activity. However, membership cannot be confirmed in isolation of the organizational activities suggested in Guideline 1. Team members are initially suggested by the target need, geographical boundaries, and target population, and later by the value and mission statements, and finally by the action plan and workscope of

---

CASE STUDY 1   Local Education Agency

Ten years ago, LEA (Local Education Agency) 1 reorganized its special education curriculum for students with severe disabilities who were in the alternative to regular placement (ARP) program. The new curriculum addressed functional academics and life skills, community-based training, and self-advocacy and self-determination training. Based on these curricular changes, LEA staff anticipated that upcoming graduates would more fully access and participate in community activities, be interested in and prepared for a wide array of employment opportunities, and adequately empowered to advocate on their own behalf.

But the curriculum reorganization also raised many questions for the LEA staff: What adult programs are available in the community? What services do these programs currently provide? Are individuals with disabilities and/or their families aware of these services? What are the eligibility requirements? How are these services and agencies funded? With no definitive answers to these and a host of other questions, the LEA staff realized that communication and contact with adult services agencies and organizations would be necessary. Recognizing that answers to their questions were beyond the scope of school district personnel, the LEA staff decided to initiate and organize a local-level interagency team. The preliminary need identified by the team initiators was narrow: the lack of comprehensive school-to-work transition services for students with severe disabilities.

The team initiators discussed invitations: Which agencies should be invited and to whom should invitations be extended? After some preliminary telephone calls and after much discussion, it was decided to send invitational letters with follow-up telephone calls to the directors of the key agencies—vocational rehabilitation services, mental retardation/developmental disabilities, and the one supported employment provider within the community. In addition, the team initiators, the director of special education in the LEA, and a high school teacher of students with severe/profound disabilities agreed to plan and chair the organizational meetings.

The team's first meetings were successful. All invited agencies sent a representative, the preliminary need was proposed and expanded, the need for additional agency representation was discussed, and all participants agreed to attend additional organizational meetings. One significant activity of these organizational meetings was the addition of two family members to the group. As an outcome of these meetings, each of the participating agencies committed to team membership and designated one individual as the official representative. The final team membership was a mixture of administrators, direct service personnel, and family members. The team acknowledged that its membership currently focused exclusively on individuals with significant service and support needs, as well as on supported employment outcomes, but agreed that additional agencies and organizations could be added over time if new and additional needs were identified.

Team meetings were scheduled monthly, with the special education administrator serving as the chair. Several team members were eager to begin addressing the needs identified in the preliminary meetings; however, other team members were unsure about how or where to begin. One team member suggested that before addressing any of these needs, team members needed to become familiar with each other's agencies, their mandates, their missions, their services, and their eligibility requirements. Although a few members complained that this would waste valuable time, the team discussed and finally agreed to spend a meeting accomplishing this activity. All members were surprised to discover how little they really knew about each other's respective agencies. They were equally relieved to confirm the compatibility of their values and missions. However, they were disturbed to learn that there were duplications, as well as gaps, in the current delivery of services.

Despite protests from a few members who felt that the team was not accomplishing anything, an additional meeting was spent exploring what each organization, as well as each individual team member, expected to gain as a result of team efforts. This discussion led to the identification of specific goals and outcomes that the team hoped would result for individuals with significant disabilities and their families.

(continued)

CASE STUDY 1 (*continued*)

As a result of these forming and initial storming activities, fundamental progress was àccomplished: (a) commitment to the teaming concept was secured and team membership was confirmed; (b) preliminary needs, goals, and anticipated outcomes were articulated; and (c) agency-specific information was shared and roles were discussed. The team then moved further into the storming stage. One team member volunteered to capture the ideas discussed thus far in draft value and mission statements to be reviewed by the team at the following meeting. With agency and personal agendas revealed, some false assumptions were dispelled and a sense of trust and ownership began to emerge. The team readily agreed that they were now closer to being able to address the needs that were identified at their initial meetings. But once again, they were faced with the question of where to begin. One team member suggested completing a needs assessment across several levels: interagency needs, single-agency needs, and consumer and family needs. Agency representatives agreed to survey individuals served by their organizations regarding needs, issues, and areas of service concern. The family representatives agreed to collect similar information from other family members. From these data, the team concluded that some needs were long-range and others were more immediate and pressing. The needs data also supported the team's focus on individuals with significant service and support needs and supported employment services. After some negotiation, the team agreed to establish an action plan with short-range (annual), as well as long-range (2- to 5-year), goals and objectives. This would allow them to expand membership and activities beyond supported employment as short-term action plan goals and objectives were accomplished.

Invigorated by their newly developed action plan, the team next recognized the need to establish operating procedures: ground rules were established, a meeting location and 12-month meeting schedule were identified, confidentiality policies were reviewed, voting procedures were determined, and the roles, responsibilities, and length of term for a chair, a vice-chair, a secretary/recorder, and a timekeeper were determined. Last, interagency agreements were developed between the school district and each of the adult services agencies to formalize collaborative activities.

The team continued to meet monthly, with the agendas being driven by their action plan. However, over time, attendance became sporadic. One of the members voiced a concern that the meetings were too heavily focused on system issues and not on individuals. She felt that there were limited opportunities for team problem solving or sharing of successful strategies. The team decided to bring individual case studies to the meetings for discussion. However, this new focus on individuals raised other issues. Nine months after adopting a case study approach, the team recognized a need to periodically review its activities. Some members began to question whether their efforts were really making differences for individuals with disabilities and/or their families. Other members questioned the impact of their activities on local- and state-level systems. However, as they began to discuss their activities and to monitor and evaluate their progress, they realized that many of their short- and long-range goals had in fact been achieved.

The team had attained the norming stage. After reviewing and appreciating these accomplishments and making some adjustments to their operating procedures, the team experienced renewed vigor. The team conducted another needs assessment, prioritized new needs, established new short- and long-term goals, and developed a new action plan.

Thus, 3 years after the team's inception, the team was functioning in the performing stage. Self-monitoring and evaluation activities were in place and, as a result of these activities, membership was expanded to include a high school teacher of students with mild/moderate disabilities, a representative of the local mental health agency, a local community college representative, and representatives from newly established supported employment agencies. Subcommittees were established to address the work scope of this larger team. Local interagency agreements were revised and appended to reflect delivery of transition services to a broader consumer base. As a result of membership changes, leadership changes also occurred and the team recognized the need to update their operating procedures.

(*continued*)

CASE STUDY 1   (*continued*)

In the ensuing years, the team returned to the storming stage. This larger team experienced meetings that ran over the time limits, with tempers flaring as conflicts arose and remained unresolved. After conferring with other local teams, the team decided to revise its structure by establishing multiple levels of membership. The core team continued to be the nucleus, represented by the key education and adult services agencies involved in transition services. It would continue to meet monthly. An associate team was also formed, represented by agencies that were less directly connected to transition services, for example, public transportation, businesses, postsecondary educational programs, and local government offices. The associate team would meet quarterly or as needed. Still, other agencies were identified to serve as resource members, to be contacted on an as-needed basis. All members agreed to serve on standing subcommittees or work teams, as requested. In addition, the team began charging participating agencies annual membership dues to offset the costs associated with postage, brochures, and other operating expenditures. A treasurer position was defined and filled. The team decided to elect co-chairs. A school district representative would serve as a permanent co-chair, but the other position would be filled on an annual basis, with rotation determined by alphabetical order of the other core agencies. New bylaws were written to formalize the new organizational structure and operating procedures of the team. As the team moved back into the norming, and ultimately the performing, stage, it recognized that the forming and storming activities empowered them to continue to meet the challenges of changing membership, new agency policies, reduced funding streams, and changing consumer and family needs.

---

the team. To ensure initial commitment of team members, teams may find it helpful to obtain agency letters of support confirming a named team member and authorizing the individual's participation in team activities. It would be a mistake for teams to assume that membership can be finalized during the first or second meeting. Instead, it must be viewed as a developmental process. In fact, Everson and Rachal (1996) found that most teams need between three and four meetings to finalize membership—both the agencies and organizations to be represented and the individuals to represent these agencies and organizations. In addition, they suggested that teams review their membership at least annually to adjust for changes in agencies and organizations, changes in team values and mission, and progress toward addressing identified needs.

By the fourth team meeting, Everson and Rachal (1996) concluded that most teams are able to proceed to the storming stage and dedicate their meeting agendas and team-building activities to addressing Guidelines 3 to 6. Most teams will find it necessary to meet monthly during these storming activities to ensure high levels of team commitment and actions.

STORMING STAGE

Guideline 3: Develop Value and Mission Statements

Develop Value Statements. Value statements are written articulations of the beliefs and principles that bind the group together. Value statements typically take between 1 and 3 hours to develop (Everson & Rachal, 1996). They may be drafted during one meeting and adopted by the entire team during a follow-up meeting. Value statements enable teams to answer one question: *What do we believe?* An example of a value statement created by one local team is: "We believe that all individuals have the right to live a full and complete life in their community and to make informed choices about education, living, work, relationships, and recreation. Full access to services and supports that respond to and respect individual needs and preferences will empower individuals to maximize their full potential and independence."

Develop Mission Statements. Mission statements are written articulations of a team's reason for being together. Like value statements, they typically take 1 and 3 hours to develop (Everson & Rachal, 1996) and may be drafted during one meeting and adopted during a follow-up meeting. Mission statements enable teams to answer two questions: *Who are we? Why are we working together?* An example of a mission statement developed by one team is: "The mission of the Expanding Horizons Team is to respond to the choices of our consumers by facilitating the collaborative development of educational and adult services and supports."

Together, the value and mission statements lay the foundation for team goal setting and action planning. Once developed, teams should consider posting them during meetings, using them on brochures and/or a letterhead, and referring to them during meetings in order to set initial team goals, as well as to assess and monitor team progress. In addition, they should be reviewed by the team each year and used to establish new goals. According to Everson and Rachal (1996), effective teams use their value and mission statements to periodically ask themselves: "Are we doing what we said we got together to do?" If the answer to this question is negative or uncertain, these authors suggested that the team must either change its value and mission statements or its goals.

Guideline 4: Conduct Needs Assessments

Before undertaking any further team activities, teams must clearly define and assess the identified needs that have brought them together. Hasenfeld (1974) suggested that comprehensive needs assessments make it easier for teams to mobilize community and fiscal support and assist with the development of a clear, goal-based course of action. Everson (1993) described several categories of needs assessment approaches, noting that they can be either time-consuming and costly or relatively simple and inexpensive. Regardless of the type of needs assessment selected (e. g., surveys or interviews with key informants; community forums; or studies of service delivery patterns and outcomes), teams should use the data to specify,

confirm, or expand the needs identified by the team initiators and to prioritize the team's needs. Everson (1993) used eight questions to guide a team's planning for needs assessment activities: (1) What is the identified preliminary need? (2) What are the goals of the needs assessment and how will we use the data? (3) What programs do we need to assess? (4) What data do we need to collect? (5) How much money do we have to spend? (6) How much time do we want to dedicate to this activity? (7) Do we have the expertise to conduct the activity? (8) What other data have been collected that we might use or expand on?

Guideline 5: Develop Team Structural and Operating Procedures

Team Structure. Several structural and operating procedures must be negotiated and finalized during the storming stage. The first set of decisions concerns structure: How will the team relate to other teams in the state, region, or locality? Will there be a "core team" of key agencies and organizations supported by a larger advisory group? Will subcommittees or work teams be used to accomplish the team's goals and work scope? Berelson and Steiner (1964) suggested that the most desirable team size is five members. Everson and Rachal (1996) found that larger teams, those of 15 or fewer members, that used subcommittees or work teams were effective, but they also noted that teams of five or more members require a greater expenditure of resources during the forming and storming stages.

Operating Procedures. The next decisions relate to operating procedures: Who is going to be the team chair? What other roles will be defined and assigned? How frequently will meetings be held and what are attendance policies? How will team decisions be made? How will conflict be managed? How will team progress be monitored and evaluated?

Everson and Rachal (1996) found that teams that opted to have co-chairs were more effective than teams opting to have only one chair or rotating chairs. As a result, they suggested that co-chairs serve 2-year terms with differentiated time frames to allow a senior chair to mentor and nurture the leadership skills of a junior chair. They also suggested that teams use "ground rules," delineated by the team and posted during meetings, to monitor team operating procedures. Ground rules may address, among other concerns, attendance policies, meeting effectiveness strategies, communication and conflict management skills, and voting or decision-making rules.

Goal Setting. Goals are written statements of a desired future state of affairs. Goals are behavioral, measurable, attainable, and have time frames. Berelson and Steiner (1964) and Everson and Rachal (1996) suggested that teams dedicate at least one meeting to setting goals that are based on assessed needs and incorporate personal as well as group agendas and needs. Further, Berelson and Steiner (1964) recommended that teams identify team maintenance goals as well as systems outcome goals. Extending their previous suggestions, Everson and Rachal (1996) guided teams into setting team maintenance goals, systems outcome goals, and case study goals. They found that teams that set 3 to 5 goals and related activities balanced across these three areas were most likely to build and maintain effective teams, that is, teams that demonstrate changes in the lives of individuals and attain changes in systems and services within a 2-year time frame.

Guideline 6: Foster Team Effectiveness

Convening and holding effective team meetings is a critical storming activity; yet it is frequently dismissed by storming teams as being unimportant, "something we already know how to do." Effective meeting strategies include both chair and team member responsibilities and may be categorized according to things that should occur before, during, and after meetings (Jay, 1977; O'Neil Group, 1990). Table 12.1 summa-

rizes suggested meeting effectiveness strategies in a checklist format that many teams have found useful as a self-assessment activity.

Communication behaviors are a critical element of team effectiveness. To become a team, members need to develop common communication behaviors and patterns, but these do not naturally occur among most team members. Proposing new ideas; expanding, agreeing, and disagreeing with others' ideas; bringing in more reticent team members; summarizing discussions; and negotiating actions to diffuse conflict are all examples of communication behaviors that are necessary in teaming models.

Kaizen is a Japanese word meaning "continuous opportunity for improvement" (M. O'Neil, personal communication, 1990). O'Neil suggested that teams use a *kaizen* chart to evaluate every meeting and use the suggestions to improve future meetings. Figure 12.2 is an example of a *kaizen* chart completed by one local-level team.

By the tenth meeting, depending on the size of the team and the frequency of meetings, Everson and Rachal (1996) concluded that most teams are able to proceed to norming activities. Teams will know that they have reached this stage when they are able and willing to dedicate more time to systems outcome and case study goals than to team maintenance goals.

NORMING STAGE

Guideline 7: Focus on Individuals

The use of regional- and local-level teams serves to focus their goals and activities on individuals as well as on team and systems needs. A focus on individuals helps prevent goal displacement, where achievement of goals becomes an end in and of itself regardless of the benefits provided to consumers. A "case study approach" (Everson & Rachal, 1996) provides a structured data collection, analysis, and communication process for teams to use. Everson and Rachel (1996)

CASE STUDY 2   Local Education Agency 2

Five years ago, in response to state-agency mandates, representatives from LEA 2 and the local vocational rehabilitation office agreed to establish a local-level collaborative interagency team. Although many of the initiation and organizational activities were similar to those addressed in Case Study 1, several differences are worth highlighting. First, membership was different. The initial team was broader and included directors from the school district, vocational rehabilitation services, a regional family advocacy/outreach agency, and the local office of mental retardation/developmental disabilities. The representative from vocational rehabilitation services agreed to serve as the initial team chair. Second, the team identified transportation and housing as the preliminary needs and identified a broader population of all transition-age youths. Several similarities between this team and the one in Case Study 1 are also worth noting. Both teams recognized the value of initial team activities, such as sharing information about program and agency services, discussing roles, conducting needs assessments, setting goals and anticipated outcomes, and developing action plans.

Although the initial organizational meetings of this team were successful, some problems became evident as the team moved into the storming stage. Some team members were unable or unwilling to move beyond their personal agendas, to communicate effectively, or to resolve conflict. As a result, tension and mistrust emerged. Value and mission statements were not articulated and the team lacked a foundation. Although annual goals and related activities were established, long-term goals were unclear. Membership was never confirmed and the roles and responsibilities of individual team members and their agencies remained vague. As a result, meeting attendance was inconsistent.

Despite these storming problems, the team continued to meet on a monthly basis and to develop operating procedures. While negotiating the logistics of these monthly meetings, the team members agreed that when the meetings were held at any of their agencies, the respective member was likely to be interrupted and/or distracted because of in-house agency issues. In order to ensure uninterrupted meetings, they agreed to hold the core team meetings away from all of their offices at a cost-free location within the community.

Although the previously mentioned actions improved meeting effectiveness, other problem areas continued to surface. Written agendas were not typically developed before meetings. As a result, the meetings often were disorganized and unproductive. The team chair agreed to develop agendas and distribute them to members ahead of time. However, despite agendas, some members consistently ignored them and monopolized meetings with their own agendas. The team chair seemed unable to facilitate good communication, resolve conflict, or focus the team's activities on action plan items. In anger, the chair resigned and a new chair was elected. In addition, for the first time, the team elected a recording secretary and identified a timekeeper.

The newly elected chair was perceived by the team as a leader, able to guide the team toward the development of value and mission statements, to assist the team in setting and attaining goals, and to facilitate communication and resolve conflict. Commitment and collaboration from the former chair became problematic as he began to miss most meetings. Meeting effectiveness was hindered as other team members became resentful of spending time updating him on the activities and decisions of previous meetings. It seemed that the current operating procedures for documenting the activities and decisions that occurred at the team meetings were not effective. Unfortunately, the team took no specific steps to address this issue.

After 9 months, the team decided to evaluate its efforts. They were disappointed to find that most of their initial goals had not been accomplished and that their needs had not been addressed. Although some members suggested that additional members might be needed to accomplish the targeted goals, a unanimous decision could not be reached on this suggestion. Two team members refused to agree to expand the membership of the team. As a result, many other team members felt overextended and resentful. Other team members suggested revising the team's goals or extending the timelines for the goals. Once again, the team was unable to reach consensus.

(continued)

CASE STUDY 2   (*continued*)

After a year of working together, most team members were complaining that their efforts were fruitless. But they were unable to determine how to redirect their efforts. Once again, the team evaluated its efforts. Despite low morale and personal conflicts among some of the members, the team decided to conduct another needs assessment and to prioritize new goals and related activities. Other storming issues, that is, value and mission articulation, operating procedures, and communication remained unresolved.

Over the next 2 years, several events occurred that took their toll on the team. Two of the original team initiators left the team, one because of a job transfer and the other because of a request to be replaced on the team by another representative of her agency. These membership changes were disastrous. What few verbal agreements had been reached between the agencies regarding the delivery of transition services were now subject to renegotiation. The resulting written agreements were not as effective as the initial verbal agreements and they were never officially signed. In addition, one of the replacement team members lacked background and experience in transition services. Because the team still lacked written guidelines regarding the delivery of transition services, the team's efforts floundered while they tried to familiarize this person with the transition process. Then, another membership crisis occurred. After consistently requesting that the team secure additional family representation, the director of the family advocacy/outreach agency withdrew the agency from team membership. And, finally, because newer members, including the providers of community services, for example, the local housing authority and public transportation agency, remained unclear about their roles and anticipated outcomes of the team, they began discussing leaving the team.

Table 12.1 Checklist of Meeting Effectiveness Strategies

Before the meeting, did our team:
- develop an agenda and distribute it to all team members?
- ask for agenda additions?
- set time limits for agenda items and identify a timekeeper?
- identify agenda items as "for information," "for discussion," or "for decision"?
- identify a recorder and keep an accurate record of the meeting?
- make certain that copies of the minutes from the previous meeting were distributed to all team members?

During the meeting, did our team:
- follow the agenda?
- follow our "ground rules"?
- make certain that our "action plan" was completed/updated?
- make certain that copies of our new "action plan" will be distributed to all team members?
- use communication skills appropriately?
- use problem-solving and conflict-resolution mechanisms as needed?
- follow our agreed-upon "case study" format?
- schedule a meeting date, time, and location for our next meeting?

After the meeting, did our team:
- complete a *kaizen* chart or other self-assessment activity?

Sources: Adapted from Jay, 1977; O'Neil Group, 1990.

Things That Worked Well in This Meeting	Continuous Opportunities for Improvement
■ Vocational rehabilitation's participation! ■ Good brainstorming of functional vocational assessment resources! ■ Meeting began and ended on time! ■ Celebration of case study progress. Kyla has a job! Luis got a great evaluation from his supervisor!	■ Dedicate 30 minutes to case study updates instead of 20 minutes! ■ Identify a family representative from the northern part of state! ■ Don't forget food for break time!

Given What We Have Done Today, What Are We Learning About Local Service Systems?

■ School personnel need to compile a vocational portfolio to send to vocational rehabilitation for each student; person-centered planning "maps" and videotapes of school training sites yield good job development and support plan information and should be part of this portfolio.

FIGURE 12.2 *Kaizen* Chart

suggested that regional- or local-level teams first identify between three and five case study individuals from IEP (Individualized Education Program) teams or other person-centered planning teams. When cases are presented to the regional- or local-level team, local policies, procedures, or service needs should be emphasized. Next, the systems and services needs of the selected individuals are discussed during team meetings and proposed team actions to address the needs are incorporated within the team action plan. Lastly, as themes and patterns are identified across all or several case studies, teams need to ask themselves, "As a result of our team's activities with Lila, Anthony, Dawn, and Luis, what are we learning about local systems?" When regional- and local-level teams identify an issue that they are unable to solve because it requires state-level attention, they present the case or cases to the state-level team for action planning.

Focusing on individuals is the one salient characteristic that teams are most likely to question or even resist. However, state- and local-level partnerships that initially attempted transition systems change without using a case study approach found their work both easier and more effective once the local-level teams began

focusing on individuals and sharing information with their state-level teams (Everson & Rachal, 1996). Highly effective teams are able to respond in rich detail to this self-evaluation question: "As a result of our team's collaborative activities, how have we changed the lives of individuals?"

Guideline 8: Develop/Implement Action Plans

Action planning is a structured, yet flexible, process that encourages teams to identify, organize, and monitor individual and team actions to accomplish desired goals, activities, and outcomes. Action planning is useful because it (a) focuses the work of the team by setting long- and short-term priorities; (b) identifies needed actions, timelines, responsible team members, and monitoring and evaluation procedures; (c) schedules follow-up meetings; (d) presents a forum for discussing both obstacles and opportunities, as well as failures and celebrations; (e) provides a framework for team maintenance, systems, and case study goals; and (f) provides a written record of team actions and accomplishments.

Action plans should be used to drive meeting agendas. For example, teams may find it useful to align the meeting agenda with the action plan, use an update of the action plan to open the meeting, use notes on flipchart paper to record actions suggested during the meeting, and close the meeting by assigning timelines and team member responsibilities to generated actions. Figure 12.3 is an example of an action plan developed by one local-level team.

PERFORMING STAGE

Performing is the highest level of team functioning. At this stage, teams are able and willing to maintain and potentially expand their efforts even in the absence of fiscal incentives (e.g., grant awards) or mandates (e.g., state regulations). They are able and willing to take risks, articulate their accomplishments and failures, and self-evaluate their efforts. Everson and Rachal (1996) found that during a 4-year period, many teams never achieved this stage; other teams achieved the stage but were unable to maintain it, slipping back to the norming or even storming stage. Importantly, those teams that did achieve this stage required a 30- to 48-month time frame to do so.

Guideline 9: Maintain a Team's Direction and Focus

Teams will face implementation challenges at every step of the systems-change process. Action plans provide teams with direction and focus from one meeting to the next, but additional strategies are needed to ensure that teams perform effectively. There is clear evidence (Weldon & Weingart, 1993) that clear, well-defined goals increase the effectiveness of teams. Attention to communication and conflict resolution skills (Weldon & Weingart, 1993; Everson, 1995) among team members is also essential for maintaining a team's direction and focus, as is coalition building, exercising influence, managing

resistance, and reassessing a team's self-regulatory processes (Everson, 1993).

Effective teams anticipate the need to revisit their values, mission statement, membership, needs assessment data, goals and outcomes, operating procedures, and action plans on a regular periodic basis and commit meeting time to these activities. Achieving the performing stage requires diligence, but maintaining the stage requires constant self-assessment and refocusing of team efforts.

Guideline 10: Monitor and Evaluate a Team's Effectiveness

Monitoring and evaluating the progress and outcomes of team activities are important activities that are frequently overlooked or underemphasized. Collecting data generated through team activities can seem overwhelming, and reviewing and interpreting these data can be both rewarding and frustrating. Nevertheless, in the absence of monitoring and evaluation, team activities might suffer from lack of guidance and have little impact on the transition outcomes attained by young adults or on systemic changes. Even when outcomes and changes are known to be positive, these activities can assist with team expansion and replication to other local sites.

Monitoring activities serve as early warning systems, which provide internal information useful for keeping team activities on course (Kettner, Daley, & Nichols, 1985). Annual team retreats using structured self-assessment activities are an excellent way for a team to monitor its activities and outcomes. Table 12.2 presents some probing questions that teams have found useful to guide their self-assessment during team retreats.

Evaluation activities are summative measures. They may provide teams with external checks on a variety of variables, ranging from numbers of transition plans written, numbers of community-inclusive job placements made and retained, and changes in student dropout rates to process variables such as changes in policies,

Action Plan

NAME: Bryon Harmon, Chair

NAME OF TEAM: Kansas City

DATE: October 15

Activity	Responsible Person	Timeliness	Evaluation Procedures
1. Contact members who were not in attendance and confirm next meeting date/location.	Marge	October 31	Telephone calls made by October 31
2. Call Kevin to confirm availability of funding for Melissa's interpreter for the job interview.	David	October 31	Funds available—interview held/contract developed for the interpreter
3. Make presentation on teams activities at Chamber of Commerce meeting.	Bryan, David	October 19	Presentation made—contacts with three new potential employers made
4. Call state department to verify Medicaid Waiver availability for Luis PCA.	David	October 31	Telephone call made—funds available and contract developed for the PCA
5. Provide assistance to Melissa's IEP team on developmet of PASS.	Marge	November 1	PASS written and waiting for approval
6. Bring food for next meeting.	Tina	November 15	Food available!

FIGURE 12.3 Sample Action Plan

funding, and personnel. Evaluation activities enable teams to make judgments about the value and worth of collaborative team activities and outcomes with respect to use of resources such as time and money. Teams may choose to evaluate their efforts using student follow-up surveys and pre- and postreviews of IEPs and statements of transition services, conducting consumer and family surveys, and by reviewing service delivery patterns.

In summary, monitoring and evaluation activities, are distinctly different in their purpose and use, but they also are interrelated and complementary activities that yield comparable data. Effective teams will consider monitoring activities during all stages of their activities, but are most likely to commit their own resources toward evaluation during the performing stage.

SUMMARY

The collaborative interagency teamwork model described in this chapter is an essential component of comprehensive statewide transition services. State-, regional-, and local-level teams addressing transition services exist in nearly every American state and territory and there are sufficient examples of effective teams to validate their usage in transition systems-change efforts. Yet, limited research attention to the dependent variables associated with effective teams has

Table 12.2 Monitoring Team Effectiveness: Questions to Help Guide a Self-Review

GOALS

Do we agree on, and are we satisfied with, our value and mission statements?

Do our goals and activities reflect our values and mission?

Are our goals measurable and attainable?

Do we have team maintenance, systems, and consumer outcome goals?

Have we scheduled time to periodically review our goals?

Are we making progress toward our goals?

ROLES

Are the roles of the co-chairs defined in writing? Do the co-chairs know what is expected and do they carry out their roles?

Do we have an assigned recorder/minute taker? Is that person's role clear? Do minutes get to team members in a timely manner?

Do we have a timekeeper? Do we need one?

Are roles rotated? How frequently?

Are there people or agencies who are not currently represented on the team whom we want to invite to be come members? Do we have adequate family and consumer representation?

Do we use subcommittee or work teams? If no, do we need them? If yes, are their goals, roles, and processes clear?

PROCESS

Does the meeting schedule meet everyone's needs? Do we need to meet more or less frequently to accomplish our goals?

Is the location of our meetings agreeable to everyone? Do we want the location to be rotated?

Do we develop an agenda for the next meeting at the end of each meeting? Does everyone receive the agenda before the meeting? Do we need to build in time for "other" agenda items (to be specified at the beginning of each meeting)?

Do we follow our agenda?

How effective are our communication and conflict-resolution skills?

How are our "case studies" being implemented? What are we learning about local systems as a result of our case studies?

Do we want and need to conduct evaluation activities?

Source: Adapted from Everson & Rachal, 1996.

frequently led to misguided efforts by team initiators and leaders and resulted in poorly functioning teams. Moreover, because of this lack of research, teams that *are* effective are frequently unable to maintain their efforts, much less expand or replicate their activities .

The goal of this chapter was to merge findings from the empirical literature with the reports of transition efforts in order to provide teams with the tools necessary to guide their efforts. The ten guidelines presented, categorized by developmental stages, represent a framework both for newly emerging and established teams to follow when implementing a collaborative interagency team-based model of transition services.

The case studies illustrate two teams that took two different paths toward teaming and demonstrate the application of these guidelines with two actual teams. Unlike the team in Case Study 1, the future of the second team remains uncertain. Many storming problems remain unresolved and without membership confirmation, role clarification, development of communication and conflict-resolution skills, and commitment to developing and following operating procedures, the team appears destined to remain an ineffective, but mandated "team." To resolve these problems, the team in Case Study 2 needs to either generate internal leadership to guide its members through these storming activities and lay a foundation for norming and performing activities or work with an external consultant or facilitator to guide its members through these activities. Either path will require hard work on the part of all team members, but if these activities are pursued, this team can realize the positive teamwork experiences, systems-change, and enhanced consumer outcomes witnessed by the team in Case Study 1.

QUESTIONS

1. What are the defining characteristics of a team? How does this definition compare and contrast with the term as it is commonly applied to educational and human services "teams"?

2. According to Tuckman (1965), what are the four stages of teaming? Why might it be useful to leadership and team initiators to view teams within this framework?

3. Why is a team's membership such a critical forming activity?

4. Why are developing value and mission statements critical storming activities?

5. Describe the characteristics of an effective team initiator.

6. What is the optimal size of a team?

7. What is "goal displacement"? Give an example of its occurrence in a team with which you are familiar.

8. How can a case study approach assist a team in focusing its goals and activities?

9. Why are monitoring and evaluating activities important team activities?

10. Troubleshoot at least three "problems" with the team in Case Study 2. Discuss each problem and suggestions for how it might be addressed.

REFERENCES

Bates, P. E., Bronkema, J., Ames, T., & Hess, C. (1992). State-level interagency planning models. In F. P. Rusch, L. DeStefano, J. Chadsey-Rusch, L. A. Phelps, & E. Szymanski (Eds.), *Transition from school to adult life. Models, linkages, and policies* (pp. 115–129). Sycamore, IL: Sycamore.

Berelson, B., & Steiner G. (1964). *Human behavior: An inventory of scientific findings.* San Diego: Harcourt Brace Jovanovich.

Brager, G., & Holloway, S. (1978). *Changing human service organizations: Politics and practice.* New York: The Free Press.

Everson, J. M. (1993). *Youth with disabilities. Strategies for interagency transition programs.* Austin, TX: PRO-ED.

———. (1995). Teamwork in the transition from special education programs to independent living and employment. In H. G. Garner (Ed.), *Teamwork models and experience in education* (pp. 199–211). Boston: Allyn & Bacon.

Everson, J. M., & Moon, M. S. (1990). Developing community program planning and service delivery teams. In F. R. Rusch (Ed.), *Supported employment. Models, methods, and issues* (pp. 381–394). Sycamore, IL: Sycamore.

Everson, J. M., & Rachal, P. (1996). *What are we learning about state and local interagency partnerships? An analysis of statewide interagency activities for students who are deaf-blind in seventeen states.* Sands Point, NY: Helen Keller National Center–Technical Assistance Center.

Guzzo, R. A., & Dickson, M. W. (1996). Teams in organizations: Recent research on performance and effectiveness. *Annual Review of Psychology, 47,* 307–338.

Hackman, J. R. (1987). The design of work teams. In J. W. Lorsch (Ed.), *Handbook of organizational behavior* (pp. 315–342). Englewood Cliffs, NJ: Prentice Hall.

Halpern, A., Lindstrom, L. E., Benz, M. R., & Nelson, D. J. (1991). *Team leader's manual. Community transition team model.* Eugene: University of Oregon.

Hasenfeld, Y. (1974). Program development. In F. M. Cox, J. L. Erlich, J. Rothman, & J. E. Tropman (Eds.), *Strategies of community organization* (2nd ed.) (pp. 42–55). Itaska, IL: Peacock.

Jay, A. (1977). How to run a meeting. In F. M. Cox, J. L. Erlich, J. Rothman, & J. E. Tropman (Eds.), *Tactics and techniques of community practice* (pp. 255–269). Itaska, IL: Peacock.

Kettner, P., Daley, J. M., & Nichols, A. W. (1985). *Initiating change in organizations and committees.* Monterey, CA: Brooks/Cole.

Kohler, P. D., DeStefano, L., Wermuth, T. R., Grayson, T. E., & McGinity, S. (1994, Fall). An analysis of exemplary transition programs: How and why are they selected. *Career Development for Exceptional Individuals. 17*(2), 187–202.

Larson, C. E., & LaFasto, F. M. (1989). *Teamwork: What must go right/what can go wrong.* Newbury Park, CA: Sage.

Mattessich, P. W., & Monsey, B. R. (1992). *Collaboration: What makes it work.* St. Paul, MN: Amherst H. Wilder Foundation Publishing Center.

Minnesota Department of Education and Institute on Community Integration. (1990). *Interagency planning for transition in Minnesota, A resource guide.* Minneapolis: Author.

O'Neil Group. (1990). *Interactive behavior skills and meeting effectiveness.* Simsbury, CT: Author.

Sundstrom, E., DeMeuse, K. P., & Futrell, P. (1990). Work teams: Applications and effectiveness. *American Psychologist, 45,* 120–133.

Tuckman, B. W. (1965). Developmental sequences in small groups. *Psychological Bulletin, 63,* 384–399.

Varney, G. H. (1989). *Building productive teams. An action guide and resource book.* San Francisco: Jossey-Bass.

Weldon, E., & Weingart, L. N. (1993). Group goals and group performance. *British Journal of Social Psychology, 32,* 307–334.

13

The Personal Career Plan

A Person-Centered Approach to Vocational Evaluation and Career Planning

BRUCE M. MENCHETTI
and VICKY C. PILAND

This chapter illustrates the use of a Personal Career Plan to match an individual's preferences, goals, and strengths to local employment opportunities. The Personal Career Plan integrates the values and methods of person-centered planning processes with a profile approach to vocational evaluation and assessment. The Personal Career Plan may be used by schools, community rehabilitation facilities, adult education, and other employment service providers interested in implementing person-centered career assessment methods. The Personal Career Plan offers a practical strategy for making vocational evaluation, job matching, job placement, and career planning person-centered.

When paradigms change, the world itself changes with them. Led by a new paradigm, scientists adopt new instruments and look in new places.

THOMAS S. KUHN

American society is in the midst of significant change in the way we view and accommodate disability. The 1990s have brought new ways of thinking about disability (Hahn, 1988; Snow, 1993; Condeluci, 1995); policies emphasizing personal choice and empowerment (e.g., the Individuals with Disabilities Education Act; the Rehabilitation Act Amendments); and the development of personalized planning and support methods (Nisbet, 1992; Bradley, Ashbaugh, & Blaney, 1994; Menchetti & Bombay, 1994).

Some of these changes are slowly being incorporated into practice by service delivery systems such as special education and vocational

319

rehabilitation. And nowhere are these changes more evident than in the practice of vocational evaluation and program planning. Recent policies, changes in program quality standards, and the emergence of person-centered planning methods have provided opportunities to transform employment planning practices and outcomes. Employment services that are beginning to change include vocational evaluation, job matching, job placement, and career planning.

NEW POLICIES

Federal, state, and local policies reflect the changing nature of vocational evaluation and program planning. New policies urge systems to develop processes that provide opportunities for people with disabilities to become equal, active partners in all career decision-making processes. Furthermore, these policies advocate evaluation methods that identify persons' interests, strengths, and preferences. This consumer-driven, capacity-based strategy is what we refer to as the person-centered approach to vocational evaluation and career planning. In this approach, the individual receiving services is the driving force in all decision making and the development of all support options. In the person-centered approach, career planning, job development, job placement, and work support are provided in a manner that demonstrates respect for people and their wishes.

Federal policies clearly call for a person-centered approach to evaluation and career planning. For example, legislation such as the Individuals with Disabilities Education Act Amendments of 1997 (IDEA; P.L. 105-17) requires that adolescents with disabilities have a statement of needed transition services on their IEP. IDEA also stipulates that IEP transition services take into account a student's preferences and interests and may include a functional vocational evaluation (Storms, DeStefano, & O'Leary, 1996). Storms and colleagues (1996) pointed out that IDEA is explicit in encouraging active participation of students in the development of their IEP transition statements.

Insightfully, Storms and colleagues (1996) suggested that the transition requirements of IDEA provide opportunities to make evaluation and planning experiences "relate directly to students' dreams and desired outcomes" (p. 3). Thus, IDEA encourages special educators to use person-centered evaluation and transition-planning methods that involve students in meaningful ways, respect their preferences, and result in a useful plan for the future.

Similar evaluation and program planning preferences are expressed in the Rehabilitation Act Amendments of 1992 (P.L. 102-569). Specifically, Section 7(22)(B) encourages use of information provided by individuals that focus on their unique strengths, resources, priorities, interests, and needs. Menchetti and Bombay (1994) suggested that person-centered evaluation and planning methods that enhance personal choice and self-determination and highlight an individual's strengths are viable strategies for complying with the Rehabilitation Act Amendments of 1992.

In some areas of the country, evaluation and program-planning policies are beginning to change on the state level as well. For example, the Florida Developmental Disabilities Act, Chapter 393.0651, requires district developmental services program offices to give priority to consumer choice and community-inclusive experiences. In response to this state policy, the Florida Department of Children and Family Services, Developmental Services Program Office, has developed rules for "support coordination." Chapter 10F-13.012 of the Florida Administrative Code requires support coordinators to work with "the individual and family in the design of the individual's support plan and assist the individual in reaching personal life goals" (pp. 55–56).

Finally, employment policies are changing locally due to the courageous efforts of a few community-based agencies. Although widespread conversion from day training programs to integrated employment remains a significant challenge nationally (Murphy & Rogan, 1995a; Wehman & Kregel, 1995), a small percentage of community agencies have begun to change their employment policies to reflect person-centered approaches. Menchetti (1992) noted that diversification would provide opportunities for community agencies to develop person-centered support roles and that these new roles would fill important niches in the changing service delivery system. Diversified agencies could offer more broadly focused services such as increasing community disability awareness and supporting consumer empowerment and self-advocacy (Menchetti, 1992). Murphy and Rogan (1995a) pointed out that diversified community agencies could develop methods that directly address new policies and standards. One method they suggested was "individualized, person-centered, community-based assessments" (p. 57).

NEW QUALITY STANDARDS

Standards for determining the quality of programs serving people with disabilities have also changed over the last 5 years. Program quality standards now require person-centered evaluation and planning methods as indicators of appropriate practice.

For example, the 1995 edition of the Commission on Accreditation of Rehabilitation Facilities (CARF) standards manual requires that all programs seeking accreditation empower the people they serve by including their points of view and allowing them active and ongoing involvement in all components of service provision (Commission on Accreditation of Rehabilitation Facilities, 1995). According to the 1995 CARF standards, programs must be planned and delivered in response to the strengths, abilities, needs, and preferences of the persons served. The CARF manual refers to these service delivery principles as "individual-centered planning, service design, and delivery" (p. 33-2.A).

Case Study 1 illustrates how one community agency has responded to the new policies and program standards. This case study demonstrates

the organizational changes that are necessary to respond to the emerging person-centered policies and quality standards.

NEW METHODS

Changes in policies and program quality standards provide interesting opportunities for special educators, vocational rehabilitation professionals, employment consultants, and others who deliver transition and employment services to people with disabilities. We can continue to use existing processes, structures, and methods to gather vocational assessment information, plan programs, and provide employment services to people. Alternatively, like Leon Advocacy and Resource Center (LARC) in Leon County, Florida, we can implement person-centered career assessment methods by embarking on "the long journey of learning to do things differently on personal, community, and organizational levels" (Mount, 1994:107).

Although such a journey will be difficult and sometimes frustrating, there are several reasons why we must take the first steps toward implementing person-centered planning. First, there are moral, legal, and methodological reasons for such a change. Because the moral and legal reasons for implementing person-centered approaches have been articulately presented elsewhere (Mount & Zwernik, 1988; O'Brien & O'Brien 1992; Wehman, 1993), this section will focus on methodological problems and the unintended negative consequences of using formal assessment and planning techniques.

Limitations of Existing Assessment and Planning Methods

Technical Problems. The methodological problems associated with using formal assessment approaches to plan employment programs for people with disabilities have been discussed for three decades (Wolfensberger, 1967; Gold, 1973; Murphy & Hagner, 1988; Menchetti & Udvari-Solner, 1990). Nevertheless, formal

---

CASE STUDY 1 How One Community Agency Has Become More Person-Centered

Partially driven by changes in policies and programmatic standards, the Leon Advocacy and Resource Center (LARC), located in Leon County, Florida, began a conversion and diversification process in June 1995. LARC provides regional services to approximately 225 people in four Florida counties. Beginning with a sincere reexamination of the agency's values, the change process resulted in philosophical changes and adoption of more person-centered approaches.

Policies and programs began to change as result of the agency redefining its basic values and service delivery philosophy. The manifestations of these changes were dramatic. First, LARC closed its sheltered workshop. In November 1995, the agency officially changed its name from the Leon Association for Retarded Citizens to the Leon Advocacy and Resource Center. The new name better reflected LARC's person-centered values and its commitment to service diversification. The agency now provides advocacy and resources to adults with developmental disabilities through three programs: supported living; supported employment, including a voucher program; and community facilitation.

Today, LARC policies and programs strive to help people become equal partners in all aspects of the service delivery process. Thus, all LARC services, including vocational evaluation and program planning, are based on the interests and preferences of the consumer. Consumers receive opportunities and support to express their wishes, demonstrate their strengths, and control all decision making. One such support is the Personal Career Plan described later in this chapter.

---

instruments and professionally controlled processes continue to be used as the primary means of gathering assessment information and planning vocational programs for people with disabilities (Menchetti & Udvari-Solner, 1990; Hagner & Dileo, 1993).

Hagner and Dileo (1993) listed four assessment procedures that are commonly used in vocational testing of people with disabilities: (1) psychological tests such as aptitude and interest batteries; (2) work samples measuring work-related traits or simulated work tasks; (3) situational assessments consisting of brief job tryouts in rehabilitation facilities; and (4) on-the-job-evaluations comprised of actual jobs in the community.

With the exception of on-the-job evaluations using actual work, Hagner and Dileo (1993) suggested that popular assessment procedures were "artificial" and of limited use for career planning for some of the following reasons: (a) these procedures captured small, isolated pieces of real jobs; (b) these procedures lacked the work pressures, social interactions, and sights and sounds of real workplaces; and (c) many

procedures did not adequately address the effects of training or positive reinforcement on task performance. Because problems such as these may compromise the reliability of any instrument, Menchetti and Udvari-Solner (1990) questioned the reliability of vocational information gathered with the popular instruments and tests. Further, these authors suggested that the commonly used vocational assessment procedures also have validity problems when used with individuals with disabilities for career planning purposes.

Many vocational assessment instruments have not been validated for the purpose of predicting the employment success of individuals with disabilities who receive adequate, personalized support. Hagner and Dileo (1993) commented, "two decades of research have established almost no relationship between vocational assessment results and eventual success on the job" (p. 52). In fact, commonly used assessment procedures often result in predictions of employment failure for people who subsequently become employed with support. Menchetti and Udvari-Solner (1990) pointed out that instruments that make incorrect predictions are, by definition, "invalid." According to some, because of the psychometric problems associated with aptitude batteries, work samples, and other formal instruments, their continued use for career planning with individuals with disabilities "would be unprofessional, unethical, and irresponsible" (Menchetti & Udvari-Solner, 1990:305).

Unintended Negative Consequences. In addition to psychometric problems, the use of formal assessment instruments and planning approaches often produces unintended consequences that seriously limit their utility for career planning with people with disabilities. For example, there may be a conflict of interest when agencies conducting formal vocational assessments also receive funding to provide employment services to the people being assessed (Hagner & Dileo, 1993; Murphy & Rogan, 1995a). Thus, studies have found that agencies tend to recommend services based on the number of available slots rather than basing career planning decisions on an individual's preferences, strengths, and needs (Hagner & Dileo, 1993).

Dileo (1991) found that formalized assessment tools often produced "the unfortunate result of stereotypes and expectations for poor performance" (p. 11). These stereotypes and low expectations usually lead to labels, self-fulfilling prophecies, and assumptions of lifelong dependency for people who are labeled. "A label can work against an individual in powerful ways. Language can stereotype a person in reducing expectations of his or her performance or potential due to preconceived notions of what labels such as 'profoundly retarded,' or 'behaviorally disordered' mean" (Dileo, 1991:12–13).

As an explanation of the negative consequences and limited usefulness of traditional approaches to planning for people with disabilities, Mount and Zwernik (1988) concluded that these approaches have tended to focus on "deficit-finding" (p. 6). Mount and Zwernik (1988) went on to identify three problems with

traditional approaches to planning: (a) the assessment process highlights deficits; (b) the process results in goals that are already part of the existing program; and (c) the process relies solely on professional judgment and decision making.

Case Study 2 illustrates the problems associated with traditional vocational assessment procedures, demonstrating how they failed to correctly predict the employment outcomes attained by two people with extensive support needs. The two persons described in this case study were assessed with psychological tests and standardized work samples that typify traditional vocational assessment procedures. It is interesting to compare the recommendations made as a result of traditional vocational testing with the actual employment outcomes attained by the two persons described in Case Study 2.

VOCATIONAL ASSESSMENT AND PLANNING CHALLENGES

Given the limitations and negative consequences of formal assessment and planning instruments, several questions must be addressed. What kind of assessment approach will function effectively to help individuals with disabilities plan for their careers? How can special educators assist students in developing IEP transition statements that are based on their interests, preferences, and strengths? How can rehabilitation counselors empower their clients to become full partners in the development of their Individualized Written Rehabilitation Programs (IWRPs)? How can adult service providers work with consumers so that Individual Support Plans reflect the consumer's desires and delineate employment supports that lead to personally satisfying career choices and life-style improvements?

Answers to these questions include adopting new assessment instruments and looking in new places for career planning information. Adopting a person-centered career assessment approach represents the first step toward meeting these challenges.

> **CASE STUDY 2   The Limitations of Traditional Vocational Assessment**
>
> *Person 1*: 30-year-old female
> *Traditional Label(s):* Infantile autism; residual state
> *Assessment Instrument(s): Wechsler Intelligence Scale for Children-Revised; Wide Range Achievement Test; Bender Visual-Motor Gestalt*
> *Recommendation Based on Testing:* Not recommended for competitive employment
> *Current Employment Status:* She has been competitively employed for 6 years in a janitorial position.
>
> *Person 2*: 42-year-old male
> *Traditional Label(s):* Organic mental disorder; personality disorder
> *Assessment Instrument(s): McCarron-Dial Assessment of Neuromotor Development*
> *Recommendation Based on Testing:* Not recommended for competitive employment
> *Current Employment Status:* He has been competitively employed for 2 years in a landscape position.

THE PERSON-CENTERED APPROACH

A new information-gathering and support-planning process has emerged as a functional way to facilitate vocational assessment and career planning. This process reflects new ways of thinking about disability and federal policies emphasizing personal choice and empowerment. Called *lifestyle planning* (O'Brien, 1987) or *person-centered planning,* this process has been used primarily with individuals who are difficult to plan for, that is, those people for whom a career is difficult to imagine. These are people who, because of the type, severity, or number of their disabilities, have difficulty expressing their preferences and interests. Usually, they have acquired traditional labels such as severely disabled, autistic, developmentally disabled, severely emotionally disturbed, and/or multiply handicapped. As discussed earlier, these labels have made career planning even more difficult by producing stereotypes and expectations for limited performance (Mount & Zwernik, 1988; Dileo, 1991). Many teachers, counselors, and employment consultants have received vocational assessment reports that stated explicitly that people were "not ready for competitive employment" or that there were "no jobs that matched the limited aptitudes of the person being assessed."

Person-centered planning refers to an entire class of planning strategies and techniques. Person-centered techniques that were not designed specifically for vocational purposes, but may be useful for career planning include personal futures planning (Mount & Zwernik, 1988); essential life-styles planning (Smull & Harrison, 1992); and group action planning (Turnbull & Turnbull, 1993). Person-centered processes specifically designed for career planning were described by Dileo (1991), Hagner and Dileo (1993), and Murphy and Rogan (1995a).

All person-centered planning strategies utilize group support and an interactive problem-solving process to assist individuals with disabilities in planning for a bright future and successful transition. In addition, the person-centered planning process is based on the assumption that all people have the right and the capacity to achieve certain essential accomplishments that are related to life-style satisfaction.

O'Brien (1987) identified five essential outcomes or accomplishments related to life-style satisfaction:

1. Participation: With whom does the person spend time? How many are nonhandicapped? What community connections or networks can the person access?

2. Presence: What community settings are frequented on a regular basis? Does the person frequent these settings alone, in small groups, or in large groups?

3. Choices/Rights: What decisions does the person make independently and which decisions are made by others?

4. Respect: Does the person behave in ways that reinforce disability stereotypes? What valued roles does the person occupy in the community each day?

5. Competence: What skills does the person have? Which of them are needed and wanted by others? What contributions does the person make to other people's lives?

O'Brien (1987) suggested that these simple accomplishments frame the basic questions of person-centered planning. He asked: "How can we identify constructive actions that will improve the quality-of-life experiences for a particular individual? How can we increase the individual's community presence, choice, competence, respect, and community participation?" (p. 178).

Common Elements of Person-Centered Planning

Menchetti and Sweeney (1995) identified the characteristics that are common to all person-centered planning strategies or techniques: (a) group facilitation and support, (b) capacity-based description, (c) positive vision of the future, (d) plan of action and commitments, and (e) respect and empowerment. Each will be briefly discussed in what follows.

Group Facilitation and Support. All person-centered planning strategies rely on the collective wisdom, energy, and resources of a group of people. Pointing out that "no single person or service can or should do everything," O'Brien (1987:176) noted that person-centered planning asks people with different perspectives and interests to agree on desirable activities and supports for the person. In person-centered planning, this group of people is often called by different names: a circle of friends; a circle of support; or simply, a support group. It is important to understand that a circle or a support group is fundamentally different from other groups required by law to plan for individuals with disabilities (e.g., IEP teams and Individual Support Plan teams). If necessary, the circle or group uses understandable formats such as colorful charts and graphics to include and involve the person with a disability in all aspects of the process.

Capacity-Based Description. The person-centered planning process, like all planning processes, requires information. In this respect, it differs from traditional planning because it focuses on the person's strengths, talents, and gifts rather than deficits. That is, person-centered planning is a capacity-finding rather than a deficit-finding process. Some have referred to it as a "treasure hunt " (Nisbet, 1992). In person-centered planning, the circle or group searches for an individual's talents and potential resources instead of limitations. Snow (1993) reminded us that everyone is gifted! It is our challenge to use person-centered planning to discover and describe the gifts and treasures in everyone.

Positive Vision of the Future. All person-centered planning strategies generate a vision of a positive future for the person. Many use terms such as "dream" or "making the impossible possible" when referring to the goals generated by circles or support groups. Through an interactive process, group members share their ideas about the person's future. A vision of a future begins to form through this kind of brainstorming, and group members are challenged to imagine ways of increasing opportunities for the person to have more positive experiences.

Plan of Action and Commitments. All person-centered planning strategies result in a plan to achieve the vision for the person. The planning process includes identification of obstacles and opportunities, delineation of priorities, development of strategies to move toward the vision, and a voluntary commitment by group members to assist in the effort. The focus is on small action steps because the future is not designed by big events but by small ones. According to Mount and Zwernik (1988), one of the pioneers of person-centered planning, John McKnight, has said that "when thinking of doing anything in community integration, think small, think face-to-face" (p. 22).

Respect and Empowerment. The value underlying all person-centered planning strategies is respect for the person's wishes, preferences, and desires. Even though it may appear impossible to plan a positive future for people who cannot communicate their own ideas in the typical manner, the person-centered planning process is unshakable in its insistence that the group find ways to understand, listen to, and respect the person. The person gets to make his or her own choices and sometimes educates other members of the group. Mount and Zwernik (1988) have suggested that the system does not make the choice but supports the person's choice. This value is another reason why person-centered planning is fundamentally different from traditional planning approaches.

Compatibility of Person-Centered Planning and Transition Planning

While fundamentally different from traditional planning approaches, person-centered planning is highly compatible with the transition-planning requirements of The IDEA Amendments of 1997 (P.L. 105-17). It provides a process for meeting the letter of the law and making transition plans truly "preference-based."

Person-centered planning and IEP transition plans have the same purposes, both seek to (a) build connections or linkages in the community; (b) support an individual's career preferences and interests; and (c) help the person achieve satisfying adult life-style outcomes.

THE PERSONAL CAREER PLAN: FIRST STEP TOWARD IMPLEMENTING PERSON CENTERED CAREER ASSESSMENT

The next section of this chapter illustrates the use of a Personal Career Plan to match an individual's preferences, goals, and strengths to local employment opportunities. The Personal Career Plan integrates the values and methods of person-centered planning processes with a profile approach to vocational evaluation (McLoughlin, Garner, & Callahan, 1987; Hagner & Dileo, 1993).

Components of the Personal Career Plan

Hagner and Dileo (1993) suggested four steps for developing a personal career profile: (1) assembling a support group; (2) facilitating a career planning meeting; (3) developing action plans; and (4) reconvening to review efforts, resources and changes. The type of person-centered career assessment suggested in this chapter extends the work of Hagner and Dileo (1993) by adding a fifth step to the process. Thus, the Personal Career Plan proposed here also includes the development of a résumé for the individual. In keeping with the person-centered approach, the résumé is jointly developed by the individual and an employment consultant. The following sections describe how the Personal Career Plan can be used by schools, community rehabilitation facilities, adult education, and other employment service providers interested in implementing person-centered career assessment methods.

1. Assembling a Support Group. The Personal Career Plan process begins when a person is referred to a school program or adult agency for supported employment. For school-aged individuals, such referrals are usually the result of transition IEP team meetings. For adults who have exited school, referrals are usually made by state agencies to adult education or community employment providers. During the IEP meeting or intake process, someone must be designated as the "employment consultant" who will work for the person referred. The employment consultant can be a teacher, a vocational evaluator, a rehabilitation technician, or any other individual who is responsible for providing vocational evaluation services. The designated employment consultant calls the person referred to introduce himself or herself and to notify the person that a referral has been received. After confirming that the person desires employment services from the school or agency, the employment consultant describes the career planning process and discusses possible times, places, and people for a planning meeting. If the person agrees, invitations are mailed to potential support group members such as vocational rehabilitation counselors, developmental services support coordinators, teachers, friends, and other people that the person wishes to attend.

2. Facilitating a Planning Meeting.

On the designated date, the support group convenes for the expressed purpose of developing a career plan with the person. The designated employment consultant, who must be trained to conduct person-centered planning meetings, acts as the group facilitator. He or she explains the purpose and format of the meeting so that everyone present understands what is about to occur. The employment consultant emphasizes the need for all group members to listen to the person, respect his or her statements, and support his or her wishes.

The employment consultant asks everyone to sign the support group page (see Appendix 13.A) and asks the person and the group for the names of other people who should be invited to attend future meetings. Using person-centered planning techniques such as drawing charts, the employment consultant helps the group gather information relevant for job matching, employment placement, and career planning. The Personal Career Plan includes several forms to guide information gathering (see Appendix 13.A). They partially consist of (a) support group description; (b) personal data; (c) employment history and personal references; and (d) education, skills, and accomplishments. After all of the information has been collected, the employment consultant reviews the data with the person and the support group and asks for clarification and changes if needed.

3. Developing Action Plans.

To conclude the support group meeting, participants complete the last form called a Personal Career Plan (see Appendix 13.A), which requires that the group assists the individual in expressing his or her employment vision or goal and developing action steps to meet that goal. After a vision is developed in the form of an "I want … " statement, the group helps the person plan target dates, identify supports and barriers, and develop strategies and tactics to get a job that matches his or her vision.

4. Reviewing Efforts.

A few days after the support group meeting, the employment consultant calls or visits the person to review the meeting, begin implementing the career plan, and answer any questions. If necessary, or if the person requests, the employment consultant will also contact other group members or individuals the group identified as needed to implement the career plan. At this time, the employment consultant makes an appointment to visit the person and help him or her write a résumé.

5. Writing a Résumé.

Appendix 13.B illustrates how a résumé can be written using the Personal Career Plan. First, based on information from the vision statement, the person writes an employment objective. The employment consultant provides whatever support is needed to assist in writing this objective. Next, the person and the employment consultant review employment history and personal reference information to complete the employment history section of the résumé. Volunteer activities and nonpaid work experiences should be presented here. Using information from the education, skills, and accomplishment section of the Personal Career Plan, the person and employment consultant then write the education and skills and accomplishment sections of the résumé. All educational experiences, training, and awards should be presented in the appropriate section. Finally, the person and employment consultant review the personal interests section of the Personal Career Plan and write the interests and hobbies section of the résumé.

Technical Adequacy of the Personal Career Plan

It is important to evaluate the technical adequacy of any assessment technique. Although relatively new, the Personal Career Plan is being evaluated for the purposes of (a) monitoring the implementation of the process and (b) continuously improving the process to ensure quality outcomes.

Table 13.1 includes information about one hundred and three individuals who completed the Personal Career Planning process. All of them are adults who were labeled developmentally disabled and referred to a community agency for supported employment services.

Future Steps

The Personal Career Plan is not intended to be a "quick fix" for schools, community rehabilitation facilities, and other employment services providers wishing to comply with new policies and/or meet recently developed program accreditation standards. Mount (1994) cautioned that in order to successfully implement the person-centered approach, professionals must be willing to do things differently on personal, community, and organizational levels. According to Mount (1994), the reason for change to a person-centered approach must go beyond the "system's demand for compliance, control, accountability, and efficiency" (p. 103).

The Personal Career Plan represents only the first, and undoubtedly the easiest step, toward full implementation of person-centered career assessment. Other, more difficult steps must be taken. Only those willing to complete a process of personal and organizational change similar to the process undertaken by the Leon Advocacy and Resource Center (see Case Study 1) can use the Personal Career Plan effectively. Full implementation will require adoption not only of new instruments, but also a new way of thinking about our roles, processes, organizations, and communities.

CONCLUSION

This chapter illustrates the use of a Personal Career Plan to facilitate vocational evaluation, job matching, job placement, and career planning. The Personal Career Plan was designed to guide the assessment of an individual's employment history, preferences, interests, skills, and goals. Developed within the context of a person-centered process, the Personal Career Plan offers a first step to schools, community rehabilitation facilities, and other employment service providers interested in implementing alternatives to traditional vocational evaluation and assessment approaches.

American society is changing the way it views and accommodates disability. These changes are beginning to transform the methods used in special education, vocational rehabilitation, and other service delivery systems. One method that embodies this transformation is person-centered career assessment. As we near the year 2000, person-centered assessment approaches represent an information-gathering and support-planning methodology that is compatible with new disability policies and emerging program standards. We believe that person-centered career assessment methods will define transition and career planning and will become the vocational assessment standard of the twenty-first century. We urge professionals to adopt new assessment instruments, such as the

Table 13.1 Outcomes of the Personal Career Planning Process

Number of people completing process	103
Number of people employed	69
Number employed in preferred job[a]	54
Average time from referral to employment	3.5 months
Average hours employed per week	
(Range: 12 hr/wk to 40 hr/wk)	24.1
Average hourly wage	
(Range: $4.75/hr to $7.00/hr)	$5.13

[a]Employed in preferred job means that the person attained the job he or she expressed during the assessment process as recorded on the Personal Career Plan.

Personal Career Plan presented here, and look in new places for solutions to vocational evaluation, job matching, job placement, and career planning. This approach clearly provides new opportunities for individuals with disabilities to move successfully beyond high school.

QUESTIONS

1. Explain how person-centered evaluation and career planning strategies are compatible with the transition-planning requirements found in IDEA?

2. How are person-centered planning strategies compatible with the evaluation and planning requirements found in the Rehabilitation Act Amendments?

3. Describe the four assessment procedures that are commonly used in vocational testing of people with disabilities.

4. When assisting individuals with disabilities with their career planning, what are the limitations of assessment procedures such as psychological tests, work samples, and other formal instruments?

5. To date, person-centered planning has been used primarily to assist which group of people?

6. Name three person-centered planning techniques that were *not* designed specifically for career assessment, but may be adapted for this purpose.

7. What are the elements or characteristics that are common to all person-centered planning strategies or techniques?

8. List five steps for developing the Personal Career Plan described in this chapter.

9. Is it true that once a school district or community agency has adopted and used a strategy such as the Personal Career Plan, it has implemented *all* the steps necessary to become person-centered. Give reasons for your answer.

10. According to the chapter authors, which assessment approach represents the future of transition and career planning?

REFERENCES

American Association on Mental Retardation. (1992). *Mental retardation: Definition, classification, and system of supports* (9th ed.). Washington, DC: Author.

Bradley, J. V., Ashbaugh, J. W., & Blaney, B. C. (Eds.). (1994). *Creating individual supports for people with developmental disabilities.* Baltimore: Paul H. Brookes.

Commission on Accreditation of Rehabilitation Facilities. (1995). *Standards manual and interpretative guidelines for employment and community support.* Tucson, AZ: Author.

Condeluci, A. (1995). *Interdependence: The route to community* (2nd ed.). Winter Park, FL: GR Press.

Developmental Disabilities Act, 2 Fla. Stat. Subsection 393.0651. (1995).

Dileo, D. (1991). *Reach for the dream! Developing individual service plans for persons with disabilities.* St. Augustine, FL: Training Resource Network.

Florida Administrative Code, Subsection 10F-13.012. (1995).

Gold, M. W. (1973). Research on the vocational rehabilitation of the retarded: The present, the future. In N. Ellis (Ed.), *International review of research in mental retardation: Volume 6* (pp. 97–147). New York: Academic Press.

Hagner, D., & Dileo, D. (1993). *Working together: Workplace culture, supported employment, and persons with disabilities.* Cambridge, MA: Brookline Books.

Hahn, H. (1988). The politics of physical differences: Disability and discrimination. *Journal of Social Issues, 44*(1), 39–47.

McLoughlin, C. S., Garner, J. B., & Callahan, M. (1987). *Getting employed, staying employed: Job development and training for persons with severe handicaps.* Baltimore: Paul H. Brookes.

Menchetti, B. M. (1992). From work adjustment to community adjustment. *Vocational Evaluation and Work Adjustment Bulletin, 25*(3), 70–74.

Menchetti, B. M., & Bombay, H. E. (1994). Facilitating community inclusion with vocational assessment portfolios. *Assessment in Rehabilitation and Exceptionality, 1*(3), 213–222.

Menchetti, B. M., & Sweeney, M. A. (1995). *Person-centered planning* (Technical Assistance Packet 5). Gainesville: University of Florida, Department of Special Education, Florida Network.

Menchetti, B. M., & Udvari-Solner, A. (1990). Supported employment: New challenges for vocational evaluation. *Rehabilitation Education, 4,* 301–317.

Mount, B. (1994). Benefits and limitations of personal futures planning. In J. Bradley, J. W. Ashbaugh, & B. C. Blaney (Eds.), *Creating individual supports for people with developmental disabilities* (pp. 97–108). Baltimore: Paul H. Brookes.

Mount, B., & Zwernik, K. (1988). *It's never too early, it's never too late: A booklet about personal futures planning.* (Available from the Minnesota Governor's Planning Council on Developmental Disabilities, 300 Centennial Office Building, 658 Cedar Street, St. Paul, MN 55155.)

Murphy, S. T., & Hagner, D. (1988). Evaluation assessment settings: Ecological influences on vocational evaluation. *Journal of Rehabilitation, 53,* 53–59.

Murphy, S. T., Rogan, P. M. (1995a). *Closing the shop: Conversion form sheltered to integrated work.* Baltimore: Paul H. Brookes.

———. (1995b). *Developing natural supports in the workplace: A practitioner's guide.* St. Augustine, FL: Training Resource Network.

Nisbet, J. (1992). *Natural supports in school, at work, and in the community for people with severe disabilities.* Baltimore: Paul H. Brookes.

O'Brien, J. (1987). A guide to life-style planning: Using the activities catalog to integrate services and natural support systems. In B. Wilcox & G. T. Bellamy (Eds.), *A comprehensive guide to the activities catalog: An alternative curriculum for youth and adults with severe disabilities* (pp. 175–189). Baltimore: Paul H. Brookes.

O'Brien, J., & O'Brien, C. L. (1992). Members of each other: Perspectives on social support for people with severe disabilities. In J. Nisbet (Ed.), *Natural supports in school, at work, and in the community for people with severe disabilities* (pp. 17–63). Baltimore: Paul H. Brookes.

Smull, M., & Harrison, S. (1992). *Supporting people with severe reputations in the community.* (Available from the National Association of State Directors of Developmental Disabilities Services, Inc., 113 Oronoco Street, Alexandria, VA 22314.)

Snow, J. (1993). Giftedness vs. disability: A reflection. In J. Pearpoint, M. Forest, & J. Snow (Eds.), *The inclusion papers: Strategies to make inclusion work* (p. 13). Toronto: Inclusion Press.

Storms, J., DeStefano, L., & O'Leary, E. (1996). *Individuals with disabilities education act: Transition requirements. A guide for states, districts, schools, and families.* Stillwater: Oklahoma State University, National Clearinghouse of Rehabilitation Training Materials.

Turnbull, A. P., & Turnbull, H. R. (1993). Empowerment and decision-making through Group Action Planning. In *Life-long transitions: Proceedings of the third annual parent/family conference* (pp. 39–45). Washington, DC: U.S. Department of Education.

Wehman, P. (1993). *The ADA mandate for social change.* Baltimore: Paul H. Brookes.

Wehman, P., & Kregel, J. (1995). At the crossroads: Supported employment a decade later. *Journal of the Association for Persons with Severe Handicaps, 20*(4), 286–299.

Wolfensberger, W. (1967). Vocational preparation and occupation. In A. A. Baumeister (Ed.), *Mental retardation* (pp. 232–273). Chicago: Aldine.

■

Appendix 13.A
Completed Personal Career Plan

Support Group

Name: _____ Gina M. _____   **Date:** 5/6/97

Who's Here Today?

Name	Relationship/Agency
Vicky C.	Employment Consultant/LARC
Bruce R.	V.R. Counselor
Jeanine M.	Mother
Gina M.	Consumer
Ann Q.	D.S. Support Coordinator

Who Should Be Here?

Name:	Relationship/Agency
Mrs. F.	Teacher
Diane M.	Grandmother
Andrew G.	Friend

Personal Data

Name: Gina M.   **Date:** 5/6/97   **Phone:** 123-4567
Address: 205 Stone Ave.
City: Tallahassee   **State:** FL   **Zip:** 32306
Social Security #: 456-78-9100   **D.O.B.:** 12/3/77
Emergency Contact: Jeanine M.   **Phone:** 123-4567

Benefits: SSI   ☐   PASS   ☐
                                 SSDI   ☐   IRWE   ☐

                                 Payee: _____

Referral Source: DS   ☐   LCS   ☐
                                 VR   ☐   Other ☐

DS Support Coordinator: Ann Q._____
VR Counselor: Bruce R._____
Other: _____

Medical Concerns:
   Gina has had seizures. However, seizures are controlled by medication.
   Depakote 250 mg (3 pills) 3 × per day.

Transportation Concerns:
   Gina is familiar with taking the city bus, but she will need additional bus training to go
   to work. Specialized transportation is an option.

Employment History and Personal References

Employer: New County Schools   **Address:** 2757 ABC Lane

Telephone: 456-7891   **Job Title:** Custodial Worker

Dates From: 01/96   **To:** 06/96

Salary Beginning: Volunteer   **Ending:** N/A

Supervisor: Ms. Smith

Reason for Leaving: Graduated from school

Employer: Dept. of Agriculture   **Address:** 120 Easy St.

Telephone: 345-6789   **Job Title:** Janitor

Dates From: 06/10/95   **To:** 07/35/95

Salary Beginning: $4.25/hr   **Ending:** $4.25/hr

Supervisor: Mr. Jones

Reason for Leaving: Returned to school

Employer: Dept. of Hwy. Safety   **Address:** 456 Safe St.

Telephone: 668-1234   **Job Title:** Clerical Aide

Dates From: 06/10/95   **To:** 07/35/95

Salary Beginning: $4.25/hr   **Ending:** $4.25/hr

Supervisor: Mr. Martin

Reason for Leaving: Returned to school

References

Name: Mrs. F   **Address:** Local H.S.   **Phone:** 123-4567   **Occupation:** Teacher

Name: Mrs. Smith   **Address:** New County Sch.   **Phone:** 456-7891   **Occupation:** Supervisor

Name: Mr. Jones   **Address:** Dept. of Ag.   **Phone:** 345-6789   **Occupation:** Supervisor

Education/Skills and Accomplishments

Education:

School Name: Local High School   **Address:** 647 Smart St.

Dates From: 8/92   **To:**   6/96

School Name: _____   **Address:** _____

Dates From: _____   **To:**   _____

School Name: _____   **Address:** _____

Dates From: _____   **To:**   _____

Skills and Accomplishments:

Good attendance, made good grades in math, good verbal communication skills—very sociable.

Personal Interests:

1. **What are your hobbies/interest?**
   I like shopping, talking on the phone, and computers.
2. **What volunteer/school activities have you participated in?**
   I volunteered at NCS for a summer work program. I also volunteered in a preschool reading program.
3. **Imagine that you could have any job in the world. Exactly what would it be?**
   I would like to work with people in an office job and wear nice clothes. I like talking on the phone.

Personal Career Plan

Vision Statement:
I want some work experience and training this summer. I would like to work for the state in an office job where the people are friendly and nice.

Target Date:
Work this summer in JTPA program. State job by Fall 1996 (or earlier if needed).

Network/Support:
VR Counselor, DS Support Coordinator, LARC Employment Consultant, Mom.

Barriers:
Transportation and limited employment opportunities for specialized position.

Plan/Tactics:
- Work with employment consultant to develop résumé
- Fill out application for JTPA program
- Meet with support group to discuss summer experience and get help with job development
- Work with support group to look for office job with state

Appendix 13.B
Sample and Completed Résumés

JOHNNY JOBSEEKER
Street Address
Tallahassee, FL 32303
(850) XXX-XXXX

Objective

The individual, together with the employment consultant, writes an employment objective. When writing this career objective, they should review and discuss the vision statement section on the form in Appendix 13.A, Personal Career Plan.

Employment History

The individual and the employment consultant review information from the Employment History and Personal References (see Appendix 13.A) to develop this section of the résumé. Information in this section should be presented like a typical résumé. That is, jobs should be listed in reverse chronological order from the most recent to the earliest. Volunteer activities and non-paid work experience should be included.

Education

The individual and employment consultant again use the data from the Education/Skills and Accomplishments form to develop this section of the résumé. All relevant education and training experience should be presented.

Skills and Accomplishments

Referring again to the Education/Skills and Accomplishments form in Appendix 13.A, the individual and employment consultant summarize skills, talents, and accomplishments. Recognition and awards the individual may have received should be included here.

Interests and Hobbies

Finally, data from the Education/Skills and Accomplishments form should be reviewed by the individual and the employment consultant when developing this section of the résumé. Specifically, the personal interests section should be reviewed. Hobbies, as well as school and community activities, should be considered. Don't forget to discuss employment desires and choices here.

REFERENCES AVAILABLE UPON REQUEST

Gina M.
205 Stone Avenue
Tallahassee FL 32306
(850) 123-4567

Objective

My career goal is to secure employment with the state of Florida in a clerical position requiring interaction with people.

Employment History

1/96–6/96   New County Schools (custodial)
Worked as a volunteer in a custodial position performing janitorial and light building maintenance duties.

6/95–7/95   Department of Agriculture (janitorial)
Employed as a janitor performing cleaning and light building maintenance duties.

6/94–7/94   Department of Highway Safety (clerical)
Employed as a clerical aide. Duties included taking phone messages, copying and collating, operating office equipment, and greeting customers.

Education

Local High School, Tallahassee, FL   1992–1996

Skills and Accomplishments

My strengths include my ability to interact well with management, co-workers, and customers. I have excellent verbal communication skills, attendance, and math ability.

Interests and Hobbies

I have enjoyed volunteering in community service programs such as school-to-work and preschool reading projects. In my spare time, I enjoy working on computers and spending time with my friends.

REFERENCES AVAILABLE UPON REQUEST

14

◉

School-Sponsored
Work Experience and
Vocational Instruction

DAVID HAGNER and
JENNIFER VANDER SANDE

School-sponsored work experiences, periods of time students are engaged in activities at a community workplace during the school day or arranged and supported by the school, are a key component of career preparation and transition. This chapter views the rationale for work experience as rooted in three interrelated trends: (1) efforts to more effectively prepare high school students to enter the work force; (2) renewed interest in community-based instruction as a more natural, more motivating context for learning for all students; and (3) the emphasis on improving postschool outcomes for students with disabilities. Several prevalent kinds of work experiences are discussed, and six key considerations for the design of a successful work experience program are outlined. Finally, considerations relevant to the successful inclusion of students with disabilities in these programs, including job instruction, co-worker and employer consultation, strategies to facilitate social inclusion, and assistive technology, are presented.

Education can be viewed in a broad sense as preparation for young people to assume adult roles in society, including roles associated with productivity and earning a living. Programs and curricular components to help students prepare in a specific way for entry into the world of work are as old as education itself (Good & Teller, 1969). This preparation has taken numerous forms, including career guidance, career education, vocational education classes, career days and job fairs, job placement services, and many others. School-sponsored work experiences, periods of time engaged in activities at the workplace, either during the school day or arranged and supported by the school and considered part of the school curriculum, have been regarded as a central component in this preparation.

Today, educators and educational theorists are taking a closer look than ever before at work experience as an integral part of secondary education, not only as a key component of vocational preparation but on nonvocational grounds as well. Work experiences can add relevance, context, meaning, and complexity to the school-based components of a secondary curriculum; can provide young people with guided exposure to the world of adult roles and expectations; can motivate students and help improve rates of graduation; and can forge closer connections between schools and their communities.

This chapter will review the background of and rationales for school-sponsored work experience and examine the kinds of work experience that are prevalent in secondary education. Considerations for implementing a successful work experience program also will be outlined. Finally, specific job-support and instructional components necessary to ensure that students with disabilities receive equal benefit from these programs will be discussed.

BACKGROUND AND RATIONALE FOR WORK EXPERIENCE PROGRAMS

The growing interest in work experience programming stems from three interrelated educational trends. First, there have been accelerated efforts to revamp school-to-work services and improve postschool employment outcomes for young adults. Second, a growing movement favoring "contextual learning" emphasizes the benefits of instruction outside of the traditional school classroom, including workplace-based learning. And, third, developments within special education have increasingly emphasized the linkages between educational programming and

achievement of quality-of-life postschool outcomes for students with disabilities. The intersection of these trends represents a powerful force for educational restructuring that benefits all students.

Preparing for the World of Work

As discussed in greater detail in Chapter 5, in the United States, vocational education was established as a national priority with the Smith-Hughes Act of 1917. The traditional focus of vocational education was on providing those students not planning to continue with postsecondary education with training for a place in the labor force following high school. The economic structure of society and the composition of the labor force have seen dramatic changes since that time, and vocational education has changed as well. A series of initiatives and reforms have resulted in the development of a complex, and for many people confusing, collection of overlapping vocational education programs and service models, including tech-prep, co-op, DECA, and many others.

Recent reforms can be traced to the 1970s, with the introduction of the term "career education" by Sidney Marland (White & Biller, 1988). The career education movement focused on improving the way students are able to relate learning in school to what they will be doing on completion of school. An explicit goal of the movement was to adapt the educational system to the changing needs of society, and to ensure that all students left school equipped with the skills and attitudes necessary to make sound career decisions. Thus, career education represented a broadening of scope and vision of career preparation by the educational system.

In the 1980s, a series of studies and reports challenged schools to further rethink and reform vocational education. For the first time, the business community became a driving force in these efforts due to a concern that schools were not adequately preparing students for the workplace in the context of an increasingly competitive global economy (Committee for Economic Development, 1985; Tilson, Luecking, & Donovan, 1994). Many employers and business leaders felt, and continue to feel, that traditional school-based learning is simply not relevant to their needs (Hill, 1995). As a result, the Commission on the Skills of the American Workforce (CSAW, 1990) recommended that the nation's schools place increased emphasis on learning that is directly relevant to the needs of the workplace, noting that learning is likely to be most relevant when it takes place within the workplace itself.

It is easy to see how businesses stand to gain from an educational process that is relevant to their needs, and how schools and communities stand to gain from greater business commitment to education (Hill, 1995). But the primary impact of a close connection between the skills and knowledge gained in school and the skills and knowledge needed in the workplace—or lack thereof—is on the young adults within our communities. Large numbers of young adults find themselves unemployed, underemployed, or floundering in the attempt to establish their careers. For example, Veum and Weiss (1993) found that the average high school graduate who was not enrolled in postsecondary education held nearly six different jobs between the ages of 18 and 27 and was unemployed almost 35 weeks. Members of minority groups within society are affected even more seriously (Raizen, 1994).

Career development theorists, emphasizing the importance of accurate knowledge of the world of work for sound career decision making, note that the most direct and powerful information about the world of work is drawn from actual work experience (Rosenthal, 1989; Isaacson & Brown, 1993). Thus, work experiences have value for students as a vehicle for exploring careers and job types, as much as for direct preparation and skill development. Students find that even the knowledge that a particular career does not suit them can be invaluable in steering them past costly mistakes later on (Reidy & Schottmueller, 1993).

Partnership between business and education and integration of school-based with workplace-based learning are central themes in current efforts to improve vocational education. Federal initiatives in this direction include the 1990 amendments to the Carl Perkins Vocational Education Act and the School-to-Work Opportunities Act of 1994. These pieces of legislation highlight work experience in a community job as a key ingredient in career preparation.

Learning in Context

A growing movement in education challenges the adequacy of traditional classroom-based learning on purely academic grounds and advocates closer attention to the value of the "community as classroom" (Thompson, 1995). In fact, Abbott (1995) argued that the emphasis prevalent in conventional classroom-based schooling on accumulating abstract knowledge is outdated and leaves students ill equipped to face the challenges of adulthood in the twenty-first century. Advocates of more nonschool-based learning cite evidence that the pace, complexity, and value of learning are enhanced when the learning takes place within a natural context (Cox & Firpo, 1993; Miller et al., 1995). For example, Christ (1995) argued that there are ample grounds for believing that information presented in a meaningful context is retained longer, suggesting that the students' question "when are we gonna need this?" ought to be taken as a serious challenge to traditional curricula. Some studies have even suggested that classroom-based learning can interfere with an individual's ability to engage in problem solving in natural situations (Raizen, 1994). As a consequence, some theorists have come to believe that excellence in secondary education requires a greater appreciation and use of "contextualized" learning (Thompson, 1995), "situated learning" (Raizen, 1994), or "connected learning" (Van Der Vorm, 1993), that is, school-sponsored learning that takes place directly within natural community environments.

Workplaces are ideal natural contexts for learning. Miller and colleagues (1995) reported that student writing skills soared when classroom instruction was integrated with workplace-based assignments such as writing reviews for publication in a magazine, preparing vignettes for display at the state visitors' center, and preparing promotional material for a theater company. The direct relevance of these tasks motivated and challenged students in ways no abstract assignment can do. Many students simply enjoy learning in the workplace more than learning in the classroom (Hamilton, 1990).

A key aspect of community-based learning is students' interaction with one or more experienced adult instructors or mentors. Theorists such as Collins, Brown, and Holum (1991) and Raizen (1994) believe that the apprentice/mentor relationship plays a major role in cognitive development and that this role has been neglected largely by the educational system. Throughout most of human history, and today in most of the world, young people master adult roles through individualized apprenticeship. Studies of the apprenticeship process (e.g., Jordan, 1989) have found that the continual interplay among watching, doing, and didactic explanation that characterizes apprentice learning represents an extraordinarily effective cognitive development strategy. Collins et al. (1991) called this strategy "making thinking visible."

Other educational reform advocates view workplace-based learning not only as part of a return to an educational program that is more motivating for students, but also more likely to build connections between students and supportive adults in the community. Thus, community work experiences are seen as a way to improve rates of school completion for students at risk of dropping out. Loughead, Liu, and Middleton (1995), Speight and colleagues (1995), and Thompson (1995) reported that a work experience program successfully lowered school dropout rates. Thompson (1995) attributed this effect in part to the presence of additional supportive adults for children who may have inadequate role models and supports at home.

Loughead and colleagues (1995) also noted that many youth living in poverty are "basically dealing with survival issues" (p. 282) and the ability to bring home a paycheck from a school-sponsored work experience can make a critical difference in the decision to remain in school. Abbott (1995) went further to suggest that not just disadvantaged or at-risk students but all children benefit from contacts with adult role models in the community other than their relatives and teachers, and that schools can play an important role in structuring such contacts.

Ensuring Successful Transition for Students with Disabilities

Within special education, work experience has long been advocated as part of a secondary curriculum based on teaching functional skills (Gaylord-Ross et al., 1988). The concept of a "functional curriculum" arose from two related sources. First, students with disabilities continued to show poor postschool outcomes even in the face of impressive evidence that they were capable of performing meaningful work in community jobs. And, second, the prevalent belief that students in special education are poorer at generalizing from one context to another suggested that these students should be taught skills in the settings where they will be performed. Entitled to an appropriate education under federal law, students, their families, and other advocates began to demand educational services geared toward establishing viable postschool employment. The Individuals with Disabilities Education Act (P.L. 105-17) requires that the Individualized Education Program for each student with an educational disability contain a statement of needed transition services, beginning by at least age 16.

Statements such as "vocational activities should form the core of the educational program for severely handicapped high school students" (Gaylord-Ross et al., 1988:192) were commonplace in the special education transition literature for many years, and very specific recommendations for the timing and structure of these vocational activities were offered. For example, Gaylord-Ross and colleagues (1988) recommended that special education students should have at least three community work experiences during the secondary years, each lasting 3 to 9 months, from 1 to 6 hours per day, 2 to 5 days per week.

Special education programs that provide work experience as a part of the secondary curriculum (e.g., Vogelsberg, Ashe, & Williams, 1986; Tilson, 1994) have reported improved rates of postschool employment for participating students. Findings from a National Longitudinal Study of Transition (D'Amico, 1991) support these reports. Special education students who had a school-sponsored work experience were significantly more likely to hold employment 12 months after leaving school (62.2 percent) than their counterparts who had not had a school-sponsored work experience (45.2 percent).

However, a parallel movement in special education advocates full inclusion of students in the same regular education curriculum as other students. Advocates for this position argue that any separation from what other students are doing decreases the chance for interpersonal relationships and positive self-esteem, and thus all kinds of normative community experiences for people with disabilities. They argue persuasively that a pattern of separation and exclusion, once begun in school, has lifelong negative effects (Falvey, Gage, & Eshilian, 1995).

Advocates of full inclusion note that inclusion need not be at the expense of postschool employment outcomes. School inclusion itself can have a positive effect on postschool employment, as students build peer networks that produce job leads and interact with other students who are in the process of making and implementing postschool plans. There is some anecdotal evidence that this occurs (Hagner, Helm, & Butterworth, 1996). In addition, some support is available from the National Longitudinal Study of Transition (D'Amico, 1991). We have seen that the relationship between work experience and postschool employment was strong. But the relationship between percentage of time

students spent in regular classes and the probability of employment after leaving school was even stronger. That is, students spending all of their time in regular classes were almost twice as likely to be employed following graduation (66.6 percent) as students spending one-third of the time or less in regular classes (34.1 percent). Undoubtedly, differences in severity of disability among those who spent different amounts of time in regular classes is a factor, but Falvey and colleagues (1995) speculated that the increased social skills and social networks of students who participate in age-appropriate settings, and possibly a higher level of academic achievement associated with attending regular classes, play a role as well.

As the functional curriculum movement and the school inclusion movement advance and develop together, the pendulum has begun to swing away from an overreliance on a separate curriculum of community-based instruction toward a more moderate approach. For example, Halpern, Dorenz, and Benz (1993) recommended that educators decrease the hours students spend in employment unless the work experience is genuinely tied to a career plan. Thus, the amount, kind, and purpose of work experience recommended for special education students is becoming more closely matching that recommended for regular education students.

It is important to emphasize that the twin goals of age-appropriate educational inclusion and a comprehensive program of school-sponsored work experience do not conflict with one another. Both can be achieved together, as school inclusion efforts join forces with the other two educational restructuring movements, focused on using workplaces as learning environments. Examples of such a convergence are already evident. When one middle school developed a work experience program for special education students (Yatvin, 1995), other students became interested and began asking if they could have jobs, too. As a result, the program was expanded to involve all students. Miller and colleagues (1995) described an "applied learning" process that was inaugurated as part of a school restructuring effort, in which special classes for students with disabilities have been discontinued and "all students attend the same classes and work together on content-infused community projects as the focus of their curriculum" (p. 22).

The community-based programming expertise and employer contact strategies developed in a special education program can be an invaluable resource to regular education. Many schools need look no further than the existing special education department for solutions to the scheduling, transportation, labor law, evaluation, and other issues associated with work experience programming for all students. Case Study 1 exemplifies an approach to school-sponsored work experience that is characteristic of schools that take seriously both the need for educational relevance and the value of including all students.

In summary, school-sponsored work experience can be considered not simply a special education issue or a service that only applies to students who are not planning to attend college. School-sponsored work experience is a powerful educational tool that benefits all students by

- improving student motivation to learn, enjoyment of learning, confidence in learning, and self-efficacy

- improving the pace and complexity of learning

- increasing the relevance of learning to applied contexts of all kinds

- providing students with access to additional adult role models and sources of encouragement and support

- improving student awareness of the world of work and of career options

- providing critical income to students who otherwise would be unable to remain in an educational program

- providing employers firsthand experiences with potential longer-term employees and greater investment in the educational process

TYPES OF WORK EXPERIENCE

Numerous types of direct exposure to the world of work, ranging from short visits to extended, paid job placements, can be made available to students as formal, school-sponsored work experiences. Many students, of course, arrange their own employment after school, on weekends, and during the summer. In fact, far more students obtain these informal types of work experience than participate in formal work experience programs. About 73 percent of high school seniors hold after-school or weekend jobs (Stern et al., 1995).

School-sponsored work experience programs are arranged in a wide array of different formats and are known by a variety of different titles. Table 14.1 lists some of the most widely used types of work experience. The selection of a particular kind of work experience should reflect the student's educational level and the purpose of the experience. Generally, shorter, less demanding work experiences are suitable for earlier grades and/or for career exploration purposes, whereas longer-term, higher-commitment work experiences are appropriate toward the end of schooling or for specific occupational preparation (Isaacson & Brown, 1993). Karma in our case study, for example, began with brief unpaid work experiences in the school office and cafeteria while in middle school. In high school, she participated in a school-based enterprise, then in the school's internship program. The predominant types of school-sponsored work experience are described in what follows.

Field Trips and Course Projects

The briefest and least intensive forms of work experience are observational visits such as field trips or industry tours conducted by a teacher in connection with a particular course, program of study, or class module. Usually, field trips or tours are arranged for groups of students. The possibilities for connections between course curricula and the world of work are limitless. One mathematics teacher takes his students to visit an

---

CASE STUDY 1   Karma

When Karma entered Brookville High School as a freshman, her records showed that she had two previous work experiences, as a cafeteria helper and in the school office as an office assistant, as part of her middle school's in-school jobs program. Expressing an interest in food preparation, Karma chose as one of her high school courses "Cafe 321," a student-run, school-based enterprise that consisted of a restaurant in Room 321 of the school, a former classroom. The cafe was open to the public as well as faculty and staff 3 days per week.

One of Karma's IEP goals that year focused on learning to deal with frustration and the confusion of multiple assignments characteristic of restaurant work. The rest of her school schedule consisted of regular education classes, with consultation on curriculum modification and instructional strategies from the special education team.

By the end of freshman year, Karma had decided to try out other types of careers. Through Brookville High's community internship program under the auspices of the guidance office, she selected a different community-based internship experience each spring semester from those made available by the school's Business Advisory Council. She built her school schedule around the hours required by each particular internship. The school provided transportation to and from the internship sites and assisted each site in assigning a particular worker to serve as Karma's mentor. Once a week Karma also attended a job-support seminar for interns.

The guidance office staff worked with Karma to select each new internship site based on her evaluation of previous experiences. An internship supervisor accompanied Karma for the first several days of each new internship and worked with the company mentor throughout the internship, particularly to consult on strategies for helping Karma with her occasional episodes of anger and frustration.

Karma's junior year internship was as a dental assistant trainee in a group dental practice. Based on this experience, she decided to enroll in a health occupations course sponsored by the vocational education department during her senior year, again with curriculum modifications developed with special education consultation. She also had an internship at a hospital for additional experience in the medical field. Following senior year and graduation with her class, Karma was offered a paid job as a dental assistant at the group dental practice. She has worked successfully for a year and a half and is looking forward to her latest assignment: mentoring a new high school student intern this spring.

---

engineering firm that designs amusement rides, and the engineers explain the importance of mathematics in the design of the rides.

Another related type of work experience is assignment of a project that requires exposure to the workplace. In one school, the students in a literature class read their book reviews over a local radio station (Winger, 1995). In another, each student is assigned to visit with and interview an employee in a career field of interest to the student. Some high schools require students to complete a senior year community project under supervision of a workplace-based mentor, for which students receive course credit (Rothman, 1995). When the projects are oriented toward meeting community needs and teaching

the value of volunteering and good citizenship, the term "service learning" is sometimes used.

Job Shadowing

Job shadowing involves visits to a business for the purpose of learning about the work tasks, industrial processes, and workplace of a specific employee (Herr & Watts, 1988). Job shadowing is useful for observing adult role models and gaining exposure to a particular type of work. The primary purpose is observation of an employee (Isaacson & Brown, 1993). However, a job shadower also asks questions of the worker and perhaps nearby workers, and may assist in performing some of the work tasks. Usually, job

Table 14.1 Common Types of School-Sponsored Work Experience

Type	Example
From **Less Intensive**	
Field trip	Math class visits environmental engineering firm to see practical uses of math in the world of work.
Course project	English class is assigned to interview an employee and write about his or her career.
Job shadowing	Students are each matched with an employee in a field of interest to spend 2 half-days observing and assisting.
School-based enterprise	School science department contracts with engineering firm for students to conduct monthly tests of local river water quality.
Career-related "camp"	Health care organization sponsors weeklong summer health occupations camp.
Apprenticeship and internship	Interested students register to spend two afternoons per week for a semester at selected local firms.
Cooperative education	Half of junior class spends 3 days per week at work sites in the fall semester; second half does the same in the spring semester.
Work-study and part-time job placement	Job orders are posted at school with cooperating businesses; "release time" is available for student jobs.
Tech-prep	School and local community college develop formal relationship for curriculum linkage leading to Associate's degree.
Career academy	School develops comprehensive engineering program consisting of academic classes linked to work at local firm.
To **More Intensive**	

shadowing is completed in 1 or 2 days, never more than 5. Although job shadowing is not as meaningful for actual vocational preparation or training as longer-term work experience, information about a large number of jobs can be obtained through job shadowing. Students often find even pure observation to be instructive and inspiring (Stern & Rahn, 1995). Student preparation for the job shadowing experience, and the debriefing afterwards, usually as a class or group, is considered essential to a successful experience (Herr & Watts, 1988).

School-Based Enterprise

School-based enterprises are activities that produce goods or services for sale to or use by customers other than other than the immediate school community (students, faculty, and staff).

These experiences can be considered legitimate "community work experiences," because they involve students in interaction with typical customers and with suppliers and others in the community (Stern et al., 1995). As with other work experiences, the content is limited only by the imagination of the individuals involved. Many schools operate lunch restaurants open to the public. Cafe 321 at Brookville High is an example of this type of project.

One school has a bank branch on the premises, used by the community as well as school personnel and staffed jointly by bank employees and students. Nationwide about fifteen high schools have their own licensed radio station (Hawkins & Jackson, 1992). Some schools have started desktop publishing operations (Thompson, 1995), and even elementary school students have successfully operated their own greeting card business (Maselow, 1995). One school operates its own home health care service (Thompson, 1995).

In 1992, it was estimated that 19 percent of secondary schools in the United States operated some form of school-based enterprise (Stern et al., 1995). Despite the popularity of this model, there have been no published formal evaluations. Most school-based enterprises grow out of vocational education and emphasize vocational preparation; yet it is interesting that the single most widely known school-based enterprise—the *Foxfire* books (Wigginton, 1986)—emerged from the academic side, as a way of motivating English class students.

Career-Related "Camp" Programs

Some schools offer career-related short-term group projects structured along the lines of a summer camp experience. For example, one high school offers a summer course involving students in constructing home modifications for individuals who are elderly or have physical disabilities. Programs such as "Spacecamp" and "Medcamp" (Speight et al., 1995) involve students in structured 1- or 2-week problem-solving experiences developed by employees within a particular career field. Because of the expense and complexity involved in their design, these latter programs are usually regional in scope rather than based in a single high school.

Apprenticeship and Internship

Apprenticeships and internships are periods of part-time work experience that may extend from several weeks to a year or more. Usually, the term "apprenticeship" is used more in connection with learning a specific occupation, often requiring certification for entrance, whereas "internship" is used in connection with a specific employer. The duration of an apprenticeship may also be longer, up to 5 years, and apprentices are usually paid. By comparison, the

term of an internship is usually one or two semesters and interns are usually unpaid. Use of either term is far from clear-cut, however (Isaason & Brown, 1993).

In the United States, apprenticeships are closely associated with organized labor and tend to be concentrated in occupations with a strong organized labor presence (Hoyt, 1994). It is estimated that no more than 8 percent of high school students are formally enrolled in youth apprenticeship or school-to-apprenticeship programs (Stern et al., 1995). Internships are far more common, although no specific estimate is available. Some schools enter into a partnership with one or more businesses to establish rotating internship "slots" for students or to identify specific opportunities in response to a specific student interest. One school, for example, has developed a relationship with a local theater company (Miller et al., 1995) with internships in costume design, set design, and business management. Similarly, Karma took advantage of Brookville High School's community internship program, consisting of a series of semester-long part-time jobs made available by the school's Business Advisory Council.

Internships and apprenticeships alternate periods of work experience with in-school time and seek to integrate the two into a coherent curriculum. The most common scheduling arrangement is morning classes and an internship job in the afternoon (Isaacson & Brown, 1993).

Cooperative Education

Cooperative education is fairly similar to an internship, in that it consists of systematically alternating periods of academic instruction and work experience within the framework of an overall school curriculum. But cooperative education (or "co-op") systems often alternate periods of study and work in full-time blocks, sometimes even alternating full-time school for a full semester with full-time work for a full semester. Another difference is that cooperative work placements are not necessarily tied to a specific career goal or vocational field, but can have an exploratory or community service focus (Gibson & Angel, 1992).

A key to the success of cooperative education, apprenticeship, or internship is the interaction between the student and a mentor or master craftsperson, who teaches and guides the individual through the experience (Hoyt, 1994). Some authors list "mentorship" as a specific type of work experience (e.g., Smith & Rojewski, 1993), but it is more properly considered as a component of any successful longer-term work experience.

Because of the critical importance of the mentor relationship, some work experience programs have developed training programs and other guidelines for mentors. Gibson and Angel (1992) described an orientation process used by the Weyerhauser Corporation for its co-op students. Mentors attend a 90-minute training session prior to the students' start date and receive a mentorship handbook clarifying expectations and procedures. Mentors record notes on their meetings with the student and the objectives they develop together on a "goals worksheet," and a monitor is available to resolve problems or "repartner" people if relationships prove unproductive. The co-op work experience lasts from 3 to 6 months and is evaluated by both parties at the end of the term.

About 8 percent of high school juniors and seniors in the United States are enrolled in a co-op program (Stern et al., 1995). Evaluation studies of the co-op model have reached mixed results. Co-op students often report that the experience was instrumental in their decision to stay in school, and co-op students are more likely to obtain a job after graduation related to their chosen field. However, longitudinal studies have found that co-op students were no more likely to be employed nor to earn any higher wages than their counterparts with no co-op experience (Stern et al., 1995). One of the difficulties continues to be the identification of high school co-op programs as "voc. ed." programs

and thus designed for students who are not planning to attend college. Paradoxically, many colleges are adopting co-op programs of their own (Van Der Vorm, 1993).

Work-Study or Part-Time Job Placement

Many high schools operate informal job placement services, where a secretary or volunteer accepts job orders from businesses and posts or circulates them to students (Isaacson & Brown, 1993). Some schools even have a job developer or job placement staff member devoted full time to developing job opportunities (Stern et al., 1995). After-school or weekend jobs, summer jobs, and permanent employment following senior year may be developed. The school guidance counselor may arrange "release time" to allow students to work during the school day, if the student is able to earn sufficient credits for graduation during their remaining in-school time. Some schools have a mechanism for awarding school credit for such outside employment on a case-by-case basis, but without the kind of formal provision for regular contacts between school and employer or a connection between the work and the student's plan of studies that would characterize the work experience as a true internship or apprenticeship.

Tech-Prep

Tech-prep programs consist of a coordinated curriculum for the final 2 years of high school with a planned transition to a postsecondary institution, usually for 2 additional years and leading to an Associate's degree in a technical or health field (Smith & Rojewski, 1993). Most tech-prep programs consist of a series of structured work experiences, closely linked to the classroom-based academic component, and increasing progressively from part time in high school to nearly full time during the final year in community college.

Development of a close partnership between high school and community college programs requires a substantial investment in planning and funds (Stern et al., 1995). The 1990 amendments to the Perkins Vocational Education Act made funding available for this purpose. These funded programs have not yet produced thorough evaluation data.

Career Academy

The term "career academy" refers to a comprehensive curriculum of vocational and academic instruction tied to a particular field of work and leading either to certification at graduation or continuing education at a 2- or 4-year college. A career academy operates semiautonomously as a "school-within-a-school." The curriculum includes a series of work experiences, including job shadowing, summer employment, and part-time internships during the school year.

Stern and Rahn (1995) noted that health careers are particularly suited to the career academy approach because of the wide variety of types and levels of certification available and the strong tradition of internship-based learning in the health professions. A key feature of the approach is its academic rigor, ensuring that students satisfy college preparatory course requirements for graduation. But because the entire program is built on a particular career emphasis, the academic content is linked closely to student work experiences. For example, a math lesson in a health career academy may involve students in analyzing forces and angles in the design of a physical therapy treatment plan (Stern & Rahn, 1995).

DESIGNING A WORK EXPERIENCE PROGRAM

Because work experience is a sound educational practice for all students, a school-sponsored work experience program should be developed in such a way that it is an integral component of the regular education program. A separate special education work experience program or a separate vocational education work experience program will shortchange all students. It is particularly critical that the program be geared toward students who are planning to attend a 4-year college as well as those who are not (Pauly, 1994). One of the most frequently noted problems with traditional vocational education has been its association with students who are not planning to attend a 4-year college (Pauly, 1994; Raizen, 1994; Stern et al., 1995).

Community work experience should be also developed as a broad-based effort involving the entire school system of a community. For example, a school system might develop a program in which middle school students begin with in-school jobs (Yatvin, 1995), whereas secondary students are placed in community jobs.

For reasons noted earlier, many special education programs operate well-designed work experience programs that can provide a foundation for a comprehensive work experience program for the entire school. However, large-scale system change will require support from regular educators, particularly the key faculty in secondary education content areas (e.g., science, math, English). These faculty will need to understand how work experience enhances student learning in their particular areas before they will buy into the idea. The same sorts of staff resistances and traditional role definitions that inhibit any organizational change will make this a complex and difficult process (Mark & Stoia, 1993).

Many work experience projects start out with a schoolwide campaign to have regular education teachers visit local employers and bring back ideas for infusing workplace problems and activities into their lessons (Pauly, 1994). These ideas easily lead to plans for field trips and class-based projects, and success with these projects can generate support and enthusiasm for further development of the work experience initiative. Another important impetus for change is the development of an ongoing partnership between the school and the local business community, such as a business advisory group or business roundtable. As noted earlier, businesses have an interest in improving the quality of preparation of the work force, and many are willing to invest financial resources in school restructuring projects. For example, businesses donate over $240 million per year to precollege education projects in the United States (Salomon, 1991).

Pauly (1994) recommended that work experience options not be designed as rigid models, but adapted to local circumstances. It is important to go beyond program labels and instead build specific desired features into each work experience program (Stern et al., 1995). Factors to consider when designing work experience program are outlined in the following section.

Because many special education students are eligible for services from the school district until age 21 (or beyond in some states), and thus may attend high school for more than 4 years, it is first necessary to distinguish between two radically different types of work experience program for these students. If sound school inclusion practices are followed, each student will be clearly identified as a freshman, sophomore, junior, or senior throughout the age-appropriate high school years (Falvey et al., 1995). Participation in the regular education program will include school-sponsored work experience activities designed for the entire school body. Normative senior year activities will include getting one's photograph taken as a senior for the yearbook, attending the senior prom, and participating in the graduation ceremony. If this senior year is followed by a period of additional eligibility for school-funded supports, such supports should have a clearly different design, focusing as much as possible on full-time employment and/or adult education and involving little or no attendance in a high school building.

For example, Andrew is an 18-year-old student at Southwood High School. At a person-centered planning meeting held in his home over the summer to plan his fourth year of high school, it became clear that Andrew considered his fourth year to be his senior year. He wanted to have his picture in the yearbook as a senior, go to the senior prom, and leave school at the end of the year and obtain paid work.

The only work experience possibilities Southwood High School could offer during his

senior year were unpaid volunteer assignments, and Andrew was not interested in work without pay. However, the school career counselor worked throughout the year to develop a job in Andrew's preferred field of carpentry or woodwork. For the following school year, an apprenticeship arrangement was developed for Andrew to build birdhouses and other wooden craft objects in the shop of a local woodworker to be sold on consignment at a gift shop. The woodworker was paid a weekly apprenticeship stipend by the school district to teach Andrew. Andrew also enrolled in a Job Search and Work Success course sponsored by the Adult and Community Education department of the school system, but he did not attend any high school classes.

Some of the key features that need to be considered in the design of a work experience program that benefits all students are outlined in what follows. Specific instructional support and other features of the program that allow equal participation for students with severe disabilities are discussed in the following section.

Considerations for Program Design

Employer Development. Perhaps the most difficult aspect of a work experience program is the work of contacting local employers, learning about the world of work and the needs of the business community, and arranging work experience sites for students. The problem is not that the activity is difficult in itself, but that it takes a great deal of time and is not typically something school personnel are trained to do or view as a part of their job. Stern and colleagues (1995) noted that paying school staff to develop work experience sites can be expensive, and schools under serious financial pressure must be convinced that this is an expense that pays off in improved education for students.

Pauly (1994) recommended that a school either employ one individual full time to outreach to the business community or provide sufficient release time for teachers and other staff to make employer contacts and arrange visits. Some schools have used funds received under the

School-to-Work Opportunities Act of 1994 to pay teachers to undertake this activity as a summer project. No research has been conducted on the relative effectiveness of the single full-time job developer strategy versus the part-of-everyone's-job strategy. It might be expected that the former approach would be more compatible with a program whose primary goal is to develop longer-term internships or paid job placements, whereas the latter approach would more closely fit an approach whose primary purpose was to integrate workplace information and resources into the academic curricula and build schoolwide support.

Businesses listen to other businesses, so many work experience projects call on current business contacts to take the lead in outreach to other businesses (Tilson et al., 1994). For example, a Business Advisory Committee could be convened to both guide a school's work experience effort and market the effort to new businesses. Some communities have organizations such as a business association or Chamber of Commerce that can be enlisted to this purpose (Pauly, 1994). Some schools are even fortunate enough to have the business community approach them (Salomon, 1991).

Marshall and Tucker (1992) suggested that schools view work experience as part of a wider initiative to establish a deep involvement of the business community in the process of education. A Business Advisory Committee or Council could take on additional initiatives to achieve this level of involvement, such as reviewing curricula for relevance to the changing demands of the workplace or sponsoring a career day for students. At Brookville High School, years of work have resulted in cultivation of a Business Advisory Council in which each participating business commits to maintaining one part-time position each semester for a student internship. The project has been so successful and well publicized that businesses compete for admission to the Council.

The possibilities for partnership projects are limitless. Through a statewide initiative in Delaware called "Hire Education" (Hill, 1995), a group of employers began requesting high school transcripts when considering applicants for jobs at their company, encouraged other employers to do the same, and worked with the schools to develop a computerized process for furnishing transcripts in a timely manner. This initiative has increased awareness of the relationship between school and work on the part of the business community and has encouraged students to take their school work more seriously.

The role of personal contacts and networks in the development of work experience sites needs to be emphasized. Christ (1995) suggested that a social networking approach be used systematically, with members of the school community—teachers, students, administrators—exploring their own connections to businesses and occupations through parents, spouses, and friends. Christ (1995) recommended that teachers begin by conducting interviews with adults in a variety of occupations to obtaining ideas for activities and other curriculum suggestions. School alumni can also be canvassed and asked to provide opportunities for job shadowing or other work experiences (Isaacson & Brown, 1993; Hagner, Butterworth, & Keith, 1995).

A school can develop marketing materials such as a brochure or portfolio with letters of recommendation to assist in its marketing efforts to employers. Often, a local company's advertising department or a local printing company can be persuaded to provide assistance as a donation to the school. For each type of work experience, the school should develop a training agreement that sets forth the purpose and the expectations of each party (Stern et al., 1995).

In Andrew's case, Southwood High's career counselor was unable to develop a suitable work experience job during his senior year. But a summer job resulted from connections made through extracurricular involvement. Andrew had a strong interest in making more friends at school, and in consultation with his planning group decided that joining the school track team might be a good way to get involved more socially with fellow students.

This extracurricular involvement accidentally led to a job for Andrew the following summer. Andrew learned that a couple of the other track team members were applying for summer jobs with the Southwood Parks and Recreation Department. Andrew's family took him to fill out an application and he obtained a job as a recreation aide. After attending graduation, Andrew worked as a recreation aide for the summer, with summer job-support services funded by the Division of Vocational Rehabilitation.

This example highlights the value that school inclusion practices, in this case active assistance to participate in typical extracurricular activities, can have on career development. However, it also speaks to the need for schools to recruit experienced and qualified job developers. The following school year, disillusioned with her lack of success in developing community work sites, Southwood High's career counselor decided to return to classroom teaching. The school administration filled the vacancy with an ex-businessperson with sales experience and rich contacts with local employers. Within 6 months twelve students were participating in paid work experiences.

Ties to School-Based Learning and Academic Development. Stern and Rahn (1995) cautioned that unless work experience is clearly linked to nonvocational subjects and a course of study that prepares students to enter a 4-year college, the program is doomed to "second-class status" within the school. Thus, forging these links is critical to success.

Workplace-based activities become linked to academic content as teachers in each specific academic subject area become accustomed to using community activities to enhance student learning of their subject. One senior-year high school English class in California requires each student to spend one period, 2 days per week off campus at a work site, write a journal of experi-

ences, and prepare a class presentation as one of the class assignments (Cox & Firpo, 1993).

In Missouri, students in one high school can elect to participate in the school's Community Learning Program and spend three periods per day, 4 days per week, for one semester at a local business (Reidy & Schottmueller, 1993). A review of each week's experiences is part of the fifth, in-school day. Students submit a journal, time log, and an individually designed project such as a paper or an exhibit and receive full academic credit for the semester. A portfolio with student products and reports from employers on work experiences should be part of the formal school transcript. An essential link between work experience and academics is the availability of credits toward graduation for the work experience.

Work experience practices have much in common with other innovative secondary education practices, such as cooperative learning, project-based learning, and portfolio assessment of progress (Armstrong & Savage, 1990). The movement toward educational relevance and "connected learning" (Van Der Vorm, 1993) also can be expressed in the creation of new courses such as "Know Your City" (Pauly, 1994). Courses that combine academic rigor with community relevance are a natural fit with workplace-based learning initiatives. Proponents of these other creative practices are natural allies in the development of a work experience program.

The secondary school curriculum for all students should aim for a balance between community-based and classroom activities and a close interaction between both components. The term "integration" is often used to describe this interaction in a different sense than most special educators are used to. In Karma's case, for example, her internships were limited to a maximum of 4 half-days per week and she was required to maintain acceptable grades in her academic courses to remain in Brookville High School's internship program.

Moderate amounts of work, whether school-sponsored or not, have a generally positive effect on grades and academic achievement. However, high numbers of hours of work are detrimental. When students work over about 10 hours of work per week, the higher the number of hours worked, the lower the student's grade-point average and overall academic performance is likely to be (Stern et al., 1995). Even the best work experiences are limited in their ability to provide a context for comprehensive learning. The tendency in a work setting will always be to emphasize "learning to do the work" as the top priority, rather than learning for its own sake or learning to think, explore, and create (Stern et al., 1995). So although the lessons learned in the workplace are invaluable, they must be part of a planned curriculum that contains other elements as well.

Administrative Support and Logistics. Off-site activities of any kind introduce a host of logistical demands, and administrative support is required to deal with the many issues involved. The most basic policy requirement is a definition of "school attendance" expansive enough to encompass attendance at school-sponsored work experience sites. Insurance and liability issues also must be resolved in connection with the program. Procedures for obtaining parent or guardian permission for students under age 18 (or over 18 with a legal guardian) must be in place. Transportation to and from work experience sites can be problematic. Many programs require students to arrange their own transportation, but not all work sites are accessible by public transportation and not all students can travel safely. In addition, if community work experience is specified in a special education student's IEP, eligibility for education will extend to eligibility for school-provided transportation to the instructional site.

Scheduling of work experiences and scheduling of staff "coverage" for both the in-class and work experience components can pose administrative complexities. When a classroom teacher accompanies a student or visits a work site, one fewer teacher is available for class instruction in the school. Teacher aides or peer tutors are often used to help resolve some of these issues (Gaylord-Ross et al., 1988). Team teaching or cluster-type staffing models also can be used as a mechanism to plan for coverage based on changing circumstances.

Further, in the United States, federal Department of Labor regulations, particularly those governing child labor and payment of commensurate wages, must be adhered to in arranging work experiences. Children are restricted in their work hours and in the types of work they may perform. One individual within a high school or school district should be responsible for knowing these regulations and keeping up with changes.

If a true employment relationship exists, payment of commensurate wages (at least the current federal minimum wage except under certain specified circumstances) and adherence to the other provisions of the Fair Labor Standards Act is required. Volunteer work is generally restricted to not-for-profit sector employers such as hospitals or preschools. However, many school-sponsored work experiences can be structured in such a way that a true employment relationship is not established and time-limited work experiences even in for-profit organizations can be unpaid. Regional offices of the U.S. Department of Labor will provide specific written guidelines covering school-related work programs on request. The Department also administers a Work Experience and Career Education Program (WECEP) and interested schools can apply to participate in this program through the regional offices of the Department. Each state also has its own Department of Labor, and state regulations must be complied with as well.

Connections with Career Development. A central purpose of work experience is to provide the student with information about the world of work that may be useful in career decision making. The information gained from early or short-term work experiences, such as a job shadowing experience in ninth grade, may serve primarily as an exposure to the world of work or an exploration of a particular field. Later and more intensive experiences, such as a senior year internship, may be for specific preparation and skill development in a chosen career area or completion of an individual project to enhance the chance of admission to a selected university (Table 14.1).

Regardless of purpose, guidance and support are required to maximize the benefit of a work experience (Pauly, 1994). As with any school assignment or project, feedback and discussions with peers and teachers help situate the experience within the overall course or curriculum. For example, in our case study, Karma's program was coordinated by the school guidance department, and consisted of a weekly job-support seminar as well as two meetings throughout the semester with her guidance counselor to review progress and plan her next internship.

Thompson (1995) emphasized that work experiences must be individualized to each student's interests. In the context of special education transition services, Halpern and colleagues (1993) echoed this view, cautioning that work experiences in themselves, without connections to career development, have little value. Thus, with the exception of brief field trips and class projects, work experiences should be for individuals, not groups of students, and should be selected based on an assessment of student interests and goals and the educational relevance of the experience within the student's overall plan of study. Information from one experience can be used to refine these interests and goals further and plan the next experience. This necessitates continuing flexibility and employer development on the part of the school. Although some sophomore- or junior-year work experiences may be selected from a pool of work experience "slots" prearranged with local employers, an individual student may well have a particular interest or need a particular accommodation that is not available among the existing slots, so a

new site must be developed. And by senior year, the specificity of most students' interests, or a desire for a paid employment, may necessitate individual job development.

In Andrew's case, his interest was in a paid job in his preferred field of carpentry or woodwork. Although no suitable work experience could be found during his senior year, an apprenticeship arrangement was developed for Andrew for the year of school eligibility following his senior year. He worked in the shop of a local woodworker building birdhouses and other wooden craft objects to be sold on consignment at a gift shop. The woodworker was paid a weekly apprenticeship stipend by the school district to teach and supervise Andrew.

In March of that year, the new career counselor developed a full-time position for Andrew with a local manufacturer of wooden crates and pallets, and Andrew successfully interviewed for and obtained the job.

Most work experience programs provide for in-school time to process, review, and problem solve in connection with the experience, and to connect the experience with other aspects of career development. Loughead and colleagues (1995) described a program involving 6 hours of work and a 1-hour career development class per day. The class component covered such topics as career planning and job-seeking skills training. Also, the internship program described by Cox and Firpo (1993) provides work experience 4 days per week, with an accompanying seminar provided on the fifth day. Almost any type of apprenticeship, internship, co-op, or tech-prep program builds in this type of component.

Mark and Stoia (1993) suggested that schools consider combining a cooperative education and a career planning and placement service in one office. Within the same office, students can obtain information about part-time or summer job opportunities, arrange a semester-long credit-bearing internship, discuss school program options and personal goals, or work on college applications. It is easy to see how a transition facilitator knowledgeable about special education and adult disability services would make a valuable team member within such an office.

Work-Site Support for Participating Businesses. Supporting a work experience involves developing a viable partnership between the school and each participating business. Central to the success of the experience is a clear definition of the role of each party. Hoyt (1994) defined three distinct roles related to supporting a work experience:

1. The Coach—a work-site employee who assists the student to learn the job

2. The Mentor—a work-site employee who initiates the student into the workplace culture and norms and may provide other support or advice

3. The Counselor—a school employee who coordinates among work, school, and home, and may advise concerning career and life goals

In supporting students with severe disabilities, we may add a fourth role, the role of consultant to the business on instructional methods and job accommodation (Tilson et al., 1994).

All students, including those in special education, should be linked with a specific co-worker for day-to-day instruction and supervision, and with a workplace-based mentor or advisor, who may be the same as the co-worker trainer or "coach" (Thompson, 1995). A written training plan should be developed outlining instructional goals and methods. And all students, including those in regular education, need the availability of school personnel to answer employer questions, help with the design of the work experience job, assist in acclimating to the workplace, and resolve problems. There will undoubtedly be differences of degree, with some employers and some students requiring far more support or more specialized support than others. Specific instructional and other supports are discussed in what follows.

If the work experience involves the employer in expanding the diversity of its work force by including individuals who have disabilities, who are members of a minority group, or who break a gender stereotype within a particular company, support might include diversity training for the other workers, such as the training described by Tilson and colleagues (1994). The school should be willing to offer a training stipend to businesses, especially smaller companies, that devote substantial amounts of staff time to coaching and mentoring a student.

When Andrew and his family told the staff at Southwood High School that he had obtained a summer job as a recreation aide, the school's career counselor, with permission from Andrew and his family, contacted the Southwood Parks and Recreation Department and offered to assist with training and job support. Also, during Andrew's woodworking apprenticeship making consignment items, the school's career counselor visited the shop several times a week to check on progress.

When finally a full-time position offering a regular paycheck was developed for Andrew with a manufacturer of wooden crates and pallets, support for this job was provided by a local supported employment agency under contract to the school district (so that job-support personnel would remain consistent when funding responsibility switched from the school to the adult service system). Support included teaching the manager of the company how best to instruct Andrew and helping Andrew handle difficulties of getting along with some of his co-workers.

Flexible Policies for Graduation. The school-to-work-movement is closely associated with the position that just as there are multiple ways to acquire knowledge, there are multiple ways to demonstrate mastery, including examinations, portfolios, and completion of community-based projects. Thus, schools serious about educating students through work experience develop flexible policies for grading assignments and issuing credit toward graduation. (For further information about assessment, see Chapter 11 in this volume.) Several states are experimenting with the idea of a "Certificate of Initial Mastery," supplemental to the high school diploma (Rothman, 1995), which requires demonstration of applied learning in one or more fields of study. Most apprenticeships and career academies are tied to certification requirements for entry into a particular occupation.

Historically, for individuals in special education, the issues of grades, class assignment, and graduation have been dealt with either haphazardly or not at all. The degree of incoherence involved can be dramatically illustrated by an experience of one of the authors, who in response to an inquiry to a high school teacher about whether a particular special education student was a junior or a senior received the reply: "He thinks he's a senior but he will be going through the rotation again." That is, the individual was to become a freshman in high school following his senior year in high school.

Continuation of eligibility beyond 4 years of high school ought to remain a viable option for all students who are progressing in their coursework but for some reason need to take a reduced number of credits per semester or who do not receive a passing grade in all their courses. But other thoughtful options should be available as well. These include (a) completion of the academic portion of high school in 4 years with continuation of educational services in the form of employment supports, either directly provided by the school or through a contract to a supported employment service; and (b) graduation after 4 years of high school with legal entitlement terminated but a school district policy of commitment to a period of co-funding support services in collaboration with a vocational rehabilitation, developmental disabilities, or other adult service funding source.

Southwood High School responded to Andrew's needs with flexibility and creativity. We have seen that Andrew was able to spend an additional year of high school first as a woodworking apprentice, enrolling at the same time in a Job Search and Work Success course sponsored by the school's Adult and Community Education department; and later, in the spring, as a full-time employee of a manufacturer of crates and pallets. During this year, Andrew did not attend any high school classes nor view himself as a high school student. Yet, the school was responsible for his job development and job support. Services were provided directly by a school employee until March and then by means of a contract with a local supported employment agency from March until June. In June, arrangements were made for Andrew to receive his full high school diploma by mail (because he had received only a Certificate of Completion at the previous June's graduation ceremony), thereby ending his entitlement to free education at age 20. By prearrangement, as part of a community-wide Transition Services Interagency Agreement, funding to the supported employment agency was assumed by the Division of Vocational Rehabilitation for 6 months, beginning the Monday following the date on the diploma, and 6 months later by the state Department of Mental Retardation for ongoing vocational services.

Work-Based Instruction and Support for Students with Disabilities

In order to ensure that students with a range of disabilities benefit equally from school-sponsored work experiences, programs need to be prepared to offer specific instructional and other support services. Four critical components that may need particular attention include job instruction, co-worker and business consultation, facilitating social inclusion, and using assistive technology.

Job Instruction. At the heart of a work experience is instruction in fulfilling the work performance demands of the job. The primary demands of the job, of course, are the specific tasks involved in producing the work. Each task in turn can be analyzed into a sequence of small steps. For example, checking incoming stock against an order form for office supplies may involve the following:

- checking the supplier name on cartons and retrieving the order from the files

- opening cartons

- removing individual items and identifying the name of the item

- counting the number of each different item

- matching each item name with names on the order form

- placing a check next to each matching line on the order form

- placing items in their proper location, such as a storage shelf

- returning the order form to the appropriate person

- notifying the supervisor of any discrepancies between what was ordered and what was received

- disassembling the carton and taking it to the cardboard recycling station

Dividing a complex task into smaller components for instructional purposes is a familiar activity for most teachers. But several unique considerations apply to the process of analyzing tasks in a natural environment, such as a community business, as opposed to in a classroom environment.

First, the natural environment is likely to have developed a customary "way we do things around here," and the way a task should be carried out is prescribed by that workplace. For example, a company might be "picky" about one aspect of work quality, yet surprisingly (to an outsider) lax about another. Suggestions as to how to do a job better or more efficiently may be welcomed or even sought out in one workplace but be perceived as "invading someone's turf" at another. School support staff need to keep in mind that they are on site to lend their expertise, but only as guests.

Second, workplaces are complex social environments usually involving a group of people completing some production activity together. This social component of each person's job is critical to success. So performing the actual job tasks might be viewed as the tip of the behavioral iceberg, the most easily visible but smaller part. White and Biller (1988) suggested viewing a job as having three additional performance requirements: (1) handling social situations in the workplace, (2) adapting to task variations and disruptions, and (3) achieving a normative degree of independence from close supervision. For example, the ability to complete an assignment without frequent prompting or to ask for assistance if one is experiencing a problem is extremely important at most work sites. A work experience may be the first opportunity for a student to experience this type of adult role expectation, and of course that is what makes the experience so valuable. In Chapter 17 in this volume, Chadsey and Shelden discuss the issue of social inclusion in the workplace.

A comprehensive plan of work-based instruction thus will include both task-related objectives and objectives in these other social and work-ethic domains. A written training plan for each student is an indispensable component of good practice (Stern et al., 1995). In addition to objectives and instructional procedures, the plan should specify who will judge whether the student has achieved each objective. The student (and parent or guardian if a minor or under guardianship), the on-site workplace supervisor, and the school work experience coordinator should sign the plan. Direct instruction can be the responsibility of either school staff, an on-site co-worker or supervisor mentor (with consultation and backup assistance by school staff, as explained in the next section) or a combination of the two in which certain tasks or certain days and times are the responsibility of each party.

Co-Worker and Business Consultation. A work experience provides a valuable opportunity for a student to interact with and learn from adults other than parents or teachers. At least one experienced individual on site should be identified as a student's mentor (Smith & Rojewski, 1993; Pauly, 1994). This mentor usually plays a role in job instruction and also can give guidance and assistance in such areas as negotiating problem social situations and determining the "politics" of an organization, meeting other employees, learning occupation-specific information, terms, and methods, obtaining career advice and contacts, and supporting the individual in dealing with school, personal, or other nonwork problems (Hagner & DiLeo, 1993; Smith & Rojewski, 1993). Hoyt (1994) recommended a division of labor at the work site between the instructional or "coach" role and the social initiation and advisor, or "mentor" role.

The traditional role of school personnel is that of direct student instruction; therefore, it is easy for school staff to fall into the role of taking responsibility for conducting all the training a student requires at a community work site. But it is important to look for opportunities to transfer at least some of training to the host business whenever possible, while remaining available to share or even take over the training if this is determined necessary for the success of an individual student.

Businesses need support and assistance, but if co-workers are shown basic training techniques, they can provide excellent training in many cases (Mank et al., 1992) and develop suitable solutions to job-related social difficulties (Baumgart & Askvig, 1992). When employment support staff hover too closely over the employee and begin making decisions, solving problems, or acting as social "chaperones" for the individual, it can be perceived by the business as interference rather than support (Bullis et al., 1994). Some staff find that students follow instructions more readily when the instructions are provided by a co-worker mentor. Experienced workers also can show the student shortcuts and tricks learned from experience, and are best able to teach a student the critical skill of how to "size up" or "read" a given situation in the workplace (Federico, 1995).

Work experience jobs should be structured in such a way that some social interaction, such as performing a task along with a co-worker, is essential to the job. Usually, there are natural points of intersection between any one job and several others. For example, in the earlier example of the job of checking in office supplies, discussion of any discrepancies with the supervisor is a social step in this task. These social parts of a job provide natural opportunities for instruction and social interaction.

The student should be coached to be appropriately assertive in seeking out information and feedback from co-workers (Rosenthal, 1989). Newcomers to a workplace are not passive recipients of training but active information seekers (Morrison, 1993). Some students may be accustomed to have information, answers to questions, and the like handed to them effortlessly in other aspects of their lives. The workplace is an ideal environment for teaching how and when to ask for help, as well as the associated behaviors of showing appreciation and reciprocating.

Selection of the right mentor is important. As Greenberger and Steinberg (1986) noted, many young people work in settings (such as retail stores or fast-food restaurants) where co-workers and even the supervisory staff are themselves young people with little work experience and possibly even poor work habits or ethics. Hagner and DiLeo (1993) suggested the following guidelines for selecting an appropriate mentor:

- Has the individual worked at the job for at least several months and does the individual know his or her job well?

- Is the individual well liked by other employees?

- Can the individual be scheduled to work when the student is present?

- Does the employee agree to accept responsibility for training and receive the necessary consultation from school staff?

Smith and Rojewski (1993) noted that the success of a mentorship is hard to predict because it depends heavily on subtle factors of personal "chemistry" between the two individuals. Work experience coordinators should be prepared to monitor mentorships closely and make adjustments or "repartner" people (Gibson & Angel, 1992) as needed.

School staff should view themselves as consultants to the employer and to the student's on-site coach and/or mentor. This means giving these individuals the tools they need to successfully train and employ the student. Some programs provide training seminars for the business staff in disability awareness, accommodations, and inclusion strategies (Tilson et al., 1994). Another approach is to orient individuals to a student's support needs and learning style on a more individual basis. Consultation should also include (a) periodically scheduled debriefing sessions to review progress and work on any difficulties, (b) backup support if a particular task is taking very long to learn or business pressures necessitate a change in the mentor's availability, (c) rapid response to any employer-initiated questions or concerns (programs should consider a beeper or call-forwarding system and car phones for work experience staff), and (d) a schedule of frequent observational visits to the work site to observe the student's work firsthand.

Work experience staff should schedule their visits during the times they are most needed in the student's work shift or to best fit with the needs of the business. Often, staff roles are neither pure training nor pure consultation, but a combination of direct training, observation, and employer consultation that suits the needs of the specific situation. Sometimes school staff go out of their way to eat lunch at a particular restaurant or have their hair cut at a particular hairdresser's shop as a way of checking on a work experience site. This practice also rewards the participating businesses.

It is important to be clear with the host business about the contact schedule and the nature of the three-way relationship among student, workplace, and school. Promises to the business to show up at a particular time, to teach a task, or whatever, must be kept scrupulously. Often staff presence is continual or nearly so at the beginning of a work experience, then gradually decreases to a "maintenance" level of periodic visits. The employer needs to be informed at each stage and, ideally, involved as a partner in making decisions. The school also must be ready to reintroduce intensive supports quickly if the situation changes.

Facilitating Social Inclusion. Most work is fundamentally and irreducibly social activity; and therefore, forming workplace relationships and negotiating social situations are important to success on the job. Moreover, the adequacy of an individual's social inclusion at work influences the individuals job satisfaction and quality of work life (Chadsey-Rusch & Heal, 1995).

Even though it may be perceived as spontaneous rather than orchestrated or programmed, social inclusion does not always simply happen by itself. Skills such as taking a turn making the morning coffee or greeting one's co-workers by name may have to be specifically taught. And even when a co-worker plays a central a role in introducing a student apprentice to other employees and showing the individual how to fit in with the rules of the workplace culture, it is likely that the co-worker initially required some assistance learning what to do or feeling comfortable in that role. A high-quality work experience program assists both students and businesses through the process of socialization and relationship formation at the work site.

After surveying a pool of national transition experts, Chadsey-Rusch and Heal (1995) identified a number of strategies widely believed useful in promoting successful workplace social inclusion for students with disabilities. Several of these strategies involve direct instruction of the student at the work site:

- Teaching the initiation of work-related social skills, such as asking for help or offering assistance

- Teaching responses to work-related initiations from others, such as answering questions or responding to criticism
- Teaching the initiation of nonwork-related social skills, such as greetings or joking
- Teaching responses to nonwork-related initiations from others, such as answering a greeting
- Teaching conversational skills, such as taking turns, and common topics, such as sports
- Teaching self-determination skills, such as being persistent
- Teaching how to interpret social situations and cues, such as in what situations joking is appropriate

Other strategies involved teaching or making a request of the individual's supervisor or co-worker:

- Requesting that co-workers or supervisors initiate social interactions with the student, such as talking about a topic they both enjoy
- Requesting that co-workers or supervisors respond to social initiations initiated by the student
- Teaching co-workers or supervisors how to implement a social skills training program
- Requesting that a co-worker or supervisor function as an advocate for the student
- Requesting that co-workers or supervisors develop a social inclusion plan for the student
- Asking a co-worker who likes the same type of recreational activities as the student to do things together outside of work
- Having individuals involved more with popular or highly regarded workers

Hagner and colleagues (1995) interviewed the staff of schools and supported employment programs nominated as exemplary to identify the strategies these individuals employed to involve co-workers and supervisors in support-ive relationships and social interactions with employees with disabilities. Strategies for involving employers or co-workers in job training and support included the following:

- Showing co-workers how to provide support —including teaching or modeling training techniques to one or more co-workers—and reinforcing co-workers for their involvement
- Arranging for the consumer to go through the same orientation process as any new employee
- Looking for situations where a co-worker shows interest or seems receptive, and fostering or nurturing the relationship
- Encouraging consumers to ask questions and go to the employer and co-worker with problems
- Explaining the support needs of the employee to co-workers and asking co-workers to assist

Strategies for facilitating social interactions with co-workers at work included the following:

- Making sure consumers are appropriately dressed and have proper hygiene and grooming for the setting
- Helping identify friendly co-workers and helping people become introduced; starting and facilitating conversations with people who might form a relationship
- Helping consumers develop social interaction skills appropriate to the setting
- Encouraging direct communication between consumers and co-workers; making sure workers can communicate effectively with one another
- Modeling appropriate interactions, showing respect, and projecting a comfortable style
- Investigating details of the workplace culture, such as the break and lunch customs

- Encouraging consumers to follow important social customs, join teams, committees, or other social activities, and use the social "hangouts" at the company

- Making sure the same work schedules, routines, and rules are part of the design of the job, and that any differences (e.g., lunch boxes) are minimized

- Exploring similarities in interests and experiences, and highlighting positive consumer attributes and interests.

Strategies for facilitating interactions with co-workers off the job included the following:

- Fostering relationships, encouraging small talk, and helping people identify common interests or an interesting, positive attribute of the consumer

- Making co-workers feel comfortable, that it is OK to start a conversation or ask things; giving "permission" and making suggestions

- Pointing out to consumers any opportunities for joining and doing things

- Arranging for transportation for consumers to activities and special events

- Inquiring about available activities and discuss possibilities with the employer, pointing out the importance of this kind of involvement

Several of the most important social inclusion strategies are summarized in Table 14.2.

Assistive Technology. Utilization of technology and other workplace adaptations is a key strategy in employing individuals with disabilities, particularly those with physical and/or sensory disabilities (Sowers, 1995). The Americans with Disabilities Act requires that companies with fifteen or more employees provide reasonable accommodations to ensure that employees with disabilities are able to perform the essential functions of a job. Students involved in paid work experience where they are considered employees of the business are protected by this statute in the same way as other employees. The

challenge for employment and transition personnel is to become knowledgeable about technology and accommodation strategies.

Sowers and Powers (1991) described three phases in workplace adaptation: initial design prior to an individual's job start, intensive adaptation during the first month, and ongoing adaptation refinement in response to problems or job changes. Both the worker and the employer should play an active role in each phase of the process, so that they and not the school or employment service staff "own" and understand the adaptation.

Numerous adaptive strategies can be devised to accommodate work demands to individual workers. For example, Brenda encounters several different types of problems in her office assistant job and must communicate them to her supervisor accurately; yet her speech cannot always be clearly understood. Potential solutions include a laptop computer or speech synthesizer, perhaps with typical problem sentences programmed in as well as a method of generating new sentences, index cards with problem statements, having Brenda and her supervisor learn relevant signs and communicate using sign language, assigning a co-worker to go over to Brenda's desk when she motions that she is having difficulty and determine the problem, as well as several other approaches. After a list of potential accommodations has been generated, a tentative solution can be identified, taking into account Brenda's preferences, the response of the workplace and co-workers to the strategy, and the cost of the adaptation (Sowers, 1995).

Piuma and Udvari-Solner (1993) described four basic types of vocational adaptation, cautioning that real-life problems often require a cluster of adjustments and modifications across more than one type.

1. *Instructional adaptations* modify the method of performing a task, the method of prompting, or the level of assistance provided during instruction. Most teachers are familiar with the process of rethinking the way a task is performed. For example, Bob was unable to

Table 14.2 Strategies to Facilitate Workplace Social Inclusion

Employee-Focused	Co-worker-Focused
Teach employee when and how to ask for help.	Ask co-workers to initiate interactions.
Teach employee when and how to offer help to others.	Ask co-workers to respond to initiations from the employee.
Teach employee to respond to initiations from others.	Ask co-workers to assist in identifying socially important rules .
Teach employee the social rules for greeting and small talk.	Look for any co-workers who share a leisure or other interest with the employee.
Make sure employee's dress and grooming are socially normative.	Investigate the workplace culture and identify .the key social customs.
Look for opportunities to step back and let people be themselves.	Identify the key social people within a setting.
Point out opportunities for the employee to attend or join something.	Look for the beginnings of a relationship and ways to foster it.
Make sure employee's work tasks are naturally interactive.	Ask co-workers to take the lead in assisting with inclusion.

fold towels neatly by grasping the outer edges and folding them forwards. By grasping the inner edges and folding away from his body, he was able to obtain an accurate alignment of the edges.

2. *Environmental adaptations* change the placement of materials or the design of a workplace or work station. For example, ramps, sufficiently wide aisles, lever doorknobs, and bathroom grab bars are common adaptations for employees who use wheelchairs. Such environmental controls as switches, voice activation, and alarm devices with both a light and a sound alert can assist employees in completing work tasks.

3. *Adapted rules, policies, and procedures* are so-called "no-tech" solutions (Sowers, 1995) that can eliminate barriers to participation. For example, Jeff was allowed to begin break 10 minutes early for lunch because he takes extra time using the bathroom and getting ready for lunch. Eric's mail clerk job was redesigned so that he was only responsible for delivering mail in one building of a multibuilding complex.

4. *Physical adaptations* modify equipment so that a student can perform a task without exter-

nal assistance. For example, timers can assist an individual in keeping track of time. Various kinds of holding devices can steady or align objects. Such "high-tech" solutions as computers and robotics (Sowers, 1995) are also easily adapted to the needs of workers with disabilities.

Roberts and colleagues (1993) generated a comprehensive system for analyzing work demands and developing workplace accommodations. They suggested that an accurate job analysis, including determination of which aspects of a job are considered "essential functions" by the employer and which are "marginal functions," is critical to the development of an accommodation strategy.

CONCLUSION

Work experience and vocational instruction can be considered an integral part of a comprehensive secondary education for all students. Adding a strong work experience component to the secondary curriculum benefits students with and those without disabilities, students planning to continue their education, and those planning to enter the work force directly from high school.

Work experience is directly relevant to and most closely associated with job preparation and school-to-work transition, but it can also be viewed more broadly as a technique for imparting academic content, as a dropout prevention tool, and as a career guidance strategy.

Numerous approaches to work experience have been developed and successfully implemented, and most schools have work experience models either in place or readily available. A great deal of local variation exists within each type and it is important to look beyond the program label—co-op, tech-prep, apprenticeship, and so on—at the specific structure of the work experience. Often, the special education department within a school has a well-developed work experience component that can be generalized to include regular education students. Key components of a successful work experience program include outreach to local employers, linkages with academic content, linkages with career guidance, administrative and logistical support, and school staff to consult with participating businesses and assist students through the process.

Students with disabilities, like other students, benefit from a series of school-sponsored work experiences. More specialized or intensive support to co-workers and supervisors may be required, and specific strategies may need to be implemented to ensure satisfactory relationships and social inclusion, or to adapt the job to an individual's capabilities. These support practices for individuals with disabilities can be linked with and infused into schoolwide efforts to improve the quality of education and educational outcomes for all students.

QUESTIONS

1. Provide an argument for why learning should occur in context and why workplaces are natural contexts for learning.

2. In addition to their value as career exploration and vocational preparation, work experiences can benefit students in several other ways. List four additional benefits.

3. An American history teacher in your community is interested in creating a workplace-based field trip or project for students in connection with a class module on the Civil War. What possibilities can you think of?

4. Why are the values of full inclusion and functional skill development in special education sometimes seen as being in conflict with one another? How do you believe this conflict is best resolved?

5. Briefly describe five kinds of school-sponsored work experience. Which would be most appropriate for allowing an exploration of many different career types? Which would be most appropriate for achieving a paid job at graduation?

6. Describe the components of a work experience program.

7. List some of the administrative and logistical issues a school must tackle in order to provide a community-based work experience program for students as part of the school curriculum.

8. It is likely that not every co-worker will make a good mentor for a student intern or apprentice. Have you had either a good or a bad experience in learning a job from a co-worker? Based on your experience, what suggestions would you give for selecting an appropriate work-site mentor for a student?

9. Why do school personnel sometimes take full responsibility for work-site instruction of students with disabilities, and what are some reasons why it might be advisable to look for ways to involve co-workers in some of the instruction?

10. Joan is responsible for distributing incoming fax documents to the appropriate staff person in her office but sometimes several documents pile up before she can get to them, making it difficult for her to sort out which pages belong to which documents. Suggest a job accommodation that might solve this problem. In case that idea does not work, develop an additional backup idea.

REFERENCES

Abbott, J. (1995). Children need communities; communities need children. *Educational Leadership, 52*(8), 6–10.

Armstrong, D., & Savage, T. (1990). *Secondary education: An introduction* (2nd ed.). New York: Macmillan.

Baumgart, D., & Askvig, B. (1992). Job-related social skills interventions: Suggestions from managers and employers. *Education and Training in Mental Retardation, 27,* 345–353.

Bullis, M., Fredericks, H., Lehman, C., Paris, K., Corbitt, J., & Johnson, B. (1994). Description and evaluation of the Job Designs Project for adolescents and young adults with emotional or behavioral disorders. *Behavioral Disorders, 19,* 254–268.

Chadsey-Rusch, J., & Heal, L. (1995). Building consensus from transition experts on social integration outcomes and interventions. *Exceptional Children, 62,* 165–187.

Christ, G. (1995). Curriculums with real-world connections. *Educational Leadership, 52*(8), 32–35.

Collins, A., Brown, J., & Holum, A. (1991). Cognitive apprenticeship: Making thinking visible. *The American Educator, 15*(3), 38–46.

Commission on the Skills of the American Workforce. (1990). *America's choice: High skills or low wages!* Rochester, NY: National Center on Education and the Economy.

Committee for Economic Development. (1985). *Investing in our children.* New York: Author.

Cox, M., & Firpo, C. (1993). What would they be doing if we gave them worksheets? *English Journal, 82*(3), 42–45.

D'Amico, R. (1991). The working world awaits: Employment experiences during and shortly after secondary school. In M. Wagner, L. Newman, R. D'Amico, E. Jay, P. Butler-Nalin, C. Marder, & R. Cox (Eds.), *Youth with disabilities: How are they doing?* (pp. 8.1–8.54). Menlo Park, CA: SRI International.

Falvey, M., Gage, S., & Eshilian, L. (1995). Secondary curriculum and instruction. In M. Falvey (Ed.), *Inclusive and heterogeneous schooling: Assessment, curriculum, and instruction* (pp. 341–361). Baltimore: Paul H. Brookes.

Federico, P. (1995). Expert and novice recognition of similar situations. *Human Factors, 37,* 105–122.

Gaylord-Ross, R., Siegel, S., Park, H., & Wilson, W. (1988). Secondary vocational training. In R. Gaylord-Ross (Ed.), *Vocational education for persons with handicaps* (pp. 174–202). Mountain View, CA: Mayfield.

Gibson, L., & Angel, D. (1992). A model mentoring program for co-op students. *Journal of Cooperative Education, 29,* 66–79.

Good, H., & Teller, J. (1969). *A history of Western education* (3rd ed.). Toronto: Macmillan.

Greenberger, E., & Steinberg, L. (1986). *When teenagers work: The psychological and social costs of adolescent employment.* New York: Basic Books.

Hagner, D., Butterworth, J., & Keith, G. (1995). Strategies and barriers in facilitating natural supports for employment of adults with severe disabilities. *Journal of the Association for Persons with Severe Handicaps, 20,* 110–120.

Hagner, D., & DiLeo, D. (1993). Working together: Workplace culture, supported employment, and persons with disabilities. Cambridge, MA: Brookline.

Hagner, D., Helm, D., & Butterworth, J. (1996). "This is your meeting": A qualitative study of person-centered planning. *Mental Retardation, 34,* 159–171.

Halpern, A., Dorenz, B., & Benz, M. (1993). Job experiences of students with disabilities during their last two years in school. *Career Development for Exceptional Individuals, 16,* 63–73.

Hamilton, S. (1990). *Apprenticeship for adulthood.* New York: The Free Press.

Hawkins, R., & Jackson, S. (1992). Using radio courses in the high school curriculum. *Tech Trends, 37*(4), 27–28.

Herr, E., & Watts, A. (1988). Work shadowing and work-related learning. *Career Development Quarterly, 37,* 78–86.

Hill, D. (1995). Hire education. *Education Week, 15* (May 10), pp. 33–34.

Hoyt, K. (1994). Youth apprenticeship "American style" and career development. *Career Development Quarterly, 42,* 216–223.

Isaacson, L., & Brown, D. (1993). *Career information, career counseling, and career development.* Boston: Allyn & Bacon.

Jordan, L. (1989). Cosmopolitical obstetrics: Some insights from the training of midwives. *Social Science and Medicine, 28,* 925–944.

Loughead, T., Liu, S., & Middleton, E. (1995). Career development for at-risk youth: A program evaluation. *Career Development Quarterly, 43,* 274–284.

Mank, D., Oorthuys, J., Rhodes, L., Sandow, D., & Weyer, T. (1992). Accommodating workers with mental disabilities. *Training and Development Journal, 46,* 49–52.

Mark, J., & Stoia, J. (1993). Anything that starts with a "C": Combining co-op with career services. *Journal of Cooperative Education, 28*(3), 42–48.

Marshall, R., & Tucker, M. (1992). *Thinking for a living: Education and the wealth of nations.* New York: Basic Books.

Maselow, R. (1995). How little tykes become big tycoons. *Educational Leadership, 52*(8), 58–61.

Miller, P., Shambaugh, K., Robinson, C., & Wimberly, J. (1995). Applied learning for middle schoolers. *Educational Leadership, 52*(8), 22–25.

Morrison, E. (1993). Newcomer information seeking: Exploring types, modes, sources and outcomes. *Academy of Management Journal, 36,* 557–589.

Pauly, E. (1994). Home-grown lessons: There is much to learn from existing school-to-work programs. *Vocational Educational Journal, 69*(7), 16–18.

Piuma, M., & Udvari-Solner, A. (1993). *Materials and process manual: Developing low cost vocational adaptations for individuals with severe disabilities.* Madison, WI: Madison Metropolitan School District.

Raizen, S. (1994). Learning and work: The research base. In L. McFarland & M. Vickers (Eds.), *Vocational education and training for youth: Towards coherent policy and practice* (pp. 69–114). Washington, DC: Organization for Economic Cooperation and Development.

Reidy, J., & Schottmueller, J. (1993). Trying out careers. *Educational Leadership, 50*(7), 46–47.

Roberts, G., Zimbrich, K., Butterworth, J., & Hart, D. (1993). *Job accommodation system.* Boston: Institute for Community Inclusion.

Rosenthal, I. (1989). Model transition for disabled high school and college students. *Rehabilitation Counseling Bulletin, 33,* 54–66.

Rothman, R. (1995). The certificate of initial mastery. *Educational Leadership, 52*(8), 41–45.

Salomon, C. (1991). New partners in business. *Personnel Journal, 58*(4), 57–62.

Smith, C., & Rojewski, J. (1993). School-to-work transition: Alternatives for educational reform. *Youth & Society, 25,* 222–250.

Sowers, J. (1995). Adaptive environments in the workplace. In K. Flippo, K. Inge, & M. Barcus (Eds.),

Assistive technology: A resource for school, work, and community (pp. 167–186). Baltimore: Paul H. Brookes.

Sowers, J., & Powers, L. (1991). *Vocational preparation and employment of students with physical and multiple disabilities.* Baltimore: Paul H. Brookes.

Speight, J., Rosenthal, K., Jones, B., & Gastenveld, P. (1995). Medcamp's effect on junior high school students' career self-efficacy. *Career Development Quarterly, 43,* 285–293.

Stern, D., Finkelstein, N., Stone, J., Latting, J., & Dornsife, C. (1995). *School to work: Research on programs in the United States.* London: Falmer Press.

Stern, D., & Rahn, M. (1995). How health career academies provide work-based learning. *Educational Leadership, 52*(8), 37–40.

Thompson, S. (1995). The community as classroom. *Educational Leadership, 52*(8), 17–20.

Tilson, G., Luecking, R., & Donovan, M. (1994). Involving employers in transition: The Bridges model. *Career Development for Exceptional Individuals, 17,* 77–89.

Van Der Vorm, P. (1993). Cooperative education and general education: A partnership with potential. *Journal of Cooperative Education, 30,* 28–33.

Veum, J., & Weiss, A. (1993). Education and the work histories of young adults. *Monthly Labor Review, 116*(4), 11–20.

Vogelsberg, R. T., Ashe, W., & Williams, W. (1986). Community-based service delivery in rural Vermont: Issues and recommendations. In R. Horner, L. Meyer, & B. Fredericks (Eds.), *Education of learners with severe handicaps* (pp. 29–59). Baltimore: Paul H. Brookes.

White, W., & Biller, E. (1988). Career education for students with handicaps. In R. Gaylord-Ross (Ed.), *Vocational education for students with handicaps* (pp. 30–64). Mountain View, CA: Mayfield.

Wigginton, E. (1986). *Sometimes a shining moment: The Foxfire experience.* New York: Doubleday.

Winger, M. (1995). Students and radio: Getting the good word out. *Educational Leadership, 52*(8), 36–38.

Yatvin, J. (1995). Middle schoolers experience the world of work. *Educational Leadership, 52*(8), 52–55.

15

◉

Supporting the Transition from School to Adult Life

CAROLYN HUGHES
and JIN-HO KIM

Providing support for students as they make the transition from school to adult life has been advocated for over 10 years. Unfortunately, little consensus exists regarding best practices that comprise a model that supports the transition from school to adult life. The purpose of this chapter is to propose an empirically based, socially validated model of support for the transition from school to adult life. First, we overview the development of the model. Next, we describe the support model in detail, providing examples of its application among secondary special education students. Using a case study approach, we illustrate the model in practice with a high school student. We conclude with recommendations for practitioners interested in implementing the model.

Despite a sustained emphasis in policy statements and the literature regarding the importance of providing student support, the outcomes facing many adolescents with disabilities as they leave high school are unemployment, economic dependence, and segregation (Hasazi, Hock, & Cravedi-Cheng, 1992; Sitlington, Frank, & Carson, 1993; Harris & Associates, 1994; U.S. Department of Education, 1995; Blackorby & Wagner, 1996). Three to five years after exiting school, less than 8 percent of young persons with disabilities are reported to be fully employed or receiving postsecondary training, active socially, and living independently in the community (Wagner, 1995). Further, less than 10 percent of special education graduates are estimated to be living above the poverty level 3 years after graduation (Affleck et al., 1990).

Analyses of postsecondary outcome studies corroborate these findings: Few students with disabilities are living independently, working full- or part-time, or enrolled in postsecondary education (Hasazi et al., 1992). These findings paint an abysmal picture of adult outcomes for secondary education students. For example, let's examine the life of Lester Anthony in Case Study 1.

NEED FOR A MODEL OF SUPPORT THAT WORKS

Unfortunately, Lester's story is not unusual. Without support, for many students, school is not a positive experience resulting in a successful transition to adult life. A promising career, satisfying personal relationships, a comfortable home, leisure-time activities—the expectations many of us hold for adulthood—do not materialize for many students when they leave high school. Some students need additional support than is typically provided by a traditional secondary school curriculum to achieve adult outcomes that many of us take for granted (e.g., a job, a car, marriage).

The importance of providing support for students as they make the transition from school to adult life has been advocated for over 10 years (Will, 1984; Halpern, 1985, 1992; Rusch & Mithaug, 1985; Rusch & Phelps, 1987). Support models that have received considerable attention in the literature include Will's (1984) "bridges" model of school to employment proposed by the Office of Special Education and Rehabilitative Services (OSERS), Halpern's (1985) model of school to "community adjustment," the 1990 Individuals with Disabilities Education Act (IDEA), which mandated support for the transition from school to a range of postschool adult outcomes, and finally the 1994 School-to-Work Opportunities Act, which addressed employment among all youth.

Although the scope of these models differs in comprehensiveness, an element common to all is a commitment to match the level and intensity of support to students' individual needs. Specifically, these models are based on the assumption that students require varying degrees and duration of support to experience full community participation as they make the transition from school to adult life (Will, 1984; Halpern,

1985; Rusch et al., 1992). Support strategies might include a co-worker giving a student a ride to work, a peer helping a student with limited use of her hands to eat lunch, or a vocational rehabilitation counselor assisting a student in developing a résumé. For discussion purposes, we define "support strategies" as any assistance or help provided directly to a student to promote a successful transition from school to adult life.

Unfortunately, little consensus exists on best practices to support the transition from school to adult life (Halpern, 1992; Rusch, 1992; Johnson & Rusch, 1993; Kohler, 1993; Greene & Albright, 1995). J. J. Stowitschek (personal communication, October 7, 1994) observed that "recent review articles have questioned what we know about what works in school-to-work transition, even after a decade of research, development, and demonstration." Similarly, Kohler's (1993) review of best practices in transition suggested that, although there is some social validation to support a relationship between current transition practices and postschool outcomes, there is limited empirical evidence identifying critical components of the transition process. Because practice constitutes the process by which desired outcomes are achieved, it is imperative to identify and validate models of support that functionally relate to favorable outcomes (Haring & Breen, 1989; DeStefano & Wagner, 1992). Without knowledge of how practice relates to outcomes, the field cannot expect that schooling systematically will improve the adult outcomes of secondary special education students (Rusch, 1992). Although the type and intensity of support that students need to make a smooth transition to adult life will differ according to individual needs (e.g., a personal care attendant for a person with quadriplegia or a communication book for a nonverbal student), we propose that there are certain critical strategies that must be incorporated into any successful model of student support.

Applied research offers some insight into critical factors that have been demonstrated empirically as supporting successful student

---

CASE STUDY 1   Lester Anthony

Lester Anthony is 16 years old and lives with his aunt, his younger brother, and his younger sister in a small apartment in a large urban housing project. An older brother and sister live out of the home. Lester's mother, who has legal custody of him, has been in and out of jail for prostitution and selling drugs for as long as Lester can remember. His elementary school teachers remember Lester as affectionate, having a good sense of humor, quick to laugh and make a joke, and good at drawing his favorite sports figures. At school, Lester made passing grades and maintained good attendance until the seventh grade when his grades and attendance rapidly began to decline. During the eighth grade, Lester was suspended for 4 days for fighting with another student, 2 days for throwing rocks, and 1 day for verbally abusing a teacher. At that time, his aunt expressed concern to Lester's teacher about her ability to cope with Lester. However, neither she, Lester, nor the rest of the family was offered any support. During the ninth grade, Lester was identified as having a learning disability and placed in a resource room for English, math, and history classes. That same year, he missed 42 days of school and spent 5 days in a juvenile detention center for possession of drugs and disturbing the peace. Lester got a job in a large supermarket at the beginning of his sophomore year, but was fired when he was caught by his work supervisor eating candy off a shelf while sitting on the floor. His resource room teacher felt that he would have been successful at work if he had had a job coach. During the first week of October of the same year, he slept through all his classes and received zeros. Lester has not been seen in school since.

---

outcomes. These factors include (a) paid work experiences during high school (Hasazi, Gorden, & Roe, 1985; Scuccimarra & Speece, 1990); (b) a network of family and friends (Hasazi et al., 1985); (c) community-based instruction (McDonnell et al.,1993); (d) parent involvement (Schalock, 1986; Heal et al.,1990); (e) social skills training (Mithaug, Horiuchi, & Fanning, 1985; Heal et al., 1990); (f) employment skills training (Hasazi et al., 1985; Mithaug et al., 1985; Schalock, 1986); (g) job match (Heal et al., 1990); and (h) follow-up support services (McDonnell et al., 1989; Wacker et al., 1989; Heal et al., 1990).

In addition, the field is beginning to establish a consensus among stakeholders regarding the essential components of a model of support. For example, policy makers and state directors of special education who participated in focus groups agreed that a transition model should support broad-based student outcomes such as personal and social adjustment, physical health, and citizenship (Ysseldyke, Thurlow, & Bruininks, 1992; National Center on Educational Outcomes, 1993). Directors of federally funded model demonstration transition pro-

grams were reported to concur that support models should address multiple outcomes of social participation, perceived and actual social support, and personal, peer, and co-worker acceptance (Chadsey-Rusch & Heal, 1995), as well as social integration, functional life skills, employment, and postsecondary education (Rusch, Kohler, & Hughes, 1992; Rusch, Enchelmaier, & Kohler, 1994). Further, parents and practitioners who were surveyed agreed that parental involvement, community-based instruction, and social and employment skills training were critical support model components (Halpern, 1985; Benz & Halpern, 1987). Persons with disabilities (Lovett & Harris, 1987b), parents (Lovett & Harris, 1987a; Epps & Myers, 1989), and teachers (Morgan et al., 1992) who responded to questionnaires advocated a broad-based model of support that targets employment, social, community, and independent living skills. Finally, professional organizations, such as the Council for Exceptional Children Division on Career Development and Transition, have published position papers that support models that address student needs and interests, self-determination, functional life skills instruction, and the demands of adulthood (Clark et al., 1994; Halpern, 1994).

The applied research and consensus literature provide an indication of practices and outcomes that may be germane to supporting a successful transition from school to adult life. However, we cannot ignore findings that indicate that secondary education has not resulted in successful adulthood for many special education students. In an era of shrinking funding allocated for disability programs (Council for Exceptional Children, 1995), it is particularly critical to identify valid models of support for special education students that may improve these otherwise dismal outcomes.

The purpose of this chapter is to propose an empirically based, socially validated model of support for the transition from school to adult life. First, we overview the development of the model. Next, we describe it in detail, providing examples of its application among secondary special education students. Using a case study approach, we illustrate the model in practice with a high school student. We conclude with recommendations for practitioners interested in implementing the model.

DEVELOPMENT OF A MODEL OF SUPPORT

We used a three-step process to develop our model by (a) conducting a review of literature, (b) developing a questionnaire, and (c) surveying the opinions of applied researchers. (See Hughes et al., in press, for a more detailed account of the process.)

The purpose of the literature review was to identify a candidate list of support model components that were supported by empirical and conceptual literature. A total of 395 articles meeting selection criteria were reviewed. All student-support model components investigated or discussed per article (e.g., social skills training, identifying students' preferences and choices, number of persons in a student's social network) were identified, and each component that met

a preestablished criterion for face validity was retained in a candidate list of critical support model components. The criterion for establishing face validity of a component included a minimum of (a) two demonstrations of empirical evidence of effectiveness and (b) one statement of support in a conceptual paper. The number of process and outcome components retained was 10 and 11, respectively.

To assess the social validity and practicality of the model, these components then were incorporated into a questionnaire and field-tested nationally among fifty-four researchers in the area of transition (response rate = 92 percent). This process was designed to establish a degree of consensus within the field regarding the acceptability of the model and the feasibility of its implementation by practitioners. Results of the survey indicated that respondents judged all components of the model as critical to the transition from school to adult life. A definition of each process and outcome component derived from the three-step process is shown in Table 15.1.

OVERVIEW OF THE MODEL OF SUPPORT

The model development process resulted in a model of student support derived from the literature and socially validated by experts in the area of transition. The following 10 process components were identified:

1. identify co-worker, peer, and family support
2. identify student's preferences and choices
3. teach choice making and decision making
4. match support to student's needs
5. teach self-management and independence
6. teach social skills
7. identify independence objectives
8. identify environmental support
9. monitor social acceptance across time
10. assess social acceptance

Table 15.1 Candidate List of Critical Support Model Components

Component	Definition
Process Components	
Teach social skills	Teach the student social behaviors that facilitate interactions with significant others in a manner considered socially appropriate in the immediate environment.
Teach self-management and independence	Teach students self-management skills that will enable them to perform expected behaviors with greater independence.
Identify independence objectives	Survey student's environments (i.e., home, community, school, work) through observation and by interviewing the student and significant others to identify areas in which the student's performance is not consistent with expectations.
Identify co-worker, peer, and family support	Identify co-workers, peers, and family members who may provide support to the student at home, school, work, and in the community.
Assess social acceptance	Assess acceptance of student's everyday performance (e.g., attendance, personal satisfaction, social interaction) via evaluations completed by the student, teacher, employer, co-worker, and significant others and by observing and comparing the student's performance to that of co-worker(s) and peers.
Identify student's preferences and choices	Identify student's expectations, choices, and preferences with respect to daily living (e.g., recreational activities, friends, types of employment) by conducting observations, interviews, and assessments (written or pictorial) with the student and by interviewing the student's significant others. In addition, assess the student's choice-making and decision-making skills.
Monitor social acceptance across time	Establish a continuous schedule by which the student, teachers, employers, co-workers, and significant others evaluate acceptance of the student's performance. Use evaluations to identify and discuss discrepancies between observed performance and expected performance and to reach consensus on social acceptance.
Identify environmental support	Identify naturally occurring cues in the student's workplace and other environments that will support the student in initiating and completing expected and desired behavior.
Teach choice making and decision making	Teach the student skills that are necessary for making choices and decisions and expressing preferences and provide opportunities to exercise choice.
Match support to student's needs	Match existing support to those areas in which a student needs support.
Outcome Components	
Quality of social skills	Quality of student's social behaviors that facilitate socially appropriate interactions as assessed by interviewing significant others, such as peers and co-workers, and by conducting direct observation.
Wages earned	Amount of earnings (e.g., hourly wages) student receives for work performed.
Length of employment	Number of days (months) student maintains employment in an integrated work setting.

(continued)

Table 15.1 *(continued)*

Component	Definition
Employer, co-worker, peer, and family satisfaction	Employer, co-worker, peer, and family satisfaction with student's independence, work performance, adaptability, social interaction, and other performance indicators as assessed by interviewing significant others.
Quality of student's performance	Quality of the student's independence, adaptability, social interaction, and other performance indicators as assessed by interviewing significant others, such as a teacher or work supervisor, and by conducting direct observation.
Level of independence	Extent to which student performs socially valued behavior without assistance or with partial assistance.
Number of hours worked	Number of hours worked by student per week.
Student satisfaction	Student's satisfaction with own daily living experiences.
Level of social integration	Extent to which student interacts with peers, co-workers, and significant others as an equal member within school, home, workplace, and community.
Job type	Type of job student maintains.
Level of choice making and decision making	Extent to which student displays a preference or choice as well as the extent to which student is able to make responsible decisions and evaluate the outcomes of decisions made.

In addition 11 outcome components were identified:

1. student satisfaction
2. level of choice making and decision making
3. level of social integration
4. quality of student's performance
5. quality of social skills
6. employer, co-worker, peer, and family satisfaction
7. level of independence
8. length of employment
9. wages earned
10. number of hours worked
11. job type

The following illustrations demonstrate the use of the model components in a student's everyday life.

Process Components

First, the process components of the model could be used to develop support in a student's environment. For example, a teacher may identify social support from employers, co-workers, peers, and family, which is available in a student's environment (see Box 15.1).

BOX 15.1   Process Component: Identify Social Support

Beth, a young woman with a visual impairment, is helped by her brother to find her bus pass, which had become lost in her purse. She then walks to the bus stop with a classmate who lives nearby. At her community job in a legal office, she confides in a co-worker, telling her at break about the frustrations she is having with her boyfriend. As she leaves for the day, her supervisor says, "See you tonight at the picnic."

BOX 15.2   Process Component: Promote Social Acceptance

James works in the laundry room of a large hotel where he stacks and bundles washcloths. He arrives at work on time every day and is an expert at his job. He has a tendency to hum and talk to himself and he walks unsteadily as he pushes his cart of bundled washcloths. James's job coach points out to the supervisor that James is an excellent and reliable worker and a valuable member of the laundry staff, even if he does have some behaviors that are different from those of his co-workers.

A job coach could also help to promote acceptance of a student within an environment (see Box 15.2).

The model's process components also could be used to increase a student's competence within his or her environment. For example, a student could be provided opportunities to learn and practice social skills (see Box 15.3).

A student also could be taught to use self-management skills to improve and maintain her daily performance (see Box 15.4).

Outcome Components

The outcome components of the model are useful in determining if the goals of a student's transition program are being met and if the amount of support is sufficient. For example, a teacher could assess the extent of a student's satisfaction (see Box 15.5).

The model's outcome components also may be used to evaluate a student's job experiences (see Box 15.6).

BOX 15.3   Process Component: Teach Social Skills

Tony began talking in one- and two-word phrases when he was 7 years old. At 16, he usually sat by himself in the lunchroom looking down at his plate of food until his teacher noticed and decided to start a peer buddy program. Now Tony eats with volunteers from general education classes who prompt and reinforce him for engaging in conversation during lunch. Tony has also joined some school clubs with his new friends and now has considerable opportunity to practice his new social skills with a variety of people.

BOX 15.4   Process Component: Teach Self-Management

Shalonda has a job cleaning equipment at a local hospital during part of her school day. She has difficulty remembering the cleaning sequence for some of the more complicated jobs, such as the I.V. equipment. Her teacher set up a picture cue system to help guide Shalonda through the job. Now she checks off each task of the cleaning job in her picture notebook as she does it and has no difficulty completing the job on her own.

BOX 15.5   Process Component: Student Satisfaction

Ms. Martin, a teacher of students with language impairments, is interested in the quality of life of her students. Because many of the students don't talk, Ms. Martin is careful to observe their affect during recreational activities and on the job. She also keeps track of whom they choose to interact with and the type of activities in which they engage. Ms. Martin knows that nonverbal signs may be a good indication of a students' satisfaction in their daily life. If she notices signs of displeasure, Ms. Martin can intervene to help.

RELEVANCE OF THE MODEL

As illustrated in the preceding examples, the support model has direct relevance for students who are making the transition from school to adult life, many of whom face unfavorable postschool outcomes. Previous literature reviews conducted by Johnson and Rusch (1993), Kohler (1993), and others did not systematically search the applied literature to identify empirically established transition-process components that support students. Consequently, Kohler, for example, identified only four transition processes supported by empirical evidence (i.e., vocational training, parent involvement, paid work, social skills training), with a range of only one to three studies cited as supporting evidence. The study reported found ten process components that were empirically demonstrated in the applied research to be effective in supporting the transition from school to adult life. These components were supported by an average of eighteen empirical demonstrations of effectiveness (range = 3 to 34).

In addition, the social validity of the empirically derived model components was established by the research community, an endeavor that was not attempted in past studies. As reported by Kohler and colleagues (1994), exemplary transition-model process components typically are identified in the field through nomination by staff or peers and evaluated through a peer review process. As a result, transition practices recommended, evaluated, and reported as exemplary frequently are not supported by empirical evidence. This model provides a degree of consensus regarding best practices that is sorely missing in the field of transition. As argued recently by the editors of *Career Development for Exceptional Individuals,* a critical issue in the field is that "little empirical evidence exists in support of what is considered 'best practices' in transition" (Greene & Albright, 1995:1).

APPLICATION OF THE MODEL

To illustrate application of the student support model, let us return to Lester Anthony who

---

BOX 15.6   Outcome Component: Work History

Mr. Francesco uses his computer to keep records of his students' job experiences during high school. Because his community-based program allows students to sample many different jobs before graduation, Mr. Francesco has much information to record regarding his students' work history. Mr. Francesco has developed a work performance evaluation form on his computer in which he records relevant data on all his students' work experiences throughout high school. He continually updates his students' work history, which he can also easily convert into student résumés.

received little support during his secondary school years and eventually dropped out of school at age 16 (see Case Study 2). How might Lester's life have been different if he had received support?

Lester and his transition team devised a support plan that would help him in his daily life now, as well as throughout his secondary school years and during his transition from school to his adult life. Let us take a look at applications of the support plan the team developed, which was based on the model of student support proposed in this chapter (see Table 15.2).

The support plan developed by Lester and his transition team was two-pronged. It called for (a) developing support in Lester's environment and (b) helping Lester develop his competence within that environment.

Developing Support

This part of the support plan comprised identifying social and environmental support and promoting social acceptance. For example, the team reasoned that, without a father or older brother in the home, Lester needed a male role model. Sherman Sanders, a member of the "100 Black Men" mentoring program in the city where Lester lived, was matched as a mentor for Lester. Mr. Sanders was a successful businessman in town who knew Lester and his family from the church they attended. Lester and his mentor spoke on the phone almost daily and attended church and school events together several times a week. If Lester needed help with his homework or someone to talk to about a problem with his friends or family, he knew whom to call.

Lester's plan called for more support at school as well. Because of his learning disability, he was eligible for special education services. Rather than pulling him out into a separate resource class, the special education consultant provided support services in Lester's regular education classes, where he could remain with his peers with whom he had grown up. The consul-

tant helped Lester with his schoolwork in the classes and helped Lester's teachers adapt his assignments to accentuate his academic strengths. The consultant helped some of Lester's classmates, too, so Lester did not feel like he was being singled out. Lester also began meeting with the school counselor weekly to help him deal with the loss of his mother at home and to improve his relationships with the rest of his family. He started attending a drug prevention support group at the school's counseling center that was designed to build students' self-esteem and coping skills.

When he turned 16, Lester became eligible for vocational rehabilitation services through the vocational rehabilitation counselor housed in Lester's high school. The counselor, Ms. Bennett, helped Lester get a job at the downtown Piggly Wiggly supermarket. When Lester had trouble pricing items with the price gun, Ms. Bennett encouraged Lester's co-workers to help out. Soon Lester caught on and was given additional responsibilities, which his co-workers assisted him in learning. Lester became especially good friends with Wally, who was a bagger at the supermarket. Wally began giving Lester a ride home after work and they often would stop off together for a soft drink on the way.

The transition team requested increased environmental support for Lester. A home visit by the school counselor revealed that Lester was spending too much time alone unsupervised before his aunt got home from work in the afternoon. By joining the Boys' and Girls' Club in his neighborhood and attending every day after school, Lester no longer was likely to run around with the rough crowd he had started hanging out with. He developed an interest in sports and even joined some of the teams at school. Eventually, he started making friends at the club and even rode home with his friends on the school bus. Lester no longer came into contact with the old crowd, who continued to get into trouble.

When Lester got his job at the supermarket in the tenth grade, his supervisor had never

---

CASE STUDY 2   Ms. Raine Helps Lester Anthony

Lester Anthony was 13 years old and in the seventh grade when his language arts teacher, Ms. Raine, noticed that her usually light-hearted, amiable student seemed "down." Lester just did not seem like his usual joking, fun-loving self. A quick look at her record book showed Ms. Raine that Lester's passing grades and good attendance had suddenly dropped. She knew she had a student who needed help!

At lunch break, Ms. Raine consulted Lester's science, math, and P.E. teachers, who all agreed that now that she mentioned it, they, too, had noticed a change in Lester's behavior. After school, Ms. Raine called Lester's home, surprised to find out that Lester was now living with his aunt—his mother having recently been arrested and jailed again. The phone call was shortly followed up with a home visit, at which time Ms. Raine found out that Lester's Aunt Gladys was also caring for Lester's younger brother and sister. Aunt Gladys was very relieved to see Ms. Raine. She had been worried when Lester recently had become unruly at home, but did not know what to do. He had always been so sweet, helpful with his brother and sister, and had attended church and other activities with the family. Maybe it was caused by drugs, which were prevalent in the neighborhood, or the rough crowd he had started hanging out with. Ms. Raine and Aunt Gladys decided that Lester needed support.

Much happened within the next 3 months. A referral to special education resulted in a transition team meeting, which was attended by Lester, his aunt, his teachers, the special education consulting teacher, the school social worker, the school psychologist, and the school principal. At the meeting, Lester was identified as having a learning disability, and he and his aunt were told he could receive special education services. The team then worked together to build a support plan for Lester that would (a) develop support in Lester's environment and (b) help him develop his competence. The team continued to monitor and implement the plan throughout Lester's secondary school years. Lester graduated at 18 from high school and began working in an auto body shop, a job that he had chosen himself. He now has many friends, enjoys sports, and attends church and social events regularly with his family.

---

hired someone with a learning disability before. The supervisor became exasperated when Lester failed to follow through on some of his tasks, especially those that required Lester to follow several steps. For example, stocking shelves required several different tasks such as checking orders in the stock room, getting and loading a cart, placing the cart out of the way in the correct aisle in the store, and facing the items correctly on the shelves.

The vocational rehabilitation counselor emphasized the accuracy of Lester's work when he followed the correct sequence and helped the supervisor devise a schedule that Lester could follow to complete his daily tasks. The supervisor also learned to make his directions very clear so that Lester no longer became confused. Lester became comfortable and confident at work and won the "Employee of the Month" award for the month of November.

Developing Competence

Lester's support plan also called for activities designed to develop his competence. These activities focused on increasing his choice-making opportunities, general skill repertoire, self-management skills, and social skills. For example, during her visits to Lester's home, the school counselor noticed that Lester had little choice regarding his clothes. It made Lester angry that his aunt wanted to pick out what he wore, just like she did with his younger brother and sister. He wanted to dress like his friends, who were wearing "baggy" clothing now that they had entered seventh grade. The school counselor helped Lester's aunt accept the changes in Lester's clothing style and the idea that Lester was old enough and responsible enough to pick out his own clothes. Lester had a "clothes allowance" and the opportunity to buy

Table 15.2 Lester Anthony's Support Plan

Component	Application
Develop Support in the Environment	
Identify social support from employers, co-workers, peers, and family	A male mentor was matched with Lester through the "100 Black Men" mentoring program in Lester's city. Lester's mentor was a businessman who spent time with Lester several days a week, talked with him on the phone almost daily, and even helped him with his homework. The special education consulting teacher provided help to Lester with his schoolwork in his regular education classes and helped his teachers adapt Lester's assignments. The school counselor helped Lester deal with the loss of his mother at home and helped Lester and his aunt improve their communication with each other. Lester started attending church again with his family and joined the church choir.
	When he entered tenth grade, Lester became eligible for vocational rehabilitation services. Lester's vocational rehabilitation counselor helped him get a job in a large supermarket and his supervisor and co-workers worked alongside him until he learned the job. Lester and his co-workers often attended sports events together at night after work.
Identify environmental support and provide needed changes within the environment	Lester's school counselor visited Lester and his aunt at home to pinpoint sources of problems within Lester's neighborhood. They identified the hours after school before Lester's aunt came home from work as when he was likely to spend time with boys who were in trouble or using drugs. The counselor helped Lester and a friend join the Boys' and Girls' Club in their neighborhood. Lester attended the club every day after school with his friend until his aunt got home from work. Soon, he became interested in playing sports. Eventually, he joined his school's track team and became assistant manager of the basketball team. With his time now spent in clubs or at team practices, Lester no longer came in contact with the rough crowd he used to hang out with. The counselor also helped Lester change his bus route to and from school so he could ride with his new friends from his sports teams.
Promote acceptance in the student's environment	Because of his learning disability, Lester had a difficult time remembering a sequence of tasks. When he got his job at the supermarket in the tenth grade, his supervisor became impatient when he failed to follow through on some of his job assignments. Lester's vocational rehabilitation counselor helped the supervisor realize that Lester's work was accurate and complete when he was sure of what his duties were. Together, the counselor and the supervisor devised a schedule Lester could follow every day and a "to-do" list so he could keep track of his sequence of tasks. Soon Lester's supervisor learned to clarify his verbal directions to Lester and Lester became one of his favorite workers.
Help Student Develop Competence	
Observe the student's opportunities for choice	During her visits to Lester's home, the school counselor observed that choosing clothes appeared to be a source of tension in the home. Lester's aunt had been selecting clothes every day for the children in the house ever since they had come to live with her. Lester's younger brother or sister did not mind, but when Lester entered seventh grade, he wanted to start wearing "baggy" clothing like the rest of his friends. The counselor helped Lester's aunt realize that Lester was old enough to start choosing some of his own clothing. His aunt began providing Lester with opportunities to pick out his own clothes when they went shopping.

(continued)

Table 15.2 *(continued)*

Component	Application
Provide opportunities for choice making	Lester liked his job at the supermarket, which he had gotten in the tenth grade. But after a few months, he wondered if he might rather work somewhere else. He was especially concerned about finding out what sort of job he might want full-time, after he finished high school. Lester's vocational rehabilitation counselor realized that Lester needed the opportunity to sample different types of jobs in order to determine his own preference. He let Lester sample many jobs throughout his sophomore, junior, and senior years of high school. Lester decided that what he really liked doing was working on cars. And on graduation, he got a job at an auto body shop.
Identify the student's strengths and areas needing support	Lester's special education consulting teacher observed Lester throughout his day and across his home, school, and work environments. She also spoke with Lester and his family, friends, teachers, co-workers, and work supervisor. She discovered that Lester had many strengths, including his sense of humor, his friendliness, his loyalty, and his desire to please others. An area in which he needed support, however, was that he was easily distracted and tended to get off-task, especially with co-workers at work or with friends during class.
Teach self-management	The special education consulting teacher helped Lester realize that getting off-task could really be a problem, especially at work when he had been asked by his boss to complete a job. If Lester lost track of what he was doing, his boss might be disappointed with his work. His teacher taught Lester to self-instruct to remind himself what he was doing. If he was in the middle of completing a task and a co-worker started to talk to him, Lester reminded himself to say "Hi. How are you? I'd like to talk to you now but I have to finish this job for Mr. Bateson first. I'll stop back as soon as I'm done." This strategy helped Lester keep on-task and finish his jobs while he maintained social interaction with his co-workers and friends.
Provide opportunities to learn and practice social skills	When Lester first was matched with his mentor, Sherman Sanders of the "100 Black Men" program, he had never had any opportunity to eat out at restaurants, use services at a bank, or ask for help in a department store. Mr. Sanders knew Lester needed some opportunity to practice the social skills required in these situations. Therefore, they frequently went out to eat together and Mr. Sanders often had Lester accompany him to the bank or on other occasions when he was conducting business. Mr. Sanders knew he was serving as a model for Lester as well as giving Lester the chance to practice the social skills he observed Mr. Sanders performing on their outings in the community.

his own clothes when he went to the shopping mall with his aunt.

Lester was also given opportunities to choose in other areas. The transition team agreed that, like all adolescents, Lester needed the opportunity to sample a range of experiences in his life in order to determine his own interests and preferences. One area in which Lester was interested in exploring different options was his career. He liked the job at the Piggly Wiggly he had during his sophomore year, but he really did not think he wanted to keep that job for the rest of his life. During Lester's sophomore, junior, and senior years, his vocational rehabilitation counselor arranged for him to sample many different jobs, such as small parts assembly, landscaping, and office work. It turned out that Lester was primarily interested in working on cars, which he got a chance to do during his senior year. After high school, Lester got a job in an auto body shop and loved it.

The special education consulting teacher knew Lester had many strengths. She had observed Lester during many different situations across many environments and had interviewed and met with family members, friends, teachers, and co-workers. Lester was friendly and easygoing, had a sense of humor, and liked to please others. One problem he did have, though, a tendency to get off-task. He was easily distracted, especially when he was around his classmates or co-workers. This was becoming a problem, especially on the job.

Together, Lester and the special education consultant developed a plan to help Lester manage his own behavior. He wanted to stay on-task and keep his job; yet, he did not want to have to stop interacting totally with his co-workers. The consultant taught Lester to use self-instruction to remind himself to complete the job before socializing at work. If a co-worker stopped to talk when he was completing a task, Lester learned to say, "Hi. Good to see you. Let me finish shelving these cans and then I'll stop back in the storeroom and talk to you." Self-instructing helped Lester stay on-task and finish the job, yet still be able to interact with his co-workers at work.

Another goal on Lester's support plan was to develop his social skills. As he was growing up, Lester had little opportunity to learn and practice social skills by eating out or getting services in the community. Mr. Sanders, his mentor from the "100 Black Men" program, became an important part of Lester's social skills support plan. By taking Lester out in the community for business and social events, Mr. Sanders was able to model good social skills and Lester had the opportunity to practice the skills he observed.

Summary

Lester's support plan was a success. Rather than dropping out of school at age 16 with a history of drugs and a record at juvenile court, Lester's outcomes were positive. Considering the warm and friendly manner in which he interacted with his co-workers on the job, you could tell that he liked his work. He had made a good choice in choosing auto body as his career. Four years after graduation, he still worked at the same shop. After several promotions, his salary was well above minimum wage and he was given more and more responsibility. Lester even had personal use of a company pickup truck. He regularly bowled with the company's team and was well liked by his co-workers. His supervisor was pleased with his work and Lester's Aunt Gladys was pleased that Lester was helping to pay the rent and some expenses of his younger brother and sister. When he is not spending time with his friends or co-workers, Lester often can be found at the Boys' and Girls' Club, shooting baskets and talking with neighborhood students who are having a rough time at school.

RECOMMENDED PRACTICES

In summary, our findings corroborate an overall model of student support that emphasizes self-determination, personal satisfaction, supportive environments, social interaction, independence, social acceptance, and employment. Other models have been proposed (e.g., Halpern, 1985). However, the one presented here is unique in that each component was derived from the empirical literature and validated by the research community as being socially important. Further, the model comprises only support components that function on the student or small group level of social interaction (e.g., helping a co-worker assist a student on a new job), rather than the organizational or community level (e.g., organizing an urban development project) (Bronfenbrenner, 1977). This feature of the model is important because it makes it more likely that service providers (e.g., teachers) can directly impact interactions that are proximal to a student (e.g., obtaining parents' input into their child's IEP), whereas they may have less immediate influence on more distal interactions, such as increasing the number of job opportunities in their community.

With sufficient resources and support, this model may provide a practical and pragmatic implementation guide for practitioners directly responsible for building supports for special education students as they make the transition from school to adult life. In an era of diminishing funds, it is essential to identify strategies in the area of transition that work and that are likely to be accepted and supported by researchers and practitioners in the field.

QUESTIONS

1. Briefly describe the common findings from studies that have investigated the adult outcomes of special education graduates.

2. Describe the differences and similarities between Will's and Halpern's transition model.

3. Describe the process components related to the model of student support.

4. Describe the outcome components related to the model of student support.

5. Briefly describe the relationship between process and outcomes of student-support models.

6. Name and briefly discuss five of ten critical factors that have been demonstrated empirically to support successful student-transition outcomes.

7. Give an example of how the outcome components of the model can be used in determining if the goals of a student's transition program are being met or if the amount of support is sufficient.

8. When assisting in the development of a support model for a student within his or her environment, there are two critical things to consider. Name and describe them.

9. In this chapter, you read two case studies about a student named Lester. List the two major components of Lester's support plan and discuss how these were implemented.

10. Briefly discuss why it is so important to enable students such as Lester to make choices in their everyday lives.

REFERENCES

Affleck, J. Q., Edgar, E., Levine, P., & Kortering, L. (1990). Postschool status of students classified as mildly mentally retarded, learning disabled, or non-handicapped: Does it get better with time? *Education and Training in Mental Retardation, 25,* 315–324.

Benz, M. R., & Halpern, A. S. (1987). Transition services for secondary students with mild disabilities: A statewide perspective. *Exceptional Children, 53,* 507–514.

Blackorby, J., & Wagner, M. (1996). Longitudinal postschool outcomes of youth with disabilities: Findings from the national longitudinal transition study. *Exceptional Children, 62,* 399–413.

Bronfenbrenner, U. (1977). Toward an experimental ecology of human development. *American Psychologist, 32,* 513–531.

Chadsey-Rusch, J., & Heal, L. W. (1995). Building consensus from transition experts on social integration outcomes and interventions. *Exceptional Children, 62,* 165–187.

Clark, G. M., Field, S., Patton, J. R., Brolin, D. E., & Sitlington, P. L. (1994). Life skills instruction: A necessary component for all students with disabilities. A position statement of the Division on Career Development and Transition. *Career Development for Exceptional Individuals, 17,* 125–134.

Council for Exceptional Children. (1995). CEC leads IDEA testimony at congressional hearings. *Today, 2,* pp. 1, 2, 3, and 15.

DeStefano, L., & Wagner, M. (1992). Outcome assessment in special education: What lessons have we learned? In F. R. Rusch, L. DeStefano, J. Chadsey-Rusch, L. A. Phelps, & E. Szymanski (Eds.), *Transition from school to adult life: Models, linkages, and policy* (pp. 173–207). Sycamore, IL: Sycamore.

Epps, S., & Myers, C. L. (1989). Priority domains for instruction, satisfaction with school teaching, and postschool living and employment: An analysis of perceptions of parents of students with severe and profound disabilities. *Education and Training of the Mentally Retarded, 24,* 157–167.

Greene, G., & Albright, L. (1995). "Best practices" in transition services: Do they exist? *Career Development for Exceptional Individuals, 18,* 1–2.

Halpern, A. S. (1985). Transition: A look at the foundations. *Exceptional Children, 51,* 479–502.

———. (1992). Transition: Old wine in new bottles. *Exceptional Children, 58,* 202–211.

———. (1994). The transition of youth with disabilities to adult life: A position statement of the Division on Career Development and Transition. *Career Development for Exceptional Individuals, 17,* 115–124.

Haring, T. G., & Breen, C. (1989). Units of analysis of social interaction outcomes in supported education. *Journal of the Association for Persons with Severe Handicaps, 14,* 255–262.

Harris & Associates, Inc. (1994). *N.O.D./Harris survey of Americans with disabilities.* New York: Author.

Hasazi, S. B., Gordon, L. R., & Roe, C. A. (1985). Factors associated with the employment status of handicapped youth exiting high school from 1979 to 1983. *Exceptional Children, 51,* 455–469.

Hasazi, S. B., Hock, M. L., & Cravedi-Cheng, L. (1992). Vermont's postschool indicators: Using satisfaction and postschool outcome data for program improvement. In F. R. Rusch, L. DeStefano, J. Chadsey-Rusch, L. A. Phelps, & E. Szymanski (Eds.), *Transition from school to adult life: Models, linkages, and policy* (pp. 485–506). Sycamore, IL: Sycamore.

Heal, L. W., Gonzalez, P., Rusch, F. R., Copher, J. I., & DeStefano, L. (1990). A comparison of successful and unsuccessful placements of youths with mental handicaps into competitive employment. *Exceptionality, 1,* 181–195.

Hughes, C., Hwang, B., Kim, J., Killian, D. J., Harmer, M. L., & Alcantara, P. R. (In press). A preliminary validation of strategies that support the transition from school to adult life. *Career Development for Exceptional Individuals.*

Johnson, J. R., & Rusch, F. R. (1993). Secondary special education and transition services: Identification and recommendations for future research and demonstration. *Career Development for Exceptional Individuals, 16,* 1–18.

Kohler, P. D. (1993). Best practices in transition: Substantiated or implied? *Career Development for Exceptional Individuals, 16,* 107–121.

Kohler, P. D., DeStefano, L., Wermuth, T. R., Grayson, T. E., & McGinty, S. (1994). An analysis of exemplary transition programs: How and why are they selected? *Career Development for Exceptional Individuals, 17,* 187–202.

Lovett, D. L., & Harris, M. B. (1987a). Identification of important community living skills for adults with mental retardation. *Rehabilitation Counseling Bulletin, 31,* 34–41.

———. (1987b). Important skills for adults with mental retardation: The client's point of view. *Mental Retardation, 25,* 351–356.

McDonnell, J., Hardman, M. L., Hightower, J., Keifer-O'Donnell, R., & Drew, C. (1993). Impact of community-based instruction on the development of adaptive behavior of secondary-level students with mental retardation. *American Journal on Mental Retardation, 97,* 575–584.

McDonnell, J., Nofs, D., Hardman, M., & Chambless, C. (1989). An analysis of the procedural components of supported employment programs associated with employment outcomes. *Journal of Applied Behavior Analysis, 22,* 417–428.

Mithaug, D. E., Horiuchi, C. R., & Fanning, P. R. (1985). A report on the Colorado statewide follow-up survey of special education students. *Exceptional Children, 51,* 397–404.

Morgan, R. L., Moore, S. C., McSweyn, C., & Salzberg, C. L. (1992). Transition from school to work: Views of secondary special educators. *Education and Training in Mental Retardation, 27,* 315–323.

National Center on Educational Outcomes. (1993). *Outcomes, 2,2.* Minneapolis: University of Minnesota, National Center on Educational Outcomes.

Rusch, F. R. (1992). Identifying special education outcomes: Response to Ysseldyke, Thurlow, and Bruininks. *Remedial and Special Education, 13,* 31–32.

Rusch, F. R., DeStefano, L., Chadsey-Rusch, J., Phelps, L. A., & Szymanski, E. (Eds.). (1992). *Transition from school to adult life: Models, linkages, and policy.* Sycamore, IL: Sycamore.

Rusch, F. R., Enchelmaier, J. F., & Kohler, P. D. (1994). Employment outcomes and activities for youths in transition. *Career Development for Exceptional Individuals, 17,* 1–16.

Rusch, F. R., Kohler, P. D., & Hughes, C. (1992). An analysis of OSERS-sponsored secondary special education and transitional services research. *Career Development for Exceptional Individuals, 15,* 121–143.

Rusch, F. R., & Mithaug, D. E. (1985). Competitive employment education: A systems-analytic approach to transitional programming for the student with severe handicaps. In K. C. Lakin & R. H. Bruininks (Eds.), *Strategies for achieving community integration of developmentally disabled citizens* (pp. 177–192). Baltimore: Paul H. Brookes.

Rusch, F. R., & Phelps, L. A. (1987). Secondary special education and transition from school to work: A national priority. *Exceptional Children, 53,* 487–492.

Schalock, R. L. (1986). Employment outcomes from secondary school programs. *Remedial and Special Education, 7,* 37–39.

Scuccimarra, D. J., & Speece, D. L. (1990). Employment outcomes and social integration of students with mild handicaps: The quality of life two years after high school. *Journal of Learning Disabilities, 23,* 213–219.

Sitlington, P., Frank, A., & Carson, R. (1993). Adult adjustment among graduates with mild disabilities. *Exceptional Children, 59,* 221–233.

U.S. Department of Education. (1995). *To assure the free appropriate public education of all children with disabilities: Seventeenth annual report to congress on the implementation of the Individuals with Disabilities Education Act.* Washington, DC: Author.

Wacker, D. P., Fromm-Steege, L., Berg, W. K., & Flynn, T. H. (1989). Supported employment as an intervention package: A preliminary analysis of functional variables. *Journal of Applied Behavior Analysis, 22,* 429–439.

Wagner, M. (1995). *Transition from high school to employment and postsecondary education: Interdisciplinary implications for youths with mental retardation.* Paper presented at the 119th Annual Meeting of the American Association on Mental Retardation, San Francisco.

Will, M. (1984). *OSERS programming for the transition of youth with disabilities: Bridges from school to working life.* Washington, DC: U.S. Department of Education, Office of Special Education and Rehabilitation Services.

Ysseldyke, J. E., Thurlow, M. L., & Bruininks, R. H. (1992). Expected educational outcomes for students with disabilities. *Remedial and Special Education, 13,* 19–30.

16

◼

Postsecondary Education

ANNA GAJAR

The number of students with disabilities seeking admission to and enrolling in postsecondary education programs has increased dramatically in the past two decades—a trend that is expected to continue in the twenty-first century. Although many of these students demonstrate success in these environments, including college, university, vocational and technical school settings, others are faced with a long and difficult transitional journey from adolescence to adulthood, primarily due to the absence of (a) a clear connection between research and practices, (b) effective transition programs, and (c) skill training in self-advocacy. This chapter presents the historical background of postsecondary education as a viable option for individuals with disabilities, current practice, and recommendations regarding the future of service provision for this population of postsecondary students.

The following vignette presents an account of a student's experiences before the passage of Section 504 of P.L. 93-112 (Rehabilitation Act of 1973). It describes some of the difficulties an individual in a wheelchair used to encounter in postsecondary settings.

As a disabled person who was educated during this time, I know how often my plans had to be modified and sometimes even abandoned because of lack of accessibility. I know how much of my energy I had to devote to figuring out how to get to class, how to use the library, how to do outside

assignments, and how to research, seek out and try to use all available resources. I know that where help was available to remove some of these handicaps. It truly liberated my mind for learning. I also believe I could have achieved far more than I did if my energy had not had to be expended to constantly fight the system. (Johns, 1984:23)

In the past two decades, the number of students with disabilities who are seeking admission to and enrolling in postsecondary education programs has dramatically increased. Enrollment figures for this population are growing at a much faster rate than for nondisabled students. Thus, the proportion of full-time freshmen with disabilities increased threefold between 1978 and 1985, rising from 2.6 percent in 1978 to 7.4 percent in 1985 (Vogel, 1993). In 1991, 8.8 percent of all entering freshman reported having a disability. A slight increase to 9.2 percent was reported in 1994 (Henderson, 1995). When the full range of students is considered (e.g., students enrolled part time, students involved in graduate programs), the proportional figure for students with disabilities increases. The most recent federal statistics indicate that 10.5 percent of all postsecondary students are identified as having a disability. Table 16.1 provides relevant demographic information about recent census data regarding students with disabilities.

According to Hughes and Gajar (1995), the dramatic increase in the number of students with disabilities seeking services is a result of four factors: (1) the enrollment of students with disabilities who received compensatory services in high school; (2) the lobbying of postsecondary institutions for increased services by disability advocacy groups; (3) the impact of Section 504 of the Rehabilitation Act of 1973 and P.L. 101-336, the Americans with Disabilities Act (ADA) (federal regulation requiring that postsecondary institutions make reasonable accommodations and permit access for individuals with disabilities); and (4) the need for postsecondary institutions to recruit nontraditional students in a time of declining enrollment for traditional (e.g., nondisabled) students (Nelson & Lignugaris-Kraft, 1989). The sharp increase in enrollment of students with disabilities has led to a 90 percent increase in the number of universities providing support services (Brinckerhoff, Shaw, & McGuire, 1993; Yost et al., 1993). The professional association of disability service personnel (**A**ssociation on **H**igher **E**ducation **A**nd **D**isability [AHEAD]) reports a 67 percent increase in membership over the past 5 years, from less than 900 to over 2,000 members. Nationally, over 900 colleges and universities offer services for students with disabilities (Mangrum & Strichart, 1988).

The increase of students with disabilities seeking postsecondary education is not limited to college and/or university settings. Postsecondary vocational education programs often provide a viable alternative to and/or a transitional step toward a college or university program. Vocational programs provide specialized training in various occupational areas. Scheiber and Talpers (1987) identified a number of technical institutions, community colleges, and area vocational technical centers that provide these services. Private or proprietary programs include trade, technical, and business schools.

DISABILITY SERVICE PROVIDERS

As the range of postsecondary options for students with disabilities has expanded, the need for qualified personnel to work with these students (especially during the transition period) has dramatically increased. In addition, service availability and the need for preparation programs that support retention and success of students with disabilities in postsecondary programs have become pressing issues. When appropriate services are provided, students with disabilities succeed at levels commensurate with their abilities and equivalent to their nondisabled peers (Gajar, Murphy, & Hunt, 1982; Dalke, 1993). Failure to provide appropriate services, however, often leads students with disabilities to achieve a grade-point average significantly lower than that of their nondisabled peers and may even lead to their withdrawal from the postsecondary program (Dalke, 1993). Because of limited services and variability in the quality of services provided in postsecondary settings, students with disabilities (although qualified at entry) are far more likely to withdraw without graduating than are their nondisabled peers (Walter & Welsh, 1986; Bursuck et al., 1989; Sitlington & Frank, 1990). Research has also shown that for individuals with disabilities, a university education is highly correlated with vocational options and financial success (Welsh & Walter, 1988). Therefore, the

Table 16.1 Demographic Statistics for College and University Students (1987)

College and University Student Group	Enrollment	% of Students	% of All Students with Disabilities
Nondisabled students	12,563,018	89.5	
Students with disabilities	1,219,229	10.5	
Learning disability	160,878	1.3	12.2
Hearing impairment	346,394	2.7	26.2
Visual impairment	514,681	4.1	39.0
Speech impairment	62,525	0.5	4.7
Physical disability	231,491	1.8	17.6
Health impairment	320,272	2.6	24.3

Source: National Center for Educational Statistics (1993).

cost of failure, both to these individuals as well as to society, is a pressing concern (Yost et al., 1993).

THE LAWS THAT IMPACT CHANGE

Three major pieces of legislation (P.L. 101-476, the Individuals with Disabilities Education Act [IDEA], P.L. 105-17, the Individuals with Disabilities Education Act [IDEA] Amendments, and P.L. 101-336, the Americans with Disabilities Act [ADA]), that were enacted during the 1990s have positively influenced the provision of transition services for the disabled from secondary programs to postsecondary education. The availability of appropriate services and the training of postsecondary service providers who possess the competencies required to recruit students with disabilities and facilitate their transition into postsecondary settings will be addressed later in this chapter.

In summary, students with disabilities are the fastest growing group of individuals in need of services at the postsecondary level of education including college, university, vocational and technical school settings. It is anticipated that this trend will continue into the twenty-first century (Shaw & Shaw, 1989; Gajar & Smith,

1996). Services and programs, however, have not kept pace with the needs of this population. The remaining sections of this chapter discuss (a) the historical background of postsecondary education as a viable option for individuals with disabilities, (b) current practices being used to facilitate the educational process for individuals with disabilities in postsecondary settings, and (c) recommendations regarding the future of service provision for this population of postsecondary students.

HISTORICAL REVIEW

Prior to the passage of P.L. 93-112, the Rehabilitation Act of 1973, and its accompanying Section 504 regulations, participation in postsecondary education for individuals with disabilities was sporadic and inconsistent. The first recorded support for postsecondary education for individuals with disabilities can be traced to the 1860s. Gallaudet, a liberal arts college, was established by federal legislation as a specialized school for students with hearing impairments. Funding was provided on a ad hoc basis until the 1950s. Regular support was authorized for subsequent years (Scales, 1986). In 1917, based on concern for the future of disabled World War I veterans, a number of acts were passed providing for their vocational rehabilitation (Smith-Hughes Act,

P.L. 64-347; Smith-Sears Act, P.L. 65-178; Smith-Fess Act, P.L. 66-236). Although the emphasis of these acts was on preparing individuals with disabilities for employment, postsecondary education was at times encompassed by this legislation (Gajar, Goodman, & McAfee, 1993). The same was true for vocational rehabilitation legislation passed following World War II and during the 1950s and 1960s. In short, the 53-year span from 1917 to 1970 included a national recognition of the needs of Americans with disabilities. However, the various programs concentrated on vocational and or rehabilitation activities. Occasionally, benefits were extended to a few individuals for postsecondary education, and a number of universities took the initiative to provide such opportunities. But funding and access were often limited (Scales, 1986; Jarrow 1987; Gajar et al., 1993). The late 1960s witnessed a rise in the number of model projects for the postsecondary education of students with disabilities. These programs were funded by the National Science Foundation and the Fund for Improvement of Postsecondary Education (Scales, 1986).

In spite of the growing awareness of postsecondary education for individuals with disabilities, a number of barriers continued to exist. Prior to 1973, with no legal backing to demand inclusion, these students were routinely denied admission to chosen professions because of "beliefs" and/or "stereotypes" held by both society and postsecondary officials: A person in a wheelchair could never be a teacher, a person with cerebral palsy would be dangerous in a laboratory setting, a blind or deaf person could not handle the rigors of an academic setting (Scales, 1986). A number of these beliefs and stereotypes still exist. Fortunately, the passage of several mandates during the 1970s and 1980s has enabled students with disabilities to legally challenge arbitrary decisions and practices.

The major turning point in the availability of higher education for students with disabilities came with the passage of P.L. 93-112, the Rehabilitation Act of 1973, and specifically Section 504 of this mandate. The wording is simple, but the intent of this mandate has exerted a lasting influence on postsecondary education for the disabled: "No otherwise qualified handicapped individual in the United States, shall, solely by reason of his handicap, be excluded from the participation in, be denied the benefits of, or be subjected to discrimination under any activity receiving federal financial assistance."

Under this mandate, which, at the time of its passage, was referred to as the "Civil Rights Act for the Disabled," postsecondary institutions are obligated to adhere to certain conditions. These conditions are pivotal in the historical review of postsecondary education for persons with disabilities, and they are addressed in university literature on disabilities as follows:

1. The institution cannot place a limitation on the number of qualified handicapped[1] students who can be admitted.

2. Preadmission inquiries as to whether applicants are handicapped or not cannot be conducted.

3. Students cannot be excluded from a course of study solely on the basis of a handicapping condition.

4. Modifications in degree or academic course requirements must be made when such requirements discriminate against qualified students who are handicapped.

5. Rules (such as prohibiting tape recorders in classrooms) must be waived for certain students who are handicapped.

---

[1] In this chapter, the word "handicapped" is used when discussing legislation in which the term handicapped is used; otherwise, the preferred term "disabled" is used.

6. Devices or aids which ensure the full participation of students who are handicapped in the classroom cannot be prohibited.

7. Alternative testing and evaluation methods for measuring student achievement may be necessary for students with sensory, manual, or speaking skill impairment. (Exceptions include areas in which these skills are being measured as an indication of achievement.)

8. Faculty members may be requested to adapt teaching techniques and use special devices (such as amplification equipment) for classes in which students who are handicapped are enrolled.

9. It is discriminatory to counsel students who are handicapped toward restrictive careers unless such counseling is justified by the licensing or certification requirements of the profession.

10. Finally, students who are handicapped and feel discriminated against have the right to process complaints through the institution's civil rights channels or to initiate legal proceedings on an individual basis. (Gajar et al., 1993:232)

IDEA

The second mandate to exert an influence on postsecondary education for the disabled was the Individuals with Disabilities Education Act (IDEA), P.L. 101-476, enacted in 1990. IDEA was amended in 1997 and is currently cited as P.L. 105-17, the new Individuals with Disabilities Education Act. The relevance of this legislation to postsecondary settings was its position that future funded projects could now include the development and dissemination of "exemplary programs and practices that meet the unique needs of students who utilize assistive

technology devices and services as such students make the transition to postsecondary education, vocational training. ..." In addition, the act directed the funding of demonstration models "designed to establish appropriate methods of providing or continuing to provide assistive technology devices and services to secondary school students as they make the transition to vocational rehabilitation, employment, postsecondary education or adult services" (National Association of State Directors of Special Education, 1990:12).

ADA

The final piece of legislation affecting postsecondary students with disabilities was the Americans with Disabilities Act (ADA), P.L. 101-336. This legislation expanded federal civil rights laws that applied to women and minorities to over 43 million Americans who have some form of disability. The legislation prohibits discrimination in employment, public services, and public accommodations and transportation, and it provides for telecommunications relay services. In short, institutions of higher learning cannot deny access to their activities, services, or programs to individuals with disabilities.

Section 504 and ADA Comparison

The regulations contained in Section 504 of the Rehabilitation Act (1973) and the Americans with Disabilities Act have exerted pressure on postsecondary institutions to accommodate the special needs of students with disabilities. The extent of such accommodations, required under the law, is debatable and has been the subject of litigation. In essence, the requirement for "reasonable accommodation" has not been operationally or consistently defined. Current practices and outcomes, in postsecondary settings, have been strongly influenced by the absence of clear definitions and structure. In addition, successful transitions into postsecondary settings by students with disabilities continue to be undermined by political, social, and economic efforts to curtail federal spending, and the unsuccessful attempts by organizations such as the American Heritage Foundation to declare mandates for the disabled, and especially the American Disabilities Act (even though these mandates are firmly founded on the 14th Amendment of the U.S. Constitution) as unfunded mandates, and, therefore, not worthy of reauthorization.

CURRENT PRACTICES

The recent influx of students with disabilities into postsecondary settings has precluded the establishment of both a body of proven practices and a clear relationship between practices and outcomes. Services have evolved sporadically and programs have been pieced together in a haphazard manner. Bursuck and colleagues (1989) found that services varied a great deal from program to program and that postsecondary guides to services were inaccurate and incomplete. Additionally, they found that access to programs was a major concern; compensatory strategies were found to be important; provision of remedial instruction was considered important; smaller institutions offered more personalized services; peer tutoring was an important component; the absence of follow-up data on the rate of graduation, vocational, and life adjustment was formidable (Gajar et al., 1993).

The following section will present an overview of the current status of students with disabilities in postsecondary settings, and describe the practices that are now considered to be essential in making the transition from secondary to postsecondary education (i.e., secondary programming for transition, referral, admissions, academic accommodations, and the

myriad of services available to all postsecondary students). This narrative will be followed by a discussion of the characteristics and services cited as necessary for specific disability populations, including the hearing impaired, visually impaired, mildly handicapped, speech impaired, health and physically impaired.

Current Status and Characteristics of Freshman[2] Students with Disabilities

Questions about disability status in postsecondary settings have been included in *The American Freshman: National Norms* since 1978. A cooperative agreement between the American Council of Education (ACE) and the U.S. Department of Education enables the HEATH Resource Center to publish a triennial series entitled *College Freshmen with Disabilities: A Statistical Profile* (1992, 1995, 1998). The following summary of the profile of freshmen with disabilities is based on the most current of these publications (Henderson, 1995).[3] Table 16.2 shows the types of disabilities reported by freshmen over three selected years.

Learning disabilities was reported to be the fastest growing category of disability between 1988 and 1994. In 1988, 15.3 percent of freshmen with disabilities cited a learning disability. In 1994, this percentage rose to 32.2 percent or close to one-third of freshmen with disabilities. The actual number of freshmen with learning disabilities rose from approximately 20,000 in 1988 to 45,654 in 1994. "Partially sighted or blind" was the most cited disability in 1988 (approximately 45,000 students). In 1994, this category was the second most common disability. Over the same 6-year period, the percent of "partially sighted or blind" students dropped

[2] A comprehensive review of the characteristics of all postsecondary students with disabilities is not available. Therefore, freshman college and university characteristics of students with disabilities are cited throughout this chapter. It is hypothesized that the characteristics of other postsecondary students with disabilities, with minor exceptions, are similar.

[3] The publication may be purchased from the American Council on Education, One Dupont Circle, Washington, DC 20036.

Table 16.2 Types of Disabilities Among Full-Time College Freshmen with Disabilities,[a] by Percentage: Selected Years

Disability	1988	1991	1994
Learning	15.3	24.9	32.2
Partially sighted or blind	31.7	25.2	21.9
Other	18.5	18.3	18.8
Health-related	15.7	14.6	16.4
Orthopedic	13.8	13.5	10.2
Hearing	11.6	10.5	9.7
Speech	3.8	5.4	3.5

Source: HEATH Resource Center, ACE. Based on unpublished data from the 1994 Cooperative Institutional Research Program, UCLA, 1995.

[a]For example, in 1994, 32.2% of students with disabilities reported a learning disability.

Note: The detail may sum to more than 100% because of multiple disabilities.

from 31.7 percent of the disability population to 21.9 percent (Henderson, 1995).

In 1994, data collected on 1,400,600 nondisabled freshmen and 159,867 freshmen reporting a disability revealed a number of similarities and some differences (Henderson, 1995). For example, freshmen with disabilities "were more likely to enroll in two-year colleges," and less likely to be enrolled in university settings. Proportions of students with disabilities were similar to peers in enrollment in 4-year colleges and in historically black colleges and universities. Gender and age revealed a number of differences. Students with disabilities were more likely to be Caucasian males. In contrast, Caucasian females with disabilities were underrepresented. Freshmen students with disabilities tended to be older than their nondisabled peers, to report lower high school grades, and to rank themselves lower on a wide range of abilities than their nondisabled peers. Educational and career goals were similar for both groups, as were a number of demographic characteristics, such as living situations, family income, and/or citizenship.

In the summary section of the HEATH report, Henderson (1995) stated the "specific programs available at certain colleges, and the advice and support of teachers and guidance counselors, were very important factors in helping students with disabilities decide among par-

ticular colleges to attend" (p. 38). A discussion of practices in secondary programming for transition, admissions, academic accommodations, and the myriad of services available to all postsecondary students follows.

Secondary Transition Programs

Research shows that transitional services and programs at the secondary level for students with disabilities are in the early stages of development. Survey data indicate that district size and wealth are tied to the level and range of transitional services provided (Fairweather, 1989). Effective practices in secondary-to-postsecondary transition are beyond the scope of this chapter; they include practices regarding teaching, independent living skills, effective learning strategies, dealing with psychological and social issues, enhancing academic skills (e.g., study skills, self-management, time management, library skills, notetaking, and exam-taking skills), preparing students for postsecondary environments, and facilitating the selection and admission process to a postsecondary setting. Dalke and Schmitt (1987) indicated that if transition practices are provided in preparing the student with disabilities for the changes in educational settings (from secondary to postsecondary programs), the following should be included.

- Provide students with an educational experience similar to what is expected in higher education.

- Assist students in obtaining a clear picture of their strengths and needs as they relate to the demands of the postsecondary environment.

- Provide opportunities for students to explore and address issues related to the emotional factors involved in losing a familiar support system of family, friends, and teachers.

- Provide students occasions to practice self-advocacy skills.

- Familiarize students with the physical environment of the campus and community.

- Identify and explain campus and community organizations, agencies, and related support services that are available to students.

- Provide instruction to students in areas such as study skills, time management, notetaking and test taking strategies and library usage.

- Provide direct instruction to students in academic areas such as reading comprehension, written language, and basic math skills.

- Provide staff with formal and informal student performance data. (Dalke, 1991:120)

Admissions

Scheiber and Talpers (1987) identified admission requirements used by various postsecondary programs for students with disabilities. Public, community and junior colleges, and vocational education schools (public and private—2 years or less) usually function under an open admission policy. Private 2-year junior colleges, 4-year colleges (public and private), universities, and technical schools usually require regular admission procedures consisting of one or more of the

following: (a) high school diploma or GED, (b) some type of entrance examination (SATs, ACTs), (c) grade-point average, and, occasionally, (d) an interview. Most programs have not yet developed specific admission standards for students with disabilities (Bowen, 1986).

During the admission process, a "catch-22" situation, such as the following, may develop:

1. An applicant who has disabilities may have difficulties or need accommodations in one or more areas of academic achievement.

2. Admission requirements may include a standardized entrance examination including academic achievement components.

3. A student may take the entrance examination under nonstandard conditions. For example, a student who is blind might take the exam orally.

4. The nonstandardized administration of the entrance examination is usually flagged by the testing service.

5. The right to confidentiality and nondiscrimination precludes admissions personnel from asking questions concerning the student's disability.

6. Under mandate, the institution must provide equal access and modified testing and accommodations for the student. If the student does not identify him/herself, the questions concerning the types of accommodations required are forbidden. The result is confusion and frustration on the part of both the applicant and the institution. (Gajar et al., 1993)

Disability Service Delivery and Accommodations

Postsecondary institutions provide students with disabilities a variety of services and accommodations. The entire range of services is not found in any one program or institution, but is usually provided on an individualized or specialized program basis. As stated earlier, one reason for this wide, sporadic, and varied range of services is the lack of an empirical basis for the effect of services on educational outcomes for this population.

Services and accommodations cited in the literature include (a) summer or presemester specialized orientation programs; (b) individualized counseling and advising; (c) priority registration and/or reduced courseloads; (d) course substitutions, course waivers, and modified materials, program or degree requirements; (e) taped textbooks, lectures, and the allowance of tape recorders in the classroom; (f) services of adjunct personnel such as notetakers, proofreaders, typists, readers, interpreters, mobility guides; (g) alternative testing accommodations such as untimed, individualized, or oral examinations; (h) assistance with study skills, self- and time management; (i) adaptive and regular technological assistance (e.g., calculators, Braille devices, reading machines, computer keyboard modifications, augmentative communication devices, modified word processors, modified telephones); and (j) accessibility adjustments, such as the removal of architectural barriers, designated parking areas, transportation assistance, and barrier guide sheets (Dalke, 1991; Gajar et al., 1993).

Institutional Services

Services available to nondisabled students are often utilized by students with disabilities. These include mental health counseling, developmental year programs, tutoring, personal or social counseling, academic or program counseling, and career or vocational counseling. A number of smaller colleges and institutions have been established for specific disabilities. For example, Gallaudet serves deaf students and Barat and the College of the Ozarks serve students with learning disabilities. These academic institutions tend

to provide more individualized, remedial, and tutorial services (Gajar et al., 1993). A number of postsecondary vocational education programs have developed support teams to work with individuals who have disabilities. Scheiber and Talpers (1987) cited California, Colorado, Georgia, Kentucky, Maryland, Missouri, and Wisconsin as states that are in the forefront of providing services via a team effort. Each of these states employs a specialist in postsecondary vocational education for those who have disabilities. This person and team members provide instructional assistance, ideas and materials, and they assist individual students in finding job sites for work experience and eventual job placement.

With regard to students who have disabilities, secondary transition programs, admission procedures and practices, service and accommodation delivery, and availability of personal academic and career counseling have evolved spontaneously. The following discussion presents unique characteristics and services required by distinct categories of students with disabilities in postsecondary settings (i.e., hearing impaired, visually impaired, mildly handicapped, speech impaired, health and physically impaired).[4]

Students Who Are Deaf or Have a Hearing Impairment

According to Henderson (1995), one out of ten freshmen in postsecondary education settings report being deaf or having a hearing impairment. About half are women and one in five is a person of color. Three out of five are enrolled in 4-year institutions and approximately two out of five are enrolled in 2-year colleges. Three percent attend Historically Black Colleges and Universities (HBCUs). Generally, students with hearing impairments report needs similar to those of other students with disabilities. However, they are more likely to live at home or with relatives and rate themselves on the same level as

---

[4] A number of questions presented in this section were obtained from the Postsecondary Disabilities Listserv (DSSHE-L) and can be accessed by subscribing to LISTSERV@UBVM.CC.BUFFALO.EDU or via http://www.netspace.org/cgi-bin/longate/DSSHE-L.

students without disabilities on writing skills and leadership ability.

Communication is the major area of difficulty for many students who are deaf or hearing impaired. "Oral" and "manual" are two ways of communication. Oral communication includes speech and lip reading. Manual communication involves the use of the American Sign Language (ASL) system. The English language is translated by gestures, hand, and arm movements. Finger spelling is used when vocabulary cannot be translated into signs. ASL is often considered by postsecondary institutions to be a language, and in many cases, students can enroll in an ASL course as a substitution for a foreign language requirement (Dalke, 1991).

There are a number of specific devices, aids, and accommodations for students who are deaf or have a hearing impairment. Accommodations include the use of interpreters, translators, and notetakers. Devices include hearing aids and various voice-amplification systems. Modern technology has greatly facilitated the communication process for these students. Close-captioned video and television presentations, computer-assisted instruction, interactive videodisks, telecommunications devices (TDD systems), the teletypewriter and printer (TTY), and real-time captioning are only a few of the most recent innovations.

TDD systems involve the relay of telephone translations via printed formats to the student. A relay telephone operator often acts as a go-between for the student and the person on the other end of the line. TTY systems allow the student to communicate by telephone with a typewriter. The system then converts the typed letters into electric signals through a modem. Real-time captioning is similar to having a court reporter present at a lecture or presentation. The recorder inputs the lecture as it is being presented and the words are shown on a screen or monitor simultaneously as the speaker is presenting. Following the presentation, the student can receive a written copy of the lecture. In addition, the system allows the student to be active in the class discussion. Students who are

deaf or hard of hearing report favorable experiences with this type of technology.

In spite of the numerous devices and methods of communication available to students with hearing impairments, some individuals encounter barriers in postsecondary education. This usually occurs because of the lack of clear and tested practices and policies. Providing accommodations, and especially technological devices, is expensive. The following are a few of the many questions that are not clearly defined: How much should interpreters, notetakers, and translators be paid? How can we determine whether a person is qualified to act as an interpreter, translator, or notetaker in postsecondary settings? Considering the expense, is it feasible to provide real-time captioning to one or two students, especially if interpreters are available? Must institutions provide the student with exactly the equipment he/she asks for or can alternative accommodations be provided?

A number of requests and questions presented by students with hearing impairments or students who are deaf have resulted in litigation. A document entitled *Legal Issues Specific to Serving Deaf Students and Students with Hearing Impairments in Higher Education* by Jeanne M. Kincaid includes a compilation of court cases on issues related to deafness. Some of these cases, along with cases addressing issues related to other disability areas, will be summarized later on in this chapter (Kincaid, 1995).

Students Who Are Blind or Have a Visual Impairment

One in five freshmen with disabilities report being partially sighted or blind. The proportion of freshman students with visual problems has decreased 10 percent over the past 7 years. The majority of these freshmen attend 4-year institutions, with 26 percent enrolled in 2-year schools and 5 percent in HBCUs. On the average, when compared with other disability groups, students who are blind or partially sighted exhibit a higher percentage of straight A's in high school, have tutored other students, have met or exceeded the requirements in English, math, foreign languages, and computer science, and have rated themselves above average on measures of academic ability, writing ability, ambition, intellectual confidence, and emotional health (Henderson, 1995).

In postsecondary settings, reading, notetaking, and mobility are the major areas of difficulty for students who are blind or visually impaired. The Braille system, a code developed by Louis Braille in 1829, is the most widely used tactile means of reading and writing. Postsecondary curriculums usually include extensive reading assignments. The amount of time needed to complete these assignments by students with visual impairments often exceeds that required by students who are sighted. The same holds true for reviewing both lecture notes and descriptions of visual materials. Extra time is also needed in learning to move around campus and to become familiar with the environment of each academic building, facility, classroom, and laboratory. When planning their daily schedule, these students need to have enough time to move safely and effectively from classroom to classroom and other campus settings.

A number of special devices, aids, and accommodations are available for students with visual impairments. Alternative student evaluation accommodations may include oral exams, readers, taped responses, and Braille translators. Aids in the area of reading include reading machines, recorded materials, Braille books, speech-synthesized computer systems, and voice-recognition software. Aids, devices, and accommodations in the areas of notetaking and descriptions of visual learning materials include the assistance of a notetaker; with subsequent conversion of written notes into audiotapes or Braille. The use of a Perkins Brailler, a slate and stylus, taped lectures, and the conversion of tapes into Braille are equivalent alternatives. Finally, a vast number of magnification, identification, and audio devices and techniques are extremely useful in postsecondary environments. Magnification lenses and screens, Braille labels, talking calculators and books, record players, and audiotape recorders are often available to both students and service and environmental access providers. Finally, in the area of orientation assistance guide dogs, canes, tactile Braille and audio cassette maps may be necessary (Dalke, 1991).

Current developments in technology for students who are blind or visually impaired include devices such as the Rose Braille Display Reader, the Opticon Scanner, a number of different Kurzweil machines (reader, music synthesizer, and voice recognition), and numerous computer adaptations. The Rose Braille Display Reader records Braille on magnetic tape cassettes rather than on paper. This reduces the bulk and storage problems associated with written Braille materials. The Opticon Scanner produces tactile reproductions of the written materials via a camera and a fingerpad. The Kurzweil machines convert (a) reading materials into synthetic speech, (b) musical compositions into synthesized music, and (c) voice recordings into printed text. The cost of personal Kurzweil machines is often prohibitive. However, their potential for reducing the need for tapes, personal readers, and recorders at the postsecondary level is vast. Manufacturers are now in the process of designing and developing less expensive models. Finally, a number of computer modifications and adaptive devices are listed in a *Resource Guide for Persons with Vision Impairments* available from the IBM National Support Center for Persons with Disabilities (1990a).

Barriers to postsecondary education for students who are blind or visually impaired are often not as formidable as they are for students with "invisible" disabilities (deaf, hearing impaired, mildly disabled). A number of organizations and resources, such as the American Foundation for the Blind, Recordings for the Blind, and Talking Books, facilitate the purchase and provision of devices and materials. However, questions concerning accessibility to campus settings and programs (such as medicine), clear and tested practices and policies, and reasonable accommodations are in the process of being decided by litigation.

Students Who Have a Health-Related Disability

One in six freshmen with disabilities report having a "health-related" condition. These include conditions such as severe allergies, cystic fibrosis, epilepsy, cancer, lupus, and multiple sclerosis. Slightly more than half of these students are women, and one in four is a person of color. These students report a shift from 2- to 4-year programs (three in five freshmen with health-related conditions); 35 percent attend 2-year colleges and 6 percent attend HBCUs. When compared to other students with disabilities, these students tend to be women, have lower median family incomes, have missed school due to illness, rank themselves lowest on a comparison of physical health, and expect to be satisfied with college (Henderson, 1995).

The extensive range of health-related disabilities (heart, lung, digestive diseases, renal disorders, asthma, sickle cell anemia, lupus, leukemia, diabetes, epilepsy, acquired immune deficiency syndrome [AIDS]) precludes an extensive discussion of accommodations, devices, and/or aids available for this postsecondary population. Students with health impairments usually require the range of services available to other students with disabilities. However, two specific accommodations are included when working with these students: (1) planning for possible periods of absence, and (2) arranging for modification of physical education requirements.

Students Who Have Orthopedic and/or Physical Impairments

One in 10 freshmen with disabilities report having an orthopedic condition. Over half of these students are women and 18 percent are persons of color. Three in five are enrolled in 4-year institutions, two in five attend 2-year schools, and 2 percent attend HBCUs. Freshmen with orthopedic problems are most likely to be 20 years of age or older, have received assistance from vocational rehabilitation funds, have

applied to only one college, and have taken more than a few months off between high school graduation and entry into college (Henderson, 1995).

Similar to the population of students with health impairments, students with orthopedic and/or physical impairments encompass a range of disabilities (e.g., different types of paralysis and/or loss of one or more voluntary motor functions). Accommodations are provided on an individual basis. In general, students included in this population need to (a) schedule extra travel time between campus settings, (b) plan for possible periods of absence, (c) request modification of the physical education requirements, and (d) request testing modifications. Assistance may also be needed for manual activities, such as laboratory experiments, notetaking, and other activities involving written and/or oral expression. Recently, dogs have been trained to assist with a number of tasks such as carrying books or opening doors, and they may accompany the student around campus (Dalke, 1991).

As with other disability populations, technology serves to facilitate the postsecondary experience for students with orthopedic and physical impairments. For example, the *Resource Guide for Persons with Mobility Impairments,* available from the IBM National Support Center for Persons with Disabilities (1990b), lists a number of computer adaptations, including numerous suggestions for keyboard modification. Motorized wheelchairs, artificial limbs, and various body-support systems are only a few of the wide range of available devices.

Accessibility is a major concern for all students with orthopedic and physical impairments. Often, if programs are accessible, students subsumed under this category require little or no supplemental services. Most postsecondary institutions have (a) attempted to modify architectural barriers to buildings (e.g., wider doorways, automatic door openers, elevators, lowered control panels, ramps); (b) installed handicapped restrooms; (c) provided handicapped parking; (d) installed reachable drinking fountains; (e) modified laboratory and classroom work areas to accommodate individuals in wheelchairs; and (f) cut curbs and installed railings in frequently used areas. However, problems arise in defining the term "accessible," as mandated by the American with Disabilities Act. Because of the expense, most institutions provide access based on minimum standards or requirements. For example, "handicapped restrooms" do not usually accommodate individuals in motorized wheelchairs. Additional questions include (a) must institutions provide transportation for all campus activities; (b) are snow routes for individuals with disabilities mandated; (c) are emergency evacuation devices required; (d) should special maps and barrier sheets be updated on a daily basis; (e) are designated residential handicapped access floors a form of discrimination; (f) is the institution responsible for providing modified computers, or information-access devices, for personal use, rather than in a computer center where more than one person can use the equipment; (g) must institutions provide single rooms (at no extra charge) to students on request? There are many questions surrounding the word "assessible," and based on the absence of established practices and policies, these questions will be answered in the future by litigation and judicial proceedings.

Postsecondary Students with Mild Disabilities

For the sake of organization, mental retardation/intellectual impairments, emotional disturbance/psychiatric disorders, and learning disabilities will be discussed under the category of "mildly disabled" students in postsecondary education.

Students with mental retardation, or who exhibit intellectual impairments, have historically been excluded from postsecondary settings (Dalke, 1991). However, because of the transition-to-work mandates and programs initiated during in the 1980s, and the School-to-Work Opportunities Act of 1994, which includes the intent of increased opportunities for further education "including education in a 4-year college or university," a number of programs (especially community colleges and vocational and technical training programs) have initiated an open door policy for students in this category (McAfee & Scheeler, 1987; McAfee, 1989). In short, services for this population have often taken the form of special programs designed to teach vocational, independent living, or social skills. The advantages of 2-year community college settings and vocational or technical training programs for this population include (a) the absence of stringent entrance requirements, (b) the availability of vocational education support teams, (c) specialized training in occupational skills, (d) individualized job placement services, and (important for the purposes of this chapter) (e) preparation for later transfer to a 4-year institution (Scheiber & Talpers, 1987; Gajar et al., 1993).

Services for students who are emotionally disturbed, or who exhibit mild psychiatric disorders, have existed in colleges for decades. These services are usually generic (e.g., personal counseling) and are available to all students. When considering accommodations for these students service providers usually work closely with therapists and mental health facilities available at their postsecondary institutions. Peer support groups, advocacy, and accessible information for faculty, staff, and peers are generally recommended practices for this group of postsecondary students.

Students with learning disabilities constitute the largest group of freshman students with disabilities in postsecondary education. About one in three students with disabilities reported having a learning disability. Two out of five students were women, and 17 percent were persons of color. Slightly more than half attend 2-year campuses, and 44 percent are enrolled at universities or 4-year colleges. A trend to attend 4-year institutions has been observed for this population over a 4-year period. Only 1 percent of these students attend HBCUs. Compared to other freshmen with disabilities, students with learning disabilities are most likely to be men, be from Caucasian families, be from families where the income exceeds $75,000, be from families where parents have earned graduate degrees, not have completed 3 years of high school math or 2 years of a foreign language, have earned C or D averages in high school, aspire to a degree that is less than a bachelor's degree, rank themselves lowest on math ability, intellectual self-confidence, and academic ability. Special programs are especially important to students with learning disabilities, because they are less likely to be offered financial assistance as an incentive to enroll in postsecondary programs, and they are less inclined to earn money from a part-time job while enrolled in school (Henderson, 1995).

Postsecondary students with learning disabilities exhibit characteristics that are heterogeneous in nature. Due to the invisible nature of the disability, and the difficulties involved in identification and assessment of this population, faculty and staff at postsecondary institutions are often less than willing to provide accommodations for this population. In a review of the literature pertaining to college students with learning disabilities, Hughes and Smith (1990) found that these students have average to above-average intelligence and exhibit difficulties in reading, math, writing, and foreign language achievement. Kahn (1980) observed that this population exhibits poor time management skills, difficulty in completing tasks, and poor study skills. In several settings, they demonstrate problems such as inappropriate communication with pertinent others and a lack of response to verbal cues (Blalock, 1982). Buchanan and Wolf (1986) cited problems with self-concept. Haig and Patterson (1980) reported problems that they identified as social immaturity. Further, coping problems, such as withdrawal under stress, were reported by Moss and Fox (1980).

Almost all of the accommodations, devices, and aids alluded to in the preceding sections have been utilized by one or more postsecondary students with learning disabilities. For example, students with reading problems may require taped texts, students with auditory perceptual difficulties may require notetakers, and students with manual problems may require oral testing. Large universities usually provide a number of instructional accommodations and assistance with study skills, as well as self- and time management assistance for this population. Other services that are available to all students include mental health, tutoring, and career counseling. Smaller colleges often provide individualized remedial and tutoring services (Gajar & Smith, 1996). Nelson and Lignugaris-Kraft (1989) reported that counseling services are cited as necessary components of model programs for this population. These services include personal or social counseling, academic or program counseling, and career or vocational counseling.

In a review of community college options for students with learning disabilities, Bursuck and Rose (1992) identified a number of support services, including faculty awareness sessions, "early availability of course syllabi, taped textbooks, permission to tape lectures, note-takers, word processing programs, proofreaders, modified exam procedures, and modified course assignment" (p. 80). Other areas of service included "individualized education plans, specialized academic advisement, regular monitoring of academic progress, advocacy, content tutoring, support groups, specialized counseling, and special courses in career awareness or learning strategies" (p. 80). In addition, remedial services are provided for basic skill areas such as reading, written language, oral language, and mathematics. In 4-year university and college settings, developmental year programs often serve as remedial service alternatives (Gajar, 1992). Many of the previously cited practices are available to students in other than community college postsecondary settings. Finally, due to the large number of students with learning disabilities, postsecondary institutions often hire specialists in learning disabilities to facilitate and coordinate services.

Students with learning disabilities face numerous barriers in postsecondary settings. They often request extended or individualized testing procedures, which raises a number of questions: (a) is untimed testing a reasonable accommodation, (b) are alternative evaluation procedures fair to other students, (c) how much time is reasonable, and (d) are professors required to provide alternative testing formats? Other questions revolve around (a) whether course substitutions or waivers jeopardize the academic integrity of a program; (b) if a student cannot read, how can he expect to pass courses in higher education; (c) how are students identified; and (d) should admission procedures be different for these students? Once again, the absence of empirical data on practice and policy is resulting in judicial rulings on these questions.

In summary, at first glance, the array of services available for students with mild disabilities in different postsecondary settings is impressive. However, the graduation rates from many programs are still low and a number of schools at all levels of postsecondary education do not provide many of the critical services (Gajar, 1992). With reference to community college settings, Bursuck and Rose (1992) stated that "although community-college level services for persons with mild disabilities are increasing overall there are not data to justify classifying existing services as anything but a good start" (p. 84). This is true for all postsecondary programs for students with disabilities.

Judicial Rulings and Litigation

The relatively recent passage of access and nondiscriminatory mandates for students with disabilities, and the virtual absence of research addressing outcomes of successful practices, has resulted in a dependence on judicial means for defining the rights and responsibilities of both the student and the postsecondary institution. Due to the lengthy appeal process, many of these cases have not yet been resolved. For citations of specific cases, the reader is directed to a compilation of recent legal decisions by Jeanne M. Kincaid, entitled *Fatal Distraction: Keeping Abreast of Legal Developments.*[5] A summary of several legal developments (Kincaid, 1995) are as follows:

1. With regard to preadmission inquiry about a student's disability: Forms suggesting that applicants needing special services should contact the Disabled Student Services office are not unlawful; forms asking whether a student has a disability and asking for a description of the disability are unlawful.

2. With regard to documentation to verify the need for accommodations: Written support obtained from physicians and psychiatrists, based solely on a student's request rather than on clinical needs, is not adequate support for testing accommodations.

3. With regard to visual impairments: A medical school's refusal to admit a blind applicant has been upheld; mandates do not require universities to provide readers immediately upon request; a Kurzweil reading machine can be provided by a university in place of a reader; requiring students to perform a number of administrative tasks, such as canceling a service that is no longer required, is not unlawful.

4. With regard to students with hearing impairments: "Public institutions must give primary consideration to the communication preferences of the individual with a disability;" neither Section 504 nor ADA is violated if a university provides an interpreter within one week of a student's request; if qualified interpreters are not available, the institution can choose alternative methods, such as

notetakers or professor assistance in providing necessary accommodations; if qualified individuals are available, the failure to provide an ASL interpreter or providing unqualified interpreters is unlawful; refusing to allow tape recorders in classroom settings is unlawful.

5. With regard to students with learning disabilities: A college cannot discriminate against students by refusing to allow them to tape lectures solely on the basis of administrative convenience (the college informed the student that a committee would have to rule on the request, and it would not meet until after the beginning of classes); colleges are not responsible for providing accommodations if students do not request these services in a timely fashion; institutions charging a fee for services are in violation of federal mandates; the refusal to provide a bar examination candidate double time and a distraction-free testing room on the basis that he did not have sufficient documentation proving that he had a disability was upheld by a federal court.

6. With regard to students with psychological disabilities: Home visits for individuals with disabilities may be required in order to provide access to vocational rehabilitation services; students may be dismissed if they are a threat to a professor, peers, or other individuals in the environment; a college's refusal to admit a student who was emotionally unstable into an Early Childhood Teaching program was upheld.

7. With regard to accessibility issues: It is unlawful to hold activities such as commencement in off-campus inaccessible facilities; if existing facilities are not accessible, a university may choose to relocate an activity to an accessible location; existing facilities must be modified or evacuation measures provided for emergency purposes; if materials are provided in off-campus facilities, such facilities must be accessible; equal experiences must be provided for students who cannot partici-

pate in an off-campus activity because it is not accessible.

RECOMMENDED PRACTICES

Providing support services for postsecondary students with disabilities is a relatively new field of endeavor. During this initial stage of program development, professionals in related fields (e.g., special educators, rehabilitation specialists, educational administrators, and policy developers) must address certain basic issues that will ultimately affect the future of service delivery for postsecondary populations with disabilities. These issues revolve around the need to (a) conduct research on current support policies and practices and the relative value of the outcomes they produce, (b) implement self-advocacy programs, (c) design and initiate comprehensive training programs for postsecondary services providers who work with individuals who are disabled, and (d) establish effective secondary-to-postsecondary transition programs for students who are disabled.

Research Needs

Access to postsecondary education for students with disabilities has finally become a reality over the past 20 years. A review of the literature indicates that investigative efforts with this population have primarily focused on the use of survey, descriptive, and group research methodologies for the purposes of identification and diagnosis. This research has served to define the characteristics of people within the various disability categories and to provide basic insights into the problems faced by postsecondary students with disabilities (Gajar, 1987a, 1987b, 1989, 1992; Dalke, 1988; Salvia et al., 1988; Gajar et al., 1989; Leonard, 1991).

Legal and legislative directives have mandated the provision of services for this population. As noted, services and practices are numerous and varied. However, research regarding the differential effects of various services and practices on retention and postsecondary outcomes is virtually nonexistent. Inadequate research in this area has resulted in an absence of data-based information on which to build effective policies and educational programs. This, in turn, has resulted in an increase in judicial involvement and time-consuming litigation. In short, basic guidelines for postsecondary programs serving students with disabilities need to be established through research. Studies need to be conducted not only on the characteristics and needs of this population, but also on the unique characteristics and demands of various postsecondary settings (community colleges, universities, vocational and technical programs).

The primary thrust of research now, and in the immediate future, should involve the development of data-based intervention techniques. In addition, it is imperative that research be conducted on the service delivery network to ensure that it is capable of maximizing effective transmission of proven interventions that facilitate success in higher education settings (Gajar et al., 1993). If these research recommendations are pursued, the answers to a number of the questions presented in the previous sections of this chapter might be found.

Based on the heterogeneous nature of the different categories of postsecondary students with disabilities and the virtual absence of data-based research regarding the effectiveness of current accommodations and practices, single-subject research is recommended (Gajar, 1996). Single-subject research designs replicate treatment effects within a subject to support the internal validity of the practice (i.e., the extent to which academic behavior can be attributed to the treatment procedure). The primary advantage of these designs is that they allow the researcher to make precise and valid statements regarding the effectiveness of specific procedures with specific subjects when homogeneous groups are not available.

At the present time, it is unlikely that group designs will result in the development of intervention procedures for specific individuals in specific postsecondary settings. It is also unlikely that, in the near future, a significant population of postsecondary students with disabilities, possessing homogeneous characteristics that can be studied as a group, will be identified. Finally, a well-established body of data-based research will facilitate student self-advocacy.

Self-Advocacy

The following quotes explain how some students who have disabilities, and are currently in postsecondary education settings, advocate for special academic accommodations:

> I try to be organized, competent, and responsible before I go talk to my professors.
>
> I have to ask professors in advance for names of texts, reading materials, and handouts so I can get them read onto tape or typed in Braille.
>
> I go see them to talk about the problem and list possible solutions, listen for feedback and alternatives, and then work out an agreement we are both happy with.
>
> If professors don't say what's on the overheads, I ask them if they could read it aloud or loan me the overhead. If they forget, I occasionally remind them.
>
> I usually say, "In case I need extra time to write the exam, I need time-and-a-half. But I'll try to finish quickly."
>
> I tell them I need handouts a week early or as early as possible. I also tell them that I may need extra time to complete assignments. (Fichten et al., 1989:23)

Merchant (1995) discussed the need for self-advocacy training for first-year college students with learning disabilities. Based on her literature review, it is hypothesized that self-advocacy skills are not only needed by students with learning disabilities, but are necessary for success in postsecondary settings for all students with disabilities. Additionally, there is little evidence that formal training in self-advocacy now exists in either secondary or postsecondary settings.

The myriad services available to students with disabilities at the postsecondary level of education has been criticized for a tendency to promote student dependence on practitioners and services. Dependency on services is facilitated by the lack of independent skill training at the high school level. After leaving high school environments where parents and school personnel are held responsible for academic and personal decisions, students suddenly find themselves in postsecondary education settings where independence is highly valued. Mandates such as P.L. 94-142 do not include the student in the decision-making process. Consequently, when students with disabilities, and especially students with "invisible" impairments, enter postsecondary academic settings, they are often reluctant to ask for, or do not feel the need to justify, accommodations. They have not been asked to do so in previous academic settings, and they have no concept of how to appropriately address the issue.

Self-advocacy and/or self-reliance is often cited as an alternative to dependence. The ability to express one's needs and the ability to make informed decisions are considered to be important skills for students with disabilities. Merchant (1995) suggested that students need the opportunity to role play in secondary and postsecondary situations. In a role-playing situation, students can describe the nature of their disability, the impact of their disability on learning, and the accommodations they need for success. The skills acquired in this manner can then be transferred to real-life situations. The self-advocacy issue will be revisited in our discussion of secondary-to-postsecondary transition programs.

Training Service Providers

A review of the literature indicates a need for developing and implementing training programs for individuals who are responsible for providing services and accommodations for students with disabilities in postsecondary settings. Neither standards nor certification requirements exist for service providers. As a result many postsecondary students with disabilities have been served by individuals who possess little or no knowledge about the nature of various disabilities or the accommodations that are needed to appropriately serve this population. This absence of knowledge can be a contributing factor in the proliferation of services and practices that lack an empirical basis. The following communication outlining the steps to be taken as a new service provider is a familiar scenario.

Judith, who has been a disability service provider for the past four years, received a call from a college friend. Ann had just accepted a position as the first disability service provider for a small private college. Knowing of Judith's work in this area, Ann asked her, "Where do I begin with this job? Please give me whatever information you can to help me get started!" Having been undergraduates together, majoring in education and rehabilitation services, Judith knew Ann was beginning the job with a good foundation, all she needed was some resources to get started.

The first step was for Ann to join the Association on Higher Education and Disability (AHEAD), which provides a wealth of information and training. Also, newly developed AHEAD Professional Standards would serve as an excellent guideline for what is expected in providing services to college students with disabilities. Once a member, Judith suggested Ann obtain the following two AHEAD publications: *Title by Title: the ADA's Impact on Postsecondary Education,* by Jane Jarrow, and *Subpart E: The Impact of Section 504 on Postsecondary Education,* by Jane Jarrow.

The other organization that would provide Ann with valuable resources to help her in her job is HEATH, the national clearinghouse on postsecondary education for individuals with disabilities, funded by the U.S. Department of Education. HEATH provides a listing of free publications on postsecondary education as well as a newsletter with additional information that would be helpful for Ann.

Since Ann has access to e-mail, a vital link to other disability service providers nationwide is the DSSHE listserv on the internet. This listserv provides daily discussions with others on issues they are facing with students with disabilities. In addition, since its inception three years ago, DSSHE has archived all of its information, which can be easily accessed through key word searches.

Hoping Ann was not feeling overwhelmed with all this information, Judith assured her that as she got settled in her job she would be more than happy to assist her in any way she could. (Ellen Long, personal communication, August 2, 1996)

According to Yost and colleagues (1993), only 28 percent of disability service practitioners have training in special education. Service providers themselves express a need for training in many critical areas (e.g., assessment, developing effective learning strategies, and legal issues).

Hughes and Gajar (1993) compiled a list of competencies that are considered to be essential for successful disability service providers. They identified these competencies by reviewing (a) job announcements placed in the *Chronicle of Higher Education* and those sent to AHEAD, in which employers specified the competencies they expected qualified disability service providers to demonstrate; (b) the competencies that disability service program directors have reported as being important for successful job performance (Norlander, Shaw, & McGuire, 1990); and (c) important competencies that have been identified by expert individuals and review panels (e.g., National Joint Committee on Learning Disabilities, 1987). The competencies that were identified in each of the three sources are presented in Table 16.3.

These sources revealed agreement on the following major competencies/qualifications necessary for administrative and/or supervisory positions in higher education disabilities programs:

1. Direct experience with individuals with disabilities
2. Administration and supervision experience
3. Communication and collaboration skills
4. Research and grant writing skills
5. Prior experience in higher education settings
6. Counseling and advising
7. Diagnostic and assessment expertise
8. Knowledge of advocacy and self-advocacy issues (including knowledge of the laws and regulations related to disabilities). (Hughes & Gajar, 1995)

Students with disabilities can succeed at levels commensurate with their abilities and equivalent to their nondisabled peers (Gajar et al., 1982; Dalke, 1993). Failure to receive appropriate services often leads to a grade-point average for postsecondary students with disabilities that is significantly lower than that of their nondisabled peers, withdrawal from the postsecondary setting, and an absence of vocational options and financial resources resulting in a high cost not only to the individual, but to society. The quality of services and the absence of trained personnel are urgent issues that must be addressed in the design and development of future service delivery programs for students with disabilities in higher education settings.

Networking with High Schools

Transition models emphasize the need for linkages between secondary/postsecondary settings. However, developers of these models are often unclear as to who is responsible for developing the necessary connections. The high school is definitely different from the university setting. Hence the need for a transition facilitator is

Table 16.3 Identification of Competencies for Personnel Serving College Students with Disabilities

	SOURCE		
Competency	Job Listings	Norlander et al. (1990)	National Joint Committee on Learning Disabilities (1987)
1. Direct experience with individuals with disabilities	X	X	X
2. Administration and supervision	X		X
3. Communication and collaboration	X	X	X
4. Research and grant writing	X	X	X
5. Prior experience in higher education	X	X	X
6. Counseling and advising	X	X	X
7. Diagnosis and assessment	X	X	X
8. Advocacy	X	X	X

imperative. It is often assumed mistakenly the secondary special education teacher will take on the responsibilities of the transition facilitator. Currently, the secondary special education teacher is required to be a consultant, tutor, curriculum developer, and the individual who can handle every transition issue. It is impossible for one person to fulfill successfully all these roles. The need for a transition specialist who has the training in secondary to postsecondary transition issues is obvious.

Palmer, Vellman, and Shafer (1985) reviewed the functions that would be required of a transition specialist. These include (a) planning and coordinating interdisciplinary efforts surrounding the transition from school to work and community living; (b) training school personnel, adult service workers, and family members; (c) job placement training and follow-up; (d) case management; and (e) advocacy. To function effectively, the transition specialist must successfully utilize the following methods of service delivery: consultation, collaboration, cooperation, advocacy, evaluation, and follow-up. Transition facilitators would provide the necessary linkages between essential settings (i.e., community, secondary school, and postsecondary settings) and setting agents, (i.e., teachers, parents, faculty members, and service providers). It

is strongly recommended that all students with disabilities who are seeking a postsecondary education have full access to a transition facilitator.

CONCLUSION

The beginning of this chapter reviewed the history of postsecondary education for students with disabilities. Today, legal and legislative mandates exist, and practices and accommodations are numerous. However, data-based research in this area is nonexistent. In essence, the link between practice and success has not been established. Service providers lack training, and transition programs from secondary to postsecondary education have not been developed.

Students with disabilities are now attending postsecondary institutions and their numbers are steadily growing. Many of them demonstrate success in these environments. However, many face the obstacles of inappropriate services and an absence of knowledgeable transition specialists. In the absence of (a) clear connection between research and practice, (b) effective transition programs, and (c) skill training in self-advocacy, this population is faced with a long and difficult transitional journey from adolescence to adulthood.

QUESTIONS

1. Identify the factors that have precipitated the increase in the numbers of students with disabilities seeking services at the postsecondary education level.

2. Describe the history preceding the passage of P.L. 93-112, the Rehabilitation Act of 1973, and how it impacts postsecondary education.

3. Name the conditions that postsecondary institutions were to adhere to under P.L. 93-112, the Rehabilitation Act of 1973.

4. Describe how P.L. 101-476, the Individuals with Disabilities Education Act (IDEA), and P.L. 105-17 impacted postsecondary education.

5. What are some of the transition practices that should be provided to help prepare students with disabilities to enter postsecondary education settings.

6. Discuss the current practices of postsecondary settings in providing services to students with disabilities.

7. Name nine common services and accommodations provided to students with disabilities.

8. Identify the major populations for students with disabilities in postsecondary education and what are the common accommodation needs of these students.

9. Define self-advocacy and its importance for students with disabilities.

10. Discuss the factors missing from postsecondary settings in providing the optimum services for students with disabilities.

REFERENCES

Americans with Disabilities Act (ADA), P.L. 101-336. (1990).

Blalock, J. W. (1982). Persistent problems and concerns of young adult with learning disabilities. In W. M. Cruickshank & A. A. Silver (Eds.), *Bridges to tomorrow: The best of ACLD* (pp. 2:35–56). Syracuse: Syracuse University Press.

Bowen, E. (1986). Good timers need not apply. *Time, 127*(16), April 21, 70–71.

Brinckerhoff, L. C., Shaw, S. F., & McGuire, J. M. (1993). *Promoting postsecondary education for students with learning disabilities: A handbook for practitioners.* Austin, TX: PRO-ED.

Buchanan, M., & Wolf, J. S. (1986). A comprehensive study of learning disabled adults. *Journal of Learning Disabilities, 14,* 404–407.

Bursuck, W. D., & Rose, E. (1992). Community college options for students with mild disabilities. In F. R. Rusch, L. DeStefano, L. J., Chadsey-Rusch, L. A. Phelps, & E. Szymanski (Eds.), *Transition from school to adult life: Models, linkages, and policy* (pp. 71–91). Sycamore, IL: Sycamore.

Bursuck, W. D., Rose, E., Cowen, S., & Yahaya, M. A. (1989). Nationwide survey of postsecondary education services for students with learning disabilities. *Exceptional Children, 56,* 236–245.

Dalke, C. (1988). Woodcock-Johnson Psycho-educational Test Battery Profiles: A comparative study of college freshmen with and without learning disabilities. *Journal of Learning Disabilities, 21*(9), 567–570.

———. (1991). *Support programs in higher education for students with disabilities: Access for all.* Rockville, MD: Aspen.

———. (1993). Making a successful transition from high school to college: A model program. In S. A. Vogel & P. B. Adelman (Eds.), *Success for college students with learning disabilities* (pp. 57–80). New York: Springer-Verlag.

Dalke, C., & Schmitt, S. (1987). Meeting the transition needs of college-bound students with learning disabilities. *Journal of Learning Disabilities, 20,* 176–180.

Fairweather, J. S. (1989). Transition and other services for handicapped students in local education agencies. *Exceptional Children, 55*(4), 315–320.

Fichten, C. S., Amsel, R., Goodrick, G., & Libman, E. (1989). *Students and their professors: A guide for the college student with a disability.* Montreal: Dawson College.

Gajar, A. H. (1987a). Foreign language learning disabilities: The identification of predictive and diagnostic variables. *Journal of Learning, 20*(6), 327–330.

———. (1987b). Performance of learning disabled university students on the Woodcock Johnson Psycho-Educational Battery, Part II: Tests of achievement. *Diagnostique, 12*(2), 87–92.

———. (1989). A computer analysis of written language variables and a comparison of compositions written by learning disabled and nonlearning disabled university students. *Journal of Learning Disabilities, 22*(2), 125–130.

————— . (1992). Adults with learning disabilities: Current and future research practices. *Journal of Learning Disabilities, 25,* 507–519.

————— . (1996). Current and future research priorities. In J. R. Patton & E. A. Polloway (Eds.), *Learning disabilities: The challenges of adulthood* (pp. 185–204). Austin, TX: PRO-ED.

Gajar, A. H., Goodman, L., & McAfee, J. (1993). *Secondary schools and beyond: Transition of individuals with mild disabilities.* New York: Charles E. Merrill.

Gajar, A. H., Murphy, J., & Hunt, F. M. (1982). A university program for learning disabled students. *Reading Improvement, 19,* 282–288.

Gajar, A. H., Salvia, J., Gajria, M., & Salvia, S. (1989). A comparison of IQ-achievement discrepancies between LD and nonLD college students. *Learning Disabilities Research, 4*(2), 119–124.

Gajar, A. H., & Smith, J. O. (1996). Service delivery models effective with adults with learning disabilities. In S. Hoy & N. Gregg (Eds.), *Adults with learning disabilities* (pp. 298–328). New York: Guilford Press.

Haig, J. H., & Patterson, B. H. (1980). *An overview of adult learning disabilities.* Paper presented at the Annual Meeting of the 13th Western College Reading Association, San Francisco. (ERIC Reproduction Service No. ED 197 563.)

Henderson, C. (1995). The American freshman: National norms. *College Freshmen with disabilities; A statistical profile.* Washington, DC: HEATH Resource Center, American Council of Education, U.S. Department of Education.

Hughes, C. A., & Gajar, A. H. (1993). *A component analysis of competencies and requirements for positions in higher education disability services programs.* Unpublished manuscript.

————— . (1995). *Postsecondary transition and higher education services for students with disabilities.* Unpublished manuscript.

Hughes, C. A., & Smith, J. O. (1990). Cognitive and academic performance of college students with learning disabilities: A synthesis of the literature. *Learning Disability Quarterly, 13,* 66–79.

IBM National Support Center for Persons with Disabilities. (1990a). *Resource guide for persons with vision impairments.* Atlanta, GA: IBM.

————— . (1990b). *Resource guide for persons with mobility impairments.* Atlanta, GA: IBM.

Individuals with Disabilities Education Act (IDEA), P.L. 101-476 (1990).

Jarrow, J. E. (1987). Integration of Individuals with disabilities in higher education: A review of the literature. *Journal of Postsecondary Education and Disability, 5*(4), 38–56.

Johns, C. (1984). The disability backlash: Is the implementation of Section 504 a matter of cost to tradition or to the treasury? Testimony presented to the House Subcommittee on the Civil Rights Restoration Act. Cited in W. Scales (1986), Postsecondary education for disabled students—Written testimony. *Bulletin of the Association on Handicapped Student Service Programs in Post-Secondary Education, 4*(1), 20–32.

Kahn, M. S. (1980). Learning problems of the secondary and junior college learning disabled student: Suggested remedies. *Journal of Learning Disabilities, 13*(8), 40–44.

Kincaid, J. M. (1995). *Fatal distraction: Keeping abreast of legal developments.* Unpublished manuscript.

Leonard, F. (1991). Using Wechsler data to predict success for learning disabled college students. *Learning Disabilities Research & Practice, 6*(1), 17–24.

Mangrum, C. T., & Strichart, S. S. (1988). *College and the learning disabled student.* Orlando, FL: Grune & Stratton.

McAfee, J. K. (1989). Community colleges and individuals with emotional disorders. *Behavioral Disorders, 15*(1) 9–15.

McAfee, J. K., & Scheeler, M. C. (1987). Accommodation of adults who are mentally retarded in community colleges: A national study. *Education and Training in Mental Retardation, 22,* 262–267.

Merchant, D. J. (1995). *A self-advocacy training program for first year college students with learning disabilities.* Unpublished manuscript.

Moss, J. R., & Fox, D. L. (1980). *College-level programs for the learning disabled.* Tulsa, OK: Partners in Publishing.

National Association of State Directors of Special Education. (1990). *Education of the Handicapped Act Amendment of 1990 (PL 101-476): Summary of major changes in parts A through H of the Act.* Washington, DC: Author.

National Center for Educational Statistics. (1993). *Digest of Educational Statistics: The 1987 National postsecondary student aid study.* Washington, DC: U.S. Department of Education.

National Joint Committee on Learning Disabilities. (1987). Adults with learning disabilities: A call to action. A position paper of the National Joint Committee on Learning Disabilities, February 10. *Journal of Learning Disabilities, 20*(3), 172–174.

Nelson, R., & Lignugaris-Kraft, B. (1989). Postsecondary education for students with learning disabilities. *Exceptional Children, 56,* 246–265.

Norlander, K. A., Shaw, S. F., & McGuire, J. M. (1990). Competencies of postsecondary education personnel serving students with learning disabilities. *Journal of Learning Disabilities, 23,* 426–432.

Palmer, J. T., Vellman, R., & Shafer, D. (1985). *The transition process of disabled youth: Literature review.* Albertson, NY: Human Resources Center.

Rehabilitation Act of 1973, P.L. 93-112, Sections 503, 504; 87 Stat. 366, 393, 394.

Salvia, J., Gajar, A. H., Gajria, M., & Salvia, S. (1988). A comparison of WAIS-R profiles of college LD and normal students. *Journal of Learning Disabilities, 21*(10), 632–636.

Scales, W. (1986). Postsecondary education for disabled students—Written testimony. *Bulletin of the Association on Handicapped Student Service Programs in Postsecondary Education, 4*(1) 20–32.

Scheiber, B., & Talpers, J. (1987). *Unlocking potential.* Bethesda, MD: Adler & Adler.

School-to-Work Opportunities Act of 1994, P.L. 103-239, 20 U.S.C. 6101 et seq.

Shaw, S. F., & Shaw, S. R. (1989). Learning disability college programming: A bibliography. *Journal of Postsecondary Education and Disability, 6*(1), 77–85.

Sitlington, P. L., & Frank, A. R. (1990). Are adolescents with learning disabilities successfully crossing the bridge into adult life? *Learning Disability Quarterly, 13*(2), 97–111.

Smith-Fess Act of 1920, P.L. 66-236.

Smith-Hughes Act of 1915–1917, P.L. 64-347, 39 Stat. 929.

Smith-Sears Act of 1918, P.L. 65-178.

Vogel, S. A. (1993). The continuum of university responses to Section 504 for students with learning disabilities. In S. A. Vogel & B. Adelman (Eds.), *Success for college students with learning disabilities* (pp. 83–113). New York: Springer-Verlag.

Walter, G. G., & Welsh, W. A. (1986). *Providing for the needs of handicapped students in postsecondary environment.* New York: Rochester Institute of Technology.

Welsh, W. A., & Walter, G. G. (1988). The effect of postsecondary education on the occupational attainments of deaf adults. *Journal of the American Deafness and Rehabilitation Association, 22*(1), 14–22.

Yost, D. S., Shaw, S. F., Cullen, J., McGuire, J. M., & Bigaj, S. (1994). Practices and attitudes of postsecondary LD service providers in North America. *Journal of Learning Disabilities, 27*(10), 631–640.

17

◨

Moving Toward Social Inclusion in Employment and Postsecondary School Settings

JANIS CHADSEY
and DEBRA SHELDEN

The purpose of this chapter is to view social inclusion in postsecondary school and employment settings from an ecological perspective. The term "social inclusion" is used in a broad sense, focusing on some of the subcomponents that may impact on social inclusion, including social skills, social integration, and interpersonal relationships. A brief historical review of the emergence of social inclusion as an outcome of transition is provided, followed by descriptions of the occurrence of social inclusion in postsecondary school and employment settings. Finally, current interventions and recommended practices for enhancing social inclusion are specified. The interventions and recommended practices maintain an ecological perspective and include practices designed to change the individual, the context or environment, and/or other people in the postsecondary educational and employment settings.

In their conclusion to answering the question: "Who is happy?" Myers and Diener (1995) suggest that the best clues related to happiness come from "knowing a person's traits, whether the person enjoys a supportive network of close relationships, whether the person's culture offers positive interpretations for most daily events, whether the person is engaged in work and leisure, and whether the person has faith that entails social support, purpose, and hope" (p. 17). Scrutiny of this list of clues reveals that social interactions and relationships with others may be a central key to one's happiness. Closely related to the concept of happiness is the concept of quality of life. In a recent review of the literature assessing the quality of life for persons with disabilities, Hughes and colleagues (1995) reported that social relations and interactions were cited most frequently as being an important dimension of one's quality of life. It makes sense then that the display of appropriate social interactions and the establishment of social supports and relationships are associated with preferred outcomes of education and transition services (e.g., Halpern, 1993).

Interactions with others, some of which may lead to the formation of relationships, may best be viewed within an ecological framework. Ecological psychology studies the interrelationships and the interdependencies among individuals, their behavior, and their physical and social environments (Barker, 1968; Schoggen, 1978). Within this perspective, behavior is viewed as a dynamic part of the interaction between the person and the environment where people and environments exert mutual influences on one another (Chadsey-Rusch & Rusch, 1988). An example of this occurs when we consider the different social behaviors we use when we are in a bar versus a church, and when we are talking to our boss versus an intimate partner. If we exhibit bar social behavior in a church, we will receive disgruntled looks and may be asked to leave. If we talk to our intimate partner like we talk to our boss, our intimate relationship may be in jeopardy. The goal, from an ecological perspective, is to maximize the fit or congruence (Thurman, 1977) between people and their environments. Harmonious interactions and relationships with others occur when expectations from others in environments are met. If incongruencies occur, then the individuals, the environment, or both the individuals and the environment need to be changed until harmony is reached.

The purpose of this chapter is to view social inclusion in postsecondary school and employment settings from an ecological perspective. Too often, students with disabilities are viewed from a deficit-remedial hypothesis (Meyer, 1991). With this hypothesis, the problem that needs to be "fixed" (e.g., lack of social inclusion) is

assumed to lie within the person with the disability. However, if one assumes an ecological perspective, it is quite clear that the environment or others in the environment also may need to be the focus of intervention efforts.

In this chapter, the term "social inclusion" is used in a broad sense; it occurs when one is a constituent or integral part of the social fabric of a particular context. With this broad definition, we will discuss literature from postsecondary school and employment settings that focuses on some of the subcomponent parts that we believe impact on social inclusion, namely, social skills, social integration, and interpersonal relationships. We will do several things. First, we will give a brief historical review of the emergence of social inclusion as an outcome of transition. Then, we will provide descriptions of the occurrence of social inclusion in postsecondary school and employment settings. Third, we will discuss current intervention practices used in these settings. And finally, we will conclude the chapter with recommended practices for enhancing social inclusion.

SOCIAL INCLUSION: A VIABLE TRANSITION OUTCOME

Ever since Halpern (1985) took issue with employment being identified as the primary outcome of transition services, social and interpersonal relationships have been designated as an important outcome. In his quest to further define quality of life, Halpern (1993) listed a number of outcomes related to social inclusion, such as personal relationships, social responsibility, and happiness.

Although not implied tacitly, the outcome of social inclusion can be inferred from the Individuals with Disabilities Education Act, (IDEA), P.L. 105-17. Transitional services have been defined as an outcome-oriented process that leads to movement from school to "integrated employment." At least within the context of employment settings, the federal government has shown a commitment to the social inclusion of persons with disabilities.

In a national longitudinal study that investigated the transition outcomes of youths with disabilities, Wagner (1989, 1992) and colleagues assessed the social involvement of young people. Noting the importance of social networks and support, Wagner stated that having a job or going to school could provide opportunities for developing or strengthening relationships with others. In particular, social support could be very important by mitigating against stress during the transition from high school to adulthood because transition periods are usually stressful (Tappe & Gaylord-Ross, 1990).

Wagner (1989, 1992) reported the social involvement of transitioning youths in a variety of ways. For youths still in high school, Wagner (1989) found that about one-third were reported by their parents as getting together with their friends more than five times per week; only 10 percent of the youths saw their friends less than once a week. In addition, almost half of the youths (43 percent) belonged to school or community group, the majority to sports teams. Overall, youths with disabilities belonged to fewer groups than youths without disabilities. Further, youths with mental retardation, emotional disturbance, and health impairments joined fewer groups than youths with speech, visual, or hearing impairments.

After youths had been out of high school for 3 to 5 years, Wagner (1992) noted a decline in the percentage of youths seeing their friends or family members. Over this period of time, the rate of contact decreased from 58 to 38 percent. Group membership in clubs and organizations also declined (28 to 21 percent). However, even though social contacts with others had declined, few youths (approximately 5 percent) were described as being socially isolated.

Of all youths, those with learning disabilities experienced the greatest social involvement 3 to 5 years after leaving school, and youths with multiple handicaps or who were deaf/blind were the least socially involved. Youths with learning

disabilities were married or living with someone of the opposite sex as frequently as youths in the general population, but they also had the dubious distinction (along with youths who were emotionally disturbed) of having the highest rates of arrest.

Wagner (1992) also reported that young women with disabilities were less socially involved than men and were twice as likely to be parents as men. African-American youths had similar patterns of social affiliation as Caucasians, but were more likely to be registered to vote and arrested. Youths who graduated from high school were more likely than dropouts to belong to social and community groups and be registered to vote.

One of the difficulties in considering social inclusion as a viable transition outcome relates to its assessment. Wagner (1989, 1992) measured social inclusion or involvement by assessing social participation rates through the number of times youths with disabilities saw their friends and parents, joined groups, got married, had children, registered to vote, and were arrested. All of these outcome variables are important and provide useful information about the social involvement of youths. However, it also seems important to know how youths themselves feel about their social situations. In addition, information from employers, co-workers, university and community college instructors, and peers on the social status of youths with disabilities in employment and postsecondary educational settings would be useful.

The transition outcome of social inclusion is complex and multifaceted, which has led to a number of proposed definitions and conceptual frameworks for the study of its component parts (e.g., Chadsey-Rusch, 1992; Chadsey-Rusch & O'Reilly, 1992; Storey, 1993; Newton et al., 1994). It is not our intent to propose a conceptual framework for assessing transition outcomes related to social inclusion; however, we will describe studies in both postsecondary schools and employment settings that have assessed this outcome in a variety of ways.

STUDIES OF SOCIAL INCLUSION IN POSTSECONDARY SCHOOLS AND EMPLOYMENT SETTINGS

What do the social lives of young adults with disabilities in postsecondary schools and employment settings look like? Do they experience social problems? What do employers, postsecondary school instructors, peers, and co-workers without disabilities think of individuals with disabilities? Do they like to work with them, teach them, or date them? The answers to these questions will be answered in what follows.

Postsecondary Schools

As a group, the enrollment rate for youths with disabilities in postsecondary schools is lower than that for the general population (Marder, 1992). Enrollment rates by disability category are even more disparate. That is, 3 to 5 years after leaving secondary schools, youths with mental retardation were found to attend postsecondary schools at a rate of 13 percent, whereas youth who were hard of hearing or deaf attended at a rate of 60 percent, which is similar to the rate attended by youth in general.

Studies investigating the social involvement of youths with disabilities in postsecondary schools have primarily involved the disability categories of deaf and hearing impairment, visual impairment, physical disabilities, and learning disabilities. As studies are discussed, particular disability categories will be mentioned because it is unlikely that some findings specific to certain categories can be generalized to all categories of disability. In addition, it is important to know that most studies took place in university or community college settings.

Do Social Problems Occur in Postsecondary Schools? Many youths who experienced social and interpersonal problems in high school continue to encounter similar problems in postsecondary schools. For example, some adults with learning disabilities have been reported to experience a negative self-concept, poor socialization skills, stress and anxiety, insecurity, loneliness, and to be at an increased risk for suicide and trouble with the law (Vogel & Forness, 1992; Brinkerhoff, Shaw, & McGuire, 1993; Bender & Wall, 1994). However, it is unknown, how widespread these problems are among adults with learning disabilities and whether they are characteristic of particular subgroups (Vogel & Forness, 1992; Bender & Wall, 1994).

In a comparison of university students with and without learning disabilities, Saracoglu, Minden, and Wilchesky (1989) found that students with learning disabilities reported significantly poorer self-esteem and personal-emotional adjustment. Mangrum and Strichart (1984) also found that college students with learning disabilities reported difficulties forming positive interpersonal relationships. This lack of competent interpersonal skills, and difficulty accepting learning disabilities, contributed to these students dropping out of college.

In an exploratory study, Mellard and Hazel (1992) compared students with and without learning disabilities from 21 of California's 106 community colleges; students completed a self-report, study-developed, adaptive behavior instrument that asked students to indicate how frequently an item applied to them. Mellard and Hazel (1992) reported that students with learning disabilities had difficulties in conversational activities, the use of pragmatics, humor, and peer relationships.

In another study that assessed student developmental levels, Benshoff, Fried, and Roberto (1990) compared 45 college students with disabilities and 45 students without disabilities. The results from their study indicated that there were no differences between the groups on developmental tasks related to autonomy, independence, and planning; the only difference occurred in the area of interpersonal skills, where college students with disabilities were found to score lower (there were no differences in scores by disability group, which included students with visual, hearing, and orthopedic impairments, and learning disabilities). Because the college years provide opportunities for building friendships and potentially choosing a marital partner, Benshoff and colleagues (1990) suggested that developmental delays in interpersonal skills could result in loneliness, isolation, and difficulties in later life.

The area of loneliness was assessed in 170 students with hearing impairment who attended eight mainstream colleges and universities in the United States (Murphy & Newlon, 1987). When these students' loneliness scores were compared to the mean loneliness scores of a hearing sample (Russell, Peplau, & Cutrona, 1980), the students with hearing impairments were found to be more lonely. Interestingly, Murphy and Newlon (1987) found no differences in loneliness scores between deaf and hard-of-hearing students, male and female students, or by year in college. Small but significant correlations showed that there were relationships between loneliness and unsatisfactory peer and parental relationships, and between loneliness and perceived comfort with communication mode.

In a study assessing the views of 102 students with visual impairments who "survived" their freshman year, McBroom, Sikka, and Jones (1994) reported that 38 percent experienced problems participating in recreational and athletic activities, dealing with teachers and professors (34 percent), experiencing loneliness (28 percent), making friends (24 percent), and getting along with their roommate (22 percent). However, in this same study, 54 percent of the students participated in social groups or organizations, including scholastic or academic organizations, religious activities, career-related organizations, political and athletic groups, and sororities and fraternities.

Positive findings related to social involvement were also reported by Greenbaum, Graham, and Sales (1995). In this study, which looked at the college experiences of 49 adults

with learning disabilities, 61 percent were involved in extracurricular activities, which included belonging to a sorority or fraternity, athletic team, band, campus club, or support group. This percentage of involvement was actually higher than that for the general student body.

Houck, Engelhard, and Geller (1989) also found somewhat positive social involvement results when they compared 54 students with learning disabilities and 54 students without learning disabilities on a self-assessment survey. Their results showed that both groups perceived little difficulty with their ability to get along with peers and adults and felt that important people in their lives supported their career goals.

Finally, in an assessment of loneliness, assertiveness, and perceived control over one's social life, Gambrill, Florian, and Splaver (1986) found few differences between college students with and without a physical disability. The only difference between the two groups occurred in the area of assertiveness; college students with physical disabilities were more assertive than those without physical disabilities. Gambrill and colleagues (1986) interpreted this finding by suggesting that students with physical disabilities were often placed in unique and challenging situations where they had to ask for help, refuse unwanted offers of help, and perhaps smooth social predicaments caused by their disability.

Summary. It is not surprising that there is no definite answer to the question, "Do social problems occur in postsecondary schools?" The majority of the studies reported here suggest that certain young adults with learning, hearing, and vision disabilities experience social problems when they attend postsecondary schools. What is most notable about these findings is that they reflect the feelings and perceptions of the individuals themselves. For example, students with learning disabilities reported feelings of poor self-esteem, poor personal-emotional adjustment, and difficulties with conversation skills.

Students with hearing and vision disabilities both reported feelings of loneliness. Yet in two studies, over half of the students with vision and learning disabilities were involved in a variety of extracurricular activities. Certainly, it is possible to participate in clubs and organizations and still feel lonely, and some students with disabilities do. However, in one study (Gambril et al., 1986), students with physical disabilities were no more lonely than students without physical disabilities. It is unclear whether these types of social problems are more associated with a particular disability type (e.g., learning disability) or with certain personality types and, therefore, individually determined. Nonetheless, it is clear that some students with disabilities do experience social problems in postsecondary schools, and these problems need to be recognized and ameliorated.

The preceding section addressed the questions of whether social problems were present in postsecondary schools and how students with disabilities perceived some of these problems. But what are social interactions like in college classrooms and how do college professors and instructors feel about their interactions with students with disabilities? Similarly, what characterizes the type of social interactions and experiences that occur outside of class and what do peers without disabilities think about these interactions? These issues are addressed in the next two sections.

Social Interactions and Attitudes in the College Classroom. Fichten and colleagues (e.g., Ansel & Fichten, 1990; Fichten et al., 1990) have a line of research investigating the social experiences and interactions of students with disabilities who attended colleges in Canada. For example, Ansel & Fichten (1990) compared professors' ratings of the appropriateness of certain behaviors for students with and without disabilities, as well as the students' ratings of appropriateness. All the participants rated the appropriateness of 32 student behaviors (e.g., "ask for extensions on assignments when course

requirements are difficult to meet") and 44 professor behaviors (e.g., "give student extensions when course requirements are difficult to meet"). All students in the study also indicated how comfortable they were with their professors and how satisfied they were with their treatment by professors.

The results showed no differences between students with and without disabilities on level of comfort with professors or satisfaction with the treatment they received from their professors. However, on the appropriateness ratings, differences were found. For example, students with disabilities generally thought it was less appropriate for them to request or accept special consideration from professors. In terms of professors' appropriateness ratings, professors of students with disabilities thought it was more acceptable for students to ask for special consideration than did professors of nondisabled students. In light of these findings, Ansel and Fichten (1990) speculated that perhaps students with disabilities were unaware of normative information concerning the views of students without disabilities. Students with disabilities may also have rated items as they did because they did not want to be viewed as different and wanted to succeed because of their abilities and not their disabilities.

In another study, Fichten and colleagues (1990) investigated students' and professors' thoughts and feelings concerning interactions in different academic contexts. Students were asked questions about their academic background, degree of comfort with their professors, and satisfaction with the way they were treated. They also answered a series of six questions concerning twelve common situations where they might interact with their professors (e.g., during the first few days of classes, when the final grade is a failure, but not due to the student's disability). Professors responded to the same twelve situations and also answered questions regarding their teaching experience and preferred method of contact and comfort with students with disabilities.

The results indicated that students were generally comfortable with their professors and satisfied with the way they were treated. However, when they had problems in class, or had to discuss concerns related to their disability, they were uncomfortable. The most uncomfortable situations occurred when students were failing and when communication problems arose because they could not understand each others' speech.

Overall, students with disabilities wanted to handle problems themselves. When they did have to talk to professors, they often felt inadequate compared to other students and worried about their credibility. Interestingly, students often found that after talking to professors, they felt much better, and that many of their fears had been unfounded.

With respect to specific academic situations, students found it useful to talk to professors about their disability and learning strengths and weaknesses during the first few days of classes. They also believed it was important to talk to professors before problems in class became monumental.

The data from the professors revealed few negative thoughts about students with disabilities; however, many professors were first concerned when they found out about the presence of a student with a disability in one of their classes. Specifically, they worried about how they would talk to the student, if they would be effective teachers, and if the student would require more time and effort.

Professors also preferred that students initiate contact with them, but this rarely occurred, and if it did not occur, professors initiated contact with the student, particularly early in the semester. Professors also found that once they talked to students about issues and concerns, they felt more optimistic about teaching them.

Similar to student results, professors were least comfortable interacting with students when they were failing, particularly if the failure was related to a disability. If this occurred, many professors reconsidered the course requirements to make certain they were essential, and tried to select a replacement requirement that was equal in importance and level of difficulty (e.g., students with a speech impairment would be allowed to submit a written rather than an oral presentation, or might be allowed to submit an audiotape recording). If the requirement had to stand, many professors felt badly about it. Professors also felt badly if students were failing for the "typical" reasons, but they rarely added more points to students' scores so they could succeed.

In addition to the work of Fichten and colleagues, a number of studies have used survey methods to assess the attitudes of faculty toward students with disabilities (e.g., Matthews, Anderson, & Skolnick, 1987). In a recent study, Bagget and Silver (1992) obtained survey responses from 422 faculty at the University of Massachusetts at Amherst. The results revealed that respondents were (a) most accepting of wheelchair users and individuals with hearing impairments and most concerned with individuals with psychiatric disabilities, communication disorders, and learning disabilities; (b) unfamiliar with university services designed for students with disabilities; (c) unfamiliar with special education legislation and litigation; and (d) believed printed resources (e.g., articles, directories) would be the most helpful resources for helping students. The data also showed that female professors had more favorable attitudes toward students than male professors. Bagget and Silver (1992) expressed concern about these results, noting that most people were reluctant to express negative attitudes toward persons with disabilities, most professors had limited knowledge about disabilities, and most wanted additional information through passive avenues (i.e., printed articles).

Summary. Although there is limited research about perceptions and social interactions between professors and students with disabilities, the studies discussed here imply a somewhat positive, but cautious note of optimism. Essentially, these studies suggest that professors have limited knowledge about disabilities and are somewhat reluctant and unsure about how to approach students to help them. And some students with disabilities are reluctant to approach professors for help for fear that they will be viewed as being weak and different. Yet, ironically, students without disabilities think nothing of approaching professors to ask for help or special consideration on academic matters. And when professors talk to and have experiences with students with disabilities, and students talk to professors, each group finds that many of their concerns were unfounded. These studies suggest, then, that knowledge about and experiences with students with disabilities may be the most helpful strategies for creating positive social relationships in the college classroom.

Social Interactions and Attitudes of College Students. In a review of the literature on the attitudes and beliefs that affect the social integration of students with physical disabilities, Fichten (1988) noted that many studies reflected a positivity or sympathy bias. That is, when nondisabled students have been asked to evaluate students with physical disabilities, and there are no personally relevant consequences involved, students with disabilities tend to receive very positive ratings even compared to nondisabled students.

This positivity bias led Fichten and colleagues to design several studies that attempted to control this bias by asking respondents to report the beliefs of similar others rather than their own views. For example, Fichten and Ansel (1986) asked nondisabled students to report others' views when assigning an extensive list of adjectives to male and female students with and without physical disabilities. The results showed that nondisabled students assigned stereotypical adjectives to female and male students with physical disabilities that were in direct opposition to those assigned to students without disabilities. For example, students with disabilities were characterized as being "aloof–introverted, lazy–submissive, and ingenuous–unassuming"

(p. 423). In addition, males with disabilities were seen to possess more characteristics in common with females with disabilities than with males without disabilities.

In another study employing similar methods, Fichten and colleagues (1991) looked at whether college students with visual impairments would have more difficulties than nondisabled peers dating peers without disabilities. Fichten and colleagues also assessed whether stereotypes influenced the impact of the ratings. The results from the study showed that 330 college students were more likely to date nondisabled peers and felt uncomfortable about dating someone with a visual impairment. In addition, students without disabilities believed that their peers would be very uncomfortable and unlikely to date a person with a visual impairment. The study also showed that even when students with visual impairments were characterized as having stereotypical traits associated with people without disabilities, this characterization did not change the thoughts, feelings, or behaviors about dating someone with a visual impairment. This led Fichten and colleagues to suggest that the presence of the disability, rather than personality traits, accounted for the negative attitudes.

Fichten and colleagues also have conducted a number of studies comparing students with and without disabilities on a variety of measures that impact social integration. For example, Fichten and Ansel (1988) compared cognitive thoughts about interacting with students who have visual, physical, or no disabilities. The results from this study showed that students with and without disabilities had similar thoughts about interacting with students without disabilities, but that students without disabilities had more negative thoughts about interacting with someone with a disability, particularly a physical disability. Similar findings were found in another study (Fichten et al., 1991); however, there were no differences in thought patterns by disabilities.

In another study, Fichten and colleagues (1989a) assessed the affect, stereotyping, and self-concept of students with visual and physical disabilities and no disabilities. Again, the results showed again that students without disabilities were uncomfortable about interacting with students with disabilities and believed that these students were different from them in a number of negative ways (e.g., in self-concept, socially anxious). Students with disabilities were comfortable interacting with students without disabilities, but interestingly, held some beliefs that were similar to those of nondisabled students. For example, students with disabilities had similar stereotyped views about their own disability group as did students without disabilities. Also, students in one disability group were uncomfortable interacting with students from a different disability group. Even though both groups of students with and without disabilities held different beliefs about one another, in reality, Fichten and colleagues found no differences among the groups on measures of self-esteem, social anxiety, dating anxiety, frequency, and satisfaction.

Summary. The work by Fichten and colleagues suggests that students without disabilities are less comfortable with their peers with disabilities than with their nondisabled peers. In addition, nondisabled students view their peers with disabilities as being different from them and tend to assign stereotypical and negative characteristics to them. Finally, nondisabled students believe that other nondisabled peers around them have more negative attitudes than they do.

Fichten and colleagues also found that students with disabilities feel comfortable around nondisabled students and do have friends without disabilities. But, interestingly, students with disabilities tend to hold stereotypical views about others in their own disability group and view others with disabilities in a somewhat negative light.

As students leave postsecondary settings for employment settings, or enter employment settings directly after high school, social inclusion plays a prominent role. Not only can workers form close social relationships with one another (Barber & Hupp, 1993), they can get fired from

their jobs for displaying inappropriate social behaviors (e.g., Greenspan & Schoultz, 1981). The next section discusses descriptive studies that have investigated the social inclusion of workers with disabilities in employment settings.

Employment Settings

How do the social skills of employees with disabilities compare to those of employees without disabilities? And what do co-workers report about their interactions with employees with disabilities. A series of studies have reported the social interaction patterns occurring in integrated employment contexts. Not only have these studies verified the occurrence of behaviors reported as being important by employers, they have also described differences in the interaction patterns between workers with and without disabilities. For example, Lignugaris/Kraft and colleagues (Lignugaris/Kraft et al., 1986, 1988) described the interaction patterns of adults with mild and moderate disabilities employed in a nonprofit business for refurbishing household goods. Lignugaris/Kraft and colleagues (1986) found that workers both with and without disabilities were very social when they were completing work tasks, and most social interactions involved co-workers rather than supervisors. Certain social behaviors occurred infrequently (e.g., requests for assistance and criticism), and others were more frequent (e.g., giving assistance and working cooperatively). The only statistically significant difference between the two groups of workers was for a nontask skill; workers with disabilities joked and laughed less than workers without disabilities.

In another study, Lignugaris/Kraft and colleagues (1988) found that commands and asking for information were the most frequently observed social skill areas. The authors also noted differences in these areas between workers with and without disabilities. Specifically, employees with disabilities were more likely to interact with other employees with disabilities, and nondisabled employees interacted more with each other. Workers with disabilities received more commands and were less involved in teasing and joking interactions. Workers without disabilities were involved in fewer greetings and were asked for information more often during work than employees with disabilities.

Chadsey-Rusch and Gonzalez (1988) also directly observed the social interaction patterns of workers with mild and moderate disabilities in seven competitive employment settings that were primarily food service. The majority of interactions were used to share information, tease and joke, ask questions, and give directions. Analyzing the differences in interactions between workers with and without disabilities, Chadsey-Rusch and colleagues (1989) found that supervisors were just as likely to interact with workers without disabilities as with workers with disabilities. However, workers without disabilities were more likely to interact with other co-workers without disabilities about nontask topics during lunch/break and during two observed work conditions.

Storey and Knutson (1989) directly observed the social interactions of high school students with moderate and severe handicaps who were receiving vocational training services. Students without disabilities were more involved in interactions with each other, interacted more with their supervisors, and received more compliments and directions than workers with disabilities. Similar findings were reported by Storey and colleagues (1991).

Parent and colleagues (1992) observed fifteen workers with mental retardation and fifteen co-workers without disabilities. Workers with mental retardation and co-workers did not differ significantly on the number of interactions. However, they did differ on the type and context of interactions. Co-workers without disabilities engaged in more frequent task-related and break-time interaction, whereas workers with mental retardation engaged in more frequent inappropriate interactions and nontask-related interactions during work periods.

Ferguson, McDonnell, and Drew (1993) also compared workers with and without mental retardation. Workers with mental retardation received more frequent directions from workers without mental retardation. Additionally, workers without mental retardation engaged in more frequent joking and teasing than did workers with mental retardation. These findings support previous research (e.g., Chadsey-Rusch & Gonzalez, 1989; Storey et al., 1991).

A series of studies reports the frequency of contact and involvement between co-workers and employees with disabilities. For example, Shafer and colleagues (1989) surveyed 212 co-workers who worked with twenty-nine workers with mental retardation. The results of their study showed that 72 percent of the co-workers had contact with supported employees on the job, whereas only 31 percent of the co-workers had contact at least weekly during break/lunch time; only 16 percent socialized with workers at least weekly after work. Similar results were reported in studies by Belcher and Smith (1994) and Butterworth and Strauch (1994).

Another series of studies conducted by Rusch and his colleagues (Rusch et al., 1989; McNair & Rusch, 1992; Rusch et al., 1995) investigated the level of co-worker involvement. The results indicated that co-workers were involved in a variety of ways with workers with disabilities (e.g., as advocates, trainers, evaluators), but few of them actually befriended these workers.

Summary. Taken together, these studies indicate that workers with disabilities do interact with workers without disabilities in employment settings; that is, a level of social integration is occurring. However, the majority of the interactions are about work-related matters rather than about nonwork activities. In addition, the majority of the interactions occur during the performance of the job rather than during lunch or break times or outside of work.

In many respects, the employment-related studies are similar to the postsecondary school studies. That is, although social integration and acceptance seem to occur on the job and in the classroom, more intimate or closer social relationships such as friendships seem to be the exception rather than the rule. Of course, this conclusion needs to be regarded as tentative, because few studies have investigated these types of relationships in either settings. In addition, the research reported in employment contexts has primarily focused on entry-level employment positions involving workers with more severe disabilities. Therefore, studies are needed that (a) investigate the social interactions and relationships of workers with mild disabilities and (b) focus upon the social integration patterns that occur in jobs that are not entry-level. The next section discusses intervention studies that have been conducted to impact social inclusion.

CURRENT INTERVENTION PRACTICES

Interventions designed to change the social relations, interactions, or skills of people are broad and varied. Whether interventions are designed for young or old, male or female, disabled or not, they seem to fall into three general types: (1) those designed to change the specific skills of the target person (individual interventions), (2) those designed to change others rather than the target person (peer interventions), or (3) those designed to change the environment or social context (contextual interventions). In most studies, a variety of outcome measures are taken to determine the effectiveness of the intervention. For example, one might measure the frequency and appropriateness of questions asked during a meal, the number of times the target person is invited over to other people's homes, how much peers like to work with the target person, or the loneliness of the target person.

Few intervention studies have been conducted in either work or postsecondary school settings. Consequently, it is difficult to state with certainty what types of interventions work. However, the lack of studies has not stopped

people from making recommendations for practice. Many of these practices have been suggested by researchers who have conducted descriptive studies (such as those discussed in the prior section), so there is some validity to them. However, until further research is conducted to test the effectiveness of the practices recommended, such practices must remain only speculative.

In the next section, we will discuss intervention studies that have been conducted in both postsecondary school and work settings. In the final section, recommendations are proposed for practices that have not been the focus of research efforts, but have been suggested by others and intuitively make sense.

Postsecondary Schools

Individual Interventions. Aune (1991) conducted an evaluation study of a model program designed to prepare students with learning disabilities for transition to postsecondary settings. Although the primary intent of the program was not to change the social behaviors of the students with disabilities, several measures did assess the effects of the program on social skills.

The transition model evaluated by Aune (1991) was implemented with students during their junior and senior years in high school and during their first year in the postsecondary setting. The focus of activities for the high school students centered on (a) understanding individual strengths and weaknesses; (b) exploring career options, learning about postsecondary requirements, and selecting a college; (c) using study strategies and accommodations; and (d) developing self-advocacy and interpersonal skills. The self-advocacy and interpersonal skills were addressed by (a) teaching students their rights and responsibilities under Section 504; (b) practicing assertive behavior through scripts and role plays; and (c) having an opportunity to practice a variety of interpersonal situations such as accepting criticism, discussing a grade, and keeping and canceling appointments. During the first year in the postsecondary setting, students received orientation services, had opportunities to practice self-advocacy skills, and participated in an academic support group. The evaluation data (from a pre–post design) showed that students' scores improved on three of the six self-advocacy items and on the interpersonal skills measure. Although the study is limited due to the lack of a control group, Aune (1991) attributed the program's success to several areas involving social behavior: (a) self-understanding, (b) self-advocacy, and (c) student participation in the planning and implementation of the transition plan.

Peer Interventions. One of the goals of an intervention study designed by Fichten, Tagalakis, and Ansel (1989b) was to assess the effects of four cognitive modeling interventions on thoughts, attitudes, affect, and self-efficacy expectations of nondisabled peers toward interacting with students with physical disabilities. The participants were fifty-three male and seventy-three female volunteer college students. The study represented a type of peer intervention because the intervention was designed to change the behaviors of the students without disabilities.

All participants listened to two 5-minute audiotape modeling interventions. In each, a hypothetical situation was described that involved a peer in a wheelchair and participants were instructed to imagine having the thoughts modeled on the tape. Participants heard two of four conditions: (1) positive thoughts were modeled, (2) negative thoughts were modeled, (3) positive thoughts were modeled that changed to negative ones, and (4) negative thoughts changed to positive ones.

The results from the intervention had no significant effect on the participants' attitudes, thoughts, or affect toward persons with physical disabilities. Although the lack of effects could have been due to the very brief intervention, Fichten and colleagues suggested that the results may have been influenced more by the lack of

practice and rehearsal. That is, one may need to practice positive thoughts many times, replace negative thoughts with positive thoughts, and generate one's own positive thoughts before changes can occur.

Contextual Interventions. Very few intervention studies in postsecondary schools have been conducted to increase the social inclusion of students with disabilities. Two studies, which were not specifically designed as intervention studies, were performed by Brown and Foster (1991) and Foster and DeCaro (1991). In these studies, qualitative methods were used to investigate the interactions of deaf and hearing students who attended classes together and lived in the same residence hall. The studies represent a type of a contextual intervention because they included a change in the environment or social activity arrangement (Chadsey-Rusch & Heal, 1995).

In the Brown and Foster (1991) study, thirty students (half of them female) were interviewed about their academic and social experiences with students who were deaf. Of these students, twenty-nine had been in one or more classes with the deaf students and fourteen had lived in mainstreamed residence halls. In general, the hearing students accepted the presence of deaf students in their classrooms and believed they had the necessary academic skills to do college work. The majority of the hearing students believed that educational support services were fair, but that interpreters limited deaf students' participation and integration in the classroom.

Although deaf students were accepted in the classroom, such acceptance did not extend to social situations such as clubs, parties, or residence halls. Some deaf students were viewed in a negative light and described as being rude, noisy, immature, and not interested in associating with hearing students. However, other deaf students were viewed positively; these were the students who were more outgoing, friendly, could speak or lip read, and in general, were more similar to hearing students. Brown and Foster (1991) concluded that the differences in perceptions between the academic and social settings could be explained by expectations. That is, classroom expectations are set by the system and if academic criteria are not met, the student will not proceed through the system. However, social criteria are less concrete and depend on cultural norms. In this study, deaf students were being judged by hearing norms, rather than by deaf norms, and were falling short.

In another study, Foster and DeCaro (1991) interviewed hearing and deaf students who had lived together on a mainstreamed floor in a residence hall. From interviews with thirty-three deaf students and seventeen hearing students, four themes emerged that explained the interactions between the two groups. First, there were perceived advantages to living on a mainstreamed floor, but none of the advantages had anything to do with building friendships with one another. Hearing students chose to live on the floor because the residence hall was one of the nicest on campus, and deaf students saw a need to live on the floor in order to learn how to get along with hearing people.

A second theme involved the difficulty of communicating with one another. Fluent communication between the hearing and deaf students was rare, although for some students, it improved over time. A factor that seemed to positively influence interactions was whether or not students showed a willingness and perseverance toward communicating with the other person.

Students' behavior toward one another was influenced by the knowledge they held about one another—the third theme in the interviews. Students came to campus with already formed expectations, beliefs, and myths; they also increased their knowledge base through observations and experiences with one another. This theme was closely related to the fourth theme, which was characterized by the attitudes and feelings about hearing or deaf people. The primary attitudes held by most students were either negative or neutral. For example, deaf students believed the hearing students were fearful because of their inability to communicate with the deaf students and their lack of knowledge about deaf culture. Hearing students, in turn, believed deaf students were rude because they did not try to communicate with hearing students. When hearing students attempted to learn sign language or dated deaf girls, they were judged positively by the deaf students; these hearing students also reacted positively to these experiences.

What can we learn from this type of contextual intervention where students with deafness lived in the same residence hall as students who could hear? Brown and Foster (1991) made three recommendations. First, they stated that interactions were likely to be most successful if they were secondary to the task. For example, one hearing student who formed a friendship with a deaf student on a ski trip would not have gone on the ski trip if the purpose would have been to promote interactions between persons with and without disabilities. In essence then, this recommendation implies that relationships cannot be forced, but natural opportunities (e.g., clubs, intramural sports) need to exist for the possibility that relationships might occur, and students with disabilities need to be encouraged to take advantage of these opportunities.

Second, Brown and Foster (1991) suggested that courses in deaf awareness, sign language, and deaf culture be offered to hearing students. This recommendation is particularly critical for students who live together, but use different communication forms.

Finally, Brown and Foster (1991) recommended that deaf students themselves need to do their part in facilitating interactions. That is, in order for successful interactions to occur, deaf students need to show an interest in hearing students and be more accepting of them.

Foster and DeCaro (1991) suggested that sometimes [contextual] arrangements can have unintended segregating effects. For example, the residence halls designed for deaf students included strobe lights for emergency warning signals, but in essence this served to reinforce the conceptual separation between the two groups of students. Consequently, before environmental arrangements are implemented, their potential side effects needed to be considered.

Foster and DeCaro (1991) also recommended that students have a voice in the design of interventions. For example, some deaf students may prefer to live with other deaf students.

While noting that there are no easy answers to creating environments that are devoid of stereotypes, Foster and DeCaro (1991) encouraged pluralism and stated that "the focus of policy and program development should be the creation of educational settings where all physical environments, services, and activities are fully accessible to all students and decisions about how to participate are made by students from a position of empowerment, choice, and equal opportunity" (pp. 199–200).

Summary. Few studies have been designed to assess the effects of intervention strategies on the social inclusion of students in postsecondary settings. In addition, the outcomes used to measure the effects have been somewhat limited in nature. Consequently, research is needed that provides evidence about the effectiveness of interventions across a broad range of important social outcomes.

Employment Settings

The employment literature related to intervention studies has been of two types: (1) studies to identify socially valid behaviors that should occur in employment settings, and (2) studies that aim to change social inclusion. These studies have been categorized according to the three types previously discussed (i.e., individual interventions, peer interventions, and contextual interventions).

What Skills Are Important to Employment Success? Two general classes of social behaviors occur in work settings: task-related and nontask-

related interactions (Kirmeyer, 1988; Lignugaris/Kraft et al., 1988; Chadsey-Rusch et al., 1989). Task-related interactions are interactions related to work and include such behaviors as following directions, requesting assistance, sharing work information, and accepting criticism (Lignugaris/Kraft et al., 1988; Chadsey-Rusch et al., 1989). Nontask-related interactions, or interactions unrelated to work, include such behaviors as teasing or joking, sharing information about sports, or asking questions about a co-worker's family (Chadsey-Rusch & Gonzalez, 1988; Lignugaris/Kraft et al., 1988).

Several studies have examined employer perceptions of important social skills. In general, employers have indicated that task-related social skills are more important than nontask-related social skills (Rusch, Schutz, & Agran, 1982; Salzberg, Agran, & Lignugaris/Kraft, 1986; Salzberg et al., 1987; Minskoff & DeMoss, 1994).

Salzberg and colleagues (1986) surveyed employers from five jobs to obtain their opinions regarding social behaviors that are important for entry-level work and behaviors that may differ in importance across jobs. The results indicated that social behaviors related to worker productivity (e.g., asking supervisors for assistance, following directions, responding to criticism, getting information before a job, offering to help co-workers) were rated higher in importance than general personal social behaviors (e.g., listening without interrupting, acknowledging and expressing appreciation to co-workers).

Salzberg and colleagues (1986) also noted contextual differences in importance ratings of social skills. For example, social behaviors were considered more important for kitchen helpers and food service workers than for janitors, dishwashers, and maids. Such differences were attributed to the fact that some jobs (i.e., kitchen helpers and food service workers) were carried out in a more social context where workers frequently interacted with co-workers and customers.

Salzberg and colleagues (1987) surveyed employers from manufacturing businesses (e.g., clothing, electronics/computers, construction, printing companies) to determine the social-vocational skills important for employment. Although the size of the sample was small ($N = 20$), their results extended the findings from previous research. Generally, employers' importance ratings were related to productivity. Task-related social behaviors, such as following directions, offering to help co-workers, getting the necessary information for a job, requesting assistance, and clarifying ambiguous or incomplete instructions, were rated most important. Nontask-related social behaviors, such as asking about others' personal affairs and praising co-workers, were rated least important.

Most recently, Minskoff and DeMoss (1994) asked 145 employers and 20 speech/language pathologists to rate 64 social skills as "essential," "helpful," or "not important" for job success. The highest rated items were categorized as compliance behaviors, including accepting supervision from a superior, following directions, asking for information or assistance when needed, and accepting constructive criticism. Although Minskoff and DeMoss (1994) did not differentiate task-related and nontask-related skills, it seems clear that these top-rated items are task-related skills. Additionally, the five lowest rated items (responds appropriately to humor; makes appropriate small talk; compliments others, but not excessively; introduces others; and accepts compliments) are nontask-related skills. Hence, the Minskoff and DeMoss (1994) study supports previous research findings indicating that supervisors value task-related skills more than nontask-related skills.

Although it is clear that employers report that task-related social skills are more critical to employment success than nontask-related social skills, the latter skills may still influence their overall perception of employees. In their survey of employers in manufacturing businesses, Salzberg and colleagues (1987) found that several nontask social behaviors (i.e., ignoring grum-

bling and complaining, praising co-workers, and expressing appreciation to co-workers) were rated low in importance, but were significant characteristics of top-ranked workers. Additionally, some social behaviors were considered positive for both top- and bottom-ranked employees (acknowledging what others are saying, using an appropriate tone of voice, using social amenities, and not being nosy). These findings led Salzberg and colleagues (1987) to conclude that workers may need a broad behavioral repertoire, including both task and nontask skills, if they want to become highly valued workers.

Summary. The preceding studies suggest that employers want to make certain that employees possess the social skills that will enable them to do their jobs, such as following directions, asking for assistance, and accepting criticism. Although nontask skills may not be regarded as crucial, there is evidence to suggest, however, that difficulties in this area could lead to job terminations (e.g., Greenspan & Schoultz, 1981). In addition, it is likely that appropriate use of nontask social skills during breaks, lunches, and after work may assist workers in forming closer relationships, such as friendships, with their co-workers.

Individual Interventions. Individual interventions center around social skills training. The intent of social skills training is to increase an individual's repertoire of appropriate social skills. The emphasis is on teaching the employee with a disability. Several components are common to most social skills training packages, including (a) a rationale explaining why the targeted behavior is desirable; (b) an opportunity to observe examples of the behavior (i.e., modeling); (c) an opportunity to practice the behavior, usually in role-play situations; and (d) feedback regarding performance (Chadsey-Rusch, 1986). The vast majority of research on strategies to promote social integration of employees with disabilities focuses on individual interventions.

Whang, Fawcett, and Matthews (1984) examined the effects of a social skills training package on the social skills of two high school students with learning disabilities. Targeted skills included accepting criticism, providing constructive criticism, explaining a problem, accepting instruction, and giving and accepting compliments. Six 35-minute training sessions were conducted, which included direct instruction, practice, and corrective feedback. Results indicated that although students demonstrated skills in both the training settings and actual work settings, skill levels declined over time.

Montague (1988) examined the effects of a group instruction package on the social skills of forty-nine high school students with mild to moderate disabilities. Social skills training was conducted in thirty sessions over 10 weeks. Based on a review of the literature and rankings by a panel of employment-related professionals, ten social skills were identified for training: (1) understanding instruction, (2) asking a question, (3) asking for help, (4) accepting criticism, (5) ordering job responsibilities, (6) accepting assistance, (7) giving instructions, (8) offering assistance, (9) apologizing, and (10) convincing others. Task analyses were then developed for each skill, along with scripted lessons, including teacher and student dialogue, explicit directions for facilitating group instruction, student cue cards to help students memorize the skill steps, and five practice activities. Modeling, active participation, questions, verbal rehearsal, cuing, visualization, role playing, guided practice, performance feedback, reinforcement, and criterion testing were the instructional strategies utilized. During the monitoring phase, student and employer job performance reports were used to identify potential problems for group problem-solving sessions. Results indicated that students acquired the targeted skills. However, generalization to and maintenance within the work environment were not demonstrated.

Several other early studies of the effects of social skills training programs on work-related social skills demonstrated that individuals with mental retardation could acquire targeted social skills but failed to report or demonstrate gener-

alization of these skills to integrated work settings (see Agran, Salzberg, & Stowitschek, 1987; Rusch et al., 1988; Wheeler et al., 1988; Agran et al., 1989). Problem-solving, or cognitive process strategies were then integrated into social skills training program to address problems with generalization and maintenance. Problem-solving strategies typically involve identifying a problem, stating a correct response from alternatives, acting on the response, and evaluating the effects of the response. Cognitive process strategies involve a generative process also intended to increase generalization of the targeted behaviors. Common components of the cognitive processes are (a) formulation of goals for social interaction, (b) interpreting salient cues, (c) deciding on overt behaviors that are appropriate in the given social situation, (d) performing the behavior, and (e) evaluating the behavior (Collet-Klingenberg & Chadsey-Rusch, 1991).

Park and Gaylord-Ross (1989) combined a traditional social skills training program with problem-solving skills to improve the social skills of three adults with mental retardation. Although role playing, verbal praise, modeling, and corrective feedback resulted in acquisition of skills, problem-solving skills were necessary for participants to demonstrate generalization and maintenance of skills.

Clement-Heist, Siegel, and Gaylord-Ross (1992) examined the effects of a social skills training package on the social skills of four high school students with learning disabilities. Targeted skills included ordering job duties, giving instructions, and conversation. Both classroom and workplace training was conducted. Classroom training occurred with a group of eight to twelve students. Weekly sessions were 2½ hours long and lasted for a semester. Training included a rationale, self-reflection, definition, self-evaluation, modeling, both correct and incorrect behaviors, role playing, and feedback. Students were also instructed to self-evaluate their performance of the skills at work. If students failed to demonstrate a target skill, further training occurred at work. Instruction included a rationale, role playing with the trainer, feedback, and targeted practice with a co-worker. Classroom instruction resulted in students generalizing eight of twelve total skills (three per four students) to the work setting. Additional in situ training resulted in generalization of four to six behaviors. Maintenance was not discussed.

Misra (1992) utilized a self-monitoring program to promote generalization and maintenance of the social skills of three adults with mild mental retardation. Target behaviors included interacting with customers (Participant 1), asking questions (Participant 2), and topic repetition (Participant 3). Individual social skills training was conducted in 10- to 20-minute sessions, four times per week. Training procedures included instruction, modeling, behavior rehearsal, feedback, prompting, and social reinforcement. The self-monitoring phase included a rationale for self-recording behavior and utilized the same training procedures as the social skills training phase. Counters were used for self-recording in generalization settings. The social skills training phase resulted in the demonstration of skills in analogue training settings. Generalization to natural settings did not occur until after the implementation of the self-monitoring training. Maintenance of skills varied among participants.

Collet-Klingenberg and Chadsey-Rusch (1991) utilized cognitive process strategies to teach three students with moderate mental retardation to respond appropriately to both personal and work-related criticism. Four processing rules were taught during 30-minute sessions, three times a week, using modeling, rehearsal, and feedback. The cognitive process included social decoding, social decision skills, social performance, and social evaluation. Two of the three students learned the strategy and generalized it to untrained scenarios in analogue settings; they did not, however, demonstrate generalization to natural work settings.

Recently, investigators have utilized recorded interactions as guides for training and self-evaluation. For example, Grossi, Kimball, and Heward (1994) used tape-recorded interactions to increase the frequency with which two workers with mild mental retardation acknowledged verbal initiations from co-workers. Types of initiations included direction, question, corrective feedback, praise, and social initiation. Both appropriate and inappropriate interactions were audiotaped and used for training. Training included a rationale for acknowledging co-worker initiations, self-evaluation of tape-recorded interactions, positive verbal feedback, corrective feedback, and role play. Tape review sessions occurred prior to the beginning of a work shift. For one participant, the audiotape review was augmented with graphic feedback of his interactions from his previous work shift. Results indicated that both participants increased their levels of acknowledgments and maintained levels equal to those of their co-workers 4 to 8 weeks later.

In two studies, Morgan and Salzberg (1992) utilized video-assisted training to improve the social skills of adults with severe mental retardation. In Study 1, the target skill was requesting assistance from a work supervisor. Based on input from the supervisor, sixteen potential problem situations were selected for training. For each problem, a correct and incorrect video scene was developed. Participants were asked to review the scene, identify the problem, identify the worker's response to the problem, and determine what else the worker should have done. Generalization to the work environment was assessed by manipulating tasks so that the participant would encounter each of the sixteen problems and have to act on them. All three participants were able to correctly identify problems and responses on video, but two of them were unable to demonstrate generalization to the work environment until they received behavioral training. Those two participants took part in a second study, in which the target behavior was responding to work problems. Four work problems were developed. Correct responses included identifying the problem, fixing it, and reporting it to the supervisor. Video training and work assessment was conducted similarly to that of the first study. Interventions included video-assisted training and video-assisted training combined with behavioral rehearsal. Results showed that after rehearsing responses to one or two of the identified problems, participants were able to learn responses to remaining problems with only video-assisted training. However, they did not demonstrate generalization to untrained work problems.

Peer (Co-Worker) Interventions. Using co-workers to support employees with disabilities is not a new concept. Indeed, there is a significant research and theoretical literature base on the various roles co-workers may assume when working with employees with disabilities (see Nisbet & Hagner, 1988; Rusch & Minch, 1988; Chadsey-Rusch & Heal, 1995). Identified co-worker roles in supported employment include advocating, associating, befriending, collecting data, evaluating, and training (Rusch et al., 1989). Of course, associating and befriending, both involving social interactions with a supported employee, are directly related to social integration. However, all of the other identified roles could be involved in social integration interventions.

Unfortunately, few studies have examined the efficacy of co-worker interventions targeted specifically toward social integration. Several studies examined the use of a co-worker advocate in comparison to or in combination with a social skills training program or a contextual intervention. These studies will be examined later in the section "Combination Interventions."

Contextual Interventions. Contextual interventions involve manipulating or accessing environments so as to facilitate greater opportunity for social interactions. For example, one might negotiate a schedule change with an employer so that an employee can take a break at the same time as co-workers with whom he or she has similar interests; an employee might change his or her work station to be nearer other employees during work periods; or one might prompt the employee to enter through the same door as other employees at the beginning of the shift.

As with interventions that involve co-workers, the use of naturally occurring contexts in a work environment is not a new concept. Most recently, the ideas have appeared in literature on natural supports (see Rusch & Hughes, 1990; Nisbet, 1992; Hagner & DiLeo, 1993). Again, however, research demonstrating the efficacy of such procedures in promoting social integration is lacking. Research does suggest, however, that integration (or interaction) opportunities do vary in differing contexts. For example, Chadsey, Linneman, Rusch, and Cimera (in press) observed that the presence of a job coach dampened actual opportunities for workers with severe disabilities to interact with their co-workers. Mank and Cioffi (1996) reported that initial findings of a study of 462 supported employees in the United States and 448 in other countries. This study indicated that employees with disabilities who were better integrated were those who worked more hours and had work roles and initial orientation and training similar to co-workers without disabilities. All of these findings suggest that we need further research on effective contextual strategies for promoting social integration.

Combination Interventions. Several studies have examined the effectiveness of intervention packages that consist of more than one type of intervention strategy. Park and colleagues (1991) examined the effects of both a social skills training program and a co-worker advocacy program on the social skills of adults with mild disabilities. Targeted behaviors varied among five participants and included both task and nontask skills. Social skills training consisted of 20- to 30-minute sessions occurring once or twice a week for 6 weeks. A self-management approach that included seven problem-solving rules was utilized. Training consisted of instruction, modeling, pre- and posttests, and practice. The co-worker advocate program involved 6 weeks of 20-minute weekly meetings between the primary investigator and a co-worker advocate. Meetings involved problem identification, generation of possible solutions, and selection of a strategy to promote social inclusion. The advocate implemented the agreed-upon strategies between sessions. Results indicate that the social skills training was more effective than the co-worker advocate program in increasing social interactions.

Gaylord-Ross and colleagues (1995) also compared the effects of a social skills training package with a co-worker intervention package. Two individuals who were both deaf and blind and had severe mental retardation participated in the study. This particular social skills training package involved active co-worker participation. Sessions lasted 5 to 10 minutes and occurred three to six times per week for 6 weeks. Training included role play, co-worker training, antecedent physical guidance, practice, corrective feedback, and positive reinforcement. The co-worker advocate phase consisted of six 20- to 30-minute sessions between the advocate and trainer. Advocates generated and implemented strategies designed to integrate the participant. Both training programs resulted in increased social interactions with co-workers for both trained and untrained interactions. The measurable effects of the co-worker advocate program were less noticeable than those of the social skills training program.

Chadsey and colleagues (in press) examined the effects of both a co-worker advocacy program and a contextual intervention program. The procedures for the co-worker advocacy program were similar to those used by Gaylord-Ross and colleagues (1995) and Park and colleagues (1991); however, multiple co-workers were involved. The contextual interventions were developed through a discrepancy analysis between (a) co-workers' involvement with the work culture, as described through co-worker interviews, job coach interviews, and observation; and (b) the supported employee's involvement in the culture, as described through a job coach interview and observation. Discrepancies

were reviewed to determine if contextual changes to bridge the differences might increase opportunities for interactions. Neither the contextual or the co-worker interventions, nor a combination of the two, had an effect on the overall frequency of interactions; however, the frequency of nontask interactions did increase. For example, for participants involved in co-worker intervention, scores on the *Co-worker Involvement Index* (Rusch et al., 1989) increased, indicating some change in the interactions between supported employees and their co-workers.

Summary. The majority of intervention studies have focused on changing the social skills of employees with mental retardation. Although these employees have learned skills, generalization and maintenance of such skills have been limited and variable. In addition, the types of skills taught have been narrow in focus and primarily task-related. Although task-related social skills are worthwhile targets for instruction, they may do little to promote social relationships and inclusion among co-workers.

Fewer studies have used peer (co-worker) or contextual interventions, or a combination of the two, and when such studies have been conducted, the results have not always been successful. These strategies have not been extensively researched to date, so a decision regarding their effectiveness cannot be made at this time. It is difficult to state with any certainty which types of strategies or practices will have a positive impact on social inclusion in postsecondary school and employment settings. Nevertheless, the next section offers some recommendations for practice.

RECOMMENDED PRACTICES

Postsecondary Schools

Although not empirically tested, a number of recommendations for practice have been made, which may improve the social inclusion of students with disabilities in postsecondary settings.

The recommendations have been organized into the three categories used before: (1) individual interventions, or those interventions designed to change the student with the disability; (2) peer interventions, interventions intended to change others; and (3) contextual interventions, those designed to change the environment or social activity arrangements. These recommended practices are listed in Tables 17.1, 17.2, and 17.3, respectively, accompanied by the source for each recommendation.

In addition to the practices recommended in Tables 17.1, 17.2, and 17.3, Fichten and colleagues (1990) discussed a number of practices that students with disabilities and professors could engage in to enhance the social functioning in classrooms. Table 17.4, which comes directly from Fichten and colleague's (1990) work, includes recommendations made by outstanding professors (who were nominated by students with disabilities) about what students

could do to facilitate the teaching-learning process; these recommendations would be considered a type of individual intervention. Table 17.5 consists of recommendations made by students about what professors could do to facilitate the teaching-learning process; these interventions would be considered a type of peer intervention, because they involve a change in someone else's behavior (i.e., professor) rather than a change in the behavior of students with disabilities.

In order for many of these recommended practices to be carried out successfully, supports and services need to be established on campuses, as discussed in Chapter 16 on postsecondary education. In particular, when students with disabilities have been asked about the kind of supports they needed, personal counseling or personal attention from someone occurs high on the list (Greenbaum et al., 1995; Getzel & Kregel, 1996). Siperstein (1988) and Vogel and

Table 17.1 Recommended Practices for Enhancing the Social Inclusion of Youths with Disabilities in Postsecondary Settings Through Individual Interventions[a]

Recommended Practice	Source
1. Teach students to be aware of their strengths and weaknesses in social areas.	de Fur, Getzel, & Trossi, 1996
2. Teach students how to discuss their accommodation needs with faculty.	de Fur et al., 1996
3. Teach students how to accept their disability and discuss it with others.	Yuker, 1988; Gerber, Livneh & Sherwood, 1991; Ginsbery, & Reiff, 1992; Gilson, 1996
4. Teach students personal social skills.	Getzel & Kregel, 1996
5. Teach students assertiveness skills, self-image, and stress management skills.	Siperstein, 1988
6. Allow students to choose the social behaviors they want to learn.	Siperstein, 1988
7. Teach students how to establish goals, make decisions, and move ahead.	Gerber et al., 1992; Greenbaum, Graham, & Scales, 1995
8. Teach students to be persistent but adaptable.	Gerber et al., 1992
9. Teach dating skills.	Fichten et al., 1991
10. Teach students how to communicate effectively	Yuker, 1988
11. Teach students how to demonstrate that they are more similar than different in attitudes and values to students without disabilities.	Fichten, 1988

[a]See other types of individual interventions in Table 17.4.

Table 17.2 Recommended Practices for Enhancing the Social Inclusion of Youths with Disabilities in Postsecondary Settings Through Peer Interventions[a]

Recommended Practice	Source
1. Teach others to focus on students' abilities rather than disabilities.	Yukor, 1988
2. Show how students with disabilities are similar, competent, and have as many positive characteristics as do students without disabilities.	Yukor, 1988
3. Teach others about the disability culture.	Brown & Foster, 1991
4. Involve students without disabilities in extended equal-status activities with students with disabilities.	Fichten, 1988; Yukor, 1988

[a]See other types of peer interventions in Table 17.5.

Forness (1992) noted that group counseling might be particularly effective because it allows students with disabilities to practice a number of social skills with peers in a structured and protected environment. However, Vogel and Farness (1992) warned that counselors needed to be familiar with the characteristics of the students (i.e., learning disabled) with whom they were working.

Greenbaum and colleagues (1995) and Getzel and Kregel (1996) also reported that students desired support groups or clubs for themselves. Although the establishment of groups or clubs that are designed to serve only disability groups seems exclusionary, it is possible that such groups will serve to enhance self-esteem and confidence so that students feel more comfortable attending mainstream activities.

Siperstein (1988) offered the idea of creating "Social Functioning Workshops" where students with and without disabilities worked on a variety of social skills together. Because it is likely that many students on campus have social skill deficits and are lonely (Cutrona, 1982), the creation of a group advertised to help all students improve their social lives might be successful.

The use of many of these recommended practices is exemplified in Case Study 1 featuring a young woman who experienced social inclusion in a university setting.

Table 17.3 Recommended Practices for Enhancing the Social Inclusion of Youths with Disabilities in Postsecondary Settings Through Contextual Interventions

Recommended Practice	Source
1. Have students with and without disabilities involved in activities that require cooperation, reciprocity, and positive consequences.	Yukor, 1988
2. Provide opportunities for students with and without disabilities to live in the same residential units, but do not have the units designated as ones being for people with disabilities.	Foster & DeCaro, 1991
3. Make certain that all campus activities (i.e., sporting events, concerts) are accessible and available to all students.	Foster & DeCaro, 1991; Gilson, 1996
4. Provide opportunities for interactions between students with and without disabilities, but make the interactions secondary to the activity.	Brown & Foster, 1991

Table 17.4 Recommendations by Outstanding Professors About What Students Could Do to Facilitate the Teaching-Learning Process

1. Approach the professor to discuss course issues—do this after class (46%) or make an appointment (4%).
2. Inform the professor about the nature of the disability (14%) and discuss how the disability is likely to affect performance and learning in the course (25%).
3. Talk to the professor early during the semester, before problems become serious (23%). Do not wait until there is a panic situation or until it is too late to solve the problem (5%).
4. Tell the professor the specific nature of any problems experienced and discuss possible solutions (e.g., extra time for exams, audiotaping needs) (16%).
5. Let the professor know what you can do (7%) and what you cannot do (7%).
6. Propose solutions to problems. Tell professors what has worked for you in the past—do not leave them guessing or trying to come up with solutions that may be ineffective (5%).
7. If you can handle problems by yourself, do so (9%). But do not fail to request assistance when you need it (9%).
8. Do not use the disability as an excuse (9%).

Source: Fichten, C. S., Goodnik, G., Tagalakis, V., Ansel, R., & Libman, E. (1990). Getting along in college: Recommendations for college students with disabilities and their professors. *Rehabilitation Counseling Bulletin, 34*(2), 103–125. Reprinted by permission.

Note: (%) = % of the fifty-seven professors who made this recommendation.

Employment Settings

Several practices have been recommended for improving the social inclusion of workers with disabilities. As is the case with recommendations for postsecondary settings, many of these recommendations have not been empirically tested. Again, three categories of recommended practices are (1) individual interventions, (2) peer interventions, and (3) contextual interventions. A listing of these recommended practices in these areas are included in Tables 17.6, 17.7, and 17.8, respectively.

As illustrated in Tables 17.6 and 17.7, Chadsey-Rusch and Heal (1995) identified several of the recommended practices for individual and peer interventions, all of them validated by a national sample of experts in the field of transition. Several of the individual interventions correspond to critical employer-identified social skills discussed previously in this chapter. Other practices identified in the literature are also included.

Recommended practices for contextual interventions are drawn primarily from natural supports theory and the literature. Many of these interventions rely on work done during job development to negotiate schedules, activities, or job designs that facilitate greater opportunities for social interactions with co-workers. These efforts often require indepth knowledge of the culture and dynamics of a workplace not often gained through traditional job analysis. Thus, Hagner and DiLeo (1993) recommended assessing workplace culture through observation and interviews.

The use of many of these recommended practices is exemplified in Case Study 2 of a young woman who experiences social inclusion in an employment setting.

Ecological and Matching Considerations

One thing that is evident from looking at the recommended practices for both work and postsecondary settings is that the majority of them involve changing the social behavior of the individual with the disability. This finding is not surprising because a historical model is still operating, which assumes that any deficits lie within the person with the disability, and that it is these deficits that need remediation. In many

Table 17.5 Recommendations by Students About What Professors Could Do to Facilitate the Teaching-Learning Process

1. Be an effective teacher to all students (e.g., make assignments clear, repeat lecture materials if you see puzzled looks, present up-to-date material, face the class while lecturing and speak loudly and clearly, write neatly on the board, be explicit in specifying material to be covered by students, encourage students to ask questions, show a sense of humor) (72%).

2. Let students know that you are available to meet with them—make it clear that you have the time (47%).

3. Talk to students about possible course concerns early during the term (3%) and encourage them to stay in touch (23%).

4. If the student has not approached you, approach the student to find out what accommodations would be helpful and to discuss what the student can and cannot do in terms of meeting course requirements (43%).

5. Do not delve into the student's medical history or inquire about his or her diagnosis. Stick to necessary information about the student's ability to function in your course (3%).

6. Do not discourage students from taking your course. If you foresee problems, discuss them but let students make their own decisions (36%).

7. If the student has a hearing or a speech impairment, be patient and take time to communicate effectively. Ask for repetition or clarification if you do not understand. In the case of a hearing-impaired student, if you are in doubt, check whether the student understood you (4%).

8. Make adjustments to allow the student an equal opportunity to learn course material (47%) and remember that identical treatment is not "equal" treatment (48%).

9. Encourage the student and comment on good work (21%).

10. Avoid embarrassing students by singling them out for special attention in class (4%).

11. Make adjustments in evaluating performance by giving students an equal opportunity to demonstrate that they have mastered the course material (31%). Do *not*, however, accept work of a lower quality from students with disabilities and do not give "unearned" marks by assigning a passing grade only because the student tried hard or because you feel sorry for him or her (3%).

12. Treat the student as you would all other students in situations where the disability is not an issue. Do not overcompensate by doing things for students with disabilities that they can and want to do on their own (33%).

Source: Fichten, C. S., Goodnik, G., Tagalakis, V., Ansel, R., & Libman, E. (1990). Getting along in college: Recommendations for college students with disabilities and their professors. *Rehabilitation Counseling Bulletin, 34*(2), 103–125. Reprinted by permission.

Note: (%) = % of the seventy-five students who made the recommendation.

cases, it is possible that the social behaviors of the person with the disability do need to be changed, and it is also possible that the person is motivated to work on these behaviors. However, even if individual social behaviors are changed, social inclusion may not be positively affected. Why?

Achieving social inclusion is a complex process. As mentioned in the beginning of the chapter, if an ecological framework is adopted, three intervention targets emerge: (1) the individual can be changed, (2) others in the environment can be changed, or (3) the envi-ronment can be changed. Sometimes, a change in one intervention target (e.g., the individual) is not powerful enough to affect change in the other areas. And sometimes, a change in one intervention target can actually result in unpleas-ant side effects in the other areas (Willems, 1977).

If one adopts an ecological framework (and we highly recommend this approach), it is important to monitor all ecological areas. But how does one decide what to change if social inclusion is not occurring? Unfortunately, we do not have a strategic blueprint to guide us. In

---

CASE STUDY 1   Successful Inclusion Practices: Postsecondary School Setting

During high school, Carol was a strong student but she had few friends in her small town. It wasn't that students were rude to her or made fun of her because she was in a wheelchair; they just pretty much ignored her. Although Carol enjoyed her academic subjects, she really loved music, particularly singing. Carol had a wonderful voice and loved singing in the chorus, but was very disappointed when she was not selected for the traveling chorus. Carol's choir teacher told Carol's mom that although she had a beautiful voice, she just didn't see how they could accommodate her on their out-of-town trips.

When Carol selected the university she wanted to attend, she picked one with a great music program. Among her other criteria was that it was barrier-free and offered a range of student services to both students with and without disabilities. In addition, the university had a strong student-run Christian youth group that was similar to the one Carol had joined the summer before she left for college.

Carol connected with the youth group the minute she arrived on campus. Immediately, she felt at ease because few of the other members of the group were the same—the group consisted of men and women from seven different ethnic groups! Although Carol was the only student with a disability, she did not feel like she was the only "different" person. As the group members introduced themselves, other members asked questions. One person asked Carol about her disability, and Carol readily explained it in matter-of-fact terms. All seemed to accept her explanation and told her that if she ever needed assistance with anything, to be sure to ask.

As Carol's semester proceeded, she grew confident and sure of herself. Two members of her youth group were also in her classes, and she developed a relationship with them. They often did things together—went to football games, attended concerts, and pulled "all-nighters" studying for tests.

Although Carol did not live in the same dorm as her friends, her residence assistant (RA) was instrumental in setting up opportunities for Carol to interact with other dorm residents. Prior to Carol coming to campus, her RA (who had experience with other students with disabilities) was specifically selected to work in Carol's dorm. The interaction opportunities set up by the RA were not designed just for Carol, but were nightly activities designed for all dorm members (e.g., popcorn and movie night). As a consequence of these opportunities, Carol developed a larger social circle of friends.

When Carol's sister (June) came to visit her, she was shocked by the change in Carol. She was also surprised to meet so many people who hung out with Carol and seemed to genuinely like her. When June asked about all these changes, Carol said that the diversity on campus, the acceptance and support by her youth group, and the university placement of her RA, who had had prior experience with students with disabilities, had all made a difference. People's acceptance of Carol made it easier to accept herself, and she now viewed her life as a series of opportunities rather than barriers.

---

many cases, one has to approach postsecondary and work environments from an ecological viewpoint and select the best intervention strategy that seems to match the needs of the setting. For example, consider the following scenario. Barb has worked in a hotel cleaning rooms for nearly a year, but has formed few social relationships with her co-workers. Although Barb is not very outgoing, she has indicated that she would like to spend more time socializing with co-workers. Barb's co-workers greet her and seem friendly, but they never spend time in an extended interaction with her.

Because Barb is not very outgoing, one idea might be to teach her different conversational topics she could initiate to her co-workers. Another idea might be to sit down with several of her co-workers and ask if they have any ideas on how best to include Barb. A third idea might be to rearrange Barb's schedule to make sure all her breaks and lunch times coincide with those of her co-workers so she would have several

Table 17.6 Recommended Practices for Enhancing the Social Inclusion of Youths with Disabilities in Employment Settings Through Individual Interventions

Recommended Practice	Source
1. Target social skills appropriate for specific work environments.	Chadsey-Rusch, 1986; Nisbet & Hagner, 1988
2. Use a multicomponent teaching package to teach social skills, including modeling, role playing, and feedback.	Chadsey-Rusch, 1986; Storey & Lengyel, 1992
3. Teach the employee to initiate work-related social skills (e.g., asking for assistance, offering assistance, providing information, asking questions).	Salzberg, Agran, & Lignugaris/Kraft 1986; Salzberg et al., 1987; Johnson, Greenwood, & Schriner, 1988; Minskoff & DeMoss, 1994;
4. Teach the employee to respond to work-related social skills (e.g., responding to criticism, answering questions).	Salzberg et al., 1986; 1987; Johnson et al., 1988; Minskoff & DeMoss, 1994; Chadsey-Rusch & Heal, 1995.
5. Teach the employee to initiate nonwork-related social skills (e.g., greetings, teasing and joking, asking questions, social amenities).	Salzberg et al., 1987; Johnson et. al., 1988; Chadsey-Rusch & Heal, 1995
6. Teach the employee to respond to nonwork-related initiations from others (e.g., greetings, answering questions).	Salzberg et al., 1987; Johnson et al., 1988; Chadsey-Rusch & Heal, 1995
7. Teach the employee conversational skills.	Chadsey-Rusch & Heal, 1995
8. Teach the employee self-determination skills.	Chadsey-Rusch & Heal, 1995
9. Teach the employee to read and respond appropriately to social cues.	Chadsey-Rusch & Heal, 1995

opportunities throughout the day for interactions.

The intervention that was tried was the following: Barb's employment specialist met with two co-workers who seemed particularly friendly to Barb and asked for their ideas on how Barb could be more included at work. The reason the employment specialist decided to start with this intervention was that she knew it was very difficult for Barb to initiate topics of conversation, but once someone talked to Barb, she could maintain a conversation for several minutes.

Table 17.7 Recommended Practices for Enhancing the Social Inclusion of Youths with Disabilities in Employment Settings Through Peer Interventions

Recommended Practice	Source
1. Ask co-workers or supervisor to initiate or respond to social interactions with the employee.	Chadsey-Rusch & Heal, 1995
2. Teach co-workers or supervisors to implement a social skills training program.	Chadsey-Rusch & Heal, 1995
3. Ask co-workers or supervisor to be the employee's advocate.	Chadsey-Rusch & Heal, 1995
4. Ask several co-workers to develop a social integration plan for the employee.	Chadsey-Rusch & Heal, 1995
5. Ask a co-worker with similar interests as the employee to do things with the employee outside of work.	Hagner, Rogan, & Murphy, 1992; Chadsey-Rusch & Heal, 1995

Table 17.8 Recommended Practices for Enhancing the Social Inclusion of Youths with Disabilities in Employment Settings Through Contextual Interventions

Recommended Practice	Source
1. Target jobs that are shared positions or similar positions as those held by co-workers.	Nisbet & Hagner, 1988; Hagner et al., 1992
2. Build overlapping or intersecting tasks into a job.	Hagner et al., 1992
3. Develop work schedules and routines that involve social times.	Hagner et al., 1992
4. Utilize co-worker mentors as trainers for new employees.	Nisbet & Hagner, 1988; Hagner et al., 1992
5. Identify common interests between the employee and co-workers.	Hagner et al., 1992; Hagner & DiLeo, 1993
6. Use knowledge of the work culture to create opportunities for social interactions.	Hagner & DiLeo, 1993
7. Limit the presence of a job coach.	Chadsey, Linneman, Rusch, & Cimera (In press)

Thus, the first sensible "match" seemed to be to start with changing the co-workers. Interestingly, when the employment specialist talked to the co-workers, they mentioned that they knew very little about Barb and her interests, and that it would be helpful for them to know more about her so they could initiate topics of conversation with her. Ideas were exchanged, and the employment specialist then talked to Barb to let her know that when her co-workers initiated conversations with her, it was very important for her to respond and show an interest in them. The employment specialist and Barb practiced this idea several times so Barb would be sure to know what to do. The employment specialist did this work with Barb because she wanted to make sure that Barb would respond to her co-workers if they initiated conversations to her. The employment specialist was taking an ecological approach and wanted to make sure that negative side effects did not occur (i.e., Barb not responding); also, the intervention was "matched" to Barb because she was more adept at maintaining conversations than initiating them, but she did require a little practice.

The employment specialist also rearranged Barb's work schedule so that her afternoon break coincided with that of the two co-workers who said they would like to get to know Barb better. This third part of the intervention was also "matched" to the setting because it allowed Barb and her co-workers one more opportunity to get to know one another.

In the scenario just described, several changes had to be made, but they all seemed to fit the needs of the setting. In some settings, it is possible that only one change will be needed to make a difference in social inclusion. The important point to remember is that multiple interventions may need to be tried, that interventions need to be matched to the setting, and that all need to be carefully monitored. The selection of the initial intervention strategy (or strategies) may depend on which aspect of the context seems to be contributing the most to the occurrence of the social problem. To be able to determine this cause, those in charge of designing interventions must be good observers and be sensitive to the nuances of the social culture. Interventionists need to study the behaviors of the target person, others in the setting, and the cultural milieu of the context. At the present time, an ecological approach seems to be the best practice to use to increase the social inclusion of youths with disabilities into work and postsecondary settings.

CASE STUDY 2   Successful Inclusion Practices: Employment Setting

At the age of 20, Angie had one more year of high school services. She was looking for a part-time position to complete the vocational component of her high school curriculum. Angie had held several short-term jobs in the past, including housekeeping, filing, fast-food work, and laundry. Her favorite positions in terms of job tasks had been in the fast-food restaurants, where she did a lot of food preparation. Unfortunately, Angie disliked her two previous fast-food jobs because of the people with whom she worked. She found them to be crude and a bit too fast-paced for her.

Angie and her job developer worked with a group of supportive individuals to help her find a new job. The group decided to continue to look at restaurants but to try to find one that was a bit calmer than most fast-food restaurants. Working with people her own age and having opportunities to do "cool" things with her co-workers were important to Angie. One of Angie's group members knew the owner of a small bar and grill and agreed to introduce Angie's job developer to the owner.

Angie's job developer, Suzan, met with the owner at the bar and grill. Suzan immediately noticed that most of the workers were in their early 20's and seemed to get along quite well. They talked frequently while completing their work, but they typically kept their conversations "clean." Suzan talked briefly with two of the waitresses about the restaurant and the people who worked there. She also spoke with Janice, an elderly woman who worked in the back and with whom Angie would have the most continuous contact if she were to be hired. While talking with Janice in the back, Suzan noticed that the other younger members of the staff made frequent quick trips to the back to drop off dirty dishes or just relax for a moment. Suzan felt positive about the restaurant's environment and the opportunities that Angie would have to interact with co-workers.

Two days later, Angie was interviewed and hired. She would be working in the back, prepping food for the salad bar and maintaining the salad bar during moderately busy shifts. Suzan worked with the owner and Janice to develop a training program for Angie; Janice had primary responsibility for training Janice. It was agreed that Suzan's presence at the restaurant would be minimum, but that she would be available to assist when new support or training needs arose.

Angie and her group members had concerns about Angie interacting appropriately with her co-workers. In the past, she had frequent angry outbursts, had thrown things at co-workers, and had insulted co-workers. Suzan intervened at the restaurant prior to Angie's first day. She met with co-workers and explained what types of comments tend to set Angie off and taught them how to redirect her if she did have an outburst. Suzan also took this opportunity to share some of Angie's interests with her co-workers.

Angie was thrilled with her first 2 weeks at the restaurant. She liked her job, the atmosphere, and her co-workers. However, after 2 weeks, she began to feel depressed. She felt that, although people were nice to her at work, they didn't include her in their activities outside of work. Angie expressed these concerns to Suzan, who met with Janice to discuss them. Janice, who was much older than the other workers, was also typically excluded from outside activities, but for her, it was by choice. She felt that the younger workers might feel that she was "responsible" for Angie. Janice agreed to talk to some of the other workers and suggest that they begin including Angie in outside activities. She also suggested that Angie spend some time having a soda after her shift to give her more opportunities to talk with her co-workers.

Within a week, Angie was invited to join her co-workers for a movie. Soon after, she was a regular member of the group and felt comfortable offering suggestions for group activities. Angie even continues her friendship with one waitress who left the restaurant several months ago!

QUESTIONS

1. What is meant by the term "ecological per-spective"?

2. Describe the types of social problems experi-enced by youths with disabilities in postsec-ondary educational settings.

3. What have been some of the concerns profes-sors have expressed about students with disabilities?

4. How do college students without disabilities feel about college students with disabilities?

5. Describe the social skill differences between employees with and without disabilities.

6. Describe the three types of interventions that could have a positive impact on the social relations, interactions, or skills of individuals with disabilities.

7. What kinds of social skills do employers value the most and what kinds of skills do they value the least in their employees? Are the least valued skills unimportant? Why or why not?

8. Describe the type of intervention that has been used the most in employment settings with employees with disabilities.

9. Describe three intervention strategies that professors could use to increase the social inclusion of students with disabilities in college classrooms.

10. What is meant by the phrase "ecological and matching considerations"?

REFERENCES

Agran, M., Fodor-Davis, J., Moore, S., & Deer, M. (1989). The application of a self-management program on instruction-following skills. *Journal of the Association for Persons with Severe Handicaps, 14,* 147–154.

Agran, M., Salzberg, C. L., & Stowitscheck, J. J. (1987). An analysis of the effects of a social skills training program using self-instruction on the acquisition and generalization of two social behaviors in a work setting. *Journal of the Association for Persons with Severe Handicaps, 12,* 131–139.

Ansel, R., & Fichten, C. S. (1990). Interaction between disabled and nondisabled college students and their professors: A comparison. *Journal of Postsecondary Education and Disability, 8,* 125–140.

Aune, E. (1991). A transition model for postsecondary-bound students with learning disabilities. *Learning Disabilities Research and Practice, 6,* 177–187.

Baggett, D., & Silver, P. G. (1992). *A study of faculty awareness of students with disabilities.* Amherst: University of Massachusetts, Center for Counseling and Academic Development.

Barber, D., & Hupp, S. C. (1993). A comparison of friendship patterns of individuals with develop-mental disabilities. *Education and Training in Mental Retardation, 28,* 13–22.

Barker, R. G. (1968). *Ecological psychology.* Stanford, CA: Stanford University Press.

Belcher, R. G., & Smith, M. D. (1994). Coworker attitudes toward employee with autism. *Journal of Vocational Rehabilitation, 4,* 29–36.

Bender, W. N., & Wall, M. E. (1994). Social-emotional development of students with learning disabilities. *Learning Disability Quarterly, 17,* 323–341.

Benshoff, J. J., Fried, J. H., & Roberto, K. A. (1990). Developmental skill attainment among college students with disabilities. *Rehabilitation Counseling Bulletin, 34,* 44–52.

Brinkerhoff, L. C., Shaw, S. F., & McGuire, J. M. (1993). *Promoting postsecondary education for students with learning disabilities.* Austin, TX: PRO-ED.

Brown, P. M., & Foster, S. B. (1991). Integrating hearing and deaf students on a college campus. *American Annals of the Deaf, 136,* 21–27.

Butterworth, J., & Strauch, D. (1994). The relationship between social competence and success in the com-petitive workplace for persons with mental retarda-tion. *Education and Training in Mental Retardation and Developmental Disabilities, 29,* 118–133.

Chadsey, J. G., Linneman, D., Rusch, F. R., & Cimera, R. (In press). The impact of social integration interven-tions and job coaches in work settings. *Education and training in mental retardation and developmental disabilities.*

Chadsey-Rusch, J. (1986). Identifying and teaching valued social behaviors in competitive employment settings. In F. R. Rusch (Ed.), *Competitive employ-ment: Issues and strategies* (pp. 273–287). Baltimore: Paul H. Brookes.

———. (1992). Toward defining and measuring social skills in employment settings. *American Journal on Mental Retardation, 96,* 405–418.

Chadsey-Rusch, J., & Gonzalez, P. (1988). Social ecology of the workplace: Employers' perceptions versus direct observation. *Research in Developmental Disabilities, 9*, 229–245.

Chadsey-Rusch, J., Gonzalez, P., Tines, J., & Johnson, J. (1989). Social ecology of the workplace: Contextual variables affecting social interactions of employees with and without mental retardation. *American Journal on Mental Retardation, 94*, 141–151.

Chadsey-Rusch, J., & Heal, L. (1995). Building consensus from transition experts on social integration outcomes and interventions. *Exceptional Children,* 165–187.

Chadsey-Rusch, J., & O'Reilly, M. (1992). Social integration in employment and postsecondary educational settings: Outcome and process variables. In F. R. Rusch, L. DeStefano, J. Chadsey-Rusch, A. Phelps, & E. Symanski (Eds.), *Transition from school to adult life: Models, linkages, and policy* (pp. 5–15). Sycamore, IL: Sycamore.

Chadsey-Rusch, J., & Rusch, F. R. (1988). The ecology of the workplace. In R. Gaylord-Ross (Ed.), *Vocational education for persons with special needs.* Palo Alto, CA: Mayfield.

Clement-Heist, K., Siegel, S., & Gaylord-Ross, R. (1992). Simulated and in situ vocational social skills training for youths with learning disabilities. *Exceptional Children, 58*, 336–345.

Collet-Klingenberg, L., & Chadsey-Rusch, J. (1991). Using a cognitive-process approach to teach social skills. *Education and Training in Mental Retardation, 26*, 258–270.

Cutrona, C. E. (1982). Transition to college: Loneliness and the process of social adjustment. In L. A. Peplau & D. Perlman (Eds.), *Loneliness: A sourcebook of current theory research, and therapy* (pp. 291–309). New York: John Wiley.

de Fur, S. H., Getzel, E. E., & Trossi, K. (1996). Making the postsecondary education match: A role for transition on planning. *Journal of Vocational Rehabilitation, 6*(3), 231–241.

Ferguson, B., McDonnell, J., & Drew, C. (1993). Type and frequency of social interaction among workers with and without mental retardation. *American Journal on Mental Retardation, 97*, 530–540.

Fichten, C. (1988). Students with physical disabilities in higher education: Attitudes and beliefs that affect integration. In H. Yuker (Ed.), *Attitudes toward persons with disabilities* (pp. 171–186). New York: Springer.

Fichten, C. S. & Ansel, R. (1986). Trait attributions about college students with a physical disability: Circumplex analyses and methodological issues. *Journal of Applied Psychology, 16*(5), 410–427.

———. (1988). Thoughts concerning interaction between college students who have a physical disability and their nondisabled peers. *Rehabilitation Counseling Bulletin, 32*, 23–40.

Fichten, C. S., Goodrick, G., Ansel, R., & McKenzie, S. W. (1991). Reactions toward dating peers with visual impairments. *Rehabilitation Psychology, 36*(3), 163–179.

Fichten, C. S., Goodrick, G., Tagalakis, V., Ansel, R., & Libman, E. (1990). Getting along in college: Recommendations for college students with disabilities and their professors. *Rehabilitation Counseling Bulletin, 34*(2), 103–125.

Fichten, C. S., Robillard, K., Judd, D., & Ansel, R. (1989a). College students with physical disabilities: Myths and realities. *Rehabilitation Psychology, 34*(4), 243–257.

Fichten, C. S., Robillard, K., Tagalakis, V., & Ansel, R. (1991). Casual interaction between college students with various disabilities and their nondisabled peers: The internal dialogue. *Rehabilitation Psychology, 36*(1), 3–20.

Fichten, C. S., Tagalakis, V., & Ansel, R. (1989b). Effects of cognitive modeling, affect, and contact on attitudes, thoughts, and feelings toward college students with physical disabilities. *Journal of the Multihandicapped Person, 2*(2), 119–137.

Foster, S. B., & DeCaro, P. M. (1991). An ecological model of social interaction between deaf and hearing students within a postsecondary educational setting. *Disability, Handicap, and Society, 6*(37), 181–201.

Gambrill, E., Florian, V., & Splaver, G. (1986). Assertion, loneliness, and perceived control among students with and without physical disabilities. *Rehabilitation Counseling Bulletin,* 4–12.

Gaylord-Ross, R., Park, Hyun-Sook P., Johnston, S., Lee, M., & Goetz, L. (1995). Individual social skills training and co-worker training for supported employees with dual sensory impairment: Two case examples. *Behavior Modification, 19*, 78–94.

Gerber, P. J., Ginsberg, R., & Reiff, H. B. (1992). Identifying alterable patterns in employment success for highly successful adults with learning disabilities. *Journal of Learning Disabilities, 25*(8), 475–487.

Getzel, E. E., & Kregel, J. (1996). Transitioning from the academic to the employment setting: The employment connection. *Journal of Vocational Rehabilitation, 6*(3), 273–287.

Gilson, S. F. (1996). Students with disabilities: An increasing voice and presence on college campuses. *Journal of Vocational Rehabilitation, 6*(3), 263–272.

Greenbaum, B., Graham, S., & Scales, W. (1995). Adults with learning disabilities: Education and social experiences during college. *Exceptional Children, 61*(5), 460–471.

Greenspan, S., & Schoultz, B. (1981). Why mentally retarded adults lose their jobs. Social competence as a factor in work adjustment. *Applied Research in Mental Retardation, 2*(1), 23–38.

Grossi, T. A., Kimball, J. W., & Heward, W. L. (1994). "What did you say?" Using review of tape-recorded interactions to increase social acknowledgements by trainees in a community based vocational program. *Research in Developmental Disabilities, 15,* 457–472.

Hagner, D., & DiLeo, D. (1993). *Working together: Workplace culture, supported employment, and persons with disabilities.* Cambridge, MA: Brookline Books.

Hagner, D., Rogan, P., & Murphy, S. (1992). Facilitating natural supports in the workplace: Strategies for support consultants. *Journal of Rehabilitation, 58,* 29–34.

Halpern, A. S. (1985). Transition: A look at the foundations. Exceptional Children, 51, 479-502.

———. (1993). Quality of life as a conceptual framework for evaluating transition outcomes. *Exceptional Children, 59,* 486–498.

Houck, C., Engelhard, J., & Geller, C. (1989). Self-assessment of learning disabled and nondisabled college students: A comparative study. *Learning Disabilities Research, 5*(1), 61–67.

Hughes, C., Hwang, B., Kim, J., Eisenman, L. T., & Killian, D. J. (1995). Quality of life in applied research: A review and analysis of empirical measures. *American Journal on Mental Retardation, 99,* 623–641.

Johnson, V. A., Greenwood, R., & Schriner, F. (1988). Work performance and work personality: Employer concerns about workers with disabilities. *Rehabilitation Counseling Bulletin, 32,* 50–57.

Kirmeyer, S. L. (1988). Observed communication in the workplace: Content, source, and direction. *Journal of Community Psychology, 16,* 175–187.

Lignugaris/Kraft, B., Rule, S., Salzberg, C. L., & Stowitschek, J. J. (1986). Social interpersonal skills of handicapped and nonhandicapped adults at work. *Journal of Employment Counseling, 23,* 20–30.

Lignugaris/Kraft, B., Salzberg, C. L., Rule, S., & Stowitschek, J. J. (1988). Social-vocational skills of workers with and without mental retardation in two community employment sites. *Mental Retardation, 26,* 297–305.

Livneh, H., & Sherwood, A. (1991). Application of personality theories and counseling strategies to clients with physical disabilities. *Journal of Counseling and Development, 69,* 525–538.

Mangrum, C. T., & Strichart, S. S. (1984). *College and the learning disabled student.* New York: Grune & Stratton.

Mank, D., & Cioffi, A. (1996). *An analysis of companies and features of supported employees.* Paper presented at the Annual Conference of the Association for Persons in Supported Employment, New Orleans.

Marder, C. (1992). Education after secondary school. In M. Wagner, D. D'Amico, C. Marder, L. Newman, & J. Blackorby (Eds.), *What happens next? Trends in postschool outcomes of youth with disabilities. The second comprehensive report from the national longitudinal transition study of special education students* (pp. 3 –1 to 3-40). Menlo Park, CA: SRI International.

Mathews, P. R., Anderson, D. W., & Skolnick, B. D. (1987). Faculty attitude toward accommodations for college students with LD. *LD Focus, 3,* 46–52.

McBroom, L. W., Sikka, A., & Jones, L. B. (1994). *The transition to college for students with visual impairments—executive summary.* Mississippi State: Mississippi State University.

McNair, J., & Rusch, F. R. (1992). The co-worker involvement instrument: A measure of indigenous workplace support. *Career Development for Exceptional Individuals, 15,* 23–26.

Mellard, D. F., & Hazel, J. S. (1992). Social competencies as a pathway to successful life transitions. *Learning Disability Quarterly, 15,* 251–271.

Meyer, L. H. (1991). Advocacy, research, and typical practices. A care for the reduction of discrepancies between what is and what ought to be, and how to get there. In L. H. Meyer, C. A. Peck, & L. Brown (Eds.), *Critical issues in the lives of people with severe disabilities* (pp. 629–649). Baltimore: Paul H. Brookes.

Minskoff, E. H., & DeMoss, S. (1994). Workplace social skills and individuals with learning disabilities. *Journal of Vocational Rehabilitation, 4,* 113–121.

Misra, A. (1992). Generalization of social skills through self-monitoring by adults with mental retardation. *Exceptional Children, 58,* 495–507.

Montague, M. (1988). Job-related social skills training for adolescents with handicaps. *Career Development for Exceptional Individuals, 11,* 26–41.

Morgan, R. L., & Salzberg, C. L. (1992). Effects of video-assisted training on employment-related social skills of adults with severe mental retardation. *Journal of Applied Behavior Analysis, 25,* 365–383.

Murphy, J. S., & Newlon, B. J. (1987). Loneliness and the mainstreamed hearing impaired college student. *American Annals of the Deaf,* 21–25.

Myers, D. G., & Diener, E. (1995). Who is happy? *Psychological Science, 6,* 10–19.

Newton, J. S., Horner, R. H., Ard, W. R., LeBaron, N., & Sappington, G. (1994). A conceptual model for improving the social life of individuals with mental retardation. *Mental Retardation, 32,* 393–402.

Nisbet, J. (1992). *Natural supports in school, at work, and in the community for people with severe disabilities.* Baltimore: Paul H. Brookes.

Nisbet, J., & Hagner, D. (1988). Natural supports in the workplace: A reexamination of supported employment. Journal of the Association for Persons with Severe Handicaps, 13, 260–267.

Parent, W. S., Kregel, J., Metzler, H. M. D., & Twardzik, G. (1992). Social integration in the workplace: An analysis of the interaction activities of workers with mental retardation and their co-workers. *Education and Training in Mental Retardation, 27,* 28–38.

Park, H. S., & Gaylord-Ross, R. (1989). A problem-solving approach to social skill training in employment settings with mentally retarded youth. *Journal of Applied Behavior Analysis, 22,* 373–380.

Park, H. S., Simon, M., Tappe, P., Wozniak, T., Johnson, B., & Gaylord-Ross, R. (1991). Effects of a co-worker advocacy program and social skills training on the social interaction of employees with mild disabilities. *Journal of Vocational Rehabilitation, 1,* 73–90.

Rusch, F. R., & Hughes, C. (1990). Historical overview of supported employment. In F. R. Rusch (Ed.), *Supported employment: Models, methods, and issues.* Sycamore, IL: Sycamore.

Rusch, F. R., Hughes, C., McNair, J., & Wilson, P. G. (1989). *Co-worker involvement scoring manual and index.* Champaign: University of Illinois, Board of Trustees.

Rusch, F. R., McKee, M., Chadsey-Rusch, J., & Renzaglia, A. (1988). Teaching a student with severe handicaps to self-instruct: A brief report. *Education and Training in Mental Retardation, 23,* 51–58.

Rusch, F. R., & Minch, K. E. (1988). Identification of co-worker involvement in supported employment: A review and analysis. *Research in Developmental Disabilities, 9,* 247–254.

Rusch, F. R., Schutz, R. P., & Agran, M. (1982). Validating entry level survival skills for service occupations: Implications for curriculum development. *Journal of the Association for Persons with Severe Handicaps, 7,* 32–41.

Rusch, F. R., Wilson, P. G., Hughes, C., & Heal, L. W. (1995). Interactions of persons with severe mental retardation and their nondisabled co-workers in integrated work settings. *Behavior Modification, 19,* 59–77.

Russell, D., Peplau, L. A., & Cutrona, C. E. (1980). The revised *UCLA Loneliness Scale:* Concurrent and discriminant validity evidence. *Journal of Personality and Social Psychology, 39,* 472–480.

Salzberg, C. L., Agran, M., & Lignugaris/Kraft, B. (1986). Behaviors that contribute to entry-level employment: A profile of five jobs. *Applied Research in Mental Retardation, 7,* 299–314.

Salzberg, C. L., McConaughy, K., Lignugaris/Kraft, B., Agran, M., & Stowitscheck, J. J. (1987). Behaviors of distinction: The transition from acceptable to highly-valued worker. *Journal for Vocational Special Needs Education, 10,* 23–28.

Saracoglu, B., Minden, H., & Wilchesky, M. (1989). The adjustment of students with learning disabilities to university and its relationship to self-esteem and self-efficacy. *Journal of Learning Disabilities, 22,* 590–592.

Schoggen, P. (1978). Ecological psychology and mental retardation. In G. P. Sackett (Ed.), *Observing behavior. Vol. I: Theory and applications in mental retardation* (pp. 33–62). Baltimore: University Park Press.

Shafer, M. S., Rice, M. L., Metzler, M. D., & Haring, M. (1989). A survey of nondisabled employees' attitudes toward supported employees with mental retardation. *Journal of the Association for Persons with Severe Handicaps, 14,* 137–146.

Siperstein, G. N. (1988). Students with learning disabilities in college: The need for a programmatic approach to critical transitions. *Journal of Learning Disabilities, 21*(7), 431–435.

Storey, K. (1993). A proposal for assessing integration. *Education and Training in Mental Retardation, 28,* 279–287.

Storey, K., & Knutson, N. (1989). A comparative analysis of social interactions of handicapped and nonhandicapped workers in integrated work sites: A pilot study. *Education and Training in Mental Retardation, 24,* 265–273.

Storey, K., & Lengyel, L. (1992). Strategies for increasing interactions in supported employment settings: A review. *Journal of Vocational Rehabilitation, 2,* 46–57.

Storey, K., Rhodes, L., Sandow, D., Loewinger, H., & Petherbridge, R. (1991). Direct observation of social interactions in a supported employment setting. *Education and Training in Mental Retardation, 26,* 53–63.

Tappe, P., & Gaylord-Ross, R. (1990). Social support and transition coping. In R. Gaylord-Ross, S. Siegel, H. Park, S. Sacks, & L. Goetz (Eds.), *Readings in ecosocial development.* San Francisco: San Francisco State University.

Thurman, S. K. (1977). Congruence of behavioral ecologies: A model for special education. *Journal of Special Education, 11,* 329–333.

Vogel, S. A., & Forness, S. R. (1992). Social functioning in adults with learning disabilities. *School Psychology Review, 21*(3), 375–386.

Wagner, M. (1989). *Youth with disabilities during transition: An overview of descriptive findings from the national longitudinal transition study.* Stanford, CA: SRI International.

———. (1992). "A little help from my friends": The social involvement of young people with disabilities. In M. Wagner et al. (Eds.), *What happens next? Trends in postschool outcomes of youth with disabilities. The second comprehensive report from the national longitudinal transition study of special education students* (pp. 6-1 to 6-43). Menlo Park, CA: SRI International.

Whang, P. L., Fawcett, S. B., & Matthews, R. M. (1984). Teaching job-related social skills to learning disabled adolescents. *Analysis and Intervention in Developmental Disabilities, 4,* 29–38.

Wheeler, J. J., Bates, P., Marshall, K. J., & Miller, S. R. (1988). Teaching appropriate social behaviors to a young man with moderate mental retardation in a supported competitive employment setting. *Education and Training in Mental Retardation, 23,* 105–116.

Willems, E. P. (1977). Steps toward an ecobehavioral technology. In A. Rogers-Warren & S. F. Warren (Eds.), *Ecological perspectives in behavior analysis* (pp. 39–61). Baltimore: University Park Press.

Yuker, H. E. (1988). The effects of contact on attitudes toward disabled persons: Some empirical generalizations. In H. Yuker (Ed.), *Attitudes toward persons with disabilities* (pp. 262–274). New York: Springer.

Glossary

School-to-Work (STW) is a new approach to learning in America's schools that links students, schools, and workplaces. Locally driven and community-based, STW is an effort to reform education that combines high-level academic achievement with a graduated understanding of the world of work. A new way of preparing young people for their ultimate entry into the workplace, STW also encourages schools at secondary and postsecondary levels to develop school-to-work systems cooperatively—together with employers, unions, civic groups, and other public- and private-sector organizations.

Enacted into federal legislation in 1994, the School-to-Work Opportunities Act provides venture capital to states and communities that compete successfully to bring school-to-work into their neighborhoods. The Act is jointly funded by the U.S. Departments of Labor and Education.

As school-to-work systems emerge throughout the country, we believe a "common language" may help to describe the elements that

Originally published by the National School-to-Work Office, 400 Virginia Avenue, S.W., Room 210, Washington, DC 20024. School-to-Work is a joint initiative sponsored by the U.S. Departments of Education and Labor.

The content does not necessarily reflect the views of the departments or any other agency in the U.S. government.

School and business staff may reproduce this product for use in their own programs.

comprise them. The Glossary offers a reference point to a multifaceted and highly decentralized movement. Like the local partnerships that bring school-to-work into communities, an intensely collaborative process among state STW coordinators and their stakeholder colleagues produced the definitions. Where available, definitions were pulled from the Act. Generally, however, most definitions are derived from the meanings the terms have acquired through use. The more complex definitions are illustrated with examples.

J. D. Hoye
National School-to-Work Office
The National School-to-Work Office is funded by the U.S. Departments of Labor and Education

Adopt-A-School: When a company or community organization "adopts a school," it connects with a particular school, group of schools, or school district to improve the quality of education services. Participation typically takes the form of fiscal, material, or human resource contributions. Adopt-a-school efforts may take a number of different forms, including the following:

- equipment donations
- office supplies
- speakers
- mentors and tutors
- receptions and parties
- seminars
- letters of support
- scholarships and grants
- company tours

All Aspects of Industry: As defined by the School-to-Work Opportunities Act, the term "all aspects" of an industry refers to "all aspects of the industry or industry sector a student is preparing to enter, including planning, management, finances, technical and production skills, the underlying principles of technology, labor and community issues, health and safety issues,

and environmental issues related to such industry or industry sector." "All aspects" also includes the array of occupations and careers that comprise an industry, from the most basic to the most advanced.

> *The National Health Care Skill Standards Project has identified four broad clusters of health care industry occupations: (1) the therapeutic cluster provides treatment over time; (2) the diagnostic cluster creates a picture of health status; (3) the information services cluster documents and processes information; and (4) the environmental cluster creates a therapeutic and supportive environment.*

All Students: As defined in the Act, the term "all students" means "both male and female students from a broad range of backgrounds and circumstances, including disadvantaged students, students with diverse racial, ethnic, or cultural backgrounds, American Indians, Alaska Natives, Native Hawaiians, students with disabilities, students with limited-English proficiency, migrant children, school dropouts, and academically talented students."

Apprenticeship (Registered): "Registered apprenticeship" describes those programs that meet specific federally approved standards designed to safeguard the welfare of apprentices. The programs are registered with the Bureau of Apprenticeship and Training (BAT), U.S. Department of Labor, or one of twenty-seven State Apprenticeship Agencies or Councils approved by BAT. Apprenticeships are relationships between an employer and employee during which the worker, or apprentice, learns an occupation in a structured program sponsored jointly by employers and labor unions or operated by employers and employee associations.

Basic Skills: Basic skills are essential academic and personal abilities that are necessary for success in school and the workplace. Traditionally referred to as the three R's—reading, writing, and arithmetic—the definition has been expanded in recent times, by both educators and employers, to include a number of cognitive and interpersonal abilities, including the capability to think and solve problems, to communicate information in oral, written, and electronic forms, to work effectively alone and in teams, and to take responsibility for one's own development.

Benchmarking: Benchmarking is the continuous process of measuring products, services, and practices against strong competitors or recognized leaders. It is an ongoing activity, intended to improve performance; it can be applied to all facets of operations; it requires a measurement mechanism so that the performance "gap" can be identified; and it focuses on comparing best practices among enterprises that may or may not be alike.

> *Students at Socastee High School in Myrtle Beach, S.C., take mathematics and science classes that are benchmarked to world standards. To set benchmarks, teachers meet with employers and educators at other schools, visit local business and industries, and use guidelines from organizations such as the National Council of Teachers of Mathematics. All students at the school take 4 years of mathematics, although only three are required for graduation. Science courses clearly describe what students are expected to know. The goal of the benchmarking initiative is to help prepare students for the next level by helping them judge their current progress.*

Block Scheduling: Block scheduling is a means of reconfiguring the school day. The traditional school day is typically divided into six or seven classes, each lasting from 45 to 55 minutes. With few exceptions, classroom instruction begins and ends within the allotted time period. Blocked courses may be scheduled for two or more continuous class periods or days to allow students greater time for laboratory or project-centered work, field trips or work-based learning, and special assemblies or speakers.

Career Academy: A career academy is typically a school-within-a-school that offers students academic programs organized around broad career themes. Often integrating classroom instruction with work-based learning, academies try to equip students with the necessary skills for both work-force entry and postsecondary admission. Staffed by a team of teachers from various disciplines, academy classes are usually block-scheduled and smaller than those in the typical high school to build students' sense of membership in the academy community. Curricula are often planned with the assistance of business partners, who suggest program structure, provide classroom speakers, host school field trips, and provide mentors for individual students. Students may be placed in jobs related to their field of study in the summer, and may spend some part of their senior year participating in a work experience program.

> The Academy for Law, Criminal Justice, and Public Administration, based in Horace Furness High School in South Philadelphia (Philadelphia, Pennsylvania), offers secondary students concentrated studies in the legal, governance, and criminal justice systems. To help students integrate their academic coursework, classes focus on yearlong projects that explore a specific legal issue. For example, in studying the topic of DNA for trial purposes, students might conduct statistical analyses of its structure for math, analyze its composition for chemistry, and write a research paper on its discovery for English. Periodic guest speakers, mock trials, role-playing sessions, and trips to law firms in the area lend context to classroom instruction.

Career Awareness: Career awareness activities generally take place at the elementary level. They are designed to make students aware of the broad range of careers and/or occupations in the world of work, including options that may not be traditional for their gender, race, or ethnicity. Ranges from limited exposure to the world of work through occasional field trips and classroom speakers to comprehensive exposure, including curriculum redesign, introduction to a wide span of career options, and integration with activities at the middle school level.

Career Days/Career Fairs: Career day activities are designed to help students think about their interests and abilities in relation to potential careers, and to meet people who can assist them in getting the necessary skills and experience for work-force success. Special events are typically held to allow students to meet with postsecondary educators, employers, or human resource professionals to learn about education and work opportunities. Information may be distributed through brochures that students receive from visiting firms or school representatives, via formal or informal discussions held in the classroom, or during tours of a business or college.

Career Development: Career development is the process through which an individual comes to understand his or her place in the world of work. Students develop and identify their careers through a continuum of career awareness, career exploration, and work exposure activities that helps them to discern their own career paths. Career development encompasses an individual's education and career-related choices, as well as the outcome of those choices.

Career Exploration: Career exploration generally takes place at the middle school level and is designed to provide some indepth exposure to career options for students. Activities may include the study of career opportunities in particular fields to identify potential careers, writing individual learning plans that dovetail with career majors offered at the high school level, or review of local labor market information.

Career Exposure: Career exposure can be defined as activities at the high school level that provide actual work experience connecting classroom learning to work.

Career Guidance and Counseling: As defined in the Act, the term "career guidance and counseling" means "programs—(a) that pertain to the body of subject matter and related techniques and methods organized for the development in individuals of career awareness, career planning, career decision making, placement skills, and knowledge and understanding of local, state, and national occupational, educational, and ongoing market needs, trends, and opportunities; (b) that assist individuals in making and implementing informed educational and occupational choices; and (c) that help students develop career options with attention to surmounting gender, race, ethnic, disability, language, or socioeconomic impediments to career options and encouraging careers in nontraditional employment."

Career Major: As defined in the Act, the term "career major" means "a coherent sequence of courses or field of study that prepares a student for a first job and that—(a) integrates academic and occupational learning, integrates school-based and work-based learning, and establishes linkages between secondary schools and postsecondary institutions; (b) prepares the student for employment in a broad occupational cluster or industry sector; (c) typically includes at least 2 years of secondary education and at least 1 or 2 years of postsecondary education; (d) provides the students, to the extent practicable, with strong experience in and understanding of all aspects of the industry the students are planning to enter; (e) results in the award of a high school diploma or its equivalent; a certificate or diploma recognizing successful completion of 1 or 2 years of postsecondary education (if appropriate); and a skill certificate; and (f) may lead to further education and training, such as entry into a registered apprenticeship program, or to admission to a 2- or 4-year college or university."

Career Map: A career map is a written plan of study that helps students select a coherent sequence of secondary (and where appropriate, postsecondary) courses and experiences to prepare them for college entry or work in a selected career cluster or area. Career maps are particularly valuable for entering high school freshmen, because they can provide them with the direction they need in scheduling their course of study in their career of choice.

Entering students at Roosevelt High School in Portland, Oregon, complete a "Freshman Focus" class that emphasizes career exposure activities. Students first rotate through each of the career clusters offered in the school, and receive life skills, self-esteem building, and group work skill instruction. Just prior to entering tenth grade, students draft career maps that identify a specific career pathway in which they will anchor their future academic studies. Mapping activities involve designing a career-related academic curriculum for the tenth, eleventh, and twelfth grades that may lead to advanced certification. Introductory courses in the sophomore year give way to more specialized coursework in the later grades. Learning programs include structured work-based placements that are guided by training plans.

Clinical Experiences: Clinical experiences are school- or work-based placements in which students are taught academic and occupational skills from school or employee instructors who supervise and evaluate their work. School-based clinical experiences typically expose students to situations and settings they might encounter once they enter their profession. Simulations and role playing allow students to hone their professional skills in school under the direction of a classroom teacher.

Work-based clinical experiences offer students real-life activities in a professional setting. These experiences, offered under the direction of a practicing employee, are designed to help students learn the skills and attitudes necessary to become a competent practitioner. Both students and clinical instructors are typically supervised by school-based coordinators or intermediary organizations who monitor placements to ensure that appropriate instruction occurs. Students successfully completing a clini-

cal experience program may qualify for industry certification or may receive credits that can be applied toward a professional degree.

Compact: Compacts are contracts among community leaders to work to initiate and sustain local educational reform. Compact representatives may include community decision makers, school superintendents, college presidents, and heads of business organizations as well as principals, teachers, parents, and unions. Compacts provide a structure of mutual accountability because all participants agree to work together and separately to support group goals. Efforts on the part of compact members may include creating employment opportunities for students, helping to restructure educational systems, and providing local labor market information.

The Boston Compact (Boston) was formed in 1982, when business leaders who felt that they could help raise the quality of high school graduates approached local authorities and educators with a proposal for school reform. In exchange for districtwide improvements in student academic performance and a reduction in the total dropout rate, business leaders promised to increase jobs and college assistance to high school graduates. Renegotiated twice since 1982, the most recent agreement in 1994 instituted new 6-year goals:

1. Easing students' transition to employment and higher education

2. Reorganizing traditional educational administrative and governance structures

3. Designing comprehensive curriculum, standards, and assessment methods

4. Providing teachers with training and professional development opportunities

5. Offering programs that help parents to support their children from birth to school

6. Creating community learning centers using school facilities

Connecting Activities: Connecting activities are programs or human resources that help link school- and work-based educational programs in the manner described in the School-to-Work Opportunities Act. Connecting activities include the following:

1. matching students with work-based opportunities

2. using school-site mentors as liaisons among educators, business, parents, and community partners

3. providing technical assistance to help employers and educators design comprehensive STW systems

4. providing technical assistance to help teachers integrate school- and work-based learning as well as academic and occupational subject matter

5. encouraging active business involvement in school- and work-based activities

6. assisting STW completers in finding appropriate work, continuing their education or training, and linking them to other community services

7. evaluating postprogram outcomes to assess program success, particularly with reference to selected populations

8. linking existing youth development activities with employer and industry strategies to upgrade worker skills.

Consortium: In reference to school-to-work, a consortium is a group of two or more agencies that enter into a cooperative agreement to share information or provide services that benefit students. Participating groups may pool their individual fiscal, human, and material resources to take advantage of economies of scale, or arrange to share staff technical expertise. Consortia may be formed within educational sectors, as when a number of secondary schools collaborate to offer advanced instructional services, or across educational sectors, as when secondary and postsecondary institutions arrange articulated programs.

Employer and community organizations may also join educational consortia, or form their own consortia, to support school-to-work system-building efforts.

Contextual Learning: Contextual knowledge is learning that occurs in close relationship with actual experience. Contextual learning enables students to test academic theories via tangible, real-world applications. Stressing the development of "authentic" problem-solving skills, contextual learning is designed to blend teaching methods, content, situation, and timing.

Cooperative Education: Cooperative education is a structured method of instruction whereby students alternate or coordinate their high school or postsecondary studies with a job in a field related to their academic or occupational objectives. Students and participating businesses develop written training and evaluation plans to guide instruction, and students receive course credit for both classroom and work experiences. Credit hours and intensity of placements vary with the course of study.

Curriculum Alignment: Curriculum alignment is linking academic and vocational curricula so that course content and instruction dovetail across and/or within subject areas. Curriculum alignment may take two forms: horizontal alignment, when teachers within a specific grade level coordinate instruction across disciplines, and vertical alignment, when subjects are connected across grade levels, in a cumulative manner, to build comprehensive, increasingly complex instructional programs.

Disability: The 1990 Americans with Disabilities Act defines individuals with disabilities as including any individual who (1) has a physical or mental impairment that substantially limits one or more of the major life activities of that individual; (2) has a record of an impairment described in paragraph (1); or (3) is regarded as having an impairment described in paragraph (1). This definition includes any individual who has been evaluated under Part B of the

Individuals with Disabilities Education Act and determined to be an individual with a disability who is in need of special education and related services; and any individual who is considered disabled under section 504 of the Rehabilitation Act of 1973. At the secondary level, counts of students with disabilities are typically based on whether a student has an Individualized Education Plan (IEP). At the postsecondary level, counts of students with disabilities are typically based on student self-reports of disabling conditions.

Dropout: The term "dropout" refers to an event, such as leaving school before graduating; or a status, such as an individual who is not in school and is not a graduate. A person who drops out of school may later return and graduate. At the time the person has left school, he/she is called a dropout. At the time the person returns to school, he/she is called a stopout. Measures to describe these behaviors include event dropout, status dropout rate, and high school completion rate.

Dual Enrollment: Dual enrollment is a program of study allowing high school students to simultaneously earn credits toward a high school diploma and a postsecondary degree or certificate. Written articulation agreements formalize programs of study, the transfer of academic and vocational credits among institutions, and the role of secondary and postsecondary instructors.

High school students in Norfolk, Virginia, can earn postsecondary credits at nearby Tidewater Technical College for selected occupational coursework. Student participation can begin as early as the sophomore year in high school or when a student first enrolls in a high school vocational-technical course that is articulated with the local college's offerings. Students take both academic and vocational courses at the high school in the morning, then additional vocational courses at the college in the afternoon. Students receive college credit for their high school work after graduating from high school, enrolling at Tidewater College, and completing 12 credit hours of study in their articulated program area.

Elementary School: An elementary school is an agency that is both classified as elementary by state and local practice, and is composed of any span of grades not above grade 8. A preschool or kindergarten school is included under this heading only if it is an integral part of an elementary school or a regularly established school system.

General Track: The general track is characterized by a broadly defined curriculum that is less rigorous in nature than the academic and the vocational track. General programs of study prepare students neither for college nor the work force.

Goals 2000: The Goals 2000 Act provides resources to states and communities to develop and implement educational reforms aimed at helping students master academic and occupational skill standards. By providing flexible and supportive options for coordinating, promoting, and building a system of educational standards to improve education, the Act aims to make the federal government a better partner in comprehensive state and local school improvement efforts.

Signed into law March 31, 1994, the federal legislation provides a framework for achieving eight National Education Goals by the year 2000. These goals are as follows:

1. School Readiness—all children will start school ready to learn.
2. School Completion—the high school completion rate will increase to at least 90 percent.
3. Student Achievement and Citizenship—all students leaving grades 4, 8, and 12 will demonstrate competency over challenging academic subjects and have skills that will enable them to function in a democratic society.

4. Teacher Education and Professional Development—increase professional development opportunities and raise the instructional knowledge and skills of the nation's teaching force.

5. Mathematics and Science—build student math and science achievement to be first in the world.

6. Adult Literacy and Lifelong Learning—make every adult American literate and equip them with the knowledge and skills to compete in a global economy and exercise their citizenship responsibilities.

7. Safe, Disciplined, and Alcohol- and Drug-Free Schools—offer a disciplined environment conducive to learning in every school, free of drugs, violence, and unauthorized firearms and alcohol.

8. Parental Participation—increase parental participation in promoting the social, emotional, and academic growth of children.

High-Performance Workplace: A workplace that employs sophisticated, technically advanced and efficient production techniques is called "high performance." In order for this type of workplace to function, workers must be equipped with advanced thinking and occupational skills that enable them to learn on the job, adapt to rapidly changing technology, and work in teams to solve problems. In addition to their economic development potential, high-performance workplaces may help drive school reform by providing educators with a set of occupational skill standards that are required for marketplace success.

> Employees of the Ritz-Carlton hotel chain, one such high-performance workplace, must successfully complete a Training Certificate to learn how to perform to the standards in their position. Hallmarks of the program include a comprehensive orientation followed by on-the-job training and job certification. Because of the nature of the industry, employees are expected to possess a number

of high-performance traits, including the ability to work together in teams and to perform a wide variety of tasks.

High School Completion: Most students complete high school by finishing the requisite secondary coursework to receive a regular high school diploma. The total number of credits, courses, or Carnegie units that must be completed varies by state. In some cases, minimum requirements for high school completion are legislated statewide; in others it is left to local districts to determine minimum course and content standards. A relatively small number of students may complete high school by receiving an alternative high school credential, such as a General Educational Development (GED) certificate, certificate of completion, or certificate of attendance. The term does not distinguish how long it takes to achieve the high school credential.

Integrated Curriculum: "Integrated curriculum" refers to instances where academic and occupational or career subject matter—normally offered in separate courses—is taught in a manner that emphasizes relationships among the disciplines. Integrated curriculum may take many forms, ranging from the simple introduction of academics into traditional occupational courses to comprehensive programs that organize all instruction around career major themes.

> Students at Sussex Technical High School (Sussex County, Delaware) choose from four technology clusters: Automotive/Diesel; Business; Health/Human Services; and Industrial/Engineering Technologies. Instruction within each cluster area emphasizes integration of academic and technical coursework. For example, students in the Industrial/Engineering program study American history by preparing written outlines and oral presentations that document construction techniques used by colonists. As an activity students actually design and build replicas of colonial cabins and canoes.

Internships:

1. Student internships are situations where students work for an employer for a specified period of time to learn about a particular industry or occupation. Students' workplace activities may include special projects, a sample of tasks from different jobs, or tasks from a single occupation. These may or may not include financial compensation.

2. Teacher internships are work-site experiences of at least 2 weeks in duration for teachers. During this time, teachers may work at a particular job at the firm to learn specific skills, or rotate throughout the firm to learn all aspects of the industry in which they are employed. Such internships may or may not include financial compensation.

Job Rotation: In job rotation, workers periodically transfer among a number of different positions and tasks that require different skills and responsibilities. Among the reasons employers rotate job tasks is to help workers understand: the different steps that go into creating a product and/or service delivery; how their own effort affects the quality and efficiency of production and customer service; and how each member of the team contributes to the process. Job rotation may require that employees possess a wide range of general and specific skills and that they undergo advanced training to enable them to perform a variety of work functions.

Job Shadowing: Job shadowing is typically a part of career exploration activities in late middle and early high school. A student follows an employee at a firm for one or more days to learn about a particular occupation or industry. Job shadowing can help students explore a range of career objectives and select a career major for the latter part of high school.

Labor Market Area: As defined by the U.S. Bureau of Labor Statistics, a labor market area is "an economically integrated geographic area within which individuals can reside and find employment within a reasonable distance, or can readily change employment without changing their place of residence." Labor markets are classified as either metropolitan or nonmetropolitan (small labor market) areas. In 1994, a total of 2,378 labor market areas were identified: 329 metropolitan areas and 2,049 nonmetropolitan areas. Labor market areas are identified in order to standardize and promote comparability for the collection and use of labor-force information in administering various government programs. Areas are reevaluated and updated every 10 years using the latest Decennial Census information.

Learning Objectives, Performance Measures, and Performance Standards: Educators sometimes develop performance measurement systems to assess student achievement, monitor school progress, and support program improvement. The terms "learning objectives," "performance measures," and "performance standards" are used to define each part of the three-part process of establishing a performance measurement system. The process begins with identifying learning objectives for students or other program participants. After identifying these objectives, it is necessary to decide how to measure their attainment. After developing appropriate performance measures, standards must then be set to represent the level of performance that is desired. The three terms are defined as follows:

1. *Learning Objectives:* Summarize the knowledge, skills, and abilities that students will be expected to achieve. A learning objective answers the question, "What do we want students to know, understand, or be able to do?"

2. *Performance Measures:* Describe how attainment of the learning objectives will be measured or assessed. Performance measures typically rely on standardized tests, performance assessments, surveys, or other methods of documenting and quantifying performance. A performance measure answers the question, "How will we measure attainment of the learning objectives?"

3. *Performance Standards:* Set the level of knowledge or skill mastery that students or schools will be expected to attain. Performance standards define the minimum acceptable level of achievement on the performance measures for each learning objective. A performance standard answers the question, "How much is enough?"

Learning objectives, performance measures, and performance standards can be developed for individuals as well as entire districts, schools, or programs. The following table illustrates how this might be done in the area of mathematics achievement.

Limited-English Proficiency: The 1988 Bilingual Education Act describes a limited-English proficient student as one who (1) meets one or more of the following conditions: (a) the student was born outside of the United States or whose native language is not English; (b) the student comes from an environment where a language other than English is dominant; or (c) the student is American Indian or Alaskan Native and comes from an environment where a language other than English has had a significant impact on his/her level of English-language proficiency; and (2) has sufficient difficulty speaking, reading, writing, or understanding the English language to be denied the opportunity to learn successfully in English-only classrooms.

Local Educational Agency: A local educational agency (LEA) is a local-level administrative unit that exists primarily to operate public schools or to contract for public school services. Its synonyms include "school district" and "local basic administrative unit."

Local Partnership: As defined by the Act, "the term 'local partnership' means a local entity that is responsible for local School-to-Work Opportunities programs and that—(a) consists of employers, representatives of local educational agencies and local postsecondary educational institutions (including representatives of area vocational education schools, where applicable), local educators (such as teachers, counselors, or administrators), representatives of labor organizations or non-managerial employee representatives, and students; and (b) may include other entities, such as—employer organizations; community-based organizations; national trade associations working at the local levels; industrial extension centers; rehabilitation agencies and organizations; registered apprenticeship agencies; local vocational education entities; proprietary institutions of higher education...; local government agencies; parent organizations; teacher organizations; vocational student organizations; private industry councils...; federally recognized Indian tribes, Indian organizations, Alaska Native villages..., and Native Hawaiian entities."

Example of Learning Objectives, Performance Measures, and Standards for Mathematics Achievement

	Student Level	District, School, or Program Level
1. Learning Objective, "What?"	Student will attain mathematics proficiency as identified for his or her grade level.	Same
2. Performance Measure, "How?"	State mathematics achievement test score.	Average score on state mathematics achievement test.
3. Performance Standard, "How much?"	Student will score at or above grade level.	At least 80% of students will score at or above grade level.

Mentors:

1. A School Site Mentor is defined in the Act as "a professional employed at a school who is designated as the advocate for a particular student, and who works in consultation with classroom teachers, counselors, related service personnel, and the employer of the student to design and monitor the progress of the School-to-Work Opportunities program of the student."

2. A Workplace Mentor is defined in the Act as "an employee or other individual, approved by the employer at a workplace, who possesses the skills and knowledge to be mastered by a student, and who instructs the student, critiques the performance of the student, challenges the student to perform well, and works in consultation with classroom teachers and the employer of the student."

National Skill Standards Board: Established under Title V of the Goals 2000: Educate America Act, the National Skill Standards Board serves as a catalyst to stimulate the development and adoption of a voluntary national system of skill standards, assessment, and certification of attainment criteria.

This system of skill standards is intended to increase the economic competitiveness of the United States by aiding

- industries in informing training providers and prospective employees of skill needs
- employers in evaluating applicants' skill levels and designing training for existing workers
- labor organizations in improving employment security and providing portable credentials
- workers in obtaining skill certification that enhances career advancement and job security
- students and entry-level workers in identifying skill levels necessary for high-wage jobs

- training providers and educators in determining appropriate training services
- government in evaluating outcomes of publicly funded training programs

Nontraditional Occupation and Employment: As defined in the Women Apprenticeship and Nontraditional Occupations Act, the term nontraditional occupations refers to occupations and jobs in which women make up 25 percent or less of the total number of workers.

Occupational Cluster: An occupational cluster is a grouping of occupations from one or more industries that share common skill requirements. Occupational clusters form the basis for developing national skill standards, organizing instruction in all aspects of an industry, establishing career academics, and creating career pathways or majors as part of school-to-work programs.

On-the-Job Training: On-the-job training is hands-on training in specific occupational skills that students receive as part of their workplace experiences.

Portfolio: A portfolio is a collection of work that documents a student's educational performance over time. Although no standard format has been established, portfolios typically include a range of materials (e.g., reports, photographs) selected by the student. A brief introduction and summary statement may describe how the portfolio was assembled and what was learned in the compilation process. Portfolios may be used for a variety of purposes, including increasing student learning opportunities; helping students demonstrate a wide variety of skills; assisting students in recognizing their own academic growth; and teaching students to take greater responsibility for their own learning and development. Instructors report that the portfolio process can increase collaboration with students, provide an alternative means of observing students' cognitive and academic progress, help drive program improvement, and foster professional development by helping teachers to organize and manage their curriculum.

Since 1991, the state of Kentucky has required all students to develop writing and math portfolios. Portfolios are intended to exhibit a purposeful selection of work that highlights a student's academic achievement. For example, a grade 12 writing portfolio must include a personal narrative or memoir, a short story, poem, or play; and three pieces of writing in which students predict an outcome, solve a problem, draw a conclusion, defend a position, explain a process, create a model, or analyze a situation. Teachers use completed projects to integrate performance assessment with instruction, to provide information for curriculum development, and to demonstrate gains in student achievement over time.

Postsecondary Educational Institution: A postsecondary educational institution is a school that provides formal instructional programs with a curriculum designed primarily for students who have completed the requirements for a high school diploma or equivalency certificate. This includes programs of an academic, vocational, and continuing professional education purpose, but excludes vocational and adult basic education programs.

Private Career School (Proprietary School): As defined by the U.S. Department of Education, a proprietary institution is "an educational institution that is under private control but whose profits derive from revenues subject to taxation." Private career schools typically include postsecondary institutions that are independently owned and operated as a profit-making enterprise.

SCANS (Secretary's Commission on Achieving Necessary Skills): The Secretary's Commission on Achieving Necessary Skills (SCANS) was convened in February 1990 to examine the demands of the workplace and to determine whether the current and future work force is capable of meeting those demands. The Commission was directed to: (1) define the skills needed for employment; (2) propose acceptable levels in those skills; (3) suggest effective ways to assess proficiency; and (4) develop a strategy to disseminate the findings to the nation's schools, businesses, and homes.

The Commission identified five *competencies* (i.e., skills necessary for workplace success) and three *foundations* (i.e., skills and qualities that underlie competencies).

- COMPETENCIES—effective workers can productively use:
  - Resources—allocating time, money, materials, space, and staff
  - Interpersonal Skills—working on teams, teaching others, serving customers, leading, negotiating and working well with people from culturally diverse backgrounds
  - Information—acquiring and evaluating data, organizing and maintaining files, interpreting and communicating, and using computers to process information
  - Systems—understanding social, organizational, and technological systems, monitoring and correcting performance, and designing or improving systems
  - Technology—selecting equipment and tools, applying technology to specific tasks, and maintaining and troubleshooting technologies
- FOUNDATIONS—competence requires:
  - Basic Skills—reading, writing, arithmetic and mathematics, speaking, and listening
  - Thinking Skills—thinking creatively, making decisions, solving problems, seeing things in the mind's eye, knowing how to learn, and reasoning
  - Personal Qualities—individual responsibility, self-esteem, sociability, self-management, and integrity

School-Sponsored Enterprise: In a school-sponsored enterprise, students produce goods or services as part of their school program. School-sponsored enterprises typically involve students in the management of a project that may involve the sale of goods for use by others. Enterprises may be undertaken on or off the school site but are always part of the school's programs.

School-to-Work Coordinator: Individuals assigned or hired to oversee and implement the required components of a school-to-work system, including school-based activities, work-based activities, and connecting activities. At the state level, school-to-work coordinators may be responsible for drafting a state plan; coordinating state efforts with other national and state legislation; organizing technical assistance, follow-up, and placement assistance for STW stakeholders; and monitoring local partnership plans and activities.

At the local level, school-to-work coordinators may be involved in drafting local plans; recruiting and coordinating business partners; organizing technical assistance, follow-up, and placement assistance for local STW stakeholders; and monitoring local partnership plans and activities for program improvement purposes. Coordinators must be knowledgeable of community resources; labor markets; school operations; and must possess negotiation, team building, leadership, and administrative skills.

School-to-Work Opportunities Program: As defined in the Act, general requirements of a "School-to-Work Opportunities program" include

- school-based and work-based learning that integrates academic and occupational learning and links between secondary and post-secondary education

- the opportunity for participating students to complete a career major

- the provision of a strong experience in and understanding of all aspects of the industry a student is preparing to enter

- equal access for students to a full range of program components and related activities, such as recruitment, enrollment, and placement activities. However, these services are not offered as an entitlement

In addition to general program requirements, a school-to-work program also must feature a school-based learning component, a work-based learning component, and a connecting activities component. At a minimum, these programs should include the following

School-Based Learning Component

1. Career awareness and career exploration and counseling programs beginning at the earliest possible age, but not later than grade 7

2. Career major selection not later than the beginning of grade 11

3. A program of study that meets the academic standards the state has established for all students, including, where applicable, standards established under the Goals 2000 Act, and meets the requirements for postsecondary education preparation and skill certificate award

4. A program of instruction and curriculum that integrates academic and vocational learning and incorporates instruction to the extent practicable, in all aspects of an industry

5. Regular evaluations of students and dropouts to identify their academic strengths and weaknesses, workplace knowledge, goals, and need for additional learning opportunities

6. Procedures that ease student entry into additional training or postsecondary education programs, and that ease the transfer of students between education and training programs.

Work-Based Learning Component

1. Work experience opportunities

2. Job training and work experiences co-ordinated with learning in school-based

programs that are relevant to students' career major choices, and lead to the award of skill certificates

3. Workplace mentoring

4. Instruction and activities in general workplace competencies, including positive work attitudes, employability, and practicable skills

5. Broad instruction, to the extent practicable, in all aspects of the industry

Connecting Activities Component

1. Matching students with work-based learning opportunities of employers

2. School-site mentors acting as liaisons among school, employer and community partners

3. Technical assistance to small and medium-size firms and other parties

4. Assistance to schools and employers in integrating school-based and work-based learning

5. Encouraging active participation of employers in cooperation with local education officials

6. Assistance to participants in finding jobs, continuing their education, or entering additional training and linking them with other community services to assure a successful transition

7. Collecting and analyzing postprogram outcomes of participants

8. Linking youth development activities in this Act with other employer and industry strategies

School Tutors: Tutors work with students to help them understand topics or concepts that need reinforcement. Tutoring activities may take place during or after school or work, and may or may not be part of a structured school program. In addition to academic coursework, tutors may work with students to address career or personal development issues. Tutors may be paid or unpaid.

Secondary School: Secondary schools comprise any span of grades beginning with the next grade following an elementary or middle school (usually 7, 8, or 9) and ending with or below grade 12. Both junior high schools and senior high schools are included.

Service Learning: Service learning is an instructional method that combines community service with a structured school-based opportunity for reflection about that service, emphasizing the connections between service experiences and academic learning. Although most service-learning activities vary by educational purpose, most programs balance students' need to learn with recipients' need for service. Students benefit by acquiring skills and knowledge, realizing personal satisfaction, and learning civic responsibility, whereas the community benefits by having a local need addressed.

> Custer High School, a construction magnet located in Milwaukee seeks to equip youth with academic and technical skills that will prepare them for work and postsecondary education. As part of a unique service-learning project, the school district has teamed with a local community development corporation to purchase and renovate boarded-up homes. Students produce cost estimates, analyze and design structures, and apply advanced carpentry, plumbing and electrical skills that they learn in school. Remodeled homes are sold to low-income families living in the community at the lowest possible cost consistent with good business practice. A diploma and Career Certificate are awarded to students upon graduation.

Skill Certificate: A skill certificate is a portable, industry-recognized credential that certifies the holder has demonstrated competency in a core set of content and performance standards related to an occupational cluster area. Serving as a signal of skill mastery at industry-benchmarked levels, skill certificates may assist students in finding work within their community, state, or elsewhere in the nation. When issued by a School-to-Work Opportunities Act program under an approved state plan, state-developed skill standards used for certification purposes must be at least as challenging as standards ultimately endorsed by the National Skill Standards Board.

Skill Standard: A skill standard specifies the knowledge and competencies required to perform successfully in the workplace. Standards are being developed along a skill continuum ranging from (1) general work readiness skills, and (2) core skills or knowledge for an industry, to (3) skills common to an occupational cluster, and (4) specific occupational skills. Standards may cover basic and advanced academic competencies, employability competencies, and technical competencies. Development of these standards is tied to efforts to certify students' and workers' skills.

State Educational Agency: As defined in the School-to-Work Opportunities Act, the term "state educational agency" (SEA) means the "officer or agency primarily responsible for the state supervision of public elementary and secondary schools." In many states, a state board of education and/or chief state school officer supervises the operation of public schools. State board members are typically appointed by the governor or elected by partisan or nonpartisan ballot. Chief state school officers (sometimes called "state superintendents") are typically appointed by the state board, or elected by partisan or nonpartisan ballot. A small number of states either rely solely on their state board of education or chief state school officer for educational governance.

Team Teaching: In team teaching, two or more instructors work together to design and teach curricula in multiple subjects that are presented to the same group of students. Merging teacher talents and knowledge of different disciplines with new instructional materials can help students to better understand relationships across and within their educational programs. Partici-

pating instructors may choose to teach classes together, or may present material individually based on a commonly agreed format. To encourage material development, teachers typically share common planning periods so that they may work together to coordinate their subject matter and participate in joint staff-development programs.

> The electronics and applied physics teachers at Allderdice High School (Pittsburgh), for example, meet regularly to write curricula that dovetail across the two classes. Weekly planning sessions are used to develop instructional plans and design units that link across subjects. Moreover, the two teachers regularly visit each other's classes to demonstrate and explain how physics and electronics interrelate. For example, the physics teacher may come to the electronics class to describe the underlying principles on which electricity is based, and the electronics teacher may share equipment and technical materials to provide applied context for academic concepts taught in physics class.

Tech-Prep: Tech-prep is the name given to programs that offer at least 4 years of sequential coursework at the secondary and postsecondary levels to prepare students for technical careers. Programs typically begin in the eleventh grade and result in an award of an associate's degree or certificate after 2 years of postsecondary training. Other tech-prep combinations are also available, depending on local consortium arrangements. Tech-prep is designed to build student competency in academic subjects and to provide broad technical preparation in a career area. Coursework integrates academic and vocational subject matter and may provide opportunities for dual enrollment in academic and vocational courses at secondary and postsecondary institutions.

Technical Education: Technical education is a program of vocational instruction that prepares individuals for positions, such as draftsman or lab technician, in different occupational areas requiring a range of skills and abilities. Technical education typically includes the study of the sciences and mathematics underlying a technology, as well as the methods, skills, the materials commonly used, and the services performed in the technology.

Thinking Skills: Thinking skills are cognitive abilities used to organize, evaluate, and process information. According to the SCANS *Report for America 2000,* thinking skills may be disaggregated into six distinct categories that are found, to a varying extent, in many occupations.

1. Creative thinking—uses imagination freely, combines ideas or information in new ways, makes connections between seemingly unrelated ideas, and reshapes goals in ways that reveal new possibilities.

2. Decision making—specifies goals and constraints, generates alternatives, considers risks, and evaluates and chooses best alternatives.

3. Problem solving—recognizes that a problem exists (i.e., there is a discrepancy between what is and what should or could be), identifies possible reasons for the discrepancy, devises and implements a plan of action to resolve it, evaluates and monitors progress, and revises plan as indicated by findings.

4. Seeing things in the mind's eye—organizes and processes symbols, graphs, objects, or other information; for example, sees a building from a blueprint, a system's operation from schematics, or the flow of work activities from narrative descriptions.

5. Knowing how to learn—recognizes and uses learning techniques to apply and adapt new knowledge and skills in both familiar and changing situations and is aware of learning tools such as personal learning styles, and formal and informal learning strategies and information.

6. Reasoning—discovers a rule or principle underlying the relationship between two or more objects and applies it in solving a prob-

lem. Uses logic to draw conclusions from available information, extracts rules or principles from a set of objects or written text, applies rules and principles to a new situation, or determines which conclusions are correct when given facts.

Vocational Education: As defined by the U.S. Department of Education, vocational education consists of "organized educational programs, services, and activities that are directly related to the preparation of individuals for paid or unpaid employment, or for additional preparation for a career that does not require a baccalaureate or an advanced degree." Secondary and postsecondary vocational coursework is typically offered in three areas:

1. Consumer and homemaking education—courses intended to prepare students for roles outside the paid labor market. Topics include child care, meal preparation, nutrition, and household management.

2. General labor market preparation—courses that teach general employment skills without necessarily preparing students for paid employment in a specific field. Instruction includes introductory word processing, industrial courses, business education, and work experience and career exploration.

3. Specific labor market preparation—courses that teach skills and provide information required in a particular vocation. Areas of specific labor market preparation include agriculture, business, marketing and distribution, health, occupational home economics (i.e., preparation for paid employment in the service sector), trade and industry, and technology and communication.

Work-Based Learning: Work-based learning experiences are activities at the high school level that involve actual work experience or connect classroom learning to work. The least intensive level of exposure to work-based learning might occur in traditional work experience and vocational programs (including cooperative education, distributive education, or vocational courses) that do not offer work site experience. The next level of exposure could entail integration of academic and vocational/occupational curricula, as is the case in tech-prep programs, but would not include work-site experience. At the highest level, there is full integration of academic and vocational/occupational curriculum with work-site experience.

Youth Apprenticeship: Youth apprenticeship is typically a multiyear program that combines school- and work-based learning in a specific occupational area or occupational cluster and is designed to lead directly into either a related postsecondary program, entry-level job, or registered apprenticeship program. Youth apprenticeships may or may not include financial compensation.

Author Index

Subject Index

Transition specialist, 197–198
    defined, 197
    planning, instruction, service responsibilities, 193
    role of, 197–198
TTY systems, 392

U.S. Department of Commerce, 21
U.S. Department of Education, 16, 18, 21, 37, 45, 81, 151
U.S. Department of Labor, 151
Universal standards, 168
University student demographics, 385

Values, 170–171
Value statements, 308
Vocational adaptations, 362–363
Vocational assessment, 115–116, 323–324
Vocational education, 101–123
    administrative structure, 107–108
    curriculum, 106–107
    defined, 102
    enrollment patterns, 107
    environment, 105–106
    evolution of, 103–110
    exemplary practices, framework of, 53
    funding, 107–108
    goals, 50, 101–102
    instructors, 106
    issues, 119–122
    legislation, 103–110
    measures, 119
    model programs, 50–52
    models, common features of, 51
    performance standards, 119
    programming expansion, 104
    program selection, 117
    public school, 102
    secondary, 105
    service delivery, 101
    for special populations, 52–53
    successful, key elements of, 52
    teachers, 106, 191–192, 197
    work-based approaches, 50
Vocational Education Act, 104
    Amendments of 1968, 63, 104
    Amendments of 1976, 105
Vocational Education Data System, 105
Vocational-oriented transition programs, 90–92
Vocational rehabilitation counselor, 194
Vocational student organizations (VSOs), 107
Vocation transition services model, 117, 118

What is my community? question, 171
Who am I in the world? question, 169–171

Whose Future Is It Anyway? program, 217–223
    case study, 222–223
    defined, 219–220
    DO IT! problem-solving strategy, 221
    field test, 221
    sections, 220–221
    sessions, 219–220
Work-based instruction, 357–363
Work-based learning, 54, 113–114
    cooperative education, 113
    implementing, 148–149
    school-based enterprises, 114
    youth apprenticeships, 113–114
Work experience, 340–364
    apprenticeship/internship, 348
    benefits of, 345
    career academy, 350
    career-related camp program, 348
    community, 347, 350
    cooperative education, 348–349
    course project, 345–346
    field trip, 345–346
    job shadowing, 346–347
    practices, 353
    preparing for, 341–342
    school-based enterprise, 347–348
    staff, 360
    support roles, 356
    tech-prep, 349–350
    trends, 340
    types of, 345–350
    work-study, 349
Work Experience and Career Education Program (WECEP), 354
Work Experience Performance Evaluations, 284
Work experience programs
    administrative support, 254
    career development connections, 354–356
    design of, 350–363
    employer development, 351–353
    graduation policies and, 356–357
    in-school time, 355
    rationale of, 341–345
    special education, 344, 350
    work-site support, 356
Work Force Development Act, 69–70
Work sectors, 146
Work-study programs, 349

Young adults
    decision making of, 25–27
    gender differences in, 27–29
    thinking of, 23–24